ISLAMIC FAMILY LAW

Series General Editor

Dr Mark S. W. Hoyle

Titles in the Series

The Islamic Law of Personal Status, (2 ed), Jamal J. Nasir

The Status of Women under Islamic Law, Jamal J. Nasir

Islamic Family Law, Chibli Mallat and Jane Connors (eds)

Arab and Islamic
Laws Series

ISLAMIC FAMILY LAW

Edited by

Chibli Mallat
&
Jane Connors

with a foreword by

Antony Allott

Graham & Trotman
A member of the Kluwer Academic Publishers Group
LONDON/DORDRECHT/BOSTON

First published by
Graham & Trotman Limited
Sterling House
66 Wilton Road
London SW1V 1DE
UK

Graham & Trotman Inc
Wolters Kluwer Academic Publishers Group
101 Philip Drive
Assinippi Park
Norwell, MA 02061
USA

Proceedings of a conference convened by the Centre of Islamic and Middle East Law, the Centre of Near and Middle Eastern Studies and the Law Department of the School of Oriental and African Studies, University of London, in May 1989.

British Library Cataloguing in Publication Data

Islamic family law. - (Arab and
Islamic Laws Series).
1. Families. Islamic law
I. Mallat, Chibli II. Connors, Jane
III. Series
340.5'9

ISBN 1-85333-301-8 Series ISBN 1-85333-414-6

Library of Congress data Cataloguing in Publication Data

Islamic family law.

(Arab and Islamic Laws Series)
"Proceedings of a conference convened by the Centre of Islamic and Middle Eastern Law, the Centre of Near and Middle Eastern Studies and the Department of Law of the School of Oriental and African Studies, University of London, in May 1989"-- T.p. verso.
Includes index.
1. Domestic relations (Islamic law)--Congresses.
I. Mallat, Chibli. II. Connors, Jane. III. University of London. Centre of Near and Middle Eastern Studies. IV. University of London. Centre of Islamic and Middle East Law. V. University of London. School of Oriental and African Studies. Dpt. of Law. VI. Series.
LAW 346.01'5'0917671 89-16387
ISBN 1-85333-301-8 342.6150917671

Printed and Bound in Great Britain by Athenaeum Press Ltd., Newcastle upon Tyne.

CONTENTS

NOTE ON THE CONTRIBUTORS

Dr Dima Abdulrahim has studied anthropology at the American University of Beirut and has received her PhD from the Department of Arabic and Islamic Studies at Exeter University. She has undertaken anthropological field work in Lebanon and In West Germany and is interested in the issues of minorities, gender, kinship and the constitution of identity. She is currently a Research Officer in Ethnic Health for the Directorate of Public Health with London Regional Health Authorities.

Michael Anderson is Lecturer in law at the School of Oriental and African Studies, University of London.

Rabbi Bernard Berkovits is a *dayan* (judge) at the Religious Court of the Federation of Synagogues in London. He was Registrar of the Court of the Chief Rabbi at London, a post he held for five years. Previously he taught Family law, Criminal law and International law (Public and Private) at the University of Buckingham. He has published numerous articles on legal matters and is an acknowledged expert in the field of Jewish law, and particularly Jewish Matrimonial law.

Jane Connors, B.A., LL.M. (Australian National University), is Lecturer in law at SOAS. She has written widely on the law relating to women and children, and specialises in the family law of South East Asia. Her most recent publication, *Violence Against Women,* was published under the auspices of the United Nations.

Anthony Dicks has lived in Hong Kong since 1974, where he practises as a barrister and arbitrator and pursues a long-standing interest in Chinese law and legal history. He is currently a part-time visiting professor in the Department of law, School of Oriental and African Studies, University of London.

Ian Edge is Lecturer in law and Director of the Centre of Islamic and Middle East Law, SOAS. He teaches Islamic law particularly of the contemporary Middle East, as well as Commercial law and International law. He practises as a barrister at Gray's Inn and frequently advises on Middle Eastern legal questions.

Dr Riazul Hasan Gilani is Deputy Attorney General for Pakistan, and has been closely associated with the Islamization process in his country in the past decade. He is Visiting lecturer in Islamic Jurisprudence, Law College at Lahore, and is the author of several works on Islamic law, including *The*

Reconstruction of Legal Thought in Islam, currently revised for a new edition.

Dr Shahla Haeri is the author of the *Law of Desire: Temporary Marriage in Shi'i Iran* (Syracuse University Press in the USA and I.B. Tauris in England). She is Assistant Professor of cultural anthropology at New York University, and has been a research fellow at the Center for Middle Eastern Studies, Harvard University, 1985-86, and 1987-89.

Andrew Huxley is Lecturer in the Laws of South East Asia at SOAS, University of London, and a barrister. He is writing books on 'Buddhism and Law' and 'Comparative Legal Theory'. He is a frequent visitor to Thailand and, until recently, Burma.

Dr Riva Kastoryano is 'chargée de receherche' at the Centre National de la Recherche Scientifique in Paris, where she is carrying on research on migrants in France and in Germany. After completing her studies in France, she taught from 1984 to 1987 at Harvard University. Her latest publications include *Etre Turc en France: Réflexions sur Famille et Communauté*, Paris, 1986 and 'Les Etats et les Immigrés', *Revue Européenne des Migrations Internationales,* September 1989.

Dr Tahir Mahmood is Professor of Law and Head, Law Centre II, University of Delhi, and Head of the Department of Islamic and Comparative Law at the Indian Institute of Islamic Studies, New Delhi. He has published several books on Islamic family law and is the editor of *Islamic and Comparative Law Quarterly.*

Dr Chibli Mallat is Lecturer in Islamic law at the SOAS, where he teaches Common law and Islamic law at undergraduate and graduate levels. He has advised on various issues pertaining to law and to the Middle East, and has published several articles in this field in Arabic, French and English. He is the editor of *Islamic Law and Finance,* London, 1988.

Dr Werner F. Menski has been lecturing at SOAS in modern South Asian laws since 1980. He is now actively engaged in research on the legal systems of Pakistan and Bangla Desh and is preparing a book on family law in India.

Dr David Pearl is Professor of Law and Dean of the School of Law at University of East Anglia, Norwich. He is also a Life Fellow of Fitzwilliam College, Cambridge. Amongst his external activities, he sits as an Immigration Adjudicator and practises as a Barrister specializing in the law from South Asia from Chambers in London.

Dr Sebastian Poulter is Reader in law at Southampton University where he has been lecturing since 1972. He is a specialist in the law relating to ethnic minority traditions and pioneered the first course in England on this subject for L.L.B. students. He has written extensively in this area and is the author of *English Law and Ethnic Minority Customs,* Butterworths, 1986, the standard work in the field.

Dr David S. Powers is Associate Professor of Islamic History at Cornell University, is a specialist in the history of Islamic law. His first book, *Studies in Qur'an and Hadith: the Formation of the Islamic Law of Inheritance,* was published by the University of California Press in 1986. Articles on various aspects of Islamic legal history have appeared in *Studia Islamica, Arabica, Journal of the American Oriental Society, Journal of Near Eastern Studies,* and *Comparative Studies in Society and History.*

Lynn Welchman is currently completing a thesis on Islamic family law in the Israeli-occupied West Bank, to be presented at SOAS. She is European Field Representative for al-Haq, the Ramallah-based Palestinian human rights organization.

FOREWORD*

Antony Allott

Emeritus Professor of African Law at the University of London
Former Head of the Law Department, S.O.A.S.

It was over twenty years ago that the Department of law at SOAS presented a series of public lectures by members of the Department on 'Family Law in Asia and Africa', in which Islamic law figured prominently. These lectures were largely the idea and inspiration of the then Head of Department, Britain's foremost scholar of Islamic law, Professor Sir Norman Anderson. He also edited the publication which flowed from this initiative.[1]

It is right that we recall these facts now, since Sir Norman and his colleagues, notably Professor Noel Coulson (so unhappily and prematurely taken from us), laid the foundations for mounting the conference which led to this book. We build on their pioneering efforts.

I may be the least qualified in Islamic law (though I have picked up a fair amount from my close association with Norman and Noel), but I would like to venture one or two brief reflections -as a layman- on the subject addressed in the book.

First of all, family law. I see family law as the core, key, and foundation of any legal system. What we are seeing in the West today is the virtual breakdown of the family and family law. Parental rights in England: now we refuse to recognise them, and insist instead on parental responsibilities. The control and authority which a parent may have over his or her children are such as may be conceded to them from time to time by a court or legal authority. Then, inheritance: from a period when English law recognised excessive individualism, when a testator could do as he pleased with his property and deprive his family of all rights, we have moved to a system of quota shares of capital and income for the benefit of dependants. The story is the same with marriage and divorce: one third of marriages now end in divorce, while young people in England and elsewhere are increasingly choosing not to get married but to enter informal relationships instead.

---

*Adapted from an opening address to the conference on 'Islamic Family Law: State Identity and Minority Rights', SOAS, 18-19 May 1989, where most of the papers included in this book were presented.

[1] J.N.D. Anderson ed., *Family Law in Asia and Africa,* London, 1968. The lectures were given in London through the academic year 1965-1966.

The developing world, with which this book is also concerned, tells an equally dismal story. Westernisation, the product both of colonialism and the pervasive effect of Western ideas, education and economic change, has imported these difficulties into Third World countries too. But in addition they have to face the problems of pluralism, largely a product of colonial rule, where the imported Western family law systems co-exist and often conflict with indigenous customary and religious systems. The world's largest under-class, women, is now emerging in many areas into greater social and legal equality. Just as the by-products of the industrial world are found today even in the pure air of the remotest Antarctic, so intellectual and social influences have radiated out from Western countries throughout the world.

So far has the process of deterioration gone that a French scholar could publish a few years ago in a legal journal an article with the arresting title of 'Requiem for the African family'.[2] We are, perhaps, in the presence of a universal phenomenon.

Islamic law is in a special position in all this. As a worldwide system it may be contrasted interestingly with another global system, that of the common law, which has spread to every continent from its country of origin. Of course, Islamic family law, founded on the shari'a, has a special character as being partly of divine inspiration and partly the product of tradition. But similar questions arise. Just as the common law is the product of a particular society but now finds itself adapting to operation in many different kinds of changing society, so with Islamic law. One of the interesting questions is the extent to which Islamic law is susceptible of adaptation and change. Islamic law must operate today in societies where it is dominant, as well as in those in which it is merely one component of a plural legal system.

Modernisation, then, is one theme which must be explored. Legal pluralism -the recognition of variant ways of living and behaving, regulated by different systems of law- is another. We face in our own country, Britain, today, the fundamental question whether growing pluralism should be expressed in legal pluralism too: the possible recognition and application of Islamic personal law here is on the agenda.

The coverage of the book is ambitiously large. I attach just two minor comments of a geographical kind. First, from my personal standpoint it is a matter of of some regret that the countries of Africa (except in so far as they are reclassified as part of the Middle East) do not figure on the agenda, when one notes that practically all the problems of rcognising, applying and developing of Islamic family law in a modern country with a plural legal system are acutely demonstrated in a country like Nigeria, where this is currently a principal legal and constitutional issue.

---

[2]Roger Decottignies, 'Requiem pour la Famille Africaine', *Annales Africaines,* 1965, pp.251-286.

Next, I note -without elaborating on the point- that a work on Islamic family law can include a discussion of the state of the shari'a in the United Kingdom. This tells us a good deal about what is going on, in legal and cultural terms, in our own country too. We are part of this particular world-scene now, like it or not.

One looks forward, with the keenest of interest, not just to reports of the present position, but to discussion and reflection on the policy and practical issues which now confront us as a result.

ACKNOWLEDGEMENTS

A work of this breadth and diversity would not have been possible without the active participation and support of several institutions and individuals. For their financial support, we would like to thank the Research and Publication Committee at the School of Oriental and African Studies, the British Academy, Clifford Chance, and the publishers. A number of dedicated supporters at the Centre for Near and Middle Eastern Studies, in particular its present and former Chairmen, Dr Richard Tapper and Professor Tony Allan, helped make the conference at the origin of the book a success. At the conference, Professor Eugene Cotran, Professor James Read and Dr Doreen Hinchcliffe offered their support and enthusiasm. The Coordinators of the Centre, Dinah Manisty and Simonetta Calderini were present whenever needed, and they were often needed. At the Centre also, we have had the editorial help of Diana Gur and Fiona McEwan, without whom this book would have long still been in the making. Mrs Catherine Lawrence has kindly provided her expertise for the map in Chapter 12. To all, our deep thanks. We are of course responsible for the mistakes and imperfections which remain.

TRANSLITERATION

We have used the standard transliteration of non-European words as adopted in the *Bulletin of the School of Oriental and African Studies,* but have omitted the diacritics. Words are italicized in each chapter only the first time they appear. For convenience, we have generally preferred Arabic words over Persian, Urdu, Chinese or Indian equivalents. Thus the word *shari'a* (Islamic law) will be, unless otherwise dictated by the context, preferred to *Shariah* or *Shariat*. Where relevant, the transliteration chosen by each contributor was retained.

1. INTRODUCTION

ISLAMIC FAMILY LAW: VARIATIONS ON STATE IDENTITY AND COMMUNITY RIGHTS

Chibli Mallat

Over the last three decades, most of the countries of the Near East and South Asia have lived a relative legislative lull in the area of family law. In Iraq,[1] Syria,[2] Lebanon,[3] Jordan,[4] Egypt,[5] Pakistan,[6] Iran,[7] and India,[8] as well in North African countries,[9] the wave of national reforms in matters most at heart of the countries' religious communities seemed to have been successfully completed.[10] In some cases, the attempt at unifying the law in a code of

---

[1]For Iraq, see in Western languages Norman Anderson, 'A Law of Personal Status for Iraq', *International and Comparative Law Quarterly,* 1960, pp.542-564; 'Changes in the Law of Personal Status in Iraq', *International and Comparative Law Quarterly,* 1963, pp.1026-1031; Y. Linant de Bellefonds, 'Le Code du Statut Personnel Irakien du 30 Décembre 1959', *Studia Islamica,* 1960, pp.79-135; in Arabic, see the references in chapter 5 in this volume.

[2]Norman Anderson, 'The Syrian Law of Personal Status', *Bulletin of the School of Oriental and African Studies,* 1955, pp.34-49; Rizkallah Antaki, 'La Question du Statut Personnel en Syrie', *Proche-Orient Etudes Juridiques,* 1968, pp.1-12; B. Botiveau, *Shari'a Islamique et Droit Positif dans le Moyen-Orient Contemporain, Egypte et Syrie,* Ph.D. Aix-Marseille, 1989, pp.193-198.

[3]Emile Tyan, *Notes Sommaires sur le Nouveau Régime Successoral au Liban,* Paris, 1960; P. Catala and A. Gervais, *Le Droit Libanais,* Paris, 1963, Vol.1, pp.53-188; A. Gemayel ed., *The Lebanese Legal System,* Washington, 1985, Vol.1, pp.267-390.

[4]Norman Anderson, 'The Jordanian Law of Family Rights 1951', *Muslim World,* xlii, 1952, pp.192-206.

[5]Abdel Fattah el-Sayed Bey, 'La Situation de la Femme Mariée Egyptienne après Douze Ans de Réforme Législative', *Al-Qanun wal-Iqtisad,* 11, 1932, pp.65-82; Y. Linant de Bellefonds, 'Immutabilité du Droit Musulman et Réformes Législatives en Egypte', *Revue Internationale de Droit Comparé,* 7, 1955, pp.1-34; Muhammad Abu Zahra, *Al-Ahwal ash-Shakhsiyya,* Cairo, 1957; and references in chapter 3 in this volume.

[6]N. Coulson, 'Reforms of Family Law in Pakistan', *Studia Islamica,* vii, 1956, pp.133-155; David Pearl, *A Textbook on Muslim Personal Law,* London, 1979, 2nd ed. 1987; and references in chapters 15 and 16 in this volume.

[7]D. Hinchcliffe, 'The Iranian Family Protection Act', *International and Comparative Law Quarterly,* 1968, pp.516-521; and references in chapter 4 in this volume.

[8]See generally Pearl, *A Textbook on Muslim Personal Law;* T. Mahmood, *The Muslim Law of India,* 2nd ed. Allahabad, 1982; and references in chapters 13 and 14 in this volume.

[9]M. Borrmans, *Statut Personnel et Famille au Maghreb de 1940 à nos Jours,* Paris, 1977; A. Colomer, 'Le Code du Statut Personnel Tunisien', *Revue Algérienne,* 1957, pp.115-239; Norman Anderson, 'The Tunisian Law of Personal Status', *International and Comparative Law Quarterly,* 1958, pp.262-279; Id., 'Reforms in Family Law in Morocco', *Journal of African Law,* 1958, pp.146-159; J. Roussier, 'Mariage et Divorce en Algérie', *Die Welt des Islams,* vi, 1961, pp.248-254.

[10]See generally T. Mahmood, *Family Law Reform in the Muslim World,* Bombay, 1972; Norman Anderson, *Law Reform in the Muslim World,* London, 1976; Y. Linant de

personal status (*ahwal shakhsiyya*)[11] has failed: Lebanon offers the example of a country which proved unsuccessful in bringing about a unified personal law for Muslim and Christian communities.[12] But on the whole, the legislative 'monuments', as Linant de Bellefonds called them,[13] had been completed. Since then, personal status legislation has remained, in the main, untouched for three decades. The only area where an effort was undertaken to bring about more reforms was influenced by the necessity of advancing women's social and legal rights, but even there, as the case of the Egyptian controversial law of 1979 suggests,[14] the process of legislative change was slow and uncertain. Still, some reforms were completed, as in Jordan and Algeria, but even in this case, the recent adoption of new codes may not have introduced significant breaks with previous legislation.[15]

The uneventful development of personal status laws was accompanied by a social peace among the religious communities which survived the emergence of the post-decolonization nation-states. But in the 1980s, the communitarian[16] lull came to an end. A date to signal the culmination of a long process could even be suggested in the completion in 1986 of the draft Code of Personal Status by a team of experts from Arab Ministries of justice.[17] In other words,

---

Bellefonds, *Traité de Droit Musulman Comparé,* 3 Vols., Paris, 1965-1973; J. Nasir, *The Islamic Law of Personal Status,* London, 1986, new ed.1990.

[11]The word 'ahwal shaksiyya' (literally personal modes or status) is currently used in Arabic for all matters related to family law, and includes marriage, divorce, filiation, custody, maintenance, as well as generally (but not always) matters pertaining to succession.

[12]It is to be noted that Lebanon has failed to unify the legislation for personal matters also between its Muslim communities. An effort in the 1960s to establish a common Shi'i and Sunni legislation on family law was thwarted in part because of the opposition of the Shi'i circles in Southern Iraq to a Lebanese Muslim unified legislation, as was related to the author by the late Mahdi al-Hakim (the son of the then leading Shi'i leader Muhsin al-Hakim): an interesting example of the interrelation in the Muslim world beyond nation-states.

[13]Linant de Bellefonds, *Traité de Droit Musulman Comparé,* passim.

[14]Repealed, then reenacted under a different form in 1985, see B. Botiveau, 'Les Récentes Modifications du Code Egyptien du Statut Personnel: Genèse d'un Débat sur le Droit de la Famille', *Bulletin du CEDEJ,* 17, 1985, pp.93-112; and his *Shari'a Islamique et Droit Positif dans le Moyen-Orient Contemporain,* pp.188-193.

[15]L. Welchman, 'The development of Islamic Family Law in the Legal System of Jordan', *International and Comparative Law Quarterly,* 1988, pp.868-886; M. Borrmans, 'Le Nouveau Code Algérien de la Famille dans l'Ensemble des Codes Musulmans de Statut Personnel, Principalement dans les Pays Arabes', *Revue Internationale de Droit Comparé,* 1986, pp.133-139.

[16]'Communitarian' refers to what can also be called sectarian, confessional, or communal. All these terms are interchangeable. In French, the word often used is 'confessionnel', in reference to '*confessions*', or sects. In English, the word confessional is a neologism, and the word sectarian has a negative connotation, whilst communal is more specifically used in India and Pakistan. We have therefore preferred the more neutral 'communitarian' in reference to the religious conmmunities, including communities of different religions, as well as communities within each religion.

[17]Ittihad al-Muhamin al-'Arab (Union of Arab Lawyers), *Mashru' Qanun 'Arabi Muwahhad lil-Ahwal ash-Shakhsiyya* (Draft unified Arab code of personal status), n.d., Cairo. The date is also true of India, as is suggested in Tahir Mahmood's *Personal Laws in Crisis*, New Delhi, 1986.

the process of *talfiq* (legislative construction drawing on rules pertaining to different Islamic schools of law and countries) was completed: the skilful legal puzzle drawn first by the Ottomans from the 'best' solutions provided by the various schools of law had reached its ultimate 'modern' form.

Far from the establishment of fully integrated states with smooth inter-communitarian relations, the early years of the 1980s have brought to many Muslim countries of the Near East a flavour of increased communitarian unease, in significant contrast to the confidence in nation-state building of the early independence era. Voices unheard of in the Near East for three decades have reemerged. They ring of a Christian-Muslim, Sunni-Shi'i, Sunni-'Alawi divide, and even within recognized Sunni rites, of the assertion of differences between Shafi'is, Hanafis and Hanbalis.

Some of the reemerging differences were perhaps due to the victory of the Islamic revolution in Iran, and to the claims of the Tehran leaders to be speaking with the voice of the whole Muslim community. The age-old Sunni-Shi'i divide was exacerbated. By bringing to power the Shi'i 'ulama, the Iranian revolution ushered in major convulsions and readjustments in the whole Shi'i ambit, with effects from Afghanistan to Lebanon, and it inevitably affected the rest of the Muslim world. For the first time in decades, once-buried antagonisms between the Sa'udi Hanbalis and the Iranian Ja'faris were even resurfacing.[18]

Apart from underlining communitarian differences, what the Iranian revolution also brought to the fore was more simply the reassertion of the *shari'a*, Islamic law, as a realisable agenda for legislation in the city. Ironically, the area least affected by the urgency of applying the shari'a was family law, as it was perhaps the one domain which had least been affected by colonialism and the necessities of modernisation.[19] But the wave of the Islamic appeal affected it indirectly, in a novel way, by exacerbating the emerging split on the world scene between Islamists and Muslims.[20] In the new picture, the 'Islamists' are those who support the full political and legal implementation of Islam (whatever exact practical modalities this may mean), in contrast to the Muslims, who do not necessarily live their 'Islam' politically.

The debate over family law was significantly affected, for within any country, the divide beween Islamists and Muslims carried on a further essential dimension, which overshadowed the strict differences amongst the communities. From a legal perspective, this divide, it is important to note, remained muted. No text has emerged where the problems across communities was addressed, and the tension remained in the subconscious and unsaid of the legislators. But its sharp exacerbation led to a major shift in emphasis in

[18]Martin Kramer, 'Tragedy in Mecca', *Orbis*, 32, 1988, pp.231-247.

[19]This argument is developed in many works on Islamic law, and finds its best expression in Anderson, *Law Reform in the Muslim World*. See contra the nuances in Botiveau's work.

[20]This separation has been clearly drawn in an address at the School of Oriental and African Studies by the Vice-President of the Lebanese Shi'i Council, Muhammad Mahdi Shamseddin, 12 July 1990. For a similar formulation see our Preface to C. Mallat ed., *Islamic Law and Finance*, London, 1988.

personal status matters. The shift affected the perception of, and interest in, family law. Until 1980, personal status was systematically considered as 'the last precinct' of the shari'a, in contrast with criminal, civil, economic, and constitutional law where it was acknowledged that the shari'a had little role to play. Indeed, on the level of legislation, little in this field was owed to the shari'a, whereas personal status rules had remained primarily shari'a-based.

But even though the family law codified 'monuments' remained, the central communitarian debate was inflicting a new direction to the perception and study of Islamic family law. The perceptible divide in the social and phenomenological sphere started affecting family law in a manner which overshadowed its traditional viewing as the last authentic precinct of the shari'a.

The new dimension can be formulated as a tug-of-war between a situation where the religious communities are left to their own family law devices, and one where a will of the state to issue an integrated unified law for all the communities concerned has prevailed. Unified personal law system v. community personal laws system has become the parameter of the new sensitive expression of what has reemerged as the state v. minorities (or communities) rights.[21]

The pattern is not restricted to the Near East and South Asia, with their sizeable Muslim populations and their centenarian tradition. By shifting the emphasis away from the strict analysis of the content of the various codes, Islamic family law was acquiring its truly international dimension. It was now enough for one Muslim community, however minoritarian, to voice its 'Islamicity', for the family law question to follow. Islamic family law has become consequently, also, a Western issue.

The essays in the present volume show that despite the centrality of the Middle East in terms of model for the development of family law, the issues that have gripped the field after a relative lull of thirty years were also important for the world at large. Indeed issues which were inexistent or dormant in Europe have come centre stage in the last decade.

It would be inaccurate to describe the revitalization, or the novel rise of communitarian or sectarian problems, solely as the result of the Iranian Islamic phenomenon of recent years. It seems inevitable that with the immigration patterns of large non-Christian groups in the second half of the century, European countries in which the dominant regime was 'Judeo-Christian' would be called into question by communities which were not brought up in the same tradition. Indeed, the Judeo-Christian tradition, in the wide Nietzschean acceptation of the term, encompasses French 'laicisme' as well as the Church of England as 'official religion' in the United Kingdom and the separation of church and state dear to American constitutionalism. Beneath

[21]The problem is naturally wider and more complicated than the legal framework of personal laws. In the societies concerned, the more basic issues of social and political representation in the higher echelons of the state constitute the abutting basis of tensions. But the issue of family law has retained some importance, however overshadowed by the larger claims to power of communities which perceive themselves to be bereaved and marginalized.

the veneer of various state traditions, the cultural bottom line was and is Judeo-Christian, and it could be expected that people reared in another culture, and now jealous of its protection irrespective of territoriality, would eventually seek the protection of the law in egalitarian terms.

To mention only France and the United Kingdom, the debate in recent years over issues pertaining to Islam and family law has been, if not significant, new.[22] The prominent political dimension of the debate has so far been relatively contained, but the passion inwhich it developed portends ill for the smooth inter-religious future of the populations in West Europe. Whether to allow or not to allow the *hijab* in the 'laic' schools of France may appear a trivial issue, but it cannot fail to indicate, were one to pierce the thin veil, that the future cannot afford avoiding forever fundamental and difficult questions on the egalitarian status of the law.

The issue can be put in several forms: it could be described, as in the overall theme of the conference at the origin of the present work, as conflict and accommodation between state identity and minority rights. To the full, integrated and uniform identity of the national as citizen of the Nation-state, contrasts the space which is, or ought to be, reserved to the rights of 'discrete and insular minorities', as a famous decision of the American Supreme Court once put it.[23] In another sense, the issue is one of equality. Is the result to be sought in a modern state an equality between the citizens or an equality between groups? Should the voice of the organized group be given the attention of the law, or should the voice of the citizen be heard independently of the group he or she belongs to?

But the debate is also between two opposing concepts from the perspective of state policy. Should the state seek integration against differentiation, and is the debate, as again often portrayed in the contrast between the British and French governments, that the latter seeks to integrate, to *franciser* its minorities, whereas the former conceives of a much wider latitude in addressing minoritarian communities? This again can be described as a wider philosophical debate between unity and variety, or in legal terms adopted from French law, as a question of *ordre public* which no right can ultimately infringe upon.

These wider perspectives are not new to the law. Quite the opposite. They will sound familiar to the citizen as well as to the legislator and policy-maker. But in the last decade, the introduction of the Islamic dimension is new to Europe, and is consequently new as an international problem.

In so far as Islam is central to the emerging issues clustered around the debate of state identity and minority rights from the perspective of family law, these issues represent variations on the theme well-known to the Middle East, of unified personal law system v. community personal laws system. Because

---

[22]See chapters 7-10 in this volume. For similar issues in Germany and the United States., see also E. Jayme, "'Talaq' nach Iranischem Recht und Deutscher Ordre Public', *IPRax*, 9, 1989, pp.223-224; D. Forte, 'Islamic Law in American Courts', *Suffolk Transnational Law Journal*, 1983, pp.1-33.

[23]*United States v. Carolene Products Co.*, 304 U.S. 144 (1938), at 152-153 n.4.

the Middle East is the cradle of the Judeo-Islamo-Christian paradigm, the sectarian milieu, as John Wansbrough put it in a fundamental book on the semantic structure of religions,[24] has remained relevant worldwide.

Intellectually, there seems to have emerged in recent years what may be seen, in a phenomenon of *longue durée*, as the revenge of the Middle Eastern paradigm: the integrationist (and intellectually simplistic) worldview of the metropolis is giving way to fractures which are on the lookout for a new model. Even a matter as powerfully ingrained as the law of the land, in its family law aspects, is being challenged, and we find ourselves in the midst of a deep wave which is restructuring legal frontiers into unknown shapes. Family law is at the centre of this remodelling.

* * *

The reader is asked to move along three directions simultaneously:

The first dimension is *diachronical*, and the studies deal with a historical span covering family law in a long historical period. From the century separating the death of the Prophet and the solidification of what we now know as inheritance law (Chapter 2), to 18th and 19th Century colonial India (Chapter 11), to the claim to a separate legal system voiced by some British Muslims (Chapter 8), the historical span has several rythms. Even in Britain, the common law knows of an intricate tradition of several hundred years of discreet family rules for the Jews, and is asked now to provide answers to British Muslims for problems that are only a few years old (Chapter 7). And so the different rythms in China, India, Europe and the Middle East.

The second dimension is *territorial*. From the Far East (China, Chapter 17, Thailand and Malaysia, Chapter 12) to West Germany (Chapters 9 and 10), passing by Pakistan (Chapters 15 and 16), Iran (Chapter 4) and Egypt (Chapter 3), one witnesses the work of Islam as a world religion in confrontation and dialogue with other world religions, but also with 'secular' cultural systems, whether in democratic Europe (Part II- Europe, Chapters 7 to 10) and India (Chapters 11, 13, 14), or in Communist China (Chapter 17). It is in this territorial dimension that the more technical comparative aspect lies. One can therefore look further into the question of the rights of non-Muslim minorities in a predominant Muslim country (like Egypt, Chapter 3), or at the history of the formation of a single family Code (as in Iraq between 1959 and 1963, Chapter 5). In the first case, the law governing Muslims and non-Muslims is the subject of investigation; in the second case, it is the intra-Muslim dimension which is at stake, with the rich variations of the shari'a in terms of sects (Sunnis and Shi'is) and schools of law (*madhaheb*, Sunni Hanafis, Hanbalis, Shafi'is and Malikis, Shi'i Ja'faris and Zaydis). The permutations are infinite, and forgotten aspects reeemerge in the process of comparative investigation.

---

[24]See his *Quranic Studies*, Oxford, 1977, and *The Sectarian Milieu*, Oxford, 1978.

The apparently deadlocked situation beween claims of a religious minority (The Palestinian Muslim family in Germany in Chapter 10, the Palestinians in the Occupied West Bank, as in Chapter 6, Muslims in Great Britain in Chapters 7 and 8, Muslims in India, as in Chapters 13 and 14) and the 'public order' or 'the integration' asserted by the Hindu or Christian majorities is perhaps not so specific of the world religions in *vis-à-vis*. The experience of Iraq shows well how the problems are also intra-communitarian: in such instances, religion as belief seems less important than forms of social belonging (religious as a whole, or communitarian as Shi‘i or Sunni) which require a legal protection that the Nation-State finds difficult to grant.

There is finally a third dimension, which is *thematic*. Family law encompasses as much marital relations as the laws of succession. This, from the lawyer's point of view. What one will discover in the book is that the issue is far from being restricted to lawyers. What is intuitively perceived as a much more sensitive issue than the strict legal relationships in the family, will be exemplified in the interdisciplinary contributions of the authors, drawn from history, anthropology, and politics. Family law is the focal point for an issue which is both wider and more significant. Beyond history and geography, this book is an appeal to intellectual comprehensiveness. The reader who reads it as a unit will find the widening of his or her horizons gratifying.

PART I

THE MIDDLE EAST

2. THE ISLAMIC INHERITANCE SYSTEM: A SOCIO-HISTORICAL APPROACH

David S. Powers

Muslim jurisprudence portrays Islamic law as a manifestation of the revealed word of God: the *shari'a* is a divinely ordained system that controls but is not controlled by Muslim society; law does not evolve as an historical phenomenon closely linked with the evolution of society, and legal history, in the Western sense, does not exist. This view has been challenged in the twentieth century by Western scholars who have sought to demonstrate that the classical theory of Islamic law was the product of a complex historical process spanning a period of three centuries and, further, that the early growth of Islamic law was closely linked to contemporary social, political and economic developments.[1] In the field of inheritance, no scholar has done more to promote a socio-historical understanding of the law than Noel J. Coulson. Although Coulson never articulated a unified, comprehensive explanation of the historical evolution of Islamic inheritance law from pre-Islamic to modern times, one does find the elements of such an explanation scattered throughout his numerous writings.[2] Coulson's explanation of the historical evolution of Islamic inheritance law may be summarized as follows:

The Qur'anic legislation and the Islamic law of inheritance (in Arabic, the *'ilm al-fara'id* or 'science of the shares') are best viewed against the background of the tribal customary law of pre-Islamic Arabia, that is, the customary inheritance practices of the nomadic Arabs living in the Hijaz prior to the rise of Islam. This tribal society was patrilineal in its structure and patriarchal in its ethos; individual tribes were formed of adult males who traced their descent from a common ancestor through exclusively male links. The tribe was bound by the body of unwritten rules that had evolved as a manifestation of its spirit and character. These rules served to consolidate the tribe's military strength and to preserve its patrimony by limiting inheritance rights to the male agnate relatives *('asaba)* of the deceased, arranged in a hierarchical order, with sons and their descendants being first in order of priority.[3]

During the century prior to the rise of Islam, the social structure of the Hijaz was undergoing a radical transformation, especially in Mecca and Medina, where the nuclear family was replacing the tribe as the basic unit of

---

[1] The pioneer in this regard was Joseph Schacht. See his *The Origins of Muhammadan Jurisprudence*, Oxford, 1950.

[2] Noel J. Coulson, *A History of Islamic Law*, Edinburgh, 1964; *Conflicts and Tensions in Islamic Jurisprudence*, Chicago, 1969; *Succession in the Muslim Family,* Cambridge, 1971.

[3] Coulson, *History*, pp. 9-10, 15-16; *Conflicts*, p. 10; *Succession*, p. 29.

society. In response to these changes, the Qur'an introduced novel inheritance rules that emphasized the tie existing between a husband and his wife and between parents and children; these rules also had the particular goal of raising the legal status of women within the nuclear family. Thus, the Qur'anic inheritance legislation came to reform the tribal customary law of pre-Islamic Arabia.[4] In Coulson's words, the Qur'an 'modified the existing customary law by adding thereto as supernumerary heirs a number of relatives who would normally have had no rights of succession under the customary law'.[5] These reforms served to strengthen the status of members of the nuclear family.

The Qur'anic reforms were shortlived. Following Muhammad's death, Muslim jurists fused together the pre-Islamic tribal customary law and the Qur'anic inheritance legislation to form the Islamic law of inheritance. The latter imposes compulsory rules for the division of a minimum of two-thirds of every estate; bequests may not normally exceed one-third of the estate and may not be made in favour of any person who stands to inherit a share. Since the bulk of the estate was often preserved for the closest surviving male agnate, Coulson concluded that the tribal component within the Islamic law of inheritance had prevailed over the Qur'anic, nuclear family component. In his view, the Islamic law of inheritance gives superior rights to the male agnate relatives and therefore 'caters for a tribal system of society'.[6] Thus, by the end of the first century A.H., the agnatic, extended family had reasserted its dominance over the nuclear family. It was the extended family that would characterise the social structure of Muslim society for the next thousand years.[7]

According to the classical view, once the Islamic law of inheritance had been created, there could be no question of any further reforms or modifications. The law of inheritance reigned supreme for over a millenium, from the ninth to the nineteenth century A.D.; the devolution of property in pre-modern Muslim societies was largely determined by these complex and unwieldy rules.[8] Legal history had ceased to exist, only to resume in the

[4]Coulson, *History*, pp. 16, 23; *Succession*, p. 29.

[5]Coulson, *Succession*, p. 33.

[6]Coulson, *History*, p. 220; *Conflicts*, p. 97.

[7]Coulson, *History*, p. 220; *Conflicts*, pp. 37, 97; *Succession*, pp. 135-36. Coulson acknowledged that in many areas of the Muslim world (e.g. Kabylie Algeria, Sumatra, Western Nigeria, India, and Java), Muslims do not adhere to the Islamic law of inheritance. He viewed this phenomenon as the triumph of local customary law over the shari'a and explained the anomaly by drawing a distinction between Arab and non-Arab Muslim societies. Islamic inheritance law, he explained, was 'largely in accord with the innate temper of Arab society'. For non-Arab Muslims, however, the reception of Islamic inheritance law 'posed serious problems, for its basic concepts.were alien to the traditional structure of their societies.' See Coulson, *History*, pp. 135-37.

[8]Thus the task of the scholar interested in the devolution of property in pre-modern Muslim societies is seemingly limited to developing a better understanding of the specific details and many intricacies of the law of inheritance. Western legal historians such as Schacht and Coulson have therefore focused almost exclusively on legal rules, to the exclusion of social processes. Anthropologists, on the other hand, tend to emphasize social processes. See, for example, Thomas Gerholm, 'Aspects of Inheritance and Marriage Payment in North Yemen,'

twentieth century when unprecedented social and economic changes assaulted the contemporary Muslim world, resulting in the disintegration of the extended family and its replacement by the more immediate family circle of parents and children;[9] within that circle the woman plays an increasingly responsible role. Egypt, Iran, Iraq, Jordan, Morocco, Pakistan, the Sudan, Syria, and Tunisia have responded to these new and unprecedented circumstances by enacting personal status laws and codes that include major reforms in the area of inheritance. The social purpose of these reforms is to strengthen the inheritance rights of those relatives who form the nuclear, as opposed to, the tribal family.[10]

From the preceding summary, it would appear that Coulson adhered to the tradition of comparative law that views the evolution of legal systems as a reflection of man's social development from primitive to modern societies: in the former, the individual was entirely subordinate to the group; in the latter, he becomes the focus of legal rights and enjoys the freedom to enter into contracts with others.[11] Coulson's understanding of Islamic inheritance law rests upon the key assumption that inheritance rules are a faithful reflection of family structure and that changes in family structure manifest themselves in changes in inheritance rules.[12] Having made this assumption, Coulson must postulate a radical change in the structure of the family every time that he perceives a change in inheritance rules. This produces the following curious results: the extended family gave way to the nuclear family during the lifetime of the Prophet; the nuclear family was replaced by the extended family within a century after the Prophet's death, and the extended family gave way to the nuclear family in the twentieth century A.D. I find these radical shifts in the structure of the Muslim family unconvincing and difficult to accept. In what follows, I shall attempt to provide an alternative model for the socio-historical development of Islamic inheritance law.

I. Background to the Qur'anic legislation

The Distinction Between Nomads and Sedentary Arabs

Coulson portrays the Islamic law of inheritance as a unilinear extension of the so-called tribal customary law of pre-Islamic Arabia. His reconstruction of the tribal customary law, however, is highly problematic. The sources that he uses to reconstruct this law are relatively late and, furthermore, inherently

in Ann E. Mayer ed., *Property, Social Structure, and Law in the Modern Middle East*, Albany, New York, 1985, pp. 129-51, especially p. 135; Martha Mundy, 'Women's Inheritance of Land in Highland Yemen', *Arabian Studies*, 5, 1979, pp.161-188; 'The Family, Inheritance and Islam: a Re-examination of the Sociology of *Fara'id* Law', in Aziz Azmeh ed., *Islamic Law: Social and Historical Contexts*, London, 1988, pp. 1-123.

9Coulson, *Conflicts*, p. 114.

10*Ibid.*, pp. 37, 97-98; *Succession*, pp. 135-36.

11For an attempt to expose the historically conditioned assumptions upon which Coulson's view is based, see Mundy, 'Re-examination', pp. 3-23.

12Coulson, *Conflicts*, p.8; *Succession*, p.3.

biased against pre-Islamic practices.[13] Adopting an uncritical approach to these sources, Coulson makes a crucial assumption, namely, that the ʻasaba of Islamic law are a carry-over from the tribal customary law of pre-Islamic Arabia, and that the order of priorities according to which the ʻasaba inherit in Islamic law is identical to the order of priorities that prevailed prior to the revelation of the Qur'an. If this assumption is correct, then the devolution of property in pre-Islamic Arabia would have been governed by the principle of direct descent from father to son.

Coulson has ignored important evidence that points in a different direction. In 1950 Robert Brunschvig published an article in which he suggested that the order of priorities according to which the ʻasaba of pre-Islamic Arabia inherited was *not* identical to that of the Islamic ʻasaba. Rather, the devolution of property among nomads in pre-Islamic Arabia was likely to have been governed by the principle of seniority, as exemplified in the maxim, 'patronage belongs to the eldest' *(al-wala' lil-kubr).* Brunschvig speculated that a group of brothers in pre-Islamic Arabia formed a kind of fraternal corporation (*fratriarcat*). As individual members of the corporation died, their rights passed horizontally to their surviving brothers. Over time, property rights became concentrated in fewer and fewer hands, until, finally, the longest-lived brother acquired exclusive control over everything. When he died, the next generation assumed control, and the process repeated itself.[14] Although the details of Brunschvig's theory have recently been criticized by two scholars,[15] the general outlines of his argument find important confirmation in external historical, linguistic, and ethnographical considerations.[16]

Was the devolution of property in pre-Islamic Arabia governed by the principle of direct descent from father to son or by the principle of seniority? The dichotomy may be a false one. In my view, uncritical reliance upon Islamic sources has resulted in an oversimplified view of the legal situation in the Hijaz on the eve of Islam. These sources portray everything pre-Islamic in terms of tribal, nomadic society. It is reasonable to assume, however, that social organization in pre-Islamic Arabia included not only nomadic but also sedentary elements. Mecca and Medina were towns, the former a commercial

---

[13]On the historiographical background to Coulson's assumption, see William Robertson Smith, *Kinship and Marriage in Early Arabia*, Cambridge, 1885; reprinted London, 1903, pp. 65-66; W. Marçais, *Des Parents et Alliés Successibles en Droit Musulman*, Thesis, Rennes, 1898, p. 35; G.H. Bousquet and F. Peltier, *Les Successions Agnatiques Mitigées: Etude Comparée du Régime Successoral en Droit Germanique et en Droit Musulman*, Paris, 1935, pp. 99, 108-109. See now also M. Habibur Rahman, 'The Role of Pre-Islamic Customs in the Islamic Law of Succession', *Islamic and Comparative Law Quarterly*, 8:1, 1988, pp. 48-64.

[14]Robert Brunschvig, 'Un Système Peu Connu de Succession Agnatique dans le Droit Musulman', *Revue Historique de Droit Français et Etranger*, 27, 1950, pp. 23-34; reprinted in idem, *Etudes d'Islamologie*, Paris, 1976, vol. 2, pp. 53-64.

[15]See Mundy, 'Re-examination', pp. 39-40; Patricia Crone, *Roman, Provincial and Islamic Law: the Origins of the Islamic Patronate,* Cambridge, 1987, pp. 81-82.

[16]For details, see my *Studies in Qur'an and Hadith: The Formation of the Islamic Law of Inheritance,* Berkeley, 1986, pp. 91-92.

settlement and the latter an agricultural oasis. Coulson acknowledged this fact, but viewed the social customs of the sedentary Arabs as an extension of those of the nomadic Arabs. It is more likely, however, that there were *two* distinct systems of social organization and law, one for the nomadic Arabs and the other for sedentary ones. Among the former, property may have been collectively owned or controlled by the elders of the tribe, and its devolution governed by the principle of seniority; among the latter, property may have been owned by individuals, who had greater freedom to determine its ultimate devolution; further, women living in towns and settlements presumably had the right to own and inherit property. In other words, Coulson and Brunschvig may have been describing two different systems, both of which existed in pre-Islamic Arabia.[17]

It is difficult to determine exactly what the inheritance practices of the sedentary Arabs of the Hijaz were, for, as stated, the sources are unreliable and tend to emphasize nomadic law. We may perhaps circumvent the bias and reticence of the sources by viewing the issue against the background of contemporary Near Eastern provincial law, that is, Roman, Syro-Roman, Egyptian, Jewish, and Sassanian legal systems.[18] All of these legal systems drew a distinction between testate succession and intestacy. With regard to testate succession, the individual had freedom - within certain limits - to determine who his heirs would be and what they would inherit. As for intestacy, Egyptian, Syro-Roman, and Jewish law limited inheritance upon intestacy to blood relatives of the deceased arranged in a series of hierarchically related classes;[19] the first three classes, in order of priority, were children, parents, and siblings.[20] Further, all of these systems awarded shares of the estate to both males and females: Egyptian law awarded a double portion to the eldest son, while treating daughters and all younger sons on a basis of equality; according to Jewish law, the first son received a double share, while daughters inherited only in the absence of a son; in Sassanian law, a son's share was twice as large as a daughter's, and all sons were treated equally.[21] Is Near Eastern provincial law comparable to any system of law that prevailed in pre-Islamic Arabia ?

---

[17]See Mundy, 'Re-examination', p. 30. A similar situation prevailed in pre-Islamic Iran, where the small, individual family co-existed with the extended patriarchal family. See A. Perikhanian, 'Iranian Society and Law', in Ehsan Yarshater ed., *The Cambridge History of Iran*, Cambridge, 1983, vol. 3, pt. 2, pp. 627-680, esp. 641ff.

[18]The following discussion is based on Powers, *Studies*, p. 106, n.46.

[19]Sassanian law awarded the widow a share of her husband's estate, on the condition that she had been assimilated into the husband's agnatic group at the time of the marriage. Perikhanian, 'Iranian Society and Law', p. 648.

[20]See also Mundy, 'Re-examination', pp. 27-29.

[21]Perikhanian, 'Iranian Society and Law', p. 668.

II. The Qur'anic Legislation: Proto-Islamic Law

At this point I must advance a speculation that may facilitate our understanding of the formation of the Islamic law of inheritance. Elsewhere I have argued that there is a discontinuity in the historical record and that the process of formation took place in a manner radically different from that represented in classical Islamic sources. Specifically, I maintain that the traditional interpretation of the Qur'anic inheritance verses and certain prophetic *ahadith* is not identical to the originally intended significance of that legislation. By means of a literary-historical analysis of key Qur'anic verses and prophetic reports, I have attempted to reconstruct the system of inheritance in which the Qur'anic verses and prophetic ahadith were originally embedded, a system that I refer to as the 'proto-Islamic law of inheritance'. I regard the proto-Islamic law of inheritance as a hitherto unrecognized stage in the formation of the Islamic law of inheritance. Let us see how the postulation of its existence provides a different perspective on legal developments during the first century A.H.[22]

The essential features of the proto-Islamic law of inheritance may be summarized as follows: proto-Islamic law made a clear distinction between testate succession and intestacy. By means of a last will and testament, a person contemplating death could designate a testamentary heir and dispose of his or her property as he or she saw fit. The testator might designate a son, daughter, or other close relative as the testamentary heir, but was also free to designate an affine, such as a wife, or daughter-in-law; in the latter case, relatives who would have inherited in the absence of a will are awarded a fractional share of the estate, not to exceed one-third, as compensation for the disinheritance (Q. 4:12b).[23] In addition to designating an heir, the testator might also bequeath up to one-third of the estate (*al-wasiyya fi'th-thulth*)[24] to parents and/or other close relatives (Q. 2:180), as well as make provision for the maintenance of his wife (Q. 2:240). To be valid, a last will and testament had to be drawn up or dictated in the presence of two trustworthy witnesses (Q. 5:105-106). Tampering with the provisions of a last will and testament was discouraged (Q. 2:181), and disagreements over the provisions of a will

---

22Powers, *Studies,* pp. 21-109.

23*Ibid.*, pp. 43-44. I argue that the original intention of Q. 4:12b was to award a small fractional share of the estate to siblings who had been disinherited by their brother in favour of persons who were not related to the latter by ties of blood; that is, the verse imposed restrictions upon the capacity to bequeath, the underlying rationale being to protect the rights of members of the testator's family vis-à-vis persons outside of the family. Viewed in this manner Q. 4:12b displays a distinct resemblance to a reform of the Roman law of inheritance instituted by Justinian less than a century prior to the revelation of the Qur'an, and provides additional support for the contention that the Arabs of pre-conquest Arabia placed restrictions on the capacity to bequeath. See William G. Hammond, *An Introduction to Sandar's Institutes of Justinian*, Chicago, 1876, pp. 285-86.

24For an analysis of the authenticity and significance of the dictum, see my 'The Will of Sa'd b. Abi Waqqas: A Reassessment', *Studia Islamica,* 58, 1983, pp. 34-53; 'On Bequests in Early Islam', *Journal of Near Eastern Studies,* 48, 1989. For a different view of the origins of the one-third restriction, see Crone, *Roman, Provincial and Islamic Law,* pp. 91-96.

were to be referred to a third party for settlement (Q. 2:182).

In proto-Islamic law, the Qur'anic rules for the division of property took effect only in the absence of a valid last will and testament and were therefore rules of intestate succession, properly speaking. The general principles of the proto-Islamic law of intestacy may be summarized as follows: the right to inherit was limited to blood relatives of the deceased (Q. 4:7). Husbands and wives did not, under normal circumstances, inherit from one another. An exception to this rule was made in the case of a wife who had not been awarded a dowry by her husband at the time the marriage was concluded; this award was made reciprocal (Q. 4:12a). The Qur'an mentions three classes of heirs who inherited according to the following order of priorities: (1) lineal descendants; (2) lineal ascendants; (3) collaterals. The inheritance verses illustrate the application of these principles to specific cases. Finally, the proto-Islamic law of intestacy drew a distinction between primary heirs, who inherited between fifty and a hundred per cent of the estate, and secondary heirs, who inherited a maximum of one-third.[25]

The proto-Islamic law of inheritance can hardly be viewed as an extension of the customary inheritance practices of the nomadic Arabs of pre-Islamic Arabia, among whom property was collectively owned and devolved in accordance with the principle of seniority. Can it be seen as a manifestation of the inheritance practices of the sedentary Arabs of pre-Islamic Arabia? And does it perhaps represent a specifically Arabian version of the contemporary Near Eastern provincial law? In order to answer these questions, we need to determine what diagnostic features of the two systems should be compared. Crone has identified two key indices of possible Near Eastern provincial influence on pre-conquest Arabian law: (1) extensive familiarity with testamentary dispositions and (2) restrictions on the capacity to bequeath.[26] Near Eastern provincial law makes a clear distinction between testate succession and intestacy and places limitations on the capacity to bequeath.[27] The same holds true for proto-Islamic law. Several Qur'anic verses (2:180-182, 2:240, 4:11-12, and 5:105-06) attest to the Arabs' familiarity with testamentary dispositions prior to the conquest of the Near East.[28] One subverse, Q 4:12b, places limits on a testator's freedom to disinherit a close blood relative, and the prophetic dictum al-wasiyya fi'th-thulth limits bequests to one-third of an estate; the Qur'anic subverse and the prophetic hadith attest to the existence of restrictions on the right to bequeath in pre-conquest Arabia.

As for the law of intestacy, both proto-Islamic and Near Eastern provincial law arrange the intestate heirs into a series of hierarchically related classes and award the right to inherit to both males and females.[29] There are

25Powers, *Studies*, pp. 87-109.

26Crone, *Patronate*, p. 93; cf. Maine, *Ancient Law* , London, 1917, chapter 6.

27Crone, *Patronate*, p. 93.

28On Q 2:180-182, and 5:105-106 see above. Q 4:11-12 mention bequests four times.

29Compare Mundy, 'Re-examination', pp. 29-30.

differences too,[30] but the similarities outweigh them. Thus, the resemblances between proto-Islamic and Near Eastern provincial law in the areas of testate succession and intestacy are striking. The proto-Islamic law of inheritance should, in my view, be regarded as an Arabian variety of Near Eastern provincial law, existing alongside and in competition with Arabian tribal law.[31] The tension between tribal and proto-Islamic law manifested itself most directly in the rules for the devolution of property. According to the former, the devolution of property was governed by the principle of seniority, while in the latter, it was governed by the principle of direct descent from father to son. The new system of inheritance seems to have angered the proponents of nomadic customary law, whose resistance to the new principle may be reflected in the concluding line of Q. 4:12b, 'Your fathers and your sons, you know not which of them is closer to you in usefulness'.[32]

III. The Islamic Law of Inheritance

The proto-Islamic law of inheritance was shortlived, giving way almost immediately to the Islamic law of inheritance. This transformation resulted not from any change in the structure of the Arab family, but rather from a series of historical factors that emerged during the course of the first century A.H. First there was the problem of succession to Muhammad. The existence in the Qur'an of a mechanism for designating an heir may have been a source of embarrassment to the early leaders of the Muslim community. One of these leaders, or his representative, eliminated this mechanism by imposing a secondary reading (*qira'a*) upon the consonantal text of Q4:12b and by redefining the word *al-kalala* that occurs in that subverse. The elimination of the sole Qur'anic reference to the possibility of designating an heir, combined with a concomitant shift of emphasis from heirs to shares, led to the fusion of several subverses into a single unit that came to be known as 'the inheritance verses' (Q. 4:11, 4:12 and 4:176). In this manner, the proto-Islamic rules of intestacy were transformed into compulsory rules for the division of property, a shift that may have promoted social cohesion during the tumultuous period of the Arab conquests, when large numbers of Muslims were dying on distant battlefields and vast wealth was being funnelled into a small number of hands. Further, the identification of the Divinity as the source of these compulsory rules would have served to reinforce the emerging conception of the shari‘a as the manifestation of God's plan for mankind.[33]

Inevitably, there were some loose ends that had to be tied up. The reinterpretation of Q. 4:12b resulted in an awkward syntactical structure that proved difficult to explain away; it also created some tricky lexicographical

---

[30]Powers, *Studies*, p. 106, n.46.

[31]Compare Mundy, 'Re-examination', p. 99, n.117.

[32]Powers, *Studies*, pp. 102-106.

[33]For a discussion of the various hermeneutical devices that were employed to effect this transformation, see *ibid.*, pp. 212-216.

problems.[34] Further, Muslim legists found it difficult to account for the apparent discrepancy between the principle that 'a male is entitled to the share of two females', stated in Q. 4:11 and 4:176, and the fact that the mother and father in Q. 4:11 and the brother and sister in Q. 4:12 are awarded *equal* shares of the estate.[35] In addition, when working out the details of the Islamic law of inheritance, the legists encountered a number of problems that compelled them to deviate from the explicit working of the Qur'an.[36] These phenomena are easily explained as unintended by-products of the transformation from proto-Islamic to Islamic law.

A. The Islamic Inheritance System: Theory

Gifts *Inter Vivos*

The transformation from proto-Islamic to Islamic law took place so early and so quickly that it left virtually no trace in the historical sources, where the secondary stage of development has been made to appear as if it were the primary one. Ironically, changes that had their origin in *ad hoc* responses to the historical circumstances confronting the Muslim community in the years immediately following Muhammad's death acquired a fixed and immutable status. At least since the beginning of the second/ninth century, neither Qur'anic revelation nor prophetic sunna could be overtly modified to reflect changing circumstances. But circumstances continued to change. As the conquests came to an end, increasing numbers of Muslims - including many non-Arab converts to Islam (*mawali*) who had formerly followed Near Eastern provincial law - found themselves burdened by a system of inheritance that not only severely constrained the freedom of the individual to determine the ultimate devolution of his property, but also resulted in the inevitable fragmentation of property. The law of inheritance itself could not be reformed or modified, but, *pace* Coulson, that does not mean that legal history came to end. Rather, Muslim jurists (*fuqaha*) provided a simple but brilliant solution to the tension between the seeming inflexibility of Islamic inheritance law and the myriad needs and desires of individual Muslims. In order to appreciate this solution, it is necessary to examine categories of Islamic law that developed subsequent to the law of inheritance, specifically, the law of gift (*hiba*). It also will be helpful to invoke a distinction that social scientists have drawn between inheritance laws and inheritance systems: inheritance laws indicate who shares in the estate and how much he or she will inherit; the term 'inheritance system' refers to the combination of laws, customs, land tenure

---

[34]On these problems, see Tabari, *Jami' al-bayan 'an ta'wil ayat al-qur'an,* Cairo, 1954-68, vol. IV, pp. 283-286; Powers, *Studies*, pp. 22-29.

[35]The discrepancy disappears in proto-Islamic law, where the Qur'anic statement, 'a male is entitled to the share of two females', applies to primary, not secondary, heirs. See Powers, *Studies*, pp. 65, 102.

[36] Examples of such deviations are *'awl* (oversubscription of the estate) and the so-called *'Umariyyatan* (two cases settled by 'Umar b. al-Khattab). On these, see *ibid*., pp. 56-78.

rights and settlement restrictions that regulate the division of land at a succession.[37]

Islamic law defines a gift as 'a liberality by means of which the donor divests himself of the possession of a thing without the intention of receiving anything in return'.[38] The jurists taught that the rules of inheritance take effect upon property owned by the deceased only at the moment of death or at the time he enters his final death sickness. This distinction is crucial because it means that a proprietor is legally free to dispose of his property in any way he sees fit prior to his final death sickness. Islamic law places no limitations whatsoever upon the amount of property that a person may alienate during his lifetime, whether in favour of his eventual heirs or anyone else. Thus, a farsighted proprietor who wanted to exercise greater control over the transmission of property than is allowed by the Islamic inheritance law might begin transmitting property to the next generation as soon as he wishes, typically soon after marrying and producing offspring. The liberality of Islamic law in this regard contrasts sharply with that of other nearly contemporaneous Near Eastern legal systems.[39]

By making a gift, the donor effectively decreases the quantum of the estate that will be divided up among his legal heirs upon his death. A gift to a child, for example, constitutes a partial disinheritance of the donor's parents and spouse. Gifts therefore enable a proprietor to tip the balance of entitlement against his parents and spouse in favour of his children. The only restriction in this regard is that the donor may not favour one child over the other, a restriction that is attributed to the Prophet.[40]

There are certain drawbacks to a gift, most importantly, the fact that a proprietor is required to formally deliver the object of the gift to its recipient, and the recipient is required to formally take possession of it. Once the transfer occurs, the original proprietor is not free to revoke the gift. This would be particularly disadvantageous in the case of a dwelling in which the proprietor himself resided or in the case of a revenue-producing property over which he wished to continue exercising effective control. Furthermore, if the formality is not observed, upon the proprietor's death, the gift reverts as inheritable property to be divided up among his heirs. The donor's heirs therefore have an interest in demonstrating that the formality was not properly observed. The tension between donees and heirs is reflected in a

---

[37]On this distinction, see Lutz Berkner and Franklin Mendels, 'Inheritance Systems, Family Structure and Demographic Patterns in Western Europe, 1700-1900', in Charles Tilley ed., *Historical Studies of Changing Fertility,* Princeton, 1978, pp. 209-224, esp. 211-212; Mundy, 'Re-examination', p. 54.

[38]Edouard Sautayra and Eugène Cherbonneau, *Droit Musulman: du Statut Personnel et des Successions*, Paris, 1873-74, vol. 2, p. 28; see also J. Schacht, *An Introduction to Islamic Law,* Oxford, 1964, pp. 157-158.

[39]Mundy, 'Re-examination', p. 45.

[40]See Shaybani, *Muwatta' Malik*, ed. 'Abd al-Wahhab 'Abd al-Latif, Cairo, 1967, vol. 2, pp. 285-86, no. 807, where the Prophet tells one of his Companions to revoke a gift of a slave that he had given to his minor son because the donor had not given each of his children a similar gift.

story told about Abu Bakr, who had reportedly given his daughter, 'A'isha, some property in al-'Aliya. 'A'isha failed to take possession *(ihtaza)* of the property, and Abu Bakr therefore declared upon his deathbed that it must be divided up 'in accordance with the Book of God' among his heirs - 'A'isha, her brother, and her two sisters.[41] The gift seems to have been motivated, at least in part, by Abu Bakr's desire to circumvent the Islamic law of inheritance, a desire that was frustrated by his daughter's failure to observe the proper legal formalities. The story serves as a warning to other would-be donors.

In practice there were several ways in which a proprietor might avoid the inconvenience of relinquishing ownership and control of a gift. For example, an exception to the rule that the recipient had to take immediate possession was made in the case of a child who was a minor and therefore did not have the legal capacity to acquire possession. In a report attributed to 'Uthman b. 'Affan, we learn that a father may bestow a gift upon his minor child and take possession on behalf of that child. The father is merely required to make a public declaration of his intention to make the gift and to summon witnesses to attest to it.[42] In this manner, the father may continue to exercise effective control over the property after the gift had been made. Indeed, he might continue to exercise control over the property even after the child reaches the age of majority, for one of several reasons: because the child is unaware of the gift; because the child is unwilling to challenge the father for control over it; or because it is understood that the child will take control of the gift upon the father's death. This tendency is reflected in a report attributed to 'Umar b. al-Khattab, who reportedly asked, "Why is it that people give gifts to their sons and then hold on to them, so that, if one of [the sons] dies, [the father] says, 'It is my property, in my possession, and I did not give it to anyone'. If [the father] dies, he says, 'It belongs to my son, to whom I gave it [and not to father's other heirs]".[43]

Gifts Inter Vivos: Some Variations

Several variations of a simple gift (hiba) could also be used to circumvent the law of inheritance. A charitable gift (*sadaqa*) is a liberality made with the intention of pleasing God. Customarily made in favour of the poor members of the community or the donor's poor relatives, a charitable gift is subject to the rules for simple gifts (hibat), with the following special features: the donor must leave no doubt as to his intention to make a charitable gift - as opposed to a simple gift or family endowment; the object of the charitable gift may not return to the donor except as an inheritance; and any donation made in favour of orphans, the poor, or female relatives is treated as a sadaqa.[44] Another

---

[41]*Ibid.*, p. 286, no. 808. Al-'Aliya was a site in the vicinity of Medina. According to a variant version, the property was located in al-Ghaba, a site on the postal route from Medina to Syria.

[42]*Ibid.*, p. 285, no. 806; cf. no. 810.

[43]*Ibid.*, p. 286, no. 809.

[44]E. Amar, 'La Pierre de Touche Extraordinaire', *Archives Marocaines*, 13, 1908, pp. 407-8.

variation of the simple hiba is a life-gift (*'umra*), by means of which the donor confers upon the recipient the usufructory rights to the object of the gift. The recipient may not sell these rights to someone other than the donor or the latter's heirs. Otherwise, the life-gift is subject to the rules of gifts.[45] The relationship between charitable gifts and life-gifts, on the one hand, and inheritance, on the other, is reflected in early legal sources.[46]

The most important variation of a gift inter vivos was the family endowment (*waqf ahli*). Like a simple gift, a family endowment provided a proprietor with a legal means to remove all or part of the patrimony from the effects of the Islamic law of inheritance, and to reduce the quantum of property available as an inheritance for ascendants, collaterals and spouses. In addition, the creation of a family endowment enabled the proprietor to establish a lineal descent group with exclusive usufructory rights to the endowment revenues, and to define the descent strategy according to which these rights pass from one generation to the next - theoretically, in perpetuity. Thus, a family endowment provides a means of ensuring that property would remain intact throughout the generations.

The tension between family endowments and inheritance is clearly reflected in the early sources. Indeed, several early Muslim jurists were opposed to certain aspects of the endowment system.[47] Shurayh (d. between 695 and 717) opposed waqf insofar as it interfered with or modified the Islamic law of inheritance; he is reported to have said, *la habs 'an fara'id Allah* ('no endowment in circumvention of God's shares'). Abu Hanifa (d. 767), who objected to the inalienability of endowment property, considered waqf to be permissible, but not binding. These arguments were rejected by the majority of Muslim authorities. Shafi'i (d. 822) refuted Shurayh's position on the ground that family endowments, a type of gift inter vivos, do not constitute an evasion of the law of inheritance because the latter takes effect on property owned by the deceased at the time of his death or when he enters his final death sickness. Other legists refuted Abu Hanifa's position on the strength of the sunna of the Prophet. It is reported that 'Umar b. al-Khattab had approached Muhammad and asked him what he should do with property belonging to him in Khaybar; the Prophet responded, 'Sequester (*ihbas*) the capital and distribute the revenues'. This dictum is considered by the great majority of Muslim jurists to have established a precedent for the institution of religious endowments. But whatever the arguments for and against the institution, there can be no denying the fact that the overwhelming majority of Muslim jurists belonging to all four schools of law approved of the institution,

---

45 *Ibid.*, p. 414.

46 See, for example, 'Abd al-Razzaq as-San'ani, *al-Musannaf*, Karachi, 1970-72, vol. 9, pp. 117-135 (sadaqat); Shaybani, *Muwatta' Malik*, vol. 2, p. 287, nos. 811 and 812 ('umra).

47 See, for example Ahmad b. 'Amr ash-Shaybani, known as al-Khassaf, *Kitab ahkam al-awqaf*, Cairo, 1322/1904; Hilal b.Yahya al-Ra'y, *Kitab ahkam al-waqf,* Hyderabad, 1355/1936; Sahnun, *al-Mudawwana al-kubra li-imam Malik,* Cairo, 1323/1905, vol. 15, pp. 98-111; Shafi'i, *Kitab al-umm,* Cairo, 1321-26, pp. 274-83. See also Muhammad b. Ahmad as-Sarakhsi, *al-Mabsut,* Cairo, 1324-31, vol. 12, pp. 27-46.

which became an integral part of Islamic law.[48]

Gifts *Post Mortem*

Islamic law does not permit a testator to leave a bequest for any person who will inherit a share of the estate according to the prescriptive rules for the division of property, a restriction that is based upon the alleged prophetic dictum, 'No bequest to an heir' (*la wasiyya li-warith*).[49] Muslim jurists developed various techniques to circumvent this restriction. Since a grandchild is excluded from inheriting by the deceased's child, a legacy in favour of the former does not violate the restriction. A proprietor who wants to favour one of his children over the others may therefore make a bequest for the benefit of his minor grandchild, the child of the person he wants to favour. As a minor, the legatee's property would be administered by his father - the desired heir. If the proprietor did not have a grandchild at the time that he drew up his last will and testament, he may leave a legacy for 'the first child born to my son' or to 'all children who will be born to his son'; in this manner, the unborn child's father will gain control of the property upon the testator's death.[50]

B. The Islamic Inheritance System: Practice

The early jurists responded to the needs of Muslim proprietors by creating what I refer to as 'the Islamic inheritance system', that is, a comprehensive system for the devolution of property in which the rules of inheritance were subordinated to other categories of law. Once the general parameters of this system are understood, the focus of historical investigation necessarily shifts from rules of inheritance, strictly speaking, to social processes. On the basis of my study of pre-modern inheritance disputes, I can make the following preliminary observations: typically, several years before he died, the head of a family will transfer title to a house or apartment to his wife or daughters in the form of a gift; designate certain fields, orchards, gardens and other revenue-producing properties as an endowment for a lineal descent group; and make other alienations of property so that little or none of the immovable property that he has accumulated over the course of a lifetime will be subject to the effects of the law of inheritance when he dies. Such

---

[48]At the end of the nineteenth and beginning of the twentieth century, French orientalists and British judges argued that family endowments were illegal from an Islamic perspective. Their arguments betray a profound misunderstanding of the historical development of Islamic law and a willingness to manipulate the historical record for political purposes. See David S. Powers, 'Orientalism, Colonialism, and Legal History: The Attack on Family Endowments in Algeria and India', *Comparative Studies in Society and History*, 31, 1989, pp. 131-171; Bernard S. Cohen, 'Law and the Colonial State in India', in June Starr and Jane Collier eds., *History and Power in the Study of Law*, Ithaca, 1989, pp. 131-152. See also Michael Anderson's contribution to this volume.

[49]For an analysis of the authenticity of this dictum, see Powers, *Studies*, pp. 158-72.

[50]Sautayra and Cherbonneau, *Droit Musulman*, 2:326-327.

decisions presumably are based upon many considerations, including individual need, personal sympathy, and regard for social and business relationships.

I maintain that the Islamic inheritance system functioned throughout the Muslim world for over a thousand years, from the ninth to the nineteenth centuries A.D. In order to substantiate this contention, I have chosen some representative examples from Ahmad al-Wansharisi's *Kitab al-Mi'yar*, a collection of *fatwas* (judicial opinions) issued in Spain, Morocco, and Tunis between the tenth and fifteenth centuries A.D.[51]

Gifts Inter Vivos

We read in a fatwa issued in the fourteenth century of a man who gave all of his property as a gift to his son *(wahaba lahu jami'a mulkihi fi hayatihi)*; subsequently, he acquired some additional property and designated it as a gift for an unrelated third party. The donor's son tried to recover the property that had been given to the non-relative.[52] In another, nearly contemporaneous case, a woman gave her brother a gift of some property that she owned; the brother accepted the gift and exercised control over it for many years. Shortly before he died, the brother issued a formal acknowledgment *(iqrar)* in which he stated that his sister had *not* given him the property in question as a gift, but had merely nominated him as the administrator of the property; if this were the case, the property would still be owned by his sister. When the brother died, the sister invoked this acknowledgment in an unsuccessful attempt to prevent the property from passing as an inheritance to her brother's children.[53]

A donor might attempt to exercise control over the subsequent devolution of a gift by imposing certain stipulations on the donee. A woman made a gift to her two daughters and stipulated that the share of the first daughter who died would revert to the other. When one of the daughters died, the latter's heirs tried to prevent the implementation of the stipulation. The case was referred to a *mufti* who noted that the donor's stipulation had the effect of concentrating the bulk of her estate in the hands of only one of her heirs, the surviving sister, thereby preventing the deceased sister's other heirs from taking the full amount of the estate to which they otherwise would have been entitled. Yet, the mufti reluctantly upheld the validity of the stipulation.[54]

The rule requiring the donor to leave his house and not return to it for a year might create a conflict between his long-term goal of arranging for the devolution of the property and his own short-term needs. In one case, a donor managed to harmonize these two conflicting interests by limiting the gift to a certain fractional portion of the house. The one-year rule therefore applied

---

51 Ahmad al-Wansharisi, *Kitab al-mi'yar al-mughrib wal-jami' al-mu'rib 'an fatawi ahl ifriqiya wal-andalus wal-maghrib*, 13 vols., Rabat, 1981-83.

52 *Ibid.*, 5:157 (fatwa of al-Yalisuti); compare *ibid.*, pp. 149-50.

53 Ibid., 5:150 (fatwa of al-Yalisuti).

54 *Ibid.*, 9:127-28.

only to the fractional share of the house that had been designated as a gift, and the donor was able to continue living in the house together with the donee without invalidating the donation.[55] In another, similar case, a man living in Cordova in the twelfth century reserved for himself ten per cent of the revenues of some property that he had given to his daughters as a charitable donation. The property was divided among the children, and ten per cent of each child's share was reserved for the father.[56]

A gift inter vivos would frequently become the subject of a dispute between the donee or donees, on the one hand, and the donor's other heirs, on the other. The latter could not contest the gift on the ground that it circumvented the Islamic law of inheritance, but they might contest it on the ground of an irregularity in its establishment. In fifteenth century Spain, a man purchased a dwelling in his own name, but paid for it with revenues of property that he had previously assigned as a charitable gift to his four minor daughters. The man paid for the house in several instalments; after paying the last instalment, he summoned witnesses to attest to the fact that he had purchased the dwelling on behalf of his four daughters. When the man died, his sister sought to have the dwelling included as part of her brother's estate on the ground that he had continued to live in the house until the day he died; thus, she claimed, the formal requirement of transfer (*hiyaza*) had not been properly observed. The mufti to whom the case was referred opined that if the father had taken possession of the dwelling on behalf of his daughters, then hiyaza had in fact taken place. It is interesting to note that the mufti concluded his fatwa by rebuking the woman for jeopardizing relations with her four nieces for the sake of an insignificant share of the estate.[57]

Another way to resolve the tension between a proprietor's short- and long-term interests was by means of a combination of a charitable gift and a life-gift (‘umra). In a case that occurred in twelfth century Spain, two close relatives, one male and the other female, held a pasture in joint-ownership. The female gave her half of the pasture to the male as a charitable gift. One year later, after transfer (hiyaza) of the sadaqa had become legally effective, the man designated the same share of the pasture as a life-gift for his female relative. As a result of these two transactions, the male now *owned* both shares of the pasture, which would pass to his heirs when he died, while the female was entitled to the usufruct of half of the pasture for the remainder of her life. This example also demonstrates how males might apply pressure on females to relinquish their property rights.[58]

A previously unmentioned method of circumventing the effects of the law of inheritance is the fictitious sale. We read, for example, of a paternal grand–mother who sold one-fourth of her estate for an unspecified but artificially

55*Ibid.*, 9:167 (fatwa of Ibn Lubaba).

56*Ibid.*, 9:167 (fatwa of Ibn al-Hajj).

57*Ibid.*, 5:38-39 (fatwa of al-Mawwaq).

58*Ibid.*, 9:166 (fatwa of Ibn al-Hajj). For a similar case, see *ibid.*, 9:146, where Ibn Zarb nullifies the arrangements because the original donee failed to wait one year before assigning a house as a life-gift for the original donor.

low price to her granddaughter's prospective husband; the sale was made on the condition that the man immediately transfer the property to his fiancée as her bride-price. At the same time, the grandmother provided the girl with a dowry by giving her one-fourth of her estate as a gift. By means of these two separate but simultaneous transactions, the grandmother had transferred half of her estate to her granddaughter and had effectively disinherited her own son (the bride's father) and daughter. The grandmother died one year after the marriage had been arranged, but before it was consummated. Upon her death, all of the interested parties became involved in litigation.[59]

The family endowment, a type of gift inter vivos, was used extensively by Muslim proprietors in pre-modern times.[60] One example may suffice. In the late thirteenth or early fourteenth century A.D., a certain Abu al-Qasim b. Bashir designated a garden outside of the Iron Gate of Fez as an endowment for the use of his son, Abu Muhammad ‘Abdallah and the latter's descendants, 'so long as they proliferate and their branches extend'. Six generations and over a hundred years later the endowment was still functioning according to the terms stipulated by the founder - despite challenges from persons outside the lineal descent group and contention among members of the descent group itself. The creation of a family endowment clearly provided the founder with a means of ensuring that his property would remain intact for generations after his death.[61]

Gifts Post Mortem

A proprietor who wants to favour one of his children over the others may leave a bequest for the benefit of his minor grandchild; if he does not have a grandchild at the time that he draws up his last will and testament, he may leave a bequest in favour of an as yet unborn grandchild. In either case, the proprietor's child, that is, the desired heir, would exercise effective control over the property when the legacy took effect.[62] We read, for example, of a case in which the testator bequeathed one-third of his property to the future offspring of his three sons, stipulating that his three sons should administer the property until such time as children were born to them or the sons despaired of leaving any issue.[63] Such an arrangement was likely to be

59 *Ibid.*, 8:102, cf. Sautayra and Cherbonneau, *Droit Musulman*, 2:23.

60 Estimates of the percentage of land that had been designated as public and private endowments in the various regions of the Ottoman Empire in the nineteenth century range from one-fifth to two-thirds of all landed property. See Fuad Köprülü, 'L'Institution du *Vakouf*: Sa Nature Juridique et son Évolution Historique', *Vakiflar Dergisi,* 2, 1942, p. 3 *(partie française)*; Gabriel Baer, *Studies on the Social History of Modern Egypt*, Chicago, 1969, p. 79.

61 Wansharisi, *Mi‘yar,* 7:486-514. For an analysis of this case, see my 'A Court Case from Fourteenth-Century North Africa', forthcoming in the *Journal of the American Oriental Society*, 110, 1990.

62 Wansharisi, *Mi‘yar*, 9:362 (fatwa of Ibn Abi Dunya); Sautayra and Cherbonneau, *Droit Musulman*, 2:326-27.

63 Wansharisi, *Mi‘yar,* 9:360 (fatwa of Abu ‘Abdallah b. Ziyadatallah).

contested by the testator's other heirs.

The notaries who drafted and served as witnesses to a last will and testament might play a crucial role in mediating between legal theory and practice. A woman on her deathbed summoned two notary-witnesses to attest to her last will and testament. She informed them that she wanted to leave one-third of her estate as a bequest for two of her daughters, Maryam and 'A'isha, to the exclusion of a third daughter, Maymuna, who allegedly detested her mother. The two notaries explained that such a stipulation violated the rule, 'no bequest in favour of an heir' (in this case, two heirs), and therefore would require Maymuna's consent to be valid. At this, the woman inquired, 'And if the bequest were for Maryam's and 'A'isha's *children*?' Such a stipulation, the witnesses indicated, would be permissible. The document was therefore drawn up in accordance with the woman's wishes. When the testator died, Maymuna unsuccessfully challenged the will on the ground that her mother had deprived her of her lawful share of the estate.[64]

As mentioned, one drawback of a family endowment that was created inter vivos was that the founder had to immediately relinquish control of the property. A person could avoid this inconvenience by creating a testamentary endowment that would become effective only upon his death; such an endowment, however, could not exceed one-third of his assets. Such an instrument was created in the year 791/1389 by a certain Fatima az-Zarhuni and her son, Abu Zayd 'Abd al-Rahman b. Khanusa. In a joint last will and testament, these two stipulated that 'one-third of their entire estate' was to be given to 'the first child born alive to the two children, 'A'isha and Muhammad, of the aforementioned 'Abd al-Rahman'. Subsequently, the bequest was to function as an endowment for the descendants of the first unborn child. A generation later, in the year 826/1422, one of Abu Zayd's agnatic relatives who was not a member of the lineal descent group initiated a lawsuit in an effort to acquire control of the endowment property.[65]

IV. Conclusion

I maintain that the Islamic inheritance system functioned throughout the Muslim world between the ninth century and the middle of the nineteenth century.[66] Its essential features were described by orientalist scholars writing betwen the end of the eighteenth and beginning of the twentieth centuries. Referring to the various modes for the transmission of property (inheritance, family endowments, donations, and testamentary dispositions) used by families in Istanbul, the eighteenth century orientalist D'Ohsson noted the flexibility of

---

[64] *Ibid.*, 9:367-68 (fatwa of Abu al-Hasan as-Saghir).

[65] *Ibid.*, 7:311-21. I am currently preparing an analysis of this case.

[66] It would perhaps be more accurate to speak of Islamic inheritance systems, in the plural. As Mundy, 'Re-examination', p. 54, notes, the Islamic inheritance system should be studied in the context of the differing political economies that have characterized Islamic society throughout its history.

the Islamic inheritance system.[67] In a treatise on Islamic law published in 1873-74, the French orientalists Edouard Sautayra and Eugene Cherbonneau concluded that the Islamic law of inheritance was rarely applied to immovable property and that the division of such property was normally carried out in accordance with the rules for family endowments; they reached this conclusion on the basis of their examination of estate inventories.[68] Similarly, Michel-Farès Boulos remarked in 1925 that 'one has only to consult the registers in which the transmission of property upon death are recorded in order to verify the almost total absence of the application of these complicated rules (viz., the Islamic law of inheritance).'[69] A decade later, G. H. Bousquet acknowledged the great practical importance of family endowments as a legal means of circumventing the law of inheritance.[70]

Beginning in approximately 1930, knowledge of the Islamic inheritance system seems to have dissipated. Although the reasons for this epistemological shift lie outside the scope of the present essay, two contributing factors may be mentioned. First, during the period of European colonial expansion, the scope of Islamic law was progressively reduced to the domain of family law (marriage, divorce, and inheritance), and colonial jurists and administrators considered themselves bound to faithfully apply the Islamic inheritance rules; they did not, however, view it as their obligation to apply other aspects of the Islamic inheritance system. Second, during the course of the nineteenth century, the system of family endowments was subjected to widespread attack. From Algeria to India, family endowments came to be viewed as an obstacle to the economic welfare and social progress of Muslim societies. Inspired by Western theories, advocates of reform marshaled economic, moral, religious and legal objections to family endowments, which were allegedly responsible for retarding socio-economic development by sequestering large quantities of a nation's capital resources. Colonial governments passed legislation intended to dismantle the institution; they received important assistance from European orientalists, who discovered that one of the best ways to justify an attack on family endowments was to discredit the institution in the eyes of Muslims themselves. These scholar-administrators propagated a negative, hostile attitude toward family endowments that came to pervade the subsequent scholarly literature. These two inter-related phenomena may provide a partial explanation for the fact that contemporary legal historians recognize Islamic inheritance law, but are largely unaware of the Islamic inheritance system.[71]

---

[67]Ignatius Mouradgea D'Ohsson, *Tableau Général de l'Empire Ottoman,* Paris, 1787-1820; cited in Mundy, 'Re-examination', p. 6.

[68]Sautayra and Cherbonneau, *Droit Musulman,* vol. 2, pp. 213, 220, 347, 399.

[69]Michel-Farès Boulos, *La Succession en Droit Musulman: son Origine et son Évolution,* Paris, 1925, p. 12.

[70]Bousquet and Peltier, *Successions*, pp. 145-150.

[71]For a more detailed analysis of this phenomenon, see my 'Orientalism, Colonialism, and Legal History'; see also Tahir Mahmood, 'Islamic Family Waqf in Twentieth Century Legislation: A Comparative Perspective', *Islamic and Conmparative Law Quarterly*, 8:1, 1988, pp. 1-20.

As historians, we must not allow contemporary realities to cloud our vision of the past. In pre-modern times, the application of the Islamic law of inheritance was often the last and least important stage in the process of transmitting property from one generation to the next. By paying greater attention to inheritance as a social process, we will gain a better understanding of the social dynamics of pre-modern Muslim societies.

3. A COMPARATIVE APPROACH TO THE TREATMENT OF NON-MUSLIM MINORITIES IN THE MIDDLE EAST, WITH SPECIAL REFERENCE TO EGYPT

Ian Edge

Introduction

Recent calls for the amendment of the English law of blasphemy[1] to protect the religious feelings of non-Christian ethnic minorities in England have given rise to debate concerning the treatment accorded to religious minorities in England. England has a single national set of courts which purport to act on the basis of the equality of its citizens before the law. In fact, recent acts of Parliament[2] have made it an offence to discriminate against portions of the population on certain grounds such as race, sex, colour and ethnic origin. However, certain unusual corners of English law still contain provisions redolent of the nineteenth century, such as blasphemous libel in which only the religious feelings of the Christian majority are protected.

The last fifty years has seen considerable demographic change in regard to the number and variety of non-Christian citizens in Britain. The independence granted to former Imperial possessions has been the main impetus behind this change although successive Nationality and Immigration Acts have gradually reduced the possibilities for inhabitants of former British colonies to come to Britain and make it their home. However, there are now an estimated 3 million non-Christian members of minority religions and communities in Britain; of which 1-2 million are Muslim.[3] Many of these non-English communities have very different religious and traditional practices and customs and the extent to which the law allows them to be practised gives

---

[1]The publication of Salman Ruhdie's novel *The Satanic Verses*, which is considered by many Muslims as insulting to the Prophet and blasphemous against Islam, cannot found proceedings for blasphemous libel, since that offence only serves to protect the Christian religion against blasphemous attacks: see *R v. Lemon* [1979] AC 617. This view has now been accepted in the High Court: see *R. v. Bow Street Magistrates Court, ex parte Choudhury, Times* 9/4/1990. Furthermore the publishers, Penguin books, were held not to have committed an offence against the Public Order Act 1986; see *R v. Richmond Magistrates Court, ex parte White* (unreported 22/3/89; available on Lexis), and *R. v. Horseferry Road Justices, ex parte Siadatan, Times* 11/4/1990.

[2]See Race Relations Act 1976 and Sexual Discrimination Act 1975.

[3]For these statistics, and generally, see S. Poulter, *English Law and Ethnic Minority Customs*, London, 1986.

rise to tension, as to forego these practices may be considered by some as tantamount to destruction of cultural identity.

English law, in the main, permits religious practices and customs where there is no conflict with the existing law; it recognises foreign rules and customs where applicable according to the rules of conflict of laws, but has only rarely allowed ethnic minority customs to permeate and alter the actual framework of the law itself. Of course, some minor historical anomalies exist, such as the privileges enjoyed by Quakers and Jews in terms of their religious practice and marriage, but these are throwbacks to the liberalism of the eighteenth and nineteenth centuries and there have been few modern analogies or extensions.[4]

The result is that for almost all of multi-cultural Britain, marriages must be celebrated, divorces sought, religious observance manifested, children educated and places of worship constructed within the bounds of an English legal regime applicable to all.

In recent years, there have been some calls for the application of ethnic minority law to minorities in Britain, particularly Islamic law to Muslims, either in separate courts or by Islamic experts attached to the present court structure. None of these has so far elicited anything other than curt rejections from the government of the day, if they were acknowledged at all. However, the ethnic minorities in Britain are fairly well served by the general law. The law of blasphemy admittedly protects only Christians, but it is an archaic offence which was recommended for abolition by the Law Commission in 1979, on the grounds that there were sufficient legal alternatives to protect insults against a person through his faith, particularly by way of the Public Order Act 1986.[5]

Many Muslim writers in the wake of the Rushdie affair wrote that English law was being unfair to Muslims in not taking further cognisance of the application of Islamic law to them and their affairs. One legal aspect of this is the question of reciprocity. In the conflict of laws some countries consider that the recognition and application of foreign law to local minorities should only occur if it is reciprocated in the treatment of minorities in foreign countries.[6] It is the contention of this article that the present treatment of minorities in England often surpasses the treatment of minorities in most foreign countries, particularly those of the Middle East, so that no real reciprocity of treatment exists. To consider separate treatment in separate

---

[4]See Poulter, *English Law and Ethnic Minority Customs,* pp. 34-39.

[5]Law Com. Working Paper No. 79.

[6]See the US Supreme Court case of *Hilton v. Guyot* (1895) 159 US 113 for a classical exposition of the reciprocity theory. It never took root in England, but has been adopted in a limited way by certain statutes as the basis for the recognition and enforcement of foreign judgements; see Administration of Justice Act 1920 and Foreign Judgements (Reciprocal Enforcement) Act 1933. Prior to the Recognition of Divorces and Legal Separations Act 1972, English law had to some extent used reciprocity as a basis for the recognition of foreign divorces; see *Travers v. Holley* [1953] p. 246. See now ss.46-54 Family Law Act 1986 in which reciprocity plays no part in the recognition of foreign divorces.

courts is to return to the worst of the nineteenth century legal babel that in fact existed in the Middle East.[7] This is not to say that minorities in England do not have grounds for grievance over certain inconsistencies that exist in English law, although the system purports to treat everyone equally. To call for separate courts or the enforcement of Islamic law (other than by consent) is however misguided and could result in curious anomalies and problems for the courts in conflict of laws cases.

An attempt to cover the treatment of religious minorities in all Muslim countries would be a vast undertaking. Consideration will therefore be confined in the main to one country, Egypt. This is chosen for a variety of reasons. First, Egypt has a large, vocal Christian minority (the Copts) and its past and present treatment of them typifies in many ways the treatment accorded to minorities in the different ages of Islam. The presence of the Copts forced Egypt to find solutions to problems which did not always arise elsewhere. Second, Egypt is recognised as a cultural centre of the Middle East and what happens there is often followed and, certainly, considered by other Arab states. Third, there is available written material on the treatment of minorities in Egypt in practically every age up to the modern day.

First, however, I will consider the position of minorities in classical Islamic law and then assess how this has been applied in practice.

What is Islamic Law?[8]

Islamic law (the *shari'a*) is that law which governs adherents of the Muslim religion. Theoretically it provides rules to cover all aspects of a person's life, within a complete moral and ethical code of conduct. All Muslims are subject to it and, in theory at least, it is a single unified system.

This ideal state has never existed in practice. After the Prophet Muhammad's death in 632 A.D., political constraints soon caused the Islamic community to splinter with the eventual result that each political community often developed its own interpretation of the law. The Qur'an acts as an important unifying document, but is neither comprehensive enough, nor specific enough in legal matters to provide more than the most rudimentary legal foundations of the faith. The *sunna*, the traditional stories of the Prophet's life, originally oral and passed from narrator to narrator until collected and written down, beginning in the eighth and ninth century A.D., make up perhaps the most important written source. However, it also suffers certain inadequacies, such as a lack of organisation and internal inconsistency, vagueness, indirectness and (in some cases) obvious forgery.

The system of law as we know it was in essence therefore worked out by medieval jurists using certain techniques, such as logic and analogy and rational reasoning and consensus. The evident divergences this produced were

---

[7]See J. Brinton, *The Mixed Courts of Egypt,* New Haven, 1968.
[8]See generally J. Schacht, *An Introduction to Islamic Law,* Oxford, 1964.

explained away in the purported hadith: '*ikhtilaf* (divergence of opinion) is a sign of the bounty of God'.

By the ninth century A.D. numerous schools of law existed and it was left to the jurist ash-Shafi'i (d. 820 A.D.) in his writings on the science of jurisprudence to prevent the total disintegration of Islamic law into many widely differing schools, by proposing a scheme of sources of law (*usul al-fiqh*) which by and large all the orthodox Sunni schools adopted. Henceforward, four Sunni schools established themselves as pre-eminent - the Hanafi, Maliki, Shafi'i and Hanbali schools- and different areas of the Muslim world gradually adopted one of the schools or became associated with it.[9]

The Shi'i adherents of the fourth Caliph, 'Ali, follow an altogether different pattern of development which for a long time was considered heterodox. This results in deep rooted differences between Shi'i and Sunni to this day.

The adoption of al-Shafi'is thesis resulted in the condemnation of innovation as a method of development of Islamic law, which eventually led to its total demise. Later jurists (with a few famous exceptions) were limited to imitation *(taqlid)* and not innovation (*ijtihad*). This was the state of affairs until the nineteenth century, when as a result of European colonial expansion and commercial exploitation Islamic law seemed to retreat in the face of western law, in all but the hinterlands of the Middle East. In some countries this caused the wholesale abandonment of Islamic law (e.g. Turkey in 1926). In the majority of countries, it resulted in the truncation of the jurisdictional areas of operation of Islamic law. Particularly in civil, commercial, constitutional and administrative law (where Islamic law was either non-existent or considered unsuitable to the modern environment) Islamic law was totally replaced. In criminal law there were wider variations. The result was that almost no country was unaffected by the import of western law and in no present day state is the Islamic law of the medieval jurists applied without any modification. Even in the area of family law almost every country has now produced codes or reforms of the medieval law.[10]

It is therefore impossible to speak of Islamic law as a single system of law. There are as many modern expressions of Islamic law as there are states in the Muslim world. Islamic law remains the core and focal point and common law of Muslim countries; but in practice Islamic law in Egypt differs from that in Pakistan which both differ from that in Malaysia and so on. This state of affairs has existed for centuries, although differences are perhaps more marked today after the widely differing political attitudes to Islamic law, its role and its reform. Some fundamental concepts will be the same. In general terms the same institutions will be found, but in detail and in operation the systems will be quite distinctly different.

---

[9]See N. Coulson, *A History of Islamic Law,* Edinburgh, 1964, Chapter 4.

[10]See the laws and materials in H. Liebesny, *The Law of the Near and Middle East,* New York, 1975.

Of course there are many movements for unification, but so far they have had little success.[11] Some Islamic theoreticians claim that unification could be achieved by adopting the Qur'an and the sunna as law. Such an approach is simplistic, misguided and dangerous - although it has a great pull with believing Muslims. By rejecting what the medieval jurists said as casuistic or even wrong the Islamic legal system itself is rejected.

There is no uniformly accepted corpus of sunna - each school reveres different collections - although the six books that make the Sunni canon are generally accepted as authentic.

Further, the material in the Qur'an and the sunna is still wholly inadequate to answer in itself all the legal problems of a modern society. (This may also be said of the medieval texts, but they at least provide a systematic approach, with recognised channels for development by analogy). Hence, interpretation is needed and in the absence of the medieval interpretations this gives immense power to the modern religious jurist. It is paradoxical that those who most condemn modern reforms or changes in Islamic law are often the most vehement supporters of a system based only on the Qur'an and the sunna, which would give extensive powers of interpretation (and mainly therefore *re*-interpretation) to modern jurists and religious leaders. The paradox becomes tragic when the modern interpretations are narrower and more illiberal than the established texts of the medieval jurists, leading to solutions which would probably have horrified a medieval Islamic jurist.[12]

Who is a Muslim?

A Muslim is anyone who professes the religion of Islam, who accepts the basic tenets of its faith, and performs the five pillars (*arkan al-islam*) of the religion; the *shahadatayn* (the two testimonies on the existence of God and the Prophethood of Muhammad), prayer, fasting in the month of Ramadan, the *zakat* (charitable tax) and the *hajj* (the pilgrimage to Mecca at least once in one's lifetime). Conversion to Islam is a relatively simple matter, involving the learning of the prayers (to be said five times a day) and some counselling about the faith, which then culminates in a simple ceremony, in which the convert recites a certain formula (known as the *shahada*) before witnesses.

---

[11] The Arab League and the Islamic Conference Organisation have both made attempts on codification. The most recent has been the Draft Code of Personal Status produced by the Council of Arab Ministers of Justice. For the text see the journal of the Society of United Arab Lawyers in Egypt, Volume 4, n.d. [1986 ?], pp.12-55. A translation is appendixed to J. Nasir, *The Islamic Law of Personal Status,* London, 1986.

[12] See the application in Pakistan of the Offence of Zina Ordinance 1979, e.g. the case of *Safia Bibi v. The State* (1985) 37 PLD (FSC) 120-126 where a blind girl raped by her landlord was convicted under the ordinance by a session court judge of zina (on the evidence of her pregnancy while unmarried) and sentenced to fine, whipping and imprisonment. The Federal Shariat Court, looking at standard shari‘a texts, reversed the decision and quashed the conviction.

The shahada includes the words *'la ilaha illa allah wa Muhammad rasul Allah'*, (the shahadatayn of the arkan) which means 'there is no God but God and Muhammad is his prophet'. Generally this recital will be before or in the presence of a religious leader (an *imam*) who is then authorised to issue a certificate (*ishhad*) that evidences the conversion. Conversion to Islam is considered a lifelong obligation and apostacy from Islam carries severe penalties in traditional Islamic law, as well as censure and obloquy in the present day.

A person may also be a Muslim by birth. A child is Muslim by birth if his or her father is a Muslim. As Islamic law does not allow marriage between a Muslim woman and a non-Muslim man then a Muslim mother will necessarily have a Muslim husband. Where, however, a Muslim father has a non-Muslim wife (as is permitted) then the children will be considered as following the father's religion. A Muslim woman who wants to marry a non-Muslim man will either cause him to convert to Islam (whence any children will be Muslim) or will herself convert from Islam to a non-Muslim faith. This latter possibility is fraught with problems and has serious consequences in an Islamic society. One modern solution is to marry in a civil, non-religious ceremony in a non-Muslim country. There has been some controversy as to the validity and enforceability of such a marriage, but some countries now accept it as valid.

Islam, however, is composed of many sects and factions with slightly different beliefs. The question of orthodoxy and how far certain beliefs are incompatible with the arkan and shahadatayn so as to transgress into the realm of the heterodox is moot. There is no effective primal authority to decide and hence each community must decide for itself. For a long time the Shi'is were regarded as a heterodox sect, but since Shi'ism was adopted by the Persian Safavid dynasty as its official doctrine, it has gained acceptance as the fifth school of law. Some smaller heterodox sects have died out, others exist in small pockets, and some modern sects consider themselves Muslims even though the majority of Muslims would not so accept them. These sects accept the arkan and shahadatayn, but either reinterpret parts of it, or accept beliefs inconsistent with them.

I will now consider some of the more important heterodox groups.

The Zahiris

This was an early school of law, now extinct, whose conservative views on the interpretations to be put on the Qur'an and the Sunna caused them to be considered as a heterodox school.[13]

---

[13] See 'Zahiris', in *Encyclopaedia of Islam I and II*.

The Khawarij

This was the umbrella term given to a group of early Muslims who claimed that anyone could lead the Muslim community and who proposed a rudimentary form of democracy. Needless to say they were condemned as heterodox and wars were fought against them. The Ibadis of Oman and Yemen are remnants of this movement, but are now certainly considered to be Muslims.[14]

The Druze

This sect reveres the Egyptian Fatimid caliph, al-Hakim, who disappeared in 1021 A.D.. It is named after Darazi, al-Hakim's minister, who after the caliph's disappearance journeyed to what is present day Palestine/Lebanon and was instrumental in founding this sect. Their rituals have elements taken from a number of religions. As they were persecuted they developed a doctrine of assimilation in which it was permitted to sham the rituals of another faith rather than be persecuted or possibly hounded to death. Their heterodoxy lies in the fact that they revere al-Hakim almost to idolatry. He is considered a prophet who is the equal of, if not greater than, the Prophet Muhammad and it is for this reason that they are generally not considered as an Islamic group by mainstream Islam.[15]

For Muslims the words *khatim al-anbiya'* (literally 'the seal of the prophets') refers to the finality of prophethood that Muhammad brought. Muhammad was the last in a line of prophets stretching back to Adam and Noah, through Moses and Abraham to Jesus Christ. He will come again, but only at the Day of Judgement. Some faiths (the Druze amongst them) interpret this phrase differently without the sense of complete finality and they accept the coming of another prophet (the *mahdi*) before the Day of Judgement.

Two sects clearly rejected by mainstream Islam, but who consider themselves to be Islamic, following prophets that they claim came after the Prophet Muhammad, are the Baha'is and the Qadianis (or Ahmediyya).

Babism and Bahaism

These sects follow two nineteenth century figures: Sayyid Ali Muhammed, known as the Bab (d.1850), and Mirza Husayn Ali Baba, known as Baha'ullah (d. 1892), the former of whom is buried in Haifa, Israel. Both claimed to be new prophets and successors to the Prophet Muhammad. Baha'ullah produced many writings including a set of new laws and

---

[14]See 'Khawarij', in *Encyclopaedia of Islam I and II*.

[15]See A. Layish, *Marriage, Divorce and Succession in the Druze Family*, Leiden, 1982.

principles.[16] The sects existed until recent times in large numbers in Iran, but since the advent of the Islamic Revolution in 1979, they have been condemned as non-Muslim heterodox groups and enemies of the state and been subjected to harsh persecution. The United Arab Republic of Egypt and Syria in 1960 proscribed their activities and sequestrated their properties.[17]

The Qadianis/Ahmediyya

This sect, mainly based in Pakistan and India, follows and reveres a late nineteenth century figure, Mirza Ghulam Ahmed, a resident of the city of Qadian in Punjab, Pakistan. They are called after him and after the place of his first teaching. He too produced many writings and claimed to be the successor to the Prophet Muhammad, bringing a new set of rules and principles for modern society. The Ahmediyya are fervent proselytizers, who consider it a religious duty to convert others to their faith; thus, it has grown to respectable proportions this century. It was, until recently, treated tolerantly by the ruling Muslim party in Pakistan and also in India.

In 1974, however, there were violent clashes in Pakistan between Muslims and Ahmediyyas and as a result of considerable pressure from traditional Muslim groups, the leader of Pakistan, Zulfikar Ali Bhutto, ensured that an amendment was made to the Constitution the effect of which was to exclude the Ahmediyya sect from being considered as a Muslim group.

A new clause 260 (3) of the Constitution was inserted which reads as follows:-

> (3) A person who does not believe in the absolute and unqualified finality of the Prophethood of Muhammad (peace be upon him) the last of the Prophets or claims to be a prophet, in any sense of the word or of any description whatsoever, after Muhammad (peace be upon him), or recognises such a claimant as a prophet or a religious reformer, is not a Muslim for the purposes of the Constitution or law.

Article 106 was also amended to include the Ahmediyyas alongside those non-Muslim groups who were to be awarded special seats in the provincial assemblies. Further, in 1984, President Zia al-Haq promulgated by presidential decree an ordinance called the 'Anti Islamic Activities of Qadiani Group, Lahori Group and Ahmadis (Prohibition and Punishment) Ordinance 1984' which makes it a criminal offence for an Ahmedi to directly or

---

[16]See generally William McElwee Miller, *The Baha'i Faith,* London, 1974. It contains an appendix of the *al-kitab al-aqdas* , the most holy book by Mirza Husayn Ali Baha'ullah.
[17]U.A.R. Presidential Decision No 263 of 1960.

indirectly pose as a Muslim; to call or refer to his faith as Islam; to preach or propagate his faith; to invite others to accept his faith or to outrage the feelings of Muslims in any way. This draconian measure is still in force in Pakistan and Prime Minister Benazir Bhutto has intimated that she does not intend to repeal it. It has produced considerable difficulties for the Ahmediyya community in Pakistan in the free expression of its views and in the celebration of its rites of worship.

Malaysia

In Malaysia, the definition of Muslim and non-Muslim has arisen in a number of contexts. Trengganu (in 1980) and Kelantan (in 1981) enacted laws for the 'control and restriction of the propagation on non-Islamic religions'. A 'non-Islamic religion' is defined in the Trengganu enactment to mean 'Christianity, Hinduism, Buddhism, Sikhism, Judaism, or any other variation, version, form or offshoot of the said religions'. The definition in Kelantan is the same, but extends to also include 'any creed, ideology, philosophy, or body of practices which has as one of its characteristics the worship of some spiritual or supernatural being or power... and which is not recognised by the religion of Islam as belonging to it'.

The definition of a non-Islamic religion is thus very specific, but wide. In comparison to this the definition of a Muslim is more vague and narrow. In both laws, however, the question of who is a Muslim is to be decided by criteria of general reputation without making any attempt to question the faith, beliefs, conduct, behaviour, character, acts or omissions of that person. Proselytizing is made an offence in a wide variety of forms, as is misuse of certain words and phrases uttered in the Muslim religion for repetition on ritual occasions. No cases are reported yet on this very recent legislation, but it is being watched with interest and a certain amount of anxious disquiet.

The Attitude of Islamic Law to Non-Muslims

From the earliest times of the Islamic era, Islam has considered and reconsidered the legal position of non-Muslims within the body politic of the Islamic Empire (*dar al-Islam*; literally 'abode of Islam'). Initially, the attitude to non-Muslims seems to have been liberal, but much depended on an individual ruler. As the Islamic Empire split, different rulers emerged and the principles hardened so that after the course of about two centuries the regime applicable to non-Muslims became increasingly limiting.[18]

The Qur'an itself has verses concerning the treatment of non-Muslims which vary in their content, some saying that non-Muslims must be given

[18] The literature is large, but see particularly A. Fattal, *Le Statut Légal des Non-Musulmans en Pays d'Islam,* Beirut, 1958.

protection, others saying that they should not be taken as friends because they are devious and only aim to lead the believer away from the true faith.

Nevertheless, we have some contemporaneous documentary evidence that the conquering Muslims made pacts or covenants with conquered non-Muslim communities whereby they were afforded the protection of the Muslim state in return for the payment of tribute. This became known as the *jizya* (poll tax). The protection was circumscribed by limiting conditions, however, which varied from covenant to covenant and which became gradually more onerous. General limitations included prohibitions on building new churches, on proselytising, on displaying non-Muslim images, on celebrating non-Muslim feasts, on building higher buildings than Muslims, and injunctions to live apart from Muslims in special city sectors, to wear special apparel or differently coloured clothes. The pact was broken if certain offences (such as striking a Muslim or insulting the Prophet or Islam) were committed or if the protection was abused. The most famous of these was known as the Pact of Umar, because it was attributed to the Caliph Umar, although most scholars now consider it to be of a later origin.[19]

Dhimmis

The permanently settled non-Muslims were known as *dhimmis* or *ahl al-kitab* (literally 'people of the book') and were accorded special privileges because they were seen as members of religious groups that preceeded Islam, with a Holy Book revealed from God by an earlier prophet. Most importantly these communities were allowed their own courts (*millet* courts) which decided cases on the basis of their own religious laws. The majority of cases dealt with by the millet courts concerned personal status matters, but they also had some civil and criminal jurisdiction. However, if a matter involved a Muslim and a non-Muslim then it automatically reverted to the shari'a court because a dhimmi could never be a judge over a Muslim. In the shari'a court a dhimmi was subject to considerable procedural disadvantages, the major one being that a dhimmi's testimony was not allowed against that of a Muslim. There were also substantive limitations in the law itself: a dhimmi man could not marry a Muslim woman, a dhimmi could not own a Muslim slave, dhimmi merchants paid more expensive tolls, dhimmis paid a special tax on land holdings *(kharaj)* as well as the poll tax, the blood money payable for causing death or injury to a dhimmi was less than that payable to a Muslim and dhimmis and Muslims could not inherit from one another.

---

[19] See A.S. Tritton, *The Caliphs and their Non-Muslim Subjects,* Oxford, 1930. The text of the Pact of Umar is given at pp. 5-6.

Musta'mins

Non-Muslims residing temporarily in a Muslim country were required to obtain the issue of a safe conduct visa called an '*aman*' hence they were known as *musta'mins*. The visa lasted for a short period of time generally not longer than a year and provided the holder with the protection of the state. Gradually it was extended from individual safe conduct to groups or communities and, later still, treaties between nation states provided for the mutual protection of their subjects by way of reciprocal rights and duties.

Harbis

Non-Muslims outside the abode of Islam were theoretically inhabitants of states in perpetual war (*jihad*) with Islam and hence took their name (*harbis*) from their place of residence: the abode of war (*the dar al-harb*). It was a controversial question whether Muslims could have relations with harbis, but it became accepted that the perpetual war could be punctuated by periods of peace created by agreement (*sulh*). In such a case mutual rights were accorded to visitors and Islamic jurists had to consider difficult questions concerning the applicability of Islamic law to Muslims in the dar al-harb and dar al-sulh.

The legal protections applicable in the Middle East to dhimmis and musta'mins were inconsistently enforced. The historical evidence shows cycles of repression and toleration. In times of toleration, non-Muslims could hold important state posts, could worship openly and even build or rebuild their places of worship. In times of repression, non-Muslims would be cast out of their positions, would be restricted in their worship, would be subject to confiscations, sequestrations and destruction of their belongings and their places of worship. At such times of repression there was considerable pressure to convert to Islam and indeed at specific times of repression one finds mass conversions taking place in order to save lives. This practice, however, is hardly surprising as the treatments accorded to non-Christian communities in Christiandom was similar to this during the Middle Ages and after. Edward I expelled all Jews from England and confiscated their property and it was not until the time of Cromwell that they were allowed back. This was after all the time of the crusades when Christian-Muslim relations were truly at their nadir.

In time, however, the privileges accorded to minority groups were put into state treaties, from about the sixteenth century onwards. These treaties provided for reciprocal privileges to be accorded to the citizens of each state in the territory of the other. By the nineteenth century these rights of privilege had grown enormously and included rights accorded to minorities to have their own courts, to exemption from taxes and dues, to special administrative process and immunities from the local law. Rights had also become less and less reciprocal and more unilateral. The Industrial Revolution, expanded European markets and political expediency, all played a part in increasing the numbers of Europeans and non-Muslims in the Middle East, without any similar increase in Muslims in Europe. As a result the capitulatory treaties in the nineteenth century helped to develop European enclaves within the dar al-Islam which eventually became unsupportable. It is no surprise therefore that it is only with their final demise this century that the Middle East attained complete legal independence from European domination.

The Special Position of Egypt

Egypt was conquered by the Arab general 'Amr ibn al-'As in 639 A.D. At that time the population was almost wholly Christian, the majority sect being the Coptic Orthodox church, a monophysite sect which split from mainstream Christianity after the Council of Chalcedon in 451 A.D. It purports to be the church founded by St. Mark the Evangelist in Alexandria and it elects its own patriarch, known as the Coptic Pope.[20] The new Arab rulers of Egypt were not immediately concerned with converting Egypt to Islam; rather they preferred to consolidate their precarious hold on the country. Copts held all the important offices of state, but often were forced to convert to keep their posts. Treatment of non-Muslims varied with the times. Under the Fatimids (a North African Shi'i dynasty) non-Muslims achieved both their highest attainments (as *wazirs* and advisers to the Fatimid caliphs) and were subject to the worst repression: al-Hakim enacted many limiting decrees as well as ordering from 1007-1012 the destruction of all Egyptian churches. Gradually, the Coptic community dwindled to a minority of the population, although as dhimmis they kept their own courts to decide legal matters and the faith survived in many monasteries in the desert. Monasticism was, in fact, the Coptic church's most important influence on the Western church.

In 1856 the Ottoman Sultan (then the official power in Egypt) promulgated a ordinance known as the *Hatt-i-Humayuni*[21] which laid down the various paths of reform which the Ottomans would instigate in order to be admitted to the Club of Europe as a 'modern' state. One of these was the ensuring of religious freedom, but it was subject to limitations similar to the Pact of Umar. One of these limitations was that the consent of *both* parties became necessary to take a case to a millet court. This measure limited their jurisdiction to a greater extent than previously.

In 1949 the Egyptian capitulatory courts (the mixed courts) were abolished and all that matters, except personal status, were henceforth to be referred to the national courts.

Finally in 1955, all the religious courts in Egypt were abolished (Jewish, Christian and Muslim) by law 462 of 1955 and since that time all legal questions have been tried in the national courts. Law 462 contains special

---

[20] See generally O. Meinardus, *Christian Egypt: Ancient and Modern,* Cairo, 2nd ed. 1977.
[21] See Liebesny, *The Law of the Near and Middle East,* pp.49-52.

principles concerning the law to be applied by the national courts in a particular case, especially where there is a mixed problem involving a Muslim and a non-Muslim.

Law 462 of 1955

The important provisions of this act are as follows:

> Article 1: The shari'a courts and the Millet courts are abolished from 1/1/56 and pending litigation is transferred to the National courts.
> Article 3: Legal proceedings which were within the jurisdiction of the shari'a courts or the Millet courts are to go to the National courts as from 1/1/56.
> Article 6: (1) Decisions relating to personal status and waqf which would have originally gone to the shari'a courts are to be decided by the national courts in accordance with Article 280 of the previous shari'a courts law of 1931.[22]
> (2) As for cases of personal status of non-Muslim Egyptians of the same sect and community (*al-muttahid at-ta'ifat wal-millat*), then *subject to public policy* (*fi nitaq al-nizam al-'am*)... they are to be decided *by their laws* (*tibqan li shari'atihim*).
> Article 7: Article 6(2) is not affected by a change of sect or religious community (*ta'ifat wa millat*) when one of the litigants leaves one sect for another during the course of litigation, except that if the change is *to* Islam then Article 6(1) shall apply.

Egyptian Civil Code 1949

The Egyptian Civil Code of 1949 has among its preliminary provisions a number of articles which also deal with personal status and which are also relevant. They are as follows:

> Article 11: The status and the legal capacity of persons are governed by the law of the country to which they belong by reason of their nationality.
> Article 12: The fundamental conditions relating to the validity of marriage are governed by the law of each of the two spouses.

---

[22]Article 280 of the Shari'a Courts Law of 1931 provides as follows: '... decisions are given in conformity with this decree, but most weight is given to the teachings of Abu Hanifa, except in cases where a law fixes that special principles are necessary...'.

Article 13: (1)The effects of marriage ... are regulated by the law of the country to which the husband belongs at the time of the conclusion of the marriage.

(2) Repudiation of marriage is governed by the law of the country to which the husband belongs at the time of the repudiation.

Article 14: If, in the cases provided for in the two preceding articles, one of the two spouses is an Egyptian at the time of the conclusion of the marriage, Egyptian law alone shall apply except as regards legal capacity to marry.

Article 16: The law of a person to be protected shall be applied in respect of all fundamental matters relating to legal and natural guardianship.

Article 23: The provisions of the preceding articles only apply when no provisions to the contrary are included in a special law in force in Egypt.

Article 28:The provisions of a foreign law applicable by virtue of the preceding articles shall not be applied if these provisions are contrary to public policy or to morality in Egypt.[23]

Conflict of Law Problems

The application by the Courts of the above articles in regard to personal status matters involving non-Muslims is extremely interesting and exhibits what conflict of laws specialists call a 'homeward trend': that is, the Egyptian courts have a strong tendency to apply Egyptian law wherever possible. This is frequently considered as practically synonomous with Islamic law.

As is clear from Article 14 of the Civil Code, in the case of a foreign mixed marriage, if one of the parties is an Egyptian national then Egyptian legal provisions will apply regardless of an otherwise applicable foreign law.These provisions will almost certainly be Islamic law.

Where neither party is an Egyptian national, the conflict of laws provisions will apply, although still subject to Egyptian public policy and morality as provided for in Article 28. The Egyptian courts seem much more willing than English courts to intervene on the grounds of public policy. Thus, in a case in 1953 concerning the validity of a secular marriage between an English Christian man and a Turkish Muslim woman, which according to the Egyptian Civil Code should have been decided according to principles of English law (the national law of the husband) under which it was valid, an Egyptian court held that the marriage was void because it contravened Islamic public policy which considers marriages of Muslim women with non-Muslim

[23]The translations of the Civil Code are taken from that of Perrott, Fanner and Sims, 1949, but amended by the author where necessary.

men a nullity. The principle of public policy plainly overrode the specific provisions of Article 13 of the Civil Code.[24]

In custody cases, particularly, the courts will almost never award custody to a foreign or non-Muslim claimant in preference to an Egyptian or, indeed, a foreign Muslim of whatever sex. Islamic law awards custody of children at an early age to their mothers, but if the mother is a non-Muslim or of reprehensible character then custody may be transferred to the father or his closest female relative (e.g. a paternal grandmother or aunt). Where one parent is Egyptian the courts will almost always prefer his or her claim over that of a non-Egyptian. Egypt is not a signatory to any unilateral or bilateral convention against child abduction and thus, once a child is present in Egypt the non-Egyptian (or non-Muslim) spouse will have virtually no method of ensuring the return of the child and access to the child may be limited or barred. Foreign decrees of custody, particularly of non-Islamic states, would not generally affect the position at all. Recently, however, France and Egypt signed a treaty of judicial cooperation[25] which provided for the mutual respecting of certain judicial decisions *inter alia* final decrees for the custody of children. It remains to be seen how effective this will be.

Domestic Cases of Mixed Religion

In purely domestic cases the use of Islamic public policy and the limited interpretation given to the wording of parts of law 462 of 1955 have also contributed to the expanded application of Islamic law even to matters among Christians. The words 'ta'ifat wa millat' have been interpreted to mean any autonomous religious group which exists within the large framework of different faiths. Thus, instead of treating all Christians as a single religious community or 'ta'ifat wa millat', each separate sect is treated separately. Hence, the Coptic Orthodox Church, the Roman Catholics, the Greek Orthodox, the Maronite, the Presbyterians, the Anglicans, are all considered as separate sects (ta'ifat).

This interpretation produces the consequence that Article 6(2) is restricted to cases where the parties are of the same individual sect. If a dispute occurs between people who are of two different (though Christian) sects, Article 6(2) does not apply and Islamic law applies as a residual law. Islamic law, therefore, may and does apply to a number of wholly Christian disputes and some unscrupulous litigants have exploited this to their own ends as is shown later.

---

[24]See Y. Linant de Bellefonds, 'La Jurisprudence Égyptienne et les Conflits de Lois en Matière de Statut Personnel', *Journal du Droit International,* 1960, pp 1-18, at p. 10.
[25]See *Bulletin of CEDEJ*, 1984.

The Effect of Religious Conversion

Problems most commonly arise where one party has undergone conversion from one religion to another, or even from one sect to another while remaining within one religious faith. Conversion is undertaken for many reasons, but often occurs in order to evade some mandatory restriction in a relevant religion. For example, a non-Muslim man cannot marry a Muslim woman without converting to Islam and this is one of the most common reasons for conversion. Another reason is to obtain the liberal provisions of another law. This is particularly true of divorce.

Christianity has a great antipathy to divorce. According to Roman Catholic and Greek Orthodox doctrine it is totally forbidden, whereas some Presbyterian and eastern sects (including the Coptic Orthodox church) permit divorce from an adulterous spouse.

Islam has always had a more liberal approach to divorce. It gives men an almost complete freedom to divorce. Thus, it has been common for Christian men, unable to obtain a divorce in their Christian sect, to convert to Islam in order to use the more liberal Islamic regime. Egyptian courts have, since the nineteenth century, accepted the validity of such a divorce, regarding the law of the Muslim husband as applicable and rejecting any argument that the status of the marriage is governed by the law of the parties at the time of the marriage and cannot be unilaterally altered by one party (as would be the case in most European laws). Islamic law considers that the marriage survives the conversion as long as the wife is a *kitabiyya* (a follower of certain revealed religions, but particularly a Christian or a Jew). Nevertheless, Islamic law would govern the effects of the marriage and the husband could use provisions for divorce.

Similarly, any children of the marriage would automatically become Muslim on their father's conversion to Islam, as a child's religion is considered to follow that of its father. The mother would therefore be unlikely to be given custody in the case of divorce. Islamic law would not consider the acquired rights of the marriage or the motive behind the husband's conversion. As we have seen, conversion is a simple and quick process subject only to objective considerations of whether the right form has been complied with.

Conversion to Islam

A 1952 case indicates clearly the way the courts exhibit a 'homeward trend' in conflict of law cases and make the application of Egyptian and/or Islamic law predominant.[26] An Englishman domiciled in England converted to Islam in order to marry a Muslim woman. The marriage took place in the Middle East, outside both Egypt and England. Under English law at that time

---

[26] Linant de Bellefonds, 'La Jurisprudence Égyptienne', pp. 10-11.

the Englishman had no capacity to enter into such a marriage. The couple lived in Egypt, but soon separated. The Englishman then met and married a Christian woman in Egypt, without revealing his previous Muslim marriage elsewhere. When the second wife discovered the true facts she applied to an Egyptian court for a declaration of nullity on the grounds of bigamy. According to Article 12 of the Civil Code her capacity to marry was governed by Egyptian Christian law, whereas the husband's capacity to marry was governed by English law. The court should have looked at English law and would have then been forced to say that English law did not recognise the first marriage for lack of capacity. This would however have meant calling into question the validity of a Muslim marriage in a Muslim state. So instead, the court said that Article 12 was always subject to Article 28 and that it was against public policy to consider the first marriage void and to cause this to affect the second marriage. Islamic law was to be applied. Thus the validity of the first marriage was accepted, and as polygamy is possible under Islam, the second marriage was also valid! In reaching this decision, the court rejected both the national law of the husband and the national (Christian) law of the wife under which they were married.

Conversion within the Christian Faith

Many Christians adhere to their faith strictly and would not countenance the legal trickery involved in conversion to Islam. For some, other pathways are open - but the courts have made these paths difficult. For example, conversion from a Christian sect which prohibits divorce to one which permits it is possible and the national courts give effect to such a change if it is properly evidenced.

A good example of the problems that arise can be seen in a case[27] that was considered by the Supreme Court (the *mahkamat al-naqd*) in 1969. Here both parties were Coptic Orthodox Christians who had married in Egypt according to the rites of that faith. The Coptic Orthodox church permits divorce on a number of limited grounds, including adultery by the other spouse.[28] The husband desired a divorce but had no grounds. So he purported to convert to the Protestant faith, which permitted divorce on wider grounds, and began attending a Protestant church. However, the courts will only allow such a conversion to carry with it the right to divorce if the other spouse belongs to a faith which permits divorce in some form, although not necessarily on the grounds claimed. The wife, therefore, knowing this, purported to convert to the Roman Catholic faith in an attempt to stymie her husband's action. The case before the Supreme Court centred on the validity of the two conversions. Conversion to the Christian faiths in Egypt requires more instruction than

---

[27] *Majmu'at ahkam al-naqd* (collection of decisions of the Supreme courts), Session 29/1/69, Year 20 (Vol.1), pp. 187-192.

[28] See Maurice Sadiq, *Al-ahwal ash-shakhsiyya li-ghayr al-muslimin fi misr*, Cairo, 1987.

Islam as well as clear motives. Further, the different church authorities issue their own authoritative certificates of conversion after the appropriate steps have been taken. The Supreme Court tested the sincerity of each conversion and the proffered documentation and decided that neither party had provided proof of proper conversion. The husband's action failed.

More recently, however, there have been instances of claimants attempting to use Article 6(2) of Law 462 so that it applies to conversions to different sects *within* one faith and the lower courts seem to have been willing to sanction this. By limiting the meaning of the words 'separate sect or community' in this way, a Christian husband desirous of divorcing his wife can effect it merely by converting to another Christian sect that accepts divorce. As the parties then differ in sect, Islamic law is applied and the full liberality of the Islamic law of repudiation (*talaq*) is available to the husband. This is a complete perversion of the spirit of Article 6(2). However, no case has come as yet to the Supreme Court on this matter and it may be that the higher courts would strike down such an interpretation. The cases themselves are not officially reported, but are mentioned in some of the heavily biased Coptic Orthodox gazettes.

One case in 1978 is of particular interest.[29] It is reported that a Coptic Orthodox husband converted to the Greek Orthodox faith and married again in that faith. The Court of Appeal in Cairo accepted as valid the argument based on Article 6(2) that Islamic law applied to determine the validity of the second marriage and that as Islamic law accepted polygamy the second marriage was valid and the Islamic law of talaq was available to the husband. Thus, the court confused the application of the laws and perverted both.

Conversion from Islam

Conversion from Islam creates even greater problems. Apostacy (*ridda* or *irtidad*) was subject to severe penalties in classical Islamic law, including in some cases capital punishment. Article 2 of the Egyptian Constitution 1980 declares that Islam is the religion of the state, but there is nothing in the Constitution concerning apostacy from Islam and there is no specific penalty attached to apostacy under the present secular law of Egypt. Recently, however, there have been occasional calls by the *'ulama* (Islamic religious scholars) for criminal penalties to be established. The last such call was in 1978 when a draft law on apostacy prepared by the University of Al-Azhar (and approved by the *maglis ad-dawla*) was published.[30] This draft law made it a criminal offence for a Muslim to convert to Christianity and for a Christian

---

[29]*Aida Mikhail v. Soliman Yousri Yousefi,* Session 21/3/78, Case 104, Judicial Year 94. I am indebted for this and other cases to Mrs Samiha Lutfallah who is researching a doctorate on the subject of the treatment of non-Muslims in Egypt.

[30]This was published by al-Azhar itself unusually in both English and Arabic. The English title is 'Ordained Penalties (*Hudud*) of the Shari'a : Draft Law and Explanatory Memorandum'.

to seek actively to convert Muslims to Christianity by proselytising. It provided various punishments including, in extreme cases, the death penalty.

The Christian community in Egypt protested strongly about its possible application. Pope Shenouda, head of the Coptic Orthodox church, led the denunciations against the law, announcing the non-celebration of Easter as an indication of Christian alarm, writing constantly against the law and seeking audience with President Sadat to indicate the dismay of the whole Coptic Community in Egypt. The result was that the draft law was delayed and eventually shelved.

In an effort to halt religious division and supposed subversion, however, Sadat proposed and the People's Assembly accepted, a law (Law 95 of 1980) which made it a crime to propagate views advocating opposition to the state's political, social and economic system and to engage in shameful conduct. It became known as the *qanun al-'ayb* (literally, the law of shame) and a special court was set up to deal with offences under it. A special office (that of the Socialist Public Prosecutor) was created to investigate such crimes. In the main it has dealt with cases of corruption and has not touched the question of apostacy or conversions.

The ordinary courts however have had to consider occasionally the civil consequences of apostacy from Islam and their attitude seems to be that any residual judicial discretion is to be exercised against the interests of the apostate.

The Coptic gazette reports an unpublished case of 1974 which came before the court of appeal of Alexandria.[31] In the case, a woman, originally a Muslim, had converted from Islam to Christianity in order to marry a Christian man in a Christian church ceremony. At the instance of local Muslims, the public prosecutor brought an action against the couple on behalf of the state calling for nullification of the marriage on the grounds that it contravened public policy. The Alexandria court, while accepting that Article 6(2) provided that the validity of the marriage should be governed by Christian law, held that it was subject to the overriding public policy provisions of Islamic law. Further, in Islamic law an apostate forfeits any civil rights on apostacy and hence, having no capacity, cannot marry. An argument based upon Article 46 of the Constitution which provides that 'the state guarantees the freedom of belief and the freedom of practice of religious rites' was rejected, as it was held to be limited by Article 2 which declares Islam to be the religion of the state.

An earlier case of the Supreme Civil Court of Egypt is reported and is couched in even stronger terms.[32] Here again a Muslim woman converted to Christianity in order to marry a Christian man in a church ceremony. A Muslim neighbour of the couple brought an action for nullity that was taken up by the authorities. The locus standi of any Muslim to bring such an action

[31] *Saleh v. the State*, Suit 25/1972, Session 9/6/74.
[32] *Majmu'at ahkam al-naqd,* Session 30/3/66, Year 17 (Vol. 2), pp. 782-791.

was upheld by the court on the basis of the Islamic concept of *hisba* which, classically, refers to the duty an individual Muslim owes to keep the shari'a and uphold the law: in effect to act as a *muhtasib*, a protector of peoples morals. The Supreme Court held the marriage between the parties null and void concluding that an apostate from Islam had no right to marry at all and that as far as her civil rights were concerned the wife should be considered as 'legally dead'. This decision, which has serious consequences for the life of the convert, stands alone in the decisions of the Supreme Court and does not seem to have been built upon or referred to in later cases. It is possible that the parties publicly and provocatively publicised the conversion, their Christianity and their new marriage. This might explain why there was so much anti-neighbourly feeling. It does, however, provide evidence of a considerable cultural prejudice against apostacy and a willingness to use legal tools to make the life of the apostate difficult. It is hard not to interpret this as being done solely as a means to deter others from following the same path.

It remains to be said that the above cases are some of the most startling examples in Egyptian case law. They are difficult to assess as they are often only isolated instances and some are not officially reported but only appear in rather partial and one-sided Christian journals.

Egypt produces law reports following the French model. There is no rule of precedent as such and only the cases before the highest courts are reported as guides to the many regional courts of appeal in the application of the law. Some judges are more traditional than others and certainly the judges in the lower courts show more traditional and more Islamic traits than their judicial colleagues in the higher courts. Thus, when the Constitution was amended in 1980 making Islamic law 'the' principal source of legislation, many first instance judges began to hand down Islamic punishments for crimes. All these judgements were reversed on appeal and the head of the Judiciary, the President of the Supreme Court (the mahkamat al-naqd) stopped this trend by issuing a judicial circular stating that the Article 2 amendment did not effect any change in the criminal law, it being for the People's Assembly to legislate on the basis of the amendment.

Succession to Property

Areas of the law of personal status, other than marriage and divorce also create problems, although a number of statutes now provide some solutions - often by the application of Islamic law.

Succession to property, whether for a Muslim or non-Muslim deceased, is governed by Law 77 of 1943 which is a codification of Islamic law with some slight amending reforms. Article 6 provides, in accordance with Islamic law, that 'there is no succession between a Muslim and a non-Muslim', but that non-Muslims can inherit from one another. Conversion can still create problems however as a Supreme Court case of 1970 shows.[33] A Christian lady of means died leaving substantial property and a number of relatives. Her nephew, who had converted to Islam some time earlier, claimed that his aunt had adopted Islam just before her death and that he was therefore her sole heir. This self-serving claim was not subjected to rigorous examination: the evidence of Muslim servants was accepted and the evidence of the non-Muslim servants rejected, as Islamic law but not modern Egyptian law requires. Hence, the nephew obtained all his aunt's property.

Church Lands

One of the most important objectives of the Free Officers Revolution of 1952 was the promotion of social and economic equality through land reform. The Agrarian Reform Law 1952 limited land holdings to two hundred *feddans* (one feddan is approximately one acre). This was reduced in 1956 to one hundred feddans. Compensation was payable but was not at a market price. The sequestered land was then distributed to peasant farmers, but the Coptic church claimed that it was only the Muslim and not the Christian rural communities which gained.

In 1947 a law of waqf had been promulgated which organised on a statutory basis the administration of waqf property - property permanently dedicated to a charitable purpose, which might also include family members of the dedicator as beneficiaries. All waqf property, Muslim and Christian, was put under the control and administration of the Minister of Waqf and Islamic affairs; thus Muslim administrators became involved in the administration of many Christian waqfs. In 1952 all private family waqf were abolished and their land holdings sequestered. Again the Coptic church claimed that the sequestered properties were only distributed to Muslim communities.

After Nasser's death in 1970, and following a famous land reform scandal known as the Kamshish affair,[34] Sadat set in train a de-sequestration process which has resulted in many cases being brought before the highest administrative courts and has caused some sequestration decrees to be overturned, but the process is long and arduous.

Under the Hatti Humayuni of the Ottoman period, still notionally in force in Egypt, there are restrictions on the building of churches (e.g. they must not be higher then neighbouring buildings and must not be near mosques) and these were further reinforced by a presidential decree of 1960 which made it a condition of building new churches or making repairs to old ones, that presidential permission was sought and obtained. This has only been sparingly given.

---

[33]Supreme Court Session 19/5/70.

[34]See H. Ansari, *Egypt: The Stalled Society*, Cairo, 1987.

Finally, the Coptic church suffered its ultimate humbling when Sadat, in his clampdown of dissidents in 1981, purported to strip Pope Shenouda III of his powers.

The Coptic church has its method of appointment of its supreme pontiff, which is effected partly by election and partly by chance. Whoever is chosen by the designated procedure becomes Pope after an investing ceremony, but for legal purposes his appointment is announced in the official gazette by means of a presidential decree. For this reason it was argued by President Sadat that the Pope was actually appointed by the President - a point of great controversy for Copts. In 1981 Sadat ordered a crackdown against dissidents under emergency legislation, which included Nasserists, communists and Muslim and Christian fundamentalists. It was by Presidential Decree 491 of 1981 that Sadat purported to depose Shenouda as Pope and appointed a five man council of bishops to rule the church in his place. Shenouda himself was also held in the monastery of Anba Bishoy in Wadi Natrun for a period of over forty months, where he lectured and wrote. Eventually, after Sadat's assassination, President Mubarak repealed in 1985 the former decree and reappointed Shenouda Pope. Shenouda and the church brought an action for damages against the President and Prime Minister for a number of wrongs, including wrongful deposing and arrest. The Council of State decided that the President did possess a power to depose, but had no power to appoint a five bishop council to run the church. It did not award damages.

Conclusion

The treatment of non-Muslim communities in the Middle East has always been an uncertain and controversial topic. The treatment has varied according to historical period and to region, but it is perhaps possible to say that on the whole the treatment historically was generally better and certainly no worse than the treatment of Muslims in Christendom. In the nineteenth century as a result of the colonially imposed capitulatory treaties, Middle Eastern countries were forced to cede considerable powers to non-Muslim communities to order their own affairs, which included allowing their own courts to operate, applying their own personal laws and granting them immunities from the local law. These privileges became intolerable and a clear sign of colonial dependence. In the modern day, these capitulations having been abolished, the position of non-Muslim communities is assimilated to that of the local people. At least as far as Egypt is concerned, the modern tendency has been increasingly to limit the application of the communities' own law and to impose Islamic law solutions on non-Islamic situations. This is generally done by subjecting the ordinary choice of legal rules in the Egyptian Civil Code to the overriding principles of Egyptian public policy, and through this means, to Islamic law.

A comparison with English law would indicate much less readiness to use English public policy[35] to undermine the application of clear choice of law rules. There is by no means reciprocity of treatment in such cases, which may be a consideration of which the English courts will take cognisance. Certainly, it may influence the way English law reacts to calls to protect Muslims further by law and make of them a particularly favoured community.

[35]See generally Dicey and Morris, *Conflict of Laws,* London, 11th ed. 1987 at chapter 6 on exclusion of foreign law, especially pp.93 seq: 'The doctrine of public policy has assumed far less prominence in the English conflict of laws than have corresponding doctrines in the laws of foreign countries.' But for the opposite view see the cases on recognition of talaq: *Zaal v. Zaal* (1983) 4 FLR 284 and *Chaudhary v. Chaudhary* (1984) 3 AER 1017 in which the lack of notice given to a wife who is the subject of a talaq was considered to be contrary to English public policy and a reason for not recognising an Islamic divorce.

4. DIVORCE IN CONTEMPORARY IRAN: A MALE PREROGATIVE IN SELF-WILL

Shahla Haeri

Much has been written on Islamic divorce and the rights and obligations of the spouses within it. In this chapter my intention is not to describe yet again variations of Islamic divorce, though this will be part of the broader aim of the present endeavour. Rather, I am interested in rendering a critique of the logic and rationale behind the institution. To do so we would have to discuss divorce within the context of the contractual structure of Islamic marriage. The mutual rights and obligations of the spouses in Shi'i Islam, in my view, essentially rest on the perception of three predetermined, reinforcing, self-legitimating, and interlocking axes, namely a legal determinism, a biological determinism, and a divine determinism.[1] Looking at the institutions of divorce and marriage within this triangle of determinisms, I wish to consider the issue, for the moment, from a male point of view. What does it mean to be a man in a society like Iran where the divinity, the nature, and the law work hand in hand to legitimate structural and conceptual inequalities between men and women? And, what are their implications for male-female relationships? Given the presumption of the ahistoricity of this cosmological model, a further question is, how has the dynamic tension between continuity and change been historically confronted? I am not claiming that there is a perfect fit between the perception of the immutability of this model and the actual male-female relationships or experiences. Nor am I saying that such structure is necessarily Islamic. Rather my critique has to do with: (a) a textual discussion of the Shi'i texts, and (b) the way structural differences have historically been invoked in order to justify sexual inequalities, or conversely, the way culturally learned gender behaviour is used as further proof of structural differences.[2] It is the contention in the present article that this model, as has been historically represented and maintained by the religious

[1]I am not setting up these as separate and distinct categories. It must be borne in mind that the boundaries of these 'determinisms' are permeable and dynamic. For the sake of analytic discussion I am treating them as if they were separate concepts.

[2]Qur'anic exegesis has been for too long the monopoly of a small group of learned men who have arrogated unto themselves its interpretation and representation to the public. Inevitably therefore their interpretation has gone through a prism of patriarchy, different only in local flavour. Muslim women, however, have recently begun to rethink issues relevant to their very existence and everyday life by going to the source of Islamic law, the Qur'an, for fresh interpretation. Their objective is to produce their own rendition, *tafsir*, of the Qur'anic verses. See R. Hassan, 'Made from Adam's Rib ? The Woman's Creation Question', *al-Mushir* (Pakistan), 27:3, 1985, pp.124-155; Id., 'Equal before Allah? Woman-man Equality in the Islamic Tradition', *Harvard Divinity Bulletin,* 17:2, 1987, pp.2-4.

scholars, provides the broader framework for variations of particular male-female behaviour prevalent in most of the Islamic cultures. As a case in point, I shall describe and discuss the Islamic regime's efforts in modifying the law of divorce in Iran. I am mainly concerned with the institutions of marriage and divorce in Shi'i Islam but my argument, I believe, is equally relevant to other schools of Islamic law.

I. Legal Determinism

The key concept in this section is that of contract, *'aqd*, which is the basis of an Islamic marriage. 'Aqd is an Arabic term meaning literally to knot or coagulate. Little has been written on the concept of contract from the point of view of Islamic jurisprudence. Schacht argues that the most common ground for an obligation is the contract, 'aqd, which is the field of 'pecuniary transactions'.[3] As in other forms of Islamic contracts, marriage is a contract of exchange, requiring agreement of *both partners*. In exchange for brideprice (and daily support, later on) that a wife receives, the husband gains a legitimate right to sexual union with her. The broader outline of a contract of marriage is divinely determined, and therefore 'laws regarding the rights of husband and wife cannot be modified by the parties at the drawing up of the contract'.[4] Conditions not contradictory to the basic tenets of the contract (e.g. reserving the right to choose marital residence), however, may be inserted in it. It is this possibility of including conditions in a marriage contract that has provided the Islamic regime in Iran, and other Islamic jurists earlier, with a legally and religiously acceptable medium for introducing modifications in the law of marriage and divorce. It is the logic of the contract that I suggest we look into in order to understand aspects of marital male-female relationships in Islamic societies.

In the seventh century A.D. the Prophet Muhammed unified the multiplicity of pre-Islamic modes of sexual unions by outlawing all but one form of marriage, namely marriage by contract. Fundamental to this rearranging of the existing social structure was the realignment of the role of husband and wife into that of the principal transacting parties. As distinct from the pre-Islamic form of 'marriage of dominion',[5] Islamic law recognised the wife - not her father - to be the recipient of the brideprice.[6] Implicit in this act is a recognition of a degree of women's autonomy and volition. As a party to the contract, it is the woman herself who has to give her consent - however nominally - for the contract to be valid. And it is the woman herself, not her father (custom aside), who is to receive the full amount of brideprice, be it immediate or deferred.

---

[3]J. Schacht, *Introduction to Islamic Law,* Oxford, 1964, pp.194-195.

[4]*Encyclopaedia of Islam*, Volume 3, Leiden, Second Edition 1960ff., p.914.

[5]W. Robertson Smith, *Kinship and Marriage in Early Arabia,* Boston, 1903, p.92.

[6]Qur'an, 4:34; A. Y. Nuri, *Huquq-i Zan dar Islam va Jahan* (Legal rights of women in Islam and in the world), Tehran, 1968, p.118; W. Robertson Smith, *Kinship and Marriage in Early Arabia*; R. Levy, *The Social Structure of Islam,* London, 1957, p. 95.

In an Islamic marriage, then, a woman is given some legal autonomy in order to bargain over her own destiny. Ironically, however, the very same structure that gives her the right to exercise her decision-making power deprives her of it as soon as she uses it. Prior to signing the contract of marriage an adult Shi'i Muslim woman is accorded a relatively independent legal autonomy, but after the conclusion of the contract she is legally associated with the object of exchange, and hence she comes under the jural authority of her husband. This *association of women with the object of exchange* is at the heart of the Islamic doctrinal double image of women (naive/cunning; sexually insatiable/innocent) as well as at the root of the ideological ambivalence towards them.

An Islamic marriage contract is of course more than a mere exchange of material goods. As with many other forms of social exchange, a contract of marriage is at once a legal, religious, economic and symbolic transaction.[7] The unique thing in the Islamic marriage contract, however, is the assumption of ownership and purchase imbedded in this kind of exchange.

Scholars of the Islamic law classify marriage, *nikah*, as a contract ('aqd), but shy away from specifying the type of contracts to which it actually belongs. This is particularly true in the works of contemporary *'ulama* who have been made increasingly aware of the implications of the assumptions of ownership and purchase in the marriage contract for male-female relationship. Noel Coulson is among the few scholars who have drawn attention to similarities between a contract of marriage and a contract of sale, *bay'*. In his view, nikah can be classified as a type of sale because it results in 'the transfer of an absolute propriety'.[8] With this view I concur. Having made this analogy, however, Coulson does not pursue the argument further. The legal, economic and social implications of such conceptualisation for marital relationship, I believe, are far reaching and profound.

Historically almost identical language is used to define the institution of Shi'i Muslim marriage. In his monumental and much quoted book, *Shara'i' al-Islam*, the thirteenth century scholar Hilli defines a contract of marriage as 'that which gives ownership, *tamlik*, over intercourse, *vatye*, not like buying a slavegirl whose ownership entitles her master a right to intercourse'.[9] In the tradition of his predecessors, Jabiri Arablu, a contemporary Iranian scholar, after giving several interpretations of the term nikah, concludes that 'nikah is a contract for ownership, tamlik, of the use of the vagina'.[10] Note here that Hilli's distinction is not between existence or lack of ownership, but between

[7] See M. Mauss, *The Gift*, New York, 1967, p.76.

[8] N. Coulson, *A History of Islamic Law*, Edinburgh, 1964, p.111.

[9] Muhaqqiq Najm ad-Din Abu al-Qasim Ja'far al-Hilli, *Sharaye' al-Islam*, Persian translation by M.T. Daneshpazuh, Tehran, 1968, p.428. Vatye literally means to stampede, as in the case of being trampled under the hooves of horses. See 'Ali Akbar Dihkuda, *Lughat Nameh*, Tehran, 1959, s.v.; and Hans Wehr, *Dictionary of Modern Written Arabic*, ed. by J. M. Cowan, London, 1976, p.1078.

[10] M. Jabiri Arablu, *Farhang-i Istilahat-i Fiqh-i Islami dar Bab-i Mu'amilat* (Encyclopaedia of Islamic legal terms regarding transactions), Tehran, 1983, p.175.

what I call a 'complete ownership', as in the case of owning a slave girl, and a 'partial ownership', as in the case of a contract of marriage. Hilli's ambivalence regarding similarities between a contract of sale and a marriage contract is underscored by yet another of his definitions of nikah. He classifies marriage as 'that type of contract which ensures domination over vagina, *biz'* (or *buz'*) without ownership, *milkiyyat*.'[11] Having said so, however, he immediately adds: "'Aqd (i.e. marriage) and ownership do not mix'.[12] This is to say, a man may marry some one else's slavegirl, but not his own. Under his ownership she can be either his concubine or his wife, but not both. Since he can already have sexual relations with his slave girl, marrying her would be redundant. The linguistic phraseology used in this injunction masks the actual legal implications of a marriage contract which entitles the man to own 'parts' of his wife's body and by extension herself.[13]

Because marriage is a contract, from an Islamic point of view, the phenomenon of intercourse, *vatye*, is inevitably intertwined with monetary exchanges. The Islamic maxims, 'sexual relations invoke either payment or punishment', and 'intercourse is respected' (*vatye muhtaram ast*), are repeatedly invoked to indicate legitimacy - or its absence - in a sexual relation.[14] The underlying assumption here is twofold. First, as 'purchasers' in a contract of marriage, men are 'in charge' of their wives because they pay for them,[15] and naturally they ought to be able to *control* their wives' activities. Secondly, women are required to submit that for which they have been paid - or promised to be paid. It follows therefore that women ought to be *obedient* to their husbands.

---

[11]Hilli, *Sharaye' al-Islam*, p.517.

[12]Ibid.

[13]Despite his vehement objection to the conceptualisation of marriage as a contract of sale, and of women as an object, Ayatollah Mutahhari writes in a moment of spontaneity: 'Islam recognises the man as the buyer, *kharidar*, and the woman as the owner of the object, *saheb-i kala*'. Murtaza Mutahhari, *Nizam-i Huquq-i Zan dar Islam* (Legal Rights of Women in Islam), Qum, 1974, p. 232.

[14]Mahdi Ghazanfari, *Khudamuz-i Luma'ih*, Tehran, 1957, vol.1, p.130; Hilli, *Sharaye' al-Islam*, p. 450; Abulfutuh Razi, *Tafsir* (Interpretation), Tehran, 1963, Vol.3, p. 362; Shaikh Abu Ja'far Muhammad Tusi, *An-Nihaya*, Persian tr. By M.T. Danishpazhuh, Tehran, 1964, p.477; see also S. Murata, *Izdivaj-i Muvaqqat va Asar-i Ijtima'i-i An* (Temporary marriage and its social effects), M.A. Thesis, Tehran University, 1974, p. 51.The exchange of this money is so indispensable that even in the case of an 'intercourse on the account of a misunderstanding', *vatye-i bih shubhih*, some money in the form of brideprice must be given to the woman in order to ensure legal and moral propriety. See Tusi, *An-Nihaya*, p.477; Hilli, *Sharaye' al-Islam*, p.520; Muhammad Ja'far Langarudi, *Huquq-i Khanivadih* (Family law), 1976, pp.28, 84; Sayyid Husain Imami, *Huquq-i Madani* (Civil Law), Tehran, 1971-1974, Vol. 4, pp. 26-27; Cf. also S. Shafa, *Tauzih al-Masa'il: Pasukhi bih Pursishhay-i Hizar Salih*, Paris, 1983, p.710-711.

[15]Qur'an, 4:34.

II. Biological Determinism

> No one can deny that most, if not all, married men have had sexual relations, legitimate or illegitimate, with other women. Is it wise then to forbid married men from having relations [of temporary marriage] with other women? Is such a law just and in accordance with human nature? Of course not. Such law has not been practical and will not be so![16]

In this section I focus on the concept of nature, *fitrat,* which forms the core of the Shi'i ideological assumptions regarding the unique nature, function, and status of man and woman and their mutual rights and obligations. The essence of human nature and the cultural differences between the sexes are believed to be rooted in biology, in human anatomy. Making a fundamental and paradigmatic analogy between humans and other 'animal pairs' in referring to man, woman, and their relationship, the Shi'i 'ulama always invoke 'the law of nature', *ain-i fitrat.*[17] The late Ayatollah Murtaza Mutahhari (d.1979), one of the most influential, articulate and prolific contemporarty Shi'i 'ulama, has argued: 'The difference between woman and man is not the result of an [historical] accident. That is why we do not need to look for its causes into historical and social circumstances [ie feudalism, capitalism] in order to learn about men's [innate] sense of protection [for women] and women's [innate] sense of seeking refuge [in men]. Women psychologically and physically want to put themselves under men's protection, *himayat*. Therefore this difference [between man and woman] is not because of historical and social causes. Rather, it is due to natural, *fitri,* reasons'.[18]

That men and women are biologically different is self evident. My objection is to muddling cultural construction of gender with law of nature, and to using physiological differences as justification for the existing sexual inequalities: for instance, in keeping women from becoming judges, or giving men licence to indulge in plural marriages or unilateral divorces. 'Nature has given the man', says Ayatollah Mutahhari,

> the key to the natural breakup of marriage. It is the man whose disinterest and unfaithfulness toward the woman sets off a similar response in his wife. On the contrary, the woman's disinterest, if it is initiated from her, has no bearing on the man's affection for her: it might even make him more eager.

16A. A. Muhajir, 'Ta'addud-i Zujat va Mut'a' (Polygamy and mut'a), in *Majallih-i Kanun-i Sar Daftaran*, 10, 1974, p.20.

17Mutahhari, *Nizam-i Huquq-i Zan dar Islam*, p.211; Sayyid Javad Mustafavi, 'Izdivaj dar Islam va Fitrat (Marriage in Islam and natural disposition)', in *Nashriyih-i Danishkadihi-i Ilahiyat va Ma'arif-i Islami-i Danishgah-i Mashhad*, Mashhad, 1972, pp.159-60; Nuri, *Huquq-i-Zan*, pp.15-37.

18Cited in *Zan-i Ruz,* 1988 (≠1169), p.11. See also *Zan-i Ruz,* 1986 (≠1164), p.12-13.

> So the man's disinterest and cooling off is the death (*marg*) of the marriage, signifying the end of family life. But a similar situation in the case of women indicates a momentary disease that can be cured. It is not an insult for a man to keep his disinclined beloved by force of law, so that he can eventually tame (*ram*) her. But it is an unbearable insult for the woman to appeal to the law in order to keep her protector and her beloved [from divorcing her].[19]

Shi'i law acknowledges male sexuality and accommodates it by principles of polygamy, concubinage, and unilateral divorce. Concubinage in the form of slave ownership is all but obsolete in most Islamic societies. Polygamy in Iran, however, takes at least two forms, permanent marriage, nikah, and temporary marriage, *mut'a*, (or *sigheh* in Persian vernacular). This is to say, a Shi'i Muslim man is permitted to marry up to four permanent wives. This he shares with men of other schools of Islamic law. Additionally, he can legitimately contract an unlimited number of temporary marriages simultaneously or serially. This is unique to Shi'i Islam. Whereas a contract of permanent marriage is similar to a contract of sale, temporary marriage structurally is similar to a contract of lease.[20] Temporary marriage is essentially a verbal contract in which a man and an unmarried woman (virgin, divorced, or widowed) agree to marry for as short or as long as they desire. In exchange for the brideprice (known as reward, *ajr*, and not *mahr*, as in permanent marriage)[21] a temporary wife receives, the man gains a legitimate right to sexual union during the time they are married. Children born of temporary unions are legally protected, though socially stigmatized. There is no divorce ceremony in this form of marriage. At the end of the specified time the marriage is automatically dissolved and the partners part company. Shi'i Muslim women, unlike men, are forbidden from engaging in more than one contract of temporary marriage at a time. After the expiration of the temporary marriage, no matter how short, women have to observe a period of sexual abstinence for two menstrual cycles or 45 days.[22]

19Mutahhari, *Nizam-i Huquq-i Zan dar Islam*, pp. 284-285.

20Theses issues are more fully argued in S. Haeri, *The Law of Desire: Temporary Marriage in Shi'i Iran*, London, 1989.

21In the Qur'an (4:24) the exchange of this money is referred to as *ajr* (literally wage or reward), in order to set it apart from brideprice (*mahr*) in the contract of permanent marriage. Many contemporary Shi'i scholars, however, have used the term mahr to refer to both forms of marriage payments. Popular usage also follows the same tendency.

22For a complete description of mut'a marriage see: Tusi, *An-Nihaya,* pp.497-502; Hilli, *Sharaye' al-Islam*, pp.515-528; Ghazanfari, *Khudamuz-i Luma'ih*, Vol.2 pp.126-134; M. H. Kashif al-Ghita', *A'in-i Ma*, Qum, 1968, p.372-392; Ayatollah Ruhullah Khomeini, *Tawzih al-Masa'il,* Tehran, 1977, para.2421-2431; Mutahhari, *Nizam-i Huquq-i Zan dar Islam*, pp. 21-52; Ahmad Bihishti, *Shinakht-i Islam,* Tehran, n.d., pp.329-335; Sayyid Husain Yusifi Makki, *Mut'a dar Islam,* Damascus, 1963; M. Shafa'i, *Mut'a va Asar-i Huquqi va Ijtima'i-i An*, Tehran, 6th ed. 1973; Imami, *Huquq-i Madani*; S. Murata, *Izdivaj-i Muvaqqat va Asar-i Ijtima'i-i An*, Tehran, 1974; M. J. Langarudi, *Huquq-i Khanivadih*, Tehran, 1976; N. Katuzian, *Huquq-i Madani-i Khanivadih,* Tehran, 1978; For English sources refer to S.

Against the Sunni ‘ulama's chronic objection to lack of moral propriety of temporary marriage and its legitimacy, the Shi‘i ‘ulama have argued in favour of temporary marriage with various degrees of intensity and conviction. The Shi‘i ‘ulama's justification for legitimacy of temporary marriage has been consistently and chiefly a sexual one. In their view, while the objective of permanent marriage is procreation, that of temporary marriage is recreation, sexual enjoyment.[23] Although the Shi‘i ‘ulama's emphasis has shifted after the revolution of 1979, their rationale all along has been that men need to have a substitute wife when they are away from their wives, or when their own wives are unavailable for whatever reason.

A contract of marriage of either form obliges a woman to be obedient to her husband. In an Islamic marriage obedience, *tamkin*, is not merely a culturally accepted behaviour for women. It is rather a binding legal obligation. Not only the logic of the marriage contract demands that from women, it is also sanctioned in the Qur'an. As the 'purchaser' in the contract (the one who pays for the woman), legal and cultural mechanisms must be provisioned so that he can take 'possession' of the object of sale.[24] The prompt payment of a wife's maintenance is tied in with her obedience, tamkin, and good behaviour towards her husband. The importance of obedience - which is legally binding on married women - is repeatedly underscored in the Qur'an, resonating in the literature of the religious elite as well as in popular culture throughout the centuries. Men are advised to treat their disobedient wives accordingly : 'As for those of whom ye fear rebellion, admonish (banish) them to the beds apart, and scourge them. Then if they obey you, seek not a way against them. Lo! Allah is ever High, Exalted, Great'.[25]

Ayatollah Khomeini's comments are indicative of the continuity of his predecessors' rationale. 'A permanent wife', he writes, 'must not leave the house without her husband's permission, and must submit, *taslim*, herself for what ever pleasure he wants... In this case her maintenance is incumbent upon her husband. If she does not obey him, she is a sinner, *gunahkar*, and has no right to clothing, housing, or sleeping...'[26] Majlisi, the most prominent seventeenth century Shi‘i scholar, relates the following sayings from the

---

Haeri, *Law of Desire*; Rubin Levy, *Introduction to the Sociology of Islam*, London, 1931-1933, Vol.2, pp.131-190; A. A. Fayzee, *Outlines of Muhamadan Law*, Delhi, 1974, pp.117-121.

[23]Tusi, *An-Nihaya,* pp.497-502; Hilli, *Sharaye‘ al-Islam,* p.524; Khomeini, *Tawzih al-Masa'il,* para.2421-2431; Mutahhari, *Nizam-i Huquq-i Zan dar Islam*, p.38.

[24]Qur'an 4:34 and 2:223.

[25]Qur'an 2:34; see also R. Maybudi, *Kashf al-Asrar va ‘Uddat al-Abrar*, Tehran, 1952-61, for an interpretation of the Sura of Women, at Vol.2, 1952, pp.401-792.

[26]Khomeini, *Tawzih al-Masa'il,* para. 2412-13; see also Khomeini, *The Practical Laws of Islam*, Tehran, 1983, p.115; Hilli, *Sharaye‘ al-Islam,* pp.715-32; Tusi, *An-Nihaya,* p.483; Imami, *Huquq-i Madani*, Vol.4, p.47; Langarudi, *Huquq-i Khanivadih*, p.173; S. Ardistani, *Islam va Masa'il-i Jinsi va Zanashu'i*, Tehran, n.d., p.239; Schacht, *An Introduction to Islamic Law,* p.166.

Prophet : 'Any time a husband wants to have intercourse with his wife she should not deny him, not even if she is riding a camel'.[27]

The law is not totally oblivious to female sexuality, however. A married man is to spend every fourth night with one of his wives, if he has more than one. This is known as the right of sleeping arrangement. If he has less than four wives he can of course spend as many nights with her as he desires. But it should not be less than every fourth night with one of his wives. While he is expected to spend his time with one of the wives, he is not required to be intimate with her (them). In fact women are often advised not to be too demanding in expecting performance from their husbands. Once every fourth month, however, a husband is legally required to have intercourse with his wife. This is called the right of intercourse, which if denied can be used as a ground for complaint by a woman.

The assumption here is that biologically, men and women have fundamentally different sexual make-ups and needs. Whereas men cannot sexually restrain themselves and must be satisfied on demand, women can and must wait for their turn. Legally, too, as 'purchaser' in the marriage contract, and as one who supports the woman, a man should have total control over the object of the sale, ie her sexuality, and by extension, herself.

III. Divine Determinism

> 'When ye (men) put away women, put them away for their (legal) period, and keep your duty to Allah, your Lord. Expel them not from their houses nor let them go forth unless they commit open immorality'.[28]
>
> 'Of all things permissible, divorce *(talaq)* is the most blameworthy.' The Prophet Muhammad.

The Ayatollah Mahdavi Kirmani, head of Family Courts in Iran and a contemporary Shi'i scholar, was asked to comment on Muslim women's rights and obligations in divorce. He related the following story,"Imam Ja'far as-Sadiq said, 'My father contracted a wife for me. She was temperamental, *bad akhlaq*. I complained to my father. He said 'What is preventing you from divorcing her ? God has given you this right."'[29]

Obedience, tamkin, is the key concept we focus on in this section. The cornerstone of the Shi'i worldview regarding social order is that of obedience. Islam means submission and obedience. Like the concepts of contract and nature, the concept of obedience has the characteristics of a 'root paradigm'.[30]

---

[27]Muhammad Baqer Majlisi, *Hulyat al-Muttaqin,* Tehran, n.d., p.76.

[28]Qur'an, Sura of Divorce:1

[29]Cited in *Zan-i Ruz,* 1985 (≠1046), pp.40-41.

[30]Root paradigms 'have reference not only to the current state of social relations existing or developing between actors, but also to the cultural goals, means, ideas, outlooks, currents of thought, patterns of beliefs..., which enter into those relationships, interpret them, and incline

The social system is based on the assumption of obedience, functioning at a series of concentric levels. Social order is thus maintained if man is obedient to God, ordinary people are obedient to the supreme leader, ie the king or the imam, women are obedient to their fathers and husbands, and children are obedient to their fathers. Constituting the dominant morality, obedience thus becomes a powerful disciplinary 'agency' in society, and ensures the smooth and proper functioning of social order. In the absence of obedience chaos will reign. Thus a disobedient woman is labeled a *nashiza*, a rebellious one who has to be punished, for her action brings about disorder and chaos.

Being a contract, an Islamic marriage inevitably has its own demise built into its structure. Although Islamic teachings generally discourage divorce, nonetheless Islamic law does give the husband the unilateral right to divorce his wife or wives. This right is sanctioned in the Qur'an and as such is divine,[31] and therefore unchanging. Divorce is but one variation, though the most important one, of the break-up of marriage. An Islamic marriage may also be brought to an end through a judicial decision, or an annulment. In addition, the logic of marriage contract entitles a husband to return the 'goods' anytime he does not wish to keep them. Theoretically nothing stands in his way. The logic of the contract gives him the right, the law of nature dictates it, and the divine law blesses it.

It might be asked here that if marriage is a contract of exchange requiring both the husband and the wife's agreement for its effectiveness, then how is it that its termination is essentially a prerogative of the man. Here lies the most important distinction between a contract of marriage and a contract of sale. A contract of sale establishes a legal relationship between any two individuals (or groups). Although it is an irrevocable contract, it may be canceled by either party only if instances of fraud, deception, defect, or others, are discovered after concluding the contract. But a contract of marriage is both irrevocable and revocable simultaneously. This is to say, as far as the husband is concerned, a contract of marriage is permissible, *jayiz*, and revocable; he can divorce his wife any time he wants. The same contract, however, becomes irrevocable, *lazim*, as far as the wife is concerned.[32] She cannot terminate the contract unilaterally; that right is reserved for her husband only. Under special circumstances, however, should she desire a divorce, she has to go to court. There her request has to be litigated upon and agreed to by her husband. In addition to a legal relation, a contract of marriage legitimates a *sexual* relation between a man and a woman. Although the husband becomes legally in charge of the object of sale (women's sexual and reproductive organs), the object in fact remains in possession of the woman herself. Conceptually, therefore, a man gains a double relation to his

---

them to alliance or divisiveness'. See V. Turner, *Dramas, Fields, and Metaphors,* Cornell, 1974, p.64.

31 Qur'an 2: 226-237, and Sura of Divorce.

32 An irrevocable (lazim) contract is the type of contract in which neither party has the right to cancel the contract unilaterally unless under special circumstances. See Aqa Muhammad Sangalaji, *Kulliyat-i 'uqud va Iqa'at va Qanun-i Riza' dar Islam,* Teheran, n.d., p.13.

wife; one to her sexual and reproductive organ as the object of sale, and the other to her as a person.[33] Acting as an intermediary between God and his wife, a husband is empowered to act autonomously. Just as divine command supersedes man-made laws, a husband's wish takes precedence over those of his wife. It follows that, although marriage is essentially a contract of sale in form and procedure, its termination does not necessarily require mutual consent.

According to Shi'i law a divorce may take several forms, the most common form of which is the revocable divorce. A revocable, *rij'i* (literally returnable), divorce is a semi-final divorce in which the bonds of marriage are not completely severed. Although the husband and wife are separated from each other, the wife cannot marry within the next three months following her divorce, and the husband has the right to return to his wife during this period and to resume his marital duties. Just as he has the right to return, she has the right to be supported. On the other hand the husband's right to return is unilateral, meaning that legally the wife's consent is not sought.[34] Islamic law stipulates that a man may divorce his wife twice and then return to her during the waiting period. But after the third time the divorce is no longer revocable. It becomes 'irrevocable'. Unlike Sunni law that permits the pronouncement of a triple 'I divorce thee' at once, Shi'i law prohibits such an act, and views it not to be legally binding.

An irrevocable (*ba'in*) divorce is when the dissolution of marriage is final from the moment of pronouncement. In this form of divorce the husband's right to return and the wife's right to maintenance are both curtailed. The wife however has to abstain from sexual intercourse by observing her allotted three months waiting period. Divorce of a woman who has been repudiated twice under the revocable kind, that of a woman past her menopause and of a girl who has not reached the age of menstruation, are all irrevocable. In the former two cases, however, the wife is also not bound to maintain abstinence after divorce.

The existence, or absence, of certain conditions in the marriage contract gives both the husband and wife an option to annul the marriage contract.[35] Because of the greater sociological dimension of marriage, Imami argues,[36] the option to annul a marriage contract is limited to three out of several other variations of cancellation specified for a contract of sale. Although the marital

---

[33]For a discussion on this point see Haeri, *The Law of Desire*, pp.66-67.

[34]Khomeini, *Tawzih al-Masa'il*, para.2525; Langarudi, *Huquq-i Khanivadih*, pp.245-248; Katuzian, *Huquq-i Madani*, p.382. Before Islam a husband could apparently return to his wife indefinitely, and could thus keep her in such a suspended state. The Prophet Muhammad put an end to this practice by limiting to three the number of times a husband could repudiate his wife and take her back again (Qur'an 2:231, see also Maybudi, *Kashf al-Asrar va 'Uddat al-Abrar*, vol.1, p. 617; Langarudi, *Huquq-i Khanivadih*, p.92).

[35]Imami, *Huquq-i Madani*, Vol. 4, p.363; Schacht, *Introduction to Islamic Law*, p.148.

[36]Imami, *Huquq-i Madani*, Vol. 4, p.363.

relation is severed, the annulment of marriage is not legally equivalent to divorce.[37]

Divorce and annulment are each other's antithesis, each reflecting the divine and secular dimensions of marriage contract respectively. Whereas divorce cuts across the law of Muslim contract of sale by being the exclusive right of the husband, the annulment of marriage follows directly the procedures and format of a contract of sale: it is a mutual right.

Since the revolution of 1979, attempts have been made to 'purify' Iranian family law, and to harmonize it with the shari'a as presently interpreted and implemented by the Islamic regime. Despite the changes made in the Iranian civil law in the early 1930s, however, Iranian family law never significantly deviated from the basic tenets of Shi'i law. It has been essentially a verbatim codification of the shari'a.[38] Because of an ongoing tension in the understanding of the law, the Islamic regime has been recently trying to adopt a policy to standardise (*vahdat-i raviyya*) different interpretations of the shari'a.[39]

Using the concept of contract as a paradigm, the Islamic regime has introduced some modifications in family law. This is to say, while the greater boundaries of the law have been left unchanged, conditions can be included in the contract to temper a man's right to plural marriages and unilateral divorce. The idea of including conditions in the marriage contract is hardly an innovation. Traditionally, alert women and concerned parents have required conditions favourable to the woman to be inserted in a marriage contract in order to safeguard her rights. On this basis, the Islamic regime has proposed twelve conditions that are to be read to the husband and wife at the time of signing the marriage contract, and every single one of them has to be signed by both husband and wife in order for them to be legally effective. In fact the major reason for many of the 'ulama's objection to the original Family Protection of Law of 1967,[40] had to do with the requirements of the contract. In the Family Protection Law of 1967 the clauses concerned with limitation of plural marriages and unilateral divorce were automatically inserted in all marriage contracts regardless of whether a man agreed to them. The 'ulama regarded this as un-Islamic and thus illegal. Instead, in the new version of family law, they have emphasised the role of the contract, giving husband and wife a chance to agree on the conditions of their marriage contract.

In the present regime's version, only those conditions that have the signature of both husband and wife are legally binding. Whether the spouses decide to sign only one, or choose to sign none of the conditions, the marriage contract is still valid. The first condition in this new set of modifications is

---

[37] Hilli, *Mukhtasar-i Nafi'*, p.238; Imami, *Huquq-i Madani*, Vol. 4, p.476.

[38] See A. Banani, *The Modernisation of Iran, 1921-41*, Stanford, 1960.

[39] See F. Qurbani, *Majmu'ih-i Kamil-i Qavanin va Muqarrarat-i Huquqi*, Tehran, 1988.

[40] See D. Hinchcliffe, 'The Iranian Family Protection Act', in *International and Comparative Law Quarterly*, 17:2, 1968, pp.516-521. The law was further modified in 1975.

specifically related to right of the woman at the time of divorce. It reads: 'In a marriage contract, if a divorce is not requested by the wife and if in the court's judgement the request of divorce is not due to her ill temper and behaviour, then the husband is required to pay her up to half of his income earned during the time they have been married together, or something equivalent to it as deemed appropriate by the court'.[41]

There are obviously several flaws in this condition. To begin with, the request must not come from the wife, since that goes under the category of divorce of the *khul'* kind with its own different set of requirements. In this case not only must a wife forgo her brideprice, she must even pay something in order to buy her freedom. Her right to apply for dissolution of marriage, however, is qualitatively different from that of the man's: she cannot implement her decision unilaterally. Not only must the demand for divorce be litigated, but her husband has to agree to it. A woman may initiate divorce and buy back, as it were, her freedom. The Qur'an puts it this way: 'It is not lawful for you that ye take from woman aught of that of which ye have given them; ....And if ye fear that they may not be able to keep to the limits of God, in that case it is no sin for either of them if the woman ransom herself'.[42]

Properly speaking, khul' means to take off, e.g. one's clothes. In a metaphorical language the Qur'an refers to man and wife as each other's 'wear', that clothe and cover one another.[43] A divorce of the khul' kind is usually initiated by a woman who feels strong repugnance towards her husband and is no longer willing to 'wear' him. Because marriage is a contract, and because some money in the form of brideprice has been exchanged, actually or symbolically, the wife therefore may obtain her freedom in exchange for some money more or less equal to her brideprice. Significantly, khul' is not a unilateral privilege for women, the same way repudiation (talaq) is for men. Rather, it is considered as a contract of exchange, in which mutual agreement and acceptance play fundamental roles. Legally speaking, therefore, khul' is not the equivalent of talaq, though it serves the same purpose. This is why the term khul' and not the word talaq is used. Although local custom may greatly influence the custom of khul', in a Muslim tradition 'khul' can never be enforced unilaterally by the wife herself'.[44] This means that the husband must agree to it, for khul' is a contract, and so requires mutual consent by both husband and wife. A divorce of the khul' kind is irrevocable: the husband and wife both forgo their respective rights to return and to maintenance during the wife's three months waiting period.[45]

---

[41]For a detailed description see *Iran Times* 1986 (≠760), 1, 11.

[42]Qur'an, 2:229.

[43]Qur'an, 2:187.

[44]N. Coulson, *Conflict and Tensions in Islamic Jurisprudence,* Chicago, 1959, p.19.

[45]Hilli, *Mukhtasar-i Nafi'*, Persian tr. by E. Yarshater and M.T. Danish Pazuh, Tehran, 1964, p.257; Khomeini, *Tawzih al-Masa'il,* para. 2528; Langarudi, *Huquq-i Khanivadih*, p.252; Robertson Smith, *Kinship and Marriage,* p.92; Levy, *The Social Structure*, p.122. Another variation on the theme of divorce is *mubara'a*, separation. Here the feeling of dislike is mutual.

Secondly, the divorce must not be caused by the wife's 'ill temperament and behaviour'. Determination of a wife's good or bad temperament is a totally subjective matter based on a husband's interpretation of her behaviour. Potentially a wife is always in danger of being accused of disobedience, *nushuz*.[46] Whereas a husband, given his unilateral right to divorce, does not need to provide any proof of the actual incompatibility of his wife's behaviour, a wife must *prove* her husband's ill treatment in order to get the court to even hear her out.[47]

Thirdly, assuming that she emerges successfully from the first two ordeals, she will receive *up to* half of his income earned during their married life. This again has left many women and men confused. It does not mean that a man will have to give half of his income to his wife automatically. Nor does it mean that it will be half of his wealth, but only up to half of his income or an amount equivalent to it as deemed appropriate by a judge. Most importantly, the whole affair is null and void if the husband refuses to sign each and every one of these conditions to begin with. According to one report,[48] in the month preceding Ramadan alone, more than a hundred marriage engagements were broken off at the last minute when the man's family came to know of the implications of these conditions. This was partly due to the fact that the 'law' was relatively new and that no concerted effort had been made to educate the public about it beforehand. Some women, on their part, knowing that there are always other women who are willing to contract a marriage without these conditions, or feeling the pressure of the moment, or facing the fear of loosing their opportunity, agree to forgo these conditions, only to leave themselves vulnerable to the built-in insecurities of the marriage contract, and to the whims of a capricious spouse. In addition, women could even be prevented from taking possession of those items that they brought to their husbands' homes at the time of their marriage if they neglect to make a list and have it signed by their husbands. The wife needs to

---

Like divorce of the khul' kind, mubara'a is an irrevocable divorce, meaning that no provisions are envisaged for the spouses during the wife's waiting period. Here, too, she has to ransom herself by paying something equal to or less than her brideprice to her husband in return for her freedom. It ought not be more than her brideprice, because in this situation neither one is happy with the marriage; see the above sources.

[46] Nushuz is a legal category meaning disobedience of one's marital duties. It includes both husband's refusal to support his wife and the wife's refusal to grant her husband's wishes, particularly in sexual matters (Langarudi, *Huquq-i Khanivadih*, p.173; Imami, *Huquq-i Madani,* vol. 4, p.453). Popularly, a 'disobedient' woman is labeled *nashizih*, which is a pejorative term. Not only is the husband spared such a pejorative cultural categorisation, he can use his discretion in interpreting his wife's disobedience and execute his privileges accordingly. One of my informants who did not share her husband's eccentric taste ('unnatural', as she put it) in matters of sexuality was denied financial support because her husband accused her of disobedience.

[47] A young woman who was physically abused by her husband was told by the court that she must provide evidence before he would be issued a warning. In other words, she had to convince the judge that her husband had been ill-treating her, before she could proceed to file for divorce; whilst her husband accused her of disobedience and refused to provide maintenance for her or divorce her. *Zan-i Ruz,* 1989 (≠1211), p.52.

[48] *Iran Times*, 3 June 1986 (≠760), p.1.

prove her ownership over her own belongings. Faced with all kinds of problems and tensions, the popular woman's weekly magazine *Zan-i Ruz* has been publishing a series of articles informing women of their rights, and emphasising the fact that unless women sign every single condition in their marriage contract, they will have no recourse in case their marriage falls apart.[49]

Knowing that divorce is their divine right, and that they do not have to provide a divorced wife beyond her three months waiting period (that is, if divorce is of the revocable kind), very few men sign these conditions voluntarily. One marriage contract is as good as any other. If a woman or her family insist that the potential husband sign these conditions, he can always cancel the marriage altogether and look for another woman. Even if some men do sign these conditions, when the time comes they may not necessarily leave it unchallenged. They still have the right to refuse to divorce their wives. Or conversely, they can make life so miserable for their wives to force them to start a divorce procedure. In this case not only does the husband not have to give his wife anything, he is even entitled to receive some compensation since the separation will fall under khul'. One can read in *Zan-i Ruz* many stories of injustices done to women at the time of divorce, and the pain many women face by denial of custody over their children, lack of proper payment, etc.

The ambivalence the 'ulama feel regarding classification of marriage as a contract stands in sharp contrast to the clarity of their position on the contractual nature of marriage as far as divorce is concerned. They put emphasis on the contractual logic of marriage in order to provide changes in the law of divorce to spell relief for women. What they have consistently chosen to neglect is the fact that men and women do not negotiate a marriage contract from a position of social, psychological, economic, or legal equality. This is where the tension lies, and where most of the confusion surrounding the spouses' expectations of marital relations arises. On the one hand the 'ulama object strongly to the notion that brideprice functions like price in a contract of a sale, or that reward in a contract of temporary marriage is like the wage earned by a lessee.[50] On the other hand, in discussing divorce and deciding its outcome they emphasise the role of contract and the sanctity of the initial agreement between the spouses. This seems to have created a genuine bewilderment in the minds of many Iranians, particularly those who must rely on oral knowledge.

The Shi'i doctrinal images of men and women as conveyed through different forms of marriage contract and divorce are determined on the basis of a set of preordained hierarchical divine commands and biological, legal, and 'natural' rights. Because of the inherent assumption of ownership and purchase in an Islamic contract of marriage, although both men and women

---

[49] *Zan-i Ruz*, 1988 (≠1178), pp.18-19, 48, and (≠1186), p.14-15; see also various issues of *Zan-i Ruz* in the period 1987-1989.

[50] See Mutahhari, *Nizam-i Huquq-i Zan*, pp.193-242.

are assumed to be partners in the contract, only men are automatically and ideologically perceived to be complete, 'full' individuals: biologically, legally, socially, and psychologically. They are considered to be independent, superior, and dominant. Ironically, however, while women are objectified and relegated to the realm of nature, and consequently considered to lack self-control, in essence, Shi'i law and ideology acknowledge the urgency, vulnerability, and unpredictability of male sexuality by legitimating sexual gratification through various institutions such as permanent marriage, temporary marriage and concubinage with one's own bond maidens, as well as through the institution of divorce.

5. SHI'ISM AND SUNNISM IN IRAQ: REVISITING THE CODES

Chibli Mallat

Introduction

Our purpose is to examine the significance of the Sunni-Shi'i unity (or divide) in Iraq upon the adoption of a unified Code of Personal Status in 1959. By way of caveat, it must be emphasized at the outset that several constraints are characteristic of any research on Iraq. Sources are scarce, and reports of the shari'a courts were not accessible. The development of case-law, which Professor Anderson had described in his seminal commentary on the Code in 1960 as central to the analysis of the status of personal law,[1] has therefore not been possible. But there were other ways which could be probed, and the present essay looks into the problems across the Shi'i-Sunni divide which the Code faced in its early days. The discovery of a treatise emanating from the Shi'i circles most opposed to the unification of the law, as well as the milieu which formed the backbone of this opposition, will serve as points of focus for a reassessment of the Iraqi family Code in its 'unified personal law system v. community personal laws' dimension.[2]

The treatise which forms the basis of the reassessment was published in Najaf in 1963. It was written by a promising young scholar, Muhammad Bahr al-'Ulum.[3] Bahr al-'Ulum, who was born in 1927, belongs to a Shi'i family famous for its scholarship in the law, and he himself continued to publish

---

[1]See Norman Anderson, 'A Law of Personal Status for Iraq', *International and Comparative Law Quarterly,* 1960, pp.542-564, at p.545; Y. Linant de Bellefonds, 'Le Code du Statut Personnel Irakien du 30 Décembre 1959', *Studia Islamica,* 1960, pp.79-135. In Arabic, a comprehensive early study is Muhsin Naji, *Sharh Qanun al-Ahwal ash-Shakhsiyya,* Baghdad, 1962. Law 188 of 1959 (*Qanun al-Ahwal ash-Shakhsiyya*) can be found in the Appendix to this book, as well in the Iraqi Official Journal, *al-Waqa'i' al-'Iraqiyya,* Issue 280, 30.12. 1959. The 1963 Amendment appears in issue 785, dated 21.3.1963. For subsequent Amendments, see the Conclusion to this chapter. On personal status in Iraq, see also 'Ala' ad-Din Kharufa, *Sharh Qanun al-Ahwal ash-Shahkhsiyya,* 2 Vols, Baghdad, 1962-1963; Muhammad Shafiq al-'Ani, *Ahkam al-Ahwal ash-Shakhsiyya fil-'Iraq*, n.p., 1970.

[2]On this question, see the Introduction to this volume.

[3]Muhammad Bahr al-'Ulum, *Adwa' 'ala Qanun al-Ahwal ash-Shakhsiyya al-'Iraqi* (Lights on the Iraqi law of personal status), Najaf, at the Na'man press, 1963. For convenience, the book will be referred to in the main text of this chapter as *Adwa'*, followed by the page number.

prolifically in various fields of the shari'a.[4] Once a *shar'i* judge,[5] Bahr al-'Ulum was propelled by Iraqi politics into opposition, then into exile. Since 1969, he has been living outside Iraq, in the Gulf, Iran, Egypt, then England, where he is recognised as a spiritual and political leader of the Iraqi Shi'i community. In the early 1960s, his already evident scholarship rendered him close to the highest Shi'i *marja'* of the time, Muhsin at-Tabataba'i al-Hakim:[6] the significance of his contribution to the debate on the Iraqi family Code stems also from the perception that he was acting as a spokesman to the higher Shi'i legal circles. Hakim's works, as well as his personal opinions to Bahr al-'Ulum, are often quoted in *Adwa'*.

Adwa' sheds an important light on the controversy over the Code of Personal Status as it was perceived in Najaf in the Ja'fari[7] circles of the 'ulama. The opposition to the Code in these circles was at the origin of the most important amendment to the 1959 text. This First Amendment to the Iraqi Code of Personal Status, which was among the immediate legislative measures introduced by the protagonists of the 1963 coup against the ruler General 'Abd al-Karim Qasem, repealed the whole section on inheritance, altered the law of polygamy, and replaced them with rules more consonent with the classical shari'a.[8] But *Adwa'*, like the Amendment, was published in 1963, and it does not fail to take into account the new legislation. In fact, the date of publication is not a coincidence. *Adwa'* came as the scholarly response of the Shi'i circles opposition in Najaf to the legislative revolution introduced by General Qasem upon coming to power in 1959. From 1959 to 1963, Najaf strongly opposed the Code, and it is partly to take this criticism into account that the new government introduced the 1963 Amendment. As a consequence, albeit a result of research pursued before the Amendment, *Adwa'* had to take into consideration the modifications of the new régime in power in 1963. The full Code, with the amendments of 1963, is the subject of *Adwa'*. Although its

[4]Muhammad Bahr al-'Ulum has written widely on Islamic law topics. His most important books are, besides *Adwa'*, *al-Ijtihad*, Beirut, 1977, *Masdar at-Tashri' li-Nizam al-Mulk fil-Islam* (The Source of legislation in the Islamic system of government), Beirut, 1977, and *'Uyub al-Irada fish-Shari'a al-Islamiyya* (Vices of consent in Islamic law), Beirut, 1984.

[5]Shar'i judge in this article is used, following the thrust of its occurrence in *Adwa'*, as the personal status judge, as contrasted with the secular judges in the civil and administrative courts. Ths system of courts is now unified in Iraq for all Muslims, but there are family law divisions which specialize in personal status matters.

[6]Muhsin al-Hakim was, until his death in 1970, recognised as the most prominent Shi'i scholar (known as marja', reference) in Iraq. In 1964, he offered his protection to Ruhullah al-Khumaini, who remained in Najaf until the beginning of the Iranian Revolution in 1978. Hakim is the author of several treatises on Islamic law, most important of which are *Minhaj as-Salihin,* 2 vols, Beirut, 1976 and 1980; *Mustamsak al-'Urwa al-Wuthqa,* 14 Vols, 4th ed. Beirut, 1971.

[7]The word Ja'fari is in reference to followers of Imam Ja'far as-Sadeq, who, among the twelve recognised Imams of the Shi'i tradition, was the most competent in legal matters. In this chapter, as in *Adwa'*, the words Ja'fari, Imami, Ithna 'ashari (Twelver) and Shi'i are interchangeable.

[8]For a full review, see Norman Anderson, 'Changes in the Law of Personal Status in Iraq', *International and Comparative Law Quarterly,* 1963, pp.1026-1031.

criticism of the section on inheritance was mooted by the adoption of the Amendment, and was thereby been significantly altered from what it could have been in the original proposal, the project undertaken by Muhammad Bahr al-'Ulum was wider and more fundamental: the whole Iraqi Code is subjected to an article by article criticism.

Before addressing the substantive and formal criticism which unravel in the work of Muhammad Bahr al-'Ulum, and in view of the importance of Najaf in the contemporary Shi'i world, it is worth describing the context of the family law controversy through a détour in the legal-theological structure of the Shi'i system. Muhammad Bahr al-'Ulum's work was the scholarly expression of a wide and significant social and educational legal structure.

I. The Legal Importance of Najaf

Najaf is associated in the Shi'i worldview with two characteristics. It is first a site for pilgrimage, with a number of shrines most important of which is the grave of 'Ali, the son-in-law and cousin of the Prophet Muhammad, as well as the first of the Imams in the Shi'i theological tradition. It is secondly a high centre of religious-legal scholarship. It is the second dimension which is central to the importance of Najaf from a legal point of view. Two manifestations of this role bear on the present analysis. The 'civil society' of Shi'ism is normally governed by the Shi'i shari'a, and makes for a distinct and autonomous legal and social system which sets the community apart in the Iraqi state, particularly as against the politically dominant Sunni group.[9] Secondly, the distinctive structure of Shi'ism is shared beyond the confines of the Nation-state. Najaf is at the centre of an international web which has put its 'ulama centre-stage, both from a legal and a political point of view, in the second half of the twentieth century.[10]

The Legal Structure of Civil Society

There are in theory two categories of persons which are recognized by modern Shi'i law: the *mujtahid*s and the *muqallid*s. A mujtahid ought 'to be able of deduction in all fields of *fiqh* (jurisprudence)' or at least in one of these fields. He is capable of *ijtihad*. The muqallid is the layman, who is devoid of such knowledge. He or she is bound to follow the mujtahid's decrees. The process of following or imitating is called *taqlid*. The rule admits no exception:

9The Arab Shi'is of Iraq form a distinct majority of the population (50 to 60%, depending on the estimates). Arab Sunnis constitute some 20% of the population, and have traditionally been the dominant group in Baghdad. The rest of the population is constituted by Kurds (mostly Sunnis), and Christian minorities. The Jewish and Yezidi constituencies are now insignificant.

10For more on Najaf, see C. Mallat, 'The Renaissance of Islamic Law', Ph.D. London, 1990, pp.53-89.

> The act of a layman (*'ammi*) who proceeds without taqlid or without *ihtiyat* [defined as 'the act which is certain in good faith when in presence of an unknown matter'] is void, except in two cases: (1) if the muqallid acts in accordance with the *fatwa* (decree) of the mujtahid he follows; (2) if the act performed is a matter of worship, in case of an approximation of the situation [i.e. its close resemblance to rituals usually performed]. Nonetheless, in the latter occurrence, it is recommended that the act be consonant with the fatwa of the mujtahid whom the muqallid should have related to at the time of performing of the act.[11]

The way a Shi'i comes out of taqlid to become a mujtahid is determined by his success and reputation after a long learning process undertaken with renowned scholars in the *madrasa*s (schools) of a given city. In the twentieth century, two such cities were dominant in the Shi'i world: Najaf and Qum.[12] Especially since the grip of the Iranian Shah had increased after the Second World War, Najaf had become a haven which was relatively free from state interference, and the scholars of the city were able to constitute a pool of talents which attracted students from all over the world, and encouraged the most promising graduates to stay in the city and, in turn, dispense their own teaching.

The graduation process of Najaf and the schools' curriculum can be assessed against the description of Shi'i civil society by the Great Ayatollah Khu'i. The essential task of the Shi'i colleges in the city was to form and train scholars who would lead the community as mujtahids. For the apprentice who becomes a mujtahid, then chooses to leave Najaf to go to Iran, India, Afghanistan, or Lebanon, a recommendation from his teachers will accompany him, and will be very influential for a position of judge or of religious leader in his country of destination. A stay in Najaf, like a stay at the Cairo Azhar for a Sunni, is very prestigious. The reputation of the scholar trained in Najaf, which is enhanced by the network of the Shi'i 'ulama, the visits to the shrines of Najaf by compatriots, and all the intricate contacts betweeen the civil society and the hierarchy of 'ulama, puts him in a position which commands respect in the society. This position is also the key to his financial survival in the city or village where he resides if he chooses to leave Najaf.

Voluntary taxation is another aspect of the network created by the legal structure. The *sahm al-imam*, which is the tax levied for the *'alim* (singular of 'ulama) in his capacity of representative of the Hidden Imam, constitutes one of the two essential revenues of the 'ulama, the other being the *khums*, which is paid to most mujtahids in their capacity as *sayyid*s, or descendants of the

[11] Abul Qasem al-Khu'i, *al-Masa'el al-Muntakhaba,* 22nd ed. Beirut, 1985, p.2-3.

[12] On the madrasas in Qum, see generally M. Fischer, *Iran: From Dispute to Revolution,* Cambridge, Mass., 1980.

Prophet through his daughter Fatima and the first Imam 'Ali.[13] The degree to which the tax is paid varies naturally with the relative wealth of the society where it is levied, and with the fame of the 'alim it is paid to. Since the state system is completely independent from the Shi'i structure, such tax cannot be enforced with the help of coercive measures. Depending on the religious commitment of the followers of a 'alim, financial support will consequently be more or less forthcoming, and there is competition among the 'ulama for the pool of financial support.

The pooling of religious taxes is obviously not structured. Lack of structure is owed in the first place to the impossibility to enforce taxation without state power. But it is also due to a combination of the international character of the Shi'i civil society system and to the absolute freedom for a muqallid to choose his or her own mujtahid.

Internationalism

Students coming from all over the Shi'i world form an international pool of graduates for the Najaf colleges. Internationalism is of the essence in the Najaf network. It also derives from the constant interaction between the 'ulama of the various parts of the Shi'i world after they have graduated from Najaf, and internationalism is enhanced on the level of the population at large by the visits and pilgrimages, as well as by a mystique surrounding the burial in Najaf, the 'valley of peace'. Najaf is in this context only the most prominent pilgrimage. In Qum and in Mashhad, flows of visitors stream to the holy places, and the structure of pilgrimages suggests a dense network of varying intensities.[14]

Legal scholarship and religiosity are peculiarly intertwined in Shi'i civil society. The pilgrimage to Najaf or to Qum depends to a large extent on the importance of the scholars in the city. This appears in remarkable contrast to the Sunni world, where the pilgrimage to Mecca is completely independent from the reputation of the city as a centre of Islamic learning. Of course, there is, in the same way as the *hajar* in Mecca, the *sahn sharif* in Najaf, where the first Shi'i Imam is believed to be resting. But the ritualistic dimension is secondary to the connection between the Najaf scholars and the Shi'i lay visitors of the city, who will have known of an eminent mujtahid to whom

[13]On khums in Shi'i law, see M.H. al-Milani, *Muhadarat fi Fiqh al-Imamiyya, Kitab al-Khums*, F. Milani ed., n.p., 1980.

[14]Political and more arcane scholarly reasons will impress upon the various flows. The most dramatic recent example is of course the barring of Najaf to Iranian visitors after the war with Iraq, but even in more relaxed times, the flow of visitors will be subject to some or the other turbulences of the Middle Eastern scene. On the scholarly level, the history of Najaf and the central Shi'i places suggests that the reputation of a particular Shi'i centre of learning will significantly affect the ebb and flow of the visitors. At the turn of the century, Karbala and Kazimiyya were more important in Iraq than Najaf, and in the thirties, the foundation of Qum as a centre of learning under the scholarship of Ayat Allah al-Ha'eri pushed Najaf momentarily into the background. Since the mid-1940s however, and until the 1970s, Najaf had recovered its importance in the Shi'i world as the most respected centre of learning.

they pay tribute (both legally and financially), and whom they may be able to see and listen to.

The choice of a muqallid by the layman is in this respect absolutely free. In theory, it is compulsory for the muqallid to choose a *living* mujtahid, and this feature of the Shi'i Usuli Schools figures as the most important distinctive mark of the School in contradistinction with the Akhbaris.[15] If Usulism compels taqlid, it does not interfere in the choice of the jurist who is imitated. As a consequence, the way a *'alim* becomes important comes not only from the superiority of his knowledge of the law as is recognized in his educational training. It is also vital that he relates to the mass of lay persons, and that they also recognize his religious leadership. Since the muqallids are free to choose the mujtahid they prefer, a mujtahid's importance will grow proportionately to the number of his muqallids. This importance is not only scholarly. The mujtahid is also rewarded financially by his muqallids as the recipient of sahm al-imam.

Internationalism is decisive in this respect, since a muqallid can choose beyond his geographical confine, and reach in his taqlid the far away 'ulama whom he knows by reputation. Thus, it is common for a Shi'i in Lebanon or in India to profess taqlid of an Iraqi mujtahid. Nationality in this respect is neutral. The Shi'i civil society transcends state boundaries.[16] Why this importance, and the number of muqallids, is disputed is partly due to the fact that the system is essentially oral. There is no register of taqlid. But were there a central register, it would be meaningless. The lay Shi'is have several ways of 'practising' their taqlid. Since there is no coercion at any level in the system, the gamut of taqlid will run from absolute passivity to hearty financial and religious commitment. The only constraint, which is the hallmark of Usulism, is the necessity of following a *living* mujtahid. This trait guarantees the smooth reproduction of the system.

The Najaf background to the family law controversy must be also understood in terms of the Shi'i 'ulama hierarchical system. As much as the number and devotion of his followers, it is the hierarchy of mujtahids of which he is now part that counts most for the Najaf graduate. This hierarchy, in the contemporary world of Shi'ism, is the key to the most important political events. Education is only part of a much wider context which transcends pure knowledge, and in societies with many Shi'i believers, the Shi'i hierarchy has offered both a social weight or corrective, and a focal organization for popular movements that have rocked the Islamic world in recent years.

The key word to understand Najaf is reputation. In the absence of a strict examination system and of an 'honours' diploma, it is the reputation of the legal competence of a student which allows him to pass from a stage to the next, and it is again his reputation, as recognized by his pairs or by other

---

[15]On Usulim and Akhbarism, see my 'The Renaissance of Islamic Law', pp.37-50.

[16]Today, it is said that the mujtahid who commands the largest number of muqallids is Abul-Qasem al-Khu'i in Najaf.

mujtahids, which decides ultimately of his right to accede the elite of the *marja'iyya*.

The importance of reputation does not stop with graduation. Its centrality from the early days of apprenticeship is recurrent through all the stages of the process of knowledge, and is even more important for the various degrees in the ladder towards supreme ijtihad.

Whether the graduate 'alim remains in Najaf or goes to another city across the Shi'i world (traditionally in the East, including Pakistan and India, but since the late 1960s also in places like Germany, the U.K.,[17] and the United States), he is part of both the educational structure and of Shi'i civil society in its legal dimension of the mujtahid-muqallid dichotomy.

From the educational point of view, he can start teaching at various levels, depending on the students who can come to him. His circle will obviously depend on the place where he professes. A 'alim in Najaf and in Qum will carry more importance than his colleague in Jabal 'Amil (South Lebanon) or in Pakistan. The competition of the various schools and *hauzas*[18] will also affect the mujtahid's educational importance and rayonnement. To this extent, and bearing in mind the flexibility built in the system of 'registration', which will allow any Shi'i to find a teacher and living means in university towns like Najaf and Qum,[19] the mujtahids as professors function only to a degree as their counterparts in Western universities.

The difference with Western teachers is notable. This is true in the educational field, in the civil society at large, as well as in the fiscal dimension of the mujtahids. Financially, as mentioned earlier, the mujtahids are independent from state support, and their revenues will vary largely according to their reputation, to the degree of religiosity of society at large, and of course, according to the wealth and commitment of their muqallids. Since the muqallids' financial support cannot be constrained, the reputation of a given mujtahid will constitute in the final analysis the criterion for taqlid, and the muqallids' financial support.

It is in this context that Bahr al-'Ulum opus must be understood. There was, in the Iraq of the 1960s, a form of autonomous scholarship which was specific to the Shi'is, and the centre of this specificity was Najaf and its colleges and hauzas. This reflected also on the legal sphere in two major ways: in the first place, there was a formal structure which was relatively independent from state control, and that was also true in the autonomy of the family courts. Each religious community had its own court, and the state recognised its decisions and implemented them, without interfering with the internal legal process which was specific to each community. This legal process, in turn, was not only formally distinct. The substance of the law was also different, as a Ja'fari judge would exclusively apply Shi'i law, and a Sunni judge Sunni law. The Code of 1959 evidently constituted a double threat for

[17]This is the case of Muhammad Bahr al-'Ulum.

[18]A hauza is a circle of scholars. It is smaller than a madrasa, and operates informally.

[19]Muhammad Jawad Mughniyya, *Tajarib* (Trials), Beirut, 1980, p.61.

Najaf: it meant that the days of Shi'i legal autonomy were over. It also meant that the whole separate process was in jeopardy. The unified personal law system would prevail over the system of community personal laws. It is therefore along these two lines that *Adwa'* is structured.

II. Formal Criticism

As mentioned earlier, the 1963 Amendment deflected the strongest arguments against the Code that were emanating from Najaf. The Amendment undermined the bold dispositions in the two sections of the Code most blatantly at variance with the traditional shari'a. This concerned some restrictions on the recognition of polygamy, and, more importantly, the rules of intestate succession. 'Abd al-Karim Qasem, who led Iraq from the 1958 Revolution to his deposition and execution in February 1963, had stood fast against '[his] brothers the men of religion' who voiced to him their absolute opposition to these sections of the 1959 Code, 'those sections, in fact, which we regard as representing forward leaps in putting in order the rights of the Iraqi family'.[20] On matters of inheritance in particular, he suggested that 'he who does not wish to be bound by the text of the Code may make a bequest while he is alive to his sons and daughters in such manner as he desires and wishes'[21] [and so circumvent the new legal rules which he may dislike].

Once Qasem was evinced, one of the first measures of the new coalition of Ba'thist and Arab nationalist in power after the 1963 Coup was to abolish these controversial provisions. The short Explanatory Memorandum, which followed the signatures of the full 22-member Cabinet, specified the reasons which led to the adoption of the Amendment:

> The most serious deviation in the legislation enacted by the governement of Qasem was the destruction of the shar'i rules of intestate devolution and their replacement by the transfer of Amiri lands.[22] This event was the cause of an outcry and a rejection which comprised all the classes of Iraqi society, because of the law's opposition to the Holy Book, whose rules Iraqi society had been applying in these matters for centuries since the rise of Islam on these lands.[23]

---

[20]Anderson, 'A Law of Personal Status for Iraq', p.562.

[21]Anderson, *Ibid.*, p. 563.

[22]The original Code of Personal Status had introduced the Civil Code's dispositions on the succession to *amiri* lands (Iraqi Civil Code, Articles 1187-1199, Code of Personal Status 1959, Art. 74) as the general system of inheritance. Amiri land, which is government land generally held on lease for an undetermined period, was distributed according to a system of classes of heirs which openly flouted the shari'a, especially in its ignorance of the principle of a male's double share of the female.

[23]*Al-Waqa'i' al-'Iraqiyya,* issue 785, 21.3.1963.

Though it had been weakened considerably, the opposition of Najaf remained, and its objections took its most sophisticated and scholarly form in Muhammad Bahr al-'Ulum's *Adwa'*.

Bahr al-'Ulum's arguments appear under three headings. The original, and most serious objection, was 'that many of the articles of the Code were contrary to the opinions of the Islamic Schools of law (*madhahib*)' (*Adwa'*, p.11). The book is a patient reconstruction of the variations, not merely of Shi'i, but of all four Sunni Schools in each unacceptable article of the law. As a unique such testimony extant in the modern literature, this will be examined in detail in the next section.

The two other objections are based on technicalities related to the legal process. Bahr al-'Ulum argues that the whole Code was unconstitutional, and that it undermined the accepted and specific role of the shar'i, as opposed to the civil, judge.

Unconstitutionality is read against the Provisional Constitution adopted in Iraq in the wake of the 1958 revolution. Article 20 of the Provisional Constitution mentioned that the 'Presidency of the Republic was constituted by a council with a head and two members', and Art. 21 stipulated that the 'Council of Ministers is responsible for the legislative power with the countersigning of the Presidential Council'. The law of 1959, argues Muhammad Bahr al-'Ulum following the then highest shar'i judge, Muhammad Sadeq as-Sadr, was adopted without the attendance of one of the members of the council who had submitted his resignation. Were one to argue that the majority of two was enough in the decisions of the council, it was necessary, before this majority takes any decision, that a proper meeting of the full council be convened.

The Amendment of 1963 might have changed the picture, admits Bahr al-'Ulum, since the constitutional process was this time fully respected. But then, the new dispositions should not be considered to be an Amendment to an unconstitutional Code. They constitute a new autonomous piece of legislation. (*Adwa'*, pp.14-17)

More interesting than the argument of unconstitutionality, which was overtaken by the events of 1963, was Bahr al-'Ulum's analysis of the danger which a unified Code of Personal Status represented to the function of the shar'i judge.

This argument is two-pronged. First, the criticism is directed to the very existence of the Code:

> It is not proper to legislate a Code of Personal Status which would be binding on the judges of all times. Such Code would be constrictive by the specific nature of its articles, and would constitute a departure from the open-ended nature [of Personal Status matters] in both the scientific and shar'i perspectives as well as an expression of the closure of the gate of ijtihad. (*Adwa'*, p. 26)

Closing the gate of ijtihad is not the sole detrimental effect of the Code. For the young ‘alim from Najaf, codified law also bars the ways of keeping to the tradition. Specific dispositions written down in the Code will prevent the practice of taqlid, and will 'constitute a form of closing the gate of taqlid to the person who imitates (muqallid) a scholar who disagrees with the Code's rules'. This constraint, he argues, affects both Sunnis and Shi‘is.

> For example, if a Hanafi repudiates his wife in a state of drunkenness or under duress, or if he repudiates her subject to a condition, the repudiation would be valid in the School's opinion; yet it is void under the Code,[24] which bars therefore the means of taqlid [to the Hanafi judge]. (*Adwa'*, p. 26)

The argument is also true *viz.* the Shi‘is, as in the presence of witnesses required for the validity of a marriage in Art.6, following the Hanafi School, even though they are not necessary under Ja‘fari law.

Under these conditions, the judge is threatened by the Code in his very competence, as his ability to practise an independent analysis is constrained by the articles. This argument is set forth independently from the judge's School of law. The mere existence of the articles suggests for Bahr al-‘Ulum that the traditional autonomy of the judge is undermined. The constraints are also true for the layman, since the Code is nefarious to the very structure of the social movement available under the muqallid-mujtahid paradigm: the muqallid will not be able to follow a mujtahid whose opinion differs from the letter of the law.[25]

To the argument that legislation inevitably limits the judge's autonomous sphere, Bahr al-‘Ulum argues that the threat to the independence of the judiciary is compounded in matters of personal status. The shar‘i judge, says Bahr al-‘Ulum, represents the quintessence of the *qadi*, as opposed to the civil judge who ought to be better known as a *hakim*, a ruler's appointee and delegate. 'This area of the law [personal status] has been [traditionally] restricted to the Islamic men of jurisprudence [*rijal al-fiqh al-islami*], especially in the ambit of the judiciary, *al-qada'*, because they are the most competent to deduce legal rules from the original sources.' (*Adwa'*, p. 24) In other words, the danger residing in a Code inspired and established by the state is to vest its administration in judges who are incapable of dispensing justice as is required by the sensitive and touchy area of personal status, which is 'the rule of a person's life from the cradle to the grave'. (*Adwa'*, p. 21)

This mistrust is no doubt the expression of the ‘ulama's worries as they saw themselves threatened in a field until then under their control. For the Shi‘i mujtahids, whose distance towards the central state was strengthened by their financial independence, a unified Code meant the end of their expertise

---

[24]Arts. 35 and 36; see infra.

[25]This, of course, is true only of the Shi‘is, but Bahr al-‘Ulum does not make a distinction between Sunnis and Shi‘is at this stage.

and the irruption on their own scene of state-appointed scholars who looked only to the text of the Code for their decisions. For when Qasem was criticizing his 'brother the men of religion' who did not fail to receive their salaries from the state taxation revenues, 'including the duties of wine',[26] this meant principally the Sunni judges. Bahr al-'Ulum, of course, insists that his reservation was 'not limited to the Ja'faris' (*Adwa'*, p. 23). All Muslims, he argues, need 'to go back for their rules to a living 'alim who is a mujtahid in one of the Schools, so that he can issue a fatwa for them in accordance with the rules of their imam [here the imam is the eponym of the School].' (*Adwa'*, p. 25)

The criticism of the establishment of a Code of Personal Status was carried further in *Adwa'*, as the argument overshadowed the strict family law matters, and appears to have been directed at the process of codification itself. After all, Bahr al-'Ulum argues, the curtailment of the diversity of the Schools of law and the restrictions on ijtihad are the result of 'arresting' the text in a fixed form. Why would the authorities [the party responsible, *al-jiha al-mas'ula*] be allowed to hold the community by the opinion of one of the Schools only, as does the Majalla?[27] And why would the courts be limited in space and time, as is specified in Art. 1801 of the Ottoman text ?

The debate becomes here fundamentally an argument for or against codification. This time, the specificity of Ja'farism is clear. In a lengthy commentary, Art. 1801 of the Majalla is faulted on the basis of the necessary independence of the judiciary, the 'alim, from the ruler, and the authority used for the argument is found in a major Ja'fari commentary on the Majalla, published in Iraq during the second world war.[28] Art. 1801 of the Majalla states:

> The judiciary is bound and limited in time and space..., the ruler in charge of judgement who is appointed for a year will rule (judge, *yahkum*) for that one year... similarly the person apppointed in a district is limited to this district... (*Adwa'*, p. 28-9)

This Article expresses clearly the ruler's (*sultan*) right to delegate his powers to appointees limited in their judgments in time, space and competence. This practice, however, is not admitted in Shi'i law. Muhammad Kashif al-Ghata''s *Tahrir al-Majalla* underlines this view. On the Majalla's chapter on the judiciary, Kashif al-Ghata' commented:

> For the Imamis, the judiciary (qada') and the administration of justice (*hakimiyya*) are a divinely-ordained position (*mansib*

---

[26]This remark by Qasem is quoted in Anderson, 'Changes in the Law of Personal Status in Iraq', p.1031.

[27]This is in reference to Majallat al-Ahkam al-'adliyya, the Ottoman Civil Code which was in vigour in Iraq until 1951.

[28]Muhammad Husain Kashif al-Ghata', *Tahrir al-Majalla,* 4 Vols, Najaf, 1940-1943.

> *ilahi*) which has nothing to do with the ruler (sultan), or anyone else. [The appointment] is done by justice (*'adl*) and the combination of conditions [i.e. the various conditions required in Shi'i law], and its cessation is achieved by the withering of essential bases of intellect (*'aql*), justice (*'adala*) and ijtihad. It is not bound in time and place... Most of the dispositions of this chapter of the Majalla have no place in the rules of the Imamis. There is no appointment, no dismissal, no delegator and no agent (*la nasb, la 'azl, la nayeb wa la manub*).[29]

From Kashif al-Ghata's comment Bahr al-'Ulum draws the conclusion that the judge (the shar'i judge in particular) will find himself bound by a Code which translates the will of the authorities, and this will leave him no room for ijtihad. As the judge is obliged to act according to the will of the sultan, he abandons his duty of ijtihad.

> The qadi meant by the Code of Personal Status is the one mentioned in the Majalla, I mean the judge appointed by the sultan or the supreme leader. He must act by the terms of his appointment as to time, place, the jurisprudential ways and the Schools of ijtihad... How could this Code be imposed on such a large number of Muslims ? (*Adwa'*, p. 32-33)

III. Substantial Criticism

The Code rejection on the basis of unconstitutionality, the refusal to impose a text on the shar'i judge, the constraints on the judiciary, the barring of both taqlid and ijtihad, all form important formal objections to the Code of Personal Status as they were voiced in Najaf. But the most crucial objection was for Bahr al-'Ulum to force a School of law, its judges and laity alike, to follow another School's precepts, when a basic principle for the judge is that 'he cannot go beyond his [School's] ijtihad by judging between the parties according to their [different community] affiliation, and against his own School. [The judge] must rule according to his own ijtihad and to follow his own fatwa.' (*Adwa'*, p. 32)

For Muhammad Bahr al-'Ulum, as for the Shi'i 'ulama of Iraq, unification represented the greatest threat to their autonomy vis-à-vis the State, and more dramatically to their legitimacy as the judges of the personal matters of their community. The rest of the book illustrates how the dispositions of the Code, even after the 1963 Amendment, ignored the Schools' diversity and specificity, and how both Sunnis and Shi'is were done harm by the unifiying dispositions of the personal status laws.

---

[29]Kashif al-Ghata', *Tahrir al-Majalla,* vol.4, pp.186-187; *Adwa'*, pp. 30-31.

The analysis in the book follows the Code article by article, and dwells on the shortcomings in each section. The text is extremely detailed, and often dwells not only on the rules considered by the five (or more when the Zaydis, Ibadis and Zahiris are mentioned) main madhahib; we will examine here the most important sections addressed by Muhammad Bahr al-'Ulum.

Marriage and Betrothal (*Adwa'*, pp. 37-55)

Polygamy. The limits on polygamy introduced by the Iraqi legislator are considered 'to have no foundation in law... Islam has permitted the freedom to marry four wives'. Art.3.4 conditions the right to polygamy on the permission of the qadi, who will grant it only if (a) the husband is financially able to support more than one wife, and (b) if a 'lawful advantage' is guaranteed.

The Ja'faris accept the first condition, ability (*kafa'a*), which is defined as 'the equality between man and woman, and belief (*iman*)'. Some modern (*muta'akkhirin*) Shi'i scholars cast doubt on financial ability. For them, this is not a condition of validity for marriage. Others, still, define the financial side of ability as providing maintenance, immediately or potentially, while some are satisfied with the mere ability to provide maintenance for the first months of marriage.

Among the Sunnis, all the Hanafis and the Hanbalis include money in their definition of kafa'a. In contrast, the Shafi'is and the Malikis do not mention it as a condition for the validity of marriage. For some of the Hanafis who consider ability to be also financial, the amount considered satisfactory is a combination of providing maintenance and dower, although maintenance plays the larger role in kafa'a. But Abu Yusuf, one of the early Hanafis, considers dower to be more important than maintenance.

To Shafi'i are ascribed three different opinions on kafa'a. It is either defined as ease (*yasar*) in general, or as ease in the sense of ability to provide dower and maintenance, or as the ability to secure maintenance with a consideration to varying degrees of wealth in society.

The second condition upon which the qadi may refuse polygamy, 'lawful interest', is deemed by Bahr al-'Ulum to be inexistent in the five Schools.

Elements and conditions in the marriage contract. (*Adwa'*, pp. 43-48). Art.6.1.d requires the testimony of two witnesses as a constituent element of the marriage contract.

The Shi'is encourage the presence of witnesses, but they do not require them for the validity of marriage. All Sunni Schools require two witnesses (or a combination of witnesses), but for the Malikis, as opposed to the three other Schools, the witnesses must be present at the consummation ceremony, not at the meeting where offer and acceptance are exchanged.

Written marriage in the absence of the prospective husband and wife is accepted in Art.6.2 on condition that the groom's offer be met with the bride's acceptance in the presence of two witnesses. But the Imamis, the Shafi'is and the Hanbalis do not accept such marriage.[30]

Conditions stipulated by the bride. Art.6.4 allows the wife to include conditions in the marriage contract which terminate it if they are not respected.

Unlike the dispositions of the Code, Imami rules differentiate between acceptable and unacceptable conditions. Conditions such as prohibition for the husband to marry again, prohibition of divorce, or retaining the right for the wife to her own divorce (*at-talaq bi-yadiha*), all negate the essence of the marriage contract for the Shi'is. In this case, the contract remains and the conditions are considered void. But if the condition is that the wife may not be forced to leave her country, or a house where she resides, then both the contract and the conditions are valid. In this case, the wife can decide that she will not follow her husband. But she cannot divorce him, though she retains all her rights under the marriage, including maintenance and dower.

In contrast Art.6.4 is consonent with Hanbali doctrine, which allows the rescission of the marriage if conditions included in the act are not respected. The other Sunni Schools, like the Ja'faris, consider the conditions to be void.

Capacity (*Adwa'*, pp. 48-49). Child marriage is forbidden in the Iraqi Code, as the capacity to contract a marriage is set at 18 for both male and female. The Schools however diverge widely on the age capacity to marry. For Ja'faris, marriage can be contracted since the age of 15 for the male, 9 for the female. For Hanafis, the capacity is set at 18 and 15 respectively, while the Malikis' minimum age of marriage is 17 for both parties, against 15 for the Shafi'is and the Hanbalis.

Registration of marriage and its effects (*Adwa'*, pp. 50-54). The acknowledgment by a man of his marriage to a woman will validate the marriage if it is uttered before her death. If the acknowledgement comes after the woman's death, the marriage will not be recognized (Art 11.2). This is consonent with modern Shi'i law. The Hanafis are uncertain over the interpretation of the acknowledgement, as Abu Hanifa does not recognize the marriage in any case, and Abu Yusuf and Shaybani acknowledge the wife whether the husband's recognition occurs before or after her death. The opinion of the other Sunni Schools is not mentioned, as Bahr al-'Ulum could not find it in his sources.

Marriage with Christians and Jews (*Adwa'*, pp. 54-55). Art.17 confirms the rule accepted by the five Schools: 'Marriage of a Muslim man with a *kitabiyya* (from *ahl al-kitab,* people of the Book, i.e. Jews and Christians) is valid, but the marriage of a Muslim woman with a non-Muslim is not accepted.' Interestingly, Bahr al-'Ulum, who otherwise passes under silence *mut'a*

[30]See contra, Anderson, 'A Law of Personal Status for Iraq', p.550, for whom the Sunni schools accept such contract, and the Hanafis accept it only if the absence is real, i.e. if the fiancés are not in the same *majlis* (sitting).

marriage (the temporary marriage accepted by the Shi'is and rejected by the Sunnis),[31] takes the occasion of the otherwise non-controversial Article 17 to introduce the topic of mut'a. He specifies that for most Shi'i mujtahids, it is forbidden for Muslim men to marry a kitabiyya by a lasting (usual) marriage, though they can do so by way of mut'a.

Marital Rights *(Adwa'*, pp. 56-70)

On dower, Bahr al-'Ulum points out that Art. 19.1, which grants a wife the right to the specified (*musamma*) dower, and in the absence of specification to the proper dower (*mahr al-mithl*), does not mention the requirement in Shi'i law that the proper dower is due on consummation. The Sunni Schools hold divergent views on this point. As to the stipulation in Art. 21 that 'the wife is entitled to the whole of the specified dower after the marriage is consummated or after either spouse has died', it takes into account only two conditions for payment. The Sunni Schools list more conditions. The Hanafis and the Hanbalis will force the payment of the full dower in case of *khulwa* (private unattended meeting of the fiancés), and the Malikis will require its payment after the wife remains a full year with her husband, whether or not the marriage is consummated.

There is little comment in *Adwa'* on the provisions for maintenance. Bahr al-'Ulum sees a fault in Art. 26, which prohibits the husband from accommodating a second wife, or any of his own relatives, in her first wife's home without her consent. The five Schools, it is suggested, are not so specific. They only require 'a decent residence' for each wife, to be consonent with her pre-marital social status.

Dissolution of Marriage

Article 34, which defines talaq as the cessation of marriage by the husband, the wife or the qadi, adopts the Sunni position by passing under silence the strict Ja'fari requirement of the presence of two witnesses. This Shi'i requirement, notes Bahr al-'Ulum by quoting modern Egyptian authorities, puts in parallel the procedure of divorce with the one on marriage, and renders repudiation less straightforward than in the Sunni sytem.

As to the limits on repudiation introduced by the Code in Art. 35 (no recognition of divorce by a person who is intoxicated, insane or imbecile, or who is under duress, or in a state of great anger, or whose discernment is affected by a sudden calamity, old age, or illness, or a patient in death-sickness, *marad al-mawt*) and in Art. 36 (no recognition of divorce on condition or on oath), Bahr al-'Ulum accepts the validity of some for all Schools, particularly intoxication, insanity or duress. Other limits are deemed

[31] On mut'a, see now S. Haeri, *The Law of Desire: Temporary Marriage in Shi'i Iran*, London, 1989.

to be contrary to the shari'a, and borrowed from modernist legislation. This is the case of old age and sudden calamity, which were copied from Art. 53 of the Moroccan Code of Personal Status. The case of illness (Art.35.2) is deemed to even lack such a precedent. 'All Islamic Schools accept the validity of the ill person's divorce.' (*Adwa'*, p. 81)

The limitations on talaq adopted in Art. 36 are only accepted by the Imamis. Conditional divorce is considered void in Ja'farism, but the Sunni Schools admit it if the conditions meet certain requirements, which are discussed at some length. Bahr al-'Ulum's discussion is in the main related to the probability or improbability of the condition being fulfilled, and to the type of formula used in the conditional divorce. (*Adwa'* , pp. 84-85)

Bahr al-'Ulum also finds faults in all the other types of separation in the relevant Code sections. Art. 41, which grants a wife the right to judicial divorce if her husband is imprisoned for more than five years, is rejected by modern Imamis like Tabataba'i and Hakim. The details on the variations related to separation are lengthy in *Adwa'*. Here, we only mention the most important remarks of Bahr al-'Ulum: the Sunnis have no provision for divorcing a convicted husband, although the Malikis and the Hanbalis leave the possibility of divorce open in case of prolonged absence (but not specifically imprisonment), whilst the Hanafis and the Shafi'is reject even this last possibility. Absence for more than two years without a lawful excuse is also ground for judicial divorce according to Art. 43. For Muhsin al-Hakim, even if maintenance is suspended, the wife must wait for the absent husband. The Sunni Schools agree on rejecting judicial divorce as per Art. 43, with some variations. (*Adwa'*, pp. 109-110)

On the the theme of dissolution of marriage, Bahr al-'Ulum discusses the shortcomings of Art. 46 in relation to *khul'* (separation by consent of the spouses, in classical law for a consideration). According to this Article, such a separation is permitted before the judge, and is effective after agreement of the tribunal. But for the Imamis, as well as for the other Schools, the constraints of the judicial process are superfluous. Furthermore the khul' in classical law is submitted to a set of conditions pertaining to the state of the spouses, and these conditions are ignored by the Iraqi law. (*Adwa'*, pp. 112-117)

'Idda

On the question of 'idda (Waiting period upon separation or death), it is again the poverty and reductionism of the Code which is Bahr al-'Ulum main object of criticism: the variations of the Schools of law on the subject are described extensively (*Adwa'*, pp.117-127), in contrast to the few words devoted by the Code: 'The 'idda for talaq is three periods (*quru'*)' (Art.48.1). Similarly, Art.48.2 requires 'idda for the time usually allotted to widowhood (4 months and 10 days), and the Code provides for the longer 'idda only if it occurs in an irrevocable talaq, or in a revocable talaq in conjunction with death sickness. This provision , Bahr al-'Ulum writes, is limited to the Hanafis and the Malikis.[32] As for the Imamis, the Shafi'is and the Malikis, they consider widowhood 'idda to be similar to the talaq 'idda. The subsequent Article of the Code, which specifies that the 'idda starts even if the wife has not been notified of the death or of the divorce, is supported by the four Sunni Schools, but stands against the provisions of the Imamis, for whom the 'idda for widowhood starts from the time a woman is notified of her husband's death.

The effects legally attached to 'idda are mentioned in Art.50: 'Maintenance of the repudiated woman is provided for by the husband, even if the woman is *nashiz* (disobedient). There is no maintenance during 'idda for death.' In contrast, the Schools have a much more complex system, including for the Imamis maintenance due in the case of irrevocable repudiation if the woman is pregnant. All the Schools reject maintenance if the woman is nashiz.

Nasab (Filiation)

Recognition of paternity in the Iraqi Code is contingent upon two conditions: '1- That the minimum period of gestation will have lapsed; 2- that the the meeting of the spouses was possible.' This is different from the Imami rules, which stipulate that automatic filiation is premised, in a normal or temporary marriage, upon penetration. There are also requirements of a mimimum gestation period, and of a maximum gestation period (9 or 10 months, or one year, depending on the authorities). The Sunni Schools have, in contrast with the Code, a set of detailed rules based on *firash* (bed), *iqrar* (acknowledgment), and *bayyina* (evidence) (See *Adwa'*, pp. 136-142).

Rida' (Suckling) and Guardianship (*Adwa',* pp.142-159)

The requirement set down in the Code (Art. 55) for a mother to suckle her baby is rejected in all the Schools. The Imamis, in particular, reject the possibility of forcing a free woman (as opposed to a slave, as in classical law), to breastfeed her child.

Guardianship in the Code is entrusted with the mother until the child reaches the age of seven, but the father has the right to control his or her education. There are several variations in the Schools of law in relation to age and custody, which are listed in extenso in *Adwa'* (pp.151-160).

Maintenance (*Adwa'*, pp.160-198)

There are in *Adwa'* lengthy discussions on the subject of maintenance, which is qualified in three ways. It is either the maintenance of the ascendants which falls upon the descendants, or the maintenance of descendants by their ascendants, or the maintenance of collaterals. Again, Bahr al-'Ulum's criticism

[32]But even for the Hanafis, there is a possibility for 'idda to extend up to 40 years, if for instance the repudiated woman had her period only once. The 'idda then extends ot the time of menopause. (*Adwa'*, p.126)

is premised on the simplification introduced by the Code's five Articles (Arts. 58-63) to a situation where several minor and major variations had been established by the law of the Sunni and Shi'i Schools.

Bequests (*Adwa'*, pp. 199-241)

Bahr al-'Ulum analyses bequests and the appointement of a testamentary executor under the same heading. A division is made in accordance with the Shi'i doctrine between the 'disposal will' (*wasiyya tamlikiyya*) and the 'contractual will' (*wasiyya 'ahdiyya*), which are defined respectively as 'the transfer of some of the praepositus' property after his death to another person', and 'granting one's rights to another's power after one's death' (*Adwa'*, p. 200-201). A parallel is then established between Art. 64, which defines a bequest as the disposal of property and its transfer after death to the legatee, and between Art. 75, which defines *isa'* (literally to bequeathe) as 'the appointment by a person of another to look into his bequest after death'.

Bequests are accepted by the Imamis and some Malikis and Shafi'is as a testament the formula of which is 'I bequeathe to X (*awsaytu* li-*fulan*)....' Appointment of an executor is achieved by the formula 'I entrust with X (*awsaytu* ila *fulan*)...' This distinction is then used to reveal the ensuing legal differences among the five Schools, and to show how the Code did not take them into account.

The Code's dispositions on bequests are deemed to be contrary to the law of the Schools in section 1 of Article 65, which stipulates that the will is valid if done in writing and duly signed or thumb-marked (and, if the value of the legacy is more than 500 dinars, it must be authenticated at the notary).

> All the *fuqaha'* [equivalent to 'ulama] of the shari'a have agreed -or almost agreed- that the establishment of a will does not require a specific form. It can be written or oral... Section 1 of Art. 65 clearly contradicts the consensus among the five Schools. (*Adwa',* p. 209-210)

It is true, Bahr al-'Ulum adds, that the significant variations included in this section are deflected by the proviso in the following paragraph, which allows oral proof of the bequest 'in case of material impediment', but the rules of the School are specific, and the Code falls short of mentioning the necessary details. The Imamis require proof of the disposal will by a number of witnesses, with a complex combination of possibilities. For the contractual will, two Muslims 'of honour' are required, though for a bequest entailing devolution of money, even the testimony of *dhimmis* (non-Muslims in Muslim land) can serve as evidence. The Sunni sources mentioned vary widely, 'but the important matter is that the details found in the opinions of the Imamis...does not exist for the other Schools'.

The status of the legatee is discussed in connection with Art. 68, which stipulates that he must (1) be alive in fact or in law when the bequest is made, as well as at the death of the legator, and (2) he must not have murdered the legator. As for other parts of the law, these dispositions are considered to constitute an unduly brief account of the dispositions of the shari'a, which are much more detailed and precise. For instance, the Imamis accept the legatee's future existence but qualify it. If the testator bequeathes to the unborn children of his son, the bequest is not valid. The Hanafis differ amongst themselves on the validity of bequeathing to 'what is incapable of acquiring property', and a careful wording of the bequest formula is essential to the validity of the act. Abu Hanifa considers a bequest 'to' a mosque or 'for the sake of God' void, but Shaybani accepts it. The Sunni Schools also differ on the important point of a bequest to an heir on the basis of hadiths of the Prophet in which he forbids bequests to an heir. Some Sunni scholars abide by the rule of the hadith but consider the full saying to be 'No bequest to an heir without the other heirs' consent'. This is the case of Ahmad Ibn Hanbal, Shafi'i and in one opinion Abu Hanifa. But scholars like Dawud az-Zahiri,[33] Malik and Abu Hanifa in another opinion reject the second part of the hadith and refuse any possible bequest to an heir.

In contrast, the Ja'faris and the Zaydis do not admit the validity of the hadith and allow bequests to heirs as well as to non-heirs to the extent of the permissible third of the estate.

A controversial disposition of the Code is the stipulation in Art. 71 validating a bequest of personal property to persons of a different religion, suggesting thereby that real property, a contrario, cannot be bequeathed to non-Muslims. This distinction has no foundation in the shari'a, as all Schools allow the bequest of any type of property to dhimmis living in *dar al-islam* (Muslim territory).

Section 3.2 of Art. 68, which excludes the person who 'kills' the testator from any right to a bequest, ignores the differences between the Schools, especially as to the intentional in contrast to the non-intentional act. Muhsin al-Hakim, for the Ja'faris, considers 'that a disposal will must be executed if murder [presumably the murder attempt] follows it'. For 'Allama Hilli, involuntary manslaughter, unlike intentional killing, does not render the bequest void. Sunnis differ widely over the validity of the bequest to the murderer of the legator, and there are conflicts within the same School. For Sarakhsi such bequest is void, but Dimashqi reports that Abu Hanifa, Malik and Ahmad Ibn Hanbal do not invalidate it. (*Adwa'*, pp. 230-231)

On the binding effect of the acceptance by the testamentary executor of his appointment during the life time of the testator, except if an option is mentioned in the contract (Art.77.1), Bahr al-'Ulum suggests that the Iraqi legislator chose the Hanafi way. Some Imamis, in contrast, allow the executor to reconsider his appointment as long as the legator is alive. In isa' also, Art. 83.2 allows the dismissal of the executor in case of his incompetence. This, again, appears to be Hanafi law; the Imamis allow dismissal only in case of betrayal.

[33]The founder of the now extinct literalist Zahiri school.

Intestate Succession (*Adwa'*, pp. 242-247)

As previously mentioned, much of the controversy in Iraq under Qasem was deflected, after his overthrow, by the new government 's repeal of the intestate succession dispositions, which, by measuring them against the Amiri land dispositions of the Civil Code, had ignored basic tenets of the shari'a such as the principle of the male double share of the legacy, and introduced a system of class which, although vaguely similar to the Shi'i division, had ignored completely the prescribed shares of the entitled heirs. The new system introduced in the 1963 Amendment was, in contrast, totally consonent with the Ja'fari system of intestate succession. But Bahr al-'Ulum's criticism, which closes his commentary on the Code, serves as the last reminder of the underlying theme of the treatise. Despite his scholarship as Shi'i, Bahr al-'Ulum remained dissatisfied with the imposition of Ja'fari law on the Sunnis of the country. In the last section of *Adwa'*, he presents the essential structure of the Sunni system, notes that there are many more complications resulting from the differences between the four Schools, and concludes that, notwithstanding the fact that Art. 89 (the main Article of the Amendment) was written in accordance with Shi'i law, no satisfaction could be found in

> the clear contradictions [of the Code] with the Islamic Schools. Forcing any School to operate in opposition with what has been accepted by its jurisprudence is faulty legally (*mushakkal shar'an*). There is no reason for a School to go back in its shar'i matters to the tenets of another School. The problems which it confronts, whether religious or social, [must be solved in accordance with its tradition], for it would otherwise result in the hindering of the march of mankind to the establishment of a better human setting for happiness and liberty in the shade of Islam.(*Adwa'*, p. 247)

Epilogue

In the controversy over unified v. community personal laws, Muhammad Bahr al-'Ulum's treatise appears as the more elaborate expression of the point of view from Najaf. Iraqi Shi'i circles were suspicious towards the whole Code, and Bahr al-'Ulum sought to marshall a systematic reading of the Code in order to show is limitations and errors. The thrust of the criticism is built as a manifesto protecting the rights of each community against the attempt of state integration.

The second characteristic of *Adwa'* is strictly related to the substance of the law. Bahr al-'Ulum offers a comprehensive analysis of the status of the shari'a against modern family law in the Near East. *Adwa'* is in effect a compact treatise of family law, and has the advantage of being based on the official text of a Code. The Ja'fari emphasis can of course be expected from a scholar trained in Shi'i colleges. But more significant perhaps is the fact that Bahr al-'Ulum appears in *Adwa'* as the mouthpiece of the whole Shi'i hierarchy.

It was not until 1978 that the next Amendment to the Code of Personal Status was introduced.[34] Some of the subsequent changes were important, and the thrust of the dispositions introduced was related to 'liberalism' and an attempt to further protect the rights of women.[35] These changes, and the atmosphere they took place in, are outside the reach of this study. For the beginning of the war with Iran in September 1980 meant that family law in Iraq was being set against a very special background, which is not typical of other countries in the Middle East. But on the whole, the Code of Personal Status of 1959 still stands as it was then conceived. The criticism voiced in Najaf, particularly in the detailed and scholarly work of Muhammad Bahr al-'Ulum, offers a forgotten agenda in Iraq, but a blueprint of a world debate to come.

[34]English Text in the Iraqi 'Official Gazette' (English version of *al-Waqa'i' al-'Iraqiyya*), issue 16, 19.4.1978: the main dispositions were seen as a progress for the legal status of women, and saluted with enthusiasm by Iraqi 'feminist' circles. See Bahija Ahmad Shehab ed., *An-naqla al-hadariyya lil-mar'a fi qanun at-ta'dil ath-thani li-qanun al-ahwal ash-shakhsiyya* (The civilizational improvement of woman in the second Amendment to the Code of Personal Status), Baghdad, 1978. Several articles of the Code of 1959 were deleted and replaced by the prohibition of forced marriages, penalties for marriages outside the Court, wider grounds for the woman to demand judicial separation, and a strenghtened right to the mother's custody of a child. These last provisions were curtailed, 'in the interests of the child', by Law 106 of 1987, *al-Waqa'i' al-'Iraqiyya,* issue 3176, 16.11.1987.

[35]See in particular the *tanzil* doctrine in Law 72 of 1979, *The Official Gazette,* issue 39, 26.9.1979; husband's sodomy as ground for divorce, Law 125 of 1981, *The Official Gazette,* issue 6, 10.2.1982; drinking as ground for divorce, Law 5 of 1986, *al-Waqa'i' al-'Iraqiyya,* issue 3081, 20.1.1986; and most significantly, Law 77 of 1983, stipulating the right to the conjugal flat for a divorced woman, a measure similar to the one which had created much controversy in Egypt in 1979. But contrast the restrictions on child custody for an Iraqi widow who marries a non-Iraqi, Law 65 of 1986, *al-Waqa'i' al-'Iraqiyya,* issue 3105, 7.7.1986.

6. FAMILY LAW UNDER OCCUPATION: ISLAMIC LAW AND THE SHARI‘A COURTS IN THE WEST BANK

Lynn Welchman

The Palestinians of the Israeli-occupied territories always constitute something of an exception when discussion is made of legal affairs in the Arab or Islamic world. Under military occupation since 1967, the body of local civil and criminal law has been changed almost out of recognition by the huge number of Israeli military orders that touch on almost every area of life. Personal status is perhaps the only real exception to this rule.

Personal status law in the West Bank is governed, as inside Israel, on the *millet* system, a relic from the Ottomans, with the separate religious communities regulating their own family affairs. The majority of Palestinians in the occupied territories are Muslim and subject in matters of personal status to the *shari‘a* courts. In the West Bank, the law applied is the Jordanian Law of Personal Status, and close links are maintained with the Jordanian system.

This paper aims to examine how the shari‘a system in the occupied West Bank has coped with the situation since 1967, and to look at some of the ways in which the occupation affects the operation of the *shari‘a* courts and the application of the law.

I. The 1967 Israeli Occupation

The Arab-Israeli war of June 1967 ended with the Israeli army in possession of the West Bank, the Gaza Strip, the Egyptian Sinai and the Syrian Golan Heights. Immediately after the formal hostilities ceased, the Israeli Military Commander in the West Bank issued Proclamation Number 2, assuming all powers of government, legislation, appointment and administration with respect to the region and its inhabitants, henceforth to be exercised by him or his delegates, who were military officials appointed for the purpose. Previous requirements of consultation or approval in any legislative matters were repealed.

In Jerusalem, the Israeli authorities took immediate steps towards integrating the Arab East of the city with the west side that had been in the Israeli state since 1948. The controversial decision to annex East Jerusalem and a number of surrounding areas came on 14 June 1967; the municipal boundaries of West Jerusalem were extended up to and beyond the former municipal boundaries of East Jerusalem and Israeli law was extended to cover the annexed area. Jordanian government and public departments were taken over, and the existing court structure was integrated into the Israeli system along with the application of Israeli laws and regulations.

In the West Bank, the legal system was subjected to Israeli military administration. The afore-mentioned Proclamation 2 provided that:

> All laws which were in force in the area on June 7th 1967 shall continue to be in force as far as they do not contradict this or any other proclamation or order made by me [the West Bank Military Commander] or conflict with the changes arising by virtue of the occupation of the Israel Defence Forces of the area.

Chapter Four of Shehadeh's *Occupier's Law* examines in detail some of the 'changes arising' in the legal system due to the Israeli occupation in so far as the regular (*nizamiyya*) court system is concerned.[1] These included the abolition of the Court of Cassation, the highest court in the four-tier Jordanian system, together with the additional functions carried out by its members, and the transfer of the Jerusalem Court of Appeal to Ramallah. An Israeli Officer in charge of the Judiciary was appointed, to whom were transferred all powers of the Jordanian Minister of Justice. The Military Governor also established a committee to whom passed the powers of the Judicial Council in appointing judges and public prosecutors. Another Military Order required all court processes to take place and all decisions to be issued 'in the name of law and justice'. The Execution Departments attached to the local regular courts were put under the administration of the Israeli military authorities.[2]

The changes to the judicial system, the Israeli occupation in general and the annexation of East Jerusalem in particular led to a strike on the part of West Bank lawyers which was estimated in 1980 to include just under half of all the qualified lawyers in the West Bank. The striking lawyers continue to boycott the regular courts, now administered by the occupation authorities, and the Military Courts which are staffed entirely by Israeli military personnel, but many do practise in the shari'a courts, which remain outside Israeli supervision.

The Shari'a Courts under Occupation

Soon after the occupation, on 24 July 1967, some twenty notable Muslim personalities in Jerusalem established a body called *al-hay'a al-islamiyya* (the Islamic Board) to administer Muslim affairs in the West Bank, in particular in East Jerusalem, in the absence of a Muslim sovereign. The body developed into *al-hay'a al-islamiyya al-'uliya*, the Supreme Islamic Board. Kupferschmidt observes that:

---

[1]R. Shehadeh, *Occupier's Law*, Washington, 1988, pp.76-101.

[2]R. Shehadeh, *The West Bank and the Rule of Law*, Geneva, 1980, pp.18-20.

> [T]he 1967 Muslim Council was established by local initiative as an outspoken act of protest against the Israeli annexation of East Jerusalem. The Israeli government has therefore withheld any formal recognition.[3]

The Acting Chief Islamic Justice, the *qadi al-qudat,* is the head of the Supreme Islamic Board and directly supervises the work of the shari'a courts still functioning under the indirect administration of Jordan, providing the link between the *shar'i*[4] systems in Jordan and the West Bank. It is likely that at least some of the motivation for the establishment of the Supreme Islamic Board and its continuing refusal to cooperate with the Israeli authorities came from a wish to avoid the records of the courts and the Department of *Awqaf* (pious endowments) coming under Israeli control. While the workings of the various Christian communities in Jerusalem suffered little obstruction from the Israeli occupation authorities, the Islamic court system was in confrontation from the start.

As noted above, the Israeli authorities assumed all supervisory functions for the regular court system after occupation. The shar'i judiciary, however, refused to accept confirmation of appointment or payment from the military authorities or to attach Israeli stamps to court documents. In East Jerusalem, the judges of the shari'a first instance court refused to countenance integration into the Israeli state system, which would involve their own appointment by the Israeli government and the swearing of an oath of loyalty to Israel.

As it became clear that the occupation was not going to be removed in a matter of weeks or even months, the shar'i judiciary maintained its stand and the Israeli authorities extended the jurisdiction of the Israeli shari'a court of Jaffa to include East Jerusalem, in an attempt to preclude recourse to the Jerusalem court by the Muslim Palestinians resident in the annexed part of the city, and so to force compliance by the judges. In August of 1969, instructions were issued to the Execution Offices of the West Bank not to execute decisions issued by the shari'a courts.[5]

This move aroused protests from the Palestinian judiciary as a whole. Just after the order was issued, a local Arabic newspaper reported that the magistrate, public prosecutor and head of the Execution Department in Jericho, Zuhayr al-Bushtawi, had sent a memorandum to the Israeli Justice Affairs Officer, in which he stated his objection to the non-execution of

---

[3] U. Kupferschmidt, *The Supreme Muslim Council: Islam under the British Mandate for Palestine*, Leiden, 1987, p.260. The Arabic title of the Supreme Muslim Council of Mandatory times uses the word *majlis* rather than *hay'a.*

[4] Adjectival form of shari'a: the branch of the judiciary which applies the shari'a exclusively.

[5] Note that there is some dispute regarding this administrative measure; some say it applied to all shari'a courts, others say only to East Jerusalem and the Shari'a Court of Appeal. The articles in the local Arabic press, however, state clearly that the instructions for non-execution affected all shari'a courts in the West Bank.

shari'a court decisions.[6] A few weeks later, the magistrate of al-Khalil (Hebron), Hussein ash-Shuyukhi, was reported by the same paper to have resigned in protest at 'the interference in the powers of the courts by the Israeli Officer in charge of the Judiciary, and his insistence on preventing the Execution Departments of the regular courts from executing the decisions of the shari'a courts'. His reasons were included in a memorandum sent to the West Bank Military Commander.[7]

Two articles published in the local paper *al-Quds* in April of 1970, one by a shar'i lawyer and one by an Islamic *qadi* (judge), stressed that the principle behind the stand being taken by the shar'i judiciary was its need for independence and for inviolability from the effects of transient political change. The first noted that even the British had not attempted to interfere politically in the shar'i judiciary, and distanced the present stand from any particular political implications:

> Although the shar'i judiciary is Jordanian, it is first and foremost Islamic....[8]

The second article, by the then qadi of Ramallah, insisted:

> The political order must have no influence upon the work of the shari'a courts, whatever the source be of such political motive: for temporal politics has no fixed constants, and its enemy today may be its friend tomorrow.[9]

By the time the above articles were published, the newspapers had reported that some Execution Offices in the West Bank were in fact executing shari'a court decisions in defiance of the orders to the contrary.[10] The first writer notes this in his article, and in an informal chronology of events compiled at the request of a local lawyer, the second, al-Husseini, notes the effect played in the matter by the objections that had come from the Arab heads of the Execution Offices in the West Bank. It should be noted here that while decisions of the shar'i courts in the West Bank, excluding Jerusalem, are nowadays executed through the regular court Execution Offices, it is not clear whether there are any written instructions countermanding the original orders for non-execution, and that Meron is at least partly right when he states:

---

[6]*Al-Quds* newspaper (Jerusalem), 25 August 1969. See also Shehadeh, *The West Bank and Rule of Law*, p.22.

[7]*Al-Quds,* 16 October 1969. See also Shehadeh, *The West Bank and Rule of Law*, p.51 note 16.

[8]Zaydan al-Jilani, *'Al-mahakim ash-shar'iyya - ila ayn?' (Whither the shar'i courts ?)* in *Al-Quds*, 24 April 1970.

[9]Muhammad As'ad al-Imam al-Husseini, *'Taswib 'ala kalimat: al-mahakim ash-shar'iyya - ila ayn?' (Correcting the article: Whither the shar'i courts ?)* in *Al-Quds,* 27 April 1970. Article written in response to al-Jilani.

[10]*Al-Quds,* 23 April 1970.

> The judgments rendered by these Qadis could certainly not be executed by the official Execution Offices, were it not for the Military Governor's decision to honour these judgments...[11]

This decision, however, would seem to have been less of a positive 'honouring' than a preference to let the issue drop rather than force more confrontation with the shar'i judiciary and the Muslim community. The military authorities certainly paid less attention to the continued defiance of the shar'i judiciary than they would have done had the regular judiciary been in a position to make a similar stand. This may be partly due to the point made by Meron in explanation,[12] that the Israeli authorities were used to the relics of the Ottoman millet system in Israel itself and were therefore prepared to take an 'abdicatory' attitude towards the jurisdiction of the religious courts. However, it probably owes just as much to the fact that the Israeli authorities saw less political advantage in controlling the courts dealing with personal status issues in the West Bank, particularly as these had no independent means of execution. The members of the shar'i judiciary who discussed this matter with the author tend to the opinion that the 'non-political', basically domestic subject matter of their jurisdiction was the important factor. It must be noted that this 'abdicatory' attitude on the part of the Israeli authorities was not followed in East Jerusalem. In administrative terms, therefore, in the West Bank, the position of the shari'a courts as described by al-Husseini in 1970 holds good still: they

> continue to be linked to His Excellency the Qadi al-Qudat and to the shar'i Judicial Council in Amman.... they are all subject to the terms of the Kingdom's Constitution... and to the laws constituting the shari'a courts, and to the authority of the Qadi al Qudat in their administration.[13]

Since 1967, the West Bank qadis have continued to be tested and formally appointed in Amman after recommendation by the Acting qadi al-qudat in Jerusalem to the shar'i Judicial Council.[14] In contrast to the Gaza Strip qadis, where the shari'a courts are under Israeli administration like the

---

[11] Y. Meron, 'The Religious Courts in the Administered Territories', Chapter 10 in M. Shamgar ed., *Military Government in the Territories Administered by Israel 1967-1980*, Jerusalem, 1982, Volume 1, p.365.

[12] Meron, 'The Religious Courts in the Administered Territories', p.356.

[13] Al-Husseini, '*Taswib*'. An article by the then qadi of Nablus that appeared in *al-Quds* on 4 February 1974 similarly emphasised the fact: 'The Jordanian Government has not relinquished responsibility for the shari'a courts.'

[14] Kupferschmidt, *Supreme Muslim Council*, p.260, states erroneously that 'qadis are appointed by a Qadi al-Qudaat in Jerusalem.' See, for example, *al-Fajr* newspaper (Jerusalem) of 8 September 1986 reporting that four West Bank Palestinians had been appointed in Amman as qadis for the three new shari'a courts just established in the West Bank.

regular courts, and who are paid by the Israeli military authorities, the qadis in the West Bank are paid by the Jordanian authorities from the shar'i budget in Amman. Court fees are sent to Amman via the Acting qadi al-qudat in Jerusalem and are taken into account in the Amman financial reports of the Department of the qadi al-qudat. The fees are levied and collected in Jordanian currency only; any attempt to pay in Israeli shekels is met with instructions to go and find a money-changer. Judgments are issued in the name of the Jordanian king, in accordance with Article 27 of the Jordanian Constitution, and each separate ruling, or *hukm*, is entered under this formula in the court records. Should the ruling be of a nature to need the services of an Execution Office, it is written out again under the heading 'In the name of God, the Merciful, the Beneficent', thus avoiding the 'law and justice' formula used in the regular courts under the terms of Military Order 412.

Perhaps the most physical evidence of Jordan's continuing supervision of the shari'a court system in the West Bank is in the fact that four new shari'a courts have been established in the area by Jordanian decree since the 1967 occupation. One was created in the town of Salfit in 1976 and three more in Tubas, Birzeit and Dura in 1986.[15] This can be usefully contrasted with the Gaza Strip, where two new shari'a courts were opened and validated by Israeli Military Orders in the 1970s.[16]

Another very clear demonstration of the continuing links with Jordan comes in the law that is applied by the West Bank shari'a courts. Here again they stand in contrast to the *nizamiyya* courts, where, due to Proclamation 2, all laws in force in the area were frozen in their pre-occupation state and where the only post-1967 legislation applicable is the vast body of Israeli Military Orders. The residents of the West Bank have in this way been deprived of the benefits of modifications to Jordanian legislation and of new legislation introduced since the occupation, including the 1976 Jordanian Civil Code, which repealed large parts of the nineteenth century Ottoman *Majalla*. The 1976 Code is not applied in the West Bank. However, the same year, 1976, saw the promulgation in Amman of a new family law, the Jordanian Law of Personal Status, replacing the Jordanian Law of Family Rights of 1951.[17] The JLPS was applied in the West Bank shari'a courts as a matter of course.

---

[15]The creation of the courts by the Jordanian authorities was announced in *al-Fajr*, 8 September 1986. See also M. Mheilan (qadi al-qudat in Jordan), *'al-qada' ash-shar'i al-urduni fi'l-'ahd al-hashimi'* (The Jordanian shar'i judiciary under the Hashemites), Amman, 1986. The new courts brought the total in the West Bank to thirteen.

[16]Meron, 'The Religious Courts in the Administered Territories', p.361. The two new courts brought the total in the Gaza Strip to five.

[17]Jordanian Law of Personal Status, Temporary Law no 61/1976, *Official Gazette* no 2668 of 1 December 1976. The law is a 'temporary' one because it was promulgated during the suspension of the Jordanian Parliament following the 1974 Rabat Summit Conference, when the Palestine Liberation Organisation was declared 'the sole legitimate representative of the Palestinian people'. Obliged to implement this resolution, the Jordanian Parliament found itself unable to cede its representation of the West Bank Palestinians unless the Constitution was amended, and accordingly suspended itself until recalled by King Hussein in 1984. All

In many ways, then, the West Bank shari'a courts can be seen to have done their best to ignore the Israeli occupation, but a closer view reveals both minor and more far-reaching effects on the shar'i system as a result of the occupation. One example of the effects in day-to-day terms can be seen in the number of persons who are classed, for purposes of a shari'a court hearing, as 'of unknown whereabouts'. In the normal process of notification for a court session, the relevant papers will be sent to the shari'a court with jurisdiction in the area where the defendant to be notified is resident. In the West Bank, because there is no regular official contact with Jordan to allow use to be made of Consular services and so on, anybody who is outside the West Bank is of unknown whereabouts. This includes anybody living in Jordan, in Israel (since there is no liaison with the shari'a courts in Israel), and in the Gaza Strip (unless the relevant qadi responds to a personal letter from a West Bank qadi, i.e. avoiding any liaison with the Israeli authorities administering the shari'a courts in the Strip); and this category seems also to include anybody held in an Israeli prison in the West Bank on a security charge, since this would involve going through the military authorities.

Another example of the practical effects of occupation lies in the fact that the West Bank shari'a courts no longer transfer those in violation of provisions of family law to the criminal courts for prosecution. The Jordanian Penal Code of 1960 lays down penalties for certain offences arising from family law, such as non-registration of a *talaq* pronounced out of court, or involvement in the marriage of an under-age woman. Before the occupation, if such an offence came to light during proceedings in the shari'a court, the court would transfer the papers of the case to the regular court system in order for a criminal prosecution to take place if appropriate. However, since the regular courts are now under the administration of the Israeli military authorities, and the shari'a courts have no contact with the authorities, this official process has now ceased. It is not clear how far this may have affected the intended deterrent effect of the penal legislation.

In terms of the application of the law, some of the accommodations made by the first instance courts to the circumstances of occupation will be discussed below in the context of the response of the Jerusalem Shari'a Court of Appeal. It must also be noted, however, that an extensive survey of the shari'a court records of both the West Bank and Jordan for comparative purposes would doubtless reveal significant differences in, for example, the types of claim raised, as a result of the different socio-economic and political factors affecting the two areas.[18]

---

legislation passed 1974-1984 was issued as temporary legislation. For a discussion of the contents of the JLPS, see L. Welchman, 'The Development of Islamic Family Law in the Legal System of Jordan', *International and Comparative Law Quarterly*, 37, 1988, pp.868-886.

[18]It should be noted that the shari'a court records in the West Bank show already considerable differences arising since the Palestinian uprising began in December 1987.

II. The Shari'a Court of East Jerusalem

The problems facing the shari'a court of East Jerusalem constitute the major disruption suffered by the shar'i system as a result of the 1967 occupation. The situation has been referred to by, *inter alia*, two Israeli writers, Layish and Meron, neither of whom however indicate the scale of ongoing disruption. Layish summarised the situation by noting that although the jurisdiction of the Israeli shari'a court of Jaffa was extended to cover East Jerusalem, this court

> is not recognised by most East Jerusalem Muslims, while the local shari'a court .....is not recognised by the Israeli authorities. East Jerusalem Muslims do not resort to the Israeli court unless they are interested in the execution of a judgment or in the performance of some act of a government office on the strength of a certificate from the court.[19]

Further reference to the non-recognition by the Muslim Palestinians of East Jerusalem to the jurisdiction of the Israeli shari'a court of Jaffa is made by Layish in his book *Women and Islamic Law in a non-Muslim State*. Meron, on the other hand, in a tone consistent with the rest of his article, 'Religious Courts in the Territories administered by Israel', sweeps the whole issue aside with the following statement regarding the Muslims of East Jerusalem:

> These Muslims, having been deprived of the services of the Moslem Court of Jerusalem, which has refused to accept nomination under Israeli law, address themselves to the Moslem Court at Jaffa, which is the the only court competent to issue judgments in family matters, executable at the Execution Offices.[20]

Meron's understanding of 'competent' is at the least questionable, given that Israel's annexation of East Jerusalem was illegal. The non-recognition by East Jerusalem Palestinians of the Israeli annexation of their city is at the base of the limited recourse had to the Israeli shari'a court in Jaffa by Jerusalem Muslims. The shar'i judiciary had additional reasons, besides their own formal ties to the Jordanian system, including a great pride in the history and prestige of the shari'a court of Jerusalem through the centuries, the eminence of its judges, and the resource material available in its centuries of records.[21] These judges demonstrated an insistent refusal to see this court administered, and themselves appointed, by non-Muslim occupying authorities.

---

19 A. Layish, 'Shari'a Court in Jordan', draft entry for revised edition of *Encyclopaedia of Islam*, drafted in 1984, p. 5/6.

20 Meron,'The Religious Courts in the Administered Territories', p.363.

21 See for example Ahmad 'Abed Ahmad, 'al-mahkama ash-shar'iyya fi'l-quds wa'l-ihtilal' in *al-Quds*, 26 April 1974.

Under the 1961 Israeli Qadis Law, Islamic judges are appointed by the Israeli president on the recommendation of an Appointment Committee, whose members may include non-Muslims, and the qadis have to swear an oath of loyalty to the State of Israel upon their appointment. After the 1967 occupation and the annexation of East Jerusalem, the Israeli authorities demanded that the qadis of East Jerusalem accept reappointment under these terms and therefore be integrated into the Israeli judicial system. The Jerusalem judges refused as a body and the Israeli authorities therefore extended the jurisdiction of the shari'a court in Jaffa to include the Muslim Palestinians of East Jerusalem, at the same time refusing recognition and execution to any documents and rulings issued by the Jerusalem court.

In the spring of 1968, the Jaffa shari'a court dealt directly with the conflicting jurisdictions in a claim raised by an East Jerusalem Muslim applying for the lifting of an order for attachment *(hajz)* placed upon his person by the East Jerusalem court in 1949 at the application of the defendants.[22]

The plaintiff's lawyer argued his claim on the basis of the Israeli Law of Legal Competence and Guardianship of 1962, which he noted had repealed all provisions relating to the attachment of property on the grounds of a person's 'profligacy' or 'squandering'. The original attachment order had been given on these grounds under Jordanian law.

The defendant's lawyer argued for dismissal of the claim or its transferral to the East Jerusalem shari'a court, on the grounds of non-competence. He claimed that the case should be heard by the same court that had placed the attachment order on the plaintiff, and challenged the administrative measures that had extended the Jaffa court's jurisdiction to East Jerusalem.

As to the question of competence, the plaintiff's lawyer submitted that the East Jerusalem qadis were not properly appointed judges under Israeli law. He referred to the Israeli Law of Shari'a Courts 1953 and the Israeli Qadis Law 1961, which detailed the methods of appointment of qadis, including the oath of allegiance to the state (Art.7 of the 1961 Law) and the publishing of appointments in the Israeli Official Gazette. Asking the question: Who is the judge?, he submitted that since the East Jerusalem qadis had gone though none of these procedures, they could not be considered judges under the law. The Jaffa qadi agreed with this argument, and also accepted the plaintiff's submission regarding the extension of the Jaffa court's jurisdiction:

> Since its establishment on 19/11/50, the Jaffa shari'a court has exercised jurisdiction in personal status matters for Jaffa and the Southern Region including Jerusalem; adding a part to the whole does not require the granting of new authority.

---

22 Case no 39/1968 in Jaffa shari'a court.

Stating that the judge is the person legally appointed by the (Israeli) authorities to fulfil the function of judge and so to decide such claims, the decision went on:

> No person or court in the eastern part of Jerusalem has the right to hear personal status claims according to the laws of the land: the Jaffa shari'a court is the court holding jurisdiction over such claims arising in East Jerusalem.

This decision was given on 31 July 1968, a little over a year after the annexation of East Jerusalem. On 26 September 1968 a 'Shar'i Statement' was issued in East Jerusalem in response to the Jaffa decision under the signatures of the Acting qadi al-qudat, eight West Bank qadis and three West Bank *muftis*, 'proclaiming the will of the Muslims in the protection of their rights, the independence of their judges and the administration of their religious affairs...' The statement quoted from the Jaffa decision, noting that it relied on laws imposed by the Israeli authorities in violation of the terms of the shari'a. It drew attention to the threat being posed to the rights of the Muslim community in East Jerusalem, noting that it would be subject to legislative provisions that were binding on the Muslims in neither statutory nor shar'i terms. The condemnation of the Jaffa decision and of the Israeli policies behind it was supported by references to international law, including the Hague Regulations, and to UN resolutions from the previous year refusing legitimacy to the Israeli annexation of East Jerusalem. Tracing the history of the Jerusalem shari'a court back to ancient times, the Statement stressed the continuity of authority from which it derived its competence, and noted:

> At no time in our history, even under the British Mandate, has any ruler interfered with the independence of the shari'a judiciary in our land, or given themselves the right to appoint Muslim qadis : all have left that to the Muslims, and acknowledged their rights to independence in their jurisdiction and in the administration of Islamic waqf and Muslim holy places...

This statement had no effect on the Israeli authorities, and two months later a local Arabic newspaper was reporting the failure of reported contacts between various Israeli governmental departments and Islamic groupings in Jerusalem aimed at finding a solution to the problem.[23] That those attempts had also failed to find an answer to the human problems involved is illustrated by the following extract from an 'Open Letter' published in a local newspaper in 1970. The letter was signed by 'A Citizen of Arab Jerusalem' and was addressed to the Israeli Minister of Religious Affairs. It described the trying times of East Jerusalem bridegrooms:

---

[23] *Al-Quds,* 27 November 1968.

> When a son of Arab Jerusalem wants to get married, he goes to the departments of the shari'a court in the city for the shar'i qadi to process the marriage. When this is over, he heads for the (Israeli) Interior Ministry to get himself registered as married. The Interior Ministry, however, refuses to acknowledge this contract because it has been issued by the shari'a court in Arab Jerusalem, and they tell him to go to the shar'i judge in Jaffa or some other qadi in Israel...
>
> So off he goes to one of these judges to ask for a new contract to be written out. The qadi starts things off again and asks for shar'i proof in order to complete the contract. The bride-groom presents them to the qadi, who then refuses the Quranic contract when he learns that the bride is under 17 years of age, saying that the law in Israel does not permit the *ma'dhun* (marriage notary) to marry a girl under 17....and this is where the problems really start! What is to be done? The groom is married and a child is on the way, but he can't register the child in his Identity Card, and he can't get a birth certificate for it....[24]

Several of the aspects of the situation under discussion are raised by this letter. Firstly, there is the imposition of secular legal provisions upon the shari'a courts in Israel; secondly there is the non-recognition of any document issued by the Jerusalem shari'a court on the part of the Israeli authorities; and thirdly, there is the burden of double recourse as referred to in the letter. These last two points are referred to in the following paragraph taken from the Reply to the above Open Letter from a Spokesman for the Ministry of Religion, published a week later in the same paper:

> It is natural that the Israeli Ministry of the Interior should not recognise marriage certificates still bearing the name of the Hashemite King of Jordan and verified by a shari'a court that will not cooperate with government institutions, despite the fact that nearly three years have passed since the city of Jerusalem was unified. Instead, they carry on as if nothing has changed, caring nothing for the alterations in the affairs of Muslims and doing nothing to help them avoid difficulties.[25]

This reply purported to correct the Open Letter in stating that for an East Jerusalem marriage to be recognised by the Interior Ministry it is not necessary for the whole marriage to be done again, but there must be

---

[24] *Al-Quds,* 5 March 1970.
[25] *Al-Quds,* 13 March 1970.

establishment (*ithbat*) of the marriage before the Jaffa court. This is somewhat misleading, as a claim to prove an existing marriage would in any case necessitate the presence of both parties, or of one partner and witnesses, in the Jaffa court, as opposed to a simple ratification of the Jerusalem contract which could be secured by the efforts of the groom alone. The claim in any case will be subject to fees in the Israeli court, just as the contract was subject to fees in the Jerusalem court, in addition to the costs involved in the transport of spouses and/or witnesses to Jaffa. This duplication of fees, and the physical problems of traveling to Jaffa, do cause problems for the Palestinians in East Jerusalem. The Israeli answer to this problem was to encourage the Muslims involved to avoid the Jerusalem court altogether, as shown by the Spokesman's reply:

> These difficulties can be avoided if those who wish to marry go to one of the two marriage notaries appointed by the Jaffa court in unified Jerusalem.

Later on, the Israeli authorities considered establishing a permanent branch of the Jaffa shari'a court in Jerusalem: in 1973 it was reported that the then Jaffa qadi was to head the branch.[26] Less than two months later, however, the same paper reported that the Israeli government had revoked that decision and was currently considering, as an alternative, the possibility of having the decisions of the East Jerusalem court recognised by the Execution Offices.[27] It also reported the Israeli Justice Ministry to be considering recognising the Supreme Islamic Board as the sole body responsible for appointments and promotions of shar'i judges in Jerusalem and the West Bank. Had this been seriously proposed and accepted by the shar'i judiciary in the West Bank, it might have led in effect to the development of a Palestinian shar'i judiciary independent of both Israel and Jordan. However, as with other attempts to find solutions to the situation, these suggestions came to nothing.

In the 1980s, moves by the Israeli authorities concentrated again on setting up a shari'a court in Jerusalem, although this time the Minister of Religious Affairs decided to set up a new Israeli shari'a court in the city, rather than just a branch of the Jaffa court. A statement issued in response to this proposal by Shaykh Sa'd ad-Din al-'Alami, Acting qadi al-qudat and head of the Supreme Islamic Board, was published on 11 February 1985 in the *ash-Sha'b* newspaper, calling on the Israeli minister to revoke his decision and instead to recognise and execute the decisions issued by the shari'a court in Arab Jerusalem. Shaykh Sa'd ad-Din went on to deplore the burden of double recourse and duplicate fees borne by East Jerusalem Muslims, which could be removed by recognition of the East Jerusalem court. Perhaps the clearest proof that little has changed since 1967 lies in the reference Shaykh Sa'd ad-

[26] *Al-Quds*, 26 January 1973.
[27] *Al-Quds*, 12 March 1973.

Din made to the 'Shar'i Statement' of 1968, of which large parts were quoted in the 1985 article, showing that the arguments therein stand unchanged.

Nevertheless, in April of last year, Radio Israel announced that a shari'a court had been established in West Jerusalem.[28] Although no research has been done into this matter yet, the establishment of this court is unlikely to affect the fundamentals of the situation as described in this article: the most it will probably do is to alleviate some of the problems and costs of using the Jaffa court for Palestinian Muslims of East Jerusalem.

Besides being subject to conflicting jurisdiction and duplicate court fees, the East Jerusalem Muslim Palestinians are also subject to conflicting legislation. In his Reply to the Open Letter quoted above, the Israeli Spokesman for the Ministry of Religious Affairs ended by saying that the qadis of East Jerusalem should try to solve the problems by means of a joint enquiry involving themselves and the Minister of Religious Affairs,

> ...given that there are no differences from a shar'i point of view between what is followed in Jerusalem and what is followed in the shari'a courts in Israel...

This final sentence is curious when compared to his earlier exhortation to the ma'dhuns appointed by the Jerusalem shari'a court:

> [t]hat now, three years after the unification of the city, they remember, when they are going about their tasks in Jerusalem, which is in Israel, that Israeli law does not allow girls under 17 to marry, and that every action in contravention of (that law) is going to create problems for those who use their services...

The difference in the age of capacity for marriage is only one of the ways in which personal status law as applied in the shari'a courts in Israel differs from that applied in the Jerusalem court and the rest of the West Bank. In 1970, when the Open letter was published, the Jerusalem court was applying the provisions of the Jordanian Law of Family Rights of 1951, which gave the ages for marriage as 18 and 17 for males and females respectively, but allowed females aged 15-17 and males 15-18 to marry with the permission of the qadi, on proof of sufficient maturity and physical development. The Israeli Age of Marriage Law 1950, on the other hand, imposes a criminal penalty on persons involved in the marriage of a girl under the age of 17.[29] While the law does not actually invalidate the marriage if it is recognised by the parties' personal law, it can be made the grounds for dissolution on application by the

---

28*Al-Quds*, 6 April 1988, quoting Radio Israel of the previous day. The anouncement stated that the court is in Jaffa Street 'near the site of the (Israeli) Shari'a Court of Appeal'.

29Article 2 of Israeli Age of Marriage Law 1950. Arabic text in M. Natur, *Al-mar'i fi'l-qanun ash-shar'i (Applicable Texts of Islamic law)*, Jerusalem, 1981, p.138-9.

girl, her parents or guardians or a Social Affairs employee, although such dissolution does not cause the penalty to lapse.[30]

The Open Letter thus describes the situation facing East Jerusalem Muslim Palestinians: a marriage that would be both shar'i and legal in the East Jerusalem court might expose the male parties involved to a criminal penalty if referred to the Jaffa court. Problems would obviously arise if the relationship proved problematic: the young wife, for example, unable to have recourse to the Jaffa court, would have her case (for example, for dower) heard in Jerusalem and would be unable to get it executed. In most cases, the establishment (*ithbat*) of marriage would be carried out at Jaffa when the bride was of legal age according to Israeli law. In this regard, Layish notes for the three years up to 1970:

> About a third of the approximately 100 marriage confirmations issued by the Qadi of Jaffa to residents of East Jerusalem (the city and the villages in its area of jurisdiction) were clear cases of offences against the Age of Marriage Law or of reasonable suspicion in such offences.[31]

There are no statistics available to indicate whether or not East Jerusalem Palestinians have been prosecuted for this offence under Israeli law, and this absence also applies to offences against the Israeli ban on polygamy. The difference between the two laws to which East Jerusalem Muslims are variously subject is perhaps sharper here. Neither the 1951 Jordanian law nor its replacement in 1976 placed any legally enforceable restrictions on polygamy, while in Israel polygamy is a criminal offence.[32] A polygamous union would be valid under the law applied in the East Jerusalem court but could not be registered in the Jaffa court and might lead to prosecution should it be discovered. This gives rise to the same potential problems regarding recourse to legal remedy and execution that apply to marriages to girls underage by Israeli law. Layish notes nine convictions on the charge of polygamy for the year 1969, but gives no details on where those nine were resident, so it is not clear whether East Jerusalem Palestinians were

[30] The original law did empower the Israeli District Court (ie a secular civil court) to permit the marriage of an under-age girl to a man by whom she is pregnant or has given birth. In 1960 an amendment extended the District Court's power to permit a 16 year old girl to marry even where these conditions did not pertain, provided there are 'special circumstances' convincing the judge of the justification for the marriage. Layish found that there was 'no indication' that Palestinians from inside Israel availed themselves of this opportunity; it is even less likely that Palestinians from East Jerusalem would use it. A. Layish, *Women and Islamic Law in a Non-Muslim State*, Jerusalem, 1975.

[31] Layish, *Women and Islamic Law*, p.28.

[32] This was achieved in 1951 by the repeal of the 'good defence' to the charge of polygamy in the Penal Code taken over from the British. In Jordanian law, the only way a woman can protect herself against her husband taking another wife is to insert a stipulation against this eventuality in her contract of marriage (Art.19 JLPS).

involved.[33] It does however seem likely that while the Israeli authorities refuse to afford any recognition or legal value whatsoever to any documents issued by the East Jerusalem shari'a court, a marriage contract issued there for a polygamous union would be used as a basis for a criminal prosecution in the Israeli courts.[34]

These and other differences in the law applied in Israel and imposed by the Israeli authorities on the Muslim Palestinians of East Jerusalem serve to fuel the indignation of those Palestinians who find themselves in this situation. The changes introduced in the shar'i provisions by the non-Muslim Israeli occupation authorities are not accepted by the shar'i judiciary. They are challenged on the grounds of being non-shar'i both in content and by dint of being issued by a legislature not empowered to issue rules for shari'a courts. Israeli law for the Palestinians of East Jerusalem has the nature of being the law of a foreign colonial power imposed forcibly on an indigenous community.

As noted above, while the Execution Offices did go back to executing decisions from the rest of the shari'a courts of first instance, the instructions for the non-execution of Jerusalem decisions have been adhered to. There has been no official execution through the normal channels of the decisions of the Jerusalem shari'a court since the instructions were issued in 1969.[35]

However, over the two decades of occupation, there have been times when decisions issued by the Jerusalem court did obtain execution by some means or other, principally through the agreement of one Jaffa qadi to verify the Jerusalem decisions, and then by the 'substitution' of the decision in another West Bank shari'a court. The first system, basically a private accommodation by the then Jaffa qadi, lasted for about two years and then came to a halt. The second proceeded unofficially for about twelve years until it too was halted in 1985 when a fresh memorandum was circulated to the West Bank Execution Offices by the Israeli military authorities stressing the non-execution of Jerusalem decisions. Since 1985, therefore, the Jerusalem court has been unable by any means to obtain execution of its decisions. This leads obviously to problems, and not always only for those resident in Jerusalem, as will be seen later.

33Layish, *Women and Islamic Law*, p.83 and pp. 73-5.

34In 1970, in Criminal Appeal Case no 135, the Israeli Appeal Court held that an Israeli Palestinian man who had married a second wife in Jenin on the West Bank could be tried for polygamy in Israel. The first instance court had ruled itself not competent to hear the case, brought by the state, as the offence had occurred outside the borders of Israel. The case is referred to by Layish in *Women and Islamic Law*, p.88 note 35. I am grateful to advocates 'Ala' and Hanan al-Bakri for the Arabic text of the decision. It would be interesting to find out whether there has ever been a prosecution of a Palestinian from East Jerusalem who contracted both marriage contracts in courts of the West Bank.

35This can be noted from Meron, 'The Religious Courts in the Administered Territories', p. 367: the statistics he sets out are drawn from the Execution Offices in the West Bank and list the numbers of decisions executed by each and the shari'a court where each decision was issued. The list of courts includes Jaffa but makes no mention of East Jerusalem.

The reverse, of course, also applies: decisions from a West Bank shari'a court cannot be executed in Jerusalem; a resident of the West Bank will not be able to execute an award made in a West Bank court against a spouse resident in East Jerusalem or in Israel. Those entitled and willing to go to the Jaffa court can, however, have their decisions executed through the Israeli-administered West Bank Execution Offices against a spouse resident there. The only place that decisions of East Jerusalem can be executed is in Jordan. Yet another quirk in this complicated state of affairs lies in the fact that decisions issued in the Israeli-administered shari'a courts of the occupied Gaza Strip must be verified in the East Jerusalem court if they are to obtain recognition and/or execution in Jordan.

Obviously, not all documents or decisions of the shari'a courts actually need execution procedures. East Jerusalem Muslim Palestinians, who are entitled to go to the Jaffa court, may well do so where there is a need for execution, or where they need a document acceptable to the Israeli authorities; otherwise, they continue to have recourse to the East Jerusalem court. Just for the record, the East Jerusalem court has been registering over 1000 contracts of marriage every year since 1975, and it is clear from a political point of view that East Jerusalem Muslim Palestinians consider the Jerusalem court to be the body competent to decide issues of personal status, despite the fact that they may be unable to obtain their rights under the JLPS due to the Israeli annexation. In the words of Shaykh Sa'd ad-Din al-'Alami: 'The shari'a court of Jerusalem is the court around which the Muslims make their stand.'[36]

III. The Shari'a Court of Appeal in East Jerusalem

Besides the shari'a court of first instance, there is also a Shari'a Court of Appeal in East Jerusalem. The only time that Jerusalem was without a permanent shari'a court of appeal was after the Jordanian annexation of the West Bank, when the 1951 Regulation of the Shari'a Court of Appeal provided that:

> There shall be one Appeal Court in the Kingdom for all the shari'a courts, with its headquarters in Amman: it may convene in Jerusalem when necessary.

After the 1967 war, the shar'i judiciary in the West Bank were cut off from the Shari'a Appeal Court in Amman, and the same Muslim notables who formed themselves into the Supreme Islamic Board also organised a Shari'a Court of Appeal in Jerusalem along the lines laid down in Jordanian law but made up of West Bank qadis under the presidency of the Acting qadi al-qudat. The measures taken against the shari'a court of first instance in Jerusalem, and to a lesser extent in the rest of the West Bank, also included this Court of Appeal, although there appears to be some confusion over this issue among

[36] *Ash-Sha'b* newspaper (Jerusalem), 11 February 1985.

certain academics. Kupferschmidt, writing in 1987, notes in passing that 'a shari'a Court of Appeal is located in Ramallah';[37] which is not, and never has been, the case. While the regular court system of the West Bank did indeed lose the Jerusalem seat of its Appeal Court, which was moved to Ramallah, the shar'i judiciary never considered a seat other than Jerusalem for their Appeal Court.

Meron, writing in 1982, pursues what seems to be a favourite theme in noting 'the liberalism shown to the Moslem Court of Appeal acting in Jerusalem under the distant auspices of Jordan.'[38] The same author notes 'some hesitation' as to the authority of the Appeal Court as a result of the administrative order of August 1969 instructing the Execution Offices in the West Bank not to execute judgements from the shari'a courts, and continues:

> This measure was probably the result of the refusal of the Qadis in Jerusalem to accept nomination under the Israeli Qadis Law of 1961, thus denying validity to proceedings held and decisions given by them ... Later, however, the administrative order was amended so as not to apply to the Moslem Court of Appeal in Jerusalem.[39]

In 1984, Layish noted 'that the shari'a courts of first instance (in the West Bank) have been left without their court of appeal, the permanent seat of which is in Amman.'[40] Having described the *ad hoc* establishment of the Shari'a Court of Appeal in Jerusalem, Layish continued:

> [A]s the Shari'a Court of Appeal of the West Bank is in Jerusalem, its judgements are not valid in the West Bank, but in day-to-day reality they are enforced there.[41]

Neither Meron in his article nor Layish in the draft text cited above addressed what must for writers on law be the fundamental question here: the legality of the Israeli annexation of Jerusalem. Their use of the term 'valid' must be assessed in that context.

Although Meron reports that the original non-execution order was amended so as not to include the Court of Appeal, any such written modification has proved difficult to trace. Layish also seems to be unaware of this, and it may be in fact that the original instructions stand in theory, forbidding execution of any decisions of any shari'a court, although amended in practice with regard to the first instance courts other than Jerusalem. The Shari'a Court of Appeal, however, has a position somewhere between that of

---

[37]Kupferschmidt, *Supreme Muslim Council*, p.26.
[38]Meron, 'The Religious Courts in the Administered Territories', p.361.
[39]*Ibid.*, p. 360.
[40]Layish, *Shari'a Court in Jordan* , p.5.
[41]*Ibid.*, p.6.

the Jerusalem first instance court and the courts in the rest of the West Bank. As Layish notes, in practice its decisions are indeed executed, but not under the name of the Appeal Court. The decision is returned to the first instance shari'a court where the appealed decision originated, is written out and submitted to the Execution Office in the relevant West Bank town as 'having reached the stage of a final decision'. No reference is made to the Shari'a Court of Appeal in East Jerusalem, and it is to be assumed that if any such mention were to be made, the decision would not be executed.

Layish's statement that the permanent seat of the Shari'a Court of Appeal is in Amman was indeed true in statutory terms for some ten years (1967-77), although the Jordanian authorities were appointing its members for some years before they made the Jerusalem Appeal Court a fact in law as well as in practice. The delay was probably due to political reservations on the implications of this, but finally in 1977 the Jordanian authorities issued the Shari'a Courts of Appeal Regulation (no 20/1977) which repealed the 1951 Regulation stipulating Amman as the permanent seat and provided that 'a Shari'a Court of Appeal shall be constituted in both Amman and Jerusalem.'[42]

Article 3 of the Regulation provided that the Amman Appeal Court would deal with decisions issued by the shari'a courts in the East Bank and that in Jerusalem with those from the West Bank. The Regulation thus provided a statutory basis for a situation that had prevailed in practice since the 1967 occupation.

The existence of two Shari'a Courts of Appeal on the two Banks of the Jordan brought about the possibility of conflicting Appeal judgments for the two areas. While no provision is made for this in the Jordanian Appeal Courts Regulation, some lawyers in the West Bank felt that the decisions of the Amman court might be considered 'stronger' than those in Jerusalem should there be a clash. There appears however to have been no case testing this point as yet, and given the mutual inaccessibility in practical terms between the two courts there would seem to be little scope for such a challenge. The collected Amman decisions are freely quoted in West Bank courts, together with decisions from the Jerusalem court.[43]

One area where the two Appeal Courts can be seen to have taken contradictory stands and where the Jerusalem decision might be seen in light of the circumstances of occupation (despite denial of such influence by the Jerusalem judges) is that of compensation for arbitrary talaq. The provision for such compensation is new, introduced in the Jordanian Law of Personal Status of 1976[44] and thus in effect only for a matter of months

---

42 Article 2 of the Regulation of Shari'a Courts of Appeal no 20/1977.

43 Selected decisions of the Shari'a Appeal Court in Amman are available in M. al-'Arabi, *Al-mabadi' al-qada'iyya li-mahkamat al-isti'naf ash-shar'iyya, (Judicial principles in the shar'i appeal court)*, Amman, Volume 1, 1973; Volume 2, 1984. The Jerusalem court has not yet published selected decisions but apparently a collection is currently in preparation.

44 Article 134 JLPS.

before the separate jurisdictions of the two Appeal Courts were formalised in law.

The case considered by the Jerusalem court originated in 1984 in the Ramallah first instance shari'a court when a woman submitted a claim for compensation for a talaq pronounced by her husband in 1983.[45] The divorce, a second revocable talaq, became final on the termination of her *'idda* without revocation of the talaq. Both the claimant and her ex-husband were residents of Beit 'Anan, a village which had been within the jurisdiction of Jerusalem before 1967 but was transferred by the Israelis outside the annexed area to the jurisdiction of Ramallah. Thus, the parties come under the Ramallah military and regular courts, and its residents carry West Bank identity cards.[46] However, the shari'a courts did not adjust their jurisdiction, and thus the villagers come under the Jerusalem shari'a court for personal status matters. At the same time, they do not qualify for consideration by the Israeli shari'a court of Jaffa, not being Jerusalem residents according to Israeli law.

The ex-husband's lawyer sought dismissal of the woman's claim on the grounds that the man was resident within the shar'i jurisdiction of Jerusalem. He quoted from the Jordanian Law of Shar'i Procedure to detail those claims that might be heard in any court without regard for the residence of the defendant:

> All courts have the right to assess maintenance...(and) to hear applications for custody, fees for suckling and accommodation.[47]

These claims constitute an exception from the general rule laid down in same article, that claims are to be heard in the shari'a court with jurisdiction over the area where the defendant lives.

The qadi of Ramallah agreed that, technically, his court was not competent to hear the claim, which belonged in Jerusalem, but pointed out that if the claim were heard in Jerusalem, the woman would be unable to gain execution of any award that might be given. He therefore held that the Ramallah court was able to hear the claim in order to avoid injury to the woman 'in view of the circumstances of occupation and the impossibility of executing decisions of the Jerusalem shari'a court'.

---

45 Ramallah case no 150/1984. Full text of original and appealed decision taken from the Appeal decision (see note 48).

46 This situation applies to around 24 villages formerly in the Jerusalem District and transferred by the Israelis to Bethlehem (around 4 villages) and Ramallah (around 20 villages) by virtue of Military Orders nos 39 and 567. I am indebted to advocate 'Ala' ad-Din al-Bakri for preparing a summary including detailed listing of the villages and Beduin settlements affected in this way.

47 Article 3(5) Law of Shar'i Procedure of 1959.

The Ramallah qadi went on to award the woman compensation and the ex-husband appealed.[48] The Shari'a Court of Appeal in Jerusalem held that the Ramallah court was indeed competent to hear the compensation claim, but had taken the correct decision on the wrong reasoning. The Appeal Court stated that claims for compensation had the characteristics of maintenance awards and thus fell within the terms of the above-quoted article of the Law of Shar'i Procedure and like maintenance claims could be heard in any court.

Besides the implications of treating compensation like maintenance, the Jerusalem Appeal Court has established in this decision a principle entirely contrary to the one previously established by at least three Appeal decisions in Amman on the same subject and dating back to 1978. These state:

> The shari'a court has no competence to consider a claim for compensation for arbitrary talaq if the defendant is not resident in its area of jurisdiction and the claim is defended on that basis.[49]

Obviously, had this principle by the Amman court been acted upon in Jerusalem, the Ramallah court would have been held not competent and the case transferred to the court of the husband's residence - Jerusalem - leading to non-execution of whatever award might have been made. The three Amman decisions establishing the Jordanian principle are published in the collected decisions of the Appeal Court, and it is tempting to view the contrary judgment as an example of how the Jerusalem Appeal Court has taken into consideration the practical circumstances occasioned by the Israeli occupation in laying down principles for the West Bank. The text of the decision itself, however, as noted above, explicitly denies any such consideration. Whatever the Appeal Court's motivation, its reasoning amounts to a novel procedural interpretation of a question of substantive law, and is very much to the benefit of women divorced without good reason in the West Bank.

The insistence of the Jerusalem court that its decision in the compensation case was not prompted by consideration of the circumstances of occupation was upheld shortly after the above case in another claim raised in Ramallah which ended up in the Appeal Court. The residential circumstances of the parties involved, a woman and her ex-husband, led to a similar situation as that described above: while the woman was a resident of Dheishe refugee camp in the district of Bethlehem, the man was a resident of Ram, which is in the shar'i jurisdiction of Jerusalem but according to the Israelis under Ramallah.

The woman was claiming her deferred dower after the termination of her 'idda from a talaq in 1983. The ex-husband's lawyer defended the claim on the basis of no competence to the Ramallah court, as dower should

---

48 Ramallah Appeals, *sijill* 77, p.177, no 25, serial no 149/1984.

49 Appeal Decisions nos 20368/1978, 20404/1978 and 21669/1981 in al-'Arabi', *Al-mabadi' al-qada'iyya*, Volume 2, p.168.

be in the exclusive jurisdiction of Jerusalem where the defendant was resident. The woman's lawyer quoted two Appeal Court decisions to argue for consideration of the claim in Ramallah: the above Jerusalem precedent on compensation, and another case from the Amman Appeal Court which had established the principle that the first instance shari'a court in Amman could hear a claim for *ta'a* (obedience) even though the defendant (the wife) was resident in Jerusalem 'because of the circumstances of occupation and the seizure of the (West) Bank by the enemy', which meant that the husband, not allowed by the Israelis to cross the bridge into the West Bank, was unable to present his claim in Jerusalem where the wife was resident.[50]

In the claim for deferred dower, the Ramallah qadi agreed with the arguments and precedents submitted by the woman's lawyer, rejected the man's defence, and held that the Ramallah court was competent to hear the claim

> given that the present occupation has prevented the execution of the decisions of the Jerusalem shari'a court, which would cause injury (to be caused by law) and that there are precedents for this decision.

Following the award of deferred dower to the woman, the husband's lawyer appealed in Jerusalem on his original submission of no competence, and this time the Jerusalem Shari'a Appeal Court agreed with the appeal.[51] The court stated that the principle of the compensation decision could not be applied to the present case, as deferred dower was not comparable with maintenance and had none of its characteristics: unlike compensation, it was not calculated in terms of maintenance, nor was it paid in installments. The court also declared that the Amman principle in the ta'a case was not applicable to the circumstances of the present case as there was no physical obstacle preventing the wife from submitting her claim in Jerusalem where the husband was resident. The decision did not discuss the physical obstacles (ie the Israeli occupation) that would prevent the wife actually obtaining her award from the shari'a court of first instance in Jerusalem.

The two cases in the Jerusalem Court of Appeal discussed above thus involved the same arguments by both sets of lawyers, with the court accepting the appeal in the dower case and rejecting it in the case of compensation by virtue of an original interpretation of the nature of compensation. As noted above, the compensation case is likely to be something of an exception in that it constitutes a contrary position to that taken in Amman: but a proper assessment of all the ways in which the

---

[50]This decision is not published in al-'Arabi's collected Amman appeals, but two decisions establishing the rule to which it constitutes the exception appear in Volume 1, p.161 (nos 13035 and 131): 'The shari'a court may not hear a claim of ta'a if the wife is not resident within the area of its jurisdiction and the claim is defended on this basis'.

[51]Ramallah Appeals, *sijill* 101, p.9 no 8, serial no 37/1984.

Jerusalem Appeal court has or has not allowed its rulings to be influenced by the occupation would require a systematic study of all the rulings made there since 1967.

IV. A Law of Personal Status for Palestine?

In conclusion, it is worth noting again that the current law, the JLPS, was passed in 1976 as a temporary law without the participation of the Jordanian Parliament and with no Palestinian representation. The legislation is based ultimately on the Hanafi school in the tradition of the Ottoman Turks, and indeed the administration of the separate communal courts for personal status is an Ottoman relic that has been abolished, for example, in Egypt.

Until now, it has not been particularly timely for West Bank Palestinians to challenge the family laws applied to them. In the women's committees, and other groups that in various Arab states have taken a leading role in analysing the family law, the national struggle in all its various aspects has been the obvious focus for energies. In addition, the Palestinians had no way of directly addressing the legislature that issued the JLPS in 1976. Furthermore, given that as a rule the West Bankers never did recognise Jordan's authority over them,[52] it would have been politically inappropriate for them to address requests for modifications to such legislation to the Jordanian authorities. Recent events have radically changed the situation.

On 31 July 1988, against the background of the continuing uprising in the occupied territories, King Hussein announced that he was cutting all legal and administrative links with the West Bank, in recognition of the Palestine Liberation Organisation as the sole legitimate representative of the Palestinian people. In the enabling legislation passed to give effect to this move, the official relationship was cut with West Bank departments of Jordanian public and governmental institutions. The only exceptions to this rule were the Ministry of Awqaf and the Department of the qadi al-qudat.[53] That is, those employees and officials working within the Awqaf and the shari'a courts retain their Jordanian appointments, their Jordanian salaries, and Jordanian supervision. It is to be assumed that neither the Jordanians nor the PLO had any wish to see the Israeli authorities step into the administrative gap left particularly in the Awqaf administration, with its reponsibilities, *inter alia*, for the Haram ash-Sharif, the al-Aqsa mosque and its surroundings. Meanwhile, after the Jordanian withdrawal, the Palestine National Council was declared as the Palestinian legislative authority; all laws and orders in force until the time of the Jordanian decision to cut ties were declared as

---

[52]The international community also refused recognition to Jordan's annexation of the West Bank, with the exception of Britain, who made a reservation regarding sovereignty over Jerusalem, and Pakistan.

[53]Regulation no 28/1988, *Official Gazette* no 3565 of 16 August 1988.

remaining in force until repealed or amended by that legislative authority.[54] In November 1988 the Palestinian state was declared.

These developments leave the shari'a courts and Islamic family law in an interesting position. At the moment of writing, a new Jordanian Law of Personal Status is being considered by various committees within the Jordanian Parliament. The draft JLPS, drawn up in its current form in 1987, is to replace the current 'temporary' JLPS and contains some interesting and useful amendments, for example in the area of compensation for arbitrary talaq.

It is to be assumed that if this new Law is passed in the near future, it might be applied by the shari'a courts on the West Bank - even though strictly speaking the law will be passed for application in Jordan only. It is also possible that the West Bank courts would continue to apply the current legislation. A third option, however, would be for the shari'a courts on the West Bank to become the first courts in the area to apply a law promulgated by the newly created legislative authority of the State of Palestine. The promulgation of a Palestinian Law of Personal Status may not be an immediate priority, but when it does take place, both the content of the law and the method of its implementation will be of great significance.

[54]Decision of Executive Committee of Palestine National Council of 22 August 1988; reproduced in *al-Ittihad* newspaper (Jerusalem), 24 August 1988.

PART II

EUROPE

7. *GET* AND *TALAQ* IN ENGLISH LAW: REFLECTIONS ON LAW AND POLICY*

Bernard Berkovits

Introduction

The purpose of this article is to consider the attitude of the English municipal law towards the Jewish form of divorce - the *get* - as reflected in common law, legislation, and case law, and to consider the extent to which it meets the reasonable expectations and requirements of the Jewish community of this country.

In an article recently published in the *Law Quarterly Review*,[1] the writer attempted a detailed analysis of the House of Lords decision in the case of *Fatima*,[2] and the implications of that decision for Jewish divorce. *Fatima*, it will be recalled, dealt with the status in English law of a 'transnational talaq', and the House of Lords decided that such a talaq was not entitled to recognition either as a domestic divorce or as a foreign decree. It was argued in the *Law Quarterly Review* that the decision was not supported either by legal arguments or on policy grounds, and that it was, in any event, not relevant to Jewish divorces as effected by the get procedure.

The *Fatima* decision, important as it is, is restricted to the relatively unusual situation of transnational divorces. More troubling, and more pressing, is the much broader question of how English law should treat Islamic and Jewish divorces in this country, and to what extent it ought to accord recognition to the internal religious systems practised by the Muslim and Jewish communities of Britain, respectively. It is this question that the present chapter seeks to address.

Whilst the main emphasis is therefore on the position relating to Jewish divorce, it will be instructive to draw certain comparisons with the attitude taken by English law to the Islamic form of divorce known as talaq.

There are considerable similarities between Judaism and Islam in relation to family law. In the first place, both systems are essentially religious in nature, as opposed to Western legal systems which are entirely secular. Both Jewish law and Islamic law are based on religious prescriptions, which are binding on all members of the faith irrespective of geographical or national links. Both systems recognise the overriding authority of the religious-legal framework, the *halacha* in Judaism, and the *shari'a* in Islam. Both consist of a basic written core -the Torah in the case of Judaism, and the Qur'an in the case

---

* This article reflects the personal views of the author, and should not be taken in any way as representative of the views of any other person or organisation.

1 'Transnational Divorces: the Fatima Decision', 104 *Law Quarterly Review*, 1988, pp.60-93.

2 [1986] A.C. 527.

of Islam- as well as an 'oral' law -the Torah *she'be'al peh* in Judaism, and the *hadith* in Islam. And in both systems of family law, divorce is extrajudicial' -it is the parties concerned (in Judaism) or the husband (in Islam) who effect the divorce, and not a judge.

Despite these similarities, however, there are also a number of striking differences between Jewish family law, as applied nowadays, and Islamic family law. These differences relate, in the main, to the degree of formality attached to the divorce procedure, as well as to the relative equality of status of the parties. Jewish divorce, as outlined below, is a highly formal procedure: it is documentary in nature, it requires valid witnesses, and it is governed throughout by numerous legal prescriptions. Halacha does not spell out any reasons for these numerous technicalities; consequently, they become requirements which cannot effectively be amended. This has the beneficial effect of preventing easy or hasty divorce.[3]

Islamic divorce, by contrast, can be effected verbally and without witnesses, and is not surrounded by any legal technicalities. Moreover, in Islamic divorce, the wife is essentially passive; it is the husband who institutes and effects the divorce, which can be effected unilaterally, and the wife's consent -or even her express objections- are not of any relevance. Whilst this was essentially the position in early Jewish law, unilateral divorce has, to all intents and purposes, been abolished in Jewish law for over a thousand years.

There are also a number of communal and socio-legal differences betwen the structure of the Jewish community in England, and that of the Islamic community, which have important practical implications in the legal sphere. The Jewish community is highly structured and well-organised; it has a Chief Rabbi and ecclesiastical courts, and a representative lay body.[4]

The Orthodox community constitutes some 78% of all Jewish adherents in England; the two main dissenting groups -Reform and Liberal Jews- are also well-organised, and their theological-legal stands are well known. Consequently, for example, it is relatively easy to establish what Jewish law says on any specific matter, as well as to the extent to which that law is accepted and practised in the community. This means that it is relatively easy to legislate on matters of specific Jewish interest, and Parliament can therefore provide, as it does for example in respect of Jewish marriages,[5] for certain matters of personal status to be determined by Jewish law.

The Islamic community in Britain, by contrast, is far more loosely organised and divided, both in terms of representative lay bodies, and in terms of ecclesiastical teachings and authorities. It is a matter of some difficulty, therefore, for any would-be legislator to determine with precision what Islamic law says in relation to any specific matter, or whether, indeed, there is such a thing as 'Islamic law'.

---

[3]Although this is not necessarily the rationale behind the law. Biblical law is treated as binding because it is the Divine will, and attempts to ascribe 'reasons' to it are generally frowned upon. See, however, Maimonides' philosophical work, *Moreh Nevuchim,* 3:49.

[4]The Board of Deputies of British Jews.

[5]See note 28, *infra.*

Were Parliament, for example, to attempt to legislate for recognition of Islamic marriages in Britain, it would first have to establish the essential features of an Islamic marriage, and also who is authorised, from a religious point of view, to celebrate such a marriage. These religious and institutional uncertainties have no doubt played a considerable part in the cautious attitude of English law to claims for greater recognition of Islamic personal law in England. [6]

In Part one of this article an explanation is given of the essential features of Jewish divorce. This is followed, in Part II, by an outline of the Jewish law of marriage, and a historical-legal consideration of the extent to which English law takes account of the Jewish law of marriage. Part III consists of an outline of English case-law relating to Jewish divorces, and an analysis of the arguments in favour of, and against, according them recognition. Part IV deals with the problems occasioned by the present dichotomy of attitude of English civil law, and considers attempted solutions to this problem in other jurisdictions, as well as the writer's suggested legislative proposal, together with a draft Bill and accompanying notes.

I. The Get Procedure

The Historical Basis

Jewish law has always recognised the possibility and permissibility of divorce, even though it is usually strongly discouraged.[7] The *fons et origo* of all Jewish Law is the Bible (more correctly the Five Books of Moses, known to Christians as the 'Old Testament'),[8] which is considered by traditional Jewish teaching to be of Divine origin and eternally mandatory. In this sense, Judaism is very much a theologically-based legal system closely akin to the

---

[6]As indicated by the total rejection of the Muslim claims in United Muslim Organization, *Why Muslim Family Law for British Muslims,* London, 1983. I am indebted for this reference to Dr Sebastian Poulter of Southampton University.

[7]In common with Islamic law which characterises all behaviour on the basis of religious-moral valuations, Jewish law divides all human conduct into a number of different categories depending on whether the specified conduct is viewed positively or negatively. The three main categories are: *mitzvah* (religiously mandatory or positive acts); *reshut* (neutral acts); and *issur* or *aveirah* (prohibited acts). Theree are also categories of *meshubach* (praiseworthy acts) and *meguneh* (reprehensible acts). In this context, divorce (known as *gerushin*) is normally in the category of meguneh, although it may sometimes be a mitzvah (e.g. if a wife is committing adultery). It should also be noted that independently of whether the actual act of divorce (the gerushin) is reprehensible or not, it is a mitzvah to follow the get procedure prescribed in Jewish law when divorce is desired.

[8] Thc term 'Old Testament' has distinctly Christological origins. It is based upon the Christian doctrine that the Divine covenant with the Jewish people was abrogated when they failed to accept Jesus, and replaced by a new covenant with the Church, which became the true Israel. Hence the Jewish scriptures became the 'old' testament or covenant, and the Christian scriptures were termed the 'new' testament or covenant. From a Jewish point of view, therefore, the phrase 'Old Testament' is a theologically objectionable one; but it is used by Jewish writers, nonetheless, because it has become so firmly entrenched in popular consciousness.

Islamic model. There is no human authority empowered to abrogate or alter the express laws of the Bible, but naturally these laws require interpretation, and this interpretation is embodied in the 'Oral law' .

In the early stages of Jewish history, this law was indeed oral in character and transmitted by word of mouth from generation to generation. Much of it is ascribed to Moses who 'received it' during the forty day period he spent on Mount Sinai, and it is in most senses as binding and authoritative as the 'Written law' (the Bible). However, it lost its oral character and was committed to writing many centuries ago -firstly in the *Mishnah*, which was designed to be a 'code' of Jewish law; subsequently in the *Gemara* or *Talmud,* which elaborated upon the rulings of the *Mishnah*; and later in Codes of law composed by leading Rabbinic figures. Prominent amongst these codes are the *Mishneh Torah* of Maimonides (twelfth century), and the *Shulchan Aruch* of Karo (sixteenth century).

The rules and regulations contained in the Codes and commentaries thereon are also supplemented by the *teshuvot,* or Responsa, of eminent Rabbinic figures to particular questions of law addressed to them. These Responsa, which deal with individual cases, are analysed for their *ratio decidendi*, which often comes to be treated as binding precedent for subsequent cases.

The Bible speaks of divorce on the grounds of 'immoral behaviour',[9] and specifies a procedure which has to be followed to effect the divorce.[10] This is the get.[11] The Oral law has amplified and developed virtually every detail of the Biblical prescription by countless complex rules and regulations, breach of which will often invalidate the get. It should be emphasised that in Jewish law the marital relationship of husband and wife is treated as a matter of the utmost importance, and the dissolution of that relationship must be very carefully controlled, lest a wife who is in reality still married in the eyes of the law contracts what is, in effect, an adulterous new marriage or relationship.

In early Jewish law, a husband could divorce his wife unilaterally -the procedure in this respect being similar to the talaq. However, around the year 1000 the leading Rabbinic jurist of the time introduced a legal edict (known as the *cherem*, or 'ban', of Rabbi Gershom) which prohibited (with rare exceptions) divorce without consent of the wife. This edict was accepted in most Jewish communities and came to have the force of a rule of law. Consequently, the get procedure nowadays is essentially consensual; it requires the mutual consent of both husband and wife. The edict of Rabbi Gershom was

---

[9]Deuteronomy 24:1. The *Talmud* records a difference of opinion as to whether this is to be construed as the sole 'ground' for divorce, or whether other grounds are acceptable . One sage is even of the opinion that a man may divorce his wife 'if he found another woman who was more beautiful'. The accepted view is that no grounds as such are necessary, but that in case of immoral behaviour, it becomes a mitzvah (see note 7 above) to execute a divorce.

[10]*Ibid.*

[11]The word get is the Aramaic translation of the Hebrew word *sefer* used in the Biblical text, which is usually translated as 'book'. See *Targum Onkelos ad loc.*

far-sighted, almost a revolutionary one for its times, and did a great deal to protect wives against unjustified rejection by their husbands.

The Get Procedure - Preliminary Stages

In contradistinction to the talaq, a get is by its very essence documentary; there is no such thing as an oral get. The Biblical verse itself speaks of writing a *sefer keritut* - 'a book of sundering apart' or ' bill of divorcement',[12] and indeed the translation of the word get (which is Aramaic, not Hebrew) is 'a document'. When used with reference to other types of legal document, however, it is always qualified by a limiting adjective; only in reference to divorce is it left unqualified.[13] This in itself illustrates the primary importance attached to the documentary nature of the divorce.

Each get document has to follow a specific legal wording, and each one must be specifically handwritten especially for the particular couple. A printed document, or even a handwritten document which was not written specifically for the particular divorcing couple, is completely invalid.[14] In theory it is the husband who is himself mandated to write the document, but in practice, because of the detailed rules regarding its writing, which demand the most exacting standards of calligraphy, and which extend to detailed specification of the manner in which each individual letter is to be shaped, a get document is never written except by a trained scribe (known as a *sofer*).

The document refers expressly to the parties by their names.[15] The relevant names are their personal names, rather than their surnames -so that the husband will be described as X son of Y, and the wife will be similarly described as A the daughter of B. Reference may be made to many different types of name. A person may have an English name and a Hebrew name; he may have an official name (which appears, for example on his or her birth certificate or passport) but which is not normally used in everyday transactions. He or she may have more than one official name, but use only one of them when signing documents. He may have an official name, but be called by another name amongst his or her friends and acquaintances. He may, indeed, be known by one name by some of his friends, and by a different name by other friends. He may once have been known by a particular name which has now fallen into disuse. He may have nicknames or familiar names of endearment.

All this has to be carefully determined to ensure that the correct names are inscribed on the document. Furthermore, the names are transliterated in the get (which is written in a mixture of Hebrew and Aramaic) not according

---

[12]The Vulgate renders the Hebrew 'libellus divortii' or 'libellus repudii'; the King James translation has 'Writing of divorcement' or 'Bill of divorcement'. See also Selden, *Uxor Ebraica,* lib.iii cap. 24.

[13]See *Tosafot* to Babylonian Talmud , Tractate *Gittin*, p. 2a, s.v. *Hamevi.*

[14]*Ibid.*, p. 24a; Maimonides, *Mishneh Torah*, Laws of Divorce 1:3 and 3:1; *Shulchan Aruch, Even Ha'ezer*, ch. 131.

[15]Maimonides, *Mishneh Torah*, 3:7 and 3:13-14; *Shulchan Aruch,* ch. 129.

to their secular spelling, but according to pronunciation. The names 'Lewis' and 'Louis', for example, will be written differently in a get , because in the former the final letter 's' is pronounced, but not in the latter. Because of the complex rules governing every stage of the get procedure, the drafting, writing and giving over of the document is always done under the supervision and control of Jewish legal experts specialising in divorce law,[16] even though in reality the get is a consensual form of divorce executed by and between the parties themselves.

The Get Procedure - The Act of Divorce

As noted above, Jewish divorce can only be effected by means of a document, which the husband is, in theory, supposed to write himself. In practice, however the scribe writes it for him. It is therefore necessary for the husband to appear before a *Beth Din* (Jewish court) in person,[17] to formally appoint the scribe and instruct him to write the document on his behalf and that of his wife. The scribe thereby becomes a duly constituted legal proxy of the husband.[18]

Since a get must be executed as a result of the parties' free will, the husband also makes a formal disclaimer in front of the Beth Din and in the presence of two witnesses stating that all the acts he is about to do are being done without duress or pressure, and invalidating any witnesses who may allege to the contrary.[19] Jewish law construes duress very widely. If, for example, at any time the husband made an oath or undertaking obliging himself to execute a get, this may be considered duress and could consequently invalidate the subsequent get proceedings. Consequently, to ensure that no such possibility arises, the husband must seek a formal annulment in Jewish law of any such oath or undertaking. This annulment requires a declaration by three persons competent to sit as a court administering Jewish law.

The get document also has to be signed by two persons who are competent to act as witnesses in Jewish law. Their signatures must be appended to the document in accordance with the precise calligraphic rules governing the writing of the document by the scribe, and they must be appended to the document with the purpose that it should serve as an instrument of divorce for the particular couple concerned. The husband, therefore, has to formally appoint the witnesses to sign the document on his behalf.

Once the get has been written and signed, it is subjected to minute word-by-word scrutiny by the scribe, and by judges of the Beth Din, to ensure that it complies in every way with the requirements of Jewish law. If it fails to

---

16 *Shulchan Aruch*, 141:30; 142: 9, and in introduction to *Seder Haget* (appendix to ch. 154).

17 Although the get nowadays requires mutual consent, technically it is still the husband who plays the active role in terms of preparation and handing over of the document.

18 *Shulchan Aruch*, ch. 120 and ch. 131.

19 *Ibid.*, ch. 134.

comply with the necessary stipulations, it may be declared invalid, thereby necessitating the repetition of the entire procedure.[20]

The actual act of divorce in Jewish law is constituted not by the writing of the document, but by its delivery to the wife. This requires an act of physical delivery into her hand;[21] divorce by post is an impossibility in Jewish law.[22] The vital legal act which severs the marriage bond is the delivery to the wife of the document. This is done either by the husband in person, or by his legal proxy[23] whom he has formally commissioned to act on his behalf. It is handed over in a fixed manner upon declaration of a prescribed formula, stating that it constitutes the instrument of divorce by means of which the marriage is to be terminated.[24]

Moreover, and in contrast to the talaq procedure, the handing over of a get requires the presence of two valid and legally-competent witnesses (as determined by the relevant rules of Jewish law). Their presence is not merely evidential -as recorders of an event which would be valid without their presence- but constitutive: without them the act of delivery of the get is of no validity, so that their presence is a *sine qua non.*[25] In addition, the delivery of the get must take place in the presence of three persons who are competent, under the requisite rules of Jewish law, to act in a judicial capacity.

It will be apparent from this description that although the get procedure is effected by the parties themselves, it is subject to numerous requirements and restrictions which impart a quasi-judicial character to the proceedings.

II. Jewish Marriages in English Law

Jewish Marriage - a Brief Outline

The theme of this paper is, as previously stated, the question of how English law deals with the get procedure. Since the get, however, is a procedure used to dissolve Jewish marriages, we have to consider the position of Jewish marriages in English law before turning to the question of dissolution of those marriages.

Jewish marriage, in legal theory, consists of two separate elements. Firstly, there is the *kidushin* ('sanctification'), or *erusin* ('tying'), as a result of which the bride becomes a 'married ' woman who is no longer permitted to any man other than the groom. In legal theory she is already married, so that

---

[20] *Ibid.*, ch. 135. The defect may invalidate the get even after it has been handed over to the wife.

[21] Or the hand of her duly-appointed agent (although, for technical reasons, it is rare nowadays for a wife to appoint an agent to receive her get on her behalf). It is, however, quite common for the husband to appoint an agent to act on his behalf and to hand the get over to his wife, and this procedure is always followed where the parties do not wish to meet one another, or where one party lives in one country (or distant town) and the other party elsewhere.

[22] *Shulchan Aruch,* ch. 138 and 139.

[23] *Ibid.,* ch. 140 and 141.

[24] *Ibid.,* ch. 136.

[25] *Ibid.,* ch.133.

she requires a get to obtain freedom from her groom. She is not , however, permitted to her bridegroom until the process of *nisu'in* ('marriage') takes place, after which she is in all respects a married woman.

In ancient times the two procedures - *kidushin* and *nisu'in* - were often separated by a period of as much as a year, but nowadays they are invariably contracted into one ceremony. The salient features of this ceremony[26] are that the groom gives the bride an object of a specific worth,[27] which in practice nowadays is the wedding ring. This object must be given to the wife in the presence of two witnesses, whose presence is, once again, not merely evidential but constitutive.

There is no requirement as such for the presence of a Rabbi or clergyman, although usually a spiritual leader will in fact be present. The giving of the object - which takes place under a canopy symbolising the matrimonial home - is accompanied by a declaration that this is the act of consecration of the marriage. Thereafter, bride and groom retire for a short while to a private room, and are secluded therein whilst two witnesses ensure that no one else enters. It is this act of seclusion which completes the marriage.

Jewish Marriage in English Law- The Present Position

English marriage procedure is today contained in the Marriage Act 1949, which provides for (a) marriage according to the rites of the Church of England (b) marriage under the superintendent registrar's certificate (c) marriage according to the usages of the Society of Friends (colloquially known as the 'Quakers') and (d) marriage according to the usages of persons professing the Jewish religion.[28]

It will immediately be noticed that this Act is unusual in the provision it makes for different forms of marriage. It is a 'pluralistic' Act, allowing for various different groups of British citizens to celebrate valid marriages in the manner in which they see fit. The two notable exceptions to what one might perhaps call this 'declaration of religious tolerance' are Catholics and Muslims. No special provision is made in the Act for their form of marriage. Of course, they may celebrate marriages according to their own religious beliefs and customs, but such marriages do not receive the official approval, or recognition of the state. A civil marriage ceremony, in addition to the relevant religious ceremony, is required in the case of these two religious groupings.

26 Jewish law is of course treated in English courts as a question of fact, which may have to be separately proved in every case. See, for example, the definition of marriage given by the late Chief Rabbi Dr. N.M. Adler in his written statement furnished to the Royal Commission on the laws of marriage appointed in 1865.

27 A *perutah* (small Hebrew coin).

28 See sections 26(d), 35(4), 43(3), 53(c), 55(1)(b), (63) and 67 of the Marriage Act 1949.

Jewish Marriage in English Law - Mediaeval Times

It is instructive to consider the position of Jewish marriages in the period before provision was expressly made for them in legislation. There was, of course, a Jewish community in England in mediaeval times, until they were expelled by Edward I in 1290. However, civil marriage apparently did not exist in those early days; the only form of generally-recognised marriage was a religious, i.e. a Christian marriage. Clearly this would have been anathema to the Jewish community, who steadfastly maintained the traditions and rules of Jewish law. And indeed, there is evidence that allowances were made for the susceptibilities of the Jewish community, and that some measure of recognition was accorded to their marriages.

Thus we read, for example, of a case decided in 1234,[29] in which a Jew born in England purchased land and married a Jewess. The husband was subsequently converted to the Christian faith, and died, whereupon his widow (who had not converted) claimed entitlement to her dower. It was resolved in Parliament that she should not have dower, because she had refused to be converted with her husband.

In a second case,[30] decided nine years after the expulsion, in 1299, an Essex jury found that Henry de Winton and his wife had married according to Jewish law, and that subsequent thereto they had both converted to Christianity. It was found that their son Thomas was the legal heir provided that the marriage solemnised before the conversion could be held to be good.

It seems that in both cases the legal question which fell for consideration was the effect in English law upon a Jewish marriage of the conversion to Christianity of one or both of the parties to it. The first case seems to establish the proposition that where only one spouse became a Christian, he or she could treat the Jewish marriage as a nullity, so that the non-converted spouse lost all rights normally conferred by marriage.[31] Presumably this was based on religious considerations: a true believer could not be expected to live in wedlock with a infidel. Where both spouses converted, however, the original marriage seems to have retained its validity, at least in respect of property claims by issue of the marriage.[32] It appears, therefore, that one may safely deduce from these two cases that a marriage of Jews who had not converted would have been accorded recognition as a valid marriage in English law -

---

[29]Co. Lit. 31b, 32a; Jenkins, 8 *Cent. of Reports,* p.3, case 2 (in the margin); Tovey, *Anglia Judaica,* p. 230.

[30]*Calend. Geneal.*,II, 563; *Inq. Post. Mort.,* 27 Edw. I, no. 12.

[31]A Jewish woman's right to dower was clearly recognised: see the addenda to Jacob's edition of Roper on *Husband and Wife,* p. 476 (note). Prynne gives a writ to the justices of the Jews in 23 Hen. III, directing them to put the two sons of a deceased Jew, Samuel, into possession of his property on payment of a fine 'salvo uxori ejusdem Samuelis rationabili dote sua, secundum legem et consuetudinem Judaeorum'.

[32]Under the rules of feudal law, which were strictly enforced, the whole of a convert's property passed to the crown upon conversion. Hence the establishment in 1232 by Henry III of the *Domus Conversorum,* in which most Jewish converts spent the remainder of their days as pensioners upon the royal bounty. Henry of Winton had presumably acquired land *after* his conversion; otherwise the question of inheritance would not have arisen.

perhaps one of the earliest examples of English legal tolerance and ecumenism!

This recognition is all the more remarkable, as observed by Henriques,[33] in view of the general requirement of English law that the presence of a Christian priest was essential to the validity of the marriage ceremony.[34] It should also be noted that even though in Church law the ecclesiastical courts would recognise a marriage created by a contract *per verba de praesenti* (i.e. where the parties acknowledged each other as husband and wife) or even a marriage created *per verba de futuro,* if followed by cohabitation, English common law[35] had from time immemorial insisted upon marriages being celebrated *in facie ecclesiae.* One can only surmise, therefore, as to the reason which led English law to grant recognition to the marriages of Jews. Possibly the fact that in most cases a Rabbi is present to conduct the marriage ceremony (even though, as indicated above, this is not a requirement of Jewish law) led the common law to treat Jewish marriages as marriages celebrated with the benefit of the clergy.[36]

Jewish Marriage in English Law- After the Restoration

It is clear that after the return of the Jews to England in the reign of Charles II, they continued to celebrate marriages in accordance with the provisions of Jewish law. The opinion current among legal writers and the profession seems to have been that these marriages were valid,[37] and that 'questions arising upon them are determined by the Jewish law'.[38] The law concerning the Jews as administered before the expulsion was applied to them after their return, as far as circumstances permitted it.[39] It was only logical for the courts to continue to grant recognition to Jewish marriages; there was no valid reason for ignoring ancient authority.

Thus, for example, in the case of *Franks v. Martin,*[40] the House of Lords interpreted and enforced a covenant contained in a settlement made on the marriage of one Isaac Franks with the daughter of Moses Hart, although the marriage was celebrated according to Jewish law. Had the marriage been

---

33*Jewish Marriages and the English Law,* London , 1909.

34See the decision of the House of Lords in *R. v. Millis* (1844) 10 Cl. & F., 534; *Beamish v. Beamish* (1861) 9 H.& C., 274; but see *contra* Lord Stowell in *Dalrymple v. Dalrymple* (2 Hag., *Cons.* 64) .

35See *R. v. Millis, supra.*

36Selden (*Ux. Eb.*, lib. II, cap. 28) ascribes the generally held view that to make a contract of marriage complete a sacerdotal benediction was necessary to imitation of pagan and Jewish customs. Note also that the clergyman whose presence was required need not be a minister of the Church of England; a person in Holy orders such as a Roman Catholic or Greek priest recognised as such by that Church was acceptable (but see *Haydon v. Gould* (1711) 1 Salk., 119).

37Roper, *Husband and Wife*, 2nd edition, vol. II, pp. 475-6.

38*Ibid.*

39See Lilly's *Practical Register,* quoted in Henrique, *The Jews and the English Law*, pp.188-189.

40(1760) 5 Brown's *Parl. Cas.* 151.

invalid, the covenant would have been unenforceable. In *Da Costa v. Villa Real*,[41] the Court of Arches seems to have overruled an argument that a suit to enforce a marriage contract between two Jews was not maintainable on the grounds that it was a Jewish marriage. And in *Andreas v. Andreas*,[42] a wife brought an action against her husband for the restitution of conjugal rights. The court ruled that even though the marriage had taken place 'according to the forms of the Jewish nation and not of the Church of England', the woman was entitled to a remedy since the marriage was binding according to Jewish forms.

The present law, expressly recognising the civil validity of Jewish marriages, dates back to Lord Hardwicke's Marriage Act of 1753.[43] The Act was the culmination of a series of measures designed to ensure greater control over the celebration of marriages. It was felt that clandestine marriages, which were commonplace, were a bad thing. Moreover, they deprived the government of an important source of revenue. Hence, for example,the enactment in 1695 of a law requiring five shillings to be paid in duties upon marriages (for the purpose of meeting the expenses of the French war), and a further enactment in this connection in the following year.[44] Penalties were imposed upon clergymen, clerks and sextons solemnizing a marriage without banns or licence. In 1711 a further Act was found necessary[45] to include clergymen without benefices. This was followed by Lord Hardwicke's Act in 1753.[46]

41(1733) Hag., *Cons*., I, p. 242.

42(1737) p. 9 of the Appendix to Hag., *Cons*. Vol. 1.

4326 Geo. 2, c. 23.

446 &7 Will. III, c. 6 , s. 52, and 7&8 Will. III, c. 35.

4510 Ann, c. 18 (c.19, Ruff.) ss. 176-8.

46It should be noted that despite the opinion of those learned in the law, there was a widespread popular view that Jewish marriages were null and void. Thus, for example, when Parliament passed the statute 6 & 7 Will. III, c.6., which imposed, *inter alia*, a tax on the marriage of every person not in receipt of alms, it was found necessary to declare expressly that all Jews 'who shall cohabit and live together as man and wife shall and are hereby made lyable to pay the several and respective duties ... as if they had been married according to the Law of England'. See also the case of *Vigevena and Silveira v. Alvarez,* tried by the Prerogative Court in 1794 (I Hag., *Cons*. Appendix, pp. 7 and 8, and note thereon); *D'Aguilar v. D'Aguilar* (1794) I Hag., *Ecc*., p. 773; *Lindo v. Belisario* (1795), I Hag., *Cons*., 216; *Goldsmid v. Bromer* (1798), *ibid*. p. 324; *Hopewell v. De Pinna* (1808), 2 Camp. 113; and see the Act 10 & 11 Vict., c. 58, which was passed expressly 'to remove doubts as to Quakers' and Jews' marriages solemnized before certain periods', and the comments thereon in *R. v. Millis,* cited *supra*, at note 34, pp.671-3.

III. Jewish Divorces in English Law

The Legal Background

As noted, English law has recognised the validity of Jewish marriages celebrated in England for over 700 years. The position regarding Jewish divorces is very different, however. Whereas we have had legislation on Jewish marriages for over 200 years, the relevant legislation covering Jewish divorce dates back only to 1971. Similarly, judicial decisions directly relating to the validity of Jewish divorces are of very recent origin, and - especially in comparison to the case-law on Jewish marriages - there is a surprising paucity of cases.

There are, of course, valid historical-legal and sociological reasons for this. Before 1857, as is well known, civil divorce did not exist as a judicial measure; the only method of obtaining a 'civil' divorce was by means of a private Act of Parliament. These were exceedingly rare: the total number of dissolutions by this method between 1715 and 1852 amounting to no more than 244.[47] All suits for divorce other than by means of a private Act were heard in the ecclesiastical courts. Clearly, observant Jews who had contracted a valid marriage under Jewish law would not have had recourse to the ecclesiastical courts, but would instead have had the matter dealt with by way of a get.

It should also be borne in mind that even after the Matrimonial Causes Act of 1857, which created, for the first time, a mechanism for civil divorce proceedings, divorce was still a relatively rare occurrence, especially where the wife was the petitioner.[48] In practice adultery (or, in the case of a wife petitioner, aggravated adultery) was the only ground for divorce until 1937. And it was only after the Divorce Reform Act of 1969 that divorce became the widespread phenomenon that it is today.

Quite apart from the legal requirements which ensured that divorce was relatively infrequent throughout England, divorce in the Jewish community was rare for sociological reasons. The Jewish family unit has always been renowned for its stability, and divorce was almost unheard of until relatively recently. Moreover, the Jewish population of Britain was relatively minute until the turn of the century, so that the number of Jewish marriages which could potentially end up in the divorce courts was never more than a handful. This accounts for the fact that the first recorded case to deal directly with the validity of a Jewish marriage was not until 1924.[49]

There are two early cases in the law reports which require some consideration. In *Ganer v. Lady Lanesborough*,[50] the defendant alleged that

---

[47]This figure is taken from the Report of the Royal Commission on Divorce of 1850.

[48]*Ibid.*, p. 4.

[49]*Sasson v. Sasson,* (1924) 1 AC 1007.

[50](1791) 1 Peake, p. 17; and see also the reference to this case in the *Sussex Peerage Case,* (1844) 11 Cl. &F. 85 at 124, and in *R. v. Hammersmith Superintendent Registrar of Marriages, ex parte Mir-Anwaruddin* [1917] 1 K.B. 634 at 638. See also the unreported case of *Friedberg v. Friedberg, the Jewish Chronicle,* 16 October 1908, to the effect that a get

she was covert of John King, which he denied. Upon proving her marriage to John King, the plaintiff proved that King had married previously, and that his former wife was still alive. Lord Kenyon admitted the evidence, saying that it proved that there was no marriage at all between the defendant and King.

The defendant thereupon offered to prove that her marriage to King was a valid one, on the grounds that both he and his former wife were Jews, and that he had divorced her at Leghorn, Italy, according to the rites and customs of the Jews there. She produced an instrument under seal of the synagogue confirming the divorce.

Lord Kenyon, however, held this to be no evidence, 'for before he could take notice of any proceedings in a foreign Court, he must know the law of the country, which was matter of evidence, and should be proved by witness'. Thereupon the defendant called upon King's former wife as a witness, who swore (without producing any documents) that she was divorced from King in front of the Rabbi at Leghorn, according to the ceremony and customs of the Jews there, and upon that basis, the defendant won the case.

The case is an interesting one, and seemingly establishes the proposition that a get which takes place abroad may be recognised in English law. It is not a safe precedent, however, for the recognition of a foreign get, (a) because it appears that the parties were domiciled in Italy, and (b) because the judgement of Lord Kenyon seems to have been based on the (somewhat dubious) supposition that the get would have been recognised under Italian law.

The next case to raise the question of the validity of a get in English law was that of *Moss v. Smith,*[51] an action for damages brought by one Mrs. Moss in respect of negligent handling or storing of dresses deposited at the defendant's warehouses. The issue of a get arose because the defendants objected to the action on the grounds that the plaintiff, being a married woman, was not entitled to sue on the contract. The plaintiff's counsel, however, undertook to show that her marriage had been solemnised according to the Jewish rituals, and had thereafter been validly terminated by a Jewish divorce.

The get in this case had been effected in England and the so-called 'high priest' of the German Jews in England (the Chief Rabbi, Dr. S. Hirschel) gave evidence as to the requirements of a valid get in Jewish law. The superintendent of the synagogue produced a Book of Divorces, containing an entry of the divorce in Hebrew.

The defendant, however, contended that in the absence of the actual document of divorce (the original get itself) there was in fact no evidence that the divorce had taken place, and even if the fact of the divorce could be established, a marriage validly contracted in England could only be dissolved by Act of Parliament. In short, the legal, as opposed to evidential, contention was that English law does not recognise the validity of a get effected in

---

effected in England is invalid in English law. There seems to have been no discussion of this point, however.

51(1840) 1 M & G 228.

England. On these facts it was found by Erskine J. that a divorce had not been established.

Once again, the decision does not seem to establish a clear precedent. It is not clear from the report whether the decision was based on the factual circumstances of the case (i.e. because the evidence of the get was insufficient), or on the legal principle that such a get has no legal validity. A comparison of this case, however, with that of *Ganer v. Lady Lanesborough* indicates a possible tendency towards non-recognition of a get effected within the jurisdiction, whilst recognising a get effected abroad under the law of the parties' common domicile.

We turn now towards the more recent and direct decisions. In considering the attitude of English law towards the validity of the get procedure, two different questions have to be considered. The first issue relates to petitions in the English courts, and is subdivided into the two questions of jurisdiction and choice of law. In other words, when will English courts assume jurisdiction to hear a divorce petition, and if they do assume jurisdiction, what law will they apply ? The second question relates to recognition: under what circumstances will our courts recognise the get procedure?

There is surprisingly little authority or even academic discussion on either of these questions. The Matrimonial Causes Act of 1857 was silent as to the jurisdiction of the newly created courts to entertain divorce petitions. The judges 'were thus left', in the words of one academic writer,[52] 'to navigate an uncharted sea without a compass'. By 1895, however, it had become established law that the domicile for the time being of the married pair affords the only true test of jurisdiction to dissolve their marriage.[53]

In view of the rule that a married woman could not acquire a separate domicile from that of her husband, hardship could be caused to a wife when her husband acquired a foreign domicile. The rule, however, was subsequently amended by Parliament to allow for cases where a wife had been deserted or deported,[54] and later again amended to include jurisdiction on grounds of residence.[55]

Assuming then, that a Jewish couple married in England under the relevant rules of Jewish law, and that they were both domiciled in England, or fulfilled the other statutory requirements, it is clear that the courts would have jurisdiction to entertain a petition for the dissolution of that marriage. What law should they apply in determining that petition?

It seems to have been assumed - without argument - ever since 1857 that the relevant law in all cases should be English law. Morris[56] maintains that until 1937 the question simply did not arise, because 'the only possible

---

[52]See Morris, *The Conflict of Laws,* 1971, p. 13.

[53]*Le Mesurier v. Le Mesurier* [1895] AC 517 at 540.

[54]S. 13 of the Matrimonial Causes Act 1937 (later: s. 18(1)(a) of the Matrimonial Causes Act 1950, and s. 40(1)(b) of the Matrimonial Causes Act 1965).

[55]S. 1 of the Law Reform (Miscellaneous Provisions) Act 1949 (later: s.18(1)(b) of the Matrimonial Causes Act 1950, and s. 40(1)(b) of the Matrimonial Causes Act 1965).

[56]*The Conflict of Laws,* p. 134.

alternative to the *lex fori* would be the law of the domicile' , and English courts did not exercise jurisdiction unless the parties were domiciled in England.

But this seems to side-step the issue. Why is the *lex domicilii* 'the only possible alternative'? In Egypt, and certain other countries in the Levant, questions of divorce are determined by the law of the relevant religion (the so-called 'millet' system) . This would mean that persons professing the Jewish religion would be subject to Jewish law in respect of their divorces. It is not immediately apparent why this should not have been considered a possible choice of law under English law, too. Nonetheless it is clear beyond any doubt that English divorce courts, in hearing any divorce petition, will apply English domestic law to the exclusion of any other system. The relevant matrimonial statutes make no exceptions for ethnic minorities.

We turn now to the second issue, that of recognition. Under what circumstances will the courts recognise the validity of a get which has been properly executed in a Beth Din in accordance with the rules of Jewish law ? This issue, too, can be subdivided into two questions: firstly, when will the courts recognise the validity of a foreign get, and secondly, when, if at all, will they recognise the validity of a get executed wholly in England?

In the Privy Council case of *Sasson v. Sasson*,[57] it was held that a get effected between two British subjects domiciled in Egypt must be regarded as a valid dissolution of their marriage. *Sasson v. Sasson*, was a case heard on appeal from an Egyptian court, and was concerned with the interpretation of an Order in Council. Although it affected the marriage of British subjects, the get itself was effected out of the jurisdiction (in Alexandria), so that the question was in reality one of recognition of a foreign divorce. In that sense it was merely an application of long-established law,[58] to the effect that a foreign divorce may be recognised in English law irrespective of the grounds on which the decree was granted, and even though it is classified as an 'extra-judicial' divorce. The decision is not directly relevant, therefore, to the question of recognition of a get executed in England.[59]

The question was considered, however, in the leading case *Har-Shefi v. Har-Shefi*.[60] In that case, the wife petitioned for a declaration that her marriage had been validly dissolved as from the date of receipt of her get. The marriage had been contracted in Israel under Israeli law, which applies Jewish law to all marriages between Jews. The wife's ante-nuptial domicile was England; the husband was continuously domiciled in Israel. After a short residence together in England, the husband was deported from the country. Before he left, he executed a get at the London Beth Din (Court of the Chief Rabbi).

---

57 See note 44, *supra* .

58 See *Dolphin v. Robins* (1857) 7 H.L.C. 390; *Shaw v. Gould* (1868) L.R. 3 H.L. 55; *Harvey v. Farnie* [1882] 8 App. Cas. 43; *Le Mesurier v. Le Mesurier* (supra, n. 47); *Pemberton v. Hughes* [1899] 1 Ch. 781; *Bater v. Bater* [1906] p. 209

59 See also *R. v. Hammersmith Marriages Registrar* (cited *supra* at n.50); *Russ v. Russ* [1963] p. 87.

60 (No. 1), [1953] p. 161.

Had the wife petitioned for a civil divorce in England, the courts would clearly have jurisdiction under the 1937 Act. But she did not; instead, she petitioned for a declaration that the get had validly dissolved her marriage. The Court of Appeal held that the divorce court had jurisdiction to make such a declaration even though no other relief was being sought, but only if the petitioner was domiciled in England.

That question, in turn, depended upon the legal effectiveness of the get: if it was effective, the petitioner would have reverted to her English domicile, so that the court would have jurisdiction to grant the declaratory judgment she sought; whereas if it was not effective, she would not be domiciled in England, and the courts would have no jurisdiction to entertain her petition. This in turn depended upon whether Israeli law (as the law of her domicile throughout her marriage) would recognise the get as a valid divorce. The divorce court, it was held, must therefore hear evidence on that question and decide for itself whether the divorce was valid under Israeli law.

Acting upon this ruling, the wife in *Har-Shefi v. Har-Shefi (No. 2)*[61] petitioned the divorce court for a declaration that her marriage had been validly dissolved by the get which had been executed in London. It was held by Pearce J. (citing *Sasson v. Sasson* as persuasive authority), that the marriage had been validly dissolved by the get, although had the parties been domiciled in England, it would have had no effect upon their marriage in the eyes of English law.[62] In other words, the case establishes the proposition that a divorce executed abroad, *or even in England*, according to the rules of the parties' domicile, will be recognised in English law as a valid divorce whatever the grounds upon which it was effected, and even if it was an 'extra-judicial' divorce.

Har-Shefi v. Har-Shefi was subsequently followed in the well-known case of *Qureshi v. Qureshi,*[63] in which Sir Jocelyn Simon was prepared to grant recognition to a talaq pronounced in England by a husband who was domiciled in Pakistan. But the hopes which this relatively liberal decision may have raised were speedily dashed. Sir Jocelyn Simon himself expressed misgivings about the mischief which might arise when the safeguards inherent in a judicially pronounced divorce were 'by-passed' in this manner. It was these misgivings which led to Parliamentary intervention in the form of s.16 of the Domicile and Matrimonial Proceedings Act 1973. Under that section, no proceeding in the United Kingdom shall be regarded as validly dissolving a marriage unless instituted in the courts of law of the United Kingdom. 'Extra-judicial ' divorces such as the talaq and get are therefore no longer recognised as capable of validly dissolving a marriage.

61[1953] p. 220.

62See also *Preger v. Preger* (1962) 42 TLR 281; *Joseph v. Joseph* [1955] 1 WLR 1182.

63[1972] Fam. 173.

Jewish Divorce in English Law- Policy Factors Against Recognition

It will be apparent from the preceding outline of the case-law relating to Jewish marriages and divorces contracted in England, that English law exhibits a contradictory attitude to the question of recognition of Jewish law and procedures. On the one hand, Jewish marriages have always been recognised as valid, and legislation has expressly provided that Jews may contract a valid civil marriage by means of their traditional religious marriage ceremony, even though it does not require the formal presence of a clergyman.

On the other hand, no recognition has been give to the Jewish divorce procedure except in certain foreign cases, and legislation has expressly provided, in effect, that no Jewish divorce procedure effected in this country has any validity, notwithstanding the fact that Jewish divorce law prescribes very many safeguards and requirements of a judicial or quasi-judicial manner. What is the justification for this striking difference in attitude ?

A number of possible explanations have been suggested. Morris, for example,[64] justifies the practice of English courts to apply English law to all choice of law situations[65] on the grounds that (a) 'it would be highly inconvenient and undesirable from the practical point of view to apply foreign law in English divorce suits', especially in undefended cases, and (b) because to require English courts 'to dissolve marriages on exotic foreign grounds would be distasteful to the judges and unacceptable to public opinion'. (These reasons, of course, do not apply in the case of marriage.)

It is submitted, however, that upon closer analysis neither of these two reasons is a sufficient explanation for the present attitude of the law to Jewish divorces. A comparison to the marriage situation will make this abundantly clear.

All marriages in England are governed by English law when it comes to questions of essential validity, or capacity to marry. It is only in respect of the formalities of marriage that provision is made for validating the Jewish procedure. By analogy, it would be quite conceivable for the formalities of divorce to be governed by Jewish law for Jews who had married under that system, whilst questions of essential validity would continue to be governed by the usual principles of English law.

The grounds for divorce, for example, would continue to be those contained in the Matrimonial Causes Act, but the divorce procedure would be the get procedure. This would immediately eliminate the objection that marriages might be dissolved 'on exotic foreign grounds'.[66] Nor would it be

---

[64]*The Conflict of Laws,* at p. 134.

[65]As assumed in *Zanelli v. Zanelli* (1948) 64 T.L.R. 556. see now s. 40(2) of the Matrimonial Causes Act 1965.

[66]English divorce law, in any event, is tending towards divorce by consent - see the Law Commission's proposal in 1988 (cited *infra* at note 86), for divorce after a period of time. As the principal ground for a get is the mutual consent of both parties, there would be no clash between the English and Jewish grounds for divorce.

necessary to prove the foreign law - a statement of law by a recognised Beth Din could be treated in all cases as sufficient evidence of the 'foreign law'.

It should be noted, moreover, that in view of the numerous technical requirements of Jewish law which govern the get procedure (including, *inter alia,* the requirement of competent Jewish witnesses) the proposal for recognition of the get procedure in England would be implemented in the Beth Din and not in the civil courts. The role of the civil courts would be to establish the existence of the statutory grounds for divorce, after which the case would be remitted to a Beth Din, who would oversee the get procedure. Consequently no problems would arise regarding 'proof of foreign law'.

A second argument often brought against application or recognition of a foreign divorce system such as the talaq or get is that recognition should not be granted to 'extra-judicial' forms of divorce. This contention has been a constant theme in the case-law, especially in relation to talaq proceedings. Thus, for example, in the *Hammersmith* case,[67] Swinfeld Eady L. J. stigmatised as 'absurd' the suggestion that if there was a country in which marriage could be dissolved without any judicial proceedings at all, merely by the parties agreeing *in pais* to separate, every other country ought to sanction a separation had *in pais* there, and uphold a second marriage contract after such a separation.[68]

But is it so absurd? Cheshire[69] comments as follows: 'It is submitted that the proposition so disparagingly rejected is perfectly sound in principle. The *lex domicilii* applicable to the husband was the law of his religion, and whether that law required a judicial decree or not was no concern of the English court, ... Moreover, it may be asked why such stress should be laid on the fact of judicial proceedings. Judicial intervention has no inherent virtue, neither is it universal'.

To this one may validly add that in the context of contemporary divorce law, judicial intervention is an essentially anachronistic and theoretical legal doctrine, since over 99 per cent of all divorces are undefended and effected by means of the 'special procedure'. The reality of the situation is that divorce has become an essentially administrative procedure.[70] It is true that there are mandatory judicial safeguards, under s. 41 of the Matrimonial Causes Act, in relation to protection of the children, but these would be applied equally irrespective of the system of law adopted in relation to the divorce itself. And in any event the numerous requirements in Jewish law relating to the get procedure give it the character, at the least, of a quasi-judicial procedure.

There are two other arguments advanced against recognition of non-judicial divorces in English law. The first is that this enables unilateral divorce, against the will of one of the parties to the marriage, and this is

---

67 Cited *supra,* at note 50.

68 See also *Warrender v. Warrender* (1835) 2 Cl. & F.488 at 532.

69 *Private International Law,* 6th edition, p. 403.

70 The doctrine of judicial intervention seems to be a residue of the days when divorce law was based on fault. Only a judge could be trusted to ascertain relative degrees of fault.

perceived as negative on grounds of general policy. Whatever merit there may be in this contention, however,[71] it does not apply to the get procedure, which almost invariably requires the consent of both parties.

The second argument is the familiar one exposed in the case of *Quazi v. Quazi* [72] - the danger that a wife or child might be divorced without adequate financial provision. This particular defect, however, has now been rectified by statute in relation to the dissolution of a marriage overseas by judicial or other proceedings,[73] and there appears to be no reason why similar legislation could not be enacted to cover the get procedure in England.

Jewish Divorce in English Law- Policy Factors in Favour of Recognition

It will be readily apparent from the discussion above that the distinction between Jewish marriages celebrated in England (which are recognised) and Jewish divorces celebrated in England (which are not recognised) is one based, essentially, on historical accident rather than on legal policy. Nor are the arguments variously advanced against non-recognition of Jewish divorces convincing.

A strong case can in fact be made on policy grounds for according recognition to Jewish divorces in England. It will be recalled that in the *Hammersmith* case the Court of Appeal gave various reasons for refusing to recognise the talaq. The talaq procedure, it was argued, was applicable only to Mohammedan marriages, and was therefore incapable of dissolving a Christian marriage. Moreover, under Indian law (the law of the parties' domicile) it seemed that the talaq was considered incapable of dissolving a Christian marriage.[74]

It is submitted that there is considerable force in this argument, and that it ought to be applied, *mutatis mutandis*, to the get procedure. Christian marriages are inherently different from Muslim marriages, and both of them are inherently different from Jewish marriages. These differences are not merely formal or procedural, but are based on different religious concepts which form the prime underpinnings of the particular form of marriage.

The get procedure, for example (as indicated at the beginning of this article), is conceived of as religiously mandatory, and as the only valid way of dissolving a recognised Jewish marriage. It is, therefore, wholly inappropriate to legislate that a Jewish marriage should only be dissolved by what is, in the

---

[71]S.8 (2)(a) of the 1971 Recognition of Divorces and Legal Separations Act clearly does not consider a divorce to be contrary to public policy simply because of lack of notice or opportunity to defend proceedings. S.8 (2)(b) maintains a general discretion to refuse recognition when it would be manifestly contrary to public policy, and a similar discretion could be applied to prevent abuses if the legislature were to recognise non-judicial divorces effected in England.

[72][1980] A.C. 744

[73]Section 12 (1) (a) of the Matrimonial and Family Proceedings Act 1984.

[74]This was the basis on which the *Hammersmith* case was distinguished in *Russ v. Russ* (see n.59 *supra)*.

eyes of Jewish law, a totally alien civil procedure, and one which has, moreover, no validity whatsoever under the rules of Jewish law, and to provide that the get procedure is a nullity in the eyes of English law.

Our present legislation is also unsatisfactory on policy grounds because it perpetuates an indefensible anomaly which arose by pure historical accident. A coherent philosophy, systematically applied, will seek to apply fundamental principles of law with uniformity. This, for example, it would be possible to legislate that English law recognises only one form of marriage ceremony (the civil ceremony), and only one form of divorce (the civil divorce).

This is, in fact, the current position in relation to Catholic and Islamic marriages (as well as other forms of religious marriage ceremony). Parties who wish to abide by the principles of their religious convictions are free to marry under Catholic or Islamic procedures, and to divorce under those procedures -but English law will take no cognisance of them. We differentiate, in other words, between state and religion.

Equally, it would be possible to legislate that all (or defined) religious groupings are allowed to contract valid marriages in English law by means of their own religious procedures, and also to have those marriages dissolved by the relevant religious procedure.[75] What we have at the moment, however, in relation to Jewish law is an intellectually indefensible and mutually contradictory system.

The state gives its approval to, and recognition of, the Jewish form of marriage, but withholds its approval from, and recognition of, the Jewish form of divorce, which alone in Jewish law can dissolve the marriage. This is analytically unsatisfactory and difficult to justify. If the religion of the parties (albeit somewhat unusually) is recognised as a basis for according validity to Jewish marriages, it should equally be recognised as a basis for according validity to Jewish divorces.

IV. Jewish Law and English Law

The Problems Caused by the Present Dichotomy

The contradiction between the law applied to Jewish marriage and that applied to Jewish divorce is not merely a matter of theory or of jurisprudential disquiet. It results in very serious and practical problems, and contributes to the creation of a new form of 'limping marriage'. Indeed, it permits one party to a marriage to unconscionably use the situation created so as inequitably to deny the other spouse certain moral and contractual entitlements.

Where, for example, a Jewish husband has married in a religious ceremony under the provisions of s.53 of the 1949 Act, he may subsequently petition for divorce under the Matrimonial Causes Act, whilst adamantly refusing to grant his wife a get. In effect he is enabled to prevent her from

---

[75]Subject to whatever safeguards may be necessary on grounds of public policy.

remarrying in accordance with her religious beliefs and the dictates of her conscience. In other words, he is using the provisions of civil law to cynically obtain for himself an unfair advantage, whilst withholding from his spouse her right to rebuild her life. By so doing, he is also effectively defeating the aim of our current divorce legislation, viz. to enable the parties to the marriage to rid themselves of the 'empty shell' of a marriage which has ceased to exist. Similar problems arise, *mutatis mutandis,* when the husband is the petitioner, and the wife refuses her consent to the get. Although there are a number of provisions under English matrimonial legislation which can sometimes be used to prevent such abuse,[76] the reality of the situation is that these solutions are only practicable in a tiny minority of cases.

Attempted Judicial Solutions

There appears to be only one reported case in which an attempt was made to ensure that a get should not be unreasonably withheld. In *Brett v. Brett*[77] the Court of Appeal made a lump sum order in favour of the wife, the amount of which was effectively determined by the husband's willingness or otherwise to give her a get. The court found that the proper award, in the circumstances of the case, was a lump sum of £30,000 payable in two instalments, i.e. £25,000 payable within 14 days, and the balance to be paid within three months if he had not granted her a get by that time. The court clearly felt that his conduct in refusing to grant her a get was a relevant factor in assessing the amount of the award.

The *Brett v. Brett* precedent, however, is of limited value. In the first place, it was an unusual order made in exceptional circumstances. The court clearly felt some sympathy with the wife. The petition was brought, under the exception to the then three-year ban, on the grounds of exceptional hardship/exceptional depravity. The husband was, moreover, a very wealthy man who claimed to have no assets, but was in reality living off capital.

The rationale advanced by the court in support of its decision was that the wife was financially prejudiced by reason of the husband's refusal to grant her a get, since she was thereby effectively precluded from remarrying and finding some other man to support her. Even though this rationale is one which could apply to all cases where a get is unreasonably withheld, the majority of husbands are probably not in a financial position which would enable significant pressure to be brought upon them in this manner. Moreover, it is possible -indeed, even likely- that the punitive nature and purpose of the order might constitute a form of duress under Jewish law, thereby bringing about the totally counter-productive effect of invalidating any get executed as a consequence of the order.

The problems occasioned by discrepancies between civil and religious divorce requirements has been considered in other common-law jurisdictions which are patterned on English law. Thus, for example, in *Re Morris and*

---

[76]See B. Berkovits, 'Jewish Divorce', *Family Law,* March 1989, pp.115-118.
[77][1969] 1 All E.R. 1007.

Morris,[78] the Manitoba Queen's bench held that an order for *mandamus* would lie under Queen's Bench Rule 536 to direct the husband to present himself before the Beth Din to institute enquiry whether a get was necessary between the parties, and to institute proceedings for the same should the Beth Din so determine. The basis for this decision was the inherent jurisdiction of the court to issue a writ of *mandamus* calling upon someone to perform a specified act which it is his duty to do, and which the court has, upon enquiry, determined to be consonant with right and justice.

The husband's duty to execute a get was inferred from the general wording of the Jewish marriage document, as explained by expert Rabbinical opinion. Other necessary conditions which the Court found to be satisfied were that the applicant has no other means of compelling the performance of the duty, and that he or she is not acting *mala fide*. The Court also found that there was no argument based upon a personal religious conviction which forbade the respondent to do what was required by the applicant, and the court was therefore not interfering in any way with the respondent's freedom of religion.

Significantly, too, the Court relied in part on the decision of the House of Lords in *Shaw v. DPP*[79] that there remains in the courts of law a residual power to enforce the moral welfare of the state. Whether English courts would be prepared to exercise such a wide jurisdiction on the basis of general principles of law and equity remains to be seen. In particular, further clarification is required on the question of the scope of the *mandamus*, and its application to enforce an essentially private moral duty.

In the American case of *Roth v. Roth*,[80] the court found that the get procedure is not a sacerdotal or religious act as such, so that a direction to execute a get does not transgress the American doctrine of separation of Church and state. The get procedure, it is true, is mandated by Jewish law, but it is not a religious act or an act of worship; it does not invoke the Deity, and it involves neither profession of creed nor confession of faith. As such, it is no more a religious act than would be the execution of a contract or promissory note in accordance with the forms and procedures of Jewish law. Indeed, the court held that the wife had a constitutional right to liberty and freedom of religion which would be defeated were the court not to use its powers to assist in the execution of a get. The wife's right to remarry was paramount to any possible intrusion upon the husband.

More recently, in the Australian case of *Gwiazda v. Gwiazda*, [81] the Court ruled that a wife be enjoined to appear before the Beth Din if and when called upon to do so by her husband, and to take all necessary steps which the said Beth Din may require in order to give validity to a Jewish divorce. Once again, the basis for this decision was a general power (under s. 114(3) of the

---

78 36 D.L.R. 447.

79 [1961] 2 All E.R. 446.

80 Michigan Circuit Court, 23 January 1980, Court file number 79-192 709 DO

81 Case number M10631 of 1982, decided 23 Febuary 1983.

Australian Family Law Act) to grant an injunction 'in any case in which it appears to the court to be just or convenient to do so'.

Having regard to the object and purpose of the Family Law Act, which is to sever the matrimonial relationship and free either party to remarry when the marriage has irretrievably broken down, the court felt that the wife's refusal to participate in a get procedure prevented the husband, 'as a matter of fact and practicability', from remarrying, even though 'as a matter of law' (i.e. of civil law) he was free to do so. The court emphasised the 'sociological' nature of the Australian divorce law: the desire to enable the parties to remarry if they so wish. This approach, concentrating as it does on the factual, as opposed to the legal, realities of the situation is a welcome and refreshing one.

Once again, however, this precedent is not of direct assistance in the context of English matrimonial legislation, which does not have a wide-ranging provision analogous to s.114(3) of the Australian Family Law Act. It is, nonetheless, a useful example of the current trend of judicial thinking.

Legislative Solutions and Proposals

The problems occasioned by the discrepancy between the positive attitude of English law towards Jewish marriages and its negative attitude towards Jewish divorces are amenable to solution by legislative means. The simplest solution would be for Parliament to provide for application of Jewish divorce law as between parties professing the Jewish faith, in the same way that legislation currently provides for recognition of Jewish marriages. The law relating to the grounds for divorce, provision for children, and financial allocation of matrimonial property and resources would remain as it is; the change would relate solely and only to the divorce procedure itself.

In effect, such legislation would provide that where parties have contracted a recognised Jewish marriage in accordance with the provisions of the 1949 Marriage Act, that marriage would be dissolved by means of a get properly effected in a Beth Din. The usual divorce procedure would be followed up to and including issue of the decree nisi, upon which the case would be remitted to the Beth Din for execution of the get procedure. Provision could be made for a decree absolute of divorce to be granted once the Beth Din had certified, in the usual manner, that a get has been validly executed.

This proposal would retain the overall framework and policy aims of English divorce legislation, and simultaneously would satisfy the legitimate expectations of the Jewish community. It would be simple to administer, and has the merit of intellectual coherence and consistency. No Western legal system, however, has as yet promulgated such legislation, and it is unlikely that such a 'radical' proposal will be enacted in the foreseeable future in Britain.

In the absence, however, of such reforming legislation, more limited and technical solutions have been proposed and enacted. Thus, for example, a law was enacted in 1984 in the State of New York[82] which provides, in effect, that nobody shall be entitled to obtain their freedom to remarry by means of a civil divorce as long as they persist in withholding a religious divorce from their spouse. The method adopted in the New York legislation is to require a respondent to civil divorce proceedings to file an affidavit that he or she has removed, or will remove, all barriers to the other party's religious remarriage which he or she is capable of removing. A similar law has also been enacted in the State of Ontario, Canada,[83] although the mechanism adopted is somewhat different.

In 1984, a bill along the lines of the New York legislation was proposed and debated in the House of Commons,[84] and it would seem that the concept has met with approval in principle. The bill would have provided that a petitioner can oppose the grant of a decree absolute if the respondent unreasonably refuses to participate in the get procedure. Such a bill, if enacted, would give effect to the policy of the Marriage Acts, which recognise the right of Jews to marry in accordance with their religious convictions. It is clear that this right must apply not only to first marriages, but also to second or subsequent marriages. It is a right which is essentially based on equitable principles, which require that a person should not disregard contractual obligations undertaken at the time of his or her first marriage. It is submitted that this is a right which should be supported by our divorce legislation.[85]

It should be noted that there is a precedent, from the purely technical point of view, for proposed legislation along the lines suggested. Section 5 of the Matrimonial Causes Act 1973 empowers the court to withhold a divorce decree in cases of s.1(2)(e) divorces if the decree would cause the respondent 'grave financial or other hardship'. There is no doubt that the grant of a divorce decree to a spouse who unconscionably refuses a religious divorce to his or her partner can cause grave hardship no less serious than that contemplated in section 5. The Law Commission, moreover, in a recent Discussion paper,[86] has put forward arguments for the retention of the power to withhold a decree absolute, and its extension to other circumstances in

---

82 Chapter 945, Laws of New York State, 1984.

83 Sections 2(4) and 56(5)-(7) of the Family Law Act 1986. It should also be noted that on December 20th 1989 the Canadian Minister of Justice and Attorney General tabled similar amendments to the 1985 Federal Divorce Act in the House of Commons.

84 On 13 June 1984. See *Hansard,* Vol.61, No.170.

85 Since religion is the recognised criterion in relation to Jewish marriages, it should also be the recognised criterion in relation to the dissolution of that marriage. There is also a strong general argument in favour of recognising religion as the criterion. People who marry under a system of law which they perceive to be Divinely-mandated will not feel free to ignore the requirements for divorce imposed by that law. Thus, for example, a Jewish couple who accept the dictates of halacha will see a get as a categorical imperative, without which they are not free to remarry. Hence religion becomes, for them, the most powerful determining factor: and it may reasonably be argued that religious law should be applied on the grounds that it is the system of law with which the parties have the closest connection. Cf the 'real and substantial connection' test cited e.g. in *Indyka v. Indyka* [1969] 1 A.C. 33 at 76-77; 105 E-F; 111G and 113 A-B.

86 'Facing the Future: a Discussion Paper on the Ground for Divorce', Law Com. No.170, May 1988.

which hardship might be occasioned by making the decree absolute. The proposal to grant courts such a power in relation to problems arising in the context of religious law is, therefore, one which accords in principle with current thinking on the policy of divorce legislation.[87]

A Proposed Draft Bill

There follows below the text of a proposed bill which, it is submitted, would effectively deal with the immediate problems of persons refusing to execute or co-operate in a get, whilst seeking to use the provisions of the civil law to gain their own freedom. The text of the proposed draft bill is followed by a section-by-section commentary.

PROPOSED BILL RELATING TO REFUSAL OF RELIGIOUS DIVORCE

REFUSAL OF DIVORCE IN RESPECT OF CERTAIN MARRIAGES ON GROUND OF BARRIER TO THE REMARRIAGE OF THE RESPONDENT

1. (1) The following provisions of this section apply where -

(a) a petition for divorce or nullity of marriage has been presented to the court in relation to a marriage registered in accordance with the provisions of section 53 (c) of the Marriage Act 1949; or

(b) a petition for divorce or nullity of marriage has been presented to the court in relation to a marriage which has taken place outside England and Wales according to usages of persons professing the Jewish religion; and

(c) the respondent opposes the grant of a decree on the ground that a barrier exists to his remarriage according to the same usages as those under which the marriage referred to in sub-section (1) (a) or (1) (b) above was solemnized and the barrier is one which it is within the power of the petitioner to remove.

(2) Where the grant of a decree is opposed by virtue of this section the court shall refuse to grant a decree as long as the barrier referred to in section 1 (1) (c) above exists and has not been removed by the petitioner.

(3) A written statement by the secretary for the time being of the synagogue in which the marriage was solemnised, that no barrier as referred to in section 1(1)(c) above exists, or that any barrier which may have existed has been removed by the petitioner, shall be accepted as evidence of that fact by the court.

(4) In the case of a marriage which has taken place outside England and Wales according to the usage of persons professing the Jewish religion, section

[87] See e.g. paras. 5.37, 5.42, amd 5.52 of the Law Commission paper, and see *supra* at n.66.

(3) above shall apply as if for any reference to the secretary for the time being of the synagogue in which the marriage was solemnized there were substituted a reference to the clergyman who solemnized the marriage or his successor in title.

(5) The court may if it thinks fit grant a decree notwithstanding the provisions of section (2) above if it appears that there are circumstances making it desirable to do so .

(6) This Act shall come into force on such day as the Lord Chancellor may appoint by order made by statutory instrument .

Commentary on Individual Sections of the Draft Bill

Section 1, subs. (1). The following provisions...where. This limits the Act to Jewish marriages recognised in English law.

Subsection (1) (a) deals with the usual case, where a marriage has been celebrated in England under s. 53 of the Marriage Act.

Subsection (1) (b) makes provision for cases where a Jewish marriage is celebrated abroad, and is recognised as valid in England. Usually this will refer to a marriage between Jews in Israel, which (under Israeli civil legislation) is governed solely by the provisions of Jewish law. If the parties, at the time of divorce, are resident in England, the problem of a Jewish divorce may well arise in the same manner as under subsection (1) (a).

Subsection (1) (c). The respondent opposes... a barrier exists. This subsection makes it clear that the Act will only apply where one of the parties petitions the court and alleges that there is a barrier to his or her religious remarriage. In other words, it will not be an automatic barrier applying to all Jewish divorces. If both parties are content to do without a religious divorce, the Act does not seek to impose one upon them. Nor does it seek to oblige the judge dealing with a divorce petition to institute enquiries of his own accord as to the possible existence of a barrier. It is limited to cases where one of the parties expressly invokes the court's jurisdiction.

Subsection (1) (c). A barrier exists... according to the same usages. There are different denominations within the Jewish community. The Marriage Act 1949 recognises these differences, and provides (as subsequently amended) for recognition of Jewish marriages celebrated under any one of three authorities. The present proposals follow that pattern, and allow for each denomination to regulate marriages under their auspices.

As the basis for the Act is the duty of persons entering into a contract (i.e. a contract of marriage) to dissolve that contract under the relevant rules of the particular contractual system, it will be obvious that reference to a barrier to remarriage must refer back to the particular contractual system of marriage entered into by the parties.

It will not, therefore, be open to a spouse who married under the auspices of one of the denominations, but has subsequently switched their allegiance to another denomination, to require the marriage to be dissolved according to the usages of the newly-joined denomination.

Subsection (1) (c). And the barrier ... to remove. A spouse who wishes to invoke the provision of the Act will have to declare that there is a barrier to his or her remarriage, and also that it is within the power of the petitioner to remove the barrier. This will limit the application of the Act to cases of genuine hardship occasioned by unreasonable refusal to execute a get. How the existence of such a barrier is to be determined is dealt with in section (3).

Section (2). Where the grant... exists. This is the principal section of the Act, conferring upon the court the power and duty (subject to the provisions of section (5)) to withhold a decree until the barrier to remarriage has been removed, i.e. until a get has been executed. The power is mandatory, so that the judge does not have to involve himself in questions of discretion as to when, and whether, to exercise the power.

Section (2). And has not... the petitioner. As soon as the petitioner has done whatever he or she can to execute a get, there is no longer any need to withhold the divorce decree. How this is to be demonstrated to the court is dealt with in the commentary to section (3) below.

Section (3). A written statement ... by the court. The purpose of this section is twofold. In the first place, it imposes a duty upon anyone seeking to invoke the provisions of the Act to substantiate their claim that a barrier to their remarriage exists. This will prevent frivolous and vexatious applications, and also frees the judge from the onus of deciding whether a barrier exists, which may require detailed knowledge of specialised Jewish law.

The section provides that a written statement by the authority responsible for celebrating the original marriage shall be sufficient evidence for the court of the existence of a barrier. As explained in the commentary to section 1(1)(c) above, the Marriage Act recognises three different Jewish denominations. This section therefore provides that the authority for the particular denomination specified in the Marriage Act should be the authority who confirms the existence or otherwise of the barrier.

Secondly, the section provides that the same authority shall be competent to certify to the satisfaction of the court that the barrier to remarriage under which the judge exercised the powers contained in section (2) has in fact been removed, i.e. that a valid get has been granted, thereby removing the barrier. Once again, the purpose of this provision is to free the judge of the burden of having to decide unfamiliar questions of Jewish law. In some cases, the certifying authority may wish to refer the question of the existence or otherwise of a barrier to remarriage to the ecclesiastical leaders of the particular Jewish denomination, but the judge need only be concerned with the certification of the authority who celebrated the marriage.

Section (4). In the case ... successor in title. As noted in the commentary to section 1(1)(b) above, the Act is also designed to cover cases of Jewish marriages celebrated abroad. This section provides that in such cases the celebrant of the marriage shall take the place of the authority referred to under the Marriage Act 1949 (as specified in section (3)) for purposes of confirming the existence or otherwise of a barrier to remarriage, as well as its removal.

Section (5). The court may... desirable to do so. This section gives the judge a discretionary power to grant a civil divorce notwithstanding the fact that the petitioner has not yet executed a get, if there are exceptional circumstances making this desirable. It is clearly desirable that the judge should have this power if need be, so that he is not totally fettered by the provisions in section (2). The power is analogous to that contained in section 5 of the Matrimonial Causes Act 1973.

Conclusion

In this paper an attempt has been made to consider the extent to which English matrimonial legislation satisfies the legitimate expectations of ethnic religious minorities in Britain. It is clear that there are gaps and lacunae which call for urgent attention. Whilst the Jewish community receives full recognition of its religious marriage ceremonies, the Muslim and Catholic communities (as well as other religious groups, such as Sikhs and Hindus) receive no such recognition. Moreover, none of these groups receive recognition of their specific form of divorce. This creates -more particularly in relation to the Jewish community- a lack of intellectual coherence and consistency. More worryingly, it allows, and in a sense condones, an inequitable situation in which people are enabled to disregard their moral and contractual obligations. It has been argued, both as a matter of policy and also of individual justice, that our matrimonial legislation should not become a vehicle for unconscionable religious manipulation of this nature. It has also been shown, moreover, that the reasons for the current unsatisfactory situation have more to do with the exigencies of historical developments and circumstances than with a carefully conceived jurisprudential philosophy.

It is submitted that the present law can no longer be justified. In relation to marriages, provision should be made to enable religious minorities to contract valid religious marriages. In relation to divorce, consideration should be given, in the long term, to the desirability of legislation recognising the validity of the get as between Jewish parties, and in the short term an Act should be passed to remove the hardships currently suffered by Jewish spouses who cannot remarry religiously. It is submitted that there is no reason, in principle, why similar legislation should not be enacted in respect of the talaq procedure, provided that adequate provision is made for safeguarding and protecting the interests of Muslim women.

8. THE CLAIM TO A SEPARATE ISLAMIC SYSTEM OF PERSONAL LAW FOR BRITISH MUSLIMS

Sebastian Poulter

During the 1970s the Union of Muslim Organisations of UK and Eire (UMO) held a number of meetings which culminated in a formal resolution to seek official recognition of a separate system of Islamic family law which would automatically be applicable to all British Muslims.[1] A proposal along these lines was subsequently submitted to various British government ministers with a view to having it placed before Parliament for approval and enactment. This paper begins with an examination of some of the considerations underlying UMO's demand, including an assessment of the adequacy of existing legal provision for Muslims in England. It then explores the possible reasons why UMO's claim ultimately proved unsuccessful, analyses their cogency and makes special reference to the human rights dimension of the issue.

I. Considerations Underlying UMO's Demand

The claim to a separate Islamic system of personal law may be seen as arising from a variety of different causes. First, in many non-Western societies and communities those traditional customs, religious beliefs, moral values and legal principles which specifically pertain to the family and matters of personal status are held in very high esteem. They are often regarded as embodying the quintessential culture of a distinctive group of people, something not to be surrendered lightly or discarded, even when members of the group are living outside their country of origin. This is perhaps especially likely to be the case when religious belief, legal principle and family relations are closely intertwined, as they are in Islamic doctrine. Hence it is hardly surprising that Muslims should not only wish to be regulated by the principles of Islamic law when they are living in a non-Muslim state but also that they should seek to formalise such an arrangement within that state's own legal system.

Secondly, it may be argued that as other aspects of Islamic law, notably in the commercial and criminal spheres, have generally given way to Western-

---

[1] See UMO, *Why Muslim Family Law for British Muslims*, London, 1983. In 1983 UMO represented over 150 different Muslim organisations.

style codes in many countries with Muslim majorities in modern times,[2] so the particular area of Muslim family law has come to seem even more precious and worthy of preservation worldwide.

Thirdly, many Muslims living in England today are familiar with legal regimes in Asia and Africa which are of a pluralistic nature and which permit family relations within different religious and tribal communities to be regulated by a variety of distinctive systems of personal law.[3] In India, to take perhaps the most obvious example, the present pattern of legal pluralism in family matters was given statutory force by the British Parliament during the days of Empire.[4] If this system was perfectly acceptable to the British authorities during the days of the Raj, Muslims see no reason why it should not prove workable in the United Kingdom itself now that the number of people belonging to religious minorities here has become really substantial.

Fourthly, many Muslims view the issue principally in terms of religious freedom and claim a proud record of religious toleration towards members of other faiths, dating back over many centuries.[5] They, therefore, expect Islam's past respect for Jewish and Christian minorities in Muslim lands to be reciprocated today in the West.

Finally, there are powerful practical reasons involving a rejection of the perceived alternatives. Muslims in England are currently presented with images (some of which are admittedly greatly exaggerated by the media) of a majority community whose scale of values in family and personal matters appears to be poles apart from their own. Sex education at school, easy availability of contraceptives, teenage love affairs, prostitution, pornography, child abuse, easy abortion, marital breakdown, extra-marital cohabitation, children born out of wedlock and neglect of the elderly all receive such prominent publicity that minorities might easily gain the impression that these are characteristic features of life in the white community which are deliberately fostered as an integral part of legal policy. Finding themselves apparently surrounded by such 'evils', many Muslims believe that a sensible method of avoiding contamination would be to operate within a system of Islamic law which lays down a higher scale of values than those prevailing in the white community for whom the principles of English law were obviously primarily designed.

In this regard, many devout Muslims sincerely believe that the best way of preserving their own families and communities from the corrupting forces at work in the wider society is to protect their women by regulating their lives rather narrowly and strictly. Family honour is of the greatest importance and women are the repositories of that honour. Men are the guardians. The structure of Muslim families has therefore long been based on ideas and practices which are strongly patriarchal and give men dominance over women.

---

[2]See J.L. Esposito, *Women in Muslim Family Law,* Syracuse, 1982, pp.49, 75-6.

[3]See eg M. B. Hooker, *Legal Pluralism*, Oxford, 1976, chaps II and III.

[4]See eg 21 Geo III c 70, s. 17; Muslim Personal Law (Shariat) Application Act 1937.

[5]See eg Faruqi, 'The rights of non-Muslims under Islam' in Islamic Council of Europe, *Muslim Communities in Non-Muslim States*, London, 1980, pp. 43-66.

However, it is important to appreciate the historical context of progressive social reform in which this rigid 'sexual divide' came about, a matter succinctly explained by Esposito:

> *Qur'anic* reforms corrected many injustices in pre-Islamic society by granting women rights to which they were entitled - the right to contract their marriage, receive dower, retain possession and control of wealth, and receive maintenance and shares in inheritance. At the same time, however, family laws were formulated to meet a woman's needs in a society where her largely domestic, childbearing roles rendered her sheltered and dependent upon her father, her husband, and her close male relations. Thus family law reflected women's dependent position. . . Since men had more independence, wider social contacts, and higher status in the world, their social position was translated into greater legal responsibilities . . . as well as more extensive legal privileges proportionate to those responsibilities . . . In its attempt to meet the needs of a particular social milieu, Muslim family law reflected the social mores of the time - the traditional roles of men and women and the function of the extended family in a patriarchal society.[6]

The allocation of separate duties and responsibilities to men and women in classical Muslim law remained virtually unchallenged until the 20th century (as indeed it did for many centuries in English law) because they closely paralleled the accepted roles of individuals and the functions of the family in a basically unchanging society. However, profound changes in the status and role of women in recent times have undermined these long established notions and it is the degree to which Muslim law and English law have responded to these developments which informs much of the discussion which follows.

II. The Adequacy of Current English Legal Provision for Muslims and their Families

The aim of this section is to describe some of the main principles and rules of English family law, with a view to contrasting them with the position under Muslim law and hence drawing attention to the degree to which they appear to be adequate or inadequate to meet the needs of Muslims living in England. The analysis will focus on 'domestic' English law rather than the conflicts of laws and thus only consider, for example, marriages and divorces occurring in England rather than those which take place overseas.[7]

---

[6]Esposito, *Women in Muslim Family Law*, p. 48.

[7]For marriages contracted overseas, see S. M. Poulter, *English Law and Ethnic Minority Customs,* London, 1986, chaps 2, 3; for divorces obtained overseas, see Family Law Act 1986, Part II, discussed by Poulter, 'Recognition of Foreign Divorces: The New Law', (1987)

A. Marriage

(i) Formalities

The basic law governing the solemnisation of marriages in England is set out in the Marriage Acts 1949-86. These Acts stipulate quite detailed rules concerning where a marriage may take place, who should conduct the ceremony, at what time of day it may occur and the nature of the celebration. However, two religious denominations are exempt from all these regulations, namely Quakers and 'persons professing the Jewish religion'.[8] Their special privileges go back, at least, as far as Lord Hardwicke's Marriage Act 1753. As a result, their ceremonies may occur at any hour of the day or night; they need not take place in any particular building; they do not require the presence of any official appointed by or notified to the state authorities; and the form of the wedding merely has to follow the usages of the Society of Friends or the usages of the Jews, as the case may be.[9]

Whereas in the 18th century the privileges accorded to Jews and Quakers reflected religious toleration, in the 20th century they symbolise religious discrimination. There can, surely, be no justification for the preservation today of what has now become a rather embarrassing historical anomaly. There is no good reason why some religious minorities should be exempt from the normal legal requirements but not others. Since in Muslim law a marriage can be contracted merely in the presence of witnesses and requires no other formalities,[10] Muslims would no doubt appreciate being accorded the same privileges in this regard as Jews and Quakers. A far greater degree of uniformity should therefore be introduced into this aspect of English law. One problem which does arise, however, is that Muslim marriages may occur without either the bride or the groom actually being present at the ceremony. The wedding *(nikah)* can take place simply through an exchange of declarations between representatives acting on behalf of the couple.[11] Proxy marriages are not at present permitted under domestic English law and it seems unlikely that abolition of this rule would be contemplated unless adequate safeguards could be introduced to ensure that both parties had freely consented to the marriage.

(ii) Capacity to Marry

English law makes no concessions to other laws or traditions in relation to capacity to marry in England. A marriage in which either party is under the age of 16 or is within the prohibited degrees of relationship as defined in

84 *Law Soc Gaz* 253. Lack of space precludes any discussion of the laws of Scotland and Northern Ireland.

[8]Marriage Act 1949, s 26(1) (c), (d).

[9]Marriage Act 1949, ss 26(1), 35(4), 43(3), 75(1)(a).

[10]D. Pearl, *A Textbook on Muslim Personal Law*, London, 2nd ed. 1987, p. 41.

[11]*Ibid.*

the Marriage Acts 1949-86, or is already married to someone else will automatically be null and void.[12] Furthermore, it seems clear that English law will completely disregard the Islamic prohibition on marriages between Muslim women and non-Muslim men and thus any such marriage entered into in England is fully valid here. Of course, in Muslim law parties may marry under the age of 16 and a husband may take up to four wives simultaneously.[13] The difficulties involved in accommodating these possibilities in England are examined further below.

(iii) Arranged Marriages and Forced Marriages

Although the British immigration rules make it unnecessarily hard in practise for parties to arranged marriages (and engaged couples) to gain entry to the UK for purposes of settlement here,[14] such marriages are treated as perfectly valid in themselves. However, if an arranged marriage taking place in England is pushed to the point of compulsion, so that the marriage is actually being forced upon one of the parties against his or her wishes, the marriage is 'voidable', with the result that the unwilling party is entitled to obtain a decree of annulment if proceedings are instituted within three years of the marriage.[15] The ground for annulment is that the party concerned did not validly consent to the marriage in consequence of 'duress'. After being restrictively interpreted by the judges for many years,[16] the concept of duress was given a far more liberal construction by the Court of Appeal in the case of *Hirani v Hirani*[17] in 1983. A Hindu girl of 19, who had been having an affair with a Muslim man, was threatened by her parents with eviction from the family home if she did not marry the Hindu husband whom they had chosen for her. The Court, in granting her an annulment after she had gone through the ceremony of marriage, indicated that the crucial question in cases of alleged duress was whether the threats or pressures which had been made or applied were so great as to destroy the reality of consent to marriage by overbearing the will of the individual concerned. In this case they had clearly done so.

Broadly speaking, the consent of both spouses is an essential element in a Muslim marriage. However, there are instances where a minor child may be validly married simply on the basis of his or her guardian's consent, without

---

[12]Matrimonial Causes Act 1973, s 11. Concern about *foreign* marriages where the bride is under 16 or where the marriage is actually polygamous has also led to changes in the immigration rules designed to prevent such couples settling in the UK- see HC 306 of 1986; Immigration Act 1988, s 2; HC 555 of 1988.

[13]Pearl, *A Textbook,* pp. 42-3, 77.

[14]For the notorious 'primary purpose' rule see HC 169 (1982-83), as amended; I. Macdonald, *Immigration Law and Practice,* London, 2nd ed. 1987, pp. 231-7.

[15]Matrimonial Causes Act 1973, ss 12,13.

[16]See eg *Singh v. Singh* [1971] P. 226; *Singh v. Kaur* [1981] 11 *Fam Law* 152.

[17](1983) 4 FLR 232.

the minor having any voice in the matter.[18] Where such a marriage does occur Muslim law grants the child the 'option of puberty' which means that upon subsequently attaining puberty[19] the minor may elect to have the marriage set aside, provided the marriage has not yet been affirmed by voluntary consummation. However, under the Hanafi school of Islamic jurisprudence, as applied in the Indian subcontinent, this option is only available to a child who has been married off by a guardian other than the father or grandfather.[20] Hence these two male relations do have the power to impose upon their issue, without the latter's consent, a fully valid and binding marriage from which there is no escape save through a divorce. This offends against English notions of freedom of choice in marriage and, as we shall see, is unlikely to prove acceptable for marriages entered into in England.

B. Divorce

Whereas under Muslim law a divorce can be obtained in a number of different ways, notably extrajudicially through *talaq* (unilateral repudiation by the husband), *khul'* (divorce at the instance of the wife with the husband's agreement and on the basis that she will forego her right to dower) and *mubara'at* (divorce by mutual consent),[21] there is only one way of obtaining a divorce in England. This is through a decree granted by a court of civil jurisdiction on the ground that the marriage has irretrievably broken down.[22] Mutual agreement may provide the foundation of a divorce, but a period of two years' separation is required to establish breakdown[23] and the parties are not free to remarry until the decree has been made absolute by the court. Current proposals for the reform of English divorce law emphasise the need to maintain the involvement of the state in questions of divorce through the medium of a judicial procedure (albeit much more restricted than in the past) and extrajudicial divorce seems unlikely to be permitted in the near future.[24] Some form of judicial process is considered essential, partly as a brake upon precipitate action by the spouses (or oppression by one of them in seeking consent to divorce) and partly as a mechanism for ensuring that the welfare of children is adequately safeguarded and that the material outcome is reasonably fair.

---

[18] J. Nasir, *The Islamic Law of Personal Status*, London, 1986, p. 46.

[19] Puberty is set at the age of 12 for boys and 9 for girls; see Esposito, *Women in Muslim Family Law,* p.16.

[20] Pearl, *A Textbook*, p. 44.

[21] See Pearl, *A Textbook*, chap. 7; Nasir, *The Islamic Law of Personal Status*, chap. 6.

[22] Family Law Act 1986, s 44(1); Matrimonial Causes Act 1973, s 1.

[23] Matrimonial Causes Act 1973, s 1(2)(d).

[24] See Law Commission Report, 'Facing the Future: A Discussion Paper on the Ground for Divorce', No 170, London, 1988.

C. Children

(i) Custody

In custody disputes, for example where the mother and father separate or divorce, the English courts determine the children's future home and upbringing on the basis that the welfare of the individual child is the first and paramount consideration.[25] A wide variety of factors are incorporated by the courts into the notion of a child's 'welfare' and there have been decisions which clearly indicate that the judges feel it is desirable for children whose parents come from different religious backgrounds to maintain links with both cultural heritages, for instance through joint custody orders and access.[26] In no reported case has a Muslim parent yet argued that upon divorce or separation the English courts should give special weight to the provisions of Muslim law which tend to allocate younger children automatically to the mother and older children automatically to the father, with the exact age of transfer between parents being dependent upon the particular school of Islamic jurisprudence applicable to the community to which the family belongs.[27] It is very doubtful if such rules would carry much weight with an English judge in view of the wording of section 1 of the Guardianship of Minors Act 1971 which expressly states that the courts shall not take into consideration whether, from any point of view other than the welfare of the child, the claim of the father is superior to that of the mother or the claim of the mother is superior to that of the father. Over recent decades the statute laws of many Arab and Islamic countries have modified classical Muslim law by raising the age at which children go to the father rather than the mother.[28]

(ii) Circumcision

The circumcision of male infants, which is current in Muslim societies, has long been perfectly lawful in England, but the circumcision of young girls (which has probably always been unlawful under English law) has recently been specifically banned by Parliament through the enactment of the Prohibition of Female Circumcision Act 1985. There is no clear authority in the Qur'an for female circumcision, but some Muslim communities in certain parts of the world do appear to justify the practisein the name of religion.[29] There are certain exceptions from criminal liability in the 1985 Act, for example where the operation is necessary for the child's physical or mental health, but no account may be taken, in assessing mental health, of the effect on the child of any belief on the part of any person that the operation is

[25] Guardianship of Minors Act 1971, s 1.

[26] See eg *Jussa v. Jussa* [1972] 2 All ER 600; *H v. H* [1975] 5 *Fam Law* 185.

[27] See Pearl, *A Textbook*, pp. 96-7; Nasir, *The Islamic Law of Personal Status*, pp. 167-9.

[28] See J.N.D. Anderson, *Law Reform in the Muslim World,* London, 1976, pp. 141-3.

[29] See S. McLean ed., *Female Circumcision, Excision and Infibulation*, Minority Rights Group Report No 47, London, 1980, pp. 6-8.

required as a matter of custom or ritual.[30] The practise of female circumcision has been castigated by most medical experts as unnecessary, damaging and dangerous and many campaigns are being waged against its continued occurrence, both nationally and internationally.[31] The risks to the child's physical and psychological health are considerable. The sexual enjoyment of women who have been circumcised is gravely impaired and they may well experience additional hazards in childbirth.

(iii) Education

Parents have a right to express a preference to a local education authority as to which school they would like their child to attend in the state sector, but the authority is only bound to comply with the preference expressed in so far as this would be compatible with the provision of efficient education and the efficient use of resources.[32] With the shift over recent years away from single-sex schools towards co-educational schools as the predominant type of institution, some Muslim parents may find that there are insufficient places at all girls' secondary schools in their areas, with the result that they are unable to give their daughters the separate education which some traditions in Muslim societies prescribe as part of the doctrine of *purdah*. This is a most unsatisfactory situation. However, it is an offence to keep a child of compulsory school age away from school and in *Bradford Corporation v Patel*,[33] a Muslim father was convicted under the provisions of the Education Act 1944 for failing, on religious grounds, to send his adolescent daughter to the co-educational school to which she was allocated by the local authority.

Muslim parents who can afford the fees for private schooling may, of course, elect to send their daughters to schools in the independent sector. Indeed a number of denominational independent schools have been established for Muslims in recent years, often with only very limited resources. So far there seems to have been a reluctance on the part of the Department of Education and Science to confer 'voluntary aided' status upon any Muslim school, perhaps through fear that to do so would be divisive. However, such status entitles a school to very substantial financial support from the local authority[34] and it is anomalous to allow the present pattern of Anglican, Roman Catholic and Jewish aided schools to continue while opposing Muslim aided schools. There is certainly no legal principle which could justify a policy which discriminated between different faiths in this manner. Voluntary aided status would certainly help to improve the quality of education offered by some of the newer independent Muslim schools.

---

[30] Section 2(1), (2).

[31] S. McLean ed., *Female Circumcision;* A. El Dareer, *Woman, Why Do You Weep?*, London, 1982.

[32] Education Act 1944, s 76; Education Act 1980, s 6(5).

[33] 1974, unreported.

[34] Education Act 1944, ss 18-19.

So far as religious education is concerned, the Education Reform Act 1988 attempts to accommodate the needs and wishes of non-Christian pupils and their parents in a variety of ways. Although all schools in the state sector must provide for daily acts of collective worship and for classes in religious education any parent may request that his child be withdrawn from either or both of these activities.[35] In Local Education Authority (LEA) schools the collective worship must be 'wholly or mainly of a broadly Christian character'[36] when judged over a period of a school term and this clearly allows for a variety of faiths to be represented on a number of days. Moreover, particular schools may obtain exemptions from this provision if the LEA's standing advisory council on religious education decides that its application to them would be inappropriate, for example because of the large proportion of Muslims in the schools in question.[37] In LEA schools classes in religious education have to follow an 'agreed syllabus' and must not be given in the form of doctrines which are distinctive of any particular denomination.[38] The agreed syllabus is decided upon by a conference of four committees representing the LEA, the teachers' associations, the Church of England and such other denominations as reflect the principal religious traditions of the area. Any new syllabus agreed after 1988 must 'reflect the fact that the religious traditions in Great Britain are in the main Christian, while taking account of the teaching and practices of the other principal religions represented in Great Britain'.[39] Muslim parents who are not prepared to allow their child to attend classes given in accordance with the agreed syllabus and want classes exclusively in their own faith instead, may request the LEA to make arrangements for such tuition either at another LEA school or elsewhere (for example at a mosque school) or at the child's own school and such a request must usually be complied with provided the cost of the tuition does not fall upon the LEA.[40]

Voluntary aided schools may, of course, determine their own form of collective worship in line with the religious denomination of the school and similarly provide tuition in accordance with the tenets of that denomination, but parents of pupils there who are not of that faith can request tuition in accordance with the LEA agreed syllabus if they so wish.[41]

English schools are not under a legal duty to provide sex education but many teachers feel under a responsibility to do so. Muslim parents are often concerned lest this may have a tendency to corrupt the morals of their children. To meet these concerns (and those of many white parents) the law obliges LEA's and school governors to take such steps as are reasonably practicable to ensure that, where sex education is available to pupils, it is given

35 Education Reform Act 1988, s 9(3).

36 *Ibid.*, ss 6, 7.

37 *Ibid.*, s 12.

38 Education Act 1944, s 26 (as amended).

39 Education Reform Act 1988, s 8(3).

40 Education Act 1944, s 26 (as amended); Education Reform Act 1988, s 9(4).

41 Education Act 1944, s 28 (as amended).

'in such a manner as to encourage those pupils to have due regard to moral considerations and the value of family life.'[42] The result should be that teachers deal with sex education in a manner which sets it in the sort of context which most Muslim parents might find acceptable.

D. Financial Provision on Divorce and Separation

The English courts possess a wide discretion, within certain guidelines laid down by Parliament,[43] to decide whether to make orders for financial provision upon separation and divorce and, if so, how large an amount should be specified. So far as a period of separation during marriage is concerned, both English law and Muslim law oblige a husband to support his wife in appropriate circumstances. Under English law a young wife without children might well be expected to go out to work herself to reduce her husband's liability and would have her notional earning capacity taken into account by the court if she refused to do so, but a Muslim wife might be able to satisfy an English court that she should not have to do this in the light of the values and practices of wives in her own family and community.[44] It is quite commonly accepted in many Muslim communities that wives should not go out to work to earn a living and that the husband is solely responsible for the family's income.

After a divorce Muslim law only obliges a husband to support his wife during the three month period of *'idda* during which she is precluded from remarriage.[45] However, he does have to pay her any deferred dower (*mahr*) due to her in consequence of the marriage contract.[46] English courts have been prepared to order the payment of such dower[47] and would undoubtedly take account of such lump sum payments in their overall assessment of what would be an appropriate division of the couple's capital and income resources and in deciding what financial and property orders should be made. Although the trend in English law is towards encouraging divorced wives to become self-sufficient and financially independent of their former husbands and thus financial orders for only a limited period are becoming increasingly common, the courts have to consider whether such orders would be appropriate in all the circumstances and what hardship might be caused to the wife by stopping all maintenance.[48] It therefore seems unlikely that they would pay specific regard to the very limited nature of the duty to maintain divorced wives under

---

[42]Education (No 2) Act 1986, s 46.

[43]Matrimonial Causes Act 1973, Part II, as amended by Matrimonial and Family Proceedings Act 1984; Domestic Proceedings and Magistrates' Courts Act 1978.

[44]Cf *Khan v. Khan* [1980] 1 All ER 497 where the court refused to take 'judicial notice' of such a Muslim custom. The decision might have gone the other way if appropriate evidence had been presented.

[45]Nasir, *The Islamic Law of Personal Status*, pp. 137-8.

[46]*Ibid.*, chap. 4.

[47]See *Shahnaz v. Rizwan* [1965] 1 QB 390; *Qureshi v. Qureshi* [1972] Fam 173.

[48]Matrimonial Causes Act 1973, as amended, ss 25, 25A.

Muslim law, save where a very substantial payment of deferred dower had already been made.

E. Inheritance

English rules govern the inheritance both of immovable property situated here and of moveable property (wherever situated) if at the time of death the deceased was domiciled here. Hence the estates of many Muslims resident in Britain may fall to be administered under the provisions of English law. Muslim law, which basically operates a very elaborate system of allocating mathematical shares to a variety of relatives, can only apply directly in respect to immovable property situated overseas or, in the case of movables, where the deceased died domiciled in a country where the Muslim law of succession is administered.

While English rules for the distribution of an estate on intestacy are far removed in many respects from the Muslim law of intestate succession, there is nothing in English law to prevent a Muslim from making a valid will bequeathing his or her property in accordance with an Islamic pattern of inheritance. The terms of such a will would, however, be open to challenge by means of a claim for 'family provision' made by relatives or dependants who were able to prove that the will did not make reasonable financial provision for them.[49] Under Muslim law the share of a surviving wife as an heir is comparatively small and only amounts to one eighth of the net estate (increased to one quarter if there are no children or agnatic grandchildren).[50] Hence a Muslim widow living in England might, in appropriate circumstances, be able to bring a successful application for family provision if she felt financially insecure. Muslim law itself allows a person to make a will, but the bequests must not exceed one third of the value of the net estate.[51] However, to a limited extent this may enable a testator to make greater provision for a surviving spouse than is available under the intestate system.[52]

III. Possible Reasons for the Rejection of UMO 's Demand

During the 1970s the response by British government ministers to the proposal submitted by UMO for the introduction by Parliament of a system of Islamic family law applicable to all British Muslims was extremely negative.[53] The proposal seems to have been rejected out of hand on the ground that the suggested legislation would not be 'appropriate'. What justification can be offered for such resistance and how convincing is it ?

---

[49]See Inheritance (Provision for Family and Dependants) Act 1975, s 1.

[50]See Pearl, *A Textbook*, p 150. If her husband's marriage had been polygamous this share has to be divided with the other widows.

[51]*Ibid.*, p. 143.

[52]In classical Sunni law, no bequest could be made to heirs, but this rule has been abolished in several Muslim countries; no such rule ever operated in Shi'i law.

[53]See UMO, *Why Muslim Family Law.*

First, it seems to have been argued that the proposal ran counter to the English tradition of a unified system in family matters in terms of which a uniform set of rules is applied to all, regardless of their origins, race or creed.[54] This would not seem to be an adequate reason in itself, especially since (as we have seen) it is not wholly accurate. However, this argument is perhaps rather more convincing if it asserts that a basically uniform system has helped in the past to create a more cohesive society and that it is still needed today, more especially as part of the process of nation-building required to integrate the newer minorities into the general framework of English life and some of its most important values. Family law relates to one of the essential organisational structures of social and legal administration and to allow one religious denomination to separate itself off completely in this manner might be felt to be unacceptable divisive.

A second problem with the proposal for the introduction of Muslim family law in England is the practical difficulty of working out which system of Muslim family law would be applicable. Apart from the fundamental division between Sunnis and Shi'is there are a number of different 'schools' of Islamic thought. Furthermore, many countries where Muslim law is applied have, during the course of the 20th century, modernised and reformed it by means of local statutes or ordinances.[55] Which of these many different versions would be administered in England? Would the choice of law in each case depend upon the nationalities, domiciles or countries of origin of the parties and, if so, what would happen to all those Muslims who were born here or who now possess a British passport and an English domicile? There are surely dangers here of introducing both immense complexity and much artificiality into the selection of the correct system for the resolution of individual disputes.

Thirdly, would cases be decided by the existing civil courts or by a specially established religious court staffed exclusively by Muslims? If the former, one can easily envisage the controversy that might surround their interpretations of the finer points of Muslim law and the resulting accusations that they were not fit to judge such cases. However, the latter solution might be just as likely to result in recrimination because the various Muslim communities in England are far from united and might well disagree with one another about whether the legal rules were being correctly interpreted and applied, even by people who were meant to be their own judicial representatives. Some idea of the divisions of the British Muslim 'community' can be gleaned from the following passage in a recent newsletter issued by the Islamic Cultural Centre attached to the London Central Mosque :

> The administrators, the *ulema*,[56] the imams and numberless committees of our mosques and organisations have failed the

[54]*Ibid.*, p 4.

[55]See generally Nasir, *The Islamic Law of Personal Status*.

[56]Muslim scholars (The Arabic original term is *'ulama)*.

> community dismally. Instead of creating a unified infrastructure for the benefit of the community and all its needs, they have fostered discord, diversity, distrust and dishonesty, which cannot be described as other than disgraceful.[57]

In the light of such practical problems it is possible that many Muslims might actually prefer to have their disputes ultimately resolved by English judges applying English law. However, this suggestion should not be taken in any way to imply that the first line of attack upon a family dispute should not be through the particular Muslim community concerned and its various welfare organisations and agencies. In many instances these should be able to offer counselling, conciliation and mediation resulting in a satisfactory settlement of the problem.

IV. The Human Rights Dimension

A fourth difficulty with the proposal for the introduction of Muslim family law into Britain is perhaps the most fundamental of all and relates to its content. It is that, at least to the Western mind, Muslim family law appears to contain a number of substantive principles and rules which violate some of the fundamental human rights and freedoms set out in international conventions such as the European Convention on Human Rights and the International Covenant on Civil and Political Rights to which the United Kingdom is a contracting party. This is especially so in relation to those Muslim provisions which seem to discriminate against women, for the achievement of sexual equality is a matter of deep concern in modern Britain. Examples of rules that are unlikely to find favour here for this reason are those permitting polygamy, forced marriages (as opposed to arranged marriages), marriages of girls before puberty and divorce through unilateral repudiation by the husband (talaq), as well as the ban on Muslim women marrying non-Muslim husbands.[58] In response, Muslims are likely to stress that international human rights treaties provide guarantees of freedom of religion and that this perspective greatly assists their cause.[59] However, the treaty provisions giving individuals the freedom to practise their religion also contain substantial limitation clauses which permit legal restrictions to be imposed if they are necessary to safeguard, *inter alia*, public morals and the fundamental rights and freedoms of others.[60] While the ambit of public morality is no doubt highly controversial, it would appear that the principle of sexual equality in relation to marriage and family life is now firmly established as a fundamental human right and the state is thus entitled to insist

---

[57]Newsletter No 39 (April 1988). On the fragmentation of the Muslim communities in Britain, see also S.M. Darsh, *Muslims in Europe*, London, 1980, pp. 78-82.

[58]See generally Poulter, *English Law and Ethnic Minority Customs*, chaps 2, 3, and 5.

[59]See eg UMO, *Why Muslim Family Law*, p. 4.

[60]European Convention, art 9(2); International Covenant, art 18(3).

that women should not be subjected to discrimination on the basis of religious beliefs propounded, interpreted and enforced exclusively by men.[61] The International Covenant on Civil and Political Rights itself provides that state parties must take appropriate steps to ensure equality of rights and responsibilities of spouses as to marriage, during marriage and at its dissolution. A similar provision on the duty to eliminate discrimination against women in all matters relating to marriage and family relations is to be found in the International Convention on the Elimination of All Forms of Discrimination Against Women, to which the UK is a contracting party. The central question thus resolves itself into whether the Muslim rules mentioned above do or do not involve such discrimination.

First, the prohibition on Muslim women marrying non-Muslim husbands while Muslim men may marry non-Muslim wives, provided they are Christians or Jews, appears transparently discriminatory. Its underlying justification in religious terms is that Islam takes it for granted that any children will assume the religious faith of their father. Hence the only way of ensuring that a Muslim woman's children will remain within the faith is for her to marry another Muslim. Can this rationale for the rule justify the distinction in terms of human rights law ? Differentiation between the sexes has been held to be permissible provided a legitimate aim is being pursued, the distinction possesses an objective and reasonable justification, and there is a reasonable degree of proportionality between the means employed and the aim sought to be realised.[62] While it would seem quite legitimate for members of any religious denomination to aim to keep their children loyal to their faith, the methods by which Muslims try to achieve this objective seem both unreasonable and disproportionate. The rule restricting intermarriage wrongly assumes that all who marry will invariably have children and the rule itself is premised on the assumption that the parent with the power to determine the child's religion should automatically be the father. Yet a Muslim woman marrying an agnostic husband might well be able to reach an agreement with him that any children should be brought up as Muslims. Equally, there is no good reason why a Christian woman who marries a Muslim husband should automatically agree to their children being brought up as Muslims.

Secondly, the acceptance by Islam of polygamy, however limited the husband's entitlement may be under Muslim law[63] and however uncommon it may be in actual practice, also appears to be discriminatory, for it allows one of the spouses to take further partners with full legal recognition and thus

---

[61]See eg European Convention, arts 12, 14; International Covenant on Civil and Political Rights 1966, art 23(4); International Covenant on the Elimination of All Forms of Discrimination against Women, art 16.

[62]See *Marckz v. Belgium* [1980] 2 EHRR 330 at 343; *Abdulaziz, Cabales and Balkandali v. UK* (1985) 7 EHRR 471, at 499.

[63]A maximum of four wives is laid down in the Qur'an. In some Muslim countries modern statutes have decreed that the permission of a court must be sought before a man takes a second or subsequent wife - see Anderson, *Law Reform*, pp. 111-114.

fundamentally change the nature of the couple's family life together, while denying such a right to the other spouse. None of the usual justifications put forward by Muslims in favour of polygamy really carry much conviction. In modern Britain there is no surplus population of women resulting from loss of men in battle which calls for spinsters to be saved from promiscuity by attachment to already married men. There is no greater reason why a husband whose wife is barren should be entitled to take a second wife than there is for a wife whose husband is impotent or sterile to take a second husband. Nor can one sensibly take it for granted that men have more voracious sexual appetites than women which can only be gratified by maintaining relationships with several partners concurrently. Furthermore, it hardly seems a sufficient response for Muslims to draw an analogy between polygamy and the existence of mistresses in Western societies.[64] This is to confuse the law with what goes on in practise- and the Western practise is non-discriminatory in this regard, for wives can take lovers on the side too.

Thirdly, the notorious form of divorce known as talaq under which a husband may unilaterally repudiate his wife without showing cause, without the need to have recourse to any court or extraneous authority and without any requirement of notification to his wife, is clearly discriminatory since it is not available to a wife. It is a weak defence to this charge for Muslims to argue either that wives can divorce their husbands in a similar manner provided they stipulate for such a right in their marriage contracts or that to pronounce a talaq may be costly for the husband in terms of his resultant liability to pay deferred dower.[65] Again this confuses law with practise and the practical realities are that few Muslim wives have sufficient bargaining power to enable them to insert such clauses in their marriage contracts and usually the amount of dower is too small to provide a major disincentive to divorce. The notion, sometimes put forward, that to pay it would commonly bankrupt the husband seems extremely far-fetched.

Fourthly, Muslim principles whereby minors may be married while still under the age of puberty and without their consent, although broadly applicable to children of both sexes, operate in practise mainly in respect of girls. In this sense they may be regarded as oppressive to women. Forced marriages are, in any event, prohibited by several human rights treaties including the International Covenant on Civil and Political Rights[66] and the Convention on Consent to Marriage, Minimum Age for Marriage and Registration of Marriages.[67]

It is vital that arguments like these, suggesting that certain aspects of Muslim personal law entail sexual discrimination and violate human rights standards, are confronted with a degree of realism and some attempt at objectivity. Accusations of discrimination are invariably wounding to those to

---

64 See UMO, *Why Muslim Family Law*, pp. 28, 42.

65 *Ibid.*, p. 27.

66 Art 23 (3).

67 Art 1(1).

whom they are addressed, yet perhaps even worse consequences are liable to follow if Muslim claims to a system of personal law are denied on other, rather bland and less persuasive grounds simply in order to spare embarrassment. No fruitful dialogue or constructive negotiation is possible in the absence of openness on both sides.

The wide gulf which exists between Muslim and Western approaches to these matters can be graphically illustrated by reference to developments with regard to the ratification by states of the International Convention on the Elimination of All Form of Discrimination against Women. The Convention, which came into force in 1981, has so far been ratified by 97 states and signed by 20 others. At least seven Muslim countries have ratified the Convention, namely Bangladesh, Democratic Yemen, Egypt, Indonesia, Iraq, Turkey and Tunisia and two others, Afghanistan and Jordan, have signed it.

So far as these Muslim countries are concerned, their practise has generally been to attach a reservation to the whole or part of article 16 of the Convention, a key provision which not only imposes a general duty on states to take appropriate measures to eliminate discrimination against women in all matters relating to marriage and family relations but also lists particular instances in relation to which this should be done. Article 16 provides as follows:

> 1. States Parties shall take all appropriate measures to eliminate discrimination against women in all matters relating to marriage and family relations and in particular shall ensure, on a basis of equality of men and women:
>
> (a) The same right to enter into marriage;
>
> (b) The same right freely to choose a spouse and to enter into marriage only with their free and full consent;
>
> (c) The same rights and responsibilities during marriage and at its dissolution;
>
> (d) The same rights and responsibilities as parents, irrespective of their marital status, in matters relating to their children; in all cases the interests of the children shall be paramount;
>
> (e) The same rights to decide freely and responsibly on the number and spacing of their children and to have access to the information, education and means to enable them to exercise these rights;
>
> (f) The same rights and responsibilities with regard to guardianship, wardship, trusteeship and adoption of children, or similar institutions where these concepts exist in national legislation; in all cases the interests of the children shall be paramount;
>
> (g) The same personal rights as husband and wife, including the right to choose a family name, profession and an occupation;

> (h) The same rights for both spouses in respect of the ownership, acquisition, management, administration, enjoyment and disposition of property, whether free of charge or for a valuable consideration.
> 2. The betrothal and marriage of a child shall have no legal effect, and all necessary action, including legislation, shall be taken to specify a minimum age for marriage and to make the registration of marriages in an official registry compulsory.

The fullest explanation of the reasoning which underlies Muslim anxieties about the content of article 16 can be found in the reservation attached by Egypt.[68] The reservation draws attention to the provision of the shari'a in terms of which women are accorded rights 'equivalent to' those of their spouses so as to ensure 'a just balance' between them. The reservation goes on to declare:

> This is out of respect for the sacrosanct nature of the firm religious beliefs which govern marital relations in Egypt and which may not be called in question and in view of the fact that one of the most important bases of the relations is an equivalency of rights and duties so as to ensure complementarity which guarantees true equality between the spouses.

The reservation then turns to the specific questions of maintenance, dower and divorce, commenting:

> The provisions of the *Shari'ah* lay down that the husband shall pay bridal money to the wife and maintain her fully and shall also make payment to her upon divorce, whereas the wife retains full rights over her property and is not obliged to spend anything on her keep. The *Shari'ah* therefore restricts a wife's right to divorce by making it contingent on a judge's ruling, whereas no such restriction is laid down in the case of the husband.

Similar reservations to article 16 have been made by several other Muslim countries. Bangladesh has indicated that it does not consider as binding upon itself sub-paragraphs 1(c) and 1(f) of article 16 'as they conflict with the Shariah law based on the Holy Qur'an and Sunna.'[69] Iraq has declared that it is not bound by any part of article 16, drawing attention to those provisions of the shari'a which accord women rights 'equivalent to' the rights of the

---

[68] See United Nations, *Human Rights: Status of International Instruments*, New York, 1987, p. 147.

[69] *Ibid.*, p 143. *Sunna* refers to the deeds, statements and sayings of the Prophet Mohammed or collectively his 'practice'.

husbands so as to ensure a 'just balance' between them, in exactly the same terms as the Egyptian reservation.[70] Jordan has attached a reservation about article 16(1)(c) in relation to the rights to maintenance and compensation arising upon the dissolution of marriage.[71] Finally, Tunisia and Turkey do not consider themselves bound by sub-paragraph (1)(c), (d) and (f) of article 16.[72]

Some other states outside the Muslim world have, however, reacted in a hostile manner to these types of reservations. During 1985-6 Mexico, Sweden and the Federal Republic of Germany all objected formally to these reservations on the basis that they were incompatible with the object and purpose of the Convention itself and therefore impermissible under article 28(2).[73] In 1987, Sweden elaborated on its reasons for taking particular objection to the Iraqi reservation in the following terms:

> If the reservations were to apply they would inevitably have the effect of discriminating against women on the grounds of sex, which is contrary to everything the Convention stands for. It should also be borne in mind that the principles of the equal rights of men and women and of non-discrimination on the grounds of sex are set forth in the Charter of the United Nations as one of its purposes, in the Universal Declaration of Human Rights of 1948, and in the International Covenants on Economic,Social and Cultural Rights and on Civil and Political Rights, both of 1966, to which Iraq is a party.[74]

If it is assumed that states generally view their public responses to human rights treaties very seriously, this pattern of reservations and objections furnishes a valuable indication of the distance separating the rival standpoints.

Conclusions

It seems reasonably clear that, for a variety of reasons, a separate Islamic system of personal law cannot and will not be introduced for British Muslims, at any rate in the foreseeable future. How then should Muslims respond to this situation? In the first place, they should bear in mind just how flexible and accommodating many of the provisions of English law are and ensure that they use the existing system to the full to suit their own purposes. This applies particularly to such issues as arranging marriages, performing weddings in mosques, organising a child's religious education at school (or elsewhere), paying *mahr* on divorce and executing a will. Furthermore, English law generally approves of the settlement of family disputes outside the courts (save

[70] United Nations, *Human Rights,* p. 152.

[71] *Ibid.*, p. 153-4.

[72] *Ibid.*, pp. 158- 9.

[73] *Ibid.*, pp. 167, 168, 171.

[74] *Ibid.*, p 171. It should be noted that Iraq had attached reservations to other articles of the Convention as well as article 16 and the Swedish objections related to all these reservations.

for the actual obtaining of a divorce). This means that there is an opportunity for family, religious and community values to come to the fore through the process of negotiation, conciliation and mediation.[75] Insofar as many of the Qur'anic precepts are in the nature of broad ethical norms capable of adaptation to meet the particular needs of time and place,[76] many Muslims should in practise find comparatively few obstacles to leading a reasonable family life in England.

However, where English law is palpably deficient in meeting the legitimate needs of Muslims, vigorous efforts should be made to reform it. Cultural pluralism must be recognised by the English legal system as an integral part of modern English society and as one of the key elements of our liberal democracy. The legislature has recently shown itself to be perfectly capable of responding speedily to remedy the grievances of Sikhs who constitute a much smaller minority in Britain than Muslims. They have pressed their claims forcefully on the basis of religious freedom and found Parliament receptive to their pleas, both in relation to the wearing of turbans by motorcyclists[77] and in respect of the carrying of knives and daggers (*kirpans*) for religious reasons.[78] Muslims have a strong case for seeking equality with Jews and Quakers in respect of the solemnisation of marriage and for asserting the right of parents to send their children to single-sex schools in the state sector. Both claims can be supported by reference to human rights law. Apart from campaigning in relation to specific issues, it is equally important that the views and values of Britain's religious minorities are borne in mind in the general process of law reform so that they influence the direction of legal change for the benefit of the population as a whole.

No doubt some British Muslims will not feel satisfied with *ad hoc* reforms in limited areas and will not rest until their demand for a separate system of personal law in England is fully met. As a first step towards achieving this goal they might profitably consider joining together to compile a unified code of Muslim law, embodying the best principles of each of the schools of Islamic jurisprudence and omitting those rules which disregard international human rights law. This would clearly have to be a long-term project, but an attempt at unification does already exist in the form of a draft 'Law for Personal Status' prepared under the auspices of the Ministry of Justice of the League of Arab States between 1977 and 1985.[79]

Early in 1989 the more conservative forces here gravely damaged the image of Islam among the white majority community by their public burning

---

[75]One should not, of course, overlook the risks of Muslim (and indeed other) women being oppressed in such informal forums for dispute settlement.

[76]See N. Coulson, *A History of Islamic Law*, Edinburgh, 1964, p. 225.

[77]See Motor-Cycle Crash Helmets (Religious Exemption) Act 1976, subsequently re-enacted in the Road Traffic Act 1988, s.16(2).

[78]See Criminal Justice Act 1988, s 139 (5)(b).

[79]An English translation of the draft is provided in an appendix in Nasir, *The Islamic Law of Personal Status*, pp. 260-313.

of Salman Rushdie's book *The Satanic Verses*[80] in Bradford and their threats against his personal safety and that of the staff of a leading bookseller. The subsequent intervention of Ayatollah Khomeini in the affair gave little encouragement to those who would wish to foster a greater respect for Islam in the UK. While Muslims in Britain should not be diffident about declaring their needs openly and asserting their legal rights, they should bear in mind the national and international context in which British public opinion is formed. In a democracy, public opinion can play a vital role in determining the pace and direction of legal change.

[80]S. Rushdie, *The Satanic Verses*, London, 1988.

9. MUSLIM MIGRANTS IN FRANCE AND GERMANY LAW AND POLICY IN FAMILY AND GROUP IDENTITY

Riva Kastoryano*

The international migrations of the second half of the twentieth century have been a response to employment opportunities generated by postwar reconstruction and economic growth.[1] Europe had to rebuild; it also had to catch up after an interwar generation of political uncertainty, depression, and hesitant technological advance. The inflow of immigrants compensated for wartime losses and persistent low fertility and provided Europe with what economists have sometimes called unlimited supplies of labour. But the European states, in defining implicit and explicit policies of immigration, have treated foreign manpower as temporary. The migrants for their part saw this adventure, before anything else, as a stage in the upward social mobility in their country of origin.

At this time, the settlement of migrants and of their families has led to forms of organisation and of solidarity that move them to act in accordance with their identities, their interests and their personal or collective motives. This situation has moved European nations to consider their political traditions, to rethink their principles of nationality and citizenship and eventually to reform certain of their institutions, in short to redefine themselves as nation-states.[2]

For all their diversity, the definitions of the nation-state are based on subjective criteria such as 'the will to live together', after Renan's famous formula, or even the 'community of fate', after Otto Bauer. In effect, because it is the product of a history, the national community is characterised by its reference to the past; it is also characterised by its attitude toward the present, which manifests itself in its fondness for national identity; and by its will to

---

* This article has been translated by Philippa Candler and revised by the author, who also wishes to thank Professor David Landes, from Harvard University, for going over the English version.

[1] D. S. Landes, *The Unbound Prometheus,* Cambridge, 1962; M.M. Postan, *An Economic History of Western Europe 1945-1964,* London, 1967. I. Svennilson, *Growth and Stagnation in the European Economy,* Geneva, 1954.

[2] Cf also W. R. Brubaker, *Citizenship and Nationhood Project Proposal for the Society of Fellows,* Harvard University, 1988.

share the same future. This implies, at least in theory or in wish, a unified community where language, race, belief and ideologies are legitimised by the state. The question is whether it is in the interest of the nation-state to encourage feelings of belonging and to preserve cultural homogeneity and integrity.

In contrast to the United States, which has been constituted by migrants of various origins (and where immigration is found at the heart of the constitution and the conception of the nation-state), the economic migrations in Europe, which in certain cases are linked to decolonisation (in France and in Great Britain), seem to be leading to a cultural mosaic perceived as a challenge to the national unity of European countries as soon as the vast majority of the latest migratory trends appears to be 'Muslim'.

Part of this is a reaction to strangeness and the immigrant claim to separateness. Some of them demand public public recognition of a cultural identity with its politico-religious characteristics.[3] In response, some members of the host population see them as a challenge to national identity, the more so as new forms of expression of identity surrounding Islam lead to a confusion between space, culture and nation and come up against public opinion which doubts the capacity of North African migrants in France and Turks in Germany to assimilate.

The comparison of social organisation and expressions of identity of immigrant populations in France and Germany allows us to weigh effects of legislation, public policy, social practices and public opinion on the forms of family solidarity and tenacity at immigrant identity in the two countries.

France and Germany established in the 1960s immigration policies (explicit in the case of the FRG and implicit in the case of France) based on the needs of economic growth, that is to say, provisional policies. Today with the de facto installation of migrants, they find it necessary, even essential, to adjust their public policies to assure integration of the immigrant population and their families; while maintaining the internal coherence of the nation. In question here are two European countries with two different state traditions and two different histories with regard to ties to migrants - the French ties to Colonial Empire and North Africa; the privileged German economic and cultural relations with Turkey and the Turks. The extent of immigration in the two countries underlines the complexity of their social structure and

---

[3]G. Kepel, *Les Banlieues de l'Islam,* Paris, 1987.

networks of relations and of social organisation of the populations in question and poses the problem of individual or collective integration.

Individual or collective integration presents a big ambiguity, with contradictions that are unique to immigration. Even if the will to perpetuate identity and to define its boundaries slows down integration, the prolonged duration of the stay promotes the acquisition of civil and civic rights in the countries of installation. The hard question is, however, to know what the real or perverse effects of public policies (on the housing of migrants, the education of their children, etc.) are on the integration of the population in question and on the expression of its collective identity.

I. 'Foreigners' in France and Germany

The system of rotation in Germany establishes a policy of *Gastarbeiter* that gives a legal status to the provisional presence of migrant workers. Other European countries, particularly France, have an implicit policy that makes no reference to length of stay and where the presence of migrant workers is justified by their economic role as workers.[4]

The recent debates on immigration in France put the emphasis on the fact that 'France is a country of immigration' and even that all reflections on the identity of France should take account of the inclusion and assimilation of foreigners.[5] From the beginning of the 19th century, France has known immigration flows from Belgium and from Germany and then from Italy.[6] The massive influx of Polish manpower goes back to 1919 (after the Warsaw Treaty) and after peaking in the 1920s, continued but at lower level during the 1930s.[7]

Immigration to France resumed after the second World War and the beginning of the 1960s and was marked by arrivals from the Iberian Peninsula, followed a much larger influx from North Africa. Owing to earlier colonial ties, and for various economic reasons, France finds itself at

---

[4]Some research on European immigration divides the policies of immigration into two categories: the rotation system (Gastarbeiter) in Germany and in Switzerland, and permanent migration in Great Britain and Sweden. Immigration in France can be placed inbetween. Cf. T. Hammar ed., *European Immigration Policy,* New York, 1986, p. 260.

[5]G. Noiriel, *Le Creuset Français,* Paris, 1988.

[6]P. Milza, 'Un siècle d'Immigration Etrangère en France', in *Vingtième Siècle, Revue d'Histoire,* 7, 1985, pp.3-17.

[7]J. Ponty, 'Une Intégration Difficile: Les Polonais en France', in *Ibid.*, pp. 51-59.

the moment with foreign manpower that is predominantly North African: 562,300 North Africans out of a foreign active population of 1,556,260 (or 36 per cent).[8]

As for Germany, even though it has been a country of emigration, industrialisation, or rather the transition from 'an agricultural state with a large industry to an industrial state with an important agricultural basis' at the end of the last century provoked, first of all, an internal migration from Prussia.[9] These migrants were of German nationality but of Polish 'ethnic' origin. Before the Great War, other Poles, coming this time from Russia and Galicia ('foreign Poles'), settled in Prussia. The movement grew with migrants from Austria, Hungary, Italy, the Netherlands and Denmark. After the 1950s, Federal Germany adopted the policy of Gastarbeiter, according to which foreign manpower, drawn by work, would stay in Germany only provisionally. Thus the Federal Republic signed bilateral agreements with different countries of the Mediterranean to organise control of foreign manpower.[10] Amongst these countries, Turkey has become the greatest provider of labour: 1,546,300 Turks have become the target of the media and the focus of Parliamentary debates in Germany.

Until 1974, immigration in France was called 'spontaneous' because of a generally laissez-faire policy, of the lack of coordination of inflows of foreign workers (in spite of the creation of the ONI, the Office National de l'Immigration and of the SSAE, the Service Social pour l'Aide aux Etrangers), and because of the heterogeneous nature of the immigrant population. This lack of a conscious and organised immigration policy led, in fact, to a policy of assimilation of the foreign elements in French society. The ex-post regularisation of illegal immigrants confirms this implicit policy. In Germany by way of contrast, the bilateral agreements with the migrants' countries of origin have underlined the provisional character of their stay. The aim has been to prevent the integration of foreign workers and their families in German society.

---

[8]Not to speak of the French whose original nationality was North African. See INSEE, *General Population Census of 1982*, Paris,1982.

[9]K. J. Bade, 'Labour, Migration and the State: Germany from the late 19th century to the Onset of the Great Depression', in K.J. Bade ed., *Population, Labour and Migration in 19th and 20th Century Germany,* Berg, 1987, pp.59-87.

[10]These agreements were signed with Italy (1955); Spain and Greece (1960); Turkey (1961); later with Portugal (1964); Tunisia (1965); Morocco (1963 and 1966) and lastly with Yugoslavia (1968); See Hammar ed., *European Migration Policy,* pp. 165-205.

Policies of Immigration

In practice, since the 1960s, the need of most migrants to secure their own accommodation demonstrates the absence of a systematic policy in France. The spontaneous and massive arrival of migrants after the fifties gave rise to the creation of shanty towns - housing improvised by the migrants. The construction of homes for a few isolated migrants (by Sonacotra in 1957, then by the FAS, the social action fund in 1959) occurred only toward the end of the sixties. The policy (not of housing but of 'rehousing') that could be seen from the beginning of the sixties with the construction of tower blocks and of suburban towns did not answer the needs of immigrant workers specifically but catered more generally to the marginalised and badly housed population of the private sector.

In Germany, the housing of 'visitors' followed the logic of the rotation system. As soon as they arrived, the Gastarbeiter were settled in homes (*Heime*) established by their employers. This paternalistic formula aimed at preventing family regrouping, since the foreign workers had to show proof of adequate housing in order to be able to bring over the members of their family. Paradoxically, these obstacles contributed to the growing ethnic solidarity. The functions of the relation networks within the immigrant groups have been reinforced thereby and contribute in effect to the segregation of immigrant families. In certain big town neighbourhoods, large concentrations of immigrants of the same nationality conjure up the image of ethnic ghettoes as defined by the Chicago School. For example in Berlin, Turkish families are concentrated in a few neighbourhoods considered by the media and public opinion as the 'Turkish ghetto'.[11]

In Kreuzberg, nicknamed *kleine Istanbul*, Turks make up 67.8 per cent of the foreigners and 16.88 per cent of the total population.[12] The neighbourhood is an expression of the Turkish community, with its abundance of mosques, its cultural activities, function rooms, all kinds of ethnic type commerce, its Turkish libraries and the existence of intermediary services between Turkey and Germany (travel agencies for Turkey and for Mecca, funeral services, banks, transport and removal firms). The frequency of signs in Turkish, windows that show Turkish products, the language

---

[11] R. Kastoryano, 'Paris-Berlin: Politiques d'Immigration et Modalités d'Intégration des Familles Immigrées Turques', in R. Leveau and G. Kepel eds., *Les Musulmans dans la Société Française,* Paris, 1988, pp.140-169.

[12] Statistics of the Berlin Senate.

spoken in the street, all point to the transplantation of a Turkish micro-society and define the boundaries of the neighbourhood.[13]

In France, because of the lack of a housing policy, the networks of inter-ethnic relations contribute to the integration of immigrant families in the urban fabric, without creating ethnic ghettoes. However these types of solidarity among national minorities lead to forms of community organisation around a common language and religion. Taking account of the evolution of immigrants in France, certain authors call these areas 'reserved' neighbourhoods.[14] France has never organised specific education for immigrant children, even if it tolerated Polish lessons by teachers of Polish origin in the 1920s. French schools are republican and secular, and they are dominated by the principle of equality of opportunity; the institutionalised logic of equality of treatment has always treated foreign children as if they were French.[15] In the Federal Republic of Germany, on the other hand, the education of foreign children, which varies from state to state *(Land)*, fluctuates from a strategy of integration to a strategy aiming at re-integration in the country of origin by the maintenance of the culture. The policy has consisted in educating the Gastarbeiters' children by sending them to classes where the teaching was in their maternal language (on the basis of the argument calling for not separating the immigrants from their original culture). Even after 1981, the only concession to the integration of children in normal secondary school classes (preparatory lessons, bilingual classes, intensive German lessons) was part of a policy of 'temporary integration' of young foreigners. These strategies have constituted one of the elements of the rotation system, and represent an application of the basic principle of immigration policy.

Integration Policies

With the end of immigration in 1974 and the settlement of foreign populations, the problem depends on the terms of integration.[16] We are

---

[13] A. Gitmer, C. Wilpert, 'A Micro-society or an Ethnic Community? Social Organisation and Ethnicity Amongst Turkish Migrants in Berlin', in J. Rex, D. Joly and C. Wilpert eds., *Immigrants' Association in Europe*, London, 1987.

[14] E. Temime uses the expression 'habitat réservé' where new solidarities are established and where cultural characteristics are found; see his 'Marseille, Villes de Migrations', *Vingtième Siècle, Revue d'Histoire,* 7, 1985, pp.37-51.

[15] S. Boulot, D. Boyzon-Fradet, 'Ecole Française: Egalité des Chances et Logiques d'une Institution', in *L'Immigration en Europe et aux Etats-Unis,* Paris, 1988.

[16] Cf. G. Tapinos, 'L'Immigration en France', *Commentaire*, 11, 1988, pp. 692-703.

presently witnessing a convergence in the definition of public policies in housing and education in France and in Germany.

The German government is forced to develop a policy of integration' for those who remain' so as to avoid a 'structural marginalisation'.[17] To disperse the migrant families in the urban fabric and reduce their prominence, the FRG has adopted a policy that limits the quota of a national population in the same town or even in the same neighbourhood to 12 per cent.[18] The surplus is directed to new housing built for the working class in order to promote social integration. These lodgings correspond, as much in construction style as in intention, to tower blocks in France.

A policy of integration has especially been established for the schooling of the children of immigrants. First of all, to reduce the linguistic barriers, the government has taken measures to limit the proportion of foreign children of the same nationality to 20 per cent. The successive regulations, after 1981, to prepare children better for normal secondary school classes (preparatory lessons, bilingual classes, intensive German classes) have had as principal aim the 'temporary integration' of young foreigners.[19] The most important measures taken with this perspective in mind have consisted of professional training in the shape of apprenticeship, with a view to giving young foreigners a technical qualification and start them in the labour market as qualified apprentices. These provisional integration strategies are already a modification of the rotation system: the principle that Gastarbeiter policy is based on.

The French in the meantime have moved a little in the other direction. An integration policy to diminish the school failure rate in France has proposed 'looking for a solution based on the cultural identity' of the recent arrivals. This motivation has led France to sign agreements with the immigrants' countries of origin and to introduce, in various ways, an education (at least a partial one) in their language and culture.

Thus, whatever the conscious or unconscious reasons, justified and formulated in different ways, of the political traditions and experiences with populations of foreign origin, Germany and France have been led to adjust their immigration policies and to redefine their integration policies. Germany

---

[17]*Parliamentary Debates,* 1973, p. 2084.

[18]L. Holzner, 'The Myth of Turkish Ghettoes: a Geographic Case of West German Responses toward a Foreign Minority', *The Journal of Ethnic Studies*, 9, 1982, pp. 65-87.

[19]R. Rogers ed., *Guests Come to Stay: the Effects of European Labor Migration in Sending and Receiving Countries,* New York, 1985, pp.1-28.

has been forced to take measures that imply the transformation of Gastarbeiter into permanent workers (immigrants), while France has taken measures that suppose that not all immigrants are trying to assimilate, and has favoured their integration by recognising their original culture.

II. The effects of Immigration Policies

The effects of the immigration policies are problematic. Research on the education of immigrant children in France, for example, shows the failure of the specific educational policies based on recognition of cultural origin (multicultural or intercultural). Migrants seem to manifest a greater will for integration and demand, in the long run, equal treatment and opportunities. In the FRG, on the other hand, the application of a multicultural policy seems to have the reverse effect of maintaining the migrants' aim of returning to their original country.

There also exists a contradictory dynamic between integration policies and the expectations of the populations in question on the one hand, and on the other hand, between the definition of these policies and public opinion. Thus the effects of public policies appear in the social organisation of immigrant groups, in the use of previous relation networks, in family and national solidarity, and in the expectations and expression of group identity.

The policies of urban, economic, cultural or even political integration fit the aspirations of the migrant when they favour social climbing. The realisation of social mobility in the immigrant country comes up against the hostility of public opinion, which situates the latest arrivals at the bottom of the social ladder. According to Michael Hechter's theories, this ethnic division of labour should lead to 'ethnic persistence'.[20] In fact, this ethnic persistence can take on for some, an aspect of collective action with the aim of maintaining identity while at the same time furthering social promotion by means of economic integration.

Social Organisation

Community organisations provide intergenerational continuity. The generation born, brought up, and educated in France is organised now around cooperatives that tend to perpetuate identity and to affirm a certain kind of

---

[20]M. Hechter, 'Ethnicity and Industrialization: on the Proliferation of the Cultural Division of Labor', *Ethnicity,* 3, 1976, pp.214-224.

presence in France. Following the law which permitted the cooperative activities by foreigners in 1981, a proliferation of cultural, religious and national institutions has occurred. This situation has, first and foremost, an ambiguous significance: does it mean of the affirmation of a cultural particularity or, on the contrary, of a will to integrate in the larger society?

At the beginning, the associative movement of North African migrants and of young people born of this immigration demanded public recognition of their identity, with religion (Islam) at the centre. In effect the regrouping in certain neighbourhoods led to collective action on behalf of Muslim families who wanted local authorities, with or without the country of origin's agreement, to permit or provide prayer rooms and Qur'anic lessons for children. Research on Islam in France shows that much money has been raised for this purpose.[21] According to de Wenden, the North African associations have a 'tendency to manipulate the zoning codes by playing on the public v. private spheres, through the extended family's control on linguistic and cultural links'.[22]

The length of stay and the forms of young people's integration, as well as their aspirations and expectations have led to changes in the associations. Youth reaction to the Commission des Sages on the reform of the Nationality Code in December 1987, to the presidential election (May 1988) and finally recently to local elections of March 1989, show a will to participate in the national political game.

The situation presents itself differently in Germany. The measures to disperse the immigrant population in towns, have paradoxically contributed to the increase of ethnic solidarity. In Berlin the efforts to avoid ghettoisation of certain neighbourhood have been thwarted by a growth in the Turkish population due to family regrouping. The Turks in Kreuzberg amount to 19.3 per cent of the general population of Berlin. In spite of the decision to limit the number of foreign children of the same nationality to 20 per cent in primary and secondary schools, the Berlin Senate has estimated this percentage to be 85 per cent in Kreuzberg.

A public opinion hostile to foreigners and a policy of 'temporary integration' (vocational training for the young that will also be useful when and if they return to their country of origin) is always a reminder of the provisional character of their stay. The difficulties encountered by young

---

[21]G. Kepel, *Les Banlieues de l'Islam*, Paris, 1987.

[22]C. de Wenden, 'Dossier: Immigration, Citoyenneté et Nationalité', *Les Cahiers de l'Orient*, 1988, pp.115-141.

people on the labour market, in spite of periods of apprenticeship probation, drive them to seek refuge in previous connections (the extended family or their parents' country of origin) or ethnic networks developed in the country of immigration (by the neighbourhood, the work place or the children's school). This leads to a closure which is manifested economically by the development of 'ethnic business'.[23] The existence of 2000 businesses or small Turkish family enterprises and 5000 employees of the same origin shows the integrative function of the relational network.[24]

Beginning in 1981, Turkish associations have proliferated. This is explained by the length of stay but also by the massive arrival of political refugees after the Turkish *coup d'état* (1980). As opposed to associative movement of the young North Africans in France, the social actions of Turkish migrants in Germany are intended to perpetuate national and religious identity. For example, Muslim associations in Berlin united under the Islamic Federation, which was created in 1981 with the aim of obtaining recognition of Islam and an end to clandestine Qur'anic lessons. Even though Turkey is a secular country, Islam in Germany is Turkish (as opposed to Islam in France, which is North African). The institutionalisation of religion in a minority situation and its public representation make observance and practices more acceptable and legitimate, especially for the young generations born and brought up in Europe.

Apart from the desire to gain religious recognition, the politisation of Islam as Turkish in a situation of migration asserts itself just as does the national identity by the transposition of Turkish political parties to Germany, with the same division and conflicts as in Turkey.[25] The associative movement, in spite of judicial restrictions in terms of the rights of foreigners, has expanded after the coup in Turkey (1980) with the arrival of the asylum seekers. All political, national and religious actions are consequently geared toward the country of origin.

The size and variety of the Turkish immigration in Germany has also led to the forming of new groups such as sporting and cultural (literature-handicrafts) associations. The actions undertaken by these organisations are

---

[23]Cf. I. Light, *Ethnic Enterprise in America,* Berkeley, 1977; E. Bonachic and J. Modell, *The Economic Basis of Ethnic Solidarity,* Berkeley, 1980.

[24]See Gitmer and Wilpert, 'A Micro-society'.

[25]Political parties in Turkey are represented by associations like the Islamic Cultural Centre (political organization of the Sülaymanci), the Independent Turk (offshoot of the Party of National Salvation) etc.

directed neither towards Turkey nor towards Germany, but towards the recognition of the presence of Turks and their rights as migrants. The mobilisation of the children Turkish immigrants to obtain from Turkey a reduction in the fine paid to serve a shorter term of military service illustrates this point.[26] The organised mobilisation of the young and their effectiveness confirm the fact that they identify with the status that has been given them from one side or another. The new bilateral agreements between the two countries appear like a type of regulation of the original rotation system, and aim to institutionalise social (even legal) marginalisation, and not to encourage integration into German society.[27]

The Expression of Collective Identities

The social organisation of the immigrant groups is carried out apart from state policies, which have limited effects on the constitution of a community and on the structuring of relational networks, in short on the formation of ethnic solidarities.[28] Even so, the expression of collective identities is the result of interaction and negotiation between the states and the groups in question. The concept of identity is a dynamic concept and varies according to circumstances and interactions with the 'other'.

The new politics of the young immigrant populations in France stresses the expectations of public recognition of their cultural particularities. This is felt by some French as a threat to the 'homogeneity' of the nation-state. Considering the French Jacobin tradition, public opinion casts doubt on the North African migrants' 'capacity' to assimilate. The French and the Germans insist here on the cultural gap, on the link between religion and politics in Islam, and on the different conceptions of private law.

The Muslim Turkish presence in Germany provokes reactions comparable to those observed in France, even though the history of relations between Germany and Turkey is different and constitutes a non-negligible element of the expression of Turkish migrants' identity in Germany

---

[26]For several years, Turkey has adopted a policy of reducing the length of military service from two years to two months, by asking the young born of immigration to pay the equivalent of 10,000 dollars in foreign currency to replenish the state budget.

[27]C. Wilpert, 'Turkish Associations in Berlin', presented to the seminar organised at the CERI (Centre d'Etudes et de Recherches Internationales) on the policies of immigration in Europe and in the United States, Paris, 21-22 April 1988.

[28]See R. Kastoryano, 'Paris-Berlin'.

The French State tradition derived from the monarchy and imbued with the principles of the 1789 Revolution, projects itself as universal, egalitarian, rational, individualistic and secular. The republican tradition seeks to absorb all the differences and ensure the political and cultural unity of the nation; political integration implies cultural integration, even the 'assimilation' of individuals. The voluntarist conception of the French nation gives national institutions the task of assimilating all foreign culture and of developing a single identity. Participation in political life relegates cultural and religious specificities to the private sphere.

The desire of the young to be integrated into French political life appears in their concern to be registered with various political parties, and for some of the immigrant leaders, to seek positions in the candidates' lists.

Joining French political parties across the spectrum shows also both the immigrants' use of their rights as French citizens and the affirmation of their Berber or Franco-North African identity. The drive towards integration into the Jacobin state in ways similar to those of the precedent waves of immigrants leads them to demand a *secular Islam* imbued with the democratic values of Republican France. In this way Islam can still constitute the basic identity of the children of the North African immigration and manifest their attachment to family and culture of origin. A secular Islam is used as a ploy, as an element of negotiation with public authorities and a way of winning acceptance as a legitimate movement within a secular country.[29]

Against the rationalist universality of the French Revolution, the German national idea is based on a community of culture, of language and of blood. The expression *Deutsches Volk* underlines the importance of belonging to the German people. This ethnocultural conception of the nation excludes all cultural differences: cultural homogeneity and the organic characteristics of the national community are inscribed in the definition of the nation. As opposed to the French case, which places the individual face to face with the state, Germany recognises the Turkish state as sole interlocutor between the German state and the Turkish immigrants, thereby confirming their foreign status.

However, to avoid indoctrination of the young by the Turkish national/religious associations, German authorities have asked themselves about the possibility of introducing Islamic religious education in the state

[29] Partial results of the research on the political participation of migrants in France, coordinated by R. Kastoryano and executed by the migration team of CERI.

schools (in the same way as Catholicism and Protestantism).[30] This approach sees the immigrant families in Germany as a group represented by formal associations with which official bodies can negotiate their religious identity.

In the same vein, the right to a local vote and dual nationality constitutes a subject of negotiation between ethnic institutions and official bodies. This has become one of the planks in the electoral campaign of some of the political parties. Even if the parties have different points of view concerning the right to a local vote, the (political) Turkish associations of various tendencies seem to expect, with equal conviction, the introduction of the concept of dual nationality into the German Nationality Code.

The importance of national identity, both Turkish and German, is thus at the basis of negotiations between Turkish immigrant groups and the German state. This duality underlines the attachment to the idea of citizenship and to political traditions in Germany on the one hand, and the attachment to the national (Turkish) identity of migrants and of their children on the other. The combination is at the heart of the debate on political integration and constitutes a new approach in dealing with the problem of immigration in the FRG.

Conclusion

In the collective action and political mobilisation of the young born in North Africa (for France) and Turkey (for Germany), immigration carries a desire to integrate by accepting the rules of the political game as much as the specificities of identity (cultural, religious and national). The negotiations between the structured groups and the state or official bodies in the integration strategies value the two forms of education of immigrants' children: family rearing and education by the national institutions of the country of immigration.

Of course, the historical foundations of the nation and the relations between Turkey and Germany on the one hand, and between North Africa and France on the other hand, explain why integration policies and immigrant expectations are different. Public opinion reacts to religious identity, i.e. Islam, as the common denominator of migrants' identity. For some who claim a secular Islam, which reserves the system of belief for the private sphere,

30 The suggestions are by the *Ausländerbeauftragten*, an official institution founded in 1980 by the cabinet of ministers whose function is to give advice to the Federal Government in matters concerning the integration of foreign workers and their families in the FRG.

there may be possibilities of negotiations with the state. But the identification of immigrant populations with their new home, even if it does not exclude the possibility of naturalisation, is based primarily on an economic calculation. As a result, the link to politics is essentially instrumental; and this is an implicit challenge to the traditional, affective basis of nationality and citizenship and the normative character of the nation-state.[31]

The evolution of immigration is part of the debate about Europe. The construction of Europe manifests itself not only by a need to affirm the national identity of each nation-state, but also by a mobilisation on behalf of the immigrant groups of transnational networks and the creation of new ethnic solidarities. What is the place of these outsiders in the new Europe?

In this regard, European countries are now examining integration of non-European populations. The answer to this question will require the harmonisation of legislation. One possible outcome would be the creation of an international status and identity with equal treatment for foreigners and nationals.[32]

For the non-European immigrant worker, it is the economic dimension of 'unified Europe' which has priority, because work justifies his presence in the country of residence. Europe runs the risk thereby of encouraging a conception of nationality or of citizenship that would be linked more to jobs and social protection than to the conscience of a common political past, present and future.[33] Beyond the idea of an economic citizenship one can see emerging the conception of citizenship through choice: the choice of the country of 'main settlement'.[34]

---

[31] R. Kastoryano, 'Définition des Frontières de l'Identité: Turcs Musulmans', *Revue Française de Sciences Politiques*, 37:6, 1987, pp.833-855.

[32] See the works of J. Costa-Lascoux on citizenship in France and in Europe: 'Filiations et Dépendances Institutionnelles: la Seconde Génération', *Revue Européenne des Migrations Internationales,* 1:2, 1985, pp.21-41; 'L'Acquisition de la Citoyenneté Française, une Condition d'Intégration?', in S. Laacher ed., *Questions de Nationalité: Histoire et Enjeux d'un Code,* Paris, 1986, pp.86-125; 'Citoyenneté au-delà du Sol et du Sang', presented at colloquium on 'l'Immigration en Europe et aux Etats-Unis', Paris, CERI, 21-22 April 1988.

[33] It is interesting to note that in the 1920s, an Argentinian named J.C. Garay proposed a partial status of citizenship of work (*jus laboris*) for immigrants. This status would confer civic rights in the country of residence without their losing citizenship in their country of origin. See E Audinet, 'The jus laboris and the automatic citizenship of foreigners', *Revue Algérienne, Tunisienne et Marocaine de Législation et de Jurisprudence,* XLIII, 1927, 1ère partie, pp. 73-77. I owe this reference to D.S. Landes.

[34] J. Costa-Lascoux, 'La Citoyenneté: un Choix?', *Hérodote,* 50-51, 198, pp.120-138.

10. ISLAMIC LAW, GENDER AND THE POLICIES OF EXILE

THE PALESTINIANS IN WEST BERLIN: A CASE STUDY*

Dima Abdulrahim

Researchers of Muslim societies have, in recent years, focused on the mutability of Islamic law, and on its variations in terms of social and temporal context as well as in relation with legislative authorities.[1] These variations reaffirm that the Pakistani, Malaysian and Bosnian families, for example, are not an elaboration of the same Muslim family, in contrast to the prevailing approach which is fashionable in the world of the media and academia, and which tends to disregard historical, socio-economic, political legal, national, ethnic and cultural variations.

It is true that in the West, Muslim communities share the Qur'an, their minority position and their relationship with a society that separates church from state. But as families in the Muslim world differ, neither the family itself nor its relationship with the household is unchanging. The *shari'a* undoubtedly plays a role in the regulation of the framework of social and gender relations, but in the historical development of particular families, gender relations are also determined by class and by social, cultural and political factors. Family law regulates social and gender relations which are not static but change in form and meaning.

The historical development of the Palestinian family in exile shows that the interpretation of family law, like the understanding of the nature of gender relations, has been subject to transformation. Over the last four decades, the family has been defined by the marginality of Palestinian refugee status, its development through participation in the national struggle and an independent state-like structure, and finally as a minority family in Western Europe.

The reaffirmation of the unequal nature of gender relations in the application of the shari'a in society is not sufficient. A social analysis of law has to focus on the historical specificities that determine the nature of such relations and the form they take. If the inequality of the sexes remains, the socio-economic and ideological conditions which define it have changed; as have the states in which it exists. If social research can contribute to legal reforms, it cannot ignore the role of the state in maintaining forms of inequality or, on the contrary, in providing conditions that make new definitions possible and legitimate.

---

*This study is based on field work in West Berlin. All names mentioned in the study have been changed.

[1]See Aziz Azmeh ed., *Islamic Law: Social and Historical Contexts*, London, 1988.

Historical Background of the Palestinian Exile

In the period following the 1948 exile from Palestine, and for around two decades, the majority of the Palestinian population in Lebanon remained marginal to the socio-economic and political make up of the Lebanese state. Their marginality was officially sanctioned, and partially defined by their status of non citizen and their exclusion from voting rights. Palestinians were placed under the jurisdiction of the General Bureau of Palestinian Affairs which regulated matters such as travel and movement from one camp to another. Coercive forces were found in the camps in the form of police stations or Lebanese army intelligence, and matters of personal status were governed by the religious courts of the various sects, in conjunction with the Bureau of Palestinian Affairs. In spite of the activities of the United Nations Work and Relief Agency (UNRWA) in the camps, including their distribution of food rations, employment was necessary from first day of exile but was restricted by Lebanese labour regulations for foreigners.

Within the camp communities, uprooted Palestinian family and village groups lived in extremely crowded conditions, but managed to regroup along such lines. The family, transported to the camp and redefined by its conditions, took on a crucial role as a social, economic and psychological security system.[2] Customary law regulated conflict independently from the Lebanese authorities and aimed at maximising cohesion in the refugee camps. This comprehensive legal system accounted for the involvement of kinship and village groups in personal disputes and gave the party of the victim the institutionalised possibility to express its grief or anger and its wish to seek revenge through *fawret ad-damm* (the overflowing of blood). Violence was however contained, as neutral mediators whose decision was binding to the two parties secured a truce (*'atwi*) before reaching a settlement.

Between the late 1960s and the 1982 Israeli invasion of Lebanon, Palestinians enjoyed, for the first time in centuries, a degree of autonomous control over their own affairs. As the Palestinian resistance movement developed in the camps, a state-like structure was created under the Palestine Liberation Organisation (PLO). This structure developed a centrally directed socio-economic infrastructure, provided political representation, employment, a legal system, a court, social benefits and a health service. Within the camp communities, a Palestinian political identity was developed and new loyalties were formed.[3]

The application of the new social and political ideology based itself, among other tenets, on the unity of the people and the promotion of integration. The PLO was represented among the camp community by local leaders of political organisations, trade unions and women's associations and popular committees. It instituted its own legal system and its own law

---

[2]See for example Rosemary Sayigh, *Palestinians: From Peasants to Revolutionaries*, London, 1979, pp. 127-130.

[3]Bassem Sirhan, 'Palestinian Refugee Life in Lebanon', *Journal of Palestine Studies,* 4, 1975, pp. 106-107.

enforcement agencies and court. A multi-faceted process of cultural reconstruction was therein identified by Peteet:

> On the one hand, new social forms were incorporated into the existing framework and thus acquired meaning; on the other hand, traditions, rather than being cast away as useless vestiges of the past, were revitalised to take on a national and progressive meaning. This social process involved not only a revitalization of some aspects of traditional culture such as folk art but also a transformation of social institutions and social relations... The national and patriotic context in which this process of reconstruction unfolded lent it an aura of legitimacy and made possible the introduction of new forms of social relations.[4]

The family was identified by Peteet and others as one of such institutions as it was transformed into a source of recruitment, mobilisation, politicisation and political education. The legitimisation given by the national context to cultural transformation was observed in the parameters of women's role in society and was seen, for example, in the parent's acceptance of the mandatory military training of high school girls a year before the 1982 Israeli invasion.[5]

As the ideological unity of the Palestinian people actively incorporated all sectors of the population, it also included women. Not only was the presence of women in the revolution and the PLO legitimate, but the revolution was perceived to be that of women, as it was that of every Palestinian. The Palestinian woman's movement was incorporated into the national movement. The relationship between the two was summarised in the closing declaration of the General Union of Palestinian Women, which called for 'participation of the Arab Palestinian woman in all aspects of the organisation and struggle, and for her equality with males in all rights and privileges for the purpose of liberating the homeland'.[6]

Slogans of 'organic' unity between the woman's movement and the national movement are considered by Rosemary Sayigh to have been essential for the legitimisation of women's involvement in the struggle, but also for blocking the development of women's conciousness of their own history. The struggle demanded the unity of the sexes, but there was no equality in this unity.[7] Except for some notable cases, a woman's role was that of support and continued being dictated by her social position. Her involvement and participation in the struggle remained determined by traditional forms of patriarchal control and domination. No radical transformation of the division

[4]Julie Peteet, 'Conflict Resolution in the Palestinian Camps in Lebanon', *Journal of Palestine Studies*, 16, 1987, p. 32.

[5]*Ibid.* p. 32.

[6]Quoted in Ghazi al-Khali, *Al-Mar'a al Filistiniyya wath-Thawra*, Beirut, 1977, p. 105.

[7]Rosemary Sayigh, 'Femmes Palestiniennes: une Histoire en Quête d'Historiens,' *Revue d'Etudes Palestiniennes*, 23, 1987, p. 7.

of labour took place, and thus no change in the asymmetrical nature of gender relations.[8]

However, while radical transformation of social relations did not take place, new socio-economic and ideological conditions redefined gender relations. Despite its reaffirmation of gender roles, the state-like structure constituted a threat to family authority by taking over its role of social and economic security system and by weakening loyalty to family and village groups. The presence of the PLO in the camps meant that an area of socio-economic activity existed outside the family and gave women legitimate activity outside the household. Loyalty to the political organisation established a new type of relation between the sexes. Political affiliation meant that legitimate contact not sanctioned by kinship or marriage ties was possible, and implied that gender relations were not necessarily defined by their sexual nature. Participation of women in the struggle often involved unsegregated activities outside the home.

The politicisation of women was itself significant as it implied their presence and activity in areas that have been defined as man's domain. Women's participation was made possible in all Palestinian refugee camps by the establishment of services such as day-care centres and nurseries. Problems of economic participation were addressed by the provision of employment and by the promotion of literacy, skills and technical training. Within the household, young women's ability to impose their own decisions was enhanced. Their ability to choose their own marriage partner increased, as did the importance of their consent to marriage.

The opposition of the family to the political participation of women was generally met with the intervention of political cadres on behalf of the women. Cadres also intervened in cases of domestic violence, the marriage of women against their will and other matters such as divorce. In the settlement of conflicts, the circumvention of Islamic and customary law by the PLO through new procedural restrictions was becoming widespread and met with little opposition.[9] However, in the development of a formal Palestinian legal structure and culture, matters of personal status were not explicitly defined: only one political organisation made polygamy grounds for expulsion.

In 1982, a Palestinian woman political leader asked the General Union of Palestinian Women to prepare legislative reforms on family law to be applied by the Palestinian revolution.[10] The reforms, however, were preceded by the Israeli invasion and the evacuation of the formal Palestinian structures and

---

[8]Hamida Kazi, 'Palestinian Women and the National Liberation Movement: a Social Perspective', *Khamsin* (Issue on Women in the Middle East), 1987, pp. 26-40.

[9]See generally J. Peteet, 'No Going Back, Women and the Palestinian Movement', *Merip Report*, 16, 1986; Yvonne Haddad, 'Palestinian Women: Patterns of Legimization and Domination', in K. Nakhleh and E. Zureik eds., *The Sociology of the Palestinians*, London, 1980. Khadijeh Abu 'Ali, *Muqaddima hawla Waqi' al Mar'a wa Tajribatiha fith-Thawra al-Filistiniyya,* Beirut, 1975. R. Sayigh and J. Peteet, 'Between Two Fires: Palestinian Women in Lebanon', in R. Ridd ed., *Caught up in Conflict*, Basingstoke, 1986.

[10]Sayigh, 'Femmes Palestiniennes', p. 20.

institutions from Lebanon. The evacuation of the PLO reduced to a very large extent the control of Palestinians over their own affairs and meant a certain dismemberment of the social, economic and legal institutions attached to the organization.

Political Asylum in West Berlin

Like many foreigners from the so-called 'Third World' in West Berlin, Palestinians were, until recently, asylum seekers. They arrived from the refugee camps in Lebanon from the mid 1970s, generally following outbursts of war or massacres.[11] Large waves of Palestinians arrived in the FRG in 1982 after the Israeli invasion of Lebanon, and were joined by other groups from Lebanon, namely Kurds and Shi'i and Sunni Muslim Lebanese. They entered the FRG, like others, by the well-documented route through East Berlin (made much more difficult and expensive after 1986, by a deal struck between the two Germanies).[12] Around 15,000 Palestinians lived in West Berlin in 1988, but accurate figures are impossible to gather.[13] Palestinians were not registered under one coherent national or other category, but were classified as 'Lebanese' - on account of Lebanese issued travel documents for Palestinian refugees - 'stateless', and more recently, *'ungeklärt'* (undetermined or unsettled).[14]

The arrival of Palestinians in the mid 1970s, like that of other asylum

---

[11]*Projekt zur Unterstützung palästinensischer und libanesischer Flüchtlingen in Westberlin,* (Report on the Situation of the Lebanese and Palestinian Refugees in West Berlin), Berlin, 1983, p.1.

[12]For more details see 'Nicht unmöglich aber... Politisches Asyl wird teurer', *Passport,* 15, 1987, p. 3-4.

[13]The unavailability of statistics on Palestinians is a result of a number of factors. Asylum seekers have been in the last two decades a sensitive issue in West German politics and were turned throughout the FRG into a major election issue. The attitude to foreign asylum seekers and that of the CDU party in power came under strong criticism. Within their own ranks, a formal working paper by parliamentary members of the CDU talked about the overdramatisation of the asylum problem and the deliberately 'sloppy' statistics of the ministry. The working paper stated that the official statistics of June 1986 listed 673,000 refugees, an estimated 200,000 more than the actual number. 'CDU Asylum Politics: Criticism from the Ranks', *Passport*, 16, 1987, pp. 7-8. Palestinians have been lumped under three different categories, making it impossible to determine accurate figures. Under the 'stateless' category, for example, it is difficult to differentiate them from Kurds, Poles and others. However, figures have been calculated by a number of organisations and estimates such as those from the Protestant Church indicate that there are probably 15,000 asylum seekers from Lebanon. *Dokumentation,* Frankfurt am Main, 1 April 1985, p.100. Another slightly higher estimate of 16,000 has been calculated by G. Dassen and U. Haupt for the *Projekt zur Unterstützung*, p. 1.

[14]In January 1985 , the Federal Authorities informed all offices concerned with foreigners that Palestinians were not stateless but ungeklärt or of 'unsettled' nationality. The change came as an indirect result of the Convention Relating to the Status of Stateless Persons of 1954, which gives the stateless individual similar rights to those of recognised refugees. Article 28 of the Convention Relating to the Status of Stateless Persons of 1954 was used by a number of lawyers to procure their clients with travel documents as it stipulates that states shall issue travel documents to stateless persons lawfully staying in their territories.

seekers from non-Christian and non-white backgrounds, coincided in the Federal Republic of Germany with the beginnings of economic recession, unemployment and a resurgence of xenophobia. Two main tenets defined asylum policy: the non-recognition of the majority of asylum seekers from the Third World as political refugees, and the establishment of difficult living conditions ('measures of deterrence' making asylum seekers want to leave voluntarily and deterring potential new arrivals).[15]

Policies of asylum aimed at segregation of asylum seekers and the circumscription of boundaries of social and economic activity. As the socio-economic integration of claimants of refugee status was 'conciously and expressly deterred',[16] asylum seekers were made dependent and easier to control. Asylum procedures aimed at the processing of individuals as fast as possible; their outcome was either the integration of the asylum seeker into the majority community through mechanisms provided for recognised refugees, or expulsion from the country.

The legal basis for determining refugee status and the grant of asylum is found in the 1949 Basic law (*Politisch Verfolgte geniessen Asylrecht)*, the 1965 Aliens Law (AslG) and most particularly the 1982 and the revised 1985 Asylum Procedure Law. The revision of 1985, like those of the laws of 1982 intended to speed up proceedings and cut back the opportunities for judicial review. This helped provide for prompt departure or removal of rejected applicants.[17]

Refugee status was determined by the Federal Office for the Recognition of Foreign Refugees (*Bundesamt für die Anerkennung ausländischer Flüchtlinge*). A federal commissioner for asylum affairs, appointed by the Minister of the Interior, however, had the right to challenge the decision of the Bundesamt in the proceedings and before the administrative court. Although there was no appeal if the application was declined, the decision remained open to review by the Administrative Court in the applicant's place of residence. A final judgement of the Administrative Court could be reached only if the appelant is given leave to appeal by that court or by the Higher Administrative Court.[18]

As the legal proceedings extended for a period of around 5 years, little or no chance existed for the recognition of Palestinians as persecuted political refugees. Their deportation, like that of Lebanese and Kurds from Lebanon, was not always possible and was often delayed by the regular closure of the Beirut airport. In the mid-1980s, and especially after attacks on Palestinians in Beirut and South Lebanon, an organised opposition to deportations was set up. This opposition provided, among other things, a sanctuary network and was

[15]See for example the report of the meeting between N. von Nieding and UNHCR officials in the report produced by the Mission to the FRG, 1 July 1983, p. 6.

[16]K. Marx, 'The Political, Social and Legal Status of Aliens and Refugees in the FRG', in C. Fried ed., *Minorities: Community and Identity*, Berlin, 1983, p. 277.

[17]See Gill Goodwin, *The Refugee in International Law,* Oxford, 1983, pp.174-178.

[18]For more details on the legal problems relating to Palestinian asylum seekers and on problems of recognitions, see Max Reinhart, *Asylrecht*, Vol. 1, 4th ed. Baden Baden, 1984.

given some legitimacy by the involvement of the Protestant church and the bishop of Berlin.[19]

As the deportation (*Abschiebung*) of asylum seekers was often temporarily halted, they were issued with Tolerance Permits (*Aufenthalsduldung* or *Duldung*), which did not give a right of residence, but a temporary permit pending deportation. Tolerance permits were generally given when expulsion orders were legally in force, but some considerations - such as wars, famines, droughts- precluded immediate deportation. Not all rejected asylum seekers were, however, given such a permit, as some were issued with a *Bescheinigung* (certificate) which neither stated what was certified exactly, nor constituted an identity document or mentioned the suspension of expulsion. This certificate, given to 'criminals' and *Pendler*, was renewed every two to four weeks and placed its holders under the most serious threat of deportation.[20] They were seen as having no status and existing in a legal vacuum.[21]

The deterring and dissuasive nature of the procedures of asylum were never hidden. Since 1978, asylum seekers had been distributed, upon arrival to West Berlin, to the various *Länder* (states) of the Federal Republic of Germany (FRG). Movement out of the allocated area without prior authorisation was illegal. The random allocation of individuals, particularly women, to various areas of the FRG often caused problems. Zeinab, for example, was allocated, on her own, to a remote rural area of West Germany although her parents and adult siblings lived in West Berlin. Living on her own was, of course, difficult and violated the community's norms. Zeinab preferred to live illegally and in hiding, and was unable to seek hospitalisation and medical treatment for a war wound.

From the 16th of January 1982, all asylum seekers were restricted to transit accommodation centres established in former military barracks, disused hospitals and schools, hotels and other such collective premises. These centres were designed to provide for the majority of the needs of the individual. They were divided into categories of preference, based, for example, on differences between those in which food rations were allocated, as opposed to those in which cooked meals were distributed in communal areas and at specific times.

Collective premises were the subject of strong national and international

---

[19]The Protestant church in Berlin not only helped in providing sanctuary from deportation, but also instituted and financed organisations oriented to the needs of the Arabic speaking asylum seekers. The Diakonisches Werk Berlin, for example, set up the *Al Muntada* (*Modelzentrum zur Beratung und Betreuung arabischer jugendlicher Flüchtlingen*) to deal with problems of Arabic speaking youth. It also financed a women's organisation. Persons in charge were Palestinians and other Arabs.

[20]Criminals were defined as individuals with a 90-day sentence or the equivalent fine. The majority of criminals have been arrested for petty theft and most particularly for the evasion of underground and bus fares. A Pendler or 'shuttler' is a person who has visited Lebanon after applying for political asylum.

[21]Interview with Ulrike Haupt, in charge of the Zentrale Beratungsstelle für Ausländische Flüchtlinge of the Arbeiterwohlfahrt der Stadt Berlin, September 1986.

criticism. Asylum seekers often lived in very bad conditions and were restricted to spaces often not exceeding 4 or 5 square meters per adult.[22] A leaked UNHCR internal report mentioned bad sanitary conditions, the serving of pork to Muslims and stated that 'the psychological climate in the centres in the FRG ... is true cause for concern'.[23]

Over the years, living conditions within these centres were improved. A three-phase system was introduced, allowing asylum seekers, after a period of 5 years, to seek privately rented apartments. In spite of general improvements, collective premises posed problems on various levels. Within the household, for example, Palestinians often complained that the small space allocated forced adolescent siblings from both sexes to sleep in the same room.

As households were established in the various rooms of the centres, asylum seekers shared collective toilets, bathrooms and kitchens. Conflict often involved the responsibility in these shared facilities for matters such as cleaning. Boundaries between households were uncertain, and public and private domains overlapped. Conflict between four of the households in a collective premise in West Berlin started, for example, because a youth regularly failed to cover his body properly when returning from the collective showers.

By 1987 the great majority of asylum seekers, having arrived before the introduction of the restriction to collective premises, lived in privately rented apartments, with the rent paid for by the asylum authorities. Apartments were predictably situated in working class areas with high foreign concentration and provided collective means of control, access to goods and food familiar to the community and to services, such as mosques or asylum welfare organisations.

Although housing available in West Berlin meant that kinship did not operate as a residential unit, regular contact with kin was maintained. Relations were also established outside the family and the village, and neighbourhood networks incorporated all Arabic speaking women. Women's networks redefined the concepts of stranger and kin, provided services and goods and acted as channels of information.

On the 18th of July 1980, asylum seekers lost the right to work for the first two years of asylum: the period was further extended to five years in 1986. Following this period, asylum seekers were only permitted to be employed in the district in which they lived, and only after a job had not been filled for a period of three months by a German citizen or the holder of a work permit. As Palestinians were effectively excluded from the labour market, they depended for their livelihood on 'Help for Survival' (*Hilfe zum Lebensunterhalt*) introduced in January 1981. Its value remained to be 20 per cent less than the amount given to non asylum seekers, although this

---

[22]Christiane Kayser, 'Le Sort Précaire des Refugiés du Tiers-Monde', *Le Monde Diplomatique*, August 1984.

[23]The UNHCR report of July 1983 (Mission to the Federal Republic of Germany, 6 to 10 June) criticised the Federal government in very strong terms and accused the FRG of acting against international laws and UN resolutions.

discrimination was declared illegal in March 1985 by the Federal authorities.

In collective premises, benefits were given as much as possible in the form of direct aid such as cooked food, food rations, clothing and vouchers to be exchanged for clothes. Individuals were also given small amounts of cash, reaching in 1987 70 DM per month per head of household. Cash covered a wide range of expenses, including lawyers' fees, transport (minimum underground fare in 1987 DM 2.3) and cigarettes (DM 4 during the same period).

Palestinians living in privately rented dwellings received their monthly allocations in the form of cash, or, for a number of years, in *Wertgutschein* or vouchers to be exchanged in shops against food and certain household items. In 1987, benefits totalled 405-410 DM per month per adult head of the household and less for other adults and children. Laws relating to asylum seekers and people on Duldung meant that their basic minimum needs were met: legal measures ensured that they were fed, clothed and housed, but that their marginality was also sanctioned.

Within the household, asylum procedures could be felt on a number of levels. The presence of the unemployed husband, for example, restricted contact between non-kin women and reduced the possibility of shared domestic activities. Jamileh, Sahar and Fatmeh, for example, complained that they often felt isolated in their household, although the three of them lived on the same street in Kreutzberg. The employment of men, they said, cannot be calculated only in economic terms, as it is perceived by women to be a 'liberation' of the household: men's absence increased access of women to each other as it increased their mobility.

The unemployment of the husband and his dependence on social benefits implied a de facto economic independence of other members of the household from him. Fathers, for example, often voiced their belief that they had 'lost control' over their adolescent daughters and related this loss to their inability to provide living means and their economic inactivity. Social benefits, however, were not the only source of income, as illegal work was a common way of increasing the cash flow. Employment was, in general, occasional, and found, in most cases, in restaurants and bars, often involving cleaning work or work in the kitchen.

The employment of the Palestinian woman in West Berlin was subject to new considerations. Work for unmarried women in the refugee camps in Lebanon was tolerated and often necessary. Social benefits distributed in West Berlin, however, meant that the unmarried woman's basic costs were covered and that her employment was not vital for the livelihood of the family. The nature of the illegal employment available also excluded her participation. It was, for example, impossible for women to work in public leisure places where alcohol was served and to work at night. Work available in the cleaning services was characterised by difficult conditions, bad pay and low status.

The economic role of the Palestinian family in West Berlin deserves a study of its own. Economic relations in the household, the family and the community, redefined in West Berlin the concept of the family and gave it a new material basis. Although the German state guaranteed the economic survival of all individuals, the family was one of the main channels through which cash, goods and services were circulated. Many of these goods and services and much of the cash were oriented towards the acquisition of consumer items, making living conditions better than those prescribed by the employment laws relating to asylum seekers.

Ali had a relatively well paid and secure legal job. He bought video recorders for his two married brothers and often gave financial help or consumer goods to other members of his family. In the community, money was often collected in from family, village and neighbourhood networks. It was used, for example, to send the bodies of dead Palestinians to be buried in Lebanon. Cash was collected from all households although households headed by women were expected to contribute less, while richer members of the family had to pay more.[24]

Throughout the last twelve years, a number of formal funds have been set on family, village or community lines. Funds were created to provide financial help and services in West Berlin at times of emergency, and they were also used to provide services to Palestinians in refugee camps in Lebanon. Thus, in the late 1970s the fund of the Khalsa village association acquired an ambulance for Palestinians in one of the refugee camps in Lebanon, and the Baalbeck fund regularly sent financial help to the camps in Beirut under military siege in 1986 and 1987.

Although the great majority of Palestinians were asylum seekers, a small number held residence and work permits, and were thus not restricted by the procedures of political asylum. Residence permits were, in most cases, acquired by asylum seekers after their marriage to a German citizen, although in a few cases, they had been given in the 1960s and early 1970s. Among these Palestinians, a number had accumulated a small capital, and sometimes managed to be self employed. Affluent Palestinians provided services to kin and to members of the community at large, by providing consumer goods, financial help and employment.

Criteria of leadership was redefined and effective leadership came, to a large extent, to be based on a man's access to the German majority. Affluent Palestinians took on, in a number of cases, the leadership of the family or village group, although, like in the case of the Musa clan, the village elder and traditional leader was present in West Berlin. Abu Akram, another example, has been living in West Berlin since the early 1970s, had a residence permit, well-paid employment and good contacts in the German society. He provided his kin with financial help, found employment, housing and helped in the legal

---

[24]Cash was also collected from neighbouring Arabic speaking households. Contributions depended on the proximity of the neighbouring household and the closeness of the relationship between its members, especially women. Palestinians from the same refugee camp in Lebanon were expected to pay larger sums and the contribution of Palestinians in general had to be larger than that given by other national groups. The flow and movement of cash, goods and services within family groups can also be observed in the payment of *nukut* (wedding present in the form of cash).

process. As the leader of the large Musa family, he replaced Abu Mahmud, an unskilled asylum seeker with no knowledge of German and little chance of employment.

The authority of a family or village leader was reaffirmed in his prestigious role as a mediator and his role in arbitration and the settlement of conflict. Mediation was based on customary law, itself redefined by the presence of the community in a Western society. Settlement of conflict generally aimed at maintaining social cohesion and minimising conflicts by providing a compromise solution between the two parties. Customary law guaranteed a certain independence in running the affairs of the community and indicated that a 'friendly' settlement was possible. The use of the German police or court by one of the parties was perceived to constitute an undue escalation of the conflict.

The settlement of conflict internally, without using the police, guaranteed the process of arbitration, especially when conflicts involved a situation compromising to one of the parties. Customary law solved the conflict between Mustafa, a Palestinian employer and Samir, his Palestinian employee working with no valid permit, without compromising the illegal position of the two. As community leaders, known for their knowledge of customary law, came to mediate between the two parties, the settlement was finally based on both customary and Federal laws. The truce or ‘atwi agreed upon was calculated on the official sick leave for industrial injury payments, while the compensation money was calculated on end of service compensation or redundancy pay.

On the first of October 1987 Palestinians and other asylum seekers from Lebanon were subject to a change of status if they fulfilled certain requirements. A more recent West Berlin Senate directive issued on the 20th of June 1989 benefited larger numbers. It gave residence permits to all asylum seekers whose asylum processes were initiated more than five years earlier and all those from countries to which persons could not be deported for humanitarian reasons, including those coming from Lebanon.

Beneficiaries of this change in status were given a right of residence: many, like Hasan, after living in the city for 15 years. Like a small number of asylum seekers who had benefited from a similar change in 1986, they were taken outside the procedure of asylum. The change in status meant that they were not going to be deported, but it did not imply that they were recognised as political refugees. Thus no legal precedent was established for potential new arrivals. But, as they moved out of the procedures of asylum, they acquired rights denied to asylum seekers such as the right to movement, easier employment conditions, the right to study and equality of social benefits.

Today the implications of the change of status were being felt with varying degrees, in different aspects of the life of the asylum seekers. The change of status of Palestinians in West Berlin implied the possibility of their relative integration in the socio-economic structure of the majority society, especially through their newly found participation in the labour market and their access to education. It increased the possibility of the development of services oriented to the community and developed by the community itself, such as community centres, language classes, organisations, and shops.

The slight improvement in the economic position of Palestinians increased the level of contact between members of the community. It was more possible to pay telephone bills or to acquire motor cars. Generally speaking, the new relative integration of the community, however small, increased its ability to provide services for its members. It thus furthered the possibility for the community of redefining its own conditions for separateness from the majority society.

The Palestinian family remained characterised, like other minority families in West Berlin, by its marginality to the socio-economic structure of the majority society and by its presence as a 'visible' minority. The new found possibility of entering the labour market has so far not changed employment patterns. As can be predicted, men continue to be employed in unskilled, badly paid work. A number of questions will also have to be answered about the employment patterns of women, both unmarried and married.

Will the employment of men come to be perceived as meaning that the employment of women is not necessary, especially if they earn good wages? As unskilled unmarried women acquired the legal possibility of working, their employment remained in badly paid jobs, often in difficult conditions and generally associated with low status. It could be found in fast food restaurants, in the cleaning services and other such activities which did not encourage women's work outside the household. This made it more difficult for women to stand up to eventual family opposition.

Muslim Women in a Non-Muslim Society

In her analysis of Turkish Muslim identity in France, Riva Kastoryano states that the immigrant family redefines the boundaries of its identity by reaffirming, among other things, the superiority of its morals over that of the majority community. Religious practices, she adds, represent means of resisting integration and acculturation.[25] The analysis of the Palestinian community in West Berlin shows that, more than anything else, women and women's sexuality, role and position have come to be perceived by the community as a means of separateness, definition of identity and expression of cultural superiority. Women were transformed into measures of the adherence to the shari'a and ways of preserving the community from assimilation.

The shift from a sexually segregated to a sexually integrated community redefined ideals in the behaviour of women as well as the concepts of shame and honour. The ideological integration of the woman in the national struggle in the camps in Lebanon was replaced in West Berlin by the definition of the integration of the sexes as promoting the sexuality of women outside the confines of marriage. The ideal Arab or Muslim woman was portrayed as

---

[25]Riva Kastoryano, 'Définition des Frontières de l'Identité: Turcs Musulmans', *Revue Française de Science Politique,* 37, 1987. See also her chapter in the present book.

everything which the German woman was not. The German woman was perceived as promiscuous: the chastity of the unmarried Arab woman and her modest behaviour took on a new importance. German culture integrated the sexes in both the private and public domains; the Arab woman was to be segregated from men.

German culture was lived as a corrupting influence on women. Contact between Arab women and men was identified as assimilation to the majority community, the loss of Islamic and national identity, ultimately leading to the destruction of the community. Preventive measures were instituted for the protection from assimilation. In the context of West Berlin, the sexuality of women was perceived as active and aggressive and the presence of a woman in a 'corrupting' environment was cause for real concern.

The interaction of women with men, especially non-kin men, was subject to very strict control. No legitimate and neutral areas of interaction existed, such as the one provided by the Palestinian political organisations in the camps. In Berlin, any contact was perceived with suspicion. The relationship of girls and adolescent women with the German society was made minimal and friendship, even with German girls, was actively discouraged.

Previously, in the camps in Lebanon, the segregation of women meant a de-facto segregation of men. Norms regulating the behaviour of women regulated the actions of men. It was not possible, for example, for a man to have a public non-marital relationship with a woman. The presence of the community in West Berlin, however, gave men the possibility to exercise freely their 'right' to relations, including sexual relations, with German women. The movement of adolescent and young men, was not subject to control. They were even able to bring their woman friends to the family household and to cohabit with them.

The corruption of women, in contrast, was perceived to be omnipresent. The school posed a particular problem, as it exposed adolescent women to subjects such as sex education and topics such as homosexuality. It placed them in the presence of men - both students and teachers - without adequate control. As the education of the children of asylum seekers was not compulsory and was subject to a number of difficulties, the withdrawal of adolescent women from school was observed in a few of cases to be a preventive measure, especially at times when their behaviour was perceived to be outside the norm.

The acquisition by asylum seekers of residence permits in 1987 and 1989 made the education of Palestinian children compulsory. Although girls could not be withdrawn from schools any more, their education continued to face difficulties. In addition to problems faced by ethnic minority children in general, the Palestinian girl and adolescent woman, especially the eldest daughter, played an important part in domestic labour. She shared with her mother the care of the other children, the baking of the bread and other household chores.

Tension caused within the household by the schooling of women cannot be ignored. Girls and adolescent women socialised in German schools, were exposed to a system which promoted a relative equality of the sexes and a

'German' understanding of relations between gender.

Conflict between the school girl and her family was often the result of differences in interpreting the norms and in understanding the nature of gender relations. Thus, interaction with a male class-mate known since childhood, was seen by the community a violation of norms, although it was lived by the young woman herself as free from any sexual connotation. Alia, for example, was heavily reprimanded after having been seen talking to a young German man in the underground station. She felt that she was unjustly accused as she 'was only saying good morning to a class mate I have known since I was eight'.

The conflict generated by the confrontation of the two sexual cultures not only affected the relationship of a young woman with her family but was often lived by her as a conflict. A number of adolescent and young women secretly violated the areas of defined movement and action, but violations generally involved social activities with a group of class mates, such as visits to the cinema, or to a coffee shop.

Social activities of this type were partially lived as 'innocent', Su‘ad, for example, rationalised it to the researcher by saying: 'I have done nothing wrong, I behaved very modestly and did not compromise my honour'. But, as activities were conducted secretly and could be the cause of severe punishment, they were defined by their illicit nature. Thus, whatever the nature of the relationship, contact with males was lived as a crime.

State provisions for the protection of women against domestic violence posed new elements in the position of the woman in the household, although their role remained limited. The threat of deportation was, for many years, one of the first restrictions against the use of such provisions. Refuge centres for youth and women provided them with immediate protection from family violence, and women were aware of the consequences of their acts after deportation to Lebanon.

In recent years, the number of women seeking refuge outside the context of the community, although still small, increased. The desertion of the family household was in the majority of cases the result of a specific incident and was not premeditated. The case of Samira is typical: the 17 year old woman ran away from the family household after being hit by her father and mother for going to a discotheque with her class mates. Taking refuge in women's centres was a statement of her weakness within the household. But it also meant a relative strength. By leaving the family household, she was potentially compromising its honour and, while protecting herself from physical assault, she imposed a neutral area for the settlement of the conflict, and guaranteed the intervention of mediators acceptable to her.

Mediation between Mariam and her family, for example, guaranteed the continuation of contact. Mediators were perceived by the family as able to guarantee minimal social control. Mediators were known both for their respect of the culture and for their liberalism. They were chosen from the kinship group, the political organisation, the Palestinian worker's or women's unions, and were used to accelerate the process of rapprochement, thus minimising the stay of the woman outside the home. For Mariam, the settlement reached by the mediators guaranteed her protection from domestic violence as long as she remained within the framework of the settlement. For the family, it guaranteed the promise of modest behaviour.

In the majority of cases, women returned to the family household, but the increasing number of exceptions is significant. Taking refuge outside the community, even if only temporarily, indicated that an alternative to family organisation existed for women. The return of the majority of women to the family household suggests however that this alternative was not viable. The total desertion by a young woman of her parent's household not only meant the loss of contact with them, but implied her ostracism from the community as a whole. Thus although the German society provided an alternative to the family, there was no real alternative to the family in the community.

Marriage

As the minimum age of marriage of a woman was determined by Federal law, the marriage of adolescent women when it was legally possible, was often perceived as a preventive measure against their corruption. Early marriages of women were encouraged by the lack of employment or further education. As the new legal status gave the right to employment and education, cultural or Islamic factors alone cannot explain early marriage. Other factors have to be looked at: literature available on working class Western families shows that early marriage is a common way for an adolescent out of difficult family situation. 50 per cent of working class women marry in their teen years.[26]

Marriages conducted in West Berlin took on an endogamous form although endogamy reflected not only descent, but village, camp, street and neighbourhood organisation. The choice of the marriage partner of the Palestinian woman and the Palestinian man - if he were married to a Palestinian woman - was generally a matter for the family and not for the two spouses involved. The consent of the woman was expected, as the rejection of suitors was perceived with suspicion as it was seen to hide an illicit relationship or the loss of virginity. Like the rejection of suitors, showing preference for a particular man caused suspicion.

The preventive and punitive role of marriage has been observed at times when women have violated norms. These marriages were arranged with a kin whose duty it was to salvage family honour. Thus, the scandal caused by the non-marital pregnancy of Hurieh, was immediately followed by her marriage to Ali her cousin. The marriage was agreed upon by the family and the consent of neither spouse was sought, as the matter was considered to be too important to be left to individual whim.

If the marriage of a Muslim man to a non-Muslim woman was possible,

---

[26]Rayna Rapp, 'Family and Class in Contemporary America: Notes towards an Understanding of Ideology', in *Rethinking the Family: Some Feminist Questions.*, New York, 1982.

it had in West Berlin an important socio-economic advantage. Marriage to a German woman gave the husband a residence and work permit and took him outside the confines of political asylum. Marriage to a German woman was also measured by the attitude of the community to German women in general. Regardless of the nature of particular relationships, marriages to German women were regarded by the community as 'temporary' and 'non serious'. Individual German women were however accepted as wives and as mothers.

Over the years, a number of German women have converted to Islam. A predictable trend can be identified: women generally converted after having been married for a number of years and having had children. Conversion was often the result of pressure by the husband or his family, but was in other cases the expression of the wish of the women to be accepted and integrated as full members of the community. Conversion of women to Islam was often observed among women who have been cut off from their own families because of their marriage to an Arab man. German wives were expected to keep regular contact with the families of their Palestinian husbands and conformed to a number of rules such as modest dress.

The marriage of women to non-Muslim men is not recognised by Islam. It immediately implied a secret relationship and was not tolerated. The control over the movement of women meant that they had little chance to meet German men and the chances of such marriages taking place were very small. A small number, however, did exist and was dealt with by the community in different ways. The alienation of women from the family played an important role in deterring these marriages. Leila ran away from home in order to marry a German man. Her desertion of the family household led, a number of years ago, to her total ostracism from the family household and community.

The same family, however, played an important role in the legitimisation of the marriage of Zeinab, another Palestinian woman, to a German man. As an Islamic marriage and a wedding took place within the community, it was justified. Zeinab presented a different problem: twice a widow, she was over 35 and a mother of a number of children, and she was not able to remarry. She, moreover, had no surviving kin, or at least male kin, able to extend his protection *(sutra)* to her. Her marriage to the German man was the only means available to secure her protection and her sutra was more important than any other consideration. Had Zeinab had brothers or other close male kin, conditions of this marriage would have been different.

When Randa decided to marry a German class mate, she was faced with the refusal of her family and, after period of conflict, left the family household. The absence of kin made the arrangement of an immediate alternative marriage impossible, and her familiarity with German culture made her desertion a real threat. Facing the choice of her desertion, and their inability to change her mind, an Islamic marriage was arranged by the family. The Islamic marriage was, of course, preceded by the conversion of the man and was interpreted to be in accordance with Islamic law. On the social level, the Islamic marriage and Palestinian wedding signaled to the community the approval and control of the family. Such marriages remain rare. The conversion of a German man to Islam for the purpose of marriage did not make such marriages totally acceptable to the community. Conversions were not taken seriously and the religious affiliation of the men were perceived as not genuine.

Polygamy

The analysis of polygamy in West Berlin must go beyond a strict interpretation of the concept. Although polygamous marriages as such were not conducted in West Berlin, they existed and were sustained by the dual interpretation of both the FRG and Islamic law. Polygamous marriages, although not very common, took place in the following way: Palestinian and other Arab women were judicially divorced in the German courts from their husbands who, in turn, married German women. The German divorce however was not recognised as such and relations, including sexual relations, with the Arab woman continued to be regulated by the rules of Islamic marriage.

These marriages were perceived by the community as polygamous. They were accepted and recognised as such, as were the children born from the Arab woman after her 'divorce'. Polygamy found in West Berlin a new socio-economic basis as the spouse of an asylum seeker acquired a residence permit and consequently rights such as work and movement. The residence permit was passed on to his children, including those born to the Arab wife after the judicial divorce. One person was not affected by the change in status brought about by this marriage: the Arab wife, who remained an asylum seeker, and, until 1987 or 1989, the only person in the household to be threatened with deportation.

Contrary to polygamous marriages elsewhere, those in West Berlin did not constitute an economic 'burden' on the man. Social benefits covered all the basic expenses of the household. As the change of status challenged the legitimacy of the need for such arrangements, the prediction of the end of such polygamous marriages as a result of this change would be wrong. Polygamous relationships have always involved a German and an Arab wife and rarely two wives from within the community. They were tolerated as they allowed for the continuation of the relationship between the man and the household, and solved problems of care, custody and education of children.

Polygamous marriages are considered to be preferable to divorce; they guarantee that fathers retain the custody of the children but that mothers are given their care. A man who deserted his household because of his marriage or relationship with a German woman was condemned severely. Despite the importance of the role of Arab mothers in the socialisation of children, it was only the father who was perceived to be able to impose any real control. Abu Walid was judged harshly for leaving his conjugal household and was subsequently blamed for the 'immodest' behaviour of Hana, his 16 year old daughter considered by the community as 'loose'.

For the polygamous man, each household took on a specialised function. Abu Isa, effective leader of one of the largest family groups in West Berlin, used the household of his Arab wife to meet with kin on an almost daily basis. In this household, the centre of the large family's activity, he received visitors and it is there that formal relationships or contracts - such as the Islamic marriage of his nephew - were conducted.

Although the household of the German wife was not used for formal community functions, it was meant for a different type of social activities. In it, Abu Isa entertained male Arab friends or kin for alcohol-drinking sessions. The attitude of the community to these marriages is ambivalent: they are, on the one hand, tolerated, while on the other, seen as a social problem. The relationship of the polygamous man with the two wifes has been described by some as contrary to Islamic law as the two women are not treated equally. Hind, a neighbour, was aggravated by the fact that Abu Isa shared domestic activities with the German wife but did not do so with his Arab wife, Umm Issa. Worse, she said, he only took the German woman on holiday to Spain!

In recent years, as a number of marriages of Palestinian men with German women have broken up, Islamic marriages were conducted before the legal pronunciation of the divorce. Islamic marriages (*katb kitab*), did not always imply the immediate formation of a household but made relations and contact between the two legitimate. They were thus able go out and be seen in public together.

Custody and Birth Control

The custody and care of children given to the divorced German mother has resulted in a very small number of cases in the 'kidnapping' of the child to Lebanon. Men's ability to take children away depended on the availability in Lebanon of close kin, especially mothers, who would be able to care for children as this depended on security conditions in the area of Lebanon in which they lived. Girls were generally not kidnapped as the responsibility for a young girl, especially one socialised in the 'loose' culture of the West, was often rejected by kin in Lebanon. The custody of the child by the German mother was perceived as the 'loss' of the child by the community.

The attitude of Palestinians in the West Berlin to birth control and abortion was ambivalent and varied. Attitudes differed, some people said it was not allowed by Islam, while others stated that some form of birth control was approved by the Qur'an. Abdul Karim, a practising Muslim and father of 13 children, stated total opposition to any contraception, and rejected the plea for abortion despite strong medical advice recommending it for his ill wife. However, except for a minority, abortion is generally tolerated if based on medical grounds.

Whatever the power the man had to enforce his attitude, contraception and birth control are, to a large extent, women's domains. Birth control before the first child was thought to cause infertility, but was later considered as providing a resting period for the woman. Among the sexually active female population in West Berlin, contraception was generally accepted after three pregnancies. A number of women interviewed reported to have hidden the contraceptives from their husbands and blamed their temporary infertility on the 'will of God'.

Matters relating to birth control and contraception were generally dealt with through women's, often neighbourhood, networks. These networks operated as information and advice centres and provided addresses of medical centres, doctors and community centres. Women accompanied each other on these visits, providing chaperonage and cover, basic translation services, and help in the use of the public transport system for new comers.

Divorce

Divorce among Arab women in West Berlin is not common and the ability of the woman to instigate it remains small. The escalation of conflict between husband and wife, often leading to the woman taking refuge outside her conjugal household, exists, but is neither uncommon nor new. The process of *harad* (sulking) and the return of the woman to the conjugal household generally followed pressure from the family and a process of mediation. Refuge was in some cases sought within neighbouring women's networks, especially when kin were not found. In many cases, the woman's return was accompanied by a detailed agreement between the spouses, specifying duties and rights towards each other: stipulations of domestic violence were often enclosed.

The deportation of asylum seekers provided, in the few cases observed, the possibility for the separation of a woman from her husband. Umm Ali, who had been wanting to get rid of her husband for a number of years, continued to live in West Berlin with her three children after his deportation. She was thus not perceived as a divorced woman although members of the community were aware of the convenience of his deportation. Instead, her position was very similar to that of a widow, which, with her age, liberated her from her sexuality, and gave her freedom of movement and manoeuverability.

Umm Jamal physically removed her husband out of the family household with the help of the German police, but her ability to do so did not imply a change in the forms of social relation. She was a 45-year old woman, and was thus not perceived as sexually active nor vulnerable. Her act was done with the approval of her adolescent son, thus giving it the legitimacy of kin male support. The husband was an alcoholic and gambler and was known to use gratuitous physical violence against members of the household. He was considered by the community as a bad example for the adolescent children. Umm Jamal's use of the police was perceived in terms of the absence of male kin able to offer protection and not as a challenge to the authority of men, the family or the community.

A number of factors defines today the attitude of women, especially young women socialised in German schools, to marriage. The conception of marriage as romantic, for example, was often in contradiction with the choice of husband in the arrangement of the woman's own marriage. Women, partially socialised by German culture, were familiar with divorce and were aware of the existence of legal means of attaining it. Rula, a 17 year old, was one of the young women, who after a few months of marriage, left the conjugal home and sought refuge in the household of her parents described by the community in general as 'very conservative'. Although Rula was able to refuse to return to the husband despite tremendous pressure, she was aware of the social implications of her act and stated: 'my life is finished... I shall become the servant of my brothers'.

The divorced woman remained, except in the unlikely event of re-marriage, the responsibility of her father or other male kin. As women were not able to live outside the context of a family and without the presence of a male kin or husband, the divorce of a woman was a collective decision taken by her kin and was dependent on their approval. A woman taking the decision of divorce without the approval of the family, faced ostracism from them and from the community at large.

Throughout the divorce negotiations, Rula was represented by a male kin who acted as her *wakil* (representative) and agreed on the conditions of the separation without consultation with her. The wakil accepted the repayment of the *mahr* (dower) to the husband, the renunciation of her *'idda* money (paid to her until her first menstruation after the divorce). Although the divorce was instigated by her, it was finally to the advantage of the man that the divorce was pronounced.

Generally speaking, in addition to the stigmas that have previously been attached to the social status of the divorced woman, the corruptive influence of West Berlin made her to be perceived as a real threat to family honour. Her status of divorcee -thus young and non virgin- placed her in a vulnerable and easily exploitable position and the possibility of her violating the norms was considered to be very real. Rula was placed under more rigorous control than her younger sisters and her movement subject to more scrutiny. Unlike them she was not allowed unchaperoned with female friends, was rarely taken to weddings, and was considered as a social disgrace to the family.

Conclusion

The role of the family and the community in preventing a young woman's access to the German judicial system and to state provisions -such as refuge centres- cannot be understated. Questions about social reforms and attempts at legal change do however stop there. As the 'corrupt' German society is seen by the community to encourage the need for the restriction of women's movement, the majority German socio-economic structure does not provide conditions that make possible the introduction of new forms of social relations and a new understanding of gender relations and the position of women. The analysis must address the socio-economic position of a minority woman in a Western society and investigate both gender and class in terms of the Palestinian woman's position in West Berlin .

If the family and the community hinder access to the German socio-economic structure, questions must be asked, first, about the relationship of the minority woman with the German state, society and economy. Palestinians in West Berlin are partially defined by their location in a state which promotes the integration of the sexes but which marginalises the asylum seekers and ethnic minority communities. In West Berlin the relationship of the minority woman to the German society is also partially defined by individual racism, institutional discrimination in education policies and employment. From the first day at school, the migrant child is disadvantaged in basic skills and falls into the vicious circle of bad school performance, lack of training and skills, badly paid jobs, and unemployment.[27]

As the segregation of the sexes takes among the Palestinian community in West Berlin a new meaning and a new importance, this segregation is reinforced by the economic marginality of the community, especially women. Work available to women does not constitute a real alternative to her public inactivity. The improvement of the economic role of women in the household will have to be based on their empowerment in the German community at large through access to education, training and better employment. This empowerment will have to be accompanied by a radical change in official FRG policy towards foreigners.

The recent upheavals in Eastern Europe, and most particularily in Germany cannot be ignored. The implications of the imminent re-unification of Germany on all foreigners will have to be observed and could possibly be cause for concern.

---

[27]For problems relating to the education of minority children in West Germany see D. Hoft, 'The Children of Aliens in West German Schools: Situation and Problems' in C. Fried ed., *Minorities*, pp. 133-157.

PART III

SOUTH ASIA, SOUTH EAST ASIA, CHINA

11. ISLAMIC LAW AND THE COLONIAL ENCOUNTER IN BRITISH INDIA*

Michael R. Anderson

> British statesmanship determines from time to time how much of Oriental precept is to be treated as Law in the English sense, how much left to the consciences of those who acknowledge it as religiously binding, how much forcibly suppressed as noxious and immoral; and when this has been determined, European scholarship sifts and classifies the Oriental authorities, the mental habits of English and Scotch lawyers influence the methods of interpretation, and Procedure Codes of modern European manufacture regulate the ascertainment of the facts and the ultimate enforcement of the rule.
>
> Sir Roland Knyvet Wilson[1]

As the tentacles of colonial rule stretched into the Indian subcontinent in the eighteenth century, the British had a minimal knowledge of Islamic legal arrangements. Yet in 1947, when the trunk of colonial power was formally chopped off, it left behind an elaborate system of administrative roots, including a working understanding of Islamic legal precepts. Since the same administrative roots have given succour to the post-colonial states of India, Pakistan, and Bangladesh, it is important to inquire into their provenance. The colonial courts charged with administering what had come to be called 'Anglo-Muhammadan law' were able to rely upon a legal scholarship that included translations of Arabic and Persian texts, a handful of commentaries, as well as the precedent of hundreds of cases.

In some senses, the corpus of Anglo-Muhammadan law was simply the inevitable by-product of the colonial encounter. But its remarkable volume, produced at considerable cost and effort to successive colonial regimes, raises questions concerning the role of law in the establishment and maintenance of colonial power. If the genesis of Anglo-Muhammadan law lay in the quest to establish a definable and reliable relation between government and the governed, it entailed more than new legal institutions. It also demanded the

---

*I am grateful to Elleke Boehmer, Avril Powell, David Powers, and Peter Robb for their helpful comments on an earlier version of this paper.

[1]R. K. Wilson, *An Introduction to the Study of Anglo-Muhammadan Law,* London, 1894, p.2. Footnotes omitted.

formulation of a body of knowledge about the legal organisation of colonised peoples, including those professing adherence to Islam. Since the formidable amount of legal scholarship that accumulated under British rule was produced in an explicit complicity with colonialism, questions of its bias and validity are bound to be asked. What role did Anglo-Muhammadan scholarship assume in defining and mobilising colonial power? By what techniques was this scholarship created? How did the process of creating the Anglo-Muhammadan law affect its substantive content and application? In which ways did the substantive content mesh with understandings of identity and social order among the colonised peoples?

I. Indigenous Law and the Early Colonial State

The imperatives of the Company's account-books required that administrators remain mindful of two broad goals: first, to extract economic surplus, in the form of revenue, from the agrarian economy, and second, to maintain effective political control with minimal military involvement.[2] For the most part, the various administrators of the East India Company, (and later, the British Crown) followed the path of least resistance, relying upon co-opted indigenous intermediaries as well as military and police power to secure control. Throughout the subcontinent, the British exercised power by adapting themselves to the contours of pre-colonial political systems, including law. The result was that in many of its structural features, as well as its substantive policies, the colonial state sustained what were essentially pre-colonial political forms until well into the nineteenth century.[3] Although lacking in military and financial power, the edifice of the Mughal empire provided a source of *de jure* authority long after its *de facto* demise. Mughal administrative ranks, honours, rituals, and terminology persisted in muted although significant form even after Crown had supplanted Durbar in 1858. Yet while recent historiography has emphasised the continuities between the *ancien regime* and the early colonial state,[4] it is clear that colonial rule brought a host of entirely new political institutions,[5] and that when indigenous mechanisms were adapted to colonial purposes, they were incorporated within new institutional fora.[6]

---

[2]See D. Washbrook, 'Law, State, and Agrarian Society in Colonial India', *Modern Asian Studies* ,15:3, 1981.

[3]See *ibid.*, and R.E. Frykenberg, 'Company Circari in the Carnatic, 1799-1859: The Inner Logic of Political Systems in India', in R.G. Fox ed., *Realm and Region in Traditional India,* New Delhi, 1978.

[4]See *ibid.*, but also the work of C.A. Bayly, *Rulers, Townsmen and Bazaars: North Indian Society in the Age of British Expansion, 1770-1870*, Cambridge, 1983; and *Indian Society and the Making of the British Empire,* Cambridge, 1988.

[5]D. Arnold, *Police Power and Colonial Rule: Madras 1859-1947*, Delhi, 1986.

[6]See the sensible discussion by N.B. Dirks, 'From Little King to Landlord: Property, Law, and the Gift under the Madras Permanent Settlement', *Comparative Studies in Society and History* 28:2, 1986.

One of these new fora was the colonial law court. The Hastings Plan of 1772 established a hierarchy of civil and criminal courts, which were charged with the task of applying indigenous legal norms 'in all suits regarding inheritance, marriage, caste, and other religious usages or institutions'. Indigenous norms comprised 'the laws of the Koran with respect to Muhammadans', and the laws of the Brahminic 'Shasters' with respect to Hindus.[7] Although the courts followed British models of procedure and adjudication, the plan provided for *maulavis* and *pandits* to advise the courts on matters of Islamic and Hindu law, respectively. By the early nineteenth century, the system of courts had been expanded, a new legal profession had been established,[8] and a growing body of statute and court practice extended the influence of the colonial state.

The actual social impact of the courts was constrained by the reluctance expressed by many colonial administrators to interfere in agrarian society unless presented with a compelling need. Moreover, the resilience of pre-colonial political systems meant that actual authority was shared among a number of entities, so that most disputes were settled at the local or community level.[9] The autonomy legal arrangements sheltered a diversity of legal norms, even among peoples professing a strict adherence to the same orthodoxy.

Nevertheless, British courts had a broad appeal to the landed gentry and other local notables. If British legal institutions appeared to have less impact at the lower levels of society, they did establish a new framework for disputes among the local and regional elite, who were able to use courts to mediate disputes among themselves and to reinforce their dominance over agrarian producers. In British India, as elsewhere, individuals with superior economic and political resources often manipulated institutions to their advantage. Early district administrators in the North, for example, were frequently able to appropriate considerable amounts of land under their political control and then have themselves recorded as the proprietors under British legal authority.[10] Personages who had held political office in the pre-colonial regime often thrived under the law of private property, exercising political control by virtue of their new legal rights.[11] The prevalence of corruption and mini-despotisms allowed the well-heeled to use Company courts when it suited their purposes, but to exercise extra-judicial power when the law was inconvenient or contrary to their interests.[12]

---

[7]Hastings' initial formulation reappeared, in modified form, in all the constitutive legal documents of the early colonial period.

[8]Bengal Regulation VII of 1793.

[9]B. Cohn, *An Anthropologist Among the Historians and Other Essays,* Delhi, 1987, chaps. 19, 22.

[10]E. Stokes, *The Peasant and the Raj* , Cambridge, 1978, p. 84.

[11]See Dirks, 'From Little King to Landlord'.

[12]For a scathing indictment of the colonial courts, see J.B. Norton, *The Administration of Justice in South India* , Madras, 1853.

Where the landed gentry and certain merchant groups were organised according to the dynastic principles of family and clan, the administration of family law played a role in broking wealth and power at the local level, ultimately underpinning the very intermediaries whose cooperation was essential to effective colonial rule. Property and labour were often regulated under the aegis of family law. The organisation of production in the family firm, including divisions of labour according to gender and age, presupposed the legal regulation of marriage, dissolution of marriage, inheritance, and endowments. For the Islamic gentry, material subsistence as well as political authority rested on the property grants of earlier rulers that were maintained under a variety of legal arrangements.[13]

In such circumstances, the administration of Anglo-Muhammadan law was more than a concession to 'native opinion'. Systems of personal law served to consolidate the authority of certain community groups, and thus incorporate community-based forms of surplus extraction into the colonial state.[14] The position of the landed gentry rested on pre-colonial patterns of family organisation. As much as it rankled the sensibilities of Macaulay and others who sought a uniform legal code,[15] Anglo-Muhammadan law conserved and even strengthened aspects of community organisation on which colonial rule rested.

Yet at the same time, colonial administration of pre-colonial personal laws brought important changes. The autonomy of intermediaries operated in the context of state patronage and the ever-present threat of armed intervention. Moreover, the hierarchies of community and family grew more onerous as they were linked to an extractive state that could make unprecedented demands for economic surplus. If company courts lacked the moral qualifications demanded by orthodox theories to interpret and enforce legal norms of Islamic inspiration, they carried the threat of a military power that, after the battles of 1818, could effectively put down any serious resistance.

Company administrators were increasingly able, as the nineteenth century wore on, to intervene in areas of Anglo-Muhammadan law that most threatened their authority. At the same time, they were less hesitant to prohibit practices which offended their sense of morality.[16] As the apparatus of the colonial state became more refined and administrators more capable of policing various forms of resistance, large portions of the Anglo-Muhammadan law were supplanted by laws of British origin. The earliest

---

[13]For contrasting views on these processes, see Bayly, *Rulers, Townsmen, and Bazaars,* pp. 129-3, 351, and G .C. Kozlowski, *Muslim Endowments and Society in British India,* Cambridge, 1985.

[14]Washbrook, 'Law, State and Agrarian Society', pp. 654-70. For a more generalised discussion of this point, see P. Fitzpatrick, 'Law, Plurality and Underdevelopment' in D. Sugarman ed., *Legality, Ideology and the State* , London, 1983.

[15]E. Stokes, *The English Utilitarians and India*, Delhi, 1959, pp. 184ff; M.P. Jain, *Outlines of Indian Legal History,* Bombay, 2nd ed. 1966, chap. 24.

[16]B. Hjejle, 'The Social Policy of the East India Company with Regard to Sati, Slavery, Thagi, and Infanticide, 1772-1858', Unpublished D. Phil. diss., Oxford University, 1958.

Anglicising trends were latent in the 1772 doctrine that in cases where indigenous laws seemed to provide no rule, the matter should be decided according to the Roman law formula of 'justice, equity, and good conscience',[17] which by 1887 was held 'to mean the rules of English law if found applicable to society and circumstances'.[18] Continual alterations of Islamic criminal law stepped up punishments for crimes against private property, while modifying other forms of punishments to conform with British preconceptions.[19] However, the most dramatic overturning of Anglo-Muhammadan law emerged by way of statute. Slavery was abolished in 1843; Islamic criminal law and procedure were replaced entirely by colonial codes in the early 1860s, and Islamic canons of evidence were supplanted by British-based rules in 1872.[20] By 1875, new colonial codes had displaced the Anglo-Muhammadan law in all subjects except family law and certain property transactions. The codes reflected a longstanding frustration with Islamic law, but they also furnished the state with a more precise and reliable legal apparatus to maintain and regulate its police power.

Nevertheless, as an administrative technique, the enforcement of separate systems of personal law was never eliminated entirely. If personal laws had been important to the early raj as a means of maintaining political control, they assumed a new significance in the emerging communal politics of the twentieth century. Throughout the colonial period, Anglo-Muhammadan law was taken seriously as a politically sensitive and technically complex subject for legal scholarship. But there was an irony in this, for what the Company courts applied as Islamic law was often more alien than familiar to putatively 'Muslim' groups. Anglo-Muhammadan scholarship often distorted its subject matter, frequently reflecting British preoccupations more accurately than indigenous norms. Indeed, colonial administrators may never have changed Islamic legal arrangements quite so profoundly as when they were trying to preserve them.

II. Anglo-Muhammadan Scholarship

Following Hasting's plan, the limited bureaucratic machinery of the Company state found itself with an urgent need for a a serviceable knowledge of indigenous legal arrangements. Apart from the language difficulties and the limitations of a small British administration juxtaposed with a substantial colonised population, the task was complicated by the fragmented and contingent quality of the sources of legal obligation.

---

17 See J. D. M. Derrett, 'Justice, Equity and Good Conscience', in J. N. D. Anderson ed., *Changing Law in Developing Countries*, London, 1963.

18 *Waghela v. Sheikh Masludin,* (1887) 14 IA 89, at 96.

19 J. Fish, *Cheap Lives and Dear Limbs: The British Transformation of the Bengal Criminal Law, 1769-1817*, Wiesbaden, 1983.

20 Act V of 1843; *Code of Civil Procedure* (act VIII of 1859), *Indian Penal Code* (Act XLV of 1860); *Criminal Procedure Code* (Act XXV of 1861); *Indian Evidence Act* (Act 1 of 1872).

Colonial scholars drew heavily upon pre-colonial legal scholarship. Adapted forms of the *shari'a* had been administered in South Asia for centuries, first by the various Sultanates, next under the authority of the strong Mughal empire, and finally by the successor states that arose during the eighteenth century.[21] Especially under the Mughals, the administration of shari'a formed an important part of the symbolisation of imperial legitimacy; its dispensation was viewed as a sacred duty. Legal scholarship thrived in these circumstances; the imperial court patronised the *'ulama,* or legal scholars, and Aurangzeb commissioned the influential *Fatawa Alamgiri*, a collection of legal decisions. On the administrative side, the shari'a was supplemented with a comprehensive set of imperial regulations as well as a cadre of officially sponsored *qadis* drawn primarily from the 'ulama.[22]

Paradoxically, the decline of the Mughal empire appears to have stimulated a moral and cultural competition among successor powers that fuelled an increase in Islamic legal scholarship.[23] A sign of some status, legal study was widespread. Predominantly of the Hanafi school, orthodox legal specialists seem to have focussed study on *al-Hidaya*, a twelfth-century text of Central Asian origin that primarily relied upon Abu-Yusuf and ash-Shaybani, the two pupils of Abu-Hanifa. Study of the Qur'an and the *hadith* seems to have been less important for the orthodox Hanafis.[24] But the cultural vitality of the period also gave rise to more innovative scholars, including Shah Wali Ullah (1703-62) who advocated an eclectic approach to the Sunni schools, insisting that the gates of *ijtihad,* or interpretive reasoning, had never closed.[25] Shi'i scholarship was also alive. In Bengal, for instance, two Nawab-supported *madrasas* drew a wide range of legal students, some form as far away as Iran.[26]

There is no reason to doubt that pre-colonial legal scholarship was coupled with an earnest effort to enforce the shari'a. Unlike the 'Hindu' *dharmasastra* texts,[27] Islamic legal theory did not formally recognise custom as an independent source of law. So although *al-Hidaya* accorded custom a role in the absence of textual norms,[28] orthodoxy frowned on deviations. Yet the social impact of Mughal legal institutions remained limited to particular groups, especially the Islamic gentry and the urban merchants based in the

[21] A. A. A. Fyzee, 'Muhammadan Law in India', *Comparative Studies in Society and History*, 5, 1963.

[22] K. M. Yusuf, 'The Judiciary in India under the Sultans of Delhi and the Mughal Emperors', *Indo-Iranica,* 18, 1965.

[23] See B.D. Metcalfe, *Islamic Revival in British India: Deoband, 1860-1900*, Princeton, 1982, chap.2.

[24] Metcalfe, *Islamic Revival*, p.31.

[25] See Mohammad Daud Rahbar, 'Shah Wali Ullah and Ijtihad', *The Muslim World*, 45, 1955, and more generally, Wael B. Hallaq, 'Was the Gate of Ijtihad Closed?', *International Journal of Middle Eastern Studies*, 16, 1984.

[26] P. J. Marshall, *Bengal: The British Bridgehead*, Cambridge, 1988, p.31.

[27] Cf. J. D. M. Derrett, *Religion, Law and State in India*, London, 1968, chaps 6, 7.

[28] T. Mahmood, 'Custom as a Source of Law in Islam', *Journal of the Indian law Institute*, 7, 1965, p.104.

qasbah towns. Many communities jealously guarded their autonomy, operating under the umbrella of imperial tolerance to retain localised institutions, practices, and norms which operated in derogation of a strict application of the shari'a.[29] Local leaders seem to have settled disputes with varying degrees of deference to textual norms.

The British confrontation with myriad forms of legal authority and variegated local practices highlighted one of the foremost problems of colonial control: how to obtain simple, reliable, and reasonably accurate understandings of indigenous social life without sacrificing great labour and capital?[30] Law and legal institutions provided a solution. Equipped with indigenous advisors, colonial courts served as mechanisms of inquiry, while the classical religious-legal texts, whatever their genuine relevance, were taken as the key to understanding colonised cultures and societies. Most British intellectuals of the early colonial period stressed the importance of law in regulating social life. 'The Rule of Law' was a common piece of ideological baggage that linked law to public sentiments as well as political order. Law was more than an arm of sovereignty: it was employed as a proto-sociology that could guide policy. Accordingly, the first century of colonial rule witnessed the birth of an Anglo-Muhammadan jurisprudence comprising legal assumptions as well as law officers, translations, textbooks, codifications, and new legal technologies.

Basic Assumptions

The Hastings plan rested on the notion that indigenous norms could be plugged into British-based legal institutions without significantly compromising the integrity of either. Coming to understand that the shari'a was authoritative for Islamic legal scholars, many British administrators glossed over its internal contradictions and finely distinguished levels of moral approbation, and set about applying it as a set of more or less homogenous legal rules.

The presumption that a single set of legal rules could apply to all persons professing adherence to Islam violated both Islamic theory and South Asian practice. Hastings had subsumed all indigenous legal arrangements under two categories: Hindu (earlier, Gentoo), and Muslim (Muhammadan).[31] From the outset, this binary categorisation was inadequate to contain the diversity of

---

29For a more general treatment of this theme in South Asia, see K. I. Ewing ed., *Shari'at and Ambiguity in South Asian Islam*, Berkeley, 1988.

30The problem took various guises throughout colonial legal history. In 1856, Lord Harris viewed one of the main functions of the new police force as 'the procuring [of] continued accurate information on the state of the country and the feelings and sentiments of the population'. Quoted in Arnold, *Police Power*, p.24. For a detailed twentieth century account, see P. Mason, *Call the Next Witness*, London, 1945.

31It seems that in the formation of this plan, Hastings simply drew on the strategy that had been adopted during the Mughal Period and remained in force in the successor states. What was new, however, was the rigid legalism that now accompanied the binary Hindu/ Muslim divide. See Fyzee, 'Muhammadan Law,' p. 402.

legal life on the subcontinent. Not only did it fail to acknowledge the distinction between Shi'is and Sunnis, and the differences among the schools within each; it also failed to address adequately the practices and beliefs of the many groups that adopted an eclectic approach to Islam and various forms of Hinduism. Backed by the literalist legalism of colonial administration, 'Hindu' and 'Muslim' became an important part of a new bureaucratic vocabulary of colonial control - a vocabulary that drew upon indigenous terms, but imbued them with a Procrustean quality as they were deployed in governance.[32]

Looking for a unified 'Muhammadan' law that could be slotted into the Company court system, administrators made the much-celebrated mistake of treating certain classical Islamic texts as binding legal texts. To apply 'the laws of the Koran with respect to Mohamedans', was a project that mistook the Qur'an for a code of law. The Qur'an, and even more specifically legal texts such as *al-Hidaya* had never been directly applied as sources of legal precept. Their legal relevance had always derived from a properly authoritative qadi whose moral probity and knowledge of local arrangements could translate precept into practice. Qadis in the Mughal period had left much to what Bayly calls 'the sense of the neighbourhood'.[33] Even the most sophisticated text-bound approach was subject to grave error, simply because texts were applied in ignorance of social circumstances.

Colonial judicial administration soon developed a more sophisticated treatment of textual sources. Nevertheless, it was accompanied by a basic prejudice that accorded primacy to text over interpretive practice.

'Native Law Officers'

Until Anglo-Muhammadan law was consolidated in textbook and precedent, court-appointed maulavis provided fatawa to guide the British judges. Collaborating with colonial rule in the most overt sense, these clerics drawn from indigenous centres of learning were charged with responding to the courts' questions on matters of Islamic law. When faced with a question of law, British judges would present the maulavi with a question formulated in a an abstract, hypothetical manner, often shorn of relevant details. The resulting fatwa, necessarily in an abstract form, was then applied to the case at hand. This procedure resulted in a highly formalised and rigid application of legal rules. In 1935, Abur Hussain wrote of the early colonial judges that they applied the law 'mechanically to the causes before them, practically on third hand information of the law from the Moulvis who sense of justice born and bred in the native social environment was not available to the Judges'.[34]

It is not surprising that the maulavis were mistrusted. British accusations of inconsistency stemmed partially from genuine questions of probity that may

---

[32]The vocabulary was systemised for training new administrators. See H. H. Wilson, *A Glossary of Judicial and Revenue Terms*, London, 1855.

[33]Bayley, *Merchants, Townsmen and Bazaars*, p. 353.

[34]A. Hussain, *Muslim Law as Administered in British India,* Calcutta, 1935, p.14.

have been linked to a low official salary.[35] More importantly, suspicions arose from the diversity of opinion that any number of legal questions might generate. Islamic legal theories had always provided leeway for judicial discretion in applying shari'a principles.[36] Operating with their own preconceptions, British judges seemed unable to accept that there might be genuine difference of opinion on a point of law. When maulavis did disagree, their opinions often simply reflected the inherent inadequacies of the British text-based approach.

Together with pandits, the maulavis of the colonial courts were gradually eclipsed by the precedent of case law and the accrual of British expertise. In 1864, under Crown rule, the Court maulavis were dispensed with altogether,[37] so that the official administration of Anglo-Muhammadan law was severed completely from the judgment of men of distinguished moral authority. Yet qadis performed a wide variety of non-legal functions, acting as marriage registers and notaries as well as providing guidance on religious matters. In the vacuum created after 1864, conflicts arose as to the proper appointment of qadis, and pressure was put on the government to reinstate appointments for non-religious matters.[38] Despite the revival of a state-sponsored system of qadis in 1876, the laity took recourse in the private 'ulama who increasingly were responsible for settling disputes at an informal level.[39]

Translations

Given the assumed centrality of legal text, and a persistent distrust of native law officers, it followed that legal administrators were eager to have Islamic texts in English translation so that indigenous laws could be applied directly by British judges. Sir William Jones, the great polymath of early Orientalism, proposed that Hastings should endeavour to compile 'a complete Digest of Hindu and Muhammad laws after the model of Justinian's inestimable Pandects'.[40] The model of the Roman legal system lent credence to the emphasis on a rule-based legality. At the insistence of Hastings, *al-Hidaya*, the influential compilation of Hanafi opinion, was translated by three maulavis from Arabic to Persian, and then into English by Charles Hamilton

[35]Wilson, *Introduction*, pp. 96-7. William Jones expressed a distrust typical of other British judges: 'I could not with an easy conscience concur in a decision merely on the written opinion of native lawyers in any cause in which they could have the remotest interest in misleading the court'. Quoted in Hussain, *Muslim Law,* p.30.

[36]Cf. J. Makdisi, 'Legal Logic and Equity in Islamic Law', *American Journal of Comparative Law* 33, 1985, and L. Rosen, 'Equity and Discretion in a Modern Islamic Legal System', *Law and Society Review*, 15, 1980.

[37]Act XI of 1864.

[38]U. Yaduvansh, 'The Decline of the Role of the Qadis in India, 1793-1876', *Studies in Islam*, 6, 1969.

[39]T. Mahmood, *Muslim Personal Law: Role of the State in the Sub-Continent,* Delhi, 1977, pp.60-69.

[40]Quoted in Hussain, *Muslim Law*, pp.30-1.

in 1791. But *al-Hidaya* lacked any treatment of inheritance, regarded by the British as the most intractable and politically important of Muhammadan law subjects. Accordingly, in 1792, *al-Sirajiyya*, a treatise on inheritance, was translated direct from the Arabic by Jones personally.

The courts continued to rely upon advice from indigenous legal specialists for some time, so the translations made little impact on colonial administration until the early nineteenth century. Their primary significance lay in the understandings they engendered of an essentialist, static Islam incapable of change from within. They established, in the crucible of colonial rule, that a proper knowledge of India - and of the Orient more generally - could be had only through a detailed study of the classical legal texts.[41]

The translations had greater legal effect as judges began to rely upon them more directly. Although produced in haste, and with imperfect language skills, the unrevised eighteenth century translations remained authoritative. A number of translating errors were discovered in *Al-Hidaya,* but corrections were made only to the Persian version in 1807. The English version remains uncorrected. The project of translating a broader range of texts, including non-Hanafi texts, never reached fruition, and was cancelled due to financial constraints in 1808. The nineteenth century saw only one additional major translation - an abbreviated version of the *Fatawa Alamgiri* and a portion of an Ithna 'Ashari (Shi'i) text, translated by Neil Baillie and published in 1865 under the title of *A Digest of Mohummudan Law*.

Together, these three translations formed the textual basis of Anglo-Muhammadan law. Their inadequacies and blatant errors have been partially recorded in court cases and commentaries,[42] but sustained research on the ideological biases of their rendering remains to be pursued. Even a basic text on the *usul al-fiqh*, or roots of jurisprudence, that would be basic to any detailed understanding of Islamic law, did not appear until 1911.[43] It is not surprising that those few texts which were translated came to be treated as authoritative codes rather than as discrete statements within a larger spectrum of scholarly debate.

Textbooks

Increasingly, the textual basis of Anglo-Muhammadan law lay with compilations of materials ordered in a thematic way. In the earliest of these, W. H. MacNaghten compiled a number of fatawa produced by the court qadis, which he published in 1825 along with his own wide-ranging generalisations

---

[41]The legal need for a settled universal rule that can be applied generally to a broad range of individuals may have given rise to a hypostasising trend in Orientalist scholarship. The institutional links between colonial legal institutions and Orientalist scholarship demand further exploration. In the meantime, for a suggestive discussion, see E. W. Said, *Orientalism*, London, 1978, pp.77-9.

[42]*Gobind Dayal v Amir Muhammad* (1885) 7 All 775: *Jafri Begam v. Amir Muhammad* (1885) 7 All 822; see Hussain, *Muslim Law*, pp. 45-52.

[43]A. Rahim, *The Principles of Muhammadan Jurisprudence*, reprint edn. Lahore, 1974.

under the title *Principles and Precedents of Mohammadan Law*. He purported to present an authoritative distillation of opinion on various subjects. The effect was to gloss over areas of problematic interpretation and present a unified rule in place of genuine differences of doctrine. In the years that followed, colonial administration gave rise to a number of textbooks,[44] which treated their subject with varying degrees of sophistication, but nevertheless following MacNaghtan's basic model. The device of the textbook organised knowledge in a way that made the most of a limited amount understanding. It minimised doctrinal difference and presented the shari'a as something it had never been: a fixed body of immutable rules beyond the realm of interpretation and judicial discretion.

Codification of Custom

Frustrated by the inadequacy of religious texts and native law officers, British administrators in the latter half of the nineteenth century began to focus upon custom as a source of law. From the early 1850s, but especially after the Punjab Laws Act of 1872, revenue collectors in the Punjab were directed to conduct surveys with a view to ascertaining customary practices in each village. The emphasis on custom remained strongest in the Punjab, but it gave rise to a reconsideration of legal administration at the All-India level. The Punjab surveys reflect a preoccupation with landholding rights since their main function was to assist in the collection of revenue.[45]

Working with preconceived notions of custom as ancient and stable within a fairly static society, administrators took custom to be a fact in the world that could be ascertained and codified, glossing over the contingent and political nature of the arrangements that they sought to understand. In practice, custom was seldom fixed and permanent. Rather, to act according to custom necessarily entailed a re-interpretation of community standards and the interpreter's position within them. More than a simple rejection or affirmation of community standards, custom often involved very real struggles over what the standards were in the first place. If even a part of the recent anthropology of custom is to be believed, what the British called 'customary law' was inherently incompatible with the epistemological dictates of codification.[46]

---

[44]Nine major textbooks were published in the British period. In addition to MacNaghten, *Principles*; Wilson, *Introduction*; and Hussain, *Muslim Law*; texts by W.H. Morley, S.G. Sircar, A. Ali, A. Rahim A.F.M.A.Rahman, and Tyabji are of note.

[45]N. Bhattacharya, 'Custom and Rights: A Conflict of Interpretations', Paper presented at Oxford University Centre for Indian Studies, 13 November 1987.

[46]See S.F. Moore, *Law as Process*, London, 1978; J. Comaroff and S. Roberts, *Rules and Processes*, Chicago, 1981, and J.Starr and J.F. Collier eds., *History and Power in the Study of Law: New Directions in Legal Anthropology*, Ithaca, N.Y., 1989. J. Scott, *Weapons of the Weak*, New Haven, 1985 is a broader study that illuminates many of the ways in which 'custom' in a local setting is essentially contested. Anthropological studies of 'custom' in South Asia abound: a somewhat dated but useful guide to the literature is Cohn, *An Anthropologist*, chap. 22.

Much codification operated by way of a search for precedent and underlying principle in what sometimes appeared to the British as the chaotic incoherence of village life. A kind of juridical homogenisation took place, so that indigenous terms were adopted to describe a wide range of discrete practices.[47] Codification distorted social life by way of selecting and interpreting material. The issue of land tenure, for instance, was a complex matter involving reciprocal rights and duties in a number of relationships; it could never be contained adequately within the simple question that preoccupied many British administrators -that of who would inherit the land.[48] Nevertheless, codes of custom were used as guidelines for the collection of revenue and the formulation of state policy. The nineteenth century saw the compilation of both district-specific and regional texts that could be used by administrators and courts alike.[49]

At the level of legal administration, a number of tests were developed to establish the content, validity, and applicability of custom. In 1868, the Privy Council affirmed that in Hindu law, custom could outweigh the written text of the law.[50] A similar doctrine was established in limited areas of Muslim law only much later.[51] Nevertheless custom operated against the general presumption in favour of Anglo-Muhammadan law, so its applicability was strictly circumscribed. In accordance with British understandings of custom, a legally binding custom had to be enforceable, reasonable, and to have existed from time immemorial; scores of decisions recorded the fussy and detailed sifting of materials that courts used to establish the validity of custom.[52] Customs that were held to be immoral, illegal according to general legal principles, or contrary to public policy were unenforceable.[53]

The jurisprudence of customary law allowed the colonial state to recognise certain aspects of social practice that were important to particular classes of groups. But its recognition was never allowed to extend beyond a point that would be incompatible with the political and economic imperatives of colonial rule. Above all, the codification and judicial application of custom

---

[47]See P. Robb, 'Law and Agrarian Society in India: the Case of Bihar and the Nineteenth-Century Tenancy Debate', *Modern Asian Studies*, 22:2, 1988.

[48]Bhattacharya, 'Custom and Rights'.

[49]For the Punjab, See A. Gledhill, 'The Compilation of Customary Laws in the Punjab in the Nineteenth Century', in J. Glissen ed., *La Rédaction des Coutumes dans le Passé et dans le Présent,* Brussels, 1962. More generally, see S. Roy, *Customs and Customary Law in British India,* Calcutta, 1911; A. Steele, *The Law and Custom of Hindoo Castes (within the Dekhun Provinces Subject to the Presidency of Bombay),* London, 1868.

[50]*Collector of Madura v. Moottoo Ramalinga* , (1868) 12 MIA 397.

[51]See S. Roy, *Customs*, chap. 10.

[52]*Abdul Hussain v. Bibi Sona Dero,* (1917), 45 IA 10. See S. Roy, *Customs*, chap. 18.

[53]For example, it was held that customary prostitution conducted as a family business was immoral and contrary to Islamic precepts. *Ghasiti v. Umrao Jan* ,(1893) 20 IA 193. See also the general discussion at S. Roy, *Customs*, chap.16.

supplied administrators with a set of devices for incorporating diverse practices within the political recognition of the colonial state.[54]

New Legal Technologies

Colonial courts introduced a set of legal technologies, primarily bureaucratic procedure and methods of inquiry, that departed significantly form pre-colonial arrangements. Most of the new bureaucratic methods worked by way of categorising and systematising indigenous phenomena. Within a centralised bureaucratic framework, procedures were established for collecting information, making regular reports, and distilling data that could be used in Calcutta or London. A hallmark of the early nineteenth century was the increased use of standardised forms in district administration. After 1857, village records and district reports supplied detailed knowledge of the colonised society.[55] On the legal side of things, perhaps the most striking innovation was the use of documentation in matters of law and evidence.

Legal documents *per se* were not new. Mughal administrative manuals are testimony to the importance of documents in the political administration of the empire in the seventeenth century.[56] So too, written contracts provided a flexibility of financial arrangements that enabled merchants to share risks and accumulate capital for participation in pan-Asian trading networks.[57]

But in matters of evidence, pre-colonial legal theory of Islamic inspiration seems to have placed a special emphasis upon oral testimony, and concomitantly, the probity of witnesses. In the evidentiary (and epistemological) theory of the shari‘a, only the spoken testimony of a morally reliable witness was admissible as evidence before the court. Theoretically, a document such as a deed or contract could serve to remind witnesses of what had transpired, but its veracity rested on actual oral deposition.[58] Accordingly, *Al-Hidaya* furnishes rules governing the admissibility of oral testimony, but makes no provision for documentary evidence. In practice, there is no reason to doubt that documents were important in Mughal and post-Mughal courts, reflecting their important role in politics and commerce.

---

[54]Although it was not long before the codification of custom was contested in political fora. See D. Gilmartin, *Empire and Islam: Punjab and the Making of Pakistan,* Berkeley, 1988.

[55]R.S. Smith, 'Rule-by-records and Rule-by-reports: Complementary Aspects of the British Imperial Rule of Law', *Contributions to Indian Sociology (n.s.),* 19, 1985.

[56]J.F. Richards, *Document Forms for Official Orders of Appointment in the Mughal Empire,* Cambridge, 1986.

[57]See A.L. Udovitch, *Partnership and Profit in Medieval Islam,* Princeton, 1970, A. Das Gupta in D.S. Richards ed., *Islam and the Trade of Asia,* Oxford, 1970, and K. N. Chaudhuri, *Trade and Civilisation in the Indian Ocean: an Economic History from the Rise of Islam to 1750,* Oxford, 1985.

[58]For a discussion of this general principle in shari‘a theory, see J. Wakin, *The Function of Documents in Islamic Law,* Albany, 1972. It is unclear how far the principle was applied in South Asia. For a comparative discussion, see B. Messick, 'Just Writing: Paradox and Political Economy in Yemeni Legal Documents', *Cultural Anthropology,* 4:1, 1989.

Nevertheless, it is clear that under British rule, the process of documentation and the role of the scribe were amplified.

Initially, colonial courts enforced the primacy of oral testimony over documentation, especially in criminal law.[59] The state slowly chipped away at the doctrine, by continually modifying the rules governing oral testimony,[60] and introducing forms of writing into adjudication. Starting in 1793, all depositions and examinations of witnesses were to be transcribed into the language of the deponent. Once taken, depositions were then to be translated into Persian, checked for accuracy by the court officers, and then communicated in English to the Magistrate.[61] In 1797, the text of the deposition, rather than the oral testimony itself, was adopted as legally binding in the record of the court.[62] Gradually, the practice of formulating English summaries of the vernacular record was adopted, and English began to displace Persian as the official language of the court.[63] With the Criminal Procedure Code 1861, and the Indian Evidence Act 1872, adapted forms of the English law of procedure and evidence were introduced in systematised form.

The insistence on documentary evidence was 'unreal in the context of a largely illiterate society', serving to make legal institutions inaccessible to most of the population.[64] Other effects were subtle but pervasive. Standardised forms for business transactions, contracts, and government agreements became more widespread. Increasingly, the government ruled by way of administrative circular order. The growth of legal-administrative categories - inscribed into codes of custom, bureaucratic orders, mandates for investigation, and after 1871, into census forms - were symptomatic of a practical and ideological need for a stable knowledge of the colonised society.[65]

III. Legal Scholarship and State Power

The devices of Anglo-Muhammadan scholarship had this in common: they served to *fix* the fluid practices of indigenous society in legal categories that could serve as a basis for political and legal decisions.[66] Even when colonial

---

59 See T.K Banerjee, *Background to Indian Criminal Law,* Bombay 1963, p. 249.

60 The shari'a rules of evidence were modified so that Hindus could testify against Muslims and the strict evidentiary requirements for *hudud* offences were modified, although hudud punishments were also abolished gradually. See Fisch, *Cheap Limbs,* and Jain, *Outline,* chap.21.

61 Regulation IX of 1793.

62 Regulation IV of 1797.

63 Banerjee, *Background,* p. 284.

64 Washbrook, 'Law, State, and Agrarian Society', p. 658.

65 Cf. Cohn, *An Anthropologist,* chap. 10.

66 See Robb, 'Law and Agrarian Society in India'.

legal institutions had minimal impact on actual social practice, they did operate to provide information about the colonised society.[67]

The reliance on texts over customary practices was a strategy that served to contain the contumacious complexities of indigenous mores. Colonial legal understandings were not strictly wrong, but they were arrested, frozen forms of representation. They often had more to do with a limited kind of textual accuracy than a genuine appreciation of the norms by which people actually lived. In simplifying indigenous legal arrangements to a form that could be administered by colonial courts, Anglo-Muhammadan scholarship reduced living norms to immutable concepts of purely divine inspiration.[68]

IV. Colonial Law and Muslim Identity

The apparatus of Anglo-Muhammadan scholarship bore the imprint of eighteenth century assumptions even as it was refined in the twentieth century. What this meant for the detailed administration of the law deserves further study. In the meantime, one point warrants sustained attention: the Anglo-Muhammadan law seems to have contributed to an environment in which a new politics of Muslim identity could flourish.

Assertions concerning ethnic and national identity warrant caution; processes of identity formation are not well understood.[69] Nevertheless, some homologies between the administration of Anglo-Muhammadan law and the consolidation of Muslim identities in the late colonial period may be selected.

Scripturalism

One of the most marked features of the late nineteenth and early twentieth centuries was the rise of a new kind of scripturalist Islam - a form of Islam that relied upon the textual sources of the Qur'an, hadith and shari'a commentaries as the only acceptable bases of religious authority.[70]

The administration of Anglo-Muhammadan law, as we have seen, proceeded on the basis of textual understanding. The focus on texts allowed administrators to ascertain general legal rules quickly, and it may have meshed with understandings of Islam found among sections of the indigenous elite, but it misunderstood the role of the shari'a in the life of most South Asian Muslims. The legalist ideology of colonial judges erred on the side of applying

[67]See M. Anderson, 'Law as Knowledge, Law as Control: Sati in Colonial India, ca. 1770-1840', forthcoming.

[68]For a more general discussion, see Homi K. Bhabha, 'The Other Question: Difference, Discrimination and the Discourse of Colonialism,' in F.Barker et al. eds., *Literature, Politics & Theory,* London, 1986.

[69]For accounts that highlight the complexity of the topic, see S. Barnett, 'Identity Choice and Caste Ideology in Contemporary South India', in K. David ed., *The New Wind: Changing Indentities in South Asia,* The Hague, 1977; and G. C. Bentley, 'Ethnicity and Practice,' *Comparative Studies in Society and History,* 29:1, 1987.

[70]The term 'scripturalism' is drawn from Clifford Geertz, *Islam Observed,* New Haven, 1967, p.65.

clear rules in a consistent manner, regardless of whether people genuinely treated them as binding.

Qur'anic precepts and the texts of classical legal scholars were not followed as strictly as colonial administrators had presumed. When harnessed to the centralised bureaucracy of the colonial state, shari'a principles were administered with a uniformity and rule-bound consistency that was unprecedented on the subcontinent. The orthodox rules of the Hanafi school spread beyond specific urban and gentry groups, as the colonial courts disseminated a unified 'Muhammadan law' to every part of British India.

But it would be a mistake to ascribe too much importance to the effects of colonial law. A number of indigenous processes were also at work. Islamic scholars in Deoband, Aligarh, and elsewhere engaged in a 'self-conscious reassessment of what was deemed authentic religion' based on a rereading of the classical texts.[71] Studies of the Qur'an and hadith gained a prominence that had been unknown during the Mughal period.[72] Popular understandings of Islam underwent profound changes during the late nineteenth and early twentieth centuries, so that a scripturalist approach to the shari'a spread from urban to rural areas, and from elite classes to middle classes.[73] Adherence to the shari'a became more widespread and was increasingly perceived to be central to the maintenance of Muslim identity.

Colonial Categories

Under the colonial state, the category of 'Muslim', or often 'Muhammadan', took on a new fixity and certainty that had previously been uncommon. In theory, each individual was linked to a state-enforced religious category. Identities that were syncretic, ambiguous or localised gained only limited legal recognition; for the most part, litigants were forced to present themselves as 'Muhammadan' or 'Hindu'. Courts repeatedly faced the problem of accommodating the diversity of social groups within these two categories.[74]

For the purposes of applying the law, who was a Muslim? It was established at a fairly early stage that the courts would recognise the important legal differences between Shi'i and Sunni Islam,[75] but what of other, more marginalised and syncretic groups? Could the Ahmadi and Wahhabi sects properly be classified as Muslims?[76] What to make of Khoja, Memon, and Mappilla groups who professed adherence to Islam but were customarily

---

[71]Metcalfe, *Islamic Revival*, p. 348.

[72]*Ibid.*

[73]See discussions in Metcalfe, *Islamic Revival*; Aziz Ahmad, *Islamic Modernism in India and Pakistan, 1857-1964*, London, 1967; and Rafiuddin Ahmed, *The Bengal Muslims, 1871-1906*, 2nd ed. Delhi, 1988.

[74]And more marginally, the categories of Christian, Parsi, and Jew, In general, see *Abraham v. Abraham*, (1863) 9 MIA 195.

[75]*Rajah Deedar Hossain v. Ranee Zuhoornussa,* (1841) 2 MIA 441.

[76]See *Queen-Empress v. Ramzan* ,(1885) ILR 7 All 461; *Ata-Ullah v. Azim-Ullah,* (1890) ILR 12 All 494; and *Hakim Khalil Ahmad v. Malik Israfi,* (1917) 2 Patna LJ 108.

governed by personal laws of Hindu inspiration?[77] Finally, in 1922, the Madras High Court affirmed the principle that anyone who accepted the prophethood of Muhammad and the supreme authority of the Qur'an would be treated as a Muslim in the eyes of the law.[78] The erroneous belief that diverse personal law arrangements could be subsumed under the two great classes of 'Muslim' and 'Hindu' was a failing inherent in Hastings' judicial plan, but despite the problems it posed for colonial courts,[79] it did provide a framework for legal rule.

Many individuals and groups thus found themselves in a position of needing to operate within their state-defined social space in order to secure the economic, political, social, and religious patronage of the state. Previous to colonial rule, communities had been able to maintain a high level of autonomy within larger political agglomerations, but increasingly, local autonomy depended upon being able to influence matters of general policy at the all-India level. The search for political allies, both vertically and horizontally, fostered the formation of new coalitions based upon, among other things, Muslim identity.[80]

The Politics Of Personal Law

The administration of Muslim law by a non-Muslim colonial power transformed personal law into a ground for organised political struggle. Not that this was entirely new in South Asia; Islamic idioms had served to translate economic discontent into focused political action for centuries.[81] But in the late nineteenth century, various groups adopted a new approach to Islam, mobilising around Muslim identity in opposition to colonial rule.[82] In this process, a particular version of Islamic law came to be juxtaposed with colonial attacks upon it.

This was first evident in the law of *waqf*, or charitable endowment. Prior to colonial rule, the term 'waqf' seems to have applied to a wide variety of royal and personal grant-giving arrangements operated among both 'Hindu' and 'Muslim' groups in South Asia. Mosques, Sufi shrines, and other religious institutions received income from the land-grants of the imperial nobility as well as the local gentry and prosperous merchants.[83] At the same time, a

---

[77]See the famous Aga Khan case: *Advocate-General of Bombay v. Muhammad Husen Huseni*, (1866) 12 Bom HCR 323.

[78]*Narantakath v. Parakkal* (1922) 45 Madras 986.

[79]Its legacy has continued to pose problems for post-colonial courts. See *Yagnapurushdasji v. Muldas*, AIR 1966 SC 1119; and comment by Derrett, 'The definition of a Hindu', (1966) 2 SCJ J 67. See also the more general discussion by M. Galanter, 'Hinduism, Secularism and the Indian Judiciary', *Philosophy East and West,* 21, 1971.

[80]See P. Hardy, *Muslims in British India,* Cambridge, 1972; F. Robinson, *Separatism among Indian Muslims,* Cambridge, 1974.

[81]See D. Arnold, 'Islam, the Mappilas and Peasant Revolt in Malabar', *Journal of Peasant Studies,* 9:4, 1982.

[82]Cf. C. Geertz, *Islam Observed* , p. 65.

[83]Kozlowski, *Muslim Endowments,* Chap.1.

variety of legal techniques were used by Muslims in South Asia and elsewhere to transmit property from one generation to the next while protecting it from political appropriation.[84] However, under British administartion, the tools of Anglo-Muhammadan scholarship were used to craft a single, shari'a-based law of waqf used primarily for settling estates.[85]

In the last century of colonial rule, disputes over waqf properties were commonplace. Reflecting inter-personal and doctrinal disputes on specific endowments, a number of cases were heard by the colonial courts in the latter half of the nineteenth century.[86] They led up to the celebrated case of *Abul Fata v. Russomoy,* in which the Privy Council affirmed a High Court ruling that the waqf in question was not of the nature of a valid charitable endowment, but simply served to aggrandise the family.[87]

The decision was symptcmatic of a broader colonial attack on waqf as a hindrance to economic growth in a market economy.[88] Despite genuine disagreements among Muslims concerning the merits of the case, the decision served as a rallying point for Muslim discontent. Following extensive agitation, Jinnah found his first major political victory in pressing for the Wakf Validating Act 1913, that purported to overturn the Privy Council decision. But for all that Jinnah and others claimed that the Act would restore the purity of Islamic law, the Act was closer to a political statement than a restoration. In a field where even the orthodox Hanafi shari'a was marked by internal contradictions, a single 'Muhammadan' law on the subject of waqf was pure chimera. The 1913 Act simultaneously affirmed a scripturalist version of Islam as it protected the economic interests of certain propertied classes.

The culmination of the scripturalist influence on law came with the Muslim Personal Law (Shariat) Application Act 1937. The act originated in the efforts, primarily among some of the 'ulama, to secure statutory enforcement of the shari'a. Their successful lobbying resulted in an Act that abrogated what were seen as 'non-Islamic' customs. The act affirmed, in the political arena, the equivalence of Muslim indentity and a certain form of shari'a. It was an act of indigenous instigation, but its form and purpose reflected a view of the shari'a that had been re-shaped in the British administration of Anglo-Muhammadan law.

Conclusion

From the outset, a deference to indigenous family laws marked colonial administration, and as a general policy, it was never set aside. And yet, despite the effectiveness of this policy, it contained the latent contradictions of

---

[84]*Ibid.*; and D. S. Powers, 'The Historical Evolution of Islamic Inheritance Law' in this volume.

[85]Kozlowski, *Muslim Endowments,* Chap.5.

[86]*Ibid.*

[87](1894) 22 LR IA 76.

[88]See D. Powers, 'Orientalism, Colonialism, and Legal History: The Attack on Family Endowments in Algeria and India', *Comparative Studies in Society and History,* 31, 1989.

a non-Muslim government administering a Muslim law, which threw up repeated instances of misunderstanding and simplification. Company administrators encountered a variety of legal norms and institutions that varied according to the determinants of locality and community life. In their search for effective and inexpensive modalities of rule, the British came to rely upon the devices of translation, textbook, and codification, to adapt indigenous arrangements to the dictates of colonial control. Given the constraints of language, financing, and a limited tradition of scholarship, colonial administrators developed a legal system that could secure the allegiance of indigenous elites and collect revenue. In these circumstances, it is not surprising that colonial judges looked less for accuracy than for certainty and uniformity.

At the heart of Anglo-Muhammadan jurisprudence lay a conviction that Islam was a matter of religious rules, of a more or less inflexible nature, which were of equal relevance to all Muslims regardless of their cultures and histories.[89] The internal contradictions, genuine differences of interpretation, and nuanced instances of discretion that often accompanied shari'a norms were, in the main, displaced by a rule-bound legal system. If Anglo-Muhammadan scholarship endorsed a scripturalist version of Islam, that same vision was transformed into an oppositional Islam that could be used in the anti-colonial struggle. It is one of the ironies of British rule that a jurisprudence which first served to implement colonial rule in the eighteenth century could give form to a part of the independence movement of the twentieth century. Meanwhile, the intimate interaction of legal administration and indigenous indentity formation lent scripturalist Islam an enduring quality that has continued into the post-colonial period.

[89]A similar assumption seems to pervade much contemporary scholarship on Islamic law. See Enid Hill, 'Orientalism and Liberal-Legalism: the Study of Islamic Law in the Modern Middle East', *Review of Middle East Studies*, 2, 1976.

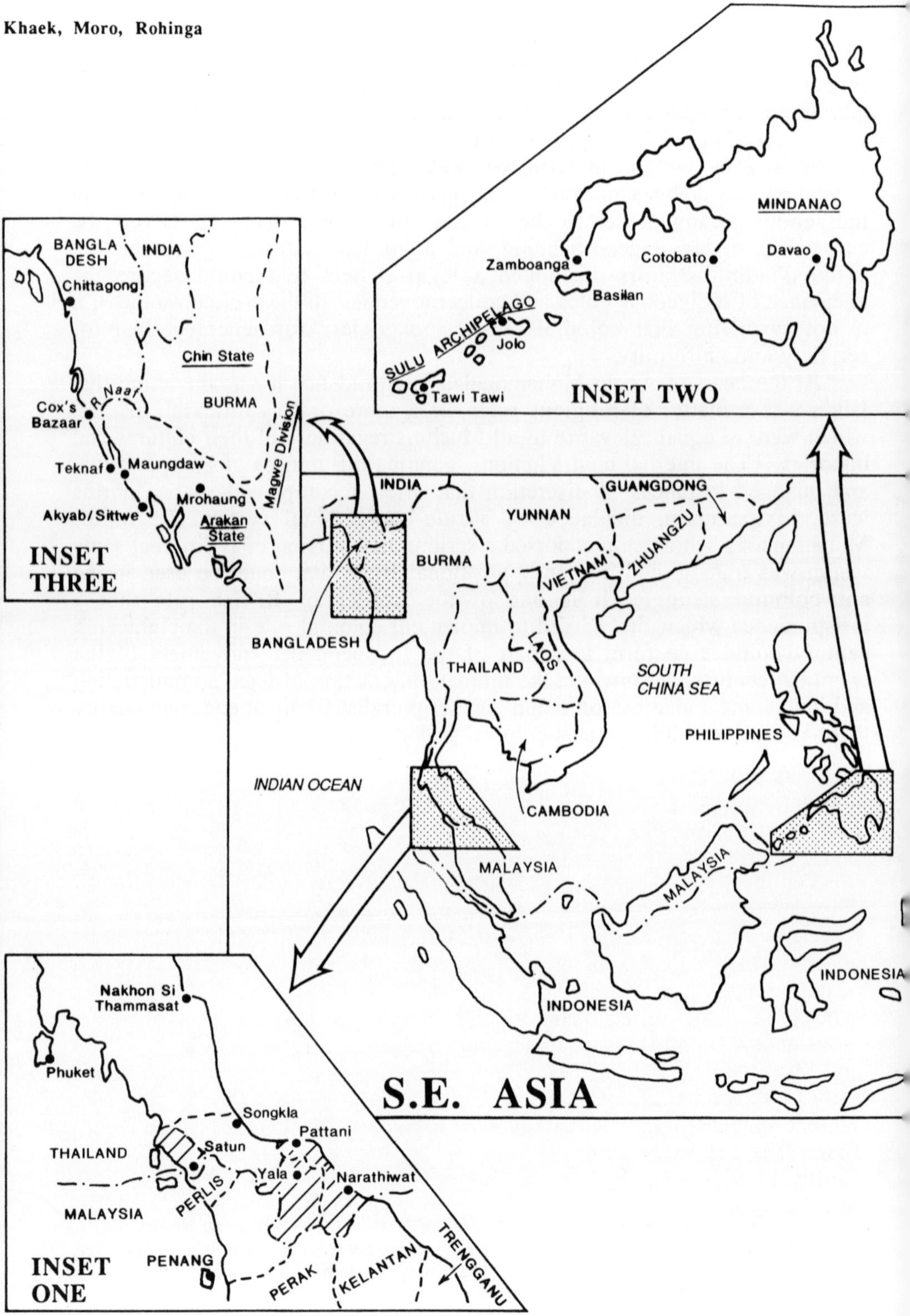
INSET TWO
MINDANAO
Zamboanga
Basilan
Cotobato
Davao
SULU ARCHIPELAGO
Jolo
Tawi Tawi
INSET THREE
BANGLA DESH
INDIA
Chittagong
Chin State
BURMA
R. Naaf
Cox's Bazaar
Teknaf
Maungdaw
Akyab/Sittwe
Mrohaung
Arakan State
Magwe Division
INDIA
GUANGDONG
YUNNAN
BURMA
VIETNAM
ZHUANGZU
BANGLADESH
LAOS
THAILAND
SOUTH CHINA SEA
PHILIPPINES
INDIAN OCEAN
CAMBODIA
MALAYSIA
MALAYSIA
INDONESIA
INDONESIA
S.E. ASIA
INSET ONE
Nakhon Si Thammasat
Phuket
Songkla
Pattani
Satun
THAILAND
Yala
Narathiwat
MALAYSIA
PERLIS
TRENGGANU
PENANG
PERAK
KELANTAN

12. KHAEK, MORO, ROHINGA - THE FAMILY LAW OF THREE SOUTH EAST ASIAN MUSLIM MINORITIES

Andrew Huxley

Some choose Muslim minority status, while others have it thrust upon them. The arguments for state recognition of Islamic Family Law are different in each case, and in this paper I shall concentrate on the latter group. A Manilan Christian or Bangkok Buddhist who converts to Islam can be said to have chosen his new religion with full knowledge of the legal consequences. Similarly a Pakistani Muslim who emigrates to central Thailand to work on a cattle ranch, or a Bengali businessman who establishes his base in Rangoon, can be assumed to have weighed the economic opportunities against the social and legal disadvantages of becoming a member of a religious minority. The position of descendants of such converts and immigrants is, of course, less clear-cut. The extent to which their parents' or grandparents' conscious choice should inhibit them from demanding special treatment must diminish with each successive generation. For economic immigrants the ties with the home country will tend to lessen with each generation, making it harder to reverse the original decision and return to Pakistan or Chinese Yunnan. In this context the Burma Citizenship Act of 1982, which I discuss in detail later, is of great interest, since it defines full citizenship as the prerogative of those families who have lived in Burma since 1824. Only the sixth or seventh generation descended from economic immigrants are to be given full civil rights.

But approximately half of the Muslims in Thailand and the Philippines, and perhaps a tenth of the Muslims in Burma, made no such initial choice. The majority Buddhist or Christian state came to them, rather than the reverse. Muslim minority status was thrust upon them in the early years of this century by the imposition of new international frontiers which reflected considerations of colonial *realpolitik* rather than religious distribution. The Khaek in southern Thailand and the Moro in the southern Philippines have become Muslim minorities through accidents of history. Moreover they live next to international frontiers across which they can see Muslim majority states. This is the classic situation out of which a secessionist or irredentist movement can emerge, and I shall summarise the military history of Khaek and Moro armed rebellion. The most intense stage of armed struggle in the early 1970s did not achieve secession, or even meaningful autonomy, but it did succeed in challenging the basis on which the state recognised Islamic Family Law. The present position in Thailand and the Philippines is that Islamic Family Law is recognised on a regional, rather than a personal, basis. A Muslim living in the four Khaek provinces of Thailand or in the Moro region of the Philippines can take advantage of special state courts administering Islamic Family Law. Conversely a Muslim living in Bangkok or Manila must obey the family law of the majority population. In both cases whether he is an economic immigrant, a convert or an ethnic Khaek or Moro is legally irrelevant. However, in order to understand how this recognition came about, the distinction between those who chose minority status and those who had it thrust upon them is highly relevant. Without Khaek and Moro agitation there would be no state recognition of Islamic Family Law in Thailand or the Philippines. An additional reason for making the distinction is that Muslim economic immigrants to the city have different attitudes towards Islamic law from their rural co-religionists in the border areas. I shall describe occasions when the majority government has been able to exploit these differences for its own, non-Islamic, ends.

The history of the Rohinga, who live on the Burmese side of the border with Bangla Desh, provides a contrast. They too are a regional Muslim minority, but their claim to have been cut off from fellow Muslims by careless drawing of the international frontier is much less persuasive. British rule in Burma favoured the Rohinga, and indeed the whole Muslim minority community. By the time the British left in 1947 the Rohinga had lost much of their ethnic identity and were ill equipped to resist the Buddhist majority's backlash. The British in Burma regarded Islamic Family Law as a personal, rather than regional, phenomenon. This approach has continued after independence, but two important statutory modifications of Burmese Islamic law have resulted in the loss of much of its practical importance.

Such are the themes of this chapter. Before I turn to a detailed exposition of the three minorities, it may prove helpful to explain how the present day distribution of Islam in S.E. Asia came about. At present, and since the beginning of the eighteenth century, a band of non-Islamic states (Burma, Thailand, Laos, Kampuchea, Vietnam, the Philippines) occupies the land between latitude 25 and latitude 5 degrees north, separating the Muslim states of Malaysia and Indonesia from the rest of the Muslim world. This strange geographical distribution of religious affiliation has its origin in the thirteenth century when Islam's overland conquest of the east halted with the Moghul conquest of Bengal in 1203 and Kublai Khan's settlement of his Turkic Muslim troops in Yunnan under the Governorship of General Shams Al Din in 1274. Any southward expansion from Bangla Desh or Yunnan would reach the populations of Burma, Laos and Thailand, where Theravada Buddhism had been adopted a century or two before as the religion both of villager and court. Neither then nor since have these populations shown any propensity to convert to Islam. But Islam's overseas expansion along the maritime trade routes linking the Gulf, South India and Bengal with the Straits of Malacca and beyond could leapfrog Buddhist mainland S.E.Asia, and proselytise more successfully in the archipelago, where the syncretic Hindism, Mahayana Buddhism and Tantra of the Javanese and Malay world was a religion espoused more by the royal court than the population at large. By the fourteenth century the early Islamic port cities of Malacca, Aceh and the central Vietnamese coast were established. Islamicisation thenceforth proceeded on three separate levels. Quite quickly it proceeded along trade routes to establish other Islamic port cities on Northern Java, on West Borneo and on Southern Sulawesi. More slowly it spread inland to the courts of the agricultural states in the island interiors. And most slowly of all it spread down from the Sultan's court to become a religion of the people. Had this process continued uninterrupted, no doubt the whole archipelago would by now be Muslim (perhaps even as far north as Taiwan?). But the arrival of the Spanish in Manila in 1565 was one of history's least predictable interruptions: for the first time in S.E.Asian history invaders came from the east, from far across the Pacific. And, unlike the other European powers in S.E.Asia who were motivated by trade, the Spanish were prodded into fulfilling their manifest destiny in the South China Seas by a particularly militant form of Christianity. In Luzon and the Visaya Islands Roman Catholicism soon became the popular religion, but in Moroland it had no success converting populations who were already Muslim, just as Islam had failed to convert in its turn populations that were already Theravada Buddhist.

KHAEK[1]

1. A Summary of Khaek History

The concept of a state bounded by fixed territorial frontiers was only introduced into the Malay peninsula this century. In describing earlier political history we must think in terms of arrangements whereby local rulers established themselves within a hierarchy. A lower king could retain his local autonomy in return for acknowledging the higher king's paramount rights by ceremonial gifts and military support. Such relationships were fluid and depended on the ambition and strength of particular kings, but certain relationships traditionally obtained. The Buddhist kingdom of Nakhon Si Thammasat usually acknowledged the sovereignty of the Thai capital (successively Sukhothai, Ayuthaya and Bangkok). And many of the Malay sultanates further south in the peninsula (particularly Pattani, Kedah, Trengganu and Kelantan) acknowledged the sovereignty of Nakhon Si Thammasat. In the thirteenth century there is some evidence that Thailand successfully claimed the whole peninsula down to Singapore. There were later centuries when the tributory patterns changed direction, and the peninsula from Nakhon Si Thammasat southwards owed allegiance to Malacca. These high level political changes did nothing to change the gradual Islamicisation of the Malay speakers in the peninsula, and in no way intruded on the local judicial and religious

---

[1]I use this term to describe the Malay inhabitants of Southern Thailand with apologies, for it is perceived by those whom it describes as highly pejorative, with overtones of 'stranger' and 'non-Thai'. They equally dislike the official Thai designation of them as 'Thai-Islam', and would prefer to call themselves simply 'Malay' or 'Citizens of Pattani'. To use the term 'Malay' risks confusion with the citizens of Malaysia, while 'Pattani' as an official geographical entity now describes only one of the four Khaek provinces.

courts dealing with Islamic Family Law. The fact that Pattani usually owed allegiance to the Thai capital at two removes did not prevent it from developing a reputation as the regional centre of Islamic learning.

The Siamese campaign of 1785 altered this position. Ostensibly launched to end the Burmese occupation of Nakhon Si Thammasat, the campaign rolled on southwards to Kelantan and Trengganu. In 1789-91 Pattani revolted, unsuccessfully, and was punished by being split into seven small states to be governed on Siamese principles.[2] Throughout the nineteenth century Thailand asserted rather more administrative control over Pattani than over Kedah, Kelantan and Trengganu. Between 1890 and 1910 the question of fixed frontiers became pressing. The Bangkok government, advised by European experts, began to modernise its local government system to maximise control and revenues. At the same time the British in Penang and Singapore were pressing the merits of a forward policy with the argument that loose Siamese control over the northern Malay states was not strong enough to protect British interests. Siam concentrated all its resources on Pattani, making six separate changes to the structure of administration within twenty years. The Malay of Pattani, seeing what was in the air, attempted an uprising in 1901, which collapsed after the Sultan's arrest, and subsequently petitioned the British, without success, to protect their interests. In 1909 the Anglo-Siamese Treaty was signed, drawing the international frontier through the middle of the Malay states. It granted the Sultanate of Pattani and Satun (the northern tip of the Sultanate of Perlis) to Thailand, and Kedah, Kelantan, Trengganu and Perlis to the British. This is the frontier recognised today, though from 1942-1945 Thailand again held the four southern sultanates as a reward from Japan for services rendered.

From 1909 until 1932, when a coup overthrew the absolute Thai monarchy, Bangkok's policy was gradually to replace Khaek institutions of government with its own bureaucratic structure. From 1939 to 1945 the policy was more urgent and brutal: Khaek language, dress and law were legislated out of existence, and the army sent in to enforce the ban. At the end of the war these policies were dropped as the Khaek lobbied hard in international forums. 'Since the frontier between Thailand and Malaya is to be redrawn for the third time this century to return the Thai war-gains of Kedah and Kelantan,' they politely asked, 'could we now be put on the Malay side of the border?' A petition to the United Nations in 1947 claimed the signatures of half the adult Khaek population. These requests were unsuccessful, and the most visible Khaek leader, Hajji Sulong, President of the Pattani Islamic Council, was arrested in 1948.[3] In 1960 Bangkok adopted a more subtle long term policy. It was now prepared to spend large sums of money improving its control over the education of Khaek children. Presumably it now believed that language, rather than custom, was the root of

---

[2]Nantawan Haemindra, 'The Problem of the Thai-Muslims in the Four Southern Provinces of Thailand, Part One', *J.S.E. Asian Studies,* 7, 1976, p. 200.

[3]Two years after his release in 1952 he disappeared (presumed murdered).

the matter, and hoped to produce a population at worst bilingual in Malay and Thai and, at best, monolingual in Thai. If increased investment was the carrot, the implicit stick was the threat of further transmigration. During the 1960s Bangkok demonstrated its ability to relocate 150,000 families from the solidly Buddhist northeast into the four Khaek provinces.

Organised Khaek resistance to Bangkok has taken many forms, mirroring the kaleidoscopic changes in the Bangkok political scene. The largest riots, or street demonstrations, or manifestations of People's Power, were in Narathiwat in 1948 and Pattani in December 1975. After the Narathiwat events some 6,000 Khaek crossed into Malaya as refugees. In 1947 a political settlement with the democratic regime of Pridi might just have been possible, but his regime was overthrown by military coup. The late 1950s, with the military firmly in power in Bangkok, saw the emergence of the various Pattani National Liberation Fronts which exist to this day. From 1973-1976, when student politics in Bangkok were of sufficient importance to be specifically mentioned in the Constitution, the South Thailand Muslim Students Group was the most influential organ of Khaek opinion. The period from 1976 to 1981, during which Bangkok once more came under authoritarian military rule, saw the most intense guerilla activity so far. The bomb attacks and murders were not limited to the Khaek provinces, but were aimed at, for example, Bangkok International Airport and the royal family itself. Since 1983 Bangkok has moved back towards parliamentary politics, and Khaek MPs have begun to play something more than a token role in national politics. In December 1988 they became part of the new coalition government, and have already received one political concession. Will this first success in pork-barrel politics offer the Khaek an escape route from what has been described recently as:

> ...an unenviable situation. They have been oppressed or ignored by the Thai administration, separatist groups have failed to give them long-term cohesive leadership or a sense of purpose, and their Muslim brothers on the world stage have not pursued their case effectively in international forums.[4]

2. Dismantling the Khaek Structure of Government

During the nineteenth century the Thai kings were content with indirect rule over the Khaek provinces. They appointed a resident Thai official to liaise with each Raja, but left the traditional Malay structure of government intact. The Raja of Pattani remained the highest political figure known to the Khaek. He continued to receive revenues from local leaders and to grant them honorific titles in return. His supremacy was not limited to the political sphere, for Malay principles of kingship placed the Raja at the apex of the Islamic community. With the senior Imams of the capital city he constituted a

[4]Cornish, 'Book Review', *Sojourn,* 3, 1988, p. 93.

body which could decide definitively on legal questions, which acted as the supreme court for disputes and which had a near-legislative power to issue authoritative recensions of Islamic law. This body delegated power down through Imams and local leaders, so that at village level family law matters were dealt with by the Imam, or by the *orang baik*, the wise elders of the village.

The first priority of the Thai was to get rid of the Raja. He was arrested in 1901, and in 1915 went into exile in Kelantan, where he died in 1933. His youngest son was prominent in business and public affairs in Kelantan: for many Khaek he and his children represent the legitimate line of Rajas of Pattani. In 1947 when Hajji Sulong organised the much publicised seven-point petition to Bangkok, his first demand was, in effect, for the restoration of the monarchy:

> 1) The appointment of a single individual with full powers to run the four provinces of Pattani, Yala, Narathiwat and Satun and in particular having authority to dismiss, suspend or replace all government servants. This individual to be local born in one of the four provinces and to be elected by the people.[5]

According to Barbara Whittingham-Jones, an English journalist who campaigned strongly for the Khaek cause, the democratic government of Pridi was willing to concede all the demands save this one. But any hope of a negotiated settlement was destroyed when Phibul overthrew Pridi in August 1947. The armed separatist groups, when they emerged in the late 1950s, put forward competing visions of how an independent Pattani might be governed. One group continued to call for the restoration of the monarchy, but others envisaged a people's democracy or a one-party state. In 1989 it is hard to imagine any situation inwhich the Sultanate of Pattani could be reinstated with its full nineteenth century powers. To this extent Bangkok has succeeded. Yet the mystique of the royal family continues, and can be harnessed for electoral ends: today the most prominent campaigner for Khaek issues in the House of Representatives is Den Tohmeena, the long serving MP for Pattani, who is a direct descendant of the last Raja of Pattani.

With the Raja safely in exile, Bangkok's second priority was to replace the middle level of the political structure with Thai bureaucrats. This was achieved more gradually during the first thirty years of this century by introducing Thai replacements only when a Malay office holder died or resigned. At the same time Thai laws which would be objectionable to the Khaek were left unenforced in the Khaek provinces. But Bangkok insisted on enforcing its revenue-collection laws, and the first evidence of the new policies at village level was the demand for increased tax payments. In 1922 the villagers, with help from the exiled Raja, organised a tax strike which

[5]Nantawan Haemindra, 'The Problem of the Thai-Muslims', p. 208.

collapsed only after widespread arrests. Since the 1930s the Khaek have consistently complained that the Thai bureaucrats sent to rule them are venal, racist and incapable of speaking Malay. In 1947 the second of Hajji Sulong's seven demands was that 80 per cent of government servants in the four provinces should be Muslims. Bangkok's response was to transfer some of the more notoriously acquisitive bureaucrats away from the region, but the complaints have persisted. Ambitious Thai civil servants regard a posting to the Muslim south as their least desirable option, and may be tempted to console themselves with the opportunities for rudeness and exploitation which such a posting offers. In 1964 the Thai government began a programme to teach the Malay language to bureaucrats posted in the south. Officials who passed a six month course at Chulalongkorn University in Bangkok were to receive a special pay increase. The pass rate, however, has been low enough to discourage civil servants from taking the course. An orientation course on Muslim culture and history is offered to new arrivals at the government's southern outpost - the 'Centre for Coordination of Administration of the Southern Border Provinces' in Yala - but this hardly lasts long enough to lead to any fluency in Malay. It appears that well meaning attempts to teach Thai bureaucrats to speak Malay have failed, and that there is no real alternative to teaching Malay speakers how to become Thai bureaucrats.

But civil servants, whatever language they speak, can hardly take up the Raja of Pattani's old role of ruling on questions of Islamic practice. Exiling the Raja had removed the embodiment of Khaek political autonomy, but it had also removed the supreme religious authority in the Khaek provinces. By the 1940s the government came to realise that it had no formal channel through which it could communicate with Muslims. Where conflicting interpretations of the demands of Islam competed for Khaek attention, Bangkok was left with no way of influencing the debate. Hence it invented the office of *Chularajamontri*, 'King of the Muslims', to stand at the head of a hierarchy of Islamic Committees under state control.[6] The *Chularajamontri* is elected for life by the Central Committee, who are in turn elected by the Provincial Committees. The organisation centres on Bangkok, and all holders of the office to date have been Muslims from Bangkok. To what extent the *fatwas*, the pronouncements, of this body are considered normative by Khaeks I do not know. But the questions which the government referred for decision in 1982 and 1983 are those that most inflame the contemporary Khaek provinces. Can Muslims join in singing the National Anthem, which starts 'We, the

[6]This was either the work of Pridi in 1947 (Surun Pitsuwan, 'The Lotus and the Crescent: Clashes of Religious Symbolisms in Southern Thailand' in *Ethnic Conflict in Buddhist Society,* 1988, p.193) or Phibul in 1943 (Michael Mastura, 'The Administration of Muslim Personal Laws in a Muslim Minority Country', *Papers and Proceedings of the First ASEAN Shari'a Administrators' Conference Workshop,* Manila, 1985, p.50). The government claims that the office dates back to the eighteenth century ('Thailand and the Islamic World', date unknown, Thai Government Publication, p.77) can be taken with pinch of salt. The 1955 Islamic Patronage Act formalised the institution.

servants of Thee, Oh Lord Buddha ...'? The Chularajamontri answered yes, provided the words are understood symbolically and not taken literally.

> Could Muslims bend their heads to pay respect to the painted image of the King? Standing upright to pay respect to the painted image is permitted. Bending one's head down, even if not as low as in Muslim prayer, is *makruh*, discouraged.[7]

The government is anxious that these questions be answered from Bangkok rather than Pattani, and by an organisation in which Thai Muslims from the rest of the country outnumber the Khaek. By the time the *fatwas* are repeated in the Khaek provinces, some of their subtleties may have been lost. See, for example, an article written in 1987 by Thawisak Da-o, head of the Muslim Relations Team of the Fourth Army Region:

> Take King Chulalongkorn Day, for example. Statues were set up. But the people here could not pay obeisance. Islam prohibits that. It's wrong to try to force people to do that. Muslims cannot pay obeisance to images. This is clearly prohibited. The solution is to use pictures instead of statues. Pictures are not prohibited. Only sculptured images are prohibited. I have told government units not to force the people and to use pictures instead. That way, there won't be any problems.[8]

---

[7]Sunan Pitsuwan, 'The Lotus and the Crescent', p.197.

[8]'Most Thai Muslims do not have problems', *Matchon Sut Sapda* (Bangkok), 12 April 1987, p.18, translated in Foreign Broadcast Information Service, *S.E.Asian Reports,* 1987, p.96.

3. The Battle for Islamic Family Law

By the 1920s the imposition of direct rule from Bangkok and the extension through Pattani of the national system of Law Courts and Police Stations forced the government to consider its policy on the Khaek use of Islamic Family Law. Thailand by then had codified and modernised its traditional Buddhist laws on marriage and divorce: bigamy had been declared illegal, and marriages now had to be registered with the state. Should Islamic law be abolished, and this national code applied to the Khaek, or should the Imams and village elders be left alone to carry out their existing dispute settlement procedures?

In 1926, shortly before the end of the absolute monarchy, the Thai king announced a wise compromise: the substance of Islamic Family Law was to be retained, while the procedure was to be brought as nearly as possible in line with procedures elsewhere in Thailand. The state's law courts were to take over the family law jurisdiction in the Khaek provinces, but they were to apply Islamic law to all disputes between Muslims concerning family and inheritance matters. The 1926 statute did not envisage that Thai judges would become expert in Islamic law. Rather they were to be joined on the bench by a *datu*, an Islamic judge whose decision on the substance of Islamic law would be final. No doubt there were Khaek who grumbled at having to use state courts for matters which had previously been settled in the village, but at least the principle that Khaek substantive law was Islamic had been established. Or so they thought.

In 1939 the ultra-nationalist Phibul came to power in Bangkok, and immediately promulgated the Thai Custom Decree. This, and subsequent regulations passed each year until 1945, attempted to dictate the day to day behaviour of the Thai people. Men were to wear shirts and ties. They were to eat noodles in preference to rice, and use cutlery in preference to chopsticks. From my western vantage point fifty years later, the regulations seem almost comic in their eccentric choice of priorities.[9] For the Buddhist majority population they must have seemed bewildering, but relatively harmless. For the Khaek minority they were an all too serious threat. The specific provision that burdens should be carried on the shoulder (Thai-style) rather than on the head (Malay-style) may not seem a matter of life and death, but everything depends on the mode of enforcement. In mid-1939 Phibul ordered units of the Thai army into the Khaek provinces to enforce the regulations. They enthusiastically arrested anyone found in the streets wearing Malay dress, and they publicly stripped Hajjis of their white robes. A year later the governor of Pattani ordered that all Khaek must pay respect to the Buddha image, as a mark of deference to the state religion. In 1944 Phibul revoked the 1926 Statute recognising the substance of Islamic Family Law. Henceforth the

[9]In a speech delivered the day after declaring war on the Allies, Phibul said 'Now more than ever it is important for our women to wear hats'.

Khaek were to obey the civil code like everybody else. All this, and more, amounted to a policy of assimilation by brute force, but before the simmering Khaek discontent could ignite into a major rebellion, the Second World War ended and Phibul was jailed as a war criminal. The incoming regime hastily restored the 1926 Statute and repealed the Thai Custom Decree. By now the Khaek leadership felt that if Bangkok could repudiate the 1926 compromise, so could they. The fourth of Hajji Sulong's 1947 demands was that Islamic Family Law should have procedural as well as substantive autonomy. He called for entirely separate Muslim courts to be set up, structurally distinct from the state courts. As we have seen, Hajji Sulong was arrested, and worse, but the Khaek petitions of 1945-7 had some effect. When Phibul returned to power in 1947 he left the 1926 statute untouched, and did not reintroduce the Thai Custom Decrees.

And that, throughout the increasing separatist violence of the next forty years, has remained the official legal position. Islamic law on family and inheritance matters officially applies to disputes between Khaek, and is administered by a secular judge and *datu* sitting together in the state courts. Some minor case law on Islamic questions has developed in the Supreme Court (the only level of the Thai judiciary whose decisions are reported). It has decided, for example, that the *Naza*, the document deeding property before death, is not recognized in Thailand since it does not fall, strictly speaking, within their definition of 'inheritance matters'. The Khaek must still be voicing objections about the 1926 compromise, since the Ministry of Justice called a conference on 'The Application of Islamic Law' in 1983.[10] The main complaint voiced at the conference was that the courts and bureaucracy were pulling in different directions. While the courts recognise the validity of an Islamic marriage ceremony, the officials - for example in the Land Registry - would only treat a couple as married if they could show a civil certificate of registration. The conference recognised that most disputes were still settled through informal village dispute settlement. A speaker at the conference suggested that present government policy was to foster local dispute settlement as an alternative to the formal system of justice. This presumably reflects a Thai concession to the Khaek demand for autonomous Shari'a courts. If people consider the government courts too secular a forum for Islamic law, they are encouraged to use the wholly autonomous, but scarcely state recognised, court of the Imam. But pressure for autonomous Shari'a courts is still being applied in the Thai parliament. Den Tohmeena, the doyen of the Muslim MPs from the Khaek provinces, has long campaigned for a separate Islamic court (and Islamic banking facilities) in Pattani. The new government elected in October 1988 owes these MPs some favours; time will tell whether an autonomous shari'a court is a concession it feels able to make.

---

[10]Vitit Muntarbhorn, 'The Aborigine in Thai Law' p.271-2 in *Law and Anthropology,* 1987.

4. The State Challenge to Traditional Islamic Education

Towards the end of the nineteenth century the Khaek organised their own education system, the *pondok* schools attached to mosques. In these the language of instruction was Malay, and the subjects taught were literacy (in the Jawi script), Arabic grammar and Islamic studies. These schools have been an influential model for Islamic education south of the Malayan border and elsewhere in Thailand. Pattani has exported both teachers and textbooks to the regional Muslim community. But sooner or later the Thai government was bound to attack them, since they produced a population for whom Malay was the first language, Arabic the second language and Thai a very distant third. By 1960, when Bangkok began to conceptualise the Khaek problem in terms of linguistic use, the pondok system stood in the way of their policy of teaching Thai as, at least, a second language. The struggle that ensued is relevant because of the important role played by the pondok in disseminating knowledge of Islamic Family Law. Fiqh was one of the most important subjects taught in the schools and Pattani has continued into the 1980s to print simple manuals of Family and Inheritance Law for use as pondok textbooks.[11] This system ensured both the efficient promulgation of the norms of Islamic law , and the continued production of potential experts who might in future years be elected as *qadi*.

The Compulsory Primary Education Act was passed in 1921, and the Thai government chose to enforce it first in the four Khaek provinces. The serious riots that followed caused the government to back off. From 1921 to 1945 they continued to build government schools, teaching in the Thai language, but did not enforce Khaek attendance. Most of the schools' rolls were Thai-speaking Buddhists; in consequence the schools boasted the best staff-pupil ratio in Thailand. Meanwhile more and more pondoks sprung up for the Malay-speaking Khaeks. The fourth of Hajji Sulong's demands in 1947 was for Malay to be the language of instruction in all primary schools. In 1948 the government offered a compromise. There would be a fixed number of hours per week of Malay language instruction. The compulsory course on Buddhist ethics would be dropped, and the history syllabus was to include an examination of Islam. During the next twelve years an increasing number of Khaek children were sent to the state schools, at least for the four compulsory years of primary education. In 1960 the government's policy changed again. Nationally, the period of compulsory education was increased to seven years (though subsequently this was not enforced in the Khaek provinces). Locally, the government moved to end the autonomy of the pondoks. They were to be registered as Private Schools Teaching Islam (PSTI), and would receive government funds to hire teachers to teach secular subjects and the Thai language. From the government point of view

[11]Matheson and Hooker, 'Jawi Literature in Pattani - the Maintenance of an Islamic Tradition', *Journal of the Malayan Branch of the Royal Asiatic Society*, 61, 1988, p.41.

> The pondoks have been reformed to become schools where both the Islamic belief and other lessons are to be taught more effectively with acceptable standards.[12]

The Khaek point of view is put in an emigre report published in Kuwait in 1970.[13] The author complains that Thai is taught three hours a day, leaving only two hours for Islam, the Qur'an and Arabic grammar. He asserts that the teachers of Thai are viewed as the eyes and ears of government in the village, and that many Khaek teachers have been arrested for teaching what is not allowed. But government control over the pondoks is still far from total. Unregistered pondoks continue to spring up in the remoter villages, though their teachers are committing a criminal offence. And the PSTIs have developed several ingenious ways of taking government money without teaching government subjects. These are revealed in a very interesting 1987 report of the 'Committee to Support Private Islamic Schools in the South'. But by and large the 1960 policy has been a success. In 1981 two thirds of Khaek children attended a PSTI, while one third attended government secondary schools.[14] But all these children were receiving lessons in the Thai language. A Thai journalist visiting Pattani last year reported that Thai was much more commonly spoken there than was the case twenty years before.[15] This contrasts strangely with the 1987 Report's statement that Muslims in Satun province, who have used Thai as a first language since the nineteenth century, have begun to speak Malay exclusively:

> Several knowledgeable people said that one of our purposes in providing general education in the private Islamic schools is to persuade them to use the Thai language in daily life. But instead, as a result of the instruction provided in these schools, the use of the Malay language is spreading to other provinces. This is very worrisome.[16]

Since 1970 the government has made strenuous efforts to open up tertiary education to the Khaeks. Previously a few students travelled to university in Saudi Arabia or Pakistan. Now two hundred places at Thai universities are reserved each year for Khaek students. The new university in south Thailand - Prince of Songhkla University - opened up with great fanfare in 1967. Only a minority of its students have been Khaek, though this may change with the

[12]'The Thai Muslims', Thai Government Publication, 1979, p.18.

[13]Translated in Walker, 'Conflict between the Thai and Islamic Cultures in Southern Thailand 1948-70', *Studies in Islam,* 9, 1972, pp. 146-7.

[14]Uthai Dulyakasem. 'Muslim Malay Separatism in Southern Thailand; Factors Underlying the Political Revolt' in *Armed Separatism in S.E. Asia*, 1984, p.233.

[15]Paisai Sricharatchanya, 'The Right to be Different', *Far Eastern Economic Review,* 26-5-1988, p.36.

[16]Narongrut Sakdannarong, *Siam Rat,* 30-6-1987, translated in Foreign Broadcast Information Service, *S.E.Asian Reports,* 1987, p.78-81.

new Thai government's announcement that the long-mooted Islamic Studies College is at last to be built on the Pattani campus.[17] Elsewhere in the Khaek provinces Teachers and Nurses Training Colleges have been set up. A far higher proportion of Khaek now receive tertiary education than did twenty years ago, but this has opened up a new focus of trouble for the government. The loudest expressions of Khaek anger in the last three years has come from the campuses: in creating Khaek students, the government has also created Khaek student dissent. In 1988, a dispute over whether female students at Teachers Training College were allowed to wear the veil bought thousands onto the streets of Yala for two months. In 1985 similar demonstrations had been sparked off by whether state schools should display Buddha images. It appears that this generation of Khaek have firmly opted into the state education system both in hope of economic advancement and because '[i]f Muslims can speak Thai, they can protect their rights'.[18]

But they are determined to fight at least a war of symbols. The students remorselessly examine aspects of majority culture, from the National Anthem to the ceremony honouring teachers for any aspect offensive to the Muslim conscience.

5. The Demands for a Better Economic Deal

Hajji Sulong's sixth demand in 1947 was that all revenue and income derived from the four provinces should be spent within them. Both before and since 1947 the Khaek have complained that they are the victims of economic exploitation. They are farmers and fishers, while the Chinese minority dominate trade and rubber production. The government replies that they are not much worse off than the other southern provinces.[19] But the Khaek compare their position not with the Buddhist provinces to the north, but with Kelantan and Trengganu to the south, and they are demonstrably worse off than their Malaysian neighbours. The powerful industrialisation of the Bangkok region has not impinged on the Muslim south. The only developments they have seen have been big tourist complexes, which are of economic assistance only to those Khaek who sell handicrafts or organise bull-fights for the tourists.[20] But this again is equally true of the Buddhist provinces in the south. The economic weapon which distinctly threatens the Khaek provinces is the land settlement program. During the 1960s the government demonstrated its ability to settle 15,000 Buddhist families from North East Thailand within the Khaek provinces. Each family received ten acres of land, and each 'self-supporting village' brought in educated Thai

[17]Paisai Sricharatchanya, 'Mollifying the Muslims', *Far Eastern Economic Review,* 3-11-1988, p.40.

[18]Uthai Dulyakasem, 'Muslim Malay Separatism in Southern Thailand', p.223.

[19]Though on the government figures of gross provincial product per person for 1980 all four Khaek provinces are beneath the average southern Thailand income per person. See Uthai Dulyakasem 'Muslim Malay Separatism in Southern Thailand', p.219.

[20]Hoang, *La Thailande et ses Populations,* Paris, 1982, p.112.

bureaucrats. Indonesia has shown the region that an aggressively pursued transmigration policy can blot out a minority problem. Both the Thai government and the Khaek know that this is the most powerful weapon, economically and demographically, against the Khaek's insistence on preserving their Malay culture.

MORO

1. Moro History in General Terms

In terms of present day international boundaries Moroland is the southern extremity of the Philippines adjacent to Indonesia in the south and Malaysian Borneo in the west. As a glance at the map will indicate, these boundaries do not follow any pressing geographical logic. Nor do they represent any ethnological or linguistic divisions among the population. They can be explained solely in terms of European colonial rivalry of a rather special kind. In 1565 when the Spanish arrived in Manila the area shown on Map Inset 2 had a certain cultural and economic unity. Culturally, a similar alphabet (of Sumatran origin) was in use in Sulawesi and Mindanao.[21] Economically, the region was dominated by China's insatiable demand for forest and sea exotica, for instance pearls, camphor and beches de mer. By 1565 this China trade was conducted from Muslim trading ports in Brunei, Jolo, Cotobatu, Eastern Borneo and Manila.[22] Quite how long these ports had been controlled by Muslim Sultans is unclear, but a Muslim gravestone has been found in Jolo dating to 1310 - the second oldest in the whole of S.E. Asia. One should not be misguided by the term 'Muslim Sultanate'. At this stage probably only the Sultan and his immediate court professed Islam. It was adopted by the majority of his subjects during the next century as a defence against the Spaniards' militant Christianity. Nor were the Sultanates 'states' in any modern sense of the word: tribal forms of organisation continued to dominate the region until this century. But Islamic ideas of government, and the memory of Malacca's brief but glorious empire, were to contribute enormously to state-formation in Moroland, Brunei and Sulawesi.

Such was the milieu into which the Spanish so unexpectedly arrived. They chose Manila for their base as the most favourably located of the existing ports for the trade with China. Thirteen years after their arrival they carried out their first attack on the rival ports of the Sulu and Maguindanao Sultans. These attacks failed, but were the first shots in a war that has smouldered intermittently to the present day. The initial reasons for this war were economic: control of the China trade seemed the only way in which the Spanish could make their new colony pay, but of course it was also a war of religion. Faced once again in their history with Muslim opponents, they applied to the new enemy the name of their oldest enemy, and once more

---

[21] Reid, 'Islamicisation and Colonial Rule in Moroland', *Solidarity,* 100, 1984, p.64.

[22] Kiefer, 'Sulu Tausug Polity circa 1840', *Solidarity,* 100, 1984, pp.75-6.

fought 'the Moro', or Moors. During the seventeenth century Spanish attacks on the Sultans of Brunei and Sulu failed, but they succeeded in capturing and fortifying Zamboanga. This was not the heartland of the Sultanate of Maguindanao, but was a highly effective base from which to prevent the China trade reaching the Sultanate's ports. Maguindanao began a slow decline into a fragmented agricultural state, but while it declined, Sulu prospered. Sulu's incessant slave raids against the Spanish controlled islands provided manpower to collect the exotica needed for the China trade. They no longer dealt directly with the Chinese, but with British and American ships desperate to find something other than precious metal which the Chinese would accept in return for tea. The great days of Sulu began to fade in the mid-nineteenth century when Spain acquired the technological advantages of steamships and modern weapons. The steamship enabled them to effectively blockade the Sulu ports and cut off the China trade from 1850 onwards. Modern weapons enabled them to attack the Sulu cities. The Sulan of Sulu capitulated for the first time in 1878. The treaty he signed in 1899 and his final capitulation in 1913 were to the USA: by this time the Spanish had ceased to operate in S.E. Asia. There is thus much force in the Moro claim that their history and Philippine history are quite distinct, since they were colonised not by Spain, but by the USA. From 1899 to 1914 the Americans ran Sulu and Mindanao as a separate political entity from the Philippines. Once the implications of the post-1914 policy of incorporation became clear, the Sulu leadership twice petitioned Washington to be incorporated into American territory. The intriguing possibility of Moroland as America's only Muslim Dependant Territory did not come about. It might have avoided the 50,000 lives lost in the subsequent Moro resistance to Philippine control. The post 1914 policy of incorporation went hand in hand with the policy of preparing the Philippines as a whole for self-rule.

To the Moro this amounted to handing control of their lives to Christians in Manila, and certainly some Americans inherited anti-Muslim attitudes from the Spanish: 'So long as Mohammedanism prevails, Anglo-Saxon civilisation will make slow headway', declared Major General Davis in 1903.[23] From this point of view it would have made sense to combine Moroland with their fellow Muslims in Borneo or Sulawesi. But such a course of action would have involved donating Moroland to either British North Borneo or the Dutch East Indies. In 1914 America was too enthusiastic about its new role as a colonial power to contemplate such a gesture.

From 1912 onwards Christian immigration into Mindanao had been encouraged, and by 1920, when the Christians were handed effective control of Moroland, the Moro had already been pushed out of half the island. The Moro claim they were cheated by the introduction of an alien system of land tenure which they did not understand. The Torrens system of land registration which the Americans introduced to Mindanao begins with a land survey and a

---

[23]Moore, 'Women and Warriors Defending Islam in the Southern Philippines', Ph.D. Thesis, 1981, p.75.

register of current ownership. The Moro did not register most of their land, they say, because they felt it belonged to the *umma*, the community, or because the land survey was conducted with undue haste and insufficient explanation. A similar survey was conducted on Jolo in 1916, but this was combined with a redistribution of land (which had all previously belonged to the Sultan) to the present inhabitants. They all received good legal title, in the Torrens sense, and have largely avoided the marginalisation which the Moro on Mindanao have suffered. The Christian influx into Mindanao continued after the Second World War, culminating in 1957 with a large group of rebel deportees from Luzon. In the same year the Manila government passed legislation which declared their policy in terms ominous to the Moro:

> The political advancement of the National Cultural Minorities [which phrase includes the Moro] must be rapidly fostered to render real, complete and permanent their integration into the body politic.[24]

These events stimulated a new, more organised form of Moro armed resistance than had existed hitherto. In the early 1960s Nur Misuari, a lecturer at the University of the Philippines in Manila, began recruiting for what was to become the Moro National Liberation Front (MNLF). Serious warfare broke out in 1968 in Mindanao, stimulated by an incident in which Manila apparently planned to use Moro troops to invade Malaysian-held Sabah. By the next year fighting had spread to Jolo and in 1972 President Marcos declared martial law throughout Moroland. The Moro had enough petro-dollars to buy sophisticated weaponry, and to ensure that the fighting was nasty, brutal and long. 50,000 are estimated to have died on each side between 1970 and the armistice of 1976. This 1976 Tripoli Agreement[25] traded a ceasefire for a promise of autonomy for Moroland 'within the realm of the sovereignty and territorial integrity of the Republic of the Philippines'. Much was promised but little has so far been delivered. In 1979 elections were held for the first experimental autonomous bodies in central and west Mindanao. But these bodies are designed for small scale local government, and have very little power or funding.[26] The current MNLF position is that although Marcos unilaterally abrogated the Tripoli Agreement in 1980 by calling for a referendum in Moroland, nonetheless all present negotiation must start from it. In the politics of the post-Marcos period, it is immensely important that Cory Aquino's late husband is on record as backing the Tripoli Agreement. A negotiated end to the Moro dispute would allow her to concentrate on the

---

[24]S.1 Republic Act no.1888 (22-6-1957), quoted in Puno 'Shari'a Courts - an Integral Part of the Justice System', in *Papers and Proceedings of the First ASEAN Shari'a Administrators' Conference Workshop*, 1985, p.12.

[25]The signatories were the MNLF, Imelda Marcos, Colonel Qadhdhafi and the Secretary of the Organisation of Islamic Conference.

[26]Macabangkit Lanto, 'Regional Autonomy: its Role in the Political Development of Mindanao', *Philippine Political Science Journal*, 15, 1982, p.1.

Philippine communist insurgency. On the other hand she may not be able to sell Muslim autonomy to her main political constituency. Her government has concluded another agreement with the MNLF. This, the Jeddah Agreement of January 1987, trades a ceasefire for the grant of autonomy to a large area 'subject to democratic processes'. One such process has taken place. The new constitution, with its explicit reference to 'Muslim Mindanao' has been approved by plebiscite. The next step, scheduled for February 1989, is an organic act of Congress giving autonomy to Moroland, which must then itself be approved by plebiscite. Meanwhile 40 per cent of the MNLF, who have formed breakaway factions on ethnic lines, are angry at being kept out of the negotiations, and the Christian majority on Mindanao is making noises of alarm. This is an interesting, but tense, year in Moroland.

2. Islamic Family Law in Moroland

The Moros have supported a literate culture since before the arrival of the Spanish. They have possessed the Qur'an for at least the last four hundred years, yet some of their religious observances would appear unorthodox in the Middle East. The daily prayers are not strictly observed and fasting takes place only at the beginning and end of Ramadan. Theologically, Sufism predominates, as elsewhere in Muslim S.E. Asia. In a 1987 discussion of Islamic Family Law, a Moro intellectual takes it for granted that Islam and Sufism march together. He calls for a court administrator to be appointed who '...knows his duty, who is knowledgeable about the Muslim way, the Sufi way.'[27]

Similarly, though the Moro had access to some, at least, of the classical Arabic works on fiqh, the Moro version of Islamic Family Law has differed both in substance and practice from the classical texts. Substantive law is very largely that of the Shafi'i school, but with the important local variant that a man must obtain his first wife's permission before taking a second wife. But that substantive law is mediated through the Sultan, who continued the Malaccan tradition of producing written codes of law for his subjects. We have a reference as early as 1744 to the Sultan of Sulu revising the laws, and I suspect these written codes go back a further two hundred years. Their production continued in full force until the American conquest of Moroland. The texts of a mid-nineteenth century code from Maguindanao and the last two codes produced by the Sultan of Sulu have survived.[28] Their short sections on marriage and divorce are orthodox, but mainly concerned with setting financial penalties for seduction, adultery and marriage by elopement. The Maguindanao text has marginal quotations in Arabic from relevant classical texts. These codes are not to be taken as evidence that the Sultan possessed a power to legislate. The 1877 Sulu code states that 'the Sultan promulgated it

---

[27]Rasul, reported in 'The Mindanao Problem - Transcript of a Seminar Held 12-7-1986', *Solidarity,* 110, 1987, p.105.

[28]Hooker, *Islamic Law in S.E. Asia,* Singapore, 1984, pp.19-27, contains a description of these texts.

with the general consent of all the datus, panglima and subordinate officers of state.' This sentence gives a good picture of Sulu dispute procedure, for judicial power and political power were not considered separate, and both were shared between Sultan and datu. The datu comprised the aristocrats, religious officials and those headmen to whom the Sultan had given titles. All of these were capable of judging a dispute, and all forwarded half the court fees to the Sultan.[29]

Such was the situation up to the American conquest. In 1903 the American Philippine Commission passed an Act directing the legislative council to enact a law that shall 'collect and codify the customary law of the Moro'. Apparently 'nothing worth admiring' was found, and no further steps to emulate the Dutch '*adat* law policy' were taken.[30] In 1905 the Americans introduced and staffed their own Tribal Ward Courts. Villagers ignored these almost totally, and continued to use the dispute settlement procedures provided by the datus. In 1914 Philippine law became generally applicable in Moroland 'under certain limitations'. Judges in the official Moroland courts were to appoint 'such Mohameddans as are versed in the local laws and cultures' as assessors and could 'modify the application of US law taking into account local laws and customs, provided such modifications shall not be in conflict with the basic principles of US law'. In 1915 the Sultan of Sulu was forced to sign a document relinquishing all power to adjudicate civil or criminal cases. Nonetheless the unofficial datu courts continued to flourish. In 1937 President Quezon exclaimed: 'These datus and Sultans should never be allowed to have anything to do with functions that are official.'

From 1899 to 1929 most Moro marriages were technically invalid for want of civil registration. In 1929 the Muslims were specifically exempted from the requirements of registration, but only for a twenty year interim period. This period was extended in 1948, 1950 and 1970,[31] but meanwhile an interesting Moro adaptation to the law gained ground. Moore reports that Tausug brides on Jolo now insist on a civil registration as well as a traditional ceremony, despite the fact that it has been legally unnecessary since 1929. Moore explains that the traditional ceremony is a secluded affair, while the civil ceremony allows the bride to parade the street in full white gown and veil.[32] From 1899 to 1949 Moro divorces were also technically invalid, since the Catholic majority abhors divorce. A 1949 Act allowed divorce among Muslims residing in non-Christian provinces to be governed by Muslim customs and practices. This Act was also expressed to last just for twenty years. It ran out in 1969 without renewal.

State recognition of Moro family law in the years from 1899 until 1968 when war broke out was grudging and haphazard. Both the Americans and

---

[29]Kiefer, *The Tausug - Violence and Law in a Philippine Muslim Society,* 1972, chap.4.

[30]Carter Bentley, 'Islamic Law in Christian S.E. Asia; the Politics of Establishing Shari'a Courts in the Philippines', *Philippine Studies,* 29, 1981, p.48 fn.9.

[31]Hooker, *Islamic Law in S.E. Asia,* p.230.

[32]Moore,'Women and Warriors defending Islam in the Southern Philippines', p.226.

the Christian government gave the strong impression that Islamic Family Law was an anomaly to be removed as soon as possible. After 1968, when President Marcos was searching for relatively painless concessions to Moro sentiments, he turned first to improving this dismal record:

> The government needed a dramatic demonstration of its constructive concern for Philippine Muslims. A Muslim Law Code fitted the requirements admirably.[33]

Reasons for such a choice could also be found in Islamic legal theory. In 1964 an American Jesuit writing in *Philippine Studies* had discussed the jurisprudential distinction between *dar al-Islam* and *dar al-harb*. The modern view, he concluded, was that dar al-harb was fundamentally a land where the legal decisions of unbelievers are regarded and those of Islam are not. The implication was that no legitimate jihad could be waged in Moroland so long as Islamic law was enforced by the state.[34] In 1968, in the context of diplomatic and perhaps financial support for the MNLF by the Organisation of the Islamic Conference, this may have been a real consideration.

This is the background to Presidential Decree No. 1083 'The Code of Muslim Laws of the Philippines'. The initial discussion, drafting, redrafting and parliamentary passage took from 1972 to 1977. In 1981 the government voted funding to bring the code into effect. By 1983 rival ministries had decided which of them was to implement it. By 1986 two of the new Islamic judges were in place in Mindanao, but none had yet reached Jolo or Tawi Tawi. In short, Manila has not rushed precipitously into over-hasty action. This unnecessary delay may now lose it valuable credibility over the autonomy question. A Moro contemplating the Jeddah Agreement could excusably foresee negotiations being dragged out into the distant future. That Michael Mastura, the present Moro spokesman to Cory Aquino (and, incidentally, a member of the Maguindanao royal family) was for fifteen years the leader of the campaign for PD 1083, guarantees at least that the Moro now have an unrivalled knowledge of Manila's techniques for procrastination.

Yet the delays in drafting and implementing PD 1083 were not entirely due to time-wasting. From 1972 to 1977 a real debate took place over the future of Moro family law. Were the unofficial courts of the datu to be given official status? Were Moro customary practices to prevail over Middle Eastern orthodoxy? An article by Carter Bentley describes this debate in compelling detail.[35] In summary, Michael Mastura's first draft code answered yes to both questions and concentrated on specifying procedures for new Shari'a Courts. Substantive law was to be codified gradually after the new courts gained experience. The government's reaction was that this

---

[33]Bentley, 'Islamic Law in Christian S.E. Asia', p.53.

[34]Gowing, 'Moros and Khaeks - the Position of Muslim Minorities in the Philippines and Thailand', Dansalan Research Centre Occasional Papers, 1975, p.17.

[35]Bentley, 'Islamic Law in Christian S.E. Asia'.

institutionalised existing practices rather than introducing progressive new practices, and they referred the draft to a new 'Presidential Commission to Review the Code of Filipino Muslim Laws'. The commission was headed by Dr Cesar Majul, a distinguished Filipino convert to Islam. The Muslim lawyers from whom it took evidence were all trained in Philippine law rather than the Shari'a, and had mostly served the government in one or another capacity. Their final draft, presented in 1975, was very different.

> Where the draft code was procedural, the final code is substantive. Where the draft code preserves Philippine Muslim customs, the final code prescribes behaviour consistent with Islam as it is practised in the Middle East. Where the draft code created a semi-autonomous judicial structure, the final code creates a small easily controlled compartment within the existing Philippine judicial system.[36]

It is Dr Majul's code which has become law as PD 1083.[37] Art. 152 states:

> Qualifications - No person shall be appointed judge of the Shari'a Circuit Court unless he is a natural born citizen of the Philippines, at least 25 years of age, and had passed an examination in the Shari'a and Islamic Jurisprudence (fiqh) to be given by the Supreme Court for admission to special membership of the Philippine Bar to practice in the Shari'a Courts.

This article was clarified at a conference in 1983 between the Chairman of the Supreme Court, Michael Mastura (by now Deputy Minister of Muslim Affairs) and others. The special Bar examination is to cover (1) fiqh and adat; (2) Persons, Family Relations and Property; (3) Succession; and (4) Shari'a procedure. The exams are open to various classes of graduates but also, crucially, to 'all high school graduates of local Islamic schools duly recognised by the government where Islamic law and jurisprudence are taught as part of the curriculum.'. The unofficial datus probably qualify under this head. A path is open, subject to passing the examination, for them to play a role in the new Shari'a Courts. In addressing an international Shari'a Administrators Workshop in Manila, Michael Mastura stressed two aspects of PD 1083. Firstly that it incorporates the principle of eclectic selection, thus allowing an area of variation within substantive Islamic law, and secondly that it spells out a role for adat. Art.5 states:

> *Proof of Muslim law and adat* - Muslim law and adat not embodied in this code shall be proven in evidence as a fact.

---

[36]*Ibid.*, pp.81-82.

[37]A full description of the law as passed is in Hooker, *Islamic Law in S.E.Asia,* pp.231-245.

> No adat which is contrary to the Constitution of the Philippines, this code, Muslim law, public order, public policy or public interest shall be given any legal effect.

And Mastura adds that 'public interest' translates the Islamic humanistic value of *maslaha*.[38]

With only two of the Shari'a Court judges in place as of 1986, it is far too early to gain any impression of PD 1083 in practice. But one's impression of its history in draft is that Christian and Philippine Muslims from outside Moroland united to convert a long overdue recognition of Moroland dispute settlement into a piece of 'progressive' law reform. The attitude underlying their alliance is summed up, in a different context, by Luis Lacar of Mindanao State University:

> We must realise that Filipino Muslims are probably one of the most isolated Muslim groups in the world, as far as the main currents of progressive Islamic thought are concerned. A progressive Muslimisation of the Filipino Muslims will be a necessary precondition for the emergence of a loyal and patriotic Filipino Muslim citizenry.[39]

ROHINGA

The Khaek and Moro have retained a strong sense of their identity and in the 1970s were able both to force concessions from their governments and to elicit international support for their cause. I discuss the case of the Rohinga to provide a contrast, since British colonial policies had the effect of diluting their identity as a distinct Muslim minority, and their rebellion following the Second World War was defeated so conclusively that neither the Burmese government nor world opinion is any longer conscious of them as a problem. From the perspective of Burmese history the Rohinga are a minority within a minority. Within Arakan they are vastly outnumbered by the Buddhist population, but the Buddhist majority in its turn has a history of independence from, and resistance to, Burmese control. Arakan is the 350 mile long coastal strip along the east side of the Bay of Bengal. Its northern boundary with Bangla Desh has always been the River Naaf, whose two mile wide estuary forms a marked geographical division between the flat coastal plain of Bengal and the mountains of Arakan. These largely impassible mountains form Arakan's eastern boundary with Burma proper. In the south the myriad watercourses of the Irrawaddy delta block easy access to Rangoon. Arakan's geography distances it from Burmese influence, but promotes maritime links with the Indian sub-continent and overland links with Bengal.

---

38 Mastura,'The Administration of Muslim Personal Laws', p.60.

39 Lacar, 'Muslim-Christian Marriages in the Philippines: some Tentative Generalisations', *Philippine Sociological Reviews*, 1985, p.83.

Little is known about the early history of Arakan, but by 400 AD a kingdom of Buddhist Burmese speakers had been established, some of whose coins and inscriptions have survived. This kingdom substantially pre-dates the foundation of Pagan, the first Burmese-speaking kingdom in Burma proper, but from the eleventh to the thirteenth century Pagan exercised some control over its older neighbour. After Pagan fell to the Mongol armies in 1287, Arakan regained its full independence until reconquered by Burma in 1785. To the present day the Arakanese retain their distinctive Burmese dialect which stays close to the language spoken throughout Burma in the sixth century.[40] Islam came into the region in 1203 when the kingdom of Bengal converted. The Rohinga arrived two centuries later when an Arakanese king deposed by the Burmese was granted military assistance to regain his throne by the Sultan of Bengal. In 1430 this Bengali army settled near Mrohaung, the new capital, built a mosque and became the first Rohinga.[41] From then until 1531, the Arakanese kings were subject to the Sultans of Bengal. Even after regaining full independence they continued to use Muslim titles (in Persian) in addition to their Buddhist honorifics. This practice reflected the increasing numbers of Muslims now living in Arakan. Many of these new arrivals were involuntary, for Arakan had become expert in maritime slave raids on the Indian coastline from Bengal to the mouth of the Ganges. In the seventeenth century, by which time the trade had become a joint venture between Arakanese and Portugese, it provoked a counter-attack from India which in turn sparked off the first Rohinga armed resistance: in 1666 a Mogul force made a punitive strike on the Arakanese naval base. As the Arakanese army retreated to Mrohaung it was harried by the local Muslim population.[42] For the next century the kingdom was weakened by interminable disputes over succession. An Afghan mercenary force brought in by one contender settled in the capital and played kingmaker for sixty years. In 1785 the Burmese annexed Arakan, only to have it snatched away by the British in 1826. Sixty years later the British controlled all of Burma.

To what extent, then, are the Rohinga a minority indigenous to Arakan? Unlike the Khaek and Moro, they are clearly not aboriginal inhabitants of their territory.[43] Their right to tolerance and recognition as a minority rests on the same arguments as apply to the Protestants in Ulster and the Afro-Americans in the USA, though their history is two hundred years older than either of those groups. They very quickly developed their own language, a patois of Bengali, Urdu and Arakanese, and their own literature, written in this language or Persian or Arabic, but these began to die out in the nineteenth century. To the British, the Rohinga appeared Arakanese in everything except religion, but this was the result of symbiosis rather than assimilation:

---

[40]In Burma proper the letters 'y' and 'r' are written differently but pronounced the same. In Arakan they have retained their separate pronounciations.

[41]There are rival theories to explain the etymology of the word *Rohinga*. Traditionally it means 'tiger from the ancient village', referring to these Bengali mercenaries.

[42]Yegar, *The Muslims of Burma,* 1972, p.24.

[43]Compare the title of Vitit Muthaborn's article on the Khaek: 'The Aborigine in Thai Law'.

Arakanese Buddhists had adopted certain Muslim customs, while the Rohinga had adopted the Arakanese language. No doubt under the King of Arakan the Rohinga developed their own procedures for applying Shari'a law, but we know nothing of what they were. Nor do we know whether the King of Arakan gave state recognition to Islamic law.[44]

Two aspects of British colonial policy were crucial in further diluting Rohinga self-identity, and both stemmed from the British insistence on treating Burma as if it were part of India. In the first place the British encouraged wholesale immigration from 'other parts of India'. Large sections of the new economy came under Indian, rather than Burmese, control and Rangoon, the centre of British government, became a largely Indian city. The cities of Burma proper already had Muslim residents and some mosques, but after the British arrival these numbers increased ten-fold. The Rohinga ceased to be a uniquely concentrated Muslim minority: to the British they became one among many immigrant groups. In Arakan itself the open frontier policy had a special effect. Bangla Desh has always been land hungry, and the British policy of encouraging seasonal Bengali workers to reap the Arakan harvests was construed by many as an invitation to settle. These settlers naturally inter-married with the Rohinga, and many Rohinga began to speak Bengali rather than Arakanese. Today, writes a correspondent from Teknaf in 1984, it is virtually impossible to distinguish a Rohinga from a Bengali.[45] The second aspect of British policy was their application to Burma of their Indian ruling that personal laws should follow religious affiliation rather than place of residence. This policy found its definitive enactment in s.1 of the Burma Laws Act 1898:

> (1) Where in any suit or other proceeding in Burma it is necessary for the Court to decide any questions regarding succession, inheritance, marriage or caste or any religious usage or institution,-
> (a) the Buddhist law in cases where the parties are Buddhists,
> (b) the Mohammedan law in cases where the parties are Mohammedans, and
> (c) the Hindu law in cases where the parties are Hindus, shall form the rule of decision, except insofar as such law has by enactment been altered or abolished, or is opposed to any custom having the force of law.

I have discussed some of the problems caused by this section elsewhere.[46] The implication for the Rohinga is that they were offered without question that which the Khaek and Moro have had to struggle to achieve - state

---

[44]The only surviving law text from this period is very similar to the oldest Pagan law texts. It concentrates on substantive norms, and gives no information about Arakanese legal practice.
[45]Linter, 'In the Dragon's Wake', *Far Eastern Economic Review,* 26-4-1984, p.36.
[46]Huxley, 'Burma - it Works but is it Law?', *J. Family Law,* 27, 1988, pp.31-4.

recognition of Islamic Family Law. Yet that recognition precluded any concept of local laws applicable to Rohingaland, such as the Khaek and Moro eventually achieved, by equating the Rohinga with all other Muslim immigrants into Burma. It has made it much easier for the present government to ignore the Rohinga's special historical claims and to apply a general policy that all Muslims in Burma are illegal immigrants unless they can prove otherwise. The 'Anglo-Mohammedan law in Burma' created by the 1898 Act has recently been analysed in great detail.[47] Suffice it to say that it was a case law subject applied by British judges following precedents from the British courts in Bengal. Many of the reported decisions concerned apostasy and conversion:

> From the reported cases it appears that people became Muslim so as to marry and very often left Islam so as to bring a marriage to an end.[48]

The commonest inter-confessional form of marriage was between a Muslim man and a Buddhist woman. In such cases the British recognition of Islamic capacity rules put the Buddhist woman in a most unfavourable position. For her marriage to be valid, she must convert to Islam. Yet when she did so, she became subject to talaq divorce and drastically curtailed rights of inheritance. Since Independence the Burmese government have made two important statutory modifications to Burmese Islamic law. The 1954 Special Marriage Act ensures that a Buddhist woman's rights on divorce are governed by Burmese Buddhist law, which has been re-established as the *lex loci*. The 1953 Burma Muslim Dissolution of Marriages Act abolishes talaq and allows husband or wife to sue for divorce on certain specified grounds. Mi Mi Khaing notes that Muslim women '...have never taken advantage of their new right, as Islamic tradition against it was too strong for women to feel bold enough to do so.'[49]

Taken together, these statutes have effectively brought the British system of personal laws to an end. Hooker concludes:

> In short, the history of Mohammedan law in Burma has been characterised by artificiality and brevity ... It was an accident of colonialism and with the demise of the latter the law, too, has fallen away.[50]

The Rohingan struggle, then, has never had to involve Islamic Family Law. The issues that roused them to rebellion since 1940 concerned ownership of land and, in later years, the struggle to avoid expulsion into Bangla Desh.

---

47 Hooker, *Islamic Law in S.E. Asia,* ch.1.
48 *Ibid.,* p.73.
49 Mi Mi Khaing, *The World of Burmese Women,* London, 1984, p.25.
50 Hooker, *Islamic Law in S.E. Asia,* p.76.

The Muslim community in general, having enjoyed favourable treatment for a hundred years under the British, was bound to suffer a backlash when the Burmese Buddhist majority inherited the state in 1948. For some Muslims, conditions in Rangoon during five years of World War and five years of civil war were a sufficient stimulus to leave. Others were expropriated by the new government's nationalisation policies. Others were ousted by inter-communal strife. In this climate the Arakan Muslims had a great deal more to fear, since for them the expulsions had started in 1942, in the wake of the British retreat. As the Japanese advanced north through Arakan, Arakanese Buddhists attacked Muslim villages, killing some and driving the others north to follow the British. In the Maungdaw region near the border the Rohinga retaliated by driving out Buddhists, and thus a de facto religious partition of Northern Arakan was created. This coincided with British war aims at the time. The Bangla Desh/Arakan border had become the principle front between Allied and Japanese armies. It suited the British to have friendly Muslims occupying both sides of the front, and rash promises were made concerning the creation, after the war, of a 'Muslim National Area'.[51] In 1945 the advancing British did leave the administration of Northern Arakan in Rohinga hands, but the future of Burma as a whole was much clearer by 1946, when the British allowed Arakanese Buddhist administrators to take over from the Rohinga. Rohingan exiles in Chittagong immediately sent a petition to Mohammed Jinnah asking him to include Northern Arakan within the boundaries of the future state of Pakistan. Meanwhile the new administration announced that Buddhists who had fled south in 1942 were to be given back their land. In August 1948 the Rohingan Mujahid preached *jihad* against the infidels. Led by Kassem, who had served with the British in the war, they conquered most of Northern Arakan by 1949. Ironically the rest of Arakan had been simultaneously conquered by a Buddhist Arakanese secessionist movement. At one stage in these years of multi-fronted civil war, the Rangoon government controlled little more than the city of Rangoon itself. But it clawed its way back into control during the early 1950s, in Arakan as in most of the rest of the country. A 1954 campaign reduced the Rohingan army from two thousand fighting men to three hundred, and these survivors promptly busied themselves with a smuggling camp on the Bengali side of the border. The Mujahid revolt was over, and Rangoon was once more in control of Northern Arakan, much of which it promptly designated a 'Frontier Area under Military Rule'. We now know that many Muslims were arrested in 1957 under the Foreigner's Registration Act for having no proof of residence and sentenced to a month in jail. Fifty of these unfortunates were released in 1984, having served over twenty years, and deported to Bangla Desh.[52] There were to be more reminders to the Rohinga of their precarious position in modern Burma. In 1977 the government took a census for the first time since Independence. The census started in those border states with a history of

[51]Fistie, *La Birmanie ou la Quête de l'Unité,* Paris, 1985, p.89.

[52]Lintner, 'Forgotten Prisoners', *Far Eastern Economic Review,* 29-8-1985, p.26.

secession, and when the census officials and army backup reached Northern Arakan 200,000 Muslims poured over the border into Bangla Desh. This drew international attention, and Rangoon was forced to negotiate with Dhaka to allow the Rohinga back. For a year the Rohinga refused to budge from their refugee camps, but most returned during early 1979. In 1981 a futher exodus took place, citing the proposed new Citizenship Act as their reason for leaving.

The Burmese Citizenship Act, passed in October 1982, takes the British concept of patriality to inspired lengths. Full citizenship is available only to those of 'pure Burmese blood', which can be demonstrated by proving that one's family was resident in Burma before the first Anglo-Burmese War of 1824. Associate citizenship, with limited civil rights, goes to those who can prove they have Burmese citizenship by the previous law, but who are descended from post-1824 immigrants. Anyone else must apply for citizenship by naturalisation - they have no better rights than any other alien. Explanation of the Act's motivation is probably best left to Ne Win himself:

> We cannot afford to accept into the organisations which hold the helm to the nation's destiny people of mixed blood who are not genuine nationals...It is not their fault. It is just a matter of parentage.[53]
>
> After Independence some of these Associate Citizens left this country leaving behind some of their family members. Some of them - *kalas* to be frank - did not go back to their home country, but went to Singapore, Hong Kong or America... They left behind a relative, say a brother, here. This brother would contact his brother in Hong Kong and his brother in England, and would smuggle goods out of our country... We are aware of their penchant for making money by all means and, knowing this, how could we trust them in our organisations that decide the destiny of our country? We will therefore not give them full citizenship and full rights. Nevertheless we will extend them rights to a certain extent. We will give them the right to earn according to their work and live a decent life. No more.[54]

The true Rohinga, the descendants of pre-1824 Arakanese Muslims, are eligible for full citizenship under the Act. But they must surely be worried by it. On what standards of proof will the government insist? Will a single Pathan great-great-grandparent who arrived with the British Army in 1825 be sufficient to taint one's 'pure Burmese blood'? The Act is far from reassuring, but in truth the Rohinga have little option but to sit it out. There

---

53 Address to the Central Committee of the Burma Socialist Programme Party (BSPP), *Forward*, 6-11-1981, December 1981, p.3.

54 Address to the Central Committee of the BSPP 8-10-1982, *Forward,* November 1982.

is no land for them in Bangla Desh. There is no support for them in the international Islamic community. A Rohinga Patriotic Front emerged in 1982, but its voice has been drowned by the longer established insurgencies elsewhere in Burma. If any consolation exists, it can only be the thought that things could have been still worse. No Islamic minority in S.E. Asia has suffered as badly as the Cham Muslims of Cambodia, the object of a determined Khmer Rouge policy of genocide.

CONCLUSIONS

In Thailand and the Philippines the demand for state recognition of Islamic Family Law has come not from the scattered community of Muslim converts and economic immigrants, but from the Muslim populations concentrated in the extreme south. The issue of Islamic Family Law has therefore become associated with other demands characteristic of a regional, rather than a religious, minority. Khaek and Moro demands can be summarised as follows:

1) Local autonomy for the traditional Muslim political and judicial institutions.
2) Formal recognition by the national legal system of the shari'a as traditionally understood at local level.
3) That the state should recognise and invest in the Islamic education system from village school pondok to post graduate level.
4) Recovery by Muslims of land 'stolen' from them and redistributed to the non-Muslim majority.
5) A better economic deal from the state for the Muslim area, either by increased investment or by less extraction of profits.

The present position is that both governments have made concessions on the second and third demands. In the Philippines the first demand is once more on the political agenda, but if local autonomy is granted to Moroland it will take some democratic form rather than restoring the Sultanate of Sulu. The fourth demand particularly concerns the Moro of Mindanao: if 'Muslim Mindanao' achieves autonomy by negotiation rather than warfare, it is unlikely that the Christian population on the island will be completely evicted to restore the distribution of population that existed in 1900. As in the dispute between Israel and Palestine, any negotiated settlement must involve each side giving up some claims to land in exchange for peace. The fifth demand is even more intractable. The commercial exploitation of Khaek and Moro natural resources has been in foreign hands for all of this century. Dispossessing Sino-Thai commercial interests in the Khaek provinces, or Japanese and Australian commercial interests in Moroland, would be an act with international ramifications. One can only see it happening if the 'other rebellions' of Thailand and the Philippines, the Communist insurgencies, were to succeed. The recognition of Islamic Family Law has come about in these countries because it is the only concession the state can make without offending non-Muslims. In both countries the recognised Islamic courts are welded into the national legal system, while the traditional autonomous forms of dispute settlement that have survived are denied official status. In both countries, also, the government is anxious to portray the Khaek and Moro as 'isolated' or 'backward' Muslims. The descendants of Muslim economic immigrants seem willing to collude in this portrayal.

In Burma, by contrast, the Rohinga were themselves immigrants, though long established. Because Islamic Family Law was recognised by the British on a personal basis, and because it was granted to all Muslims without a struggle, Rohingan self-identity was much reduced. Whether the Burmese government remains under military control or becomes a democracy, the Rohinga now face the distinct possibility of expulsion.

13. THE REFORM OF ISLAMIC FAMILY LAW AND A UNIFORM CIVIL CODE FOR INDIA

Werner F. Menski

I. Introduction

My topic involves two closely interrelated issues in the study of modern Indian laws, basically:

(a) the extent of reforms to Islamic family laws in India, and

(b) the difficult question of the desirability of a Uniform Civil Code for India, with particular reference to the position of the Islamic family laws in this context.

Following the introduction, section II considers the place of Muslims in modern India and takes up, in that context, some crucial issues in the study of Islamic law (the *shari'a)* in general and in the subcontinent in particular. In section III we consider the situation of Islamic family law in India generally and then focus on a number of specific issues that have brought controversy or debate, above all the contentious question of maintenance provisions for divorced Muslim wives, which is the one area of law in which the inherent conflicts between Islamic notions of law and modern India's professed desire for greater legal uniformity have violently clashed in the very recent past. As we shall see, this issue remains unresolved, with case-law appearing to assist the cause of legal uniformity, but at the same time taking particular account of shari'a principles.

Section IV briefly focuses on the question of the desirability and, more important, practicality of a Uniform Civil Code in India. Such a Code would either have to override Muslim concepts and principles of law, thus creating more communal tension than there is already, or it would take Muslim notions specifically into account, in which case other sections of the Indian population are likely to feel aggrieved. As we shall see, this is a dramatic constellation, in which the protagonists have to choose between the lesser evil; disagreements will remain and cannot be resolved easily.

There is, in my view, no realistic possibility of a truly uniform Civil Code for India, but I shall argue that India can - not only as a matter of political expediency - devise a Uniform Civil Code that will allow Muslims to follow the shari'a, Hindus to follow *dharma,* and will in fact give any citizen discretion to follow his or her conscience or notions of appropriateness; provided, however, that a national legal/moral/ethical framework is maintained and better defined than it is at present. This will mean that India must abandon her uncritical and quite unjustified continued dependence on Western legal models of development. In this wider context, as I see it, an acceptance of the underlying principles of Islamic law as an integral part of the Indian legal system in the twenty first century is inevitable.

This should not be seen as a victory for the Islamic chauvinists, nor as a sign of retreat of Hindu chauvinism, but will hopefully be seen as a victory for common sense in a professedly secular democracy. It is unrealistic for the Muslim minority in India, however large it may be, to expect that in a Hindu-dominated state one can expect to be governed by a totally Islamic legal system. I see many parallels here with the current situation in Britain. In India, furthermore, the constitutional guarantee of freedom of religion for all citizens, provided we know what we mean by 'law' and by 'religion' (for this reason section II is important here), remains relevant.

That Muslims as a minority in a non-Muslim country often face problems of 'split loyalty' has been noted by many writers.[1] Allott also indicated that the Indian case only *appears* to be different from the British one; the problems for the Muslim individual, in whose mind a solution to the conflict has to be found, are remarkably similar. Muslim individuals in Britain are told, often in unequivocal terms, that they have to abide by the law of the land; they might not even expect, as Indian Muslims do, that their personal law should be applied to them.

Modern India seems to have adopted, initially, a strategy of reducing traditional diversity, by seeking to replace the personal laws with a secular, generally applicable legal system that treats citizens as autonomous individuals. This approach has led to criticism, in particular from the Muslim minority. It now seems obvious that a totally uniform system of law is, for a number of reasons, unsuitable for India (as for many other countries), a fact that we may not like, but which is becoming increasingly apparent.[2]

The real problem for modern Indian law today, then, is not so much the tense relationship between Hindus and Muslims vis-à-vis legal uniformity, but the extent to which Western legal concepts are to be followed by the state. One tends to blame communalism for stirring up trouble for the Indian state, but to a large extent it may actually be the modern Indian state itself, with its continued unreflected reliance on Western concepts of law, that is the root cause for many communal tensions. The sooner this is admitted officially, and action in terms of legal policy-making taken, the better for India as a whole.

To a certain extent, thus, renewed respect for Islamic law in India (as for all 'religious laws' in the country) will remain an integral part of the Indian legal system, which can and will never, therefore, be truly uniform and secular in its application. The creation of an actually uniform Civil Code, a splendid idea for nation-making in theory, does not seem to be worth the effort any more.

---

[1]See A. N. Allott, *The Limits of Law*, London, 1980, pp. 142-143.
[2]T. Mahmood, *Personal Laws in Crisis*, New Delhi, 1986.

II. Muslims in India and the Wider Context of Islamic Legal Studies

Already before Independence (14 August 1947) it was apparent that, whereas Pakistan would become a country mainly for Muslims, the vast area of Hindustan, since 1950 the Republic of India, would remain the home of many million Muslims too. Tragic events in 1947 led to a huge exchange of Muslim and Hindu/Sikh population between India and Pakistan, mainly in certain border areas of Panjab, Gujarat/Sindh and Bengal. A total of more than 18 million people were uprooted in this way.[3] The current migration of Hindus from Bangladesh, who are then confronted by Indian Muslims,[4] and attempts by the Hindu and Sikh minorities in Afghanistan to leave that country help to keep this aspect of Indian communal relations in high visibility.

The 1971 Census of India counted 61.42 million Muslims, 11.2% of the total population.[5] The total number of Muslims and also their percentage of the Indian population have gone up since.[6] The 1981 Census counted 75.512.439 Muslims, 11.39% of the population.

There is a common perception by Hindus, who constitute the overwhelming majority (82.7% in the 1971 Census, 82.64% in the 1981 Census), that the Muslim population is growing faster than average. This is true, as Muslims appear more opposed than other Indians to the various methods of birth control, and as they continue to gain by conversions. The well-publicised conversion of a whole village in South India some years ago rekindled Hindu fears of the Muslim 'threat'. Violent clashes have erupted in the last few years over the Ramjanmabhumi-Babri Masjid issue, a derelict building in North India which is claimed both as a mosque and as a Hindu temple.

Locally, communal tensions between Muslims and non-Muslims are not infrequent; there are several points of potential conflict, including legal matters:

> Muslims are found in every nook and corner of the country. In some parts of India their population is larger than the national average. In forty districts of India the Muslim population is over twenty per cent.[7]

---

[3]Memory of this is strong also today and is reinforced by scenes in Attenborough's film on Gandhi and in the popular Indian TV soap opera *Buniad*.

[4]*India Today*, 15 April 1989, pp.53-54.

[5]Bangladesh has a Hindu minority of more than 12%, 17.5 million people (*India Today*, 15 April 1989, p.53). The parallel case of the Hindu minority in Bangladesh provides an instructive example for comparative study. Some useful material can be found in W. F. Menski and T. Rahman, 'Hindus and the law in Bangladesh' in *South Asia Research*, 8, 1989, pp.111-131.

[6]T. Mahmood, *The Muslim Law of India*, Allahabad, 1982, tells us that there were nearly 70 million Muslims, over 12% of the total population.

[7]*Ibid.*, p.4.

As in Britain today, we therefore find that Muslims may be a dominant group locally, while they remain a minority group nationally. At various levels and to varying degrees, flexibility is required to allow Muslims to continue their way of life. As now in Britain, Indian Muslims have traditionally organised themselves into local communities concentrated in certain neighbourhoods (*mohallas*), a common feature throughout India, but by no means unusual in view of traditional Indian patterns of segregation. Despite this partial segregation, it remains a fact that Muslims are a highly visible and virtually omnipresent Indian minority, especially in the areas of former Muslim princely states, such as Hyderabad, in Kerala, certain parts of Gujarat and Maharashtra, and in many areas of the North Indian 'Hindi belt'.

Politically, Muslims have traditionally been part of the Indian Congress structure, which sees Muslims as an important vote bank. India has twice had a Muslim president (1967-69 and 1974-77), many Muslim Supreme Court judges, and there is considerable Muslim representation in other high public offices. There are some Muslim parties, but they do not seem very important in electoral terms. In socio-economic matters, the Indian Muslims do not appear to differ significantly from the Hindu majority. There is a growing urban middle class and a large percentage of poor, uneducated people - as among the Hindus. Job opportunities in the Middle East have given an important bonus to many Indian Muslims, with spectacular results especially in Kerala, but Hindus and Christians have benefited too from such economic chances for people with the right skills (and connections) rather than because they belong to a particular religion.

In a situation of perennial scarce commodities, though, fierce competition locally can easily look like, or be portrayed as, Hindu-Muslim clashes. This happened apparently in Gujarat in 1985, when Hindu-Muslim riots erupted as a result of disagreements over the preferential treatment of certain backward classes in the state.[8] In a climate of continuing tense communal relations, such distortions and considerable mistrust have to be reckoned with by any law reformer.

Now, before we begin to look at Islamic law in India, I find it important to consider the position of Muslims in India in the wider context of Islamic legal studies, for two reasons:

(i) Indian Muslims and the Indian Government's attitude to them continue to be influenced by developments in the Islamic world. There can be no doubt that Pakistan's steps towards Islamisation and the adoption of Islam as state religion in Bangladesh (1988) have been influencing developments in India.

(ii) Islamic legal studies continue to emphasise the religious nature of Islamic law.[9] A secular democracy such as India with a strong constitutional mandate to strengthen secularism could be perceived as a perennial threat to Islam and to the continuation of Islamic law. Therefore,

[8] J. V. Vyas, *The Role of Caste in the Development of Modern Indian Politics: A Study of the 1985 Gujarat Caste Riots,* Stirling, Unpublished B.A. dissertation, 1989.

[9] See J. Schacht, *An Introduction to Islamic Law,* Oxford, 1964, p.1, and D. Pearl, *A Textbook on Muslim Law,* London, 2nd ed. 1987, p.1. [Hereinafter Pearl 2nd ed.]

before we talk about the Indian situation, we need to reflect on the perception of Islamic law as a religious law.

Here we need to ask, in particular, why it is that Muslims all over the world seem to find it difficult to reconcile state identity and individual Muslim identity. These difficulties arise even in Muslim countries; but how much stronger will the conflicts of identity be when the state does not represent and promote the values of an Islamic society, when it is manifestly un-Islamic, or even anti-religious in general terms ? Muslims, we are told virtually everywhere, cannot accept a separation between law and religion. The underlying reason for this appears to be that Islam, quite unlike other Asian and African religions, is based on a strictly binding core of religious dogmas that all believers have to accept without qualification. From the core of Islamic belief, that there is one God, and that the Prophet Muhammad is his messenger and last Prophet, follows a third axiom, namely that the Qur'an is God's word. Any deviation from this is bound to lead to accusations of heresy. For example, the Ahmadiyyas of Pakistan, who have their own version of who God's last Prophet is, were promptly declared non-Muslims. However, it is a somewhat difficult and uncomfortable truth for many Muslims that they cannot, among themselves, agree more fully about anything than some very elementary fundamentals of their religion. All the rest, whether we take the common believer or the highly sophisticated jurist of Islamic law, is a matter of considerable diversity of opinion and of religious practice.

From this central Islamic belief system developed the concept of shari‘a, the good or right path, which is actually not dissimilar to the Hindu dharma.[10] But while in Islam much emphasis is put on the relationship between the individual believer and God, Hinduism, although it later developed important theistic trends, sees every individual (including the non-Hindus) in a much wider socio-religious context, as part of the macrocosmic and microcosmic environment, thereby telling every individual that he/she has a role to play as part of the cosmic whole and is responsible, to an extent, for the future development of this whole. The real nature of God, the Hindus admit, is not known, but there is a supernatural order in full operation. The Hindu gods may have huge supernatural powers, but there is a much more diffused power structure within Hinduism than we find in Islam with its centralising focus on one God. This has a number of important consequences for our present discussion.

In Hinduism and Hindu law, it is explicitly admitted, though somewhat reluctantly and by no means everywhere, that dharma is a matter of individual conscience. This leaves very limited scope for central, let alone state regulation of an individual's way of life. Islam, too, appears to give importance to the individual's conscience, but focuses the believer's attention on judgment by an almighty God who has given man an ideal system to follow. In Islamic law, the jurists have tended to belittle the importance of individual discretion. For only slightly different reasons than in Hindu law,

---

[10]See P. Diwan, *Muslim Law in Modern India*, Allahabad, 1977, p.16.

the Muslim ruler is denied the power to make his own laws. The later (compared to Hinduism) and much more juristically refined Islamic system of law seems to say that God has made laws for all people and for all times to come, covering all situations, thus leaving little or no room for individual discretion.

Thus, Muslims the world over have got themselves into considerable difficulties - with non-Muslims and among themselves - over the claim that where God himself has legislated, man has no right to make laws. In other words, the Qur'an as God's word is seen as a complete code of law, an all-encompassing Uniform Civil Code, which provides guidance in all matters of human existence, alike in the seventh and in the twentieth century.

Let us now turn to books on Islamic law to see how this wide claim of Islamic law has been operationalised. One of the leading Indian textbooks states the central matter thus :

> According to classical belief of the Muslims the word of God is law and law is the command of God. This law is known as sharia. In the word of God is included, of course, the Koran, but the Divinely inspired sunna of the Prophet ranks equal. These two are immutable and the only room for the exercise of human reason is in their understanding. These two sources, namely, the Koran and sunna may thus be said to form the fundamental roots of Islamic law.[11]

Here we find the commonly accepted tradition that not only God's word in the Qur'an, but also the sunna possesses supreme authority. The author indicates the human duty, to be exercised by jurists only,[12] of discovering the right principle and understanding the basic sources correctly. The text does not help us in assessing how individual Muslims are to ascertain what is right or wrong in their life-situations and how much flexibility will be allowed. The author does indicate, in the context of his discussion of *ijma'*, that the law may need to change with the changing times and that new facts may require new decisions,[13] but we are not told how this is to be done and are left with a defensive summary refutation of Western writers who "have derisively described ijma as a means of 'Muslims shaping Islam' instead of 'Islam shaping Muslims'".[14]

Similarly, another leading textbook on Indian Islamic law introduces us briefly to the basic concepts of the shari'a:

> Muhammadan law as it exists today is the result of a continuous process of development. According to the classical

[11] D. F. Mulla, *Mulla's Principles of Mahomedan law*, 18th ed. by M. and A. Hidayatullah, Bombay, 1982, p.xxiv. [Hereinafter *Mulla's Principles*]

[12] *Mulla's Principles*, p.xxvi.

[13] *Ibid.*, p.xxiv.

[14] *Ibid.*

> theory, it consists of the express injunctions of the Koran; of the legislation introduced by the 'practice' (sunna) of the Prophet; and of the opinions of lawyers. Islamic law is not a systematic code, but a living and growing organism; nevertheless there is amongst its different schools a large measure of agreement, because the starting point and the basic principles are identical.[15]

These basic principles are again taken up in a short discussion of the origin of Islamic law, in which the author points out the intimate connection of Islamic law with religion and the moral qualities of shari'a.[16] This concept of shari'a, "embraces all human actions. For this reason it is not 'law' in the modern sense; it contains an infallible guide to ethics".[17]

There is, thus, a tendency towards religious evaluation of all the affairs of life, and the shari'a is depicted as 'totalitarian; all human activity is embraced in its sovereign domain'.[18] These various indications of the importance of the moral and ethical elements in Islamic law are not further explained; the reader is again left to his/her own devices and all we learn is that,

> Obviously, moral obligation is quite a different thing from legal necessity, and if in law these distinctions are not kept in mind, error and confusion are the inevitable result.[19]

Other Indian textbooks on Islamic law in modern India contain small but instructive sections on the concepts and sources of Islamic law. A good discussion can be found in Diwan.[20] The author shows that Muslims see the Qur'an as 'the very words of God', but come to a rapid disagreement on the indirect or internal revelations, i.e. about the authenticity of the sunna.

By stressing the ethical principles underlying the basic notion of shari'a, by suggesting that the Qur'an is more important for its spiritual value than for its legal content, and by accepting Schacht's distinction between the purely religious sphere and the sphere of law proper, the author also notes that:

> [i]t is a unique feature of Muslim law that there has been a constant divergence between theory and practice. There are several areas where a mere lip-service is paid to theory and the practice is allowed to have its way. Even in matters which are considered to be closely linked with religion, evasion of theory has been allowed.[21]

---

[15]Fyzee, *Outlines of Muhammadan Law*, New Delhi, 4th ed. 1977, p.1.
[16]*Ibid.*, pp.14, 15.
[17]*Ibid.*, p.16.
[18]*Ibid.*, p.17.
[19]*Ibid.*
[20]Diwan, *Muslim Law in Modern India*, pp. 16-19, 26-32.
[21]*Ibid.*, p.18.

The indisputable claim that the Qur'an is of divine origin is, however, commonly used as an argument against reforms. Diwan shows that the Indian Muslims have taken precisely this position to protect their personal law from state interference, despite the difficulty in reading the Qur'an chiefly as a code of law.[22]

Nor could the solution to this difficulty be found in the works of Muslim scholars. In Tahir Mahmood's several major studies on the Muslim personal law in India,[23] there is little emphasis on classical Islamic law. The author's preference for 'Muslim law' as the most appropriate term for the personal law of the Indian Muslims is considered in some detail.[24] In this context, little more than a few hints are dropped that Islamic law is something more than merely a personal law or family law. Shariat (which is distinguished from the Arabic shari'a) is depicted as the 'Islamic code of life'.[25] Later on, the classical sources of Islamic law are briefly considered,[26] but this is a perfunctory textbook treatment without analytical input. In his most recent study, we find a forceful lecture on 'Shariat - The misunderstood law of Islam'[27] which contains strong criticism especially of colonial misrepresentations and deliberate distortions of Islamic law in India. Mahmood, however, makes only a passing reference to the shari'a as 'a complete legal system'.[28]

European writers on Islamic law, who were severely criticised by Mahmood,[29] have more recently contributed much to the study of Islamic laws. But their works, too, seem to lack clarity regarding the relationship of law and religion, probably because the common distinction (so important to Western lawyers) of the religious and the legal has prevented them from considering the Islamic perspectives to the fullest possible extent. A prominent British expert on Islamic law started his discussion in the following manner:

> The essential feature of the Qur'an, the Holy book of Islam revealed to Mohammed, is that it is not a code of law. Only some eighty verses refer to legal topics and even in these verses there are both gaps as well as doubts as to whether the legal injunction is obligatory or permissive, as indeed whether it is subject to public or to private sanctions. Indeed, the very

---

22 *Ibid.*, p.28.

23 T. Mahmood, *Muslim Personal Law. Role of the State in the Subcontinent*, New Delhi, 1977; Mahmood, *The Muslim Law of India*; Mahmood, *Personal Laws in Crisis*.

24 Mahmood, *The Muslim Law of India*, pp.5-8.

25 *Ibid.*, p.7.

26 *Ibid.*, pp.13-14.

27 Mahmood, *Personal Laws in Crisis*, pp.49-94.

28 *Ibid.*, p.49.

29 See especially Mahmood, *Ibid.*, pp. 53ff.

> nature of the Qur'an is such that it could not possibly be a comprehensive code of law.[30]

These clear-cut statements, repeated more recently[31] and no doubt sensible from the viewpoint of a Western lawyer, are then immediately qualified by saying that what has just been cited above here 'should not in any way be seen as a challenge to the divinity of the Qur'an. Indeed, the reverse is intended.'[32]

How these arguments are to be reconciled we are not told. Clearly, the author is aware that there is more to Islamic law then legal rules. The morality of Islam is mentioned as an element,[33] but this point is not elaborated. By arguing in terms of 'the Qur'anic legislation which was subsequently interpreted by succeeding generations.' and by depicting the Caliphs as 'filling in the gaps to the Qur'anic legislation',[34] the author seems to employ Western legal terminology, ignoring in the process the ethical dimensions of Islamic law.

A more recent British textbook on Islamic family law begins by explaining the principal terms and concepts. Having defined shari'a as the path of the believer, the way which God wishes man to pass, the author tackles the central issue:

> The Shari'a is a divine law. Islam is essentially a religious code of conduct of which law in the western sense occupies but a small part. The Shari'a covers all aspects of a Muslim's life and makes little distinction between moral, ethical and [in a western sense] legal questions... Because it is a divine law a substantial part of the writings on the Shari'a concerns matters which one would not expect to see in a western legal textbook and treats them in exactly the same manner as the more familiar 'legal' topics. The obverse of this is that the Shari'a pervades the whole of Islam, which is a religion of the law.[35]

The author then proceeds to outline the theory of how the classical system works:

> The divine nature of the Shari'a denies the existence of any legislative authority on earth, conceding at most the capacity of political authorities to make administrative regulations to procure the implementation of the Shari'a. If there is a

---

30 Pearl, *A Textbook on Muslim Law,* London, 1st ed. 1979, p.1. [Hereinafter Pearl 1st ed.]
31 Pearl 2nd ed., p.1.
32 Pearl 1st ed., p.1; Pearl 2nd ed., p.1.
33 Pearl 1st ed., p.4.
34 *Ibid.,* p.6; Pearl 2nd ed., p.6.
35 K. Hodkinson, *Muslim Family Law. A Sourcebook*, London, 1984, p.1.

> divergence between the provisions of the Shari'a and the actual circumstances of society, then it is society not the Shari'a which must change.[36]

Some indications are given that this supremacy of revelation is to an extent theoretical, that administration of law and local custom have been allowed to prevail at times, but this is not further elaborated and the impression is maintained that Shafi'i's theory, as the principal cause of the rigidity of the shari'a, is also the principal obstacle to its reform.[37] Later on, the author elaborates on the importance of the moral and ethical precepts in the Qur'an and takes up the issue of law and morality again in more detail. This time it is clearly stated that the influence of local and tribal customary laws cannot be ignored and that the theoretical proposition is an exaggeration in view of practical realities:

> It is true that the doctrine of the Shari'a has often not been applied in practice, but this does not deprive it of the character of law and reduce it to the level of a moral code. The sanctions for breach remain; it merely happens that the political authorities do not enforce it.[38]

With respect, I find the suggestion of 'reduction' to a moral code misconceived, probably because of the undue emphasis on the Western legal perspective that is used here. In the end, this instructive debate, too, leaves too much unsaid. A lucid exposition remains Coulson's series of lectures on conflicts and tensions in Islamic jurisprudence.[39] Though both debates centre on the nature of law, Coulson distinguished the discourse on Islamic law from that on Western law:

> Islam means total submission and surrender to Allah. It is therefore the will of the Muslim God, and that will alone, which determines the ultimate values and purposes of human life. The fundamental question of the nature of law is answered for Muslim jurisprudence, in terms that admit of no compromise, by the religious faith itself. Law is the divinely ordained system of God's commands. To deny this principle would be, in effect, to renounce the religious faith of Islam.
> But while law in Islam may be God-given, it is man who must apply the law. God proposes: man disposes. And between the original divine proposition and the eventual human disposition is interposed an extensive field of intellectual activity and

[36] *Ibid.*, p.1-2.
[37] *Ibid.*, p.3.
[38] *Ibid.*, p. 11.
[39] N. J. Coulson, *Conflicts and Tensions in Islamic Jurisprudence*, Chicago, 1969.

> decision. In short, jurisprudence in Islam is the whole process of intellectual activity which ascertains and discovers the terms of the divine will and transforms them into a system of legally enforceable rights and duties. It is within, but only within, these strict terms of reference that the tensions and conflicts of Islamic legal thought arise.[40]

Coulson explains that these tensions have been starting from a very early stage in Islamic legal history with the conflict between *ra'i* and *hadith*, which was resolved in favour of the latter by the well-known theory of Shafi'i in the 9th century. The effect was to confirm that 'the role of human reason must, therefore, be entirely subordinate to the principles established by divine revelation'.[41] However, ra'i re-asserted itself, 'now dressed up in more sophisticated terminology'.[42] In principle, though, the classical theory remained unshaken:

> In sum, therefore, the classical legal theory expresses to perfection the notion of law as a comprehensive and preordained system of God's commands.[43]

Since 'it was axiomatic that justice was identical with the terms of the religious law',[44] there could not reasonably remain any contradiction. Further, an in-built system of equity ensured flexibility[45] so that, '[i]n this light, Islamic law is both a divine law and a jurists' law. In the contemplation of Islamic jurisprudence these two descriptions are complementary and not contradictory'.[46]

Though he does not say so explicitly, Coulson here accepts that, for a Muslim, the overriding ethical/moral nature of the shari'a precludes the separation of the legal and non-legal spheres. In the fifth lecture, focussing on law and morality,[47] these issues are taken up again:

> The Islamic Shari'a is, in our terminology, both a code of law and a code of morals. It is a comprehensive scheme of human behavior which derives from the one ultimate authority of the

40 *Ibid.*, pp.1-2.

41 *Ibid.*, p.6.

42 *Ibid.*, p.7.

43 *Ibid.*

44 *Ibid.*, p.17.

45 Coulson refers here to the comparable conflict in English law between common law and equity (at p.17). This debate is remarkably similar to the one on whether judges make law. It is now much more openly accepted that they do, and certainly in Oriental jurisdictions there is ample evidence of judicial creativity, which in modern India has made a very prominent issue out of 'judicial activism'.

46 Coulson, *Conflicts and Tensions in Islamic Jurisprudence*, p.19.

47 *Ibid.*, pp.77-95.

> will of Allah; so that the dividing line between law and morality is by no means so clearly drawn as it is in Western societies generally.[48]

There is no clear and consistent distinction between the moral and the legal rule:

> In theory, the Shari'a has always been a totalitarian and comprehensive code of conduct covering every aspect of human life and regulating the individual's relations with God, with the state, with his neighbor, and with his own conscience on the same single basis of the dictates of the divine command. Thus, any human activity, any social institution in Islam has in the final analysis a religious significance.[49]

By indicating that this is so 'in theory', Coulson left the way open to consider next that, 'in practice, a broad division between the religious duties that the individual owed to God and the social duties that he owed to his fellow men'[50] began to emerge. Islamic law, thus, does allow flexibility in the judgement of human action and Coulson shows that the real values and standards by which a Muslim society lives need not be the same as the ones that the court of the state will enforce.[51] Though the problem of Muslim minorities in non-Muslim states is not addressed here, we can see that there are possibilities of co-existence within the moral/ethical framework of the shari'a.

Looking back at the variety of attempts by expert authors to express the shari'a ambit, I remain concerned about lack of clarity. From a Muslim perspective, as we have seen, the ethical/moral framework of the revealed law is the supreme element of the shari'a. By using the term 'law', alone or in various combinations, authors have often confused us and themselves about the ambit of Islamic law (as, I may add as a comparative lawyer, has happened in the case of other Oriental legal systems). It appears that a fairly recent jurisprudential study can throw some light on the debate about the nature of law in our present context. Three kinds of this universal phenomenon have been distinguished:

> LAW = the general idea or concept of legal institutions abstracted from any particular occurrence of them.
>
> Law = a coherent, total, particular legal system prevailing in a given community or country.

---

48 *Ibid.*, p.79.
49 *Ibid.*, p.81.
50 *Ibid.*, p.82.
51 *Ibid.*, p.84.

law = a particular normative provision of a Law; a rule or norm of a given legal system.[52]

This distinction shows that shari'a encompasses LAW as well as Law. Since LAW is an abstraction that exists in the minds of people, it cannot really be abolished by Law, i.e. by a state legal system that may reject, as a matter of ideology, the moral/ethical framework of a particular perception of LAW. In other words, as long as a Law guarantees freedom of conscience, which would include freedom of religion, there can be no cries of 'religion in danger' from either Muslims or non-Muslims. Western obsession with the separability of law and morality induces us to overlook that, in Oriental legal contexts, there are different forms of tension at work.[53]

In a situation where, because an individual is a Muslim, a particular kind of LAW is presumed to exist, Law need not, in principle, be Islamic at all. The Muslim-ness of an individual is clearly a matter of belief, as we have seen above, much less, if at all, a result of following a particular kind of Law.[54] Of course, the ideal is that a Muslim way of life be followed, whatever that may mean in detail. But there are Muslims who follow shari'a ideals faithfully, and those do not,[55] and Islamic law makes many provisions for that all too common situation. Clearly, there are good Muslims and bad Muslims, but there is (like for Hindus) no such thing as automatic excommunication from the faith as long as the individual believes, or claims to believe, in the absolute essentials of Islam. People may well be excommunicated from a sect or a particular group, but not from Islam altogether. Cases of actual or purported excommunication of Muslims show, as the Ahmadiyya example, the dangers of non-orthodoxy and of dissent, and prominently demonstrate the invasion of politics into the realm of religion. Since the core of the orthodox essentials of Islam is so very small, albeit all-important, what we see is tremendous diversity within the framework of shari'a, and immense tension in cases of actual or perceived divergence from the 'true' path.

Muslim scholars have, for good reasons, paid much attention to the treatment and position of non-Muslim minorities in an Islamic state. Comparatively little has been written about how Muslim minorities in non-Muslim countries should work out a compromise between their LAW and the Law of the state in which they live. It seems perfectly manageable and acceptable for Muslims to live in a non-Muslim state as Muslims; it is, thus, possible to reconcile being a Muslim and living in a non-Muslim country with a secular legal system. It may, in fact, be easier for Muslims to live in a

---

[52]Allott, *The Limits of Law*, p.2.

[53]See also Coulson, *Conflicts and Tensions in Islamic Jurisprudence*, p.1.

[54]Here is, actually, a major difference between Islam and Hinduism. To be a Hindu, one need not believe in any particular central Hindu doctrine, but one may choose from a large variety of doctrines. The real test appears to be the acceptance by a community, i.e. the adoption of a particular way of life rather than belief.

[55]See Coulson, *Conflicts and Tensions in Islamic Jurisprudence*, p.83.

secular state than in one dominated by a particular religion. The onus for achieving this difficult reconciliation lies with every Muslim individual, but we shall see below how crucially important in this context communal considerations and power politics have become. Lawyers should not be fooled by claims that God's word 'laid down the law' for every Muslim and for all times, though of course Islamic law does provide an ethical framework of reference that is absolutely supreme and is designed for all times. We have seen how important it is to ask how one interprets the word 'law'. It is clear that reform in Islamic law is not impossible.[56]

III. Islamic Law in India

A. The Problem

Whenever I speak about the Indian legal system, I constantly come across people who live in the past and think that Indian law is a somewhat undeveloped appendix to English law. Nothing could be further from the truth.

India operates a very complex, modern legal system, with many problems and much talk of crisis,[57] but also with fascinating new developments that are beginning to generate more interest in Indian legal studies worldwide.

A few words on the structure of the modern Indian legal system will be helpful here. Apart from the generally applicable Indian law, which binds all Indians irrespective of their religion, we find, mainly in the area of family and succession laws, a system of concurrent personal laws applying to members of different communities. Part of this 'personal law system' is a largely optional system of 'secular' family law that is also called 'general' law, but is not very important in practice. Precisely this law, however, is the protagonist of an optional Uniform Civil Code for India. In this wider context, Islamic law continues to apply in certain areas of the law to Indian Muslims.

The modern law is dominated by the Constitution of 1950, which contains an extensive list of Fundamental Rights (Part III) and a wide range of Directive Principles of State Policy (Part IV), one of which (Art.44) shall interest us here in particular. Modern Indian law is actually a civil law system with a significant amount of British-made legislation and an impressive mass of case-law. Many new laws have been introduced since 1947, often superseding or modifying the colonial legislation and case-law. As a result, Indian law today is much less English than many scholars like to admit and

[56] *Mulla's Principles*, pp.xxxiii.

[57] See U. Baxi, *The Crisis of the Indian Legal System*, New Delhi, 1982.

whatever has remained of the Anglo-Indian heritage has, also in the area of the general law, almost completely been superseded today.[58]

Increasing consciousness by the Indian law-makers (especially an activist judiciary) about their role in creating an Indian legal system, in which law fits and serves the country and its people, must naturally take into account that India is the home of many million Muslims. Since the promulgation of the Constitution with its implied threat to the personal law system, and thus to the continuation of Islamic law in India, Muslims have felt under pressure. The state's reaction has been to choose a secular path, involving equidistance from all religions found in India; in practical terms, as we saw already, the personal law system has been allowed to continue.

Today, the big question continues to be whether the modern secular Indian legal system can do justice to the Muslims of India who 'generally have deep emotional feelings for their law which they regard as one of their distinctive religion-based possessions'.[59] The Directive Principle in Art. 44 of the Constitution, containing the message that Indian law-makers should work towards legal uniformity for all Indians by providing that 'The state shall endeavour to secure for the citizens a uniform civil code throughout the territory of India' is therefore seen as a particular threat.

In this chapter we shall discuss to what extent Islamic law in India has been modernised and reformed in various areas of the law. We will see that there is a very complex picture, but that certain prominent topics have emerged, with important political and legal consequences. Of particular interest will be the way in which scholarly discussion of particular reforms has developed.

B. Reforms of the Muslim Personal Law in India

A short and superficial treatment of this issue could result in a somewhat cryptic statement that there are no reforms worth mentioning, since the shari'a applies to Indian Muslims today. For example:

> In our country where, for various reasons, reform of Islamic personal law has been difficult at the best of times, it has become non-existent, although there is strong public opinion that progressive ideas, in keeping with the march of time should find place in the social life of Muslims.[60]

Mulla suggests that reforms to Islamic law, though continuously resisted, have been made in many Muslim countries and expresses hope that in due course 'the same measures will be introduced in India also'.[61]

---

[58] Thus, for example, the rule in *Rylands v. Fletcher*, which dominated also Indian tort law, was explicitly rejected for India in *M.C. Mehta,* AIR 1987 SC 1086, at 1098-1099.

[59] Mahmood, *The Muslim Law of India,* p.4.

[60] *Mulla's Principles*, p.xxix-xxx.

[61] *Ibid.*, p.xiv.

Diwan, in his preface, attempts to explain the underlying problem in a wider perspective:

> A writer on Muslim law in modern India is at once beset with the problem of looking at Muslim law, which, to a great extent, still continues to be based on the Koran, the sunna, the ijma; ... objectively - how much of Muslim law is still based on ancient sources and how much of it has been changed or mutated during the course of its administration by the British Indian courts and the Privy Council, and thereafter, and how much of it is in conformity with the contemporary social needs and modern thought. The problem is not of merely saying that polygamy and talak [repudiation] are out-moded (even most Muslim agree that it is so), but of looking at the entire gamut of Muslim law more deeply and dispassionately.[62]

All writers on the subject agree that Islamic law in India is different from other Islamic laws.[63] This difference is also marked by the use of shariat for South Asian Islamic law instead of shari'a. It may be argued that these differences in the law make the people to whom it applies no less Islamic than other Muslims. Tahir Mahmood, in particular, has criticised the grave distortions of the shari'a in India, whose 'pitiable story of a gravely misunderstood law' has recently been told in much detail.[64] Mahmood forcefully accuses the British, in particular, of clever scheming and wilful distortions, leading to a more or less total corruption of the true shari'a principles.[65]

Since, as we have seen, Muslim jurists cannot agree, anyway, on what pure Sharia law actually was or is, there seems little point in advocating a 'return' to an unadulterated state, as it were. There will be no agreement on this point within India because of well-recognised differences between various Muslim communities in terms of school tradition, Sunni/Shi'i divergencies, and also local customary traditions. Rather than arguing over the past, we should attempt a forward-looking, constructive approach. Whether this can lead us towards advocating a Uniform Civil Code for India remains to be seen.

C. Islamic Family Laws in India

All authors on the subject agree, though in different terms, that the Islamic family law of India in its considerably corrupted 'Anglo-Muhammadan' form has not been much interfered with in modern,

---

[62]Diwan, *Muslim Law in Modern India*, p.5.

[63]*Ibid.*, p.6; Fyzee, *Outlines of Muhammadan Law*, p.2; *Mulla's Principles*, p.viii; Hodkinson, *Muslim Family Law*, p.12; Pearl 1st ed., p.21; Pearl 2nd ed., p.20; Mahmood, *The Muslim Law of India*, p.vii.

[64]Mahmood, *Personal Laws in Crisis*, pp.49-94.

[65]*Ibid.*, pp.49-63.

independent India. The reason has not been satisfaction with the way Islamic law operates in modern India, but concern to avoid offence to Muslim sentiments; political scientists are likely to see concern to preserve the Muslim vote bank as a major factor. It appears, prima facie, that Indian governments have accepted, to a large extent, the contention that Islamic law is a religious law that cannot be subjected to extensive reform by a modern secular state.

A detailed debate on what has often been referred to as Anglo-Muhammadan law is not within the brief of this contribution. Attention may here be drawn to Michael Anderson's contribution in this book, and particularly to Mahmood,[66] where a detailed study is found, and to Diwan[67] and again Mahmood[68] for a lucid summary of the issues.

Tahir Mahmood has also written quite extensively on the constitutional principles of modern Indian law under which the Islamic law continues to be applied as a personal law.[69] If we want to know about Islamic law in India today, we have a number of authoritative sources that may be used, sometimes with diverging results.

Most writers agree that the Indian shari'a cannot be found by courts today in the Qur'an and sunna,[70] i.e. they deny Indian courts the power of ijtihad. A list of sources actually tapped by the Indian courts is found in Mahmood:

> (a) legislative enactments applicable, if any; (b) certain books of jurisprudence (fikh) of the medieval ages, now available in English translation; (c) some modern reference books which have in the course of time attained a position of authenticity; and (d) judicial precedent.[71]

Listing these sources does not mean that one finds the situation satisfactory. Mahmood has continued to be critical of the undue emphasis on the British contribution to Indian Islamic law[72] and has attacked the pattern of the courts' reliance on a variety of authoritative textbooks as improper[73] and contributing further to the distortion of Islamic law.[74] There is no doubt, though, that the widespread absence of legislative enactments on Islamic law in India has left the field wide open to judicial interpretation. The Indian judges, thus, have a most important function in developing the Indian Islamic law. Of course, there is no system of kazi's courts in India, and so the development of

---

[66]Mahmood, *Muslim Personal Law. Role of the State in the Subcontinent*, New Delhi, 1977.
[67]Diwan, *Muslim Law in Modern India*, pp.26-39.
[68]Mahmood, *The Muslim Law of India,* pp.1-17.
[69]Mahmood, *Personal Laws in Crisis,* especially, pp.3-30; See also A. M. Bhattacharjee, *Muslim Law and the Constitution*, Calcutta, 1985.
[70]E.g. *Mulla's Principles*, p.30.
[71]Mahmood, *The Muslim Law of India,* p.15.
[72]*Ibid.*, p.8; Mahmood, *Personal Laws in Crisis,* pp.49-53.
[73]Mahmood, *The Muslim Law of India,* p.17.
[74]Mahmood, *Personal Laws in Crisis,* pp.53-55.

Indian Islamic law takes place within the context of a secular democratic republic.

(i) Islamic Law of Marriage in India

Various sub-topics are traditionally distinguished and covered in detail by standard textbooks. I shall identify here those issues which are relevant in the context of the debate on the Uniform Civil Code in India.

The concept of marriage. The traditional approach to the definition of a Muslim marriage is that it is a civil contract.[75] This seems oversimplified, and is probably the result of the fact that Hindu marriages have traditionally[76] been seen as sacramental.[77] Fyzee indicates that there are several important aspects of marriage and distinguishes legal, social and religious ones.[78] Regarding the latter, marriage is seen as a 'sacred covenant'[79] or even a 'religious sacrament'.[80] Diwan maintains that Muslim marriage is 'essentially a contract',[81] but discusses both views. More recently Hodkinson has concluded that 'it would be absolutely wrong to say that it is a purely civil contract'.[82] Mahmood speaks of a 'solemn pact':

> As a matter of fact it is only the form of the Muslim marriage that is contractual and non-ceremonial; marriage itself, as a concept, is not merely a contract.[83]

This is taken up in his more recent study where, deploring the misunderstandings of the non-Muslim intelligentsia and the distortions of British-Indian judges, Mahmood shows that already the Qur'an describes marriage as a sacred covenant between a man and a woman, a sacred partnership, which has, he argues, correctly been described in a recent Supreme Court judgement[84] as a 'sacrosanct contract'.[85]

The prevailing opinion today, thus, appears to be that a Muslim marriage is more than a plain civil contract and that there are religious elements to it -

---

[75]E.g. *Mulla's Principles*, p.282.

[76] Whether this is correct is a complex question that cannot be debated here. There is certainly much evidence of contractual elements in Hindu marriages. The ease with which customary divorces continue to be available to many Hindus throws serious doubts on the idea that all Hindu marriages are of a sacramental nature. There can be no doubt, at the same time, that the Hindu *ideal* model is that of a sacramental union.

[77]Hodkinson, *Muslim Family Law*, p.90; Mahmood, *Personal Laws in Crisis*, p.65.

[78]Fyzee, *Outlines of Muhammadan Law*, p.88.

[79]*Ibid.*, p.89.

[80]*Ibid.*, p.90.

[81]Diwan, *Muslim Law in Modern India*, p.40.

[82]Hodkinson, *Muslim Family Law*, p.90.

[83]Mahmood, *The Muslim Law of India*, p.45.

[84]*Sirajmohmedkhan*, AIR 1981 SC 1972, at 1974.

[85]Mahmood, *Personal Laws in Crisis*, p.64.

but then, we have already seen that any action of a Muslim is liable to be seen as having a religious aspect.

Solemnisation of marriage. Whereas under Hindu law in India, the legal validity of a marriage is mainly determined by the performance of certain customary rituals,[86] Islamic law neither prescribes nor requires any ritual of marriage solemnisation.[87] A Muslim marriage can take place without any ceremonial,[88] but there are legal requirements for the execution of the marriage contract, which take the form of a legal ritual.[89] These rituals are treated as the 'essentials of a marriage'.[90]

Many authors indicate that apart from the legally required rituals there are certain ceremonies and customs peculiar to Indian Muslims,[91] which 'almost always' accompany the religious ceremonial.[92] There is nothing in the law specifically prohibiting them,[93] but they are 'superfluous as far as the theory of Islamic law is concerned'.[94] However, such customs are typically Indian. Only Mahmood admits that these customary rituals have not only 'great social significance',[95] but have, in fact, become very important in India in determining the legal validity of a Muslim marriage: they have 'come to acquire an evidentiary value recognized by the courts'.[96] Mahmood insists, however, on the arguments that customs must continue to be seen as extra-legal, otherwise this 'would strike at the very root of the Islamic legal concept of marriage'.[97]

State law, thus, has not had much influence here, nor has it sought to superimpose legal rules that are to be followed by all Indians uniformly. The solemnisation of Muslim marriages has remained a matter of shari'a law in theory, coupled with customary rituals, which are, in reality, a major focus of attention for South Asian Muslims. It must be noted that resistance against

[86] This law is now codified in section 7 of the Hindu Marriage Act 1955, which has, in fact, left the field wide open to custom and so is, at best, codified customary law. On some of the problems see W.F. Menski, 'Solemnisation of Hindu Marriages: the Law and Reality', *Kerala Law Times,* 1985, Journal, pp.1-10.

[87] Fyzee, *Outlines of Muhammadan Law*, p.90; Diwan, *Muslim Law in Modern India*, pp.40-41 and 47; *Mulla's Principles*, p.283; Mahmood, *The Muslim Law of India,* p.52; Mahmood, *Personal Laws in Crisis,* p.65.

[88] Fyzee, *Outlines of Muhammadan Law*, p.91.

[89] For details see *Ibid.*, p.91-92; Mahmood, *The Muslim Law of India,* pp.52-54; Diwan, *Muslim Law in Modern India*, p.47.

[90] *Mulla's Principles*, p.283.

[91] Fyzee, *Outlines of Muhammadan Law*, p.92-93; Diwan, *Muslim Law in Modern India*, p.48; Mahmood, *Personal Laws in Crisis,* p.65; See also S. A. Hussein, *Marriage Customs Among Muslims in India*, New Delhi, 1976.

[92] Pearl 2nd ed., p.42.

[93] Mahmood, *The Muslim Law of India,* p.52.

[94] *Ibid.*, pp.54 and 55; Mahmood, *Personal Laws in Crisis,* p.65.

[95] *Ibid.*, p.65.

[96] Mahmood, *The Muslim Law of India,* p.54.

[97] *Ibid.*, p.55.

state interference, as shown by Mahmood's arguments, protects not only the principles of the shari'a, but also the Indian Muslim customary law with its very diverse local manifestations.

Registration of marriages. The publicity of traditional forms of marriage solemnisation brings with it public registration of the factum of a marriage. The various requirements in Islamic law regarding witnesses may be seen to serve a similar purpose, though there is not much concern with the wider public or community. We have already seen, however, that customary 'extra-legal' ceremonies take care of that aspect.

Under classical law, an oral contract of marriage is seen as perfectly valid and there is no need for formal registration.[98] In India, it has become customary for a qazi or a *mulla* to help solemnise the marriage.[99] They keep registers of the marriages to which they were invited[100] and may issue 'marriage certificates' to the parties.[101] In fact, in some parts of India, as also in some Muslim countries,[102] the registration of Muslim marriages has been regulated by statute. The current picture is very diverse, with some old Acts like the Kazis Act 1880 and recent legislation side by side. Jammu and Kashmir passed a Muslim Marriages Registration Act in 1981.[103] Except in Jammu and Kashmir, registration of Muslim marriages is not compulsory anywhere in India. Non-registration of a marriage does not affect its legal validity.

It is important to note that marriages registered under any of these Acts remain subject to Islamic law. Muslims in India have the option to register their marriages under the Special Marriage Act 1954, with the effect that a secular regime of divorce and succession laws will then apply to the couple. As far as we know, few Muslims register their marriage under that Act; Hodkinson indicates widespread ignorance of the Special Marriage Act 1954.[104] However, Pearl claims that quite substantial numbers of urban middle-class Muslims have used the Special Marriage Act 1954, invoking a monogamous regime on the union.[105]

Several authors insist on the need to have definitive proof of the existence of marriages. Pearl sees registration as 'of paramount importance',[106] but also indicates that attempts to introduce it have met opposition among Muslims in the subcontinent, though several Muslim countries have made registration compulsory. Diwan points to opposition by the 'ulama against compulsory registration and recommends the enactment of a central statute for the

98 *Ibid.*.
99 Diwan, *Muslim Law in Modern India*, p.47.
100 Fyzee, *Outlines of Muhammadan Law*, p.92.
101 Mahmood, *The Muslim Law of India*, p.55.
102 Hodkinson, *Muslim Family Law*, p.92.
103 For details see Mahmood, *The Muslim Law of India*, pp.55-56.
104 Hodkinson, *Muslim Family Law*, p.22.
105 Pearl 1st ed., p.74; Pearl 2nd ed., p.83.
106 Pearl 1st ed., p.43; Pearl 2nd ed., p.42.

compulsory registration of all Indian marriages.[107] Such unrealistic[108] enthusiasm was apparently encouraged by Tahir Mahmood's earlier advocacy,[109] but it is significant that Mahmood's recent work[110] does not even contain a reference to this issue. It appears, here again, that a legal regulation introduced by the secular state is being opposed as a matter of principle.

Marriage guardianship. Complex and divergent Islamic law rules on the subject have become part of the Indo-Muslim case-law,[111] and there is evidence of few post-independence cases.[112] The topic should be of much less interest now, since the legal minimum age for marriage in India (except Jammu and Kashmir) was raised in 1978 to 18 for women and 21 for men.[113]

Marriage age. The Islamic law rules on this issue have also clearly been superseded by general Indian law. In the previous section we saw the legal requirement for minimum age for marriage. However, child marriages solemnised in violation of the 1978 Act continue to be valid marriages[114] and in cases where Muslim minors do get married, the Islamic law rules on marriage guardians are likely to continue in full operation. Tahir Mahmood now pleads for the introduction of a general minimum marriage age of 18 for both sexes and compulsory parental consent. At the same time, it is recommended that in cases of violation of the minimum age rule 'all matrimonial relief otherwise available in law' should be denied to such couples.[115] This, I submit, would not be much of a deterrent for Muslim couples; in fact, it would have the opposite effect, i.e. keeping them out of the ambit of state law, and re-inforcing an option which is favoured by Indian Muslims.

Option of puberty. The well-known classical Islamic law rule, relating to both sexes, has been retained in India. In addition, the option is available to the minor wife only, under the provisions of the Dissolution of Muslim Marriages

---

[107]Diwan, *Muslim Law in Modern India*, p.48.

[108]It is unrealistic because compulsory registration will never work in Indian conditions.

[109]Diwan, *Muslim Law in Modern India*, p.48 n.39.

[110]Mahmood, *Personal Laws in Crisis*.

[111]For details see esp. Mahmood, *The Muslim Law of India*, pp.46-51; Diwan, *Muslim Law in Modern India*, pp.50-52

[112]*Ayub Hasan,* AIR 1963 All 525 and two cases of 1967 and 1970 from Kerala, on which see Diwan, *Muslim Law in Modern India*, pp.50-51.

[113]In a section entitled 'Farewell to Marriage-Guardians' (*Personal Laws in Crisis*, pp.113-115) we find a strong attack by Professor Mahmood on the legislative overdosis in this area of the law. Without explicit reference to Islamic law rules Mahmood's argument appears to be that the Child Marriage Restraint (Amendment) Act 1978 does not apply to Muslims in India, even though it does. Mahmood is noticeably silent on the Muslim situation here and seems to deplore, without saying so directly, that the modern secular law has been able to virtually wipe out this large area of Islamic law.

[114]*Lila Gupta,* AIR 1978 SC 1351.

[115]Mahmood, *Personal Laws in Crisis,* p.115.

Act 1939.[116] Interestingly, an almost identical rule was introduced into the modern Hindu law of India by the Marriage Laws (Amendment) Act 1976.[117] Here is, thus, an area of law without much difference between Hindu and Islamic law; a uniform provision might easily be devised. It has been suggested that the option should be made available to both men and women and keep intact the traditional Islamic law rule.[118] To retain the option will, no doubt, suit current Indian thinking on making divorce more easily available, on as many grounds as possible, yet without introducing, formally, the 'breakdown principle'.

Capacity to marry. Apart from the guardianship and consent debate, this issue relates prominently to the religion of the spouses.[119] Ideally, two Muslims should marry, but Islamic law allows, generally speaking, Muslim males to marry *kitabiyya* women ('women of the Book', mainly Jews and Christians). In the secular set-up of modern Indian law, though, the Islamic law relating to inter-religious marriages is no more enforceable.[120] Modern secular law has here overridden personal law. An interreligious marriage must be registered under the Special Marriage Act 1954, and the couple's legal relations are, then, governed by the 'general' secular system of personal law. As indicated above, two Muslims marrying under that Act would also take themselves out of the ambit of their personal law, while remaining Muslim by religion.

Prohibited relationships. Muslim jurists have excelled in deriving very complex rules relating to consanguinity, affinity and fosterage.[121] While not specifically addressing the question under Islamic law, nor considering how Islamic law could be brought under a general legal regime, Mahmood criticises the current Indian law on the subject as confused and arbitrary.[122] The Special Marriage Act should prohibit 'only those marriages that are universally recognized as incestuous',[123] while in all other cases personal law rules, often customary, should be considered decisive. Again, this argument amounts to a covert plea for the continuation of Islamic law rules.

---

[116]For details, see Fyzee, *Outlines of Muhammadan Law*, p.94-96; Diwan, *Muslim Law in Modern India*, pp.97-99; Pearl 1st ed., pp.44-45; Pearl 2nd ed., pp.44-46; *Mulla's Principles*, p.297-299; Mahmood, *The Muslim Law of India*, pp.64-67.

[117]Mahmood, *Personal Laws in Crisis*, p.126.

[118]*Ibid.*, p.115.

[119]See Mahmood, *The Muslim Law of India*, pp.56-57; *Mulla's Principles*, p.287-288; Fyzee, *Outlines of Muhammadan Law*, pp.96-101; Diwan, *Muslim Law in Modern India*, pp.53-54.

[120]Mahmood, *The Muslim Law of India*, p.57; Pearl 1st ed., p.50; Pearl 2nd ed., p.52.

[121]For details see esp. Diwan, *Muslim Law in Modern India*, pp.54-56; Mahmood, *The Muslim Law of India*, pp.60-63.

[122]Mahmood, *Personal Laws in Crisis*, pp.117-119.

[123]Mahmood, *Ibid.*, p.119.

Mut'a marriages. The unusual character of mut'a (temporary) marriages may have added attraction for scholarly discussions.[124] It has been argued that this form of Muslim marriage has been given undue importance by some authors[125] and Mulla's textbook, in particular, has been attacked for deliberately maligning Islamic law.[126] Mahmood seeks to show that such form of marriage is only allowed to a small minority of Muslims and is virtually obsolete. Formally, this argument may be correct, but if mut'a was a device to avoid *zina* (unlawful sexual relationship), at least to an extent, one wonders how Muslims in India today justify extra-marital alliances. Mahmood himself[127] points out that mut'a is better than Western forms of extra-marital cohabitation or the notorious maitri karars among Gujaratis. One wonders whether a uniform legal regulation of this matter is possible and/or desirable at all in modern India.

Presumption of marriage. Mahmood rightly points out that the essentially informal nature of Muslim marriage registration may occasionally give rise to doubts over the legal validity of a marriage.[128] All authors outline three situations in which a presumption of marriage normally arises.[129] There is a considerable body of Anglo-Indian case-law on this subject, and we find reference to a number of post-Independence cases in India involving prostitutes who entered into Muslim marriages.

As argued earlier, a system of compulsory registration of marriages (as in English law) will not help to avoid all legal insecurities, especially if large numbers of people prefer informal cohabitation to formal marriage.[130] The problem is similarly acute in Hindu law with its myriad variations of informal customary forms of marriage, which are in danger of being denied legal recognition.[131] The example of English law shows that even a strict system of compulsory registration will not create legal uniformity.[132]

(ii) Polygamy

This is a very contentious issue in India, since Hindu law, which allowed unlimited polygamy to men till 1955, now enforces strict monogamy (as do Christian and Parsi laws), while Muslim husbands in India are still allowed to

[124] On which see Fyzee, *Outlines of Muhammadan Law*, pp.117-121; Diwan, *Muslim Law in Modern India*, pp.43-45; *Mulla's Principles*, p.293-294.
[125] Mahmood, *The Muslim Law of India,* p.46.
[126] Mahmood, *Personal Laws in Crisis,* p.71.
[127] Mahmood, *Ibid.,* p.72.
[128] Mahmood, *The Muslim Law of India,* p.56.
[129] See *Ibid.*; Diwan, *Muslim Law in Modern India*, p.49; *Mulla's Principles*, p.291-292.
[130] See also Allott, *The Limits of Law*, pp.259-286.
[131] See Menski, 'Solemnisation of Hindu Marriages'.
[132] Menski, 'English Family Law and Ethnic Laws in Britain', *Kerala Law Times,* 1988 (1), Journal, pp.56-66.

have up to four wives, a rule which seems to violate all modern ideas of equality before the law and of the desirability of uniform legal provisions.

Scholarly debate reflects these tensions well. Mulla[133] is content to state the basic rules of Islamic law, which apply in their uncodified form in India today. Thus, a Muslim husband may have up to four wives at the same time, but no more, while no Muslim woman is allowed more than one husband at the same time. Reference is made to a considerable body of Anglo-Indian case-law on the position of wives who violate this basic rule.[134] Such concern about female chastity, which seems typically Indian, is strongly reflected by the way Mahmood treats the subject.[135] It is also reflected in recent cases from Pakistan that punish such women for zina and in a few Indian cases that make such women liable to punishment under sections 494-5 of the Indian Penal Code 1860.[136] A Muslim man who marries more than four wives does not become liable to similar punishment, but Mahmood has tried to argue that in certain cases men should also be punished for entering patently void marriages.

Diwan accepts that the basic rules on Muslim polygamy were, at some point in the past, a definite step towards the improvement of the position of women in Islam, but seeks to show that even the Prophet was in favour of monogamy and that the polygamy rule is a permissive one. He also indicates that it may be impossible altogether to treat co-wives alike.[137] Indeed, as we know from some Muslim countries, polygamy has been restricted and even totally prohibited on that ground.[138]

In India, all authors concur, there has been no legislative reform on the subject of Muslim polygamy. Diwan[139] writes that no court in India could issue an injunction prohibiting a Muslim man from taking a second wife. Mahmood vaguely states that the capacity of a Muslim male in India to enter into bigamous unions is 'for inexplicable reasons'[140] not justiciable. A frequently cited case that seems to indicate judicial resentment of Muslim polygamy[141] has not been accepted in Pakistan[142] and must probably be seen as exceptional.[143] It has been pointed out that, in India, the provisions of the Dissolution of Muslim Marriages Act 1939 would enable a wife to seek divorce from her bigamously married husband on the ground of cruelty,[144]

---

[133]Mulla, *Mulla's Principles of Mahomedan law*, p.285.
[134]See also Fyzee, *Outlines of Muhammadan Law*, p.96.
[135]Mahmood, *The Muslim Law of India,* pp.58-59.
[136]For details see *Ibid.*, p.59.
[137]Diwan, *Muslim Law in Modern India*, p.41.
[138]See Pearl 1st ed., pp.69-73; Pearl 2nd ed., pp.77-81.
[139]Diwan, *Muslim Law in Modern India*, p.41.
[140]Mahmood, *The Muslim Law of India,* p.59.
[141]*Itwari,* AIR 1960 All 694.
[142]Pearl 1st ed., p.74 n.8.
[143]Diwan, *Muslim Law in Modern India,* p.42 n.11.
[144]*Ibid.*, p.42; Pearl 1st ed., p.74; Mahmood, *The Muslim Law of India,* pp.87-88.

but it could be argued that this is a remedy which operates too late to avoid real mischief.

It has been indicated that the only protection, at the time of the marriage, may be a stipulation in the marriage contract that the husband shall not take a second wife.[145] This would then give some relief to Muslim women under the 1939 Act.[146]

A lively debate has focused on Muslim resistance in India against the control of bigamy. Diwan[147] argues forcefully that 'modern India should not allow any one of its people to practise it' and lambasts the apologists of polygamy, who try to say that there is no real problem,[148] since very few Muslim men actually wish to marry several wives. Even though Mahmood[149] refuses to be seen as an apologist, there can be no doubt that his discussion of 'the myth of polygamy'[150] becomes rather emotional and seeks to veil the real issue, namely insistence by Muslims that to have several wives is a matter of religion, as is pointed out in a good systematic discussion of the issue by Hodkinson.[151] Muslim defensiveness has also taken the form of arguing that reforms must come from within the Muslim community itself and must be approved by the ‘ulama.[152]

Whether one is for or against bigamous marriages in principle, it is sometimes recognised that there are situations in which women may be better off married bigamously than seeking to exist independently from men.[153] Mahmood incorporates this into his defence of polygamy, almost acknowledging that such practice may be un-Islamic, even though he had earlier admitted that bigamy often amounts to cruelty.[154] More forcefully than Hodkinson,[155] who finds the debate theoretical and agrees that polygamy does not exist on a large scale among Indian Muslims, Mahmood argues that to allow bigamy in certain situations is much more honest than the Western form of serial monogamy, which may amount to repeated discarding of wives.[156] Mahmood's argument, as that of Derrett many years earlier,[157] is that qualified bigamy, involving the approval of an existing wife or wives, would be a suitable way for India to regulate the thorny problem of bigamous

[145]Pearl 1st ed., p.74; Pearl 2nd ed., p.83.

[146]See also Mahmood, *The Muslim Law of India,* p.88.

[147]Diwan, *Muslim Law in Modern India*, p.42.

[148]See e.g. Mahmood, *Personal Laws in Crisis,* pp.70-71.

[149]*Ibid.,* p.69.

[150]*Ibid.*, pp.68-71.

[151]Hodkinson, *Muslim Family Law,* p.107.

[152]Diwan, *Muslim Law in Modern India*, p.42.

[153]Hodkinson, *Muslim Family Law,* pp.107-108 and 246.

[154]Mahmood, *Personal Laws in Crisis,* pp.70-71; Mahmood, *The Muslim Law of India,* p.87.

[155]Hodkinson, *Muslim Family Law,* p.108.

[156]Mahmood, *Personal Laws in Crisis,* pp.115-117; See also Hodkinson, *Muslim Family Law,* pp.107-108 and parallel evidence from modern Hindu law.

[157]J. D. M. Derrett, 'The Indian Civil Code or Code of Family Law: Practical Propositions', in N. Khodie ed., *Readings in the Uniform Civil Code*, Bombay, 1975, pp.21-38.

marriages by a uniform law: 'Much more effective than legislative abolition of bigamy would, in fact, be its judicial control.'[158]

The Islamic argument appears to be, thus, that modern Indian law should relax the absolute prohibition on bigamy under non-Islamic personal laws, with the effect (i) that Islamic law need not be interfered with by the legislature and (ii) India would abandon her rather unreflected copying of the West (which has been severely criticised by Mahmood and others).[159]

(iii) *Mahr* and Dowry Problems

The Islamic institution of mahr is well-known as an integral part of marriage and is covered in great detail in all textbooks. Modern Indian legislation has explicitly provided for its recognition in two ways: (i) In the Dowry Prohibition Act 1961 mahr is exluded from the definition of dowry and mahr transactions are thus, not hit by that Act, also in its amended form; (ii) In S. 127 of the Criminal Procedure Code 1973 it has been recognised, in the context of post-divorce maintenance (at least until the case of *Bai Tahira*[160]) that receipt of 'customary dues', i.e. the deferred mahr by the divorced wife, would exonerate a Muslim husband from continued responsibility for the maintenance of his ex-wife.

We could, thus, say that modern Indian law has not interfered with the Muslim institution of mahr. The fact, however, that dowry problems now exist as much among Indian Muslims as among other Indians[161] is a different matter. Several authors have emphasised that dowry and mahr are very different concepts.[162] Indeed, the craving for status and consumerist self-indulgence which is the hallmark of the dowry problem in India today, with its accompanying vices of bride-burning and suicides, has nothing to do with mahr. However, this traditional Islamic institution has not been left unaffected by the dowry issue. While mahr is traditionally seen as a mark of respect for the wife,[163] the size of the mahr has often become a matter of status,[164] leading to absurd rules[165] and 'sham dowers, publicly announced, behind which exist private agreements for much smaller sums.'[166] Pearl reports that this practice is by no means restricted to Indian Muslims and discusses the new legal problem of ascertaining whether the sums stipulated are actually intended to be paid.[167] He also shows that Pakistan legislated on the size of marriage

---

158 Mahmood, *Personal Laws in Crisis,* p.117.

159 *Ibid.*, pp.70 and 115-116.

160 AIR 1979 SC 362.

161 Diwan, *Muslim Law in Modern India*, p.60 did not find such evidence.

162 *Ibid.*; Mahmood, *The Muslim Law of India,* p.69; Mahmood, *Personal Laws in Crisis,* pp. 66-67.

163 Fyzee, *Outlines of Muhammadan Law*, p.133.

164 *Mulla's Principles*, p.309; Mahmood, *The Muslim Law of India,* p.77.

165 See Fyzee, *Outlines of Muhammadan Law*, p.135.

166 Hodkinson, *Muslim Family Law,* p.137.

167 Pearl 1st ed., p.59.

transactions.[168] There is some recent evidence that India has incorporated a few of these reforms in the amended dowry law without specific reference to Muslims. While ostentatious display of wealth may be seen as un-Islamic, mahr in general and excessive mahr in particular may have a number of useful functions for Muslim women. The deferred mahr serves a twofold purpose: it puts a check on the husband's capricious use of the talaq[169] and it gives a 'provision for a rainy day'[170] to the wife, especially after divorce or the death of the husband.[171] Both Hodkinson[172] and Pearl[173] emphasise that the law of mahr must always be seen and judged in this context.

There is a vigorous debate on the Muslim divorced wife's position in terms of maintenance.[174] Indian courts, too, have become involved in this debate, and the matter is not yet resolved in modern Indian law, where controversy has raged over the issues raised in the *Shah Bano* case.[175]

In India, there is some limited local legislation to regulate the wife's right to claim mahr.[176] Neither in India nor Pakistan have there been attempts at regulation on the national level. Pearl indicates some statutory attempts to abolish or control dower, but 'all these attempts have come to nought'.[177] Mahmood does not even mention reforms, and we must assume that there is only limited scope here for interference with the Muslim mahr.[178]

(iv) Divorce Law

The Islamic law of divorce has generated much academic writing and is probably the largest aspect of Muslim matrimonial law,[179] with a split attitude among the scholars, resulting from tension between religious ideals and social reality. The current Muslim divorce law may well be an improvement on the pre-Islamic situation,[180] and has been seen as a 'rational, realistic and modern law of divorce' by a prominent Indian judge who favours the 'breakdown principle'.[181] On the other hand, there is a differential treatment of husbands

---

[168] *Ibid.*; see Hodkinson, *Muslim Family Law,* pp.138-143 for the text of these enactments.

[169] Fyzee, *Outlines of Muhammadan Law*, p.133; *Mulla's Principles*, p.309; Hodkinson, *Muslim Family Law,* p.136

[170] Fyzee, *Outlines of Muhammadan Law*, p.133.

[171] Hodkinson, *Muslim Family Law,* p.136; Pearl 1st ed., p.59.

[172] Hodkinson, *Muslim Family Law,* p.136.

[173] Pearl 1st ed., p.60.

[174] Fyzee, *Outlines of Muhammadan Law*, pp.143-144; *Mulla's Principles*, pp.316-324; Diwan, *Muslim Law in Modern India*, pp.67-70.

[175] See below.

[176] See Mahmood, *The Muslim Law of India,* pp.76-77; Hodkinson, *Muslim Family Law,* p.137.

[177] Pearl 1st ed., p.60.

[178] Mahmood, *The Muslim Law of India,* pp.66-68.

[179] Diwan, *Muslim Law in Modern India*, p.72.

[180] Fyzee, *Outlines of Muhammadan Law*, p.146.

[181] See Mahmood, *The Muslim Law of India,* p.94, all too pleased about such assessment.

and wives,[182] which may be seen as unjustifiable today,[183] and the effect of which is, in real life, that divorce is easier for a Muslim husband than for a Muslim wife.[184]

Different attitudes also result from the way divorce per se is perceived by Muslims. It is seen, since early times, as the most detestable of all permitted things,[185] but in practice, whatever Mahmood and other apologists argue, the law remains heavily weighted in favour of the husband,[186] who may divorce his wife whenever he desires and without giving any cause.[187] Repeated assertions that the Islamic divorce system does not give unbridled discretion to the husband, and that in fact, 'the true law on talaq' is a pro-wife law[188] remain unconvincing. Pearl's terse comment on the leading case on this matter in the subcontinent demonstrates the tension: 'Such a repudiation is good in law, though bad in theology'.[189]

We are not concerned here with details of the Islamic law of divorce. All scholars recognise the husband's right to talaq and this area of the law has, in India, remained almost exclusively a matter of extra-judicial regulation,[190] although there is some evidence of disturbed judicial consciences.[191] The 'triple talaq', also 'good in law though bad in theology' is common in India.[192] Mahmood, emphasising the complicated nature of Muslim divorce law,[193] also shows that Indian Muslims themselves are confused about the different forms of divorce.[194] Such confusion, coupled with ignorance of Muslim wives about their rights (a point generally and frequently made for Indian women) and lack of judicial supervision, makes it easy for men to discard women when and as they like. The fact that a good Muslim should shun divorce will, as we saw already, not come to the rescue of Muslim wives. Thus, Mahmood's attempts to paint a positive picture of 'the notorious talaq'[195] ignore the real life situation of Muslims in India today. It is not sufficient to blame the judiciary and books of law for their distortions without proposing ways for Muslim wives to be better protected against capricious divorces.

---

[182]Diwan, *Muslim Law in Modern India*, pp.40 and 72.

[183]Pearl 1st ed., p.93; more conciliatory Pearl 2nd ed., p.106.

[184]Pearl 1st ed., p.89; Pearl 2nd ed., p.100; Hodkinson, *Muslim Family Law*, p.246.

[185]Fyzee, *Outlines of Muhammadan Law*, p.146-147; Diwan, *Muslim Law in Modern India*, p.72; Mahmood, *The Muslim Law of India,* p.114.

[186]Hodkinson, *Muslim Family Law,* p.245; Fyzee, *Outlines of Muhammadan Law*, p.150.

[187]*Mulla's Principles*, p.325.

[188]Mahmood, *Personal Laws in Crisis,* p.76.

[189]Pearl 1st ed., p.92.

[190]Diwan, *Muslim Law in Modern India*, p.72

[191]*Ibid.*, pp.73 and 87; Mahmood, *The Muslim Law of India,* p.119; Mahmood, *Personal Laws in Crisis,* p.80.

[192]Diwan, *Muslim Law in Modern India*, p.75.

[193]Mahmood, *The Muslim Law of India,* p.95.

[194]*Ibid.*, pp.116-117; Mahmood, *Personal Laws in Crisis,* p.76-77 also blames ill-advised maulvis.

[195]*Ibid.*, pp.75-77.

Apart from talaq, the Muslim wife's right to divorce (*khul'*) is largely a matter of extra-judicial regulation. Mahmood is concerned to portray khul' as extremely liberal and he argues that it has been distorted by Muslim men and by scholars alike, so that the courts in India now treat this right 'as if it were totally non-existent'.[196] While Pakistan and Bangladesh have taken a more liberal approach,[197] the Indian courts do not dissolve marriages at the request of Muslim wives as liberally as they ought to.[198] Thus, reform in India has taken the wrong path, and Mahmood seeks to encourage the judiciary to develop liberal application of the 'breakdown theory' (see below). Quite how Indian courts can do this, since hardly any cases on khul' come before them, is not clear. Apart from maintenance problems (see below), there are only a handful of reported recent cases under the Dissolution of Muslim Marriages Act 1939.

This seems to confirm what Mahmood had reported earlier, namely that, while judicial divorce by the wife is fully recognised, 'the Muslim law in India recognises several forms of extrajudicial divorce - those to be effected (a) by the husband, (b) by the wife, and (c) by the husband and the wife jointly'.[199] Although the author at once submits that this does not fully represent the law of Islam, he makes no comment on the frequency of divorce by wives and we are left to wonder to what extent it is taken up at all.

Mahmood also writes that a Muslim wife may reserve the right for herself to dissolve her marriage in certain circumstances.[200] Apparently, this is becoming increasingly common,[201] and again this does not require a judicial proceeding. Thus, judicial divorce among Muslims is really only needed when either party resists the dissolution of the marriage.[202] Quite how a wife can resist a talaq is not clear, so judicial divorces among Muslims in India would only arise when the husband totally opposes his wife's desire for divorce. But the Dissolution of Muslim Marriages Act 1939 could only come to the rescue of very few Muslim women anyway. This is not to deny that it extended the rights of Muslim wives,[203] but that Act has not been in practice very effective.

What Muslim leaders in India fear is a state system of divorce law that requires some form of judicial proceeding for every divorce. In Pakistan and Bangladesh, the Muslim Family Laws Ordinance 1961 has brought some measure of state supervision; authors disagree on how successful this has been, but this is not our concern here. India, on the other hand, has done nothing to control abuses of the talaq system, so that the classical law remains fully in

---

196*Ibid.*, p.78.

197*Khurshid Bibi*, PLD 1967 SC 97; on subsequent developments, seeking to be more restrictive, see esp. Pearl 2nd ed., pp.123-130.

198Mahmood, *Personal Laws in Crisis*, p.78.

199Mahmood, *The Muslim Law of India*, p.95.

200For details see *Ibid.*, pp.122-123; Mahmood, *Personal Laws in Crisis*, p.77.

201Diwan, *Muslim Law in Modern India*, p.76; Mahmood, *The Muslim Law of India*, p.124.

202*Ibid.*, p.95.

203Diwan, *Muslim Law in Modern India*, p.83.

force.[204] While it is correct to say that 'almost everywhere, Muslims are making efforts to bring the law in accord with modern ideas of social justice',[205] and that 'in all Muslim countries there has been pressure to introduce reforms which will safeguard the wife's rights',[206] we must note that in India,

> All attempts to reform this area of Muslim law, as indeed other areas as well, have been met by allegations of interference in the political and religious rights of the Muslim minority community.[207]

David Pearl[208] has more recently distinguished between legislative attempts, which have indeed been resisted as indicated, and some judicial decisions which have sought to restrict the husband's unfettered right to repudiation.

One particular issue continues to be vigorously debated in India and is important for our present discussion. Authors like Diwan devote much attention to breakdown of marriage as a ground of divorce in a modern legal system and argue further that India should have a uniform divorce law based on the principle of irretrievable breakdown. Diwan was somewhat surprised to find that the breakdown principle had been 'discovered' recently by a judge in the High Court of Kerala.[209]

The Muslim response to this is significant. Firstly, Mahmood and others claim that divorce by mutual consent (which was introduced into modern Indian law by the Special Marriage Act 1954 and by the Marriage Laws (Amendment) Act 1976 into the Hindu Marriage Act 1955) has all along been provided for by Islamic law, so that 'the Shariat is undoubtedly the parent law.'[210] Secondly, Mahmood argued some years ago that "the true Islamic law in fact stood for what is now known as the 'breakdown theory of divorce'."[211] He has recently developed this argument, writing about the Oriental origin of the breakdown theory, and refuting the commonly held belief that it is a modern Western concept. In fact,

> The law-giver of Islam had laid down a superb law of dissolution of marriage, laying its foundations on what is now known as the 'breakdown theory' of divorce.[212]

---

[204]Hodkinson, *Muslim Family Law*, p.221.
[205]Fyzee, *Outlines of Muhammadan Law*, p.148.
[206]Pearl 1st ed., p.93.
[207]*Ibid.*, p.101.
[208]Pearl, 2nd ed., p.119.
[209]Diwan, *Muslim Law in Modern India*, p.83.
[210]Mahmood, *Personal Laws in Crisis,* p.79.
[211]Mahmood, *The Muslim Law of India*, p.95.
[212]Mahmood, *Personal Laws in Crisis,* p.126.

I am not in disagreement on this point, but it is suggested in the wake of this argumentation that Hindus should acknowledge the advanced position of Islamic law rather than follow Western-based laws. Thus, the most prominent academic spokesman of the Indian Muslims argues that the reformers of the Hindu law should from the beginning have followed the pattern of the 'breakdown principle'.[213] Other writers, too, have argued with deceptive persuasiveness that Hindu divorce law needs to be made easier, following Islamic models.[214] Mahmood turns communal tables by asking:

> What is wrong if the Islamic concept of breakdown-based divorce creeps into the modern personal law of the majority community ?[215]

As perceptive observers will have noted some time ago, Mahmood no longer argues for a Uniform Civil Code, and his recent book may be seen as a vigorous attack on it. Where this leaves other eager proponents of legal uniformity we shall see in section IV. My conclusion here is that Professor Mahmood's scheme of introducing the breakdown principle as the 'grundnorm' of modern Indian divorce law, provided the law reformers could be persuaded to retain extra-judicial divorces, will leave the shari'a fully intact in modern India. In fact, with some glee, the father of this clever scheme could be credited with giving a Muslim legal system of divorce to the whole of India. Communal bickerings aside, where this would leave Indian women must remain a matter of serious concern. I am totally opposed to 'easier' divorce laws in India, as social reality has shown that modern divorce law reforms have worked much to the disadvantage of women.[216] As we shall see immediately below, especially how to ensure maintenance for women after divorce remains a major problem in modern India.

(v) Maintenance after Divorce

In classical shari'a, the ground rule is that the husband must provide maintenance to the wife during *'idda*.[217] There are a number of detailed rules applying in different schools and various situations, but we are not concerned with those here.

---

[213] *Ibid.*, p.125-126.

[214] W.F. Haq, 'Amend the Laws and Make Divorce Easy for Hindus', *Kerala Law Times*, 1988 (1), Journal, pp.45-47, on which see W.F. Menski, 'Hindu Talaq: On a Progressive Divorce Law for India', *Kerala Law Times*, 1989 (1), Journal, pp.23-30.

[215] Mahmood, *Personal Laws in Crisis*, p.126.

[216] R. Mehta, *Divorced Hindu Woman*, New Delhi, 1975; Derrett, *The Death of a Marriage Law*, New Delhi, 1978; V. Dhagamwar, *Women and Divorce*, Bombay, 1987.

[217] Fyzee, *Outlines of Muhammadan Law*, p.186; Diwan, *Muslim Law in Modern India*, p.130; *Mulla's Principles*, p.301.

Legislative enactments and case-law in British India have largely respected this principle of Islamic law while, as we shall see below, modern Indian state law has attempted wide-ranging interference to assist women.

Section 488 of the Criminal Procedure Code 1898 allowed Muslim wives to claim maintenance during the continuation of the marriage in certain situations, including when the husband had taken another wife. This was objected to by the Muslims as an interference with the shari'a, but most High Courts in India held that as a general law, the Criminal Procedure Code applied to all Indians, despite the Muslim Personal Law (Shariat) Application Act 1937.[218]

The common answer[219] to an order made under Section 488 was for the husband to divorce his wife, leaving her after the 'idda period to fend for herself.[220] This had to be accepted by the courts.[221] Also the Dissolution of Muslim Marriages Act 1939 left the traditional position undisturbed.[222] Recently, Mahmood has sought to explain that this is a reasonable way of dealing with the issue, since:

> As a natural corollary to its concept of marriage and policy on divorce, after the dissolution of a marriage Islam does not keep the parties tagged to each other for the rest of their lives. It encourages both of them... to get remarried... there being no taboo in Islamic law or culture. The law keeps both parties to a dissolved marriage wholly free to look after their new responsibilities....This arrangement eminently conforms to Islam's own concepts of marriage and divorce and its unique theory of equality of sexes which is different from those other systems.[223]

The Indian legislature, however, was not satisfied with this and thus caused what Mahmood has recently called 'a Shariat vs. Cr.P.C. war in the judicial corridors of this country'.[224] One could argue that this is the result of a history of distortions, but no author explains why the law was changed, although the reasons are all too apparent. A detailed study of this complex topic will be more widely available in the near future.[225]

In 1974, the re-cast Criminal Procedure Code 1973 threatened to do away with an established rule of Islamic law. Section 125 of the new Code included a divorced wife in the definition of 'wife', so that Muslim husbands became

---

[218] Mahmood, *Personal Laws in Crisis*, p.82.

[219] Even Mahmood, *Ibid.*, p.83 admits of 'several cases'.

[220] Diwan, *Muslim Law in Modern India*, p.132.

[221] Mahmood, *The Muslim Law of India*, p.131.

[222] *Ibid.*, p.130.

[223] Mahmood, *Personal Laws in Crisis*, p.87.

[224] *Ibid.*, p.82.

[225] N. T. Murphy, 'Maintenance for Divorced Muslim Wives in India', in W.F. Menski ed., *Family Law in India*, London, forthcoming.

potentially liable to maintain their divorced wives beyond the ‘idda period, until death or re-marriage. A maximum of Rs.500/- per month could be awarded.[226]

The Indian legislature did not, however, dare to fully implement such sweeping reforms. In order to protect the Islamic law relating to a divorced wife's right to maintenance,[227] and obviously as a result of 'political pressure'[228] which was exercised in Parliament by the Indian Muslim leadership,[229] Section 127(3)(b) was included in the Code,[230] with the effect that Muslim husbands would not be liable to pay continued maintenance if the wife had received 'the whole of the sum which, under any customary or personal law applicable to the parties, was payable on such divorce', as the relevant section provided.

The meaning of this section was initially unclear.[231] The 'customary dues' would seem to include the deferred mahr,[232] so that a wife who had received it, no matter how small the amount, would not be entitled to further maintenance. Conversely, a Muslim husband who divorced his wife, maintained her during the ‘idda period and paid the whole of the deferred mahr to his ex-wife would be absolved from any further liability.

In such a situation the importance of agreeing a sufficiently high deferred mahr is quite apparent. It would also be very expedient for Muslim wives to include ante-nuptial agreements about maintenance in certain cases.[233] Subsequent events show that there must have been continued evidence of Muslim women receiving mere pittances which were totally insufficient to maintain them.

Pearl anticipated a decision by the Indian Supreme Court;[234] indeed, in the same year a novel interpretation by Mr. Justice Krishna Iyer (as he then was) was given in the important case of *Bai Tahira*.[235] The learned judge, true to his image as the Indian Lord Denning, placed the facts before him in a wide constitutional and socio-economic context, speaking of Section 125 as a benign provision enacted to help discarded divorcees, i.e. a welfare law whose true purpose must be allowed to override legal technicalities. This judgement meant that any customary sums paid under Section 127(3)(b) of the Code would have to be sufficient to help the divorced wife to keep body and soul

---

[226]Diwan, *Muslim Law in Modern India*, p.131; Hodkinson, *Muslim Family Law,* p.150.

[227]Mahmood, *The Muslim Law of India,* p.132.

[228]Pearl 1st ed., p.66.

[229]Mahmood, *Personal Laws in Crisis,* p.83.

[230]For details see Pearl 1st ed., p.66; Pearl 2nd ed., p.71; Mahmood, *The Muslim Law of India,* p.132.

[231]See Pearl 1st ed., p.66; Pearl 2nd ed., p.71-72; Mahmood, *The Muslim Law of India,* pp.131-132.

[232]See also Hodkinson, *Muslim Family Law,* p.150.

[233]See Diwan, *Muslim Law in Modern India*, pp.130-131; Hodkinson, *Muslim Family Law,* p.150-151.

[234]Pearl 1st ed., p.67.

[235] AIR 1979 SC 362; on the text see also Hodkinson, *Muslim Family Law,* pp.199-204.

together. What counted was the fulfilment of a social obligation, not a ritual exercise rooted in custom.

This was a powerful reminder to Muslim men that they had some reponsibilities towards the women that they chose to divorce. *Bai Tahira* was not so much seen as an attack on Islamic law (though there were many dissenting comments), but was hailed as a 'liberal ruling and conforms to the spirit of Islamic law on the subject'.[236]

Bai Tahira was followed in a number of cases, and within a few years its effects were felt as Muslim women, if they could afford to go to court, could claim better maintenance if their deferred mahr was insufficient. The male reaction to this became apparent when in 1985 the *cause célèbre* of *Shah Bano* opened another chapter in the 'war' between state law and Muslim sentiments of the sanctity of personal laws.

In what seems to be a heavily engineered and manipulated leading case, a rich lawyer sought to argue that he had no further liabilities towards his wife, then aged over 70, whom he had divorced after more than 40 years of marriage and given a meagre mahr. A bench of two Supreme Court judges, evidently impressed by the husband's arguments, could not agree on how to deal with this case and referred it to a larger bench. Mahmood alleges that the then Chief Justice became worried about 'an eventual affirmation of the supremacy of Islamic law over the Cr.P.C. rules'[237] and engineered a particular bench composed of five Hindu judges, which, as is implied in the criticism, led to an inadequate and biased treatment of the Muslim personal law.

The *Shah Bano* case[238] strongly affirmed that the Criminal Procedure Code as a general Indian law overrides the Muslim personal law. No court in India and no bench, however composed, could have held otherwise. The court firmly stated that the provisions of Section 125 did not supplant the personal law of individuals, but the prophylactic nature of the provisions was a moral edict of a secular nature.[239] In other words, no Muslim husband need get in conflict with Section 125; all he would have to do was to ensure that his divorced wife was properly maintained.

The court also addressed the question whether there is any conflict between Section 125 and the Muslim personal law. The court concluded that there was no such conflict. The judges looked at the textbooks on Islamic law and found them inadequate in dealing with the situation of a divorced wife unable to maintain herself. Thus the court found that Muslim personal law does not envisage a situation that a wife is unable to maintain herself after divorce; therefore there must be an implied liability on Muslim husbands to ensure maintenance of the ex-wife beyond ‘idda.

---

[236] Mahmood, *The Muslim Law of India,* p.132.

[237] Mahmood, *Personal Laws in Crisis,* p.89.

[238] *Mohd. Ahmed Khan,* AIR 1985 SC 945.

[239] *Ibid.,* at pp. 948-9.

The judges also took support from the Qur'an itself (verses 241-2 of chapter II), looking at a wide range of translations and comments. The fact that five Hindu judges 'exercised neo-ijtihad', by re-interpreting the Qur'an in modern secular India has been identified by Mahmood as 'fatal to the future of Islam in this country'[240] and as 'a victory of a Hindu-Christian doctrine over Islamic matrimonial culture'.[241]

In fact, what the Supreme Court did - apart from its rather unwarranted and superfluous comments on the Uniform Civil Code-[242] makes sound sense in modern Indian law, especially in the context of maintenance laws generally. Having found that the Qur'an expects every Muslim[243] to ensure maintenance provision for his divorced wife, the court could not find a conflict between the Muslim personal law and section 125.

Finally, the court disagreed with *Bai Tahira*'s case only to the extent that mahr was not a customary due payable on divorce. As a result, a general rule was thus laid down: henceforth every Muslim husband in India would be fully responsible for the maintenance of his divorced wife until her death or remarriage.

Muslim reaction against this judgement was no doubt fuelled by a combination of resentment against interference with the Muslim personal law and male opposition against continued obligations towards ex-wives. Recent criticisms of the Indian law of maintenance go in this direction, and Professor Mahmood has argued that the Indian judiciary, taken by 'over-enthusiasm for the so-called feminist cause',[244] 'is gradually turning divorce into a sort of an insurance deal offering far more lucrative benefits than available in marriage'.[245] Although he is concerned with divorced women starving,[246] one may wonder how divorced wives in modern India, Muslim as well as non-Muslim, can be enabled to survive in dignity if there is neither a state welfare system nor any obligation on the ex-husband to contribute to their maintenance.

Indian Muslims took part in protest marches in various parts of India. As an immediate reaction, the Muslim Women (Protection of Rights on Divorce) Act 1986 was passed hurriedly to appease the demonstrators. The effect of the Act, so one thought, was to render nugatory what the Supreme Court had said in *Shah Bano* and *Bai Tahira*, to take Muslims out of the ambit of section 125 of the Criminal Procedure Code and to place a liability on the divorced woman's natal family or children for her maintenance. Should that prove impossible, and in the absence of a state welfare system, the State Wakf Boards were to look after such women (the Wakf Boards promptly protested,

240 Mahmood, *Personal Laws in Crisis*, p.90.

241 *Ibid.*, p.91.

242 AIR 1985 SC at 954-955.

243 But note the 'shuffling plea' (at p. 951 of the judgement) of the All India Muslim Personal Law Board that this rule applies only to the more pious Muslims.

244 Mahmood, *Personal Laws in Crisis*, p.129.

245 *Ibid.*, p.127.

246 *Ibid.*, p.130.

claiming lack of funds!). The Muslim husband was absolved from all responsibility beyond the 'idda period.

The dispute seems to have ended with a victory of the shari'a, helped by the Indian government itself. The ideal of legal uniformity had been disregarded, it appeared, with the state bowing to Muslim demands for the recognition of rules of their personal law. To make an Act of Parliament specifically for the Muslims in an area of the general law, thus, in effect, taking Indian Muslims out of the ambit of a general legal provision, was contrary to the ideal behind Article 44 of the Indian Constitution and a departure from the stated policy of seeking to achieve legal uniformity.

But the Indian judiciary, recently much noted for its activist stance in many areas of the law, has not yet conceded defeat in this battle. There are, to date, two very recent cases from the High Court of Kerala, traditionally alert to personal law issues, which, if upheld on appeal to the Supreme Court, would virtually re-instate the *Shah Bano* decision.

The two cases[247] were filed under section 3(1)(a) of the 1986 Act to ascertain the extent of the liability of a Muslim husband for his divorced wife's maintenance during the 'idda period. This liability, both cases upheld on a close scrutiny of the wording of the Act, includes (a) the uncontroversial duty of the husband to maintain the woman during 'idda and (b) a duty to make fair and reasonable provision for her maintenance after the 'idda period, but before that period expires. The judges based their reasoning on established principles of statutory interpretation and found that section 3(1)(a) of the 1986 Act, speaking of 'reasonable and fair provision and maintenance to be made and paid to her within the 'idda period by her former husband', intended to protect divorced Muslim women from destitution. A Muslim wife in Kerala may, thus, file a petition under section 3(1)(a) of the 1986 Act rather than under section 125 of the Criminal Procedure Code, which does not apply to Muslims at present.

If the 1986 Act, which is being challenged as unconstitutional before the Supreme Court, is upheld, the recent Kerala cases point the way to a morally acceptable and uniform regulation of the problem. How the Muslim husband's ancient, but newly discovered obligation is to be discharged remains to be ascertained.

In summary, after much controversy modern Indian law seems to have found a way, in the area of maintenance law, of regulating a difficult issue not through application of a strengthened general law (which proved objectionable to Indian Muslim men in principle), but by a legislative reform of the Muslim personal law. Anger about the recent Kerala cases is only just beginning to get articulated; the issue is likely to remain controversial for some time.

[247] *Ali,* 1988[2] KLT 94 and *Aliyar,* 1988[2] KLT 446.

IV. Islamic Family Laws and a Uniform Civil Code in India

A. The Issue

It is hard to conceive a uniform legal system for more than 800 million people spread over an area several times the size of Britain, with many different ethnic groups, religions and ways of life. In contrast to Bangladesh, with its greater ethnic homogeneity and compactness,[248] a uniform system of family law for India will remain not only a 'distant mirage',[249] but a dangerous 'red herring' that the state would be ill-advised to push too far. Not only do Muslims resent greater uniformity, but also the Sikhs are calling for the re-instatement of their personal law. Even at state level, there is resentment against enforced centralisation.

Many supporters of legal uniformity in India have started distancing themselves from euphoric and futuristic debates. The Indian leading Islamic law scholar's change of attitude towards a Uniform Civil Code is indicative of the Islamisation-related trends in the subcontinent, but is also symptomatic of a growing realisation in India today that legal uniformity is one of those Western concepts that may be unsuitable for complex Third World legal systems.[250] There is, albeit in different contexts, a convergence in the appreciation of legislative overdoses and their interference with personal laws.[251] It is becoming increasingly questionable whether legal uniformity as an ideal model is maintainable, and whether it is useful even for European and North American jurisdictions.[252]

The debate about law reform and integrated civil codes must be seen in a wider context. There is, indeed, a false search for uniformity in modern Indian law,[253] and the exclusive focus on Muslim resistance and 'obstinacy' is incorrect and counterproductive.

---

[248] I have pointed out (supra footnote 5) that Bangladesh represents a very comparable case in terms of Hindu-Muslim percentages, only exactly in reverse, the worried minority being the Hindus in this case.

[249] Allott, *The Limits of Law*, p.216.

[250] Contrast the writings of Mahmood in 1976, 1977 and 1978 with his *Personal Laws in Crisis*, published in 1986. When, a decade ago, Professor Mahmood spoke to my students of Law and Society in South Asia at the University of London, a development could already be noted over his earlier writings.

[251] See e.g. Mahmood, *Personal Laws in Crisis*, p.112; W. F. Menski, 'Legislative Overkill and the Kerala Joint Hindu Family System (Abolition Act) 1975', in *Kerala Law Times*, 1986, pp.17-20, and W. F. Menski, 'Legislative Overkill - A Rejoinder', in *Kerala Law Times*, 1986, pp.63-65.

[252] See Menski, 'English Family Law and Ethnic Laws in Britain'.

[253] Mahmood, *Personal Laws in Crisis*, p.45.

B. The Constitutional Set-up

The wider constitutional set-up has been well-researched.[254] For some scholars, Article 44 of the Indian Constitution has remained wholly ineffectice and meaningless.[255] An earlier study partly explains why this may be so.[256] The constitutional limitations themselves are fairly obvious if we note that the Directive Principles of State Policy in Part IV of the Indian Constitution, although fundamental to the governance of the country, are non-justiciable. Article 44 is one of those non-justiciable Principles, and even if the Indian judiciary has from time to time, as in the *Shah Bano* case, called the attention of the nation to the issue, the envisaged reforms have probably been too controversial to be dealt with in one broad sweep. Indian governments have had more important tasks than the creation of legal uniformity. But even in the case of the call for integration, a huge country such as India finds it difficult to operate a uniform legal system of any kind. The Indian Constitution provides in this area little more than an ethical framework for the governance of modern India. Legal realities are to be worked out with flexibility and expediencies of all kinds, and offer fertile ground for political economists.

C. The Uniformisation of Modern Indian Family Laws

As a result of its inability to create legal uniformity in personal laws, India continues the pre-colonial and colonial model of a system of incongruous concurrent personal laws (Hindu, Muslim, Christian, Parsi, Jewish), to which a largely optional general scheme of family law has been added: the general law of the country.

It was easier to unify the law of the largest sector of the population, but the process proved more complex than previously thought. Hindu law was uniformised and secularised, in fact almost completely de-Hinduised.[257] It was made not only applicable to all Hindus, but also to Sikhs, Buddhists and Jains. But the codification of personal law did not automatically produce uniform laws. Several matters of Hindu law continued to be governed by custom, even under the modern statutes, especially for the solemnisation of marriage and much of the law of divorce.[258] With uniformity impossible to establish *within* a system of personal law, how much more difficult the creation of uniformity *between* personal laws!

---

[254] See e.g. Mahmood, *Muslim Personal Law. Role of the State in the Subcontinent*, pp.83-109; Mahmood, *Personal Laws in Crisis*, pp.12-30; Bhattacharjee, *Muslim Law and the Constitution.*

[255] Mahmood, *Personal Laws in Crisis*, p.43.

[256] Mahmood, *An Indian Civil Code and Islamic Law*, Bombay, 1976.

[257] Derrett, *The Death of a Marriage Law*; Mahmood, *Personal Laws in Crisis*, p.106.

[258] The former is explicitly saved by statute for all Hindus, and the latter for many more than was commonly thought. See S. Beckwith, 'The Hindu Customary Law of Divorce', LL.B Essay, SOAS, 1988, to appear in Menski ed., *Family Law in India.*

A number of important reforms to the Hindu law have, more recently, created a rapprochement between the provisions of the Hindu Marriage Act 1955 and those of the Special Marriage Act 1954, fuelling Muslim apprehensions of further unification. But heated court battles indicate the absence of consensus over how Hindu law should be regulated. One learns from experience that the potential for diversity would fill more than the researcher's diary can hold.[259]

Indian Islamic law, as we saw, remained almost entirely untouched by statute in modern India. Indian Christian law continues to be regulated by seriously outmoded 19th century Acts that cry for reform and have already partly been modified by recent cases. The Parsi law, which applies to less than 100,000 people in India, used to be similarly outmoded, but the Parsi community leaders decided to update their personal law and bring it in line with general Indian law. The Parsi Marriage and Divorce (Amendment) Act 1988 reads over long passages as a verbatim copy of the Hindu Marriage Act 1955 in its de-Hinduised post-1976 form. The Parsi case shows an astute strategy of a small community more concerned than the Indian Muslims about its distinct identity, to pre-empt the creation of a Uniform Civil Code. The idea that Muslims, too, should get together and codify their personal law on modern lines was suggested a long time ago, but there is little progress in that direction.

For India as a whole, gone is the hope (apparent in the underlying rationale of Article 44 in the Indian Constitution) that the personal laws of the minorities would wither away and that people would learn to use a general law. More than forty years after Independence, there is resignation that this hope may never materialise.

Rather than waiting for the miracle of a Uniform Civil Code, it seems more likely that all Indian personal laws will be reformed separately, but along similar lines. The Parsi case shows that this is already happening now. But many Muslims continue to see any reform to their personal law as a threat.

D. Muslim Personal Law and the Uniform Civil Code

A major motivation behind Professor Mahmood's search for legal uniformity in India has been that the Muslim personal law, rather than being altogether replaced by a common civil code, would be merged into it and that 'Islamic concepts, devoid of their time-worn traditional interpretations, can be a potential component of the emerging Indian civil code'.[260] More recently, he re-stated this conviction in a plea to the nation over the appropriate treatment of the Indian shari'a:

---

259 See Menski, 'Solemnisation of Hindu Marriages: the Law and Reality'; Menski, 'Legislative Overkill and the Kerala Joint Hindu Family System (Abolition Act) 1975'; Menski, 'Legislative Overkill - A Rejoinder'.

260 Mahmood, *An Indian Civil Code and Islamic Law*, p.xiii.

> The law of Islam, seen in its true perspective and purged of all its distortions, can be an asset for the emerging family code of India. What is required is that our judges and lawyers should stop looking at Islamic law through the spectacles of the British-Indian courts and their past and present rapporteurs. Those who are its followers and love it must arrange to get its principles re-written in their true perspective for the benefit of the contemporary law-men. Those who are misusing its noble principles must stop denigrating it by their conduct and learn to practise it according to its true spirit. Their law, they must understand, may not need repeal or even substantive reform - as others say - but it is surely in need of restoration of its principles. To fulfil this need of the hour is the most sacred duty of every follower of Islam in this country.[261]

This is as much an appeal to Muslims to get their house in order as to non-Muslims to be patient. One could of course question how the re-writing of Islamic principles is to take place in modern India, and to what extent the author thinks the common Muslim in India will want to follow scholarly exegesis of the 'true' Islamic law.

Given that Muslim public opinion in India is, to a large extent, 'deadly opposed to the replacement of their personal law by a common civil code',[262] the above approach seems not only a courageous, but also a feasible one. The extent of reforms to Islamic law in Muslim countries shows that modernisation is possible; it also points the way to the realisation that being Muslim and being Indian is not conflictual, even though India remains a secular democracy. What Mahmood suggests is to devise a uniform family law for India that respects the personal laws and respects Indianness rather than blindly aping the West. Devising detailed rules will, in some cases, be difficult. But Mahmood shows the way, for example, when he argues that monogamy must remain the norm in Indian law,[263] but that polygamy should be allowed in certain circumstances.[264] Independent India must build its own legal culture.[265] This is happening in other areas of the law, e.g. recently in tort law[266] and in public interest litigation.[267]

Following this path does not lead to a Uniform Civil Code - but then, specialists on Indian law as a species (endangered as it may have seemed a decade ago, but now happily growing in number) are bound to concur that uniformity may have little value per se. One can, of course, argue that a

---

261 Mahmood, *Personal Laws in Crisis*, pp.93-94.

262 Mahmood, *An Indian Civil Code and Islamic Law*, p.3; See to the same effect Diwan, *Muslim Law in Modern India*, pp.38-39; Pearl 1st ed., p.101.

263 Mahmood, *Personal Laws in Crisis*, p.116.

264 *Ibid.*, p.117.

265 *Ibid.*, pp.111-113.

266 See supra note 60.

267 See e.g. Mr. Justice Krishna Iyer in *Rattan Lal* (1976) 2 S.C.C. 103, at 114-115.

formally uniform legal system can still respect and allow diversity, as the modern codified Hindu law does, for example. It is certainly essential for modern India to create a legal system that suits the socio-economic conditions of her people and their religious perceptions of themselves and their place in the world. The one-sided politically motivated quest for a truly uniform family law for India is, several decades after the Constitution was promulgated, perhaps no longer a realistic aim.[268] It has been defeated by the persistence of traditional Indian preferences for diversity and flexibility, and by the mere size of the country and the diversity within its population.

The sore point in the conflict between Islamic law and the state in India is the state insisting (though markedly less vigorously now) on the rather ill-conceived ideal of legal uniformity for all Indians. The new-found respect for Islamic law (as indeed for all personal laws) must, however, not be confused with the recent phenomenon of political Islamisation. India is not a predominantly Muslim country, and Muslims are likely to remain a large but important minority. Because of the nature of Islamic law, it is unlikely that the problems would ever completely disappear. But if Indian Muslims are ready to acknowledge that they can continue to develop an Islamic legal system as part of Indian law, thereby following shari'a and the Indian law at the same time, conflicts and tensions would diminish significantly.

[268] See now V. Dhagamvar, *Towards the Uniform Civil Code,* Bombay, 1989.

14. ISLAMIC FAMILY LAW LATEST DEVELOPMENTS IN INDIA

Tahir Mahmood

Since the publication of *Personal Laws in Crisis,*[1] the most significant development in the field of Islamic law in India has been the enactment of the Muslim Women (Protection of Rights of Divorce) Act 1986. In the background of this Act was the controversy that followed the Supreme Court decision in the well known *Shah Bano* case.[2] The Act has at the moment of writing been in force for nearly three years, but its future is still as uncertain as its scope and purview. While the highest court of the nation has yet to give its judgment on its constitutionality, the high courts are viewing it from different, and sometimes mutually conflicting, angles. At the same time representatives of those sections of the Muslim community to whose demands the Act was the answer are preparing for its revision to make it more Islamic.

I. Jurisprudential and Historical Perspective

In Islamic law and sociology, women can be described as belonging to one of two categories:

(i) women who are living in matrimony; and

(ii) women who are not living in matrimony.

Women who have never been married are called in Islamic terminology '*bikr*'; and those who were once married but whose marriage is no longer subsisting (whether on account of the husband's death or due to divorce) are called *'thayyib'*. Islamic law places both bakir and thayyib women in the general category of *ghayr mutazawwija* (i.e., women not living in matrimony), and does not differentiate between them in any respect. It simply provides that a thayyib (i.e., a woman who was once married but whose marriage is no longer subsisting) has the same rights, privileges and status as a bikr (i.e., a virgin). The concepts of 'widowed women' and 'divorced women' are foreign to the family jurisprudence in Islam.

If a woman was once married but has lost her husband, Islam does not put on her the label of misfortune of widowhood. Similarily, if a woman's marriage is dissolved, whether at her own insistence or at the insistence of her husband, Islam does not put on her the stigma of being a divorcee. For both these cases Islam has provided a short waiting span called "*idda* '; and in Islamic law and sociology a woman may remain what we call a 'widow' or a 'divorcee' only during that short period - which in no case can extend to more

[1] T. Mahmood, *Personal Laws in Crisis*, Delhi, 1986.
[2] AIR 1965 SC 945.

than a few months. After its expiry she is regarded in Islam as the mother of her sons and daughters, if she has any. In the absence of children, like a bikr (i.e. a virgin), she is regarded as the daughter of her parents or, in their absence, as the granddaughter of her great grand parents or the sister of her brothers and sisters, the niece of her uncles and aunts - and so on. In no case, however, once the ‘idda period is over is any woman to be regarded in Islam as the 'widow' of a deceased man or the 'divorced wife' of a living man. The label of widowhood which reminds the woman herself and the society at large of her past misfortune, and the label of being a divorcee which badly stigmatises the woman and subjects her to social indignities, both are foreign to Islamic law and sociology. Both are repugnant to the Islamic concepts of women's honour, self-respect, social status, dignity and freedom.

It is in the light of these characteristics of Islamic law that one should try to comprehend the issue of the so-called 'divorced' Muslim woman. The rights of Muslim women who, as per non-Islamic legal cultures, may be placed in the categories of widowed and divorced women, are unknown to Islamic ideology, which has no place for such categorisation.

For a Muslim woman whose marriage is no more subsisting (for any reason whatsoever), maintenance rights will be governed by the following rules:

i) If she has children who have income or property, the liability of her maintenance would be exclusively for those children - whether male or female;

ii) If she has no children (or if her children are minor or have no property or income), her maintenance would be a sacred legal liability of her parents - notably both father and mother - or the survivor among them;

iii) If her parents are dead (or unable to maintain her), she would stand in the position of an orphaned virgin girl and, like the latter, shall be maintained by her nearest blood relatives; and

iv) If a woman has no children, no parents and no blood relatives, her maintenance would be a charge on the collective resources of the Muslim community as a whole.

In no situation however should a woman be left unprotected and unprovided for. This indeed is the true law of Islam. To appreciate the desire of the Muslim community to protect this principle one has to keep in mind certain features of the vaster legal history of mankind.

As is well known, the Christian religion expressly prohibited divorce. To meet the exigencies of time the Christian world legalised divorce in the 19th century A.D. and, while doing so, evolved a new law on divorced women's maintenance - which it newly introduced as the liability of the divorcing husband, mainly since divorce (though legalised) was theologically regarded as sinful. In India, the concept of divorce was unknown to the ancient Hindu law, and marriage was regarded under that law as a sacrament and as a perpetual union. When legalising divorce for the Hindu society during the middle of the twentieth century,[3] the State adopted the model evolved a little earlier in the Christian West in relation to post divorce rights for women.[4] This was in keeping with the general trend of looking mostly towards the West for every required legal reform.

Muslim society was different. Since the seventh century A.D. it had had a detailed matrimonial law of its own, which was based on the contractual theory of marriage and the breakdown theory of divorce, and which offered comprehensive protection to women at every stage of life. So when it came to legalising divorce in the nineteenth century the West evolved a new law on divorced women's rights, that new law could have no relevance for a Muslim society which already had a diferent law of its own on the subject. As the State in India adopted in the middle of the twentieth century that new western model, Muslim society found it unnecessary to give up its own law on the subject in favour of that model, especially since the model conflicted with Islam's basic concepts of family, marriage, divorce and domestic relations.

Of late there has been a demand in India that Indian Muslims should give up their own law on the subject (which they already had when the western model came into existence) despite its virtues and advantages, only because that western model has been accepted by the state in India for the majority community which never had a law of its own on the subject. This demand has been viewed by the Muslims as unfair to them and their religion and law. Enactment of the Muslim Women (Protection of Rights on Divorce) Act 1986 was a step towards accepting the point of view that Muslims need not be compelled to give up their own law on divorced women's rights in favour of another system.

II. *Shah Bano:*[5] Background and Aftermath

The new Criminal Procedure Code 1973 had generally extended its law on wives' maintenance to divorced wives but had, on the demand of the Muslims, accommodated to some extent the traditional Islamic law concerning the husband's financial liablity to his divorced wife.[6] Ever since then a section of jurists have been expressing the view that the general law of the Code (treating an ex-wife as a wife for the purpose of maintenance) could be well reconciled with Islamic legal norms. Among them was Justice Krishna Iyer of the Supreme Court of India who, while having profound respect for Islam's one-time revolutionary laws,[7] has also been extremely sensitive to the demand of gender justice. During 1979-80 he handed down two successive judgments -

---

[3]Divorce was first legalised for the Hindus by local legislation in Baroda, Madras, Bombay and Saurashtra. Later, the Hindu Marriage Act 1955 introduced it for nearly all Hindu citizens of the country.

[4]See section 24-25 of the Hindu Marriage Act 1955.

[5]Supra n.2.

[6]Section 125-127b of the Criminal Procedure Code 1973.

[7]The Islamic law on divorce is 'surprisingly rational, realistic and modern', the judge had observed in *Yusuf Rawthan v. Sowramma,* AIR 1971 Ker, p.271.

Bai Tahira[8] and *Fuzlunbi,*[9] in which he made an attempt to restrict the scope of the special provision of the 1973 Criminal Procedure Code which partly accommodated the traditional Islamic law on the subject. This was done without denigrating Islam and Muslims. Later, in the well-known *Shah Bano* case, Chief Justice Y.V. Chandrachud, going far beyond Justice Iyer's thinking, made the said special provison of the Code wholly ineffective. In his opinion that provision as well as its interpretation by Justice Iyer was based on a misunderstanding of the true Islamic law. In the hope that this would bring credibility to his thinking in Muslim circles, he tried to link his opinion with certain verses of the Qur'an as available in literal English translation in certain non-legal works. At the same time he reprimanded the custodians of the State for their failure to bring about a uniform civil code in accordance with the terms of article 44 of the Constitution.

The reaction to the *Shah Bano* judgment was unfavourable in Muslim circles. What mainly alarmed the Muslims was the alleged attempt of the judge to 'interpret' certain Qur'anic verses and his admonition to the State in respect of uniform civil code - this latter aspect of the judgment, in their view, amounting to a judicial stricture on Muslim personal law as a whole. While the Muslims were so viewing the judgment quietly, anti-Muslim elements, of whom there is no dearth in India, went into swift action, and, blowing the judgment out of proportions, projected it as a virtual death warrant on Islamic law. Involved in this game were, consciously or unconsciously, many eminent public figures, prominent lawyers and academics as well as various organisations and institutions. As a result, religious sentiment of the Muslims were badly hurt, not so much by the ratio of the *Shah Bano* judgment as by its projection by others as an anti-Islamic law ruling of the highest court of justice in the country. They, then, decided to coordinate their response. Under the leadership of the All India Muslim Personal Law Board, Muslim organisations and individuals started a country-wide agitation and evolved a near consensus of the predominant majority of Muslim citizenry of India in favour of the move to demand statutory protection of their personal law.

Prime Minister Rajiv Ghandi soon realised the gravity of the situation. Like many others, he had originally found in the *Shah Bano* ruling relief for some distressed Muslim women. The marathon speech which one of his young Muslim ministers delivered in Parliament in support of *Shah Bano* (reportedly with his blessings) reflected this initial thinking of the Prime Minister. But the growing agitation of the Muslims across the country prompted a reassessment, and he consequently initiated discussion on the issue with the Muslim leadership. Convinced that the Muslims had a case, the Prime Minister made up his mind to put his weight on their side. Law Minister A.K. Sen then introduced in the Lok Sabha the Muslim Women (Protection of Rights of Divorce Bill) 1986.

[8]AIR 1979 SC 362.
[9]AIR 1980 SC 1730.

Introduction of the Muslim Women Bill in Parliament struck with a thunderstorm all the loud-hailers of the *Shah Bano* judgment for its so-called anti-shari'a bias. Their ego was badly hurt and they came out to misrepresent the newly proposed law to ignorant laymen as a frightful national calamity. Passing of this Bill would, in their opinion, herald India's doomsday. Loud criticism of the Bill was made without even caring to read its provisions and understand the political will and the legislative intention behind it. The Bill was described as a 'fraud on the Constitution', 'a slap on the face of Indian secularism' and an unwise step that would provoke the majority community to 'communal frenzy'. Its supporters were freely called 'anti-national, orthodox and lunatic'. The Bill remained before Parliament for nearly three months and during this period it assumed the colour of a serious minority-majority conflict. It became for Muslims a symbol of their legal and constitutional equality with the majority community, whereas the latter viewed it as a symbol of victory for a religious minority which had 'no right to claim equality of rights and status' with them. To make things worse, this thinking on the part of the majority community was supported and defended by many heavyweights among its intellectuals and public figures. It was in these difficult circumstances that many Muslim academics found it advisable to lend their weight to the communities' struggle for the recognition and protection of their legal status and rights on an equal footing with the majority community. I have no hesitation in saying that I was one of them.

During the days of the hectic debate on the Bill I was portrayed in a section of the press as one of its architects and drafters. This is not true. I did not suggest to anybody, in or outside the government, any particular step that could be taken to satisfy the outraged Muslim community. Nor had I ever furnished to any person any draft of any law for this purpose. Of course, in my writings and speeches I explained the true principles of Islamic personal law (especially on the subject at issue). As regards the Bill, like all others, I read its text in the press after the introduction in the Lok Sabha. Soon after reading it I sent to some prominent spokesmen of the Muslims an extensive list of amendments which I thought were necessary in order to bring its provisions in strict conformity with the shari'a as I understood it. The All India Muslim Personal Law Board discussed all the proposed amendments at an emergency meeting was convened at Delhi in May, at which I was present as a special invitee. I was later told that as the government had a feeling that too many amendments would amount to rewriting the Bill, which might make things difficult for it, it had suggested to the Board to press only for the 'bare minimum'. When the Bill was eventually passed very few of the suggested amendments had found a place in its provisions.

The Muslim Womens Bill is now on the statute book under the title 'Muslim Women (Protection of Rights on Divorce) Act 1986'. By enacting it the government has, from the Muslim viewpoint, demonstrated its respect for the equality of all religions in the country and its regard for the religious rights of the minorities. The opponents of the Act, however, think otherwise.

III. The Muslim Women Act 1986: Major Provisions[10]

In section 3(1)(a) of the Act one finds two different expressions: 'provision' and 'maintenance'. Use of two different verbs 'made' and 'paid' in the clause suggests that the Act is speaking of two entirely different things: a provision to be made and maintenance to be paid - both, notably, 'within the ‘idda period'. The setting of this whole clause is confusing. Does the Act mean to enact a 'reasonable and fair provision' in addition to maintenance as a justifiable entitlement of the divorced wife? And, if so, is this based on the controversial interpretation of the word *mata‘* in verse 241 of chapter II of the Qur'an? In case this is true, what will be the meaning of the expression 'within the ‘iddat period ' with reference to 'provision to be made' ? How can a court which decides a case after the expiry of the divorcee-applicant's ‘idda enforce it? Moreover, making payment of mata‘ a judicially enforceable right of every divorced woman may indeed not be acceptable to those who had opposed the Supreme Court desision in the *Shah Bano* case and sought its repeal through the Act under comment. Doubtless, the intention of the legislature behind clause (a) of section 3(1) is not clear. In my opinion, payment of a 'fair and reasonable provision' to the divorced wife by the former husband should be regarded as a remedy which the court may in its discretion award in suitable cases - not an absolute right of all divorced women irrespective of circumstances that led to divorce; and where a court finds it is equitable to award it, the law must provide proper guidelines for the determination of its quantum. An amendment of the Act to this effect will make its principle of 'fair provision' a clearly Islamic provision resting on the Qur'anic injunction concerning *mata‘ at-talaq* which, in the opinion of the jurists, is an indemnity for arbitrary divorce (*talaq at-ta‘assuf*).

By section 3(3)(a) judicial enforeability of the divorced wife's right to 'provision' and 'maintenance' has been subjected to the condition of the husband 'having sufficient means'. So far as his ability to pay ‘idda is concerned, this liability under the principles of Islamic law is unconditional and is not to be regulated by the financial means of the husband. To this extent the reference to the husband's means in the Act is unwarranted. However, if the reference to 'provision' in the Act is to be read as a separate entitlement of the divorced wife in addition to maintenance of her ‘idda, the sufficiency of means may be a relevant factor for that matter.

According to an established rule of Islamic law, if a divorced woman is breast-feeding a child of her husband at the time of divorce she is entitled to maintenance from her husband for herself, not merely for the ‘idda period, but for the remaining duration of the legally prescribed feeding period which ends when the child, male or female, attains the age of two years. By virtue of the same rule, if a child of the former husband is born to the divorced wife after divorce (in which case her ‘idda will end with the birth of the child) her entitlement to receive maintenance from her former husband (for herself) will

---

[10] See text of the Act in Appendix I.

be extened to the entire duration of the feeding period (i.e., two years). These rules of Islamic law speak of the maintenance of the divorced woman, and not of her child - the latter in any case being the absolute responsibility of her former husband (i.e. the child's father).

These rules of Islamic law have been confused in the senseless drafting of section 3(1)(b) of the Act. This clause begins with the expression 'where she herself maintains the children' and speaks of a 'reasonable and fair provision and maintenance' which she must get while each child remains under the age of two. This is irrelevant to Islamic law. Where a divorced woman is actually herself maintaining a child, irrespective of the age of the child, she can legally claim reimbursement, and not 'a fair and reasonable provision and maintenance'. What the shari'a provides for her by way of maintenance of feeding period (*nafaqat ar-rada'a*) will come in addition to such reimbursement. Her own maintenance (reasonable and fair) is to be paid by her former husband while she breast-feeds her child. The confusion on the part of the drafters of the Act inherent in section 3(1) (b) is remarkable. It is a pity that an amendment suggested by me to put the law on its head had become a casualty of the apprehension that too many amendments would kill the Bill.

In Islamic law the mother is entitled to the custody (*hadana*) of her children up to a specific period in preference to all other relations of the child, including the father. This duration is different for boys and girls and also differs from school to school. In Hanafi law the mother is entitled to the custody of a male child until he attains the age of seven years, and of a female child until she attains puberty. In Shafi'i law her right to the custody of the female child extends until she gets married. In Ithna 'Ashari (Shi'i) law the female child will remain in her mother's custody up to the age of seven years, while a male child will remain with her till he attains the age of two years. The right of the mother to keep the custody of the child as per these rules, whatever be the legal duration of custody, is called hadana. According to the jurists of Islam, where a woman is divorced but is not deprived of the custody of the couple's children, for the entire duration of the custody her own maintenance (not the child's which, in any case, is incumbent upon its father) is to be paid by her former husband. This means for instance, that a divorced Hanafi mother wo retains the custody of a son is entitled to maintenance from her former husband so long as he does not attain the age of seven years.

The Act of 1986 takes no notice of these rules of Islamic law. In view of the fact that in many cases of divorce in India, minor children do remain with the divorced mother, inclusion of these rules of Islamic law into the Act would have been extremely beneficial to women. It will be seen that the husband's unconditional liability to maintain his divorced wife during 'idda may, more often than not, be suplemented by a duty to pay her maintenance of *rada'a* (duration of feeding period) and hadana (the duration of custody of children). The silence of the Act on these possible obligations of the husband is unjustified.

Section 3(1) (c) of the Act makes payable to the divorced woman 'an amount equal to the sum of *mahr* or dower agreed to be paid'. This confusing expression leads to awkward situations :

i) Is an amount equal to the agreed mahr payable on divorce even if the whole amount of agreed mahr (*mahr musamma*) has already been paid before the divorce (a strict interpretation of the statutory provision would seem to warrant it)?

ii) Where the agreed mahr has been partly paid (being 'prompt') should this payment be ignored and the full amount of agreed mahr paid again (a strict interpretation would again allow this) ?

iii) Where no mahr was ever agreed upon between the parties (in which case proper dower, *mahr al-mithl*, is payable under the shari'a) what is the entitlement of the wife under the statutory provision ?

iv) Where no mahr was ever agreed upon between the parties, but as per rules of Islamic law, the husband has already paid during the subsistence of marriage, the whole or part of 'proper dower', how will the relevant statutory provision be enforced?

Furthermore, in certain situations of divorce, according to Islamic law either no mahr is payable or only a specified portion of it is to be paid. Section 3(1)(c)of the Act fails to accommodate any such situation, and because of its unqualified language apparently makes mahr payable in every case of divorce. This is legally incorrect. The fact is that the provisions of the Act relating to mahr are poorly drafted and do not represent the correct principles of Islamic law.

Section 3(1)(d) of the Act relates to what is known in common parlance as *jahez*. The scope of this statutory provision is quite wide. Jahez here would include properties given to the woman before, at the time of, or after, marriage by :

a) her parents, other relatives or friends;
b) her husband;
c) her husband's parents, relatives or friends.

This means that section 3(1)(d) of the Act will cover :

i) The items of jewellery, clothes, furniture and gadgets, etc., given to the woman by her own parents and guardians (and this is what, strictly speaking, the Urdu word jahez means),

ii) All items of '*bari*' (i.e. jewellery and clothes, etc., given to the bride before or at the time of marriage by the groom or his parents),

iii) Marriage gifts given to her either by her own relatives and friends or by the husband's relatives and friends.

The restoration of all such properties to the divorced woman would be one of her 'entitlements' specified by section 3. This is clearly a pro-women provision and if properly enforced will be extremely beneficial to divorced wives.

A single provision in section 3 provides the procedure for the judicial enforcement of all the statutory entitlements of a divorced woman. An application is to be made in this regard to the magistrate who is required to dispose of it within one month and is empowered to direct the former husband to enable the wife to have each of these statutory entitlements enforced in full. The period of one month prescribed by section 3 is open to extension by the magistrate if he finds abiding by it 'impracticable'. Very obviously almost every magistrate will find it 'impracticable ' to dispose of an application under section 3 within one month and therefore the fate of this statutory limitation is likely to be the same as the use of a similar provision relating to interim injunctions under the provisions of the Civil Procedure Code.

Most striking is the placement in the jurisdiction of the criminal courts of the power to order and secure payment of mahr and return of jahez, etc., to the divorced wife. Hitherto only a civil court had this power, and there the time and expense required are indeed prohibitive. If the criminal courts now armed with this power do act swiftly, the new statutory provision can provide a true advantage for divorced Muslim women.

After the expiry of ‘idda (which, in fact, should mean when no maintenance - either of ‘idda or of rada‘a or hadana - is payable by the former husband), the liability to maintain a divorced woman who is unable to maintain herself will, according to the Act, fall on the following relatives in the following order:

i) Her children, both male and female, married or unmarried if any,
ii) Her parents,
iii) Other relatives entitled to inherit her property on her death.

Notably, the Bill referred originally only to 'blood relatives' - children and parents were specified (to precede other relatives) on the basis of an amendment which I had strongly suggested.

As regards children's liability, it is laid down in the Act that if there are children of the divorcee who are unable to provide maintenance for her, the liability will pass on to the parents. As regard parents, both the father and the mother have been made liable. Among other relatives, initially the liability will correspond to their nominal shares in the property of the divorcee, but where one of them is unable to discharge his liability, the magistrate may transfer it to another relative. These provisions of the Act conform to various principles of Islamic law - those relasting to the maintenance of women after divorce, maintenance in general and maintenance of dependants. Their enforcement under the Act could, I feel, have been made more practicable by adding to section 4(1) some additional suitable provisions, by-passing wherever necessary the details found in the old books of law.

In my opinion, it would not have been repugnant to the principles of Islamic law to provide that where a divorced woman has no children, no parent and no other close relatives having means to maintain her - whereas, at the same time, her former husband does have sufficient means - he should be directed to pay maintenance to her as long as necessary and to the extent of bare necessities of life. This opinion has never been acceptable to our religious leaders. On their suggestion the Act, therefore, transfers the liability of maintenance of totally destitute divorced women to the waqf boards.

According to the principles of Islamic law a member of the society who is unable to maintain himself or herself is the liability of the State. Where the Muslims are not the rulers and therefore the State cannot be compelled to fulfill this legal obligation, this liability passes on to the Mulim community in general. Drawn from this general provision of Islamic jurisprudence, an innovation requiring the local waqf boards to provide maintenance to a divorced woman who has none else legally bound to maintain her has found a place in the Act under comment.

Emanating from a last-minute amendment made in the Bill in the Lok Sabha a divorced woman and her husband may by mutual consent (which they can express either jointly or separately) opt out of the provisions of the Act and give their choice to be governed by sections 125-128 of the Criminal Procedures Code. This is seemingly meant for the consumption of those Muslim men and women who suppported (or may support) the *Shah Bano* judgment and opposed (or may oppose) the Muslim Womens Bill. Some critics have suggested that this option should have been given to the divorced woman only, and not to her and her former husband jointly. This argument overlooks the following two basic factors :

i) The choice of law to govern a particular marriage during its subsistence or after its dissolution can be made (generally at the time of marriage) only by mutual consent of the parties. In any case once the marriage has come into existence, either party cannot be allowed to make a unilateral option of marriage law other than that opted for at time of marriage.

ii) It is a false notion that opting for the Criminal Procedure Code law will always be to the advantage of women and disadvantage to men. On the contrary, it may be found less stringent for men. An unscrupulous husband who wants to avoid fulfilling his obligations under the shari'a which the Act enforces, may opt for the Criminal Procedure Code law. On the other hand, a divorced Muslim woman who wants to secure payment of her mahr and mata' due under the shari'a, and the restoration of her jahez and marriage gifts, under prompter magisterial order (instead of roaming about in the civil court for many costly long years), might prefer to be governed by the present Act.

From the shari'a viewpoint the option given by section 5 of the Act is not objectionable. Afterall a man who wants to provide maintenance to his divorced wife periodically for the rest of her life is not prevented from so doing by any provision of the shari'a. The shari'a only stops the divorced wife from claiming from him after his liability has ceased as per the shari'a (i.e., when he is unwilling to do so and there are others bound by the shari'a and in fact able to provide maintenance for her). Payment of monthly maintenance to the divorced wife by her former husband is, of course, not forbidden.

The New Law: Challenges and Objections

The Muslim Women Act 1986 has been strongly opposed by a large number of politicians, lawyers and academics on the following grounds:

i) That by subjecting divorced Muslim women to a law different from the maintenance law under the Criminal Procedure Code 1973 (applicable to all other divorced women) the Act has introduced an unconstitutional discrimination in the law;

ii) That the Act does not fully, adequately and correctly codify the correct Islamic legal principles regarding divorced women's rights.

On ground (i) stated above, viz, the alleged unconstitutionality of the Muslim Women Act 1986, a number of writ petitions filed before the Supreme Court of India were based. Though in all these petitions the Union of India is the respondent, the All India Muslim Personal Law Board (which is a co-respondent only in one case) and some Muslim leaders individually, have sought the status of intervener; this was opposed by some petitioners on the ground that the Board, etc. have no locus standi. To date all these petitions are awaiting their disposal by the Supreme Court. Since these were filed there has been a change in the constitution of the court (including the chief justiceship). Little progress has, however, so far been made in respect of these petitions.[11] The court had at the very beginning refused to stay the operation of the Muslim Women Act sought by some of the petitioners. The Act, therefore, came in force and remains fully in force until today.

On ground (ii) stated above, viz, defects of the Muslim Women Act 1986 from the Islamic judicial viewpoint, some Islamic lawyers, including myself, have been pointing out the inherent flaws of many of its provisions. In my opinion the following provisions of the section 3 of the Act of 1986 mainly require reconsideration and amendment:

i) Section 3(1)(a): This is the clause concerning 'reasonable and fair provision' - which, should be made discretionary for the courts with proper guidelines;

ii) Section 3(1)(b): This is the clause concerning children's maintenance - which is out of place in this Act and should be replaced with the divorced mother's own maintenance by her former husband while she is breast feeding his child or keeping its custody; and

---

[11]The following writ petitions against Muslim Women Act are at present pending before Supreme Court :
i) *Danial Latifi and Sona Khan* v. *the Union of India.*
ii) *Tara Ali Beg and others* (Anupam Mehta, Lotika Sarkar and Upendra Baxi) *v. Union of India.*
iii) *Susheela Gopalan and others* (Rukhsana Begum, Sarvari Khatun, Hasina Begum, Ramlu, Nazeeran, Ayisha Bi, Sugharbi and Aishabi) *v. Union of India.*
iv) *Islamic Sharia Board v. Union of India and All India Muslim Personal Law Board.*
v) *National Federation of India Women v. Union of India.*
vi) *Shahnaz Sheikh and others* (Kamila Tyabji, Anees Sayyad) *v. Union of India.*
vii) *Rashidaben v. Union of India.*

iii) Section 3(1)(c): This is the clause concerning dower - the amount of which should be left to be ascertained in each case according to the principles of the settled law allowing 'stipulated' or 'proper' dower as the case may be.

The All India Muslim Personal Law Board set up some time ago a committee to review the Muslim Women Act 1986 in order to point out its shortcomings from the Islamic angle and to suggest proper remedies. This committee is yet to give its report. Working on it are some eminent lawyers led by the Advocate Yusuf Muchhala of Bombay. They are reportedly reviewing the Act in the light of the decisions so far given by the courts under its provisions and in consultation with experts.

In the meanwhile a well-known member of Parliament has already moved a private member's bill for the amendment of the Muslim Women Act 1986. The bill seeks extensive modification of the Act.[12] Though it may never be passed, it reflects the thinking of a particular section among the Muslims. At least some provisions of the bill go very much against the thinking of some critics of the Muslim Women Act 1986. I feel that the proposed bill would further distort Islamic law.

IV. Judicial Verdicts under the New Act

The Muslim Women Act 1986 has, despite all objections to its validity under the Constitution of India and tenability under the Islamic principles, remained fully in force. During the past three years it has come up for enforcement and interpretation before various courts - both lower and higher. In the process we have had a number of significant judicial decisions under, or relating to, the Act. I will briefly analyse here some leading judgments.

The first decision under the Muslim Women Act 1986 which attracted attention of the observers and critics across the country was, perhaps, the one given by a lady magistrate of Lucknow, Rekha Dixit. A divorced Muslim woman was in this case awarded a huge sum of money by way of : (i) 'reasonable and fair provision', and (ii) maintenance of ‘idda. In effect the learned magistrate held that these two reliefs were separate from each other, simultaneously available to all divorced women under the Act of 1986. This decision, as reported in the press, threw open the following important questions:

i) Did the Muslim Women Act 1986 in fact entitle divorced women to seek from their divorced husbands a 'reasonable and fair provision' in addition to maintenance for ‘idda ?

ii) Was this 'additional relief' claimable by all divorced women irrespective of the circumstances leading to divorce ? and;

iii) Was this relief the same as is known in the Qur'anic terminology as mata‘ at-talaq ?

---

[12]Bill No. 83 of 1988 moved in the Lok Sabha on 12 August 1988 by Syed Shahabuddin. See text in Appendix II.

These questions were long discussed, and concerned people seemed to be divided in their response. Following the Lucknow decision of Ms. Dixit, huge amounts of money were reportedly granted to divorced women also by some other lower courts in different parts of the country in the name of 'fair and reasonable provision' referred to in the Muslim Women Act 1986.

Next came from Bihar a significant decision relating to the Muslim Women Act 1986 given by Justice A.P. Sinha of the Patna High Court. In *Md. Yunus v. Bibi Phenkani*[13] the court had to decide whether an order of maintenance passed in favour of a divorced Muslim woman under section 125 of the Criminal Procedure Code before the commencement of the Muslim Women Act 1986 lapsed after its commencement, or whether it could still be executed under the said Code. Deciding that such an order could no more be executed, Justice Sinha asserted that being in the nature of a 'non-obstante clause' the substantive provisions of the Act would override the contrary provisions of the Criminal Procedure Code in their application to Muslims. The judgment carefully compared the provisions of the maintenance law under section 125-128 of the Criminal Procedure Code and the Muslim Women Act and concluded that the two could not simultaneously apply to Muslim women to any extent. Surprisingly, in its comparison of the law under the two statutes the judgment made no reference to the 'fair and reasonablc' clause under section 3 of the Muslim Women Act 1986.

A year after the decision of the Patna High Court, Justice Pareed Pillay of the Kerala High Court came out with a ruling which went wholly against the judicial thinking in the former case. In a brief judgment given in *Mohammad Haji v. Rukiya*[14] Justice Pillay ruled that:

i) The provision of section 7 of the Muslim Women Act 1986 would aply only to the maintenance applications under section 125 of the Criminal Procedure Code pending the date of commencement of the Act; and

ii) Section 7 would not apply to the execution procedings initiated under the Criminal Procedure Code (regarding maintenance orders passed before the commencement of the Act of 1986).

In other words, an order of maintenance passed in favour of Muslim women under the Muslim Women Act 1986 was, in the opinion of the Kerala High Court, not nullified by this Act; it could still be executed under section 128 of the Criminal Procedure Code. The judgment was diametrically opposed to the Patna ruling analysed above.

By the end of 1987 these were the only judicial rulings available on the controversial Act of 1986. During 1988-89 different High Courts have decided many other cases concerning the Act. The most striking judgment among them has been that of Justice M.B. Shah of the High Court of Gujarat given in the case of *Arab Ahmad bin Abdulla v. Arab Dail Mahmuna*

---

[13] (1987) Mat LR 214 (Pat) decided on 4-9-1986.

[14](1987) Mar LR 16 (Ker) decided on 3-9-1987 reportedly confirmed later by a division bench of the same court.

Saidadbhai and another.[15] It was a long judgment which sought in effect to change the whole scope of the Muslim Women Act 1986 and its impact on the maintenance law under the Criminal Procedure Code. After a lengthy discussion of the provisions of the Act of 1986 Justice Shah drew the following conclusions:

i) The Act of 1986 did not nullify orders of maintenance in favour of Muslim women passed under the Criminal Procedure Code since none of its provisions took away the vested rights crystallised by court-orders;

ii) The Act of 1986 did not supersede the Supreme Court decision in the *Shah Bano* case since there was nothing in it showing Parliament in fact so intended;

iii) Under the Act of 1986, maintenance payable to a divorced woman by her former husband was not limited to the period of 'idda; and

iv) The maintenance law relating to divorced women under the Criminal Procedure Code did not become inapplicable to the Muslims by reason of the enactment of the Act of 1986.

The reasoning adopted in this judgment went wholly against the verdict of Justice Sinha in the Patna case, while it partly agreed with the decision of Justice Pillay in the Kerala case (regarding the maintainability of execution proceedings under section 128 of the Criminal Procedure Code in respect of maintenance orders passed for Muslim women under the said Code). Expectedly, it received both brickbats and bouquets from different quarters.

The question whether the Muslim Women Act 1986 has a retrospective effect so as to nullify orders already passed under section 125 of the Criminal Procedure Code in favour of Muslim women has also been examined by the Rajasthan High Court. In the case of *Abid Ali v. Raisa Begum,*[16] a division bench of the High Court, after a thorough examination of section 3, 5 and 7 of the Muslim Women Act, concluded that a maintenance order passed in favour of a divorced Muslim woman under the Criminal Procedure Code before the commencement of the Muslim Women Act could no more be executed. The court observed :

> A comparative look at the provisions contained in Chapter IX of the Code of Criminal Procedure and those contained in the Act of 1986 would show that there is no saving clause provided under the Act of 1986 by which any order passed in favour of the divorced Muslim women under section 125 of the Code of Criminal Procedure could be validated or liability created on the husband in this regard could be held valid or enforceable. . . The Act of 1986, as stated earlier, does not contain any saving clause for the right created of orders passed in favour of a divorced Muslim woman. However, the Act has completely obliterated the right of such women to get

[15](1988) 24 Reports (Guj) 288; AIR 1988 Guj 141.

[16](1988) Raj LR 104.

> maintenance. The repeal without saving such right means that such women had never acquired such right and, in this view of the matter, the said right now cannot be enforced under section 125, Criminal Procedure Code. Therefore if a Muslim woman divorced prior to the coming into force of the Act in whose favour an order of maintenance has been passed and has become final or is pending revision or in other court is being challenged by the husband, if such an order is held to be executable then it will be, in our considered view, in complete contravention of the intention of the legislature and will amount to frustrate the very object of the Act of 1986 for which it has been enacted.

Another case having a bearing on the scope of the Muslim Women Act 1986 was decided by a single judge of the High Court of Madhya Pradesh, who took a view contrary to the Patna ruling in Bibi Phenkani's case and the Rajasthan decision in Abid Ali's case. In *Kadar v. Saira,*[17] deciding the applicability of the Act to the case of a Muslim woman who had obtained a maintenance order under section 125 (i) of the Criminal Procedure Code, the judge held that there was no question of the applicability of the Act of 1986. Specifically disagreeing with the Patna ruling, the court observed that the learned judge in the Patna decision had not taken note of section 6 of the General Clause Act 1987 (relating to the effect of repeal of enactments). Later the High Courts of Allahabad and Kerala came out with their new rulings on the Muslim Women Act 1986. In the Allahabad case of *Ghulam Sbir v. Rayeesa Begum,*[18] it was explained - rightly - that maintenance right of Muslim wives (not divorced) continued to be governed by sections 125-127 of the Criminal Procedure Code, the Act of 1986 being confined in its scope to divorced wives. In *Chelangadan Ali v. Sufaira,*[19] the High Court of Kerala stressed the availability, under the Act of 1986, of the twin reliefs of mata' (reasonable and fair provision) and maintenance - both being simultaneously allowable under the statutory provisions (this confirmed the interpretation of the Act by the magistrate Rekha Dixit).

In another Kerala decision, *Alekutty,*[20] it was decided that a past order of maintenance in favour of a Muslim divorcee was outside the scope of section 7 of the Muslim Women Act 1986. Justice A.C. Sen's decision in the Calcutta case of *S.K. Mohammad Ali,*[21] saying that the Muslim Womens Act 1986 did not bar exection of a maintenance order passed before its commencement in favour of a Muslim divorcee, in effect agreed with the earlier Madhya

---

[17](1988) HLR 365.

[18](1988) All LJ 873.

[19](1988) 24 Reports 448 (Ker).

[20](1988) HLR 108 (Ker).

[21](1988) 24 Reports 486 (Cal).

Pradesh. To the same effect was the 1989 ruling of the Gauhati High Court in *Idris Ali*.[22]

In a very important judgment given in *Haji Farzand Ali*,[23] M.C. Jain, Justice of Rajasthan High Court rightly explained that the Muslim Women Act 1986 had nothing to do with the maintenance of children (including those of divorced couples): its scope was confined to rights of divorced women. This is what I have been pointing out ever since the Act became law in 1986.

Conclusion

Conflicting judgments have been given by diferent High Courts regarding the nature, objectives, scope and impact of the Muslim Women Act 1986 and its relationship with the Criminal Procedure Code 1973. Three different opinions seem to have been expressed so far:

i) The Muslim Womens Act 1986 has repealed the law on the divorced woman's maintenance under the Criminal Procedure Code in its application to Muslims so that the latter are now governed only by the said Act (unless a divorced couple opts out of it as per the statutory procedure);

ii) The Muslim Women Act 1986 and the Criminal Procedure Code (i.e., the provisions on divorced women's maintenance found in section 125-128) simultaneously apply to Muslims and there is no conflict between them;

iii) Cases of Muslim divorced women already under the Criminal Procedure Code will continue to be governed by the executory provisions of the Code, but cases pending at the time of the commencement of the Act of 1986, as well as cases arising in the future, will be governed only by the Act of 1986 (subject to the provisions of section 7 of the Act).

The exact legal position of the statutory rights of divorced Muslim women in India is, thus, in a state of uncertainty and confusion.

On the other hand, critics continue to point out how incompatible the Muslim Women Act 1986 is - or at least some of its provisions are - with the rights and reliefs available to divorced Muslim women under Islamic law; and there still are people who regard the Act as a 'retrograde step' violating the Constitution of India.

The judicial rulings under the Act have not generally changed the thinking of those who have earlier bitterly criticised the Act. Until now all the writ petitions pending before the Supreme Court remain intact; none of these has been withdrawn.

In these circumstances the long-awaited decision of the Supeme Court in the writ petitions against the Act becomes extremely important. In the interest of all concerned and with a view to effecting uniformity and certainty in the law, the court must pronounce its descision before too long. In the fitness of rulings, if the Supreme Court upholds the constitutional validity of the Muslim Women Act 1986, its ruling should be quickly obtained also on the important

---

[22] AIR 1989 Gau 24.

[23] 1988 Cri LJ 1421 (Raj)

question as to which of the various conflicting judgments of the High Courts regarding the scope of the Act is jurisprudentially tenable. Till this is done the crisis will remain unresolved.

Finally, Islamic law on post-divorce reliefs (which the Act of 1986 purports to codify) should be applied only in the cases where divorce itself has been properly given or obtained in strict conformity with the correct provisions of the shari‘a; and for this purpose I recommend a proper codification of the Islamic divorce law as early as possible.

APPENDIX I

THE MUSLIM WOMEN (PROTECTION OF RIGHTS ON DIVORCE) ACT, 1986

[Act 10-C of 1986]*

An Act to protect the rights of Muslim women who have been divorced by, or have obtained divorce from, their husbands and to provide for matters connected therewith or incidental thereto.

Be it enacted by Parliament in the thirty-seventh year of the Republic of India as follows:-

1. Short title and extent

(1) This Act may be called the Muslim Women (Protection of Rights on Divorce) Act, 1986.

(2) It extends to the whole of India except the State of Jammu and Kashmir.

2. Definitions

In this Act, unless the context otherwise requires,-

a) 'divorced woman' means a Muslim woman who was married according to Muslim law, and has been divorced by, or has obtained divorce from, her husband in accordance with Muslim law;

b) "iddat period' means, in the case of a divorced woman,-

i) three menstrual courses after the date of the divorce, if she is subject to menstruation;

ii) three lunar months after her divorce, if she is not subject to menstruation; and

* Passed by the Lok Sabha on 6 May, 1986 and by the Rajya Sabha three days later; assented to by the President on 19 May, 1986.

iii) if she is enceinte at the time of divorce, the period between the divorce and the delivery of her child or the termination of her pregnancy, whichever is earlier;

c) 'Magistrate' means a Magistrate of the first class exercising jurisdiction under the Code of Criminal Procedure, 1973 in the area where the divorced woman resides;

d) 'prescribed' means prescribed by rules made under this Act.

3. Mahr or other properties of Muslim woman to be given to her at the time of her divorce.-

1) Notwithstanding anything contained in any other law for the time being in force, a divorced woman shall be entitled to -

a) a reasonable and fair provision and maintenance to be made and paid to her within the 'iddat period by her former husband;

b) where she herself maintains the children born to her before or after the divorce, a reasonable and fair provision and maintenance to be made and paid by her former husband for a period of two years from the respective dates of birth of such children;

c) an amount equal to the sum of mahr or dower agreed to be paid to her at the time of her marriage or at any time thereafter according to Muslim law; and

d) all the properties given to her before or at at the time of her marriage or after her marriage by her relatives or friends or the husband or any relatives of the husband or his friends.

2) Where a reasonable and fair provision and maintenance or the amount of mahr or dower due has not been made or paid or the properties referred to in clause (d) of sub-section (1) have not been delivered to a divorced woman on her divorce, she or anyone duly authorised by her may, on her behalf, make an application to a Magistrate for an order for the payment of such provisions and maintenance, mahr or dower or the delivery of properties, as the case may be.

3) Where an application has been made under sub-section (2) by a divorced woman, the Magistrate may, if he is satisfied that-

a) her husband having sufficient means, has failed or neglected to make or pay her within the 'iddat period a reasonable and fair provision and maintenance for her and the children; or

b) the amount equal to the sum of mahr or dower has not been paid or that the properties referred to in clause (d) of sub-section (1) have not been delivered to her,

make an order, within one month of the date of the filing of the application, directing her former husband to pay such reasonable and fair provision and maintenance to the divorced woman as he may determine as fit and proper having regard to the needs of the divorced woman, the standard of life enjoyed by her during her marriage and the means of her former husband or, as the case may be, for the payment of such mahr or dower or the delivery of such properties referred to in clause (d) of sub-section (1) to the divorced woman:

Provided that if the Magistraste finds it impracticable to dispose of the application within the said period, he may, for reasons to be recorded by him, dispose of the application after the said period.

4) If any person against whom an order has been made under sub-section (3) fails without sufficient cause to comply with the order, the Magistrate may issue a warrant for levying the amount of the maintenance or mahr or dower due in the manner provided for levying fines under the Code of Criminal Procedure, 1973, and may sentence such person, for the whole or part of any amount remaining unpaid after the execution of the warrant, to imprisonment for a term which may extend to one year or until payment if sooner made, subject to such person being heard in defence and the said sentence being imposed according to the provisions of the said Code.

4. Order for payment of maintenance-

1) Notwithstanding anything contained in the foregoing provisions of the Act or in any other law for the time being in force, where a Magistrate is satisfied that a divorced woman has not remarried and is not able to maintain herself after the 'iddat period, he may make an order directing such of her relatives as would be entitled to inherit her property on her death according to Muslim law to pay such reasonable and fair maintenance to her as he may determine fit and proper, having regard to the needs of the divorced woman, the standard of life enjoyed by her during her marriage and the means of such relatives and such maintenance shall be payable by such relatives in the proportions in which they would inherit her property and at such periods as he may specify in his order:

Provided that where such divorced woman has children, the Magistrate shall order only such children to pay her maintenance to her, and in the event of any such children being unable to pay such maintenance, the Magistrate shall order the parents of such divorced woman to pay maintenance to her:

Provided further that if any of the parents is unable to pay his or her share of the maintenance ordered by the Magistrate on the ground of his or her not having the means to pay the same, the Magistrate may, on proof of such inability being furnished to him, order that the share of such relatives in the maintenance ordered by him be paid by such of the other relatives as may appear to the Magistrate to have the means of paying the same in such proportions as the Magistrate may think fit to order.

2) Where a divorced woman is unable to maintain herself and she has no relatives as mentioned in sub-section (1) or such relatives or any one of them have not enough means to pay the maintenance ordered by the Magistrate or the other relatives have not the means to pay the shares of those relatives whose shares have been ordered by the Magistrate to be paid by such other relatives under the proviso to sub-section (1), the Magistrate may, by order, direct the State Wakf Board established under section 9 of the Wakf Act, 1954, or under any other law for the time being in force in the State, functioning in the area in which the woman resides, to pay such maintenance as determined under sub-section (1) or, as the case may be, to pay the shares of such of the relatives who are unable to pay, at such periods as he may specify in his order.

5. Option to be governed by the provisions of section 125 and 128 of Act 2 of 1974.-

If, on the date of the first hearing of the application under sub-section (2) of section 3, a divorced woman and her former husband declare, by affidavit or any other declaration in writing in such form as may be prescribed, either jointly or separatley, that they would prefer to be governed by the provisions of section 125 to 128 of the Code of Criminal Procedure, 1973, and file such affidavit or declaration in the court hearing the application, the Magistrate shall dispose of such application accordingly.

Explanation.- For the purpose of this section, 'date of the first hearing of the application' means the date fixed in the summons for the attendance of the respondent to the application.

6. Power to make rules. -

1) The Central Government may, by notification in the Official Gazette, make rules for carrying out the purposes of this Act.

2) In particular and without prejudice to the foregoing power, such rules may provide for-

a) the form of the affidavit or other declaration in writing to be filed under section 5;

b) the procedure to be followed by the Magistrate in disposing of applications under this Act, including the serving of notices to the parties to such applications, dates of hearing of such applications and other matters;

c) any other matter which is required to be or may be prescribed.

3) Every rule made under this Act shall be laid, as soon as may be after it is made, before each House of Parliament, while it is in session, for a total period of thirty days which may be comprised in one session or in two or more successive sessions, and if, before the expiry of the session immediately following the session or the successive sessions aforesaid, both Houses agree in making any modification in the rule or both Houses agree that the rule should not be made, the rule shall thereafter have effect only in such modified form or be of no effect, as the case may be; so, however, that any such modification or annulment shall be without predjudice to the validity of anything previously done under that rule.

7. Transitional provisions.-

Every application by a divorced woman under section 125 or under section 127 of the Code of Criminal Procedure, 1973 pending before a Magistrate on the commencement of this Act, shall, notwithstanding anything contained in that Code and subject to the provisions of section 5 of this Act, be disposed of by such Magistrate in accordance with the provisions of this Act.

APPENDIX II

MUSLIM WOMEN (PROTECTION OF RIGHTS ON DIVORCE) AMENDMENT BILL 1988

Bill No. 83 of 1988

A bill to amend the Muslim Women (Protection of Rights on Divorce) Act, 1986.

Be it enacted in Parliament in the thirty-ninth year of the Republic of India as follows :-

1. Short title and commencement

1) This Act may be called the Muslim Women (Protection of Rights on Divorce) Amendment Act, 1988.

2) It shall come into force at once.

2. Substitution of a new long title for the existing long title

In the Muslim Women (Protection of Rights on Divorce) Act, 1986 (hereinafter referred to as the principal Act), for the long title, the following long title shall be substituted, namely :-

'An Act to codify and enforce the right of divorced Muslim women under the Shari'at and to provide for matters connected therewith or incidental thereto'.

3. Amendment of section 2

In section 2 of the principal Act, for clause (b), the following clause shall be substituted, namely :-

'(b)'iddat period' means, then period for which the divorced woman is prohibited from re-marriage under the Shari'at;'.

4. Amendment of section 3

In section 3 of the principal act, -

(i) for sub-section (1), the following sub-section shall be substituted, namely :-

'(1) Notwithstanding anything contained in the Code of Criminal Procedure, 1973, a divorced woman shall be entitled to -

a) a reasonable and fair maintenance for the 'iddat period to be paid to her within the 'iddat period by her former husband;

b) a reasonable and fair provision to be made by her former husband to her for education and upbringing of their children for a period of two years from the respective dates of birth of such children, provided she exercises her option of custody:

Provided that nothing in this clause shall affect the entitlement of any minor child in the custody of the mother to receive a reasonable and fair maintenance from his/her father in accordance with the Shari'at ;

c) an amount equal to the sum of mahr or part thereof which remains unpaid on the date of the divorce; and

d) all her properties including gifts made to her before or at the time of marriage by her relatives or friends or the husband or any relatives of the husband or his friends';

(ii) after sub-section (1), the following sub-sections shall be inserted, namely :-

'(1A) Where the marriage has not been consummated, a divorced woman shall be entitled only to a reasonable gift as determined by a Magistrate, if no mahr had been agreed upon, or if agreed, remained unpaid at the time of divorce.

(1B) Where the divorce had been given at the instance of the wife, terms agreed to at the time of divorce shall prevail.';

(iii) for sub-section (2), the following sub-section shall be substituted, namely :-

'(2) Where a reasonable and fair maintenance or mahr as due has not been paid or a reasonable and fair provision has not been made for the maintenance of the children, or her properties, referred to in clause (d) of sub-section (1), have not been delivered to a divorced woman on her divorce, she or anyone duly authorised by her, on her behalf, may make an application to a Magistrate for an order for payment of such maintenance, mahr or provision or the delivery of such properties, as the case may be.'; and

(iv) in sub-section (3), for the words 'Where an application has been made under sub-section (2) by a divorced woman, the magistrate may, if he is satisfied that... have not been delivered to her' the words 'Where an application has been made under sub-section (2) by a divorced woman, the magistrate may, if he is satisfied that the former husband has failed to pay mahr or any part thereof or a reasonable and fair maintenance for the ‘iddat period or has failed to make a fair and reasonable provision for the maintenance of children or to deliver the properties' shall be substituted.

5. Amendment of section 4

In section 4 of the principal Act,

(i) for sub-section (1), the following sub-section shall be substituted, namely :-

'(1) Notwithstanding anything contained in the Code of Criminal Procedure, 1973 or in any other law for the time being in force, where a Magistrate is satisfied that a divorced woman has not remarried and is not able to maintain herself after the ‘iddat period, he shall make an order directing her blood relatives, in the following order, to pay for her maintenance in the proportion in which they would inherit her property on her death:-

i) her children, if any;

ii) in case there are no children or the children have not attained majority or having attained majority do not have the means to maintain her, her parents;

iii) in case the parents are not living or do not have the means to maintain her, her brothers and sisters; and

iv) if none of the above are able to maintain her, her nearest living blood reative who, in the opinion of the magistate, has the means to maintain her.'; and

(ii) In sub-section (2), :-

a) for the words 'under the second proviso to sub-section (1)', the words 'under sub-section (1)' shall be substituted;

b) the words, 'out of its own funds earmarked for general charitable purposes or a special fund consisting of donations, if any, received for the purpose.' shall be added at the end.

6. Substitution of new section 5

For section 5 of the principal Act, the following section shall be substituted, namely :-

'5. *Option to remain out of the purview of the Act*

At the first hearing of the application under sub-section (2) of section 3, a divorced woman and her former husband by a joint affidavit may opt out of the application of this Act.'.

7. Substitution of the new section for section 7

For section 7 of the principal Act, the following section shall be substituted, namely:-

'7. *Transitional provisions*

(1) Any application, appeal or proceeding in the question of maintenance of a divorced woman under the provisions of the Code of Criminal Procedure, 1973 pending immediately before the commencement of this Act, shall be disposed of and decided in accordance with the provisions of this Act.

(2) All orders, decisions, decrees made prior to the commencement of this Act for payment of maintenance by the former husband to the divorced woman under the provisions of the Code of Criminal Procedure 1973, shall cease to operate from the date of the commencement of this Act.

(3) It shall be open to the divorced woman to make a fresh application for maintenance under the provisions of this Act.

(4) It shall not be open to the former husband to claim refund of the amount already paid.'

15. THREE DECADES OF EXECUTIVE, LEGISLATIVE AND JUDICIAL AMENDMENTS TO ISLAMIC FAMILY LAW IN PAKISTAN*

David Pearl

Introduction

It is now more than 28 years ago since Ayub Khan, then President of Pakistan, introduced into Pakistan law the Muslim Family Laws Ordinance 1961. This Ordinance has played a very significant role in the domestic and political life of that country and, indirectly, in the political battles which have accompanied legislative and judicial pronouncements on Muslim family law in neighbouring India. The purpose of this paper is to review the impact of this Ordinance on the family laws of the Muslim community in Pakistan, by placing the Ordinance into the framework of the ideological commitment to an Islamic state. This commitment is apparent to a degree in Pakistan from the beginning of its independence, although its manifestation became more central on the accession to power of President Zia in 1977. As we shall see, the Enforcement of the Shari'ah Ordinance 1988 (Revised: Ordinance XXI of 1988) has brought the whole edifice of the Muslim Family Laws Ordinance crumbling down. It is clear that any changes which Prime Minister Benazir Bhutto will introduce to reverse the trend of Zia's ideology will be slow and moderated.

It is necessary at the outset to describe in brief the main aspects of Hanafi family law as applied in Pakistan, and then to describe the changes introduced by the Muslim Family Laws Ordinance 1961.

I. Hanafi Family Law

The classical Hanafi law as applied on the sub-continent can be outlined in brief as follows.[1] The husband has the right to marry four wives, so long as he feels able to treat them equally. In this regard, equality is traditionally defined in the context of external criteria; namely food, clothing, support etc. The husband has the capability of divorcing his wives unilaterally and extra-judicially (*talaq*). There are different forms or modes of talaq, but historically the most often used in Pakistan amongst the Hanafi is the three-fold pronouncement which, first, renders the divorce irrevocable from the moment of the pronouncement; second, the parties become incapable of remarrying

---

* An earlier version of this paper was delivered at the University of Washington, Seattle, USA in 1987.

[1] See generally D. Pearl, *A Textbook on Muslim Personal Law*, London, 2nd ed. 1987.

each other unless and until the wife has been married to another man and this marriage has been consummated and she is divorced from him. The wife has no corresponding right although she can initiate a separation process from her husband known as the *khul'*. However, the husband must give his consent, and, in addition, the wife usually provides compensation. Since 1939, the wife can obtain a divorce from a court on grounds based to a large part on the culpability of the husband. In Hanafi law, the marriage is a contract effected by an offer by one side followed by an acceptance on the other side. There must be witnesses: two male Muslim witnesses or one male and two females. No other formalities are technically necessary. Once a girl attains the age of puberty, she has the capacity to contract herself in marriage. Before puberty, her guardian (usually the father or the paternal grandfather) has the right to contract the marriage for her on her behalf. A girl married in such circumstances can terminate the marriage as soon as she obtains the age of puberty. This right is now regulated, to an extent, by the Dissolution of Muslim Marriages Act 1939. Consummation with her consent will terminate her right to exercise the option of puberty and avoid the marriage.

Inheritance is of course a major area in its own right. Suffice it to say that the Hanafi law provides little in the way of support for the orphaned grandchild out of the estate of his grandfather if he is in competition with a closer survivor, for instance a brother or a son of the deceased.

II. The 1961 Muslim Family Laws Ordinance

In common with many other Muslim countries, Pakistan in the 1960s experienced a wave of governmental intervention in family law. Earlier, in the 1950s, a Commission had been appointed to consider reform in this area. The Commission had recommended far-reaching reforms based to a very large extent on social need. But it was not until Ayub Khan assumed power that many of these recommendations were introduced into law by the Muslim Family Laws Ordinance 1961. This Ordinance rests on two political concepts; first, local responsibility; and second, the principle of arbitration. Local officials are given a major role in adjudicating domestic disputes in their neighbourhood within the spirit in effect of the preservation of the peace in that district.

By section 5(1) of the Ordinance, marriages solemnized under Muslim law are to be registered in accordance with certain procedures laid down by the Ordinance. Lack of registration does not render the marriage void, although in certain circumstances it may well be difficult to prove its existence. By section 6, a married man is permitted to marry a second wife only when the approval has been given to him by an Arbitration Council comprising a representative of his first wife and his own representative together with a neutral Chairman, who is the Chairman of the local administrative unit known as the Union Council. If the Arbitration Council is satisfied that the proposed second marriage is necessary and just in accordance with the Rules laid down, then a second marriage is permitted. Otherwise, it will be refused. Rule 14 states that in making a judgement on what is 'just and necessary' and without prejudice to its general powers, the Arbitration Council should have regard to the following circumstances: sterility, physical infirmity, physical unfitness for the conjugal relationship, wilful avoidance of a decree for the restitution of conjugal rights, and insanity on the part of the existing wife. Although a second marriage solemnized without approval remains a valid marriage, the husband is liable to criminal penalties and the first wife has the *locus standi*, if she so wishes, to petition the court for a divorce under an amendment to the Dissolution of Muslim Marriages Act 1939. The second marriage however cannot be registered, and the lack of registration may make it difficult to prove the existence of a valid marriage.

Arguably by far the most contentious provision is that dealing with the right of talaq. The Ordinance by section 7 establishes the position that a talaq can always be revoked regardless of its mode of pronouncement. Subsequent to the pronouncement, the husband must inform the Chairman of the appropriate Union Council.[2] The purpose of the notification is to 'freeze' the effect of the talaq for a period of 90 days. During this time the Chairman of the Union Council summons an Arbitration Council made up of himself and two representatives, one from either side, to attempt a reconciliation. After the expiry of the 90 day period, the talaq becomes operative unless a reconciliation has been successful or the husband has in any event revoked the talaq. No further procedure is required and no order from a court or the Arbitration Council is necessary. One of the interesting aspects of these provisions concerns the marital status of the parties when the husband does not inform the appropriate Chairman that he has pronounced the talaq. It has been argued by some that the introduction of notice is contrary to the Qur'an and the sunna. The Pakistan Courts have consistently taken a different view, and the position is established that notification to the Chairman is mandatory.[3]

III. The Ordinance in Practice

Divorce

Pakistan courts have considered the implications of the divorce provisions of the Ordinance on many occasions.[4] One of the first cases was the Supreme Court decision in *Syed Ali Nawaz Gardezi v. Lt. Col. Muhammad Yusuf.*[5] The Ordinance was reviewed in the context of a matrimonial dispute which resulted in a husband suing in a civil action another man accused of enticing

---

[2]Section 7(1) MFLO 1961. The appropriate Chairman is laid down by the West Pakistan Rules, Rule 3.

[3]*Syed Ali Nawaz Gardezi v. Lt. Col. Muhammad Yusuf,* 1963 PLD SC51; *The State v. Tauqir Fatima,* 1964 PLD (WP) Kar 306; *Fahmida Bibi v. Mukhtar Ahmad,* 1972 PLD Lah 694; *Abdul Mannan v. Sufaran Nessa,* 1970 SCMR 845; *Ghulam Fatima v. Abdul Quyyum,* 1981 PLD SC 460. See however *Chuhar v. Ghulam Fatima,* 1984 PLD Lah 235.

[4]For further discussion see Pearl, *A Textbook.*

[5]See footnote 3.

his wife away. The alleged enticer defended the action by suggesting that the husband had in fact divorced his wife. The court was obliged to consider the purpose of the 1961 Ordinance. The Supreme Court stated:

> The object of section 7 is to prevent hasty dissolution of marriages by talaq, pronounced by the husband unilaterally, without an attempt being made to prevent disruption of the matrimonial status. If the husband himself thinks better of the pronouncement of talaq and abstains from giving a notice to the chairman, he should perhaps be deemed, in view of section 7, to have revoked the pronouncement and that would be to the advantage of the wife.

The Supreme Court is insistent in this case that notice delivered to the Chairman is mandatory. If the husband abstains from giving notice, then the court takes the view that the husband must be presumed to have revoked the talaq. This opinion has been followed on many occasions in the Pakistan courts. For example, in *The State v. Tauqir Fatima*,[6] the court said: 'As no notice had been given (to the chairman) the talaq could not have become effective'.

There have been two recent authorities which have adopted a different position. The first case which requires some discussion is *Chuhar v. Ghulam Fatima*.[7] This case concerned the question of legitimacy of a child. A previous pronouncement of divorce bringing to an end the mother's first marriage was clearly of relevance but only as a preliminary point. The court said that 'as the main object of section 7... is to prevent hasty dissolution of marriage by talaq', the object would not be defeated in this case by the clear evidence that no notice had been given. The case is certainly understandable on its own facts, for the talaq had been pronounced some 15 to 18 years earlier. The law leans in favour of legitimacy, and an over-reliance on the technicality of section 7 would have had an adverse effect. Nonetheless, the case certainly runs counter to the earlier authority.

The second case which adopts a similar approach is the criminal case *Noor Khan v. Haq Nawaz*,[8] which will be discussed in more detail later. The Federal Shariat Court thought that the provisions on notice in the Ordinance are too cumbersome when there is evidence that the wife and the second husband have been living together without challenge for many years. Thus for the purposes of legitimacy and the criminal prosecution of *zina* (illicit sexual relations), undue emphasis on the mandatory obligation to inform the Chairman might produce a harsh result. In these circumstances the court is willing to waive the strict application of the Ordinance. In other cases, however, where the issue is simply the effectiveness of the divorce between

---

[6] See footnote 3.
[7] See footnote 3.
[8] 1982 PLD FSC 265

the two principles, there would seem to be a uniform approach that notification to the Chairman is mandatory. This pragmatic interpretation of the words of the Ordinance fits into the Islamic notions of interpretation, as well as providing a sensible distinction between the effectiveness of a talaq at the time of the pronouncement or shortly thereafter, and the legitimacy of any child born out of a subsequent *nikah* (marriage).

The Ordinance states that the husband shall supply a copy of the notification to the Chairman to the wife. Is this mandatory? In a Lahore case, *Inamal Islam v. Hussain Bano* [9] the court gave mandatory force to the need to inform the wife: 'The supply of a copy of notice to the wife is a necessary part of the requirement of service of notice to the chairman.'

In contrast, a Karachi court, *Parveen Chaudhry v. VIth. Senior Civil Judge,*[10] has expressed itself in a slightly different way:

> The only impediment to immediate effectiveness of the divorce is information to the Chairman and the forming of the Arbitration Council. To such extent it is very clear to us that the mere fact of absence of communication of the divorce before moving the Chairman under subsection (i) of section 7 of the Ordinance does not invalidate the divorce.

Did the court mean that it is not mandatory to inform the wife of the divorce (which is indeed the position in classical law and has not been changed by the Ordinance) or alternatively that it is not mandatory to inform the wife of the notice to the Chairman? It is submitted that the former view is the more appropriate interpretation.

A final matter deals with the formation of the Arbitration Council by the Chairman. The thrust of Pakistan decisions in this area is that the formation of the Arbitration Council is a matter for the Chairman alone. Failure to summon the Council, either because of negligence on the part of the Chairman or for some other reason, does not in any way invalidate the effectiveness of the talaq; that is 90 days after notification being delivered to the Chairman.[11]

Judicial and legislative developments have also produced important developments in the law relating to khul‘, traditionally the consensual extrajudicial separation initiated by the wife. Here however it has been the court which has led the way. After some hesitation, the Supreme Court in *Khurshid Bibi v. Muhammad Amin*[12] decided that khul‘ could be effected without the consent of the husband, so long as the wife can show to the satisfaction of the court that married life has in effect irretrievably broken

---

[9] 1976 PLD Lah 1466.

[10] 1976 PLD Kar 416.

[11] *Sobhan v. Ghani,* 1973 *Dacca Law Reports* 227; *Fahmida Bibi v. Mukhtar Ahmad,* 1972 PLD Lah 694; *Maqbool Jan v. Arshad Hassan,* 1975 PLD Lah 147; *Akhtar Hussain v. Collector Lahore,* 1977 PLD Lah 1173; *M. Zikria Khan v. Aftab Ali Khan,* 1985 PLD Lah 319.

[12] 1967 PLD SC 97.

down. The involvement of the arbitral procedures is ensured by section 8 of the Muslim Family Laws Ordinance.[13]

The question of culpability has occupied the Pakistan courts. In *Siddiqui v. Sharfan,*[14] where the wife was wholly to blame for the breakup of the marriage, the court refused to grant the wife a khul' divorce, for to do so was seen to be contrary to the policy of Islam. However, in *Hakim Zadi v. Nawaz Ali,*[15] where admittedly the wife was not at fault, it was stated by the court that it would not be necessary to prove that each and every allegation was in fact true. More recently, in *Rashidan Bibi v. Bashir Ahmad,*[16] the judge stated:

> The principle of khul' is based on the fact that if a woman has decided not to live with her husband for any reason and this decision is firm, then the court, after satisfying its conscience that not to dissolve the marriage would mean forcing the woman to a hateful union with the man, it is not necessary on the part of the woman to produce evidence of facts and circumstances to show the extent of hatred to satisfy the conscience of the Judge, Family Court or the Appellate Court.

The legal decisions relating to divorce provide a valuable case study of how the courts, using as their text the reformist provisions of the 1961 Ordinance, have gradually introduced a law of divorce which to an extent is more 'even handed' than the traditional Hanafi law. Arbitration, which plays such a significant role in Islamic law, is introduced into the Hanafi law; the disapproved forms of talaq are rendered ineffective in any event; nonetheless a man is not prohibited from divorcing his wife unilaterally and extrajudicially. Although such movements in the law can be criticized for being contrary to the strict interpretation of Hanafi jurisprudence, the thrust of the case law is broadly welcomed by many sections of Pakistan society.

Polygamy

Section 6(1) of the 1961 Ordinance states:

> No man, during the subsistence of an existing marriage, shall, except with the previous permission in writing of the Arbitration Council, contract another marriage, nor shall any such marriage contracted without such permission be registered under this Ordinance.

The section on polygamy illustrates how the Ordinance has steered a path

[13]*Princess Aiyesha Yasmien Abbasi v. Maqbool Hussian Qureshi,* 1979 PLD Lah 241.
[14]1968 PLD Lah 411.
[15]1972 PLD Kar 540.
[16]1983 PLD Lah 549.

midway through the outright abolition of polygamy, even when based on interpretations of Qur'anic verses,[17] and simply leaving matters as they were and relying on the combined effect of education and the economic realities to reduce the impact of polygamy. The Ordinance is in effect a guideline provision: polygamy is discouraged, Islamic arbitral techniques are introduced, evidential difficulties and criminal sanctions act as a deterrent, but at the end of the day the possibility of polygamy still exists. The criminal sanction may not deter many but it has been used even when the first marriage was solemnized in civil form in the United Kingdom.[18]

Succession

The final example concerns the approach taken in relation to section 4, the section on inheritance. It is indeed in this area that most of the criticism towards the Ordinance has been directed, not only because the provision interferes with the Hanafi law of succession in a clear disregard of Hanafi jurisprudence, but also because it does not in any event solve the alleged social problems it was designed to alleviate. This provision states:

> In the event of the death of any son or daughter of the propositus before the opening of succession, the children of such son or daughter, if any, living at the time the succession opens, shall *per stirpes* receive a share equivalent to the share which such son or daughter, as the case may be, would have received if alive.

A recent case is *Kamal Khan v. Zainab.*[19] The case involved the distribution of the estate of Sufaid Khan (P) who died in 1972. Subsequently, in 1977, the entire estate was transferred to the surviving granddaughter (Z) of a predeceased son (R). The action challenging this distribution was brought by a nephew (K). K was the son of P's brother. The court held that Z could not receive more than half of the estate of her father, and the remaining half must revert to K. The Judge said:

> The legislature never intended to give greater benefit to the grandchildren of a predeceased parent than would have been his (sic) due, if the grandparent was alive.

He distributed the estate in the following manner:

> The starting point is that notionally the off-spring of the propositus is deemed to be alive for the purpose of succession

[17]As in Tunisia in 1956.
[18]*Fauzia Hussain v. Khadim Hussain*, 1985 PLD Lah 166.
[19]1983 PLD Lah 546.

> at the time of the death of the propositus, and the succession of the grandchildren is to be calculated again notionally as if the parent of the grandchild died after the death of the original propositus.

Some would say that the decision undermines the whole basis of section 4. However, it is as clear a judicial reflection as one has on how the Ordinance will inevitably be interpreted in such a way as to reflect the fundamentals of Hanafi distribution in cases involving Hanafis. Thus, in *Iqbal Mai v. Falak Sher*,[20] although the Supreme Court refused to consider the issues on the particular facts of that case, the court raised (although it did not answer it) the question whether it was the intention of the lawmaker to provide the opportunity for the orphaned grandchild simply to obtain the 'Islamic share', and not to provide a system of strict representation. Judicial interpretation on Islamic principles would appear to be the way the law will develop in this area. A very similar result was actually reached in *Muhammad Fikree v. Fikree Development Corporation*.[21]

We must now turn our attention to the Constitutional Provisions which have had a profound impact on the administration of family law in Pakistan.

IV. The Constitutional Debate from Partition to 1977

It has been suggested that one reason why Pakistan did not move quickly toward the introduction of Islamic laws was that regional differences and divisions tended to dominate the scene.[22] This was true of Bengal and the same phenomenon, although perhaps to a lesser extent, was apparent also in Baluchistan. The religious groupings themselves were hopelessly divided by sectarian differences. One illustration of the problem is the attempt faced by Pakistan from the start, to define and delimit the borders of Islamic adherence. The issue has appeared in its starkest form in the treatment of the Ahmadi community with its unorthodox interpretation of the doctrine of the 'seal of the prophets'. After disturbances against that community, an Inquiry was constituted to consider the reasons for the disturbances and the implications for the community at large.[23] The members of the Inquiry were unable to draw a satisfactory definition of the term 'Muslim'. Neither did they believe that any two *'ulama* (scholars of the shari'a) would necessarily agree as to the definition of a Muslim. Given such divisiveness, it is little wonder that the early period of Pakistan ignored to a very large extent the implication of the meaning of the peculiar feature of Islam as the legal basis, as opposed to

---

[20] 1986 PLD SC 228. See also *Farid v. Mst. Manzooran* 1990 PLD SC 511

[21] 1988 PLD Kar 446.

[22] See R. Russell, 'Strands of Muslim Identity in South Asia', *South Asia Review*, 6, 1972, p. 21.

[23] The Munir Report. See E. I. J. Rosenthal, *Islam in the Modern National State*, Cambridge, 1965, pp. 23-25. See also C. J. Adams, 'The Ideology of Maulana Maududi' in E. D. Smith ed., *South Asian Politics and Religion*, Princeton, 1966, p. 371.

the political and religious basis, for its existence as a separate entity.

If the ultra religious groups had difficulty at that time in impressing on the body politic of Pakistan the need to introduce a programme of full Islamicisation, it must be stated also that communism had never been a serious contender for political power. Three reasons can be given for this. First, there has always been a spirit of competition amongst the peoples of Northern India, making communism an unlikely flower; secondly, the doctrine of free trade was by now firmly planted; thirdly, Islamic ideology contains much which cannot exist side by side with communism. The disturbances which led to the resignation of Ayub Khan in 1969 were not designed to introduce a communist society; nor did this happen. The hero of the hour of course was Z. A. Bhutto, who had been detained by Ayub Khan under the Defence of Pakistan Rules. Bhutto wrote the following, in an affidavit sworn before the High Court in Lahore on February 5th 1969:

> I want to hold high the banner of the Quaid[24] and Iqbal[25] to show to the world that this Islamic State of 120,000,000 gallant people can rise to the pinnacles of glory and translate into reality the ideal of free and equal men with which Islam lit the torch of civilization...Pakistan is [a] formidable fortress of the millat of Islam, serving oppressed mankind everywhere.

These were not the words of a communist. Iqbal saw the Islamic ideal as a 'spiritual democracy'; dynamic in nature and conscious of social needs. Jinnah's Muslim state was based on the concept of the separate development of the Muslims on the subcontinent; Bhutto's 'Islamic socialism' was no more than a continuation of these traditions.

The creation of Bangladesh strengthened the hand of those who wished Pakistan to go in a direction far beyond Bhutto's vision and create an Islamic State governed by the shari'a. It was accurately stated by one observer that the 'cry of Islam betrayed' is something that no politician in Pakistan can afford to dismiss lightly.[26] It was indeed for reasons such as these that the 1973 Pakistan Constitution prescribed a time-limit of seven years for a Council of Islamic Ideology to submit a report recommending steps to give effect to appropriate injunctions of Islam and for making suggestions to bring all existing laws into conformity with those laws. The Council was given four functions. By Article 230, the Council is empowered to make recommendations to legislative bodies as to the ways and means of enabling and encouraging the Muslims of Pakistan to order their lives in accordance with the principles and concepts of Islam as enunciated in the Qur'an and the sunna. Secondly, the Council advises Government on any question which is referred to it and which bears on whether a proposed law is or is not repugnant to the injunctions of Islam.

[24]Muhammad Ali Jinnah, the first President of Pakistan.

[25]The famous Indian philosopher.

[26]Michael Hornsby writing in the *Times*, 15 July 1973.

Thirdly, it has the duty to make recommendations as to the measures for bringing existing laws into conformity with the injunctions of Islam and the stages by which such measures should be brought into effect. Finally, it is obliged to compile such injunctions as can be given legislative effect. It is in the context of this process of Islamicisation that the family laws of the Muslims must be reviewed.

V. The Constitutional Debate from 1977 to 1989

When Zia came to power in 1977, he moved quickly in the direction of Islamicisation. A federal Shariat Court was created by Article 203(C) of the Constitution. The powers, jurisdiction and functions are set out in Article 203(D):

> (1) The Court may, on the petition of a citizen of Pakistan, of the Federal Government or a Provincial Government, examine and decide the question whether or not any law or provision of law is repugnant to the injunctions of Islam as laid down in the Holy Quran and the Sunna of the Holy Prophet, hereinafter referred to as the Injunctions of Islam.
> (2) If the Court decides that any law or provision of the law is repugnant to the Injunctions of Islam, it shall set out in its decision -
> (i) the reason for its holding that opinion; and
> (ii) The extent to which such a law or provision is so repugnant; and specify the day on which the decision shall take effect.
> (3) If any law or provision of law is held by the Court to be repugnant to the Injunctions of Islam -
> (i) the President in the case of a law with respect to a matter in the Federal Legislative List or the Concurrent Legislative List, or the Governor in the case of a law with respect to a matter not enumerated in either of those Lists, shall take steps to amend the law so as to bring such law or provision into conformity with the Injunctions of Islam; and
> (ii) such law or provision shall, to the extent to which it is held to be repugnant, cease to have effect on the day on which the decision of the Court takes effect.

A very important point to mention about Article 203 (C) is that the word 'law' for the purposes of the Article includes any custom or usage having the force of law, but does *not* include the Constitution itself, Muslim personal law, or any law relating to the procedure of any court or tribunal. This last proviso, however, did not prevent the introduction in 1984 by the Qanun-e-Shahadat Order of the Islamic rules of evidence.

The Constitutional mechanisms mentioned so far, however, are to an extent limited. This can be illustrated by a consideration of *B. Z. Kaikus v. President of Pakistan*.[27] In this case, the Supreme Court had to consider the relationship between the judiciary on the one hand and the executive and the legislature on the other hand in the context of the process of Islamicisation. The petitioner, a retired Judge of the Supreme Court of Pakistan, sought a declaration and an injunction from the Court. He argued as follows:

> [The Muslims of Pakistan] being bound only by the divine law, ie the Shari'a, the Shari'a is the only law in this State, the status of the so-called remaining laws including the Constitution being only that of orders whose validity depends on their acceptance as Allah's will by the judicial ulama or the judiciary, and that any order or so-called law including the Constitution which is in conflict with any part of the Holy Qur'an and Sunnah... including the directions relating to justice and righteousness is null and void.

The Supreme Court refused to grant the relief sought. The Court placed the process of Islamicisation firmly in the hands of Government. In its view no Court had jurisdiction to interfere with that process except to the limited extent laid down by the Constitution itself:

> [T]he point which we want to emphasize is that the job... is of a legislative and political character to be performed by the State by enacting the necessary laws for Islamicisation of the existing laws or even to promulgate new laws on that pattern but within the hemisphere of the Holy Qur'an and Sunnah.

President Zia was not slow to introduce such changes. Four important Ordinances on criminal law were introduced as long ago as 1979; those relating to zina (illicit sexual relations), *qazf* (false allegations of unchastity), drinking and theft. The banking infrastructure has been progressively placed on an interest-free basis for both Pakistan and foreign banks.[28] As we have already stated, Islamic laws of evidence have been introduced.[29]

Perhaps of most significance was the introduction into the Constitution in 1985 of the new Article 2A which places into the Constitution proper as a substantive provision, the Objectives Resolution passed by the Constituent Assembly in March 1949. Article 2A is worth reciting in part. The important provisions state:

> Article 2A. The principles and provisions set out in the

---

[27] 1980 PLD SC 160.

[28] See T. Ingram, 'Islamic Banking: A Foreign Bank's View', in *Islamic Banking and Finance*, London, 1986.

[29] Qanun-e-Shahadat Order (10 of 1984).

> Objectives Resolution reproduced in the Annexure are hereby made substantive part of the Constitution and shall have effect accordingly.
>
> *The Objectives Resolution*
>
> Whereas sovereignty over the entire universe belongs to Allah Almighty alone and the authority which He has delegated to the State of Pakistan, through its people for being exercised within the limits prescribed by him is a sacred trust;
> This Constituent Assembly representing the people of Pakistan resolves to frame a Constitution for the sovereign independent state of Pakistan;...
> Wherein the State shall exercise its powers and authority through the chosen representatives of the people;
> Wherein the Muslims shall be enabled to order their lives in the individual and collective spheres in accordance with the teachings and requirements of Islam as set out in the Holy Qur'an and the Sunnah;
> Wherein adequate provision shall be made for the minorities to profess and practise their religions and develop their cultures;...

Another critical change introduced by Zia was Ordinance XX of 1984. This is referred to as the Anti-Islamic Activities of Qadiani Group, Lahori Group and Ahmadis (Prohibition and Punishment) Ordinance 1984. In effect, it amends the Pakistan Penal Code of 1860. A new section, namely 298C, makes it a criminal offence for any Ahmadi to directly or indirectly pose himself as a Muslim, to call or refer to his faith as Islam, preach or propagate his faith, or outrage the religious feelings of Muslims. Although this Ordinance can be seen as a political response to anti-Ahmadi feeling, the tone is draconian and is a rather unhappy example of the policies of President Zia. At the time of writing none of the legislative innovations of Zia which have been discussed so far have been changed by the new regime.

The most important provision from the Zia era, however, is the Enforcement of Shari'ah Ordinance 1988.[30] Section 3 of the Ordinance states:

> Shari'ah shall be the supreme source of law in Pakistan and Grundnorm for guidance for policy and law-making by the State and shall be enforced in the manner and as envisaged hereunder.

So far as Muslim personal law is concerned, the High Court is

---

[30] The Enforcement of Shari'ah (Revised) Ordinance was actually published on 15th October 1988 and is reproduced in 1989 PLD Central Statutes 18.

empowered with the jurisdiction to consider whether a law is repugnant to the shari'a. Further, if the High Court decides that any such law is repugnant to the shari'a, it shall set out in its decision (a) the reasons for its holding that opinion; and (b) the extent to which the law is so repugnant. The High Court is likely to be aided in this responsibility by the appointment to it of 'ulama (or at least by the appointment of such persons as amicus curiae) and in addition, by the creation of the position of *mufti* to aid the court. Given the views of such persons about the nature of the Family Laws Ordinance 1961, it is hardly surprising that the view in Pakistan at the present time is that the Ordinance cannot survive the Enforcement of Shari'ah (Revised) Ordinance 1988, unless there is further intervention. This is most unlikely at the present time.

VI. The Constitution and the Family Laws Ordinance in the Courts

The constitutionality of section 7 of the Muslim Family Laws Ordinance was considered by the Federal Shariat Court in *Noor Khan v. Haq Nawaz,*[31] a case which we have already mentioned briefly. This was a case brought under the provisions of the Offence of Zina Ordinance 1979. On 18 November 1979, Noor Khan filed a report in a police station alleging that some ten years before that date, the wife of his uncle Fatah Khan had gone on to her fields to cut grass when a certain Haq Nawaz forcibly took her away. It was stated by Noor Khan that the woman, Naziran Bibi, had given birth to three children and that Haq Nawaz was the father. The complainant further stated that Haq Nawaz had not returned the woman to Fatah Khan and that he had continued to commit zina. Fateh Khan himself told the police that he had married Naziran Bibi some thirty years before and that she had borne him children, five of whom were still alive. He stated that he had not divorced Naziran Bibi. The accused was acquitted by the Additional Sessions Judge. This judge formed the view that Fatah Khan had divorced Naziran Bibi. It was clear that notification to the Chairman had not taken place, yet nevertheless the judge held that the provisions of s.7 of the Ordinance were inapplicable as the section was contrary to the injunctions of Islam 'to the extent of giving notice of the talaq to the Chairman by the husband and in respect of the notice becoming effective within ninety days.' The judge relied on Article 227 which obliges the Pakistan law maker to bring all laws into conformity with Islam as laid down by the Qur'an and sunna. In appeal, the Federal Shariat Court rejected this proposition:

> Article 227 of the Constitution is controlled by Article 230 and unless Parliament enacts laws in accordance with the recommendations of the Islamic Council the provisions of Article 227 do not have the effect of rendering existing laws unIslamic automatically... This view that s.7 of the Muslim Family Laws Ordinance is unIslamic is evidently unjustified.

---

[31] 1982 PLD FSC 265.

Unfortunately, this aspect of the judgement is *obiter*. The court decided that none of the parties was aware of the requirements of notice under s.7. The Court stated:

> It would be making a technicality of the provisions of notice under section 7 of the Muslim Family Laws Ordinance too cumbersome on the parties who have been living together as husband and wife without any challenge for 10/12 years.

Another attempt to attack the validity of section 7 on the ground that it is contrary to Qur'an and sunna failed in *Aziz Khan v. Muhammad Zarif.*[32] Aftab Hussain J said:

> ...[I]t is not within our jurisdiction to declare s.7 of the Muslim Family Laws Ordinance as repugnant to the Holy Qur'an in view of the embargo placed on our jurisdiction in this respect by Article 203(B) of the Constitution.

Constitutional objections to the Ordinance finally succeeded before Tanzil-ur-Rehman J in the Karachi High Court in *Qamar Raza v. Tahira Begum.*[33] The new Article 2A was the trump card. Tanzil-ur-Rehman J stated:

> By insertion of Article 2A in the Constitution of Pakistan the Objectives Resolution of 1949 which was initially inserted as preamble to the Constitution of 1973 as also in 1956, 1962 and 1972 Constitution, has been accorded enforcibility... In this scheme and order of things, it becomes evident that all laws prevailing in Pakistan are firstly to conform to the Constitution whereas the Constitution and all such laws are then amenable to be tested on the touchstone of the Qur'an and Sunnah...

The facts before the Judge in this case were a little peculiar. The husband, who was a Shi'i Muslim, was seeking relief by virtue of a Constitutional Petition for a declaration that a talaq pronounced by him and, in compliance with the Ordinance, communicated both to the wife and to the Chairman of the Union Council was valid in law. The Judge decided that no valid divorce had been pronounced by the husband. In a significant judgement spreading over several pages, the Judge concluded that section 7 was contrary to Article 2A. In particular, the requirements to notify a Chairman of the talaq and the suspending of the effect of the talaq for 90 days from the date of receipt of the

---

32 1982 PLD FSC 156.

33 1988 PLD Kar 169. See also *Messrs Bank of Oman Ltd. v. Messrs East Trading Co. Ltd. and others* 1987 PLD Kar 404; and another case of Tanzil-u-Rehman J, *Shaukat Hussain v. Rubina* 1989 PLD Kar 513.

notice are both against the injunctions of the Qur'an and the sunna. The judge concluded:

> I, therefore, refuse to recognize section 7 of the Muslim Family Laws Ordinance to the effect that the receipt of the petitioner's notice of talaq dated 10-2-1982 by the Chairman and the expiry of 90 days from the date thereof has ipso facto made the divorce effective, in derogation of the provisions of the Qur'an and Sunnah relating to talaq.

Interestingly, the Pakistan press responded to this judgement with some dismay. For example, the *Frontier Post* on January 25th 1988 asked rhetorically in an editorial:

> In view of changing circumstances, Islam had made provision for ijma and ijtihad. The Family Laws had been in force for over a quarter of a century, and all the religious scholars and devouts as well as the laity had accepted and practised them without reservation. If that is not ijma, what is?

A rearguard action has been fought by the Lahore Bench in *Kaniz Fatima v. Wali Muhammad*.[34] However, the approach of Tanzil-ur-Rehman J was in effect upheld by the Federal Shariat Court in *Muhammad Sarwar v. The State*[35] where it was stated that the pronouncement of written talaq could not be held invalid for the reason that no notice of it had been served on the Chairman of the Union Council. The conclusion must be therefore that the Ordinance is, at the time of writing, no longer sustainable as the governing law even though it has not been repealed or abrogated by any enactment.

The other provision of the Ordinance which has been discussed in the courts in the context of its constitutionality is section 4. The provision has met considerable criticism in any event. For instance, Noel Coulson argued that although the section was intended to operate within the framework of the traditional law, its effect was actually so far reaching that he wondered whether all its implications were fully appreciated.[36] Likewise Sir Norman Anderson considered that the section made chaos of the Islamic law of succession.[37] For example, if a man were to die leaving an orphaned son's daughter and a full brother, in classical Hanafi law, the son's daughter would inherit one half of the estate and the brother would receive the other one half as the agnatic heir. In Pakistan, however, the son, if alive, would have excluded the brother; thus the son's daughter takes the entire estate to the exclusion of the brother.

---

[34]1989 PLD Lah 990.

[35]1988 PLD FSC 42.

[36]See for example *Succession in the Muslim Family*, Cambridge, 1971, pp.13 ff.

[37]Norman Anderson, *Law Reform in the Muslim World*, London, 1979, p. 155.

The religious elements in Pakistan are equally disturbed by the provision.[38] Their main concern is that children of daughters are introduced into the line of inheritance as primary heirs. Thus distant kindred are converted into sharers in contravention of the principles of Hanafi succession law.[39]

An attempt was made to attack the basis of section 4 as contrary to the principles of Islam as laid down in the Qur'an and sunna. However, this failed; the Supreme Court in *Federation of Pakistan v. Farishta*[40] holding that the Ordinance was a special statutory Ordinance intended to be applied only to Muslim citizens of Pakistan and therefore the Court was without jurisdiction to review its provisions constitutionally. As Keith Hodkinson has said:

> *Farishta* reduces the potential role of the judiciary in Islamicisation by excluding from its scrutiny almost all the controversial legislation in matters of family and succession law.[41]

We have already however seen how the courts have been able to limit the effectiveness of section 4 without any necessity to strike it down as unconstitutional.

Conclusion

The conclusion to the examination of the case law on divorce, polygamy and succession suggests that the courts reflect public opinion in Pakistan to a very great extent. There is little resistance to the provision on polygamy, there was once a consensus that talaq should be controlled and that rights for women should be acknowledged in that area, and the system of representation introduced by section 4 was seen by most observers as a flagrant breach of Islamic mores. The judicial determinations, at least up until 1988, fit neatly into the consensus views. Whether the various enactments of the Zia era will survive is of course a matter of intense speculation both abroad and in Pakistan as well. The generally held view however is that there will be no headlong rush into the repeal of the Enforcement of Shari'ah (Revised) Ordinance 1988, and that the position of Tanzil-ur-Rehman J is likely to be the orthodox view of the fate of the Muslim Family Laws Ordinance 1961 at least for some considerable time to come. [42] In many ways, the focus of the debate

---

[38]See for example A. B. M. Sultanul Alam Choudhury, 'Problems of Representation in the Muslim Law of Inheritance', *Islamic Studies,* 3, 1964, p. 375.

[39]Choudhury states: 'If for the sake of finding a short-cut to these problems, we amend and abrogate the divorce law for our convenience, then the sacrosanctity of and reverence fo the devine law will be gone forever'.

[40]1981 PLD SC 120.

[41]*Cambridge Law Journal,* 40, 1981, p.248.

[42]Guarded support for this view is to be found in the judgment by Wajihuddin Ahmad J in *Aijaz Haroon v. Inam Durrani* 1989 PLD Kar 304.

has once again shifted. Initially, attempts to undermine the Family Laws Ordinance were concentrated in the political arena. It was the failure to move along that road which persuaded certain judges to declare invalid, sections of the Family Laws Ordinance. Those who would wish to reinstate its provisions must look to political initiatives from the present Prime Minister. But one thing is certain. The Family Laws in Pakistan will continue to play a key role on the stage in Pakistan in its search for the appropriate Islamic nature of laws.

16. A NOTE ON ISLAMIC FAMILY LAW AND ISLAMIZATION IN PAKISTAN

Riazul Hasan Gilani

In Pakistan family law has moved, and continues to move, from the Anglo-Muhammadan form towards the Fundamental Islamic form. In this context, the term 'Anglo-Muhammadan' includes judge made law as well as statutory law, when they modify the provisions of Islamic law in the light of the principles of equity, justice and good conscience.

In the Anglo-Muhammadan tradition, a judge or a legislator may by incorporating his own interpretations render the law, as interpreted, binding. This is in contradistinction to Islamic jurisprudence which does not give jurisdiction to judges *(qadis)* or legislators *(ulul-amr)* to introduce radical changes to the injunctions of the Qur'an and the *sunna*. A clear example of the work of judges and legislators in constructing Anglo-Muhammadan law can be seen in the context of inheritance.

Pakistan came into being in 1947. Before that the law of succession and alienation of ancestral immovable property was governed by native custom, which had its origins in Hindu law. According to that custom the right of succession devolved on the male agnate. The power of alienation was restricted to cases of legal necessity and the consent of the male descendants or male collaterals.[1] The Punjab Laws Act was enacted in 1872, section 5 of this enactment providing:

> In questions regarding succession, special property of females, betrothal, marriage, divorce, dower, adoption, guardianship, minority, bastardy, family relations, wills, legacies, gifts, partitions, or any religious usage or institutions, the rule of decision shall be -
>
> a) Any custom applicable to the parties concerned, which is not contrary to justice, equity or good conscience, and has not been by this or any other enactment altered of abolished, and has not been declared to be void by any competent authority;
>
> b) The Muhammadan Law, in cases where the parties are Muhammadans and the Hindu Law, in cases where the parties are Hindus, except in so far as such law has been altered or abolished by legislative enactment, or is opposed to the

[1] Om Prakash Aggarwal, *Customary Law in the Punjab*, Lahore, 1939, pp.15-18, 251-258.

> provisions of this act, or has been modified by any such custom as is above referred to.

Thus Clause (b) indicated that in cases where the parties were Muslims, the decision was governed by Muslim law. However, this was subject to the condition that the law had not been modified by any custom. Under these circumstances, in questions regarding succession, the decision was dictated by customary law. Accordingly, the immovable property left by the ancestors vested in the male agnate following the principle of primogeniture. However, he was not deemed to be the absolute owner of that property: the property was ordinarily inalienable except for legal necessity or with the consent of the male descendants or, in the absence of descendants, with the consent of male collaterals or persons issued from the common ancestor who originally held that land. An alienation effected in violation of this principle was liable to be challenged in a court of law at the instance of any reversionary heir. Any decision of the court in such a case was to ensure that the reversionary heirs could claim possession of the alienated property.

This position was to be replaced by the Islamic law of inheritance. The first and central enactment to achieve this was the Muslim Personal Law Shariat Application Act of 1937, which made Islamic law applicable where the parties were Muslims. This law, however, provided exceptions in the context of succession to agricultural land. Thus Section 2 states:

> Notwithstanding any custom or usage to the contrary in all questions *(save questions relating to agricultural land)* regarding intestate succession, special property of females, including personal property inherited or obtained under contract of gift or any other provision of Personal Law, marriage, dissolution of marriage, including talaq, ila', zihar, li'an, khula' and mubara'at, maintenance, dower, guardianship, gifts, trusts and trust properties and waqfs (other than charities and charitable institutions and charitable and religious endowments) the rule of decision in cases where the parties are Muslims shall be the Muslim Personal Law (Shariat).

The next relevant piece of legislation, the West Punjab Muslim Personal Law Shariat Application Act, which applied the Islamic law of inheritance to all matters, including agricultural land, was enacted after the creation of Pakistan in 1948.

The superior courts of Pakistan, however, held that the Islamic law of inheritance could not be given retrospective effect. Thus where a person had acquired the property before 1948, his rights would be governed by the limitations of customary law. This was made clear in *Muhammad Asghar v. Muhammad Gulsher Khan*:[2]

> It might be added that the Act does not by one stroke of pen, convert owners of property with restricted powers of alienation into full and absolute owners whose powers of alienation were wholly unfettered. The Act nowhere says that all Muslim male owners had by virtue of the Act become absolute owners in the same sense as they would have been if Muhammadan Law had applied and they had succeeded in accordance with Muhammadan Law. The estate of a person who took it under customary law would continue to be subject to the limitations imposed by it till its devolution is made under the Act of 1948 i.e. after the 15th March, 1948.

In 1962, the West Pakistan Muslim Personal Law (Shariat) Application Act which extended the application of the Islamic law of inheritance was enforced. Nevertheless, under Section 2 of this Act, successions occurring before 1948 were subject to the restrictions imposed by customary law:

> 2. *Application of the Muslim Personal Law.*
> Notwithstanding any custom or usage, in all questions regarding succession (whether testate or intestate) special property of females, betrothal, marriage, divorce, dower, adoption, guardianship, minority, legitimacy or bastardy, family relations, wills, legacies, gifts, religious usages or institutions, including waqfs, trusts, and trust properties the rule of decision, subject to the provisions of any enactment for the time being in force, shall be the Muslim Personal Law (Shariat) in cases where the parties are Muslims.
>
> 2-A. *Succession prior to Act-IX of 1948.*
> Notwithstanding anything to the contrary contained in Section 2 or any other law for the time being in force, or any custom or usage or decree, judgement or order of any Court, where before the commencement of the Punjab Muslim Personal Law (Shariat) Application Act, 1948, a male heir had acquired any agricultural land under custom from the person who at the time of such acquisition was a Muslim: -

---

[2]PLD 1949 Lah 116.

> a) he shall be deemed to have become, upon such acquisition, an absolute owner of such land, as if such land had devolved on him under the Muslim Personal Law (Shariat);
>
> b) any decree, judgement or order of any Court affirming the right of any reversioner under custom of usage, to call in question such an alienation of directing delivery of possession of agricultural land on such basis shall be void, inexecutable and of no legal effect to the extent it is contrary to the Muslim Personal Law (Shariat) Act;
>
> c) all suits or other proceedings of such a nature pending in any Court and all execution proceedings seeking possession of land under such decree shall abate forthwith:
>
> Provided that nothing herein contained shall be applicable to transactions past and closed where possession of such land has already been delivered under such decree.

This continued until 1980 when a radical change took place. An amendment was incorporated into the Constitution of the Islamic Republic of Pakistan, and the Federal Shariat Court was established. The Federal Shariat Court was given the juristiction to set aside any law on the ground of repugnancy to the tenets and injunctions of Islam. The relevant parts of the constitutional amendment state:

> 203A. The provisions of this Chapter shall have effect notwithstanding anything contained in the Constitution.
>
> 203C. (1) There shall be constituted for the purposes of this Chapter a court to be called the Federal Shariat Court.
>
> (2) The court shall consist of not more than eight Muslim (Judges), including the (Chief Justice) to be appointed by the President.
>
> (3) The Chief Justice shall be a person who is, of had been or is qualified to be, a Judge of the Supreme Court or who is or has been a permanent Judge of a High Court.
>
> (3A) Of the Judges, not more than four shall be persons each one of whom is, or has been, or is to be, a Judge of a High Court and not more than three shall be Ulema who are well-versed in Islamic Law.
>
> 2203D. (1) The Court may (either of its own motion or) on the petition of a citizen of Pakistan of the Federal Government or a Provincial Government examine and decide the question

whether or not any law or provision of law is repugnant to the Injunctions of Islam, as laid down in the Holy Quran and the Sunnah of the Holy Prophet (s.a.w.s.), hereinafter referred to as the Injunctions of Islam.

(1A) where the court takes up the examination of any law or provision of law under clause (1) and such law or provision of law appears to it to be repugnant to the Injunctions of Islam, the Court shall cause to be given to the Federal Government in the case of law with respect to a matter in the Federal Legislative List, or to the Provincial Government in the case of law with respect to a matter not enumerated in either of those lists, a notice specifying the particular provisions that appear to it to be so repugnant, and afford to such Government adequate opportunity to have its point of view placed before the Court.

(2) If the Court decides that any law or provision of law is repugnant to the Injunctions of Islam, it shall be set out in its decision: -

(a) the reasons for its holding that opinion; and

(b) the extent to which such law or provision is so repugnant; and specify the day on which the decision shall take effect.

(3) If any law or provision of law is held by the Court to be repugnant to the Injunctions of Islam: -

(a) the President in the case of a law with respect to a matter in the Federal Legislative List of the Concurrent Legislative List, or the Governor in the case of a law with respect to a matter not enumerated in either of those Lists, shall take steps to amend the law so as to bring such a law or provision into conformity with the Injuctions of Islam; and

(b) such law or provision shall, to the extent to which it is held to be so repugnant, cease to have effect on the day on which the decision of the Court takes effect.

203F. (1) Any party to any proceedings before the Court under Article 203D aggrieved by the final decision of the Court in such proceedings may, within sixty days of such decision, prefer an appeal to the Supreme Court.

203G. Subject to Article 203D and 203F, any decision of the Court in the exercise of its jurisdiction under this Chapter shall be binding on a High Court and on all courts subordinate to a High Court.

Thus, the court's jurisdiction may be invoked by any citizen, by the federal or a provincial government or it may act on its own motion. Where it decides that any law is repugnant to the injunctions of Islam, it is directed to set out its reasons for holding such opinion, the extent to which it is repugnant and the date on which the decision is to take effect. Following such a decision, the law must be amended so as to bring it into conformity with the injunctions of Islam. Any provision repugnant to such injunctions ceases to have effect to the extent it is repugnant on the day on which the decision of the court takes effect.

The decisions of this court are binding on the High Court and all the subordinate judiciary of the country. Appeal, however, lies from the judgement of the Federal Shariat Court to the Supreme Court of Pakistan.

Pursuant to the new provisions, a petition was filed in the Federal Shariat Court. The petition contended that the customary law in the Punjab according to which the system of agnatic succession was followed, was the rule of law followed amongst Hindus, but was foreign to Islam where the estate of a deceased person devolves on agnates and cognates including widows and distant kindred. Consequently, it was contended that section 5 of the Punjab Laws Act, 1872, which preserved the restraints of the customary law in questions of the alienations of the land inherited before 16-3-1948, was against the Injunctions of the Qur'an and sunna and was thus void.

In its judgement dated 19-5-1981, the Federal Shariat Court upheld this contention, observing that a customary estate differs from an estate under Islam, insofar as Islamic law confers absolute property on the heirs, both male and female, and does not recognise the difference between ancestral or non-ancestral property or between male and female heirs. Each heir receives the portion of his or her inheritance fixed by the shari'a with the absolute right to dispose of it freely.

This decision was appealed against unsuccessfully by the Federal Government, where the Full Bench of the Supreme Court of Pakistan observed:[3]

> Thus we cannot accept the contention of the learned counsel of the appellant, Syed Riazul Hassan Gilani, that restrictions on the right of alienation imposed by Custom of persons inheriting agricultural land before 16-3-1948 can be imposed in Islam because the Hadith cited by him is in a different context and is not attracted here; and that for this reason it is not necessary to go into the other question of tis authenticity or conflict with the Holy Quran in this case.
>
> The result is that there is no force in this appeal which fails and is dismissed hereby.

---

[3]Shariat Appeal no.16 of 1981 *(Federation of Pakistan v. Muhammad Ishaq).*

> We would accordingly, uphold the direction of the Federal Shariat Court that the necessary amendment should be carried out in the West Pakistan Muslim Personal Law (Shariat) Application Act 1962. This was ordered to be done by the 30th of June, 1981. However, this direction was stayed by this court pending the disposal of the appeal. Since the appeal has been dismissed the necessary amendment should now be carried out by the 30th of June, 1983.

Thus, customary law has ceased to have effect in this context which is now governed entirely by Islamic law.

Note should also be taken of Section 4 of the Muslim Family Laws Ordinance (XIII of 1961) which relates to inheritance:

> *4. Succession.* In the event of death of any son or daughter of the propositus *before the opening of succession* the children of such son or daughter, if any, living at the time the succession opens, shall *per stirpes* receive a share equivalent to the share which such son or daughter, as the case may be, would have received if alive.

This provision is generally thought to be contrary to classical Islamic inheritance law, a view put forward by both Norman Anderson[4] and Noel Coulson,[5] and expressed by the Peshawar High Court in the case of *Farishta v. The Federation of Pakistan.*[6]

I am, however, of the view that Section 4 of the Muslim Family Laws Ordinance, 1961 and the classical law of inheritance are not inconsistent, as the orphaned grand children have not been given the status of legal heirs. Here the use of the formulation *per stirpes* is significant. Had the orphaned grand children been made the legal heirs the words *per capita* would have been used. In fact, the section creates a notional charge on the estate of the praepositus of which the orphaned grand children have been made the beneficiaries.

This charge must be satisfied, like loan and will, before the distribution of the estate among the legal heirs. In creating this charge for the benefit of the orphaned children on the estate of the praepositus, the legislature has acted upon Qur'an IV, 8: 'And when kinsfolk and orphans and the needy (who are not heirs) are present at the division (of the heritage) bestow on them therefrom'.

The heirs have been reminded in this verse that the non heir orphan kins should not be ignored when the estate is distributed, and an Islamic state, as in

---

4*Law Reform in the Muslim World*, London, 1976, p. 155.

5*Succession in the Muslim family,* Cambridge, 1971, pp. 143 ff.

6PLD 1980 Pesh 47.

the promulgation by Pakistan of Section 4 or the Muslim Family Laws Ordinance of 1961, can implement such obligation by legislative or executive action.

This view is indirectly supported by a judgement of the Lahore High Court:[7]

> *Per stirpes* referred to in Section 4 is the antitheses of *per capita*. This means a share according to the stock or the root or the family as against *per capita* which means share per head.
>
> This assumes greater importance only where the propositus leaves behind a number of grand children whose parents died during the lifetime of the propositus. The principle of succession in such a case will not be inheritance *per capita* but *per stirpes*, i.e. in accordance with the root or stock to which the grandchild belongs, and [thus the grandchild] will only get the share to which [he] is entitled through his parents. In the event of there being a single surviving grandchild the principle *per stirpes* is pushed to the background but cannot be employed to support a principle which militates against the Islamic Law of Inheritance.

[7] *Kamal Khan v. Mst Zainab*, PLD 1983 Lah 546.

17. NEW LAMPS FOR OLD: THE EVOLVING LEGAL POSITION OF ISLAM IN CHINA, WITH SPECIAL REFERENCE TO FAMILY LAW

A. R. Dicks

With a population of more than 20 million people professing Islam,[1] the People's Republic of China has a Muslim minority which is by any standards substantial. Yet the few vestigial traces of Islamic jurisprudence which are to be found in the legal system of China as it exists today are the negative imprints of attempts at repression, and it is only in very recent times that the study of Islamic law has been brought explicitly within the purview of officially sanctioned legal research. This paradox is compounded when the special position of the Muslims as members of national minorities in the formal structure of the Chinese state for the last forty years is considered.

China is a country where the issues of state identity and minority rights are (and, terminology apart, have always been) of crucial importance to the Muslim communities. The condition of Islam and its followers in China today is characterized by diversity and fragmentation - ethnic, cultural, linguistic, political and economic. Even to refer to 'a Muslim minority' in China is misleading, for in reality there is not one but a series of different Islamic minorities or, as they are called in China, nationalities. Accordingly, in order to understand the legal dimensions of the nature of Islam in modern China it is necessary to bear in mind not only the policy of the Communist Party and the State towards Islam as a religion and as a value system, but also the political and administrative organization of the Muslim minorities as nationalities or ethnic groups. Although in practical terms the issues of religion and nationality can hardly be separated in Chinese Islam, the communist rulers of the People's Republic have endeavoured to confine them in separate political and philosophical compartments.[2]

Of the fifty-five national minorities recognized by the law of the People's Republic of China, ten (listed below) are regarded as Muslim. Some of these can be easily identified by ethnicity and language, but some, in particular the

[1]This is a conservative estimate. Before the Second World War, some estimates for the total Muslim population of China, including Xinjiang, were as high as 50 million. See, e.g., J. Gernet, *A History of Chinese Civilization,* Cambridge, 1982, p. 380-381.

[2]For an admission of the practical difficulties in maintaining this distinction, see *Minzu Quyu Zizhifa Jianghua (Talks on the Law on National Regional Autonomy)*, comp. by the Editorial and Writing Group of the Staff Office of the Nationalities Committee of the National People's Congress and the Nationalities Department of the Central People's Broadcasting Station, Peking, 1985, p. 90.

Hui, represent groups which are linguistically and culturally largely assimilated to the Han majority, but which are nevertheless by reason of their religion set apart from the Han Chinese majority and regarded (not least by themselves) as a separate race.[3] In 1956 the State Council (then presided over by Zhou Enlai) made an attempt to clear up this confusion by legal means:

> In the areas of our country inhabited by the Han nationality the religion of Islam is usually referred to as 'the Hui religion', which means that this religion is the religion in which the Hui nationality believes. Newspapers and journals, following the established practice, also frequently use the expression 'Hui religion'. This is incorrect. Islam is a religion of an international character and the expression Islam is the name used internationally for it. In our country the believers in Islam, apart from the Hui nationality, also include nine other nationalities, namely the Uighurs, Kazakhs, Uzbeks, Tajiks, Tartars, Khalkas, Dongxiang, Salars and Baoan, comprising approximately 10 million people. For this reason, henceforth the expression 'Islam' shall always be employed in relation to the religious faith of Islam, and the expression 'Hui religion' must not be used.[4]

Since 1949 it has been the avowed policy of the Communist Party and government to preserve the cultural and ethnic identities of all the national minorities. Although the implementation of this policy in the last forty years has been very far from consistent or smooth, one of its lasting results has been the establishment of a number of 'autonomous' territorial units of government within which one or more national minorities are recognised as constituting the 'predominant' nationality.[5] These autonomous territories vary in size and importance from those which are equivalent to provinces to those which are no more than counties, depending on the numbers of the predominant

---

[3]Similarly, the Baoan and Dongxiang are communities which but for their adherence to Islam would be regarded as Mongols: L. J. Newby, 'The Pure and True Religion in China', *Third World Quarterly*, 10, 1988, p.924.

[4]*Notice of the State Council Regarding the Question of the Expression 'Islam',* issued 2nd June 1956 *(Zhonghua Renmin Gongheguo Fagui Huibian (Collected Legislation of the People's Republic of China* - hereinafter '*FGHB*'), Peking, Vol. 3, 1956, p. 584.

[5]The expression 'predominant' must be read in a special sense, for the 'predominant' nationality is by no means always the most numerous. In Ningxia Hui Autonomous Region, for example, the predominant Hui nationality is smaller in number than the Han majority; it is estimated that by the end of the century Huis will represent 38 per cent of the population, which includes 28 other nationalities. Sun Xun, 'Implement the Regional Autonomy Law and Promote Economic Take-off in Ningxia', *Ningxia Ribao (Ningxia Daily)*, 10th October 1984, translated in FBIS-China Report No. CPS-84-090, 20th December 1984, p.135.

nationality living in reasonably compact and distinctive communities.[6] Muslim national minorities predominate in two out of the five autonomous regions at the level of provinces,[7] in five out of the thirty-one autonomous prefectures and in sixteen out of eighty autonomous counties.[8]

This constitutional pluralism has been matched by a more limited pluralism in legal matters. Although the autonomous areas have certain legislative powers, in areas where believers in Islam are the predominant nationality the extent to which these powers have been used to enhance the position of Islamic law is so small as to be negligible. In the field of marriage and family law, where the national legislation has long provided for possible variations to suit the circumstances of national minorities,[9] minimum ages of marriage lower than those applicable to Han people have been permitted and existing customary forms of marriage ceremony and inheritance customs were preserved for a few years for Muslim communities by local legislation.[10] However, prominent features of Islamic family law which are in sharp conflict with the values officially attributed to the nation as a whole, such as polygamous marriage or divorce by *talaq*, were almost from the outset characterized as 'extremely unreasonable' and made unlawful.[11] As a distinguished commentator in this field of law observed of this compromise two decades ago, although the technique and the tempo may be different, the degree of autonomy given to the national minorities amounts to little more

[6]The smaller units known as 'national villages', of which there are several thousand scattered throughout the country, are too small to qualify for autonomy, but are organized under separate legislation, currently the *Notice of the State Council Regarding the Question of the Establishment of National Villages*, promulgated 29th December 1983 (*FGHB* [1983], p.93).

[7]*Viz.* Ningxia Hui Autonomous Region and Xinjiang Uighur Autonomous Region. In each of these regions there are smaller autonomous units (prefectures or counties) in which other minorities, some but not all of them Muslim, predominate.

[8]For a full list of autonomous territorial units at the regional, prefectural and county levels in which the dominant nationality traditionally adheres to Islam, see Appendix, pp.386-7 below. Neither the Uzbeks nor the Tartars have yet established autonomous areas. Xie Liangjun, '10 smallest ethnics surveyed', *China Daily,* 30th January 1990.

[9]*Marriage Law of the People's Republic of China,* promulgated 30th April 1950, entered into force 1st May 1950 (text in *Zhongyang Renmin Zhengfu Faling Huibian (Collected Laws and Decrees of the Central People's Government* - hereinafter *'FLHB'*) Peking, 1952-1955, Vol. 1, 1949-1950, pp.32-36; English translation in *Marriage Law of the People's Republic of China,* Peking, 1950), Article 27: this provision was replaced by the similar provision of the *Marriage Law of the People's Republic of China,* promulgated 10th September 1980, entered into force 1st January 1981 (*FGHB,* [1980], pp.6-12; English translation in *Laws of the People's Republic of China,* Beijing, 1987 (hereinafter cited as *'Laws'*), Vol. 1, p.184), Article 36.

[10]See for example the set of regulations promulgated in Xinjiang on 18th January 1952 for the Uighur, Kazakh and other minorities translated in M.J. Meijer, *Marriage Law and Policy of the Chinese People's Republic,* Hong Kong, 1971, p.245-246, Articles 1, 9 and 10. These regulations are now replaced by others discussed below.

[11]*Ibid.*, Articles 3 and 6.

than the expression of a policy that these communities 'should to some extent follow their own road to communism.'[12]

Although the terminology and form in which the elements of this compromise of the claims of Islamic law find their expression are characteristic of the modern Marxist-Leninist state, its essence is as old as the history of Islam in China. The monopolistic and bureaucratic character of successive Chinese regimes, since the accession of the Ming dynasty (1368) at least, has tended to impede the fragmentation of authority which is implicit in a formal system of legal pluralism. Nevertheless, the size, continuity and vitality of the Muslim populations of China over many centuries bear witness to a de facto pluralism which has enabled them, with varying degrees of success, to preserve at least a minimum knowledge and observance of the law which is an inseparable part of the Islamic faith.

It is to the changing nature of this accommodation between the Chinese and the Islamic legal systems, particularly as it affects family law, that the present study is directed.

A full investigation of this complex question, which touches on many aspects of the long and sometimes tumultuous history of Han-Muslim coexistence other than law, would be a more ambitious undertaking than can be attempted in what is essentially a preliminary survey. In order to provide a context for the legal evolution, however, some reference will be made to the various peoples who comprise the Muslim population of China, together with the political and legal position of the Muslims (especially the Muslims of China proper, the Hui), over several centuries. There is a brief examination of some of the evidence of the exercise of quasi-autonomous jurisdiction by Muslim communities over their members, and the resulting development by the close of the Qing dynasty (1644-1911) of a recognized body of Islamic customary law in some parts of China. This exemplifies the state of Islamic law in China on the eve of the modernization of the legal system. It is followed by a short survey of the replacement of this customary law, first, by a civil code along West European lines, and secondly, by the current legal regime based on the dialectical materialist and atheist philosophy of Marxist-Leninism.

---

[12]Meijer, *Marriage Law* , p.243-244. A somewhat similar compromise appears to have been reached in more recent times with the renascence of the policy of national autonomy following its virtual destruction in the Great Proletarian Cultural Revolution (1966-1976); this is considered below, although it is too early to attempt a thorough assessment of its nature or success. See, for example, Newby, 'The Pure and True Religion in China', p.942. For the desirability of such a compromise from the point of view of at least one section of Chinese Muslim opinion, see Ibrahim Ma Zhao-chun, 'Da'wah in the Chinese Context', *Journal of the Institute of Muslim Minority Affairs,* 9, 1988, p.33.

The Muslim Populations of China

The Hui Nationality

Although the Hui have been in various parts of China for many centuries, there is some dispute regarding their origins. It seems clear that some of the earliest Islamic communities reached China by sea, for ancient mosques as well as long established existing communities in Canton and Quanzhou attest to their presence in these south eastern ports as early as the 7th century. Some at least of the larger communities in central and western China, however, probably owe their origin in large measure to an event sanctified by tradition as the beginning of Chinese Islam, namely the settlement in China, at the invitation of a grateful emperor, of the Abbasid troops[13] who had been sent to Gansu in 756 AD to assist the Tang government in the suppression of the great rebellion of An Lushan.

These soldier settlers appear to have initiated what was to become an important factor in the spread of Islam in China by marrying Han Chinese women. They also appear to have been given land grants, and much of the Hui population has remained in rural communities, principally in the north west of China proper, but also in pockets in other provinces, such as Henan, Shandong, Sichuan and Yunnan.

Many Muslims, however, appear to have adopted urban occupations, as traders and artisans, and large Hui communities still exist in many cities such as Peking, sometimes dominating particular trades, as with the silversmiths of Shanghai. In addition to the communities thought to be of Arab origin in the maritime cities of the south east, by Song and Yuan times Muslim communities elsewhere in China included prosperous merchants, and even money-lenders,[14] who appear to have come overland from Central Asia. In the political system of the Yuan empire, with its elaborate system of racial discrimination, Muslims both in China proper and in Inner Asia were specially trusted by the Mongol rulers and occupied important official posts as well as having a virtual monopoly in the profitable business of tax collecting with the aid of the Mongol troops.[15] These privileges and advantages were to cost them dear in the future, however, for it is almost certain that it was at this time that the destructive stereotypes of Muslim behaviour which for generations have been

---

[13]Probably in fact of Persian and Iraqi, rather than Arab, origin; see Gernet, *A History of Chinese Civilization,* p. 288.

[14]The Muslim usurers in the former Southern Song capital of Hangzhou were highly organized with special privileges under the Mongols, which enabled them to finance the Central Asia caravan trade; their notoriously high interest rates earned them the hatred of the Han people, however; see E. Balazs, *Chinese Civilization and Bureaucracy,* New Haven, 1964, pp. 76-77, 80-81.

[15]Gernet, *A History of Chinese Civilization,* p.368-9. A Muslim was normally the deputy governor, under a Mongol, of each province; in 1274 a Muslim native of Bukhara became governor of Yunnan.

used to justify hatred and violence towards them began to be formed as cultural attitudes in the minds of their Han neighbours.[16]

The Muslims of Inner Asia

When the armies of the Qianlong Emperor conquered large parts of Inner Asia north and south of the Tianshan Mountains in the 1750's, they established the new imperial dependency of Xinjiang (the 'New Territory' or 'New Dominion', also romanized as Sinkiang). The Chinese policy in these remote areas was one of minimal interference in the internal affairs of the various native peoples, most of whom were Turkic-speaking Muslims.[17]

However, the Chinese also encouraged settlement in the agricultural parts of Xinjiang by Han Chinese and Hui, or Chinese Muslim, families from China proper. By 1800 there were hundreds of thousands of these immigrants, attracted by the government's offer of 30 *mu* of land for each family,[18] among whom by far the largest group were Chinese-speaking Muslims from Shaanxi, Gansu and Sichuan. These people, known in Turkestan as 'Donggans', were orthodox Sunnis. The majority, as in China proper, appear to have adhered to the Hanafi school of jurisprudence,[19] but some were of the Shafi'i school.[20] Their language and appearance was a barrier between them and other Muslims in Inner Asia, who regarded them as Chinese.[21]

At the peak of the administration was a Chinese military governor based in Ili, who had command of the vast garrison, with direct civil jurisdiction over various areas, particularly cities, as well as over the immigrants from China proper. Beneath this level the structure of this largely indirect government was far from uniform, however. In some places, such as the oasis-states of Hami and Turfan in Eastern Turkestan, local principalities survived until Xinjiang became a province in 1884 and were supported by the

---

[16] R. Israeli, *Muslims in China, A Study in Cultural Confrontation,* London, 1980, p. 21 *et seq*. Chinese hostility to the 'Saracens' whom the Great Khan set over them was the subject of contemporary comment by Marco Polo. It should be said that R. Israeli's profound study of the religious and cultural interactions between the Han and the Hui left the writer of this paper in his debt to a greater extent than a few isolated references might suggest.

[17] For details, see J. Fletcher, 'Ch'ing Inner Asia c. 1800', Chapter 2 in J. K. Fairbank ed., *The Cambridge History of China,* Vol. 10, *Late Ch'ing, 1800-1911,* Part 1, Cambridge, 1978 (hereinafter '*CHC,* Vol. 10'), pp. 58-60.

[18] *Ibid.*, p.65; 30 *mu* is approximately 4.5 acres, or 2 hectares.

[19] *Cihai (The Sea of Words),* separately published part of 1975 edition on 'Religion', Shanghai, 1980, p. 1342, entry *'Hanaifeipai - al-Hanafiyah'*. There is no mention of China in relation to entries for the other major schools of jurisprudence, *ibid.*, p.132-133.

[20] *Ibid.*, p.66. In 1867, during the rebellion of Yaq'ub Beg, he declared a *jihad* against the Donggans on the basis that they were Shafi'is; K.C. Liu & R.J. Smith, 'The military challenge: the north-west and the coast', Chapter 4 in J.K. Fairbank & K.C. Liu ed.,*The Cambridge History of China,* Vol. 11, *Late Ch'ing 1800-1911,* part 2, Cambridge, 1980, hereinafter *'CHC,* Vol. 11', p. 223.

[21] *CHC,* Vol. 10, p.68; their reputation for incorruptibility led the Qing government to value their services.

Chinese authorities.[22] Much of the rest of Xinjiang was ruled through lesser indigenous officials called *begs,* who formed part of the Qing administrative hierarchy and were appointed by a Qing official at Kashgar who was himself responsible to the military governor at Ili.

The Qing government interfered very little in the lives of the local population. The bureaucracy of begs[23] and *akhunds*[24] governed the population in much the same way as their predecessors before the arrival of the Chinese. They administered the law of the Hanafi school, by all accounts strictly, and even disputes between local Muslims and Manchu or Chinese troops and other non-Muslim inhabitants were apparently tried in accordance with Islamic law.[25]

Like Xinjiang, the former Tibetan province known in Chinese as Qinghai was annexed by the Qing in the 18th century. Now a separate province, it was originally administered by China as a dependency of the province of Gansu. Like the rest of Gansu it contained numerous Hui or Chinese Muslims, and was also the principal domicile of a Turkic - speaking Muslim people called the Salars, who in cultural and religious matters were akin to the Turkish peoples of Eastern Turkestan.

Religious Life

The conventional view has long been that with few exceptions the Chinese Muslims, including both the Hui and most of the various ethnic groups in

[22]Like their counterparts in Mongolia these rulers were partly integrated into the Manchu system of nobility, and thus in a sense 'bought' by their Qing overlords. Details of the elaborate titles conferred on them by successive emperors of the Qing dynasty are set out in the regulations of the Li Fan Yuan, or 'Court of Colonial Affairs', *Qinding Da Qing Huidian Shili (Imperially Authorized Institutes and Precedents of the Great Qing [Dynasty]),* Guangxu Edition (1886) (hereinafter '*Huidian Shili*'), *jüan* 972, p. 14a (Turfan), p. 14b (Hami).

[23]These were appointed civil officials who held office for life. The Qing use of the title thus departed from the previous practice in Inner Asia whereby it designated a landed aristocracy. The most senior *'hakim begs'* were very much under the influence of the Qing government, which paid them a stipend; they dressed in Chinese official costume, wore queues, and attended the Confucian temples at regular intervals to kotow to the portrait of the emperor; they in turn required the kotow from their subordinates.

[24]The akhunds (in Chinese *ahong*) were ecclesiastical officials organized in each district under a chief judge *(a'lam akhund),* with judges *(qadi akhund)* and *muftis (mufti akhund).* See W.F. Mayers,*The Chinese Government,* 3rd edition revised by G.M.H. Playfair, Shanghai, 1897, p. 104.

[25]*CHC,* Vol. 10, p.77. East Turkestan, unlike other parts of Xinjiang, was largely agricultural, and land rights were thus of crucial importance, not least for purposes of taxation, long before the arrival of the Chinese colonists. After the Chinese conquest, the patterns of land tenure remained much as they had been earlier and were similar to those prevailing in other parts of Muslim Central Asia (*CHC,* Vol. 10, p.74). This meant among other things that the *waqf,* or religious endowments under Islamic law, continued to enjoy legal protection, and, it seems, freedom from tax *(Ibid.,* p.75).

Inner Asia, are adherents of Sunni orthodoxy,[26] though long before the Qing conquest the Muslims of Inner Asia were much influenced by Sufism and *tariqa* brotherhoods played an important part in religious life.

Two main branches of the faith exist in China, known as the 'Old Teaching' (*Laojiao* or *Jiujiao* in Chinese), and the 'New Teaching' *(Xinjiao)*, the latter first propagated by the Sufi Ma Mingxin (d. 1781). Various offshoots of the latter were particularly influential in the late 18th and 19th centuries and are probably still of considerable importance today.[27] There is controversy about the exact meaning of these terms and their relation to movements in the rest of the Islamic world.[28]

What the New Teaching sects probably did have in common was a strong element of revivalism, aiming at the purification of Chinese Islam from such Confucian accretions as the veneration of ancestors. Viewed retrospectively by Chinese Muslims in Taiwan in the third quarter of the twentieth century, the controversy, while not wholly dead, had been largely resolved in favour of the New Teaching.[29] In some parts of China the degree of contentiousness between the Old Teaching and New Teaching is probably much stronger, even if latent for long periods.

---

[26]The Tajiks, people living mostly in the mountainous areas south of the Tarim basin, and speaking a language of Iranian derivation, who are Shi'is, constitute the principal exception to the rule. More recently, however, this view has been challenged, and it seems likely that among the many strands which have gone to make up the somewhat tangled skein of Chinese Islam, Shi'ite or 'proto-Shi'ite' beliefs have been much more influential than was previously thought. R. Israeli, 'Is there Shi'a in Chinese Islam?' *Journal of the Institute of Muslim Minority Affairs,* 9, 1988, pp.49-66. The term 'proto-Shi'ite' is Israeli's.

[27]For a recent call by a Chinese Muslim for the end of sectarian rivalry 'in order to properly conduct the affairs of Islam in China', see Ibrahim Ma Chao-chuen, 'Da'wah in the Chinese Context', p.33.

[28]Israeli, *Muslims in China,* Chapters XII-XIV, especially pp.157-161, where this question is fully discussed.

[29]Barbara L.K. Pillsbury, "Factionalism Observed: Behind the 'Face' of Harmony in a Chinese Community", *China Quarterly* , 74, 1978, pp. 258-259. One of the issues which still divided adherents of the two sects among the Muslim community in Taiwan which is the subject of the article was the (Old Teaching) custom of privately obtaining the services of an ahong to 'walk the grave' and recite Qur'anic passages for the benefit of the ancestors of a particular family, one of the ways in which the Hui traditionally accommodated their religion to the Confucian values of the society in which they lived. See Pillsbury, pp. 259-260.

Legal and Jurisdictional Autonomy in the History of Chinese Islam

The Hui Minority and the Imperial Administration: Historical Evolution

Like their Byzantine and Arab contemporaries in Western Asia, the Tang and Song emperors appear to have favoured a system of indirect rule for governing the earliest recorded foreign communities in China. The earliest Muslim settlers, residing in China for the purposes of trade, were allowed, or required, to live apart from their Chinese hosts in special quarters designated *fan fang*[30] or 'foreign zones', which were autonomous enclaves of a quasi-extraterritorial kind, usually in the immediate vicinity of a port.[31] Protected by the Chinese government, they were subject to the jurisdiction of a 'foreign' (Arab) official selected by the community but appointed by the imperial authorities and supplied by the latter with a *yamen*[32] and Chinese official costume.[33] These officials exercised considerable autonomy in judicial matters, and cases in which both parties were foreigners were referred by the Chinese authorities to the foreign official to be judged in accordance with their own law.[34]

How far this account, based on reports by Arab travellers, is accurate is difficult to judge[35] in the absence of further evidence, but it seems to accord with the legislative approach of the Tang dynasty (618-905).

In accordance with the *Tang Code*,[36]

> Offences committed between people outside civilization[37] who are of the same race shall be judged in accordance with their

[30]It seems possible that the idea was brought to China by the Arabs, who according to one authority, 'insisted' on such privileges in countries where they resided as foreigners and obtained them in China. See Nasim Souza, *The Capitulatory Régime of Turkey: its History, Origin and Nature,* Baltimore, 1933, pp.45-46; see also pp.39-40.

[31]J. Escarra, *La Chine et Le Droit International*, Paris, 1931, p.6, citing an article by Chang Hsin-hai in *North China Herald,* 10th February 1931. The most famous of these settlements was Quanzhou in modern Fujian province, known to the Islamic world as Zaytun; there was also such a settlement at Canton.

[32]I.e. an administrative compound containing both offices and a residence which was the headquarters of any territorially based official.

[33]Escarra, *La Chine et Le Droit International.*, p. 6.

[34]*Ibid.*, where there are further details.

[35]Compare the account given by Israeli, *Muslims in China,* p. 81.

[36]*Tanglü shuyi,* 48th article. For a full translation of the first fifty-seven articles with the commentary, see W. Johnson tr., *The T'ang Code, Vol. I, General Principles,* Princeton, 1979.

[37]I.e., non-Chinese, though possibly resident in China. Johnson, *The T'ang Code,* p.252, translates this simply as 'foreigners'.

> customs. Offences committed between barbarians of different races shall be judged in accordance with [Chinese] law.[38]

A similar rule was found in the code of the Song dynasty (960-1278) which followed the Tang.[39]

In the Yuan dynasty (1280-1341), China and Inner Asia were subject to the government of the alien Mongols, who had their own customary law. As might be expected in such a large and diverse empire, the potentiality for conflicts of laws seems to have been more acute, and the bias in favour of Chinese law built into the solution adopted by their Tang and Song predecessors was politically unacceptable to the Mongol rulers. A series of conflict rules of a much more sophisticated kind than those used by the Tang and Song were incorporated into the codes. The large population of Central Asians, many (though by no means all) of whom observed their own Islamic law, were placed under the ultimate jurisdiction of the *Du-hu-fu* or 'Bureau of Guardianship'.[40]

Where Muslims lived in compact groups, however, the quasi-extraterritorial system applied by the Tang and Song authorities appears to have persisted well into the 14th century, when the Arab traveller Ibn Battuta visited Yuan China (1324-1325 AD). He mentioned numerous cities with Islamic communities, each led by a *Shaikh-ul-Islam* or leader of the Islamic community and a *qadi* or judge, and expressed the belief that all Muslim merchants in the country were organized into such communities.[41]

With the accession of the Ming dynasty (1368-1644) and the expulsion of the Mongols, China turned its back on cosmopolitanism, at all events in legal matters. A single provision in the *Ming Code* required that

> All people outside civilization who commit crimes shall be judged in accordance with [Chinese] law.[42]

---

[38]Words in square brackets supplied. These provisions are explained in the Commentary, as translated by Johnson: 'Foreigners refers to persons of those barbarian countries who have their own rulers and leaders. They each have their own habits and customs and their regulations, and the laws are not alike. In cases involving those of the same nationality who have committed crimes against each other, the court must ask about the regulations in their native country and sentence the offence following their customs and laws. In all cases involving those of different nationalities who have committed crimes against each other, such as one person from Koryo and another person from Paekche [countries in the Korean peninsula], Chinese law will be used to sentence and decide the punishment.'*The T'ang Code*, p.252. This has been interpreted as meaning that while it is easy to choose the applicable law in the situation where both parties share the same law, the application of Chinese law in a mixed case obviates the need to make a difficult choice. See A. Bonnichon and F. X. Tcheng Yong-tai, 'Le Conflit des Lois dans le Droit Chinois Ancien', *Mélanges Juridiques de l'Université L'Aurore,* Shanghai, n. d., p.206.

[39]*Ibid.*, at p.207.

[40]P. Heng-chao Ch'en, *Chinese Legal Tradition under the Mongols,* Princeton, 1979, pp.80-83.

[41]Cited in M. Broomhall, *Islam in China: A Neglected Problem,* London, 1910, pp. 53-55.

[42]*Minglü jijie fuli* (1610 edition reprinted 1908, repr. Taipei, 1969), 1st *jüan,* p.84b.

The expression 'people outside civilization',[43] according to the Commentary on the *Ming Code,* included peoples who had submitted as tributaries to Chinese suzerainty as well as prisoners of war and other foreign inhabitants of China, all of whom were

> subjects of the Emperor... if they commit crimes, whether serious or not, they must be examined and judged according to the ordinary law, to show that the Emperor does not discriminate against foreigners.[44]

Within the provinces of China proper, therefore, the Ming sought to govern the Hui-hui in accordance with the same laws as they applied to their Chinese subjects.

The reasons for non-discrimination given by the author of the Commentary, admirable as they may at first sight seem, conceal an important deterioration in the political status of Muslims of all kinds in China. In Tang and Song times, all Muslims in China were regarded as 'Arabs' from the great empires of the Abbasids and their successors, and they derived political benefits from this reflected glory. The Mongols, however, as well as conquering China had overthrown the Islamic empires of Central and Western Asia.

Although the political results of these events were temporarily obscured by the fact that the Mongols treated the Muslims on the whole with great favour, after the overthrow of the Yuan the Muslims in China had no external protector with which they could identify.[45] They were now in all senses permanent residents of China, subjects of the Ming. However, not only were they still considered by their rulers to be outside the pale of 'civilization', that is to say, Chinese culture, they were now saddled with the opprobrium of having been the principal lieutenants of the hated Mongols.[46] It is not surprising that what one scholar has aptly summarized as the 'self-effacing process' of Muslim acculturation in China[47] has its roots in this period.

---

[43] It is difficult to do full justice to the expression *hua-wai* in translation, but it may also be rendered as 'outside (Han) Chinese society'.

[44] Quoted in Bonnichon & Tcheng, 'Le Conflit des Lois dans le Droit Chinois Ancien', p.207: text in *Minglü jijie fuli*, 1st *jüan,* 85a.

[45] Israeli, *Muslims in China,* pp.80-83, where the author analyses the results of this change.

[46] For examples of Muslim clans which adopted new Chinese surnames and migrated to different parts of China in the Ming period, see Huang Tianzhu & Liao Yuanquan, 'An Informal Talk on the Muslim Descendants of the Arabs of the Quanzhou Region and their Inheritance', in *Quanzhou Yisilanjiao Yanjiu Lunwenxian (Symposium on Islam in Quanzhou)*, Fuzhou, 1983, p.204; also examples in papers on particular clans in the same work at pp.210-212 and 217-219.

[47] Israeli, *Muslims in China,* p.31; he continues: 'The Muslims could, by camouflaging their culture from the hostile eyes of the Chinese, play the semblance of being Chinese'. For

In legal terms, the practical effect in China of this geopolitical reverse was tangible enough to be obvious even to a foreign observer. We learn from the Jesuit Benedict Goes, who travelled in China in the last decade of the sixteenth century, something of the legal position of the Muslim merchants in the city of 'Socien' (Xian) in 'the province of Scensi' (Shaanxi):

> . . . they are much in the position of the Portuguese, who are settled at Amacao, in the province of Canton, but with this difference, that the Portuguese live under their own laws and have magistrates of their own, whereas the Mohammedans are under the government of the Chinese. Indeed they are shut up every night within the walls of their own quarters in the city, and in other matters are treated just like the natives, and are subject in everything to the Chinese magistrates. The law is that one who has sojourned there for nine years shall not be allowed to return to his country.[48]

Not only did the Ming declare their intention to govern the Muslims according to Chinese law; they sought to assimilate those of foreign origin permanently.[49]

From Ming times, the Muslims in China seem to have lived a double life, appearing on the outside to compromise with the host culture, yet living the life of their own uncompromising faith and law behind the walls and shutters of their own, sometimes segregated, quarters in the cities, or within their enclosed, frequently fortified, villages. The famous mosque at Xian (substantially a Ming structure) provides an apt metaphor for the political posture of its worshippers, with its discreetly Chinese architecture and Chinese inscriptions giving way to Arabic only in the interior. Like all temples and mosques in Qing times it contained an altar table with a tablet in honour of the emperor,[50] to which worshippers were supposed to kotow. Various expedients were used whereby such outward forms could be observed. Thus, of the considerable number of Muslims who took the imperial examinations and rose sometimes to the highest ranks in the civil and especially the military service of the empire, it was said by an observer writing in 1910:

---

illuminating excerpts from the later special genre of Muslim apologetic literature in which Confucian values were discovered in Islamic teaching, see *ibid.*, chapter III, especially at pp.32-35.

[48]Translation in H. Yule, *Cathay and the Way Thither,* quoted in Broomhall, *Islam in China,* p.56.

[49]Strict border control was probably the rule throughout Chinese history; see for the Qing period the detailed discussion in R. Edwards, 'Imperial China's Border Control Law', *Journal of Chinese Law,* 1, 1987, pp.33-62, especially with regard to foreigners at pp.55-57.

[50]It bore the imperial honorific formula 'To His Imperial Majesty, Ten thousand years, Ten thousand years, Ten thousand times ten thousand years!' - a form of salutation also shouted at Chairman Mao by the Red Guards during the Cultural Revolution.

> Their attitude as students or as officials towards the worship of the Emperor and of Confucius, or even of idolatry, is that of compromise. Compelled by law to conform, they excuse themselves by saying that they only do so outwardly and not in heart. In prostrating themselves before the Emperor's tablet or idol they will avoid bringing the head in contact with the ground, which they do when worshipping Allah, and they thus satisfy their consciences that the true significance of the rite has been avoided, or that it has been merely an empty official ceremony.[51]

The Qing Period: Persecution and Pluralism

The decline in the legal status of the Muslim population of China proper under the Ming helps to place in perspective the traumatic events of the succeeding dynasty, when, by a series of interacting developments which are still not fully understood, increasingly repressive laws were met with growing Muslim resistance which ultimately in the 19th century led to several massive rebellions in various parts of the Chinese empire.[52] The uprisings were suppressed by the imperial forces (which included many Muslims among both generals and soldiers) for the most part with great savagery, so that by the fourth quarter of the 19th century many millions of followers of Islam had been massacred and whole areas of Muslim settlement devastated.

In the light of this sombre chapter in Chinese history, the Muslims have not unnaturally tended to place the whole of the blame for the tragedies of their 19th history on the Qing and to regard the whole of the previous history of Islam in China as a sort of golden epoch. It seems very doubtful however whether this simple picture adequately reflects the complex historical reality.

The Manchu Qing (1644-1911) were a dynasty of foreign emperors, who penetrated the Great Wall from their native Manchuria as the conquerors of China. Their aggressive colonial policy, leading to the rapid acquisition of enormous tracts of Muslim Inner Asia, as well as Tibet and Mongolia,

---

[51] Broomhall, *Islam in China,* p.228.

[52] For accounts of these events see Fletcher, 10 *CHC,* pp.360-375, 385-395; K. C. Liu, 11 *CHC,* pp.211-243. The term 'rebellion' conceals some of the political and institutional achievements of the rebels, short-lived though they were. In Yunnan, the separate Islamic sultanate of Pingnan ('Pacification of the South'), organized however on Chinese lines and including many non-Muslim officials and ordinary people, was established under Du Wenxu from 1856-1872 and was engaging in diplomatic overtures to London before its collapse. Yaq'ub Beg, whose monarchy dominated much of Xinjiang from 1867 until his death ten years later, was recognized as an *emir* by the Sublime Porte in 1873. Ma Hualong, the main leader of the New Teaching in the second half of the 19th century, never established a compact autonomous state; instead he led a partly military regime in Gansu, Shaanxi and elsewhere in the north west, adopting the Chinese title of 'Grand Marshal' of Ningxia Prefecture and various other areas and appointing civil officials on this basis. His real political strength, however, was religious, in that he was regarded as a *shengren* (saint) in the Sufi tradition by his followers. See K. C. Liu, p.219.

necessitated a considerable degree of pluralism in legal administration.[53] As already noted above, the Muslim populations of Inner Asia as a result of this policy were in effect subject to Islamic law for most purposes from the time of the Chinese conquest up to the collapse of the Qing dynasty in 1911.

The policy of the Qing emperors towards the Muslims in China proper did not explicitly admit of legal pluralism, but it seems to have been much less consistently oppressive than post-rebellion Muslim opinion would allow.[54] A number of imperial edicts in the 18th century refer to the Muslims in essentially benevolent terms, drawing attention to their good qualities and the attainments of those promoted to high rank, while forbidding local officials to discriminate against them on various grounds and thus in effect giving them protection.[55]

In fact, provided that they did not offer a challenge to the authority of the Confucian state, it was an important strategy of Qing government to refrain as far as possible from interfering directly in the lives of local communities. Despite the impressive semblance of uniformity suggested by the imperial codes and the hierarchy of local, provincial and national government, the fabric of the Chinese legal system was in some respects well-suited to harbour the growth of autonomous legal regimes within particular local communities.

Two aspects of the policy of minimal intervention are relevant for present purposes. In the first place, the imperial officials at the lowest administrative level - the *xian* or county - encouraged the people under their jurisdiction to

---

[53] A decade or two before their conquest of China they had set up an office to supervise the government of Mongolia, which they had already conquered, to which in 1638 was given the title Li Fan Yuan, literally the Bureau for the Administration of Border Regions, sometimes referred to as the 'Court for Colonial Affairs'; Cf Bonnichon and Tcheng, 'Bureau des Territoires Soumis' ('Le Conflit des Lois dans le Droit Chinois Ancien', p.211). It contained six departments, including those in charge of judicial and religious affairs: see *Cihai (Sea of Words),* 1975 edn., Vol. 2, p.2777. Its jurisdiction extended to Tibet and ultimately to the largely Muslim territories of Xinjiang as these were brought under Chinese control. The outlines of Qing legal administration under the supervision of the Li Fan Yuan in these areas have already been indicated above in the discussion of the Muslims of Inner Asia. One of the functions of the Li Fan Yuan in the field of law was to resolve conflict of laws problems which occurred in the territories under its control, especially in criminal matters.

[54] There were however a number of discriminatory laws, under which Hui criminals were punished more severely than Hans, e.g. for cattle-stealing. For a translation of a ruling concerning the application of discriminatory laws against Hui, see D. Bodde and C. Morris, *Law in Imperial China Exemplified by 190 Ch'ing Dynasty Cases,* Cambridge, Mass., 295, No. 144. See also E. Alabaster, *Notes and Commentaries on Chinese Criminal Law,* London, 1899, p. LII. In view of the nature of the traditional legal system, in which the formal hierarchy of law and precedent was largely concerned with criminal matters, it is not surprising that most of the Qing decisions affecting Muslims which have been recorded relate to the application of the discriminatory penal laws.

[55] See in particular the edicts in the 7th and 8th years of the Yongzheng Emperor (1729 and 1730) concerning the Muslims in Shaanxi, quoted extensively in Israeli, *Muslims in China,* pp.130-133, where the emperor reacted angrily to suggestions by Chinese officials and gentry that the Hui should be treated more harshly. The policy of the Qianlong Emperor (whose favourite concubine was a Muslim) was also mainly well disposed towards the Hui, as evidenced by the documents quoted (*ibid.,* pp.134-135), even sparing Muslim books from his famous literary inquisition. For changes in this policy, see *ibid.,* pp.135-142.

settle their own disputes, both those of a civil nature[56] and also many of the less serious criminal cases. This policy had the strong support of the imperial government in the Qing period.[57]

This quasi-autonomous exercise of jurisdiction by local bodies was of course conditional. It was neatly summarized in a famous field study of a village in eastern Guangdong in the 1920s which the author found to enjoy 'local autonomy so long as it pays its taxes and commits no crime'.[58]

Secondly, where the seriousness of a case or the intransigence of the parties to a dispute did require the intervention of the formal legal system in the person of the county magistrate, great caution was exercised by the latter to avoid so far as possible applying the formal law in such a way as to conflict with local custom, even in some cases where this was manifestly contrary to law. This policy of expediency, although obviously not formally incorporated into the law, was nonetheless tacitly approved, as can be seen from the advice given to magistrates and their legal secretaries by the various handbooks which existed for this purpose.

In one of the most famous and authoritative of such works, written by a man who had been an outstanding legal secretary[59] for many years and eventually became a magistrate,[60] the following passage occurs:

---

[56]It should be pointed out that there was no demarcation line in traditional Chinese law which corresponded precisely to the Western distinction between civil and criminal matters, although references to cases described as *'hu hun tianlu qianchai'* (cases concerning 'family and marriage, landed property and monetary obligations') appear in codes and other official documents of the Qing, and describe a class of cases where the criminal element is unimportant. Nevertheless there was a roughly equivalent difference the nature of which has only begun to be explored fully by modern scholarship. See, e.g., S. Shiga, 'Criminal Procedure in the Ch'ing Dynasty', *Memoirs of the Research Department of the Toyo Bunko,* 32, 1974, pp.1-45 (pt. 1) and 33, 1975, pp.115-138 (pt. 2); Shiga's view is that the distinction is one only of degree: see excerpt in part 1 at pp.3-5.

[57]Liu Guangan, 'Family Laws and Clan Regulations in Ming and Qing Times', *Zhongguo Faxue (Legal Science of China),* 1, 1988, p.109.

[58]D. H. Kulp, *Country Life in South China: the Sociology of Familism,* New York, 1925, p. 134.

[59]The importance of this officer, who was privately employed by each magistrate, can scarcely be overestimated, since magistrates had no training in or knowledge of law; T'ung-tsu Ch'u, *Local Government in China under the Ch'ing,* Stanford, 1969, pp. 94-101.

[60]Wang Huizu (1731-1807), who only succeeded in obtaining an official appointment as a magistrate in 1786 when he was 55, having failed the necessary examinations many times. His fame rests on his career as a legal secretary and on his publications. See A. W. Hummel et al., *Eminent Chinese of the Ching Dynasty,* Washington, 1944, pp. 824-826.

> *You must respect local customs*
>
> The primary study for a legal secretary is to know the code,[61] but skill in its application depends still more on being in sympathy with the ways of the people. Now as customs often vary from place to place, it is essential to find out all about them, without preconceptions, and make it your chief concern to abide by them. If you never act on a penal law or an edict without first seeing that it does not conflict with what local custom values, then there will be harmony between yamen[62] and people, the magistrate's fame will spread, and his secretary's prestige will increase accordingly, whereas applying the law rigidly on every occasion would probably give rise to much dissatisfaction and complaint. There is an old saying: only by common consent can you promote good and dispel evil. This has stood the test of experience and should be born in mind.[63]

The operation of these two principles of Qing legal administration - the quasi-autonomous jurisdiction of local groups and the flexible application of the Qing law in the light of local customs - may now be examined in relation to the Muslim population of China proper.

Quasi-Autonomous Jurisdiction of Muslim Communities in the Qing Period

There is a description of this quasi-autonomy in operation in a Muslim community almost as pithy as that of Kulp[64] in the account of a 19th century Muslim traveller, who wrote of the Salar Turks in Gansu that 'they administer their own laws in all matters except murder'.[65]

Although a pedantic legal secretary would certainly have added other serious crimes to the list of offences in respect of which a clan or village was supposed to make a report and hand over the offender to the local magistrate, crimes involving loss of life were no doubt the most important examples in the

---

[61] I.e., the penal code of the Qing dynasty, see *infra,* n. 78.

[62] *Supra,* n. 32.

[63] Excerpt from *Zuozhi Yaoyan (Precepts for Local Administrative Officials),* translated in S. Van der Sprenkel, *Legal Institutions in Manchu China,* London, 1962, p. 150.

[64] *Supra,* n. 58.

[65] Abdul Aziz of Kuldja, 'The Muslims of China' (in Turkish) published in an Istanbul newspaper, date unknown; from an apparently unpublished translation quoted (without date, but probably c. 1900) in Broomhall, *Islam in China,* p.262. Abdul Aziz also reported that in the seminaries of the Salars grammar, logic, interpretation and law were all taught from Arabic books imported from India, and that 'their women retain their ancient customs and use the veil' (*ibid.).*

eyes of the local population, and subject to this qualification there is no reason to doubt the fundamental accuracy of Abdul Aziz's report.

A more illuminating example is found in an anonymous 'proclamation' by a mid-19th century Chinese Muslim scholar urging his community to respect the law of God. He listed a number of the main prescriptions and prohibitions of Islam and warned Muslims to abide by them and to avoid observing Chinese customs:

> If someone does not obey these religious laws, the Three Ecclesiastics [the *imam,* the *khatib* and the *muezzin*] shall jointly impose upon him a penalty. If he does not submit to this penalty, the community will punish him. If he does not accept this punishment, the Three Ecclesiastics will send him with a document to the local mandarin, leaving him to the justice of the State.[66]

This passage suggests very clearly the mechanism of the quasi-autonomous communal jurisdiction functioning in almost exactly the same manner as for a Han lineage[67] or village. For the leaders of an ordinary Chinese clan or village, however, the religious leaders are substituted, and, even more significantly, in place of the traditional Chinese customary law, the basic laws of Islam.

The handing over of offenders to the justice of the state, with or without exclusion from the genealogy or expulsion from the clan, was one of the most characteristic sanctions of written clan rules, particularly in the case of repeated offences, or where for other reasons the clan had lost effective control over one of its members.[68] It seems probable that where the Muslim communities in China proper were organized in clans, exhortations or rules of the kind referred to in the 'proclamation' quoted above would have applied within the clan.[69] Clan rules constituted an important body of normative material in traditional China.[70]

---

[66]Quoted by Israeli, *Muslims in China,* p.45, from the translation by R. Lowenthal, *sub nom. Islam in China,* of V. P. Vasil'ev, *Magometamstvo v Kitae,* St. Petersburg, 1900. The explanations in square brackets are those of Israeli.

[67]Hui-Chen Wang Liu, *The Traditional Chinese Clan Rules,* Locust Valley, N.Y., 1959, pp. 36-39.

[68]*Ibid.*, p.143; see also the appendices in which different punishments for different offences against clan rules are tabulated, *ibid.*, pp. 222-264, *passim.*

[69]In the absence of the Chinese original it is difficult to attempt any precise assessment of the style and nature of this text, which may well turn on the Chinese expression translated as 'community'. It is not impossible that the 'proclamation' was in fact the body of rules of a Muslim clan or village.

[70]See generally, H. C. W. Liu, *The Traditional Chinese Clan Rules,* pp.7-9.

The published material, sparse as it is, on Muslim clans[71] does in fact suggest that like their Han counterparts, they not only maintained careful records of their genealogies (an internal matter) but to the outside world at least exhibited other clear signs of clan solidarity. Recently published research[72] in Quanzhou and the two neighbouring counties of Hui'an and Jinjiang in Fujian province has uncovered many traces of at least five large Muslim clans in and around the city, as well as several less numerous lineages. For example, a number of families named Jin are still living in close proximity to several ancestor halls[73] identified with the Jin clan in the city and its suburbs.[74] In a complex of lineage villages at Chendai live more than 16,000 people of the Ding clan, known locally as the 'Ten Thousand Dings'.[75] Elsewhere in the region are the 'Nine Guo Villages'.[76] These symbols of clan solidarity and strength, whatever their religious significance,[77] are a strong indication of tight-knit, well-organized and autonomous lineage groups.

---

[71]The discussion based on known institutions must unfortunately be confined to lineage groups. There is insufficient evidence at present available to consider mixed-lineage Muslim villages, although these were no doubt very numerous. Even material on Han village institutions and regulations is much less plentiful than is the case with clans: for one or two examples of village regulations, see J. Hayes, *The Hong Kong Region 1850-1911: Institutions and Leadership in Town and Countryside,* Hamden, Conn., 1977, p. 120 and footnotes. Urban institutions, especially gilds, are in general better documented, but the only material available to the writer on a Muslim gild is a brief description of the Mutton Butchers' Gild in Peking, which was founded in 1921 after the failure of the butchers in the city (all of whom were Muslims) to prevent an increase in the tax on sheep: J. S. Burgess, *The Guilds of Peking,* New York, 1925, p. 259. By this date the disciplinary powers of the gild 'courts' had been greatly curtailed (after the Peking police forbade them to use corporal punishment - *ibid.*, p.200), but the Mutton Butchers nonetheless had a procedure for the expulsion of members *(ibid.,* p.146).

[72]The results of this research in which archaeological, historical, topographical and ethnographic evidence has been drawn upon, are published in *Quanzhou Yisilanjiao Yanjiu Lunwenxian (Symposium on Islam in Quanzhou),* edited by the Quanzhou Foreign Maritime Museum and the Quanzhou City Institute for Research in the History of Quanzhou (Fuzhou, 1983) (hereinafter cited as '*Symposium*').

[73]*Citang,* the standard expression for a hall or shrine where the Confucian rites in honour of lineage ancestors were performed. Typically of such institutions, in front of one of the Jin halls there were formerly displayed honorific boards inscribed with the names of distinguished or worthy members of the clan.

[74]Huang Tianzhu and Liao Yuanquan, 'An Informal Talk on the Muslim Descendants of the Arabs of the Quanzhou Region and their Inheritance', *Symposium,* p.203.

[75]Their ancestor hall in Chendai, constructed of granite, with a floorplan in the shape of the character for 'Hui' (two concentric rectangles), is still standing; *ibid.*, p.204; see also p.205, where the Ding lineage is traced back to a family from Bukhara, now in Soviet Central Asia. See also 'A Study of the Jin Clan at Chendai', *ibid.*, pp.207-212.

[76]*Ibid.,* p.204. Not all the communities were exclusively lineage-based, for as in ordinary Chinese rural areas, there were mixed villages, where lineages of different surnames and religions coexisted.

[77]Informants stated that in ancestor worship in these clans no paper was burned, implying however that the Muslims did practise some form of ancestral rite; it is possible, however, that the ancestor halls were in fact camouflaged mosques.

In the context of traditional Chinese society, it seems safe to infer that strong lineages of this kind were the delegated agencies of law and government among the Hui exactly as their equivalents were among the Han.

Application of Islamic Law in the Qing Period

When the Qing came to promulgate a new penal code, they largely followed precedent. Thus the core of the *Da Qing Lü,* the original penal code of the dynasty first promulgated in 1646,[78] consisted of the *lü* or statutes of the Ming dynasty including the provisions[79] for resolving possible conflicts between the laws of minorities and others 'outside civilization' and those of the Han majority:[80] within China proper the code was to apply to everyone without exception.[81]

A literal interpretation of this provision would suggest that any further inquiry as to the application of Islamic law would be otiose. That this is not the case, however, is demonstrated by the hard evidence of Islamic customary law which was brought to light within a few years of the overthrow of the dynasty, some 200 years after this provision was re-enacted. Shortly before the collapse of the old order, the imperial government appointed a commission to draw up a new civil code along modern, western lines. One of the commission's initiatives was to order the collection of customs having legal force in each province of China. Although temporarily halted by the Revolution of 1911, the commission continued its work, and although it was never completed, the results were eventually published in unedited form by the Ministry of Justice of the Republic of China in 1930.[82]

---

[78]There were some modifications and additions, and in later editions (after 1740 entitled *Da Qing Lüli),* a gradual reduction in the number of *lü* matched by an ever increasing number of *li* added under the appropriate *lü* to add to, modify or in some instances virtually nullify their effect. On this process, see Bodde and Morris, *Law in Imperial China,* pp.59-75. The text of the code referred to in this paper is taken from *Da Qing Lüli Zengxiu Tongzuan Jicheng (Laws and Regulations of the Great Qing [Dynasty], Enlarged and Revised with Comprehensive Annotations*), Shanghai, 1906.

[79]*Supra,* text at n. 42.

[80]A translation of this lü will be found in Sir G. Staunton, *Ta Tsing Leu Lee; being the Fundamental Laws of the Penal Code of China,* London, 1810, pp. 36-37.

[81]The sole modification to the original text was the inclusion of the words 'who come to submit', taken from the Commentary to the *Ming Code (supra,* text at n. 43) to clarify the meaning of the lü. This is followed, however, by a new sentence making it clear that this rule does not apply in the territories (in 1646 only Mongolia) under the supervision of the Li Fan Yuan (*supra,* text at n. 53), where the Mongolian law was to continue in force. The text is found in *Da Qing Lüli,* 5th *jüan,* p.34a.

[82]*Min-Shang-Shi Xiguan Diaocha Baogaohu (Report of an Inquiry into Customs in Civil and Commercial Matters),* compiled by the Ministry of Judicial Administration of the Republic of China, 1930 (reprinted, Taipei, 1969), 3 vols. with continuous pagination (hereinafter *'Report on Customs'*).

Unwieldy and incomplete[83] as it is,[84] the *Report on Customs* has a number of features worthy of note. In the first place, it was compiled largely, if not exclusively, by legal specialists, in many localities by members of the local judiciary who were professionally involved in the practical application of the law. Secondly, it was avowedly concerned with customs which had legal force, as many of the various individual returns clearly show. Thirdly, doubtless following instructions, those responsible for compiling the reports at the local level in many instances expressly referred to divergences from the lü, that is, the statute law embodied in the *Da Qing Lüli*.[85] These features combine to give the *Report on Customs* a degree of legal authority which is largely if not wholly lacking in the surveys of customs and usages found in local gazetteers and works of ethnography.

With few exceptions, all of the customs explicitly referable to Muslim minorities appear[86] to have been reported from north west China, almost exclusively from the then province of Gansu, part of which has since been incorporated into the new province of Qinghai, and part of which now belongs to the Ningxia Hui Autonomous Region.

The customs reported fall within the area of family law. Five apply to marriage (three to re-marriage of widows), one to adoption and one to guardianship. For the present purpose, two examples of the marriage customs will serve as illustrations.

Of all the rules of Islamic family law, probably the best known in China is the rule which forbids Islamic women to marry unbelievers, a rule which perhaps more than any other continues to have important repercussions in China today. The rule is particularly significant in relation to the principle of traditional Chinese law (now abolished) whereby a woman was deemed to leave her own family on marriage, for Muslims in China from early times frequently married Chinese women. The Islamic rule thus brought about a one-way flow from the Han Chinese into the Islamic sphere.

---

[83]Not all the provinces of China proper made returns (Guangdong for one) and with the exception of Chahar in Mongolia and some of the Manchurian provinces, none of the Inner Asian territories did so.

[84]For a brief description of the *Report on Customs*, see E. Kroker, 'The Concept of Property in Chinese Customary Law', *Transactions of the Asiatic Society of Japan* (3rd Series), 7, 1959, p.123.

[85]Following the Revolution of 1911 the *Da Qing Lü Li* remained temporarily in force as a source solely of civil law until the eventual entry into force of the *Civil Code of the Republic of China* in 1930-1931.

[86]Having regard to the unwieldy nature of the *Report on Customs* and the absence of any analytical index a degree of diffidence is appropriate in relation to any claim to having exhausted the 3,432 individual customs listed in the collection: see Kroker,'The Concept of Property in Chinese Customary Law', p. 125.

A microcosmic illustration of this system in operation is provided by the custom said to have prevailed throughout the former territory of Jehol,[87] described as follows:

> *Marriage between various nationalities*
>
> Beyond the Great Wall, Hans, Manchus, Mongols and Huis live in proximity to each other, and marriages between Hans, Manchus and Mongols now all follow the ceremonies of the Han nationality and there is very little difference between these mixed marriages, which are daily becoming more numerous. However, the barrier which prevents the women of the Hui people from marrying men of the Han nationality remains extremely strict.[88]

Not surprisingly the same rule was stated even more emphatically in the less cosmopolitan environment of Gansu, where it occurs in the context of the discussion of another custom said to have prevailed throughout that province, namely, marriage between persons of the same surname. This appears to represent less the application of Islamic ideas than the disregard of the fundamental rule of surname exogamy in traditional Chinese law.[89]

> *Marriage between persons of the same surname*
>
> Although marriage between persons of the same surname is not permitted by the Code,[90] many of the people in Gansu do not avoid marriages between persons of the same surname even though it is undeniably prohibited by law.
>
> The foregoing custom is stated in accordance with the report of Councillor Liu of the First Chamber of the Superior Court of Gansu Province, based upon examples which have arisen in litigation such as Wang marrying Wang, Li marrying Li, and Zhang marrying Zhang, which are frequently

---

[87]Jehol and its environs formed a part of the old Manchu dominions lying immediately beyond the Great Wall north east of Peking; the extensive imperial estates and hunting lodges made it in a sense the Balmoral of the Qing state. It is now largely comprised in Changde Prefecture, Hebei Province.

[88]*Report on Customs,* Vol. 3, 1804. There is no indication of the authorship of this particular entry.

[89]For the statutory rule see next footnote.

[90]I.e. by lü: see *Da Qing Lüli*, 10th *jüan*, p.26a. The lü is translated in Jamieson, *Chinese Family and Commercial Law,* Shanghai, 1921, p.38: 'If any marriage takes place between persons of the same surname, the principals negotiating the marriage on either side shall be liable to 60 blows and the marriage shall be null and void. The woman shall return to her family and the marriage presents shall be forfeited to Government'. See also Staunton, *Ta Tsing Leu Lee,* p.114 (where the author's comments on the inconvenient results of this rule may be noted) and Boulais, *Manuel du Code Chinois*, Shanghai, 1924, pp.277-278.

> encountered, among others. Furthermore there are a very large number of Hui people in Gansu Province and among the Hui people eight or nine out of ten have the surname Ma. As between Huis and Hans, although there are cases of Han women marrying Hui men, no Hui woman will under any circumstances marry a Han. If Hui people were to avoid marriages to persons of the same surname it would inevitably reach the point where women would have no possibility of marrying any man. It is the impossibility of marriage that has given rise to the countless number of cases of Ma marrying Ma, in compliance with an established practice which cannot be altered.[91]

Another very obvious divergence between Islamic law and the law of traditional China lay in the different attitudes to polygamy. The Islamic rule, enabling a man to have up to four wives at one time, provided that he is able to treat them alike, is quite contrary to traditional Chinese thinking, which always restricted a man to one wife. The fact that the law in effect also allowed a Chinese to take an unlimited member of concubines did not prevent bigamy being subject to criminal penalties. Far from equality as between wives (*qi*) and concubines (*qie*) being encouraged, it was strictly forbidden to confuse the two types of status, which were considered as a matter of law to be quite distinct:

> A wife cannot be degraded to the position of a concubine, nor can a concubine be raised to the position of wife so long as the wife is alive, under a penalty of 100 or 90 blows respectively. If any one marries a wife a second time while the first wife is alive, he shall be liable to 90 blows, and the parties shall be separated.[92]

---

[91]*Report on Customs,* Vol. 3, 1768-1769. It will be noted that there is no suggestion that the Muslim population were responsible for the breach of surname exogamy, merely that they were the main beneficiaries. In fact disregard of this rule was noted by the Board of Punishments as being not unusual among the common people in a case from Hunan decided in 1789, and in some places it had to be disregarded - e.g. in parts of Fujian where almost the whole population bore the surname Lin and an official dispensation was in force. See Boulais, *Manuel du Code Chinois,* p. 281-282.

[92]*Da Qing Lüli,* 10th jüan, p. 13a, lü, as translated in Jamieson,*Chinese Family and Commercial Law,* p.35. Cf. Staunton, *Ta Tsing Leu Lee,* pp.110-111; Boulais, *Manuel du Code Chinois,* 268-269. There was a customary quasi-exception to this rule in the case of man who, being an only son and having one or more paternal uncles without any other male successors, took one or more additional 'wives' to enable two lines of successors to be established in physically separate households (*jiantiao*); but even in this exceptional case the imperial authorities refused to accept the full legal implications of this well established custom and only regarded one of the consorts as a qi. See H. McAleavy, 'Chinese Law in Hong Kong: the Choice of Sources,' in J. N. D. Anderson ed., *Changing Law in Developing Countries,* London, 1963, pp. 262 ff.

In Gansu the Muslims appear to have been able to disregard this rule in favour of their own:

> *The system of polygamy of the Hui religion*[93]
>
> According to the religion of the Hui, a man may mârry four principal wives[94] all whom as regards their title and formalities are of equal status; if he marries a fifth woman, then the fifth and any subsequent [consorts] are called concubines.[95] The concubines cannot have equal status with the principal wives, but where a vacancy occurs among the four principal wives then the fifth [consort] can be promoted to be a principal wife.
>
> The foregoing comes from the report of Councillor Xu of this Commission.[96]

This rule, which seems to have offered the best of both worlds, applied to all the Muslims of Gansu.

Other Sources of Islamic Customary Law

These few passages and others in the *Report on Customs* by no means exhaust the evidence of the operation of Islamic law within the traditional Chinese legal system. There are numerous references to the application of Islamic law scattered in general descriptions of Muslim communities in China. Leaving on one side the older descriptions found in the accounts of Western travellers and missionaries,[97] several recent Chinese studies of national minorities in general and the Islamic minorities in particular contain retrospective studies of minority customs, including customs of legal relevance.[98] Further research might well produce a considerable body of

[93]*Huijiao;* this has been translated literally, but according to the usage of that time Huijiao also stood for Islam in general.

[94]Qi.

[95]Qie.

[96]*Report on Customs,* Vol. 3, p.1791. Words in square brackets supplied.

[97]E.g., P. Dabry de Thiersant, *Le Mahométisme en Chine et dans le Turkestan Oriental,* 2 vols., Paris, 1878, Vol. 2, *passim.* Another potentially important source of information on Islamic Law in North China and Manchuria, largely neglected by Western writers, is represented by the survey data compiled by the research department of the South Manchurian Railway when the latter was controlled by Japan; see Tatsuo Chikusa, 'Succession to Ancestral Sacrifices and Adoption of Heirs to the Sacrifices: As seen from an Inquiry into Customary Institutions in Manchuria', in D.C. Buxbaum ed., *Chinese Family Law and Social Change in Historical and Comparative Perspective,* Seattle, 1978, pp.151-152.

[98]E.g. Yan Ruxian ed., *Zhongguo Shaoshu Minzu Hunyin Jiating (Marriage and Family among the Minority Nationalities of China)* Peking, 1986, pp. 80-101, 110-122, 133-156,

evidence of the prevalence of Islamic legal notions in many parts of China in the first half of the 20th century.

The Modern Fate of Islamic Customary Law

Republican China: Pluralism Abolished

Dr Sun Yat Sen's celebrated three-stage *Programme of National Reconstruction* included provision for the assistance of the national minorities towards self-government and self-determination, but only in the third stage, which assumed the completion of a long (second) stage of 'political tutelage'. This point had not been reached when Nationalist rule was extinguished in the Chinese mainland in 1949.[99] Although in the first Nationalist Constitution[100] Article 2 provided that 'All persons who, according to law, enjoy the nationality of the Republic of China shall be citizens of the Republic of China', and Article 6 provided for equality before the law of all such citizens, 'irrespective of sex, race, religion or caste', with the exception of Tibet and Mongolia, which were not regarded as provinces of China proper, the national minorities as such were in effect largely neglected in that document.

Thus the Nationalists only evolved a policy of special treatment for those minorities, including Muslim minorities, which occupied the frontier areas of the country. Minority groups such as the Hui, living amongst the Han majority in China proper (or among majorities of other races in Mongolia or Tibet), in theory at least, formed part of the ordinary citizenry, to be assimilated in the course of time.

This policy of assimilation is echoed in the legal development of the period. The modernization of Chinese criminal law and procedures in the last days of the Qing and the early years of the Republic gradually brought about the abolition of the whole structure of discriminatory penal law,[101] including

---

167-172, and 188-192; each of these studies is followed by an epilogue suggesting that most of the customs described have been extensively changed since 1949. See also Huan Qiurun, 'An Informal Discussion of the Customs of the Hui Nationality at Quanzhou', *Symposium*, pp.177-200.

99For an account of some aspects of the political life of the Hui community in Taiwan after 1949, see Pillsbury, 'Factionalism Observed', pp.241-272.

100*Provisional Constitution of the Republic of China for the Period of Political Tutelage*, promulgated by the National Government of the Republic of China, 1st June 1931; text in William Tung, *Political Institutions of Modern China*, The Hague, 1964, pp.344-349.

101A major step in this direction was taken with the abolition of the special privileges of the members of the 'banners', descendants of Manchu, Mongolian and Chinese troops who had fought on the side of the Manchus against the Ming. The rule against intermarriage of bannermen with ordinary Chinese was removed in 1902, and all the legal and jurisdictional privileges of the banners (long a source of Han discontent) were abolished in 1907. See M.J. Meijer, *The Introduction of Modern Criminal Law in China*, Hong Kong, 2nd ed. 1967, pp. 44-45 (hereinafter *Introduction*).

those directed specifically at the Hui,[102] and the introduction of the first of a series of criminal codes based on modern European principles.[103]

The codification and modernization of the civil law was a longer process, chiefly as a result of the strong conservative forces opposed to any weakening of the Confucian family system. It was only brought to fruition[104] after the accession to power of the Nationalist Party (Kuomintang).[105] In the earlier drafts prepared by the codification commission which was established by imperial decree in 1907 and continued its work after 1911, stress was placed on making allowance for the diversity of customs in China.[106] Not surprisingly, however, having regard to the spirit of the age and to the European sources from which the codifiers increasingly drew their inspiration, the eventual emphasis in the *Civil Code* was on rules of universal application. While Articles 1 and 2[107] contained provisions enabling the courts to fill the gaps in the law by reference to custom, these provisions certainly did not extend to the wholesale incorporation of minority legal systems into the *Civil Code*.[108] Only in the fields of commercial law and land law was a wider application allowed to local custom.[109]

102In another of the steps towards revision of the criminal law, in the *Qinding Xianxing Xinglü (Imperially Promulgated Criminal Laws at Present in Force)*, promulgated by the Imperial Government in 1910, and essentially a revision of the *Da Qing Lüli*, the section on *Huawairen fanzui* ('Offences committed by people outside civilization' - *supra*, n. 80) was changed to *Mengu ji ruguoji* or 'Offences committed by Mongols and [People who have] Acquired Chinese Nationality', the last term referring to non-Han peoples within the borders: see Meijer, *Introduction*, p.55. The abandonment of the ancient term did not signal a change in the formal legal policy of uniform application of law dating from 1368, however.

103*Provisional Criminal Code of the Republic of China*, promulgated 10th March 1912 (translated text, Peking, 1919).

104Book I (General Principles) of the *Civil Code of the Republic of China* came into force on 10th October 1929; Books II (Obligations) and III (Rights over Things) came into force on 5th May 1930, and Books IV (Family) and V (Succession) entered into force on 5th May 1931. For the text in English see *infra*, n. 109.

105For details of the codification process, see J. Escarra, *Le Droit Chinois*, Peking, 1936, pp.106-113, 168 et seq., and also M.H. van der Valk, *An Outline of Modern Chinese Family Law*, Peking, 1939, Chapters V-XI.

106Van der Valk, *An Outline of Modern Chinese Family Law*, p.25. This policy was the *raison d'être* of the *Report on Customs* (*supra*, n. 82).

107'*Article 1*: In civil matters if there is no provision of law applicable to a case, the case shall be decided according to custom. If there is no such custom, the case shall be decided in accordance with the general principles of law.' '*Article 2:* A custom is applicable in civil matters only when it is not contrary to public order or good morals'

108Although Escarra (*Le Droit Chinois*, pp.125-127) and others emphasize the importance of custom in the eyes of the successive codification commissions, the jurisprudence of the Chinese courts both before and after the adoption of the *Civil Code* discloses a more negative view of attempts to enforce customary rules, and several examples can be found in which long established customs in the fields of family law and succession were rejected as unlawful in that they contravened either the old statute law or the *Civil Code*. None of the prominently reported cases appear to have concerned Islamic customs, but there is no indication that they would not have suffered the same fate. Not too much significance should be attached to the apparent

Thus it may be seen that the formal Republican system of substantive law made no provision for minority communities and largely ignored the existence of substantial segments of the population who continued to live in accordance with their own traditional laws. That Islamic law continued largely to prevail among the Muslim peoples of Chinese Inner Asia,[110] as Mongolian and Tibetan law prevailed in other regions, was due to the political dislocation of China rather than to any constitutional or legal provision.[111]

The Islamic Minorities in Communist China

One of the foremost political lessons the Communist leaders learned during the prosecution of their far-ranging campaigns against both the Nationalists and the Japanese was the value of good relations with the diverse local populations of the regions through which they passed, many of them non-Han. This realization, coupled with the application of Marxist social analysis, according to which some of the more 'backward' minorities were still living in the 'feudal' or 'slave' stages of societal development, with economic bases and social superstructures different from those of the Han, necessitated the development of a much more elaborate policy towards these groups than that which had been adopted by the Kuomintang.[112] This was set out in various provisions of the *Common Programme of the Chinese People's*

---

failure of the Muslims to test the definition of custom in the Republican *Civil Code* in the courts, however, for it must be remembered that even in the brief heyday of the Nationalist regime the effect of its legislation beyond the confines of the Yangtze valley and the coastal cities was very limited; much of the country and most of the Muslim population was still only nominally subject to the new laws. See H. McAleavy, 'Some Aspects of Marriage and Divorce in Communist China', in J.N.D. Anderson ed., *Family Law in Asia and Africa,* London, 1968, p.75.

[109]For the rejection of many of the numerous exceptions in favour of local custom suggested by the Commission for the Codification of the Civil Law in the 1925 Peking Draft of the *Civil Code,* see the introduction to the semi-official translation of the Civil Code by Dr. Foo Ping-sheung, the Chairman of the Commission under the Kuomintang, *The Civil Code of the Republic of China,* Shanghai, 1931, p. xv-xvi.

[110]Escarra wrote in 1936 of Xinjiang as having '... une très forte population musulmane obéissant dans une certaine mesure au droit coranique ...'; *Le Droit Chinois,* p.244. The attempts to establish an independent Islamic republic in Eastern Turkestan in 1933-4 and in the 1940s as a reaction to nationalist attempts at the assimilation of the Muslim populations in Xinjiang is beyond the scope of the present study: see for a brief account Newby, 'The Pure and True Religion in China', pp.932-933.

[111]The law on conflicts of laws provided only for international conflicts; the existence of internal conflicts of laws was not formally admitted; *Ordinance on the Application of Laws,* promulgated 5th August 1918; text in *China Law Review*, 1, 1922, p. 61; Escarra, *Le Droit Chinois,* p.244.

[112]In the draft constitutions of the Soviet Republic of China in 1931 and 1934 there were even provisions for self-determination for the national minorities, with an option of secession; see Newby, 'The Pure and True Religion in China', p.935.

Political Consultative Conference.[113] After designating the national minorities as one of the components of the 'Chinese people's democratic united front' in the Preamble, the text refers to 'the democratic dictatorship led by the working class ... uniting all nationalities in China' (Article 1); it also calls for freedom of religious belief among other freedoms, and provides for equal rights and duties for all nationalities (Article 9).

There was also a provision which abolished the whole legal system of the former Republic of China in the following terms:-

> *Article 17.* All laws, decrees and judicial systems of the Kuomintang reactionary government which oppressed the people shall be abolished. Laws and decrees protecting the people shall be enacted, and the people's judicial system shall be established.

A whole chapter of the *Common Programme,* consisting of four articles, set out the policy of the new state towards national minorities. For present purposes it is necessary to note Article 53:

> *Article 53.* All national minorities shall have freedom to develop their dialects and languages, to preserve or reform their traditions, customs and religious beliefs. The People's Government shall assist the masses of the people of all national minorities to develop their political, economic, cultural and educational construction work.[114]

This formal link between the religious beliefs of the national minorities and their freedom to preserve or reform their traditions and customs in theory, at least, was of particular significance to the Muslim minorities. The legal association between national minority autonomy and religion did not last long, however, for it was omitted from the *Constitution of the People's Republic of China* which appeared in 1954, although freedom of religious belief was still one of the fundamental rights accorded to individual citizens.[115] Nevertheless, up to the time of the leftist movement associated with the 'Anti-

---

[113]Adopted by the First Plenary Session of the CPPCC, 29th September 1949. The *Common Programme* served both as a manifesto and as one of the components of the provisional constitution of the new People's Republic until the adoption of a more formal constitution in 1954. For the text see *FLHB,* Vol. 1, 1949-1950, pp.17-27; for an English translation, see A.P. Blaustein, *Fundamental Legal Documents of Communist China,* South Hackensack, N.J., 1962, pp.34-53.

[114]*FLHB,* Vol. 1, 1949-50, pp.26-27; Blaustein, *Fundamental Legal Documents of Communist China,* p.51.

[115]*Constitution of the People's Republic of China,* promulgated 20th September 1954, *FGHB,* Vol. 1, 1954, p.4; English translation in Blaustein, *Fundamental Legal Documents of Communist China,* p.1 (hereinafter 'the Constitution of 1954'), Article 88.

Rightist Campaign' in 1957[116] and the 'Great Leap Forward' in the following year, a policy of qualified religious liberty prevailed in relation to the national minorities.

In legal terms it appeared to bear immediate fruit in several items of legislation, of which the most important was the law governing the Land Reform, which was a cornerstone of early communist policy, although it was not applicable at first in autonomous areas. Mosques and waqf lands, i.e. those dedicated to the religious and charitable purposes of Islam, were given exceptional treatment, as may be seen from the following provision:

> *Article 3*. The rural land belonging to ancestral shrines, temples, monasteries, churches, schools and organizations, and other land owned by public bodies shall be requisitioned. But local people's governments should devise appropriate measures to solve the financial problems facing such schools, orphanages, homes for the aged, hospitals, etc., that depend on the income from the above-mentioned land for their maintenance.
>
> Land owned by mosques may be retained according to circumstances with the consent of the Moslems residing in the places where such mosques are situated.[117]

Other legislation followed which was designed to alleviate Muslim grievances, particularly in respect of dietary restrictions. In December 1950 for example, the Government issued a general order to all provinces to remit the slaughter tax on animals killed for the three major annual Muslim festivals.[118] A few years later the Ministry of Commerce issued special

---

[116]The 'Anti-Rightist Campaign' against 'bourgeois rightists' was initiated on 8th June 1957 in response to the sharp criticisms of the Communist Party made by many intellectuals and non-Party people when, during the period named after Mao Zetong's slogan 'let a hundred flowers blossom and a hundred schools of thought contend', they were invited by the Party to help it to rectify its shortcomings.

[117]*Law on Land Reform of the People's Republic of China,* promulgated and entered into force 30th June 1950 (text in *FLHB,* Vol. 1, 1949-1950, p.43; English translation in Blaustein, *Fundamental Legal Documents of Communist China,* p.276). The exception in favour of mosques and waqf land was repeated in various local land reform regulations, but this did not prevent some serious abuses occurring at the hands of local Party officials - whether out of excessive zeal or anti-Muslim prejudice, or a combination of the two, is unclear. For an account of an uprising in Gansu in 1952 following distribution of land said by officials to have been 'voluntarily' surrendered by a Muslim religious community, see M. Rafiq Khan, *Islam in China,* New Delhi, 1963, p. 68. For other instances of confiscation of waqf land, see *ibid.*, p.80 (where the author draws comparisons with Soviet policy in Central Asia in 1928-9), also pp.95, 99, 110, 118 and 131. According to Khan, before 1949 'almost every mosque had waqf property dedicated to it'.

[118]*General Order of the Government Administration Council that the Collection of Slaughter Tax should be Remitted and that Standards of Inspection should be Relaxed in respect of the Slaughter of Cattle and Sheep by People of the Islamic Faith for their own Consumption on the Three Major Festivals,* 2nd December 1950, (text in *FLHB,* Vol. 1, 1949-1950, p.185).

regulations to protect and encourage the trade of small Muslim merchants in *halal* foods and to ensure that such foods were supplied to Muslim consumers.[119] Legislation of this kind was re-enacted at the local level in areas where there was a substantial Muslim population, and was not confined to areas of national autonomy.[120] The intention was no doubt to ensure that the national legislation was made known and carried out at the local level,[121] but it is far from clear that this objective was achieved.[122]

Despite these conciliatory gestures, Islam, in common with the other religions with a following in China, soon began to feel the effects of government by a party committed to the atheistic beliefs of dialectical materialism as the Communist Party's policy towards religion evolved from control and restriction to persecution. The details of this policy and its social results are beyond the scope of this article. During the first stage, however, it should be noted that the China Islamic Association was formed in 1952 as a means of organizing 'patriotic Muslims' under Party leadership as part of the 'united front of all patriotic forces', which was the main vehicle through which the Party both enlisted the support of non-communists in the early days of the People's Republic and sought to exercise control over them while eliminating other forms of religious organization. Having regard to the inherent strength and prevalence of the loosely organized tariqa brotherhoods both in China proper and in Xinjiang before 1949, not to mention the sectarian rivalries of the Old Teaching and the New Teaching, it is very doubtful how far the second of these objectives could ever have been achieved.

Relations between the State and the religious minorities were conducted at first through the State Commission for National Minority Affairs and its local branches, but with the establishment of the Bureau of Religious Affairs under

---

[119]*Instruction of the Ministry of Commerce of the People's Republic of China regarding Arrangements for Muslim Small Traders and making Proper Allowance for the Customs of [Minority] Nationalities in Food Supply Work,* issued 15th July 1955 (text in Shi Yun, *Minzu Falü Fagui Gaishu (A General Review of National Minority Laws and Regulations)*, Peking, 1988, p.156-157. Note also an instruction dated 26th September 1955 requiring slaughter to be carried out with a knife by an ahong, or if none were available, by a Muslim worker, *ibid.*

[120]E.g., the Shanghai Municipal Government enacted regulations exempting animals slaughtered for the three major festivals from tax: *Procedures of the Municipality of Shanghai for Remission of Slaughter Tax and Relaxation of Standards of Inspection for the Slaughter of Sheep and Cattle by People of the Islamic Faith for their own Consumption on the Three Major Festivals,* 16th October 1951, *Shanghaishi Fagui Guizhang Huibian (1949-1985) (A Collection of Legislation and Regulations of the Municipality of Shanghai 1949-1985)* Shanghai, 1988, p. 205.

[121]Some of this legislation was of a surprisingly detailed kind and required the cooperation of departments not normally regarded as being directly involved in religious affairs. For example, the Yangtze Navigation Bureau under the Ministry of Communications issued regulations requiring all passenger vessels of more than 500 tons operating below Yichang to be equipped with dining saloons, complete with their own stoves and utensils, to meet the needs of Hui passengers; see 'Respecting the Customs of the National Minorities: the Yangtze Regional Navigation Bureau Issues Regulations Regarding the Dietary Customs of Hui People' *(Xinwen Ribao) (Daily News),* Shanghai, 5th August 1951.

[122]*Supra,* n. 117.

the State Council,[123] responsibility for Islam was placed under the joint administration of the local departments of minority affairs and religious affairs.[124] By 1957 these arrangements had aroused sufficient discontent to add Muslim voices to the widespread criticisms of the regime during the 'Hundred Flowers' period.[125]

In 1958 the China Islamic Association was dissolved and there began an era of intermittent religious suppression and persecution which only closed with the end of the Cultural Revolution in 1976.[126] Moreover, during the Cultural Revolution itself, the concept of national autonomy became little more than an empty shell,[127] and the senior Party leaders identified with the policy (particularly those who were themselves members of national minority races) disappeared from sight for a number of years.[128] Only with the fall of the Gang of Four in 1976 were the constitutional protection of minorities and the national autonomy system, as well as qualified freedom of religion, gradually restored.[129]

The current legal basis for the policy towards national minorities in general and for the autonomy of the areas of national autonomy within what is defined as a unitary state in particular is set out in Article 4 and in Articles 112-122 of the *Constitution of the People's Republic of China.*[130] Article 4 provides as follows:

> *Article 4*. All nationalities in the People's Republic of China are equal. The state protects the lawful rights and interests of the minority nationalities and upholds and develops a relationship of equality, unity and mutual assistance among all of China's nationalities. Discrimination against and oppression

---

[123]This is believed to have occurred in 1954 but the statutory basis for the Bureau has not been traced.

[124]*Notice of the State Council Regarding the Management and Organization of Religious Work,* 1st December 1955 (*FGHB* Vol. 2, 1955, p. 111), Paragraph 1.

[125]*Supra*, n. 116. See for example complaints regarding the Government's failure to give promised assistance for the upkeep of mosques, reported in the *Guangming Ribao (Guangming Daily),* 25th May 1957, cited by Khan, *Islam in China,* p.75.

[126]For an unfavourable account of developments up to 1962, see Khan, *Islam in China, passim;* also Kao Hao-jen, *The Imam's Account,* Hong Kong, 1960.

[127]In the *Constitution of the People's Republic of China* promulgated 17th January 1975 ('the Constitution of 1975'), it was provided that national autonomous areas 'exercise autonomy in accordance with law' and that minorities can use their own languages (Articles 4, and 24). (For the English text see J.E.-P. Wang ed., *Selected Legal Documents of the People's Republic of China,* Vol. 1, Arlington, Va., 1976, p. 63).

[128]Notable examples are the late Panchen Lama (Bainqen Erdini Qoigyi Gyaincaia) of Tibet, and Ulanfu, a Mongolian who prior to being purged in 1967 was a Vice-premier, Minister of the Commission on Nationalities and member of the Central Committee of the Party.

[129]*Constitution of the People's Republic of China,* promulgated 5th March 1978 ('the Constitution of 1978') (English text in J. E.-P. Wang ed., *Selected Legal Documents of the People's Republic of China,* Vol. 2, Washington D.C., 1979, p. 125), Articles 4 and 38-40.

[130]Promulgated 4th December 1982 (hereinafter 'the Constitution of 1982') (Text in *FGHB* [1982], p. 1, English text in *Laws*, Vol. 1, p. 1).

> of any nationality are prohibited; any act which undermines the unity of the nationalities or instigates division is prohibited.
> The state assists areas inhabited by minority nationalities in accelerating their economic and cultural development according to the characteristics and needs of the various minority nationalities.
> Regional autonomy is practised in areas where people of minority nationalities live in concentrated communities; in these areas organs of self-government are established to exercise the power of autonomy. All national autonomous areas are integral parts of the People's Republic of China.
> All nationalities have the freedom to use and develop their own spoken and written languages and to preserve or reform their own folkways and customs.

Among the powers granted to the 'organs of self-government' of the national autonomous areas by Part VI of Chapter III of the Constitution of 1982, is a limited power of legislation:

> *Article 116*. The people's congresses of national autonomous areas have the power to enact ordinances on the exercise of autonomy and other special ordinances in the light of the political, economic and cultural characteristics of the nationality or nationalities in the areas concerned. The ordinances on the exercise of autonomy and other special ordinances of autonomous regions shall be submitted to the Standing Committee of the National People's Congress for approval before they go into effect. Those of autonomous prefectures and counties shall be submitted to the standing committees of the people's congresses of provinces or autonomous regions for approval before they go into effect, and they shall be reported to the Standing Committee of the National People's Congress as a matter of record.[131]

[131] This provision (foreshadowed by Article 70 of the Constitution of 1954 and by Article 39 of the Constitution of 1978, but omitted in the Constitution of 1975) may be compared with Article 100, which sets out the legislative powers of the people's congresses of provinces and municipalities (such as Peking and Shanghai) which are directly under the Central Government, and which '... may adopt local legislation *(fagui)* which must not contravene the Constitution, the statutes or administrative rules and regulations, and they shall report such local regulations to the Standing Committee of the National People's Congress as a matter of record.'

In Article 19 of the *Law of the People's Republic of China on Regional National Autonomy* enacted two years later, the provisions of Article 116 were re-enacted almost word for word without further elaboration.[132]

Freedom of religion was also gradually restored.[133] Article 36 of the Constitution of 1982 now provides:

> *Article 36.* Citizens of the People's Republic of China enjoy freedom of religious belief.
> No state organ, public organization or individual may compel citizens to believe in, or not to believe in, any religion; nor may they discriminate against citizens who believe in, or do not believe in, any religion.
> The state protects normal religious activities. No one may make use of religion to engage in activities that disrupt public order, impair the health of citizens or interfere with the educational system of the state.
> Religious bodies and religious affairs are not subject to any foreign domination.

Since 1978 many features of the religious and social life of the Muslim populations have in fact been restored. Mosques have been repaired and reopened, the Qur'an has been reprinted after many years of being unavailable, some seminaries have been re-opened and festivals are once more publicly celebrated.[134] Numerous books on Islamic subjects have been published and Islamic studies are now pursued in some universities.[135] A number of Muslims from various nationalities are once again permitted to make the pilgrimage to Mecca.[136]

---

[132]Adopted at the Second Session of the Sixth National People's Congress and promulgated 31st May 1984, came into force 1st October 1984. (Text in *FGHB* [1984], p. 1; English translation in *Laws,* Vol. 2, p. 87). Thus although this law contains significant provisions in relation, e.g., to economic development, it appears to add nothing to the legal concept of autonomy as such.

[133]Compare the Constitution of 1975 (no mention of religion or religious freedom) with that of 1978, Article 46 of which provides: 'Citizens enjoy freedom to believe in religion and freedom not to believe in religion and to propagate atheism'.

[134]For a further examination of some of these developments, see Newby, 'The Pure and True Religion in China', pp.938 ff..

[135]The revival of the study of Islamic (and other) theology was marked by a conference held at Kunming in 1979; see G. Braybrooke, 'Recent Developments in Chinese Social Science, 1977-79', *China Quarterly,* 79, 1979, pp.604-605.

[136]These include a leading member of the Communist Party of Hui nationality, Haji Hussein Hei Boli, currently Deputy Party Secretary and Chairman of the People's Congress of the Ningxia Hui Autonomous Region; see A. Barker, 'Where Islam, Marxism meet', Reuter report in *South China Morning Post,* 11th September 1985. Mr. Hei's evidently relaxed attitude to the apparent conflict between the dictates of his Islamic faith and his Marxist conscience is shared by a number of Party members in Ningxia and possibly elsewhere, and has been attributed by some outsiders to the need to minimize overt ideological conflicts in order to attract foreign investment from Islamic countries; *ibid.*

The China Islamic Association was reorganized in 1980 and has resumed its function of acting as an intermediary between the Party and the people. Something of the flavour of its activities emerges from an account of a meeting of the committee of its Xinjiang constituent, the Xinjiang Islamic Association, in Urumqi in April 1982:

> Through the study of the party's religious policies, the participants in the meeting further distinguished between legal and illegal religious activities. They expressed their determination to give full play to the role of the association, do well in the democratic management of the mosques by Muslims themselves, and channel the religious activities into the right course as allowed by policies and laws, and properly handle the relationships among the religious people and the relationship between religious believers and nonbelievers.
> Responsible comrades of the autonomous regional Chinese Communist Party (CCP) committee, the Standing Committee of the regional people's congress, regional people's government and the regional CPPCC visited the delegates to the meeting.
>
> Ismail Amat, secretary of the regional CCP committee and chairman of the regional people's government, spoke at the meeting. In his speech, he emphasized the party's religious policies. He particularly stressed: 'Respecting and protecting the freedom of religious belief is by no means a temporary expediency but the party's basic policy on the religion issue.' He said: 'We must strictly distinguish between legal and illegal religious activities as well as between religious activities and feudal superstitious activities. We must protect normal religious activities and curb all illegal religious activities. We must deal blows at all violations of law, crimes and counter-revolutionary sabotage carried out under the cloak of religion.'[137]

Some of the 'illegal religious activities' to which Amat was referring were no doubt of a grave nature, for there had been serious anti-Chinese rioting in Kashgar in 1981,[138] and an armed uprising is said to have taken place in one of the rural counties of Xinjiang in the early 1980s.[139] Other

---

[137] 'Ismail Amat Addresses Xinjiang Islamic Meeting', translation of broadcast from Urumqi in Mandarin, 26th April 1982, FBIS-China Report - No. PSM-302, 20th May 1982, p.106.

[138] Andrew Roche, 'Muslims warned in Xinjiang', Reuter report in *South China Morning Post,* 11th August 1988. Since this paper was completed (February 1990) there have been reports of serious clashes between Muslims and government forces in Xinjiang.

[139] *Ibid.* With tens of thousands of refugees from Xinjiang living in Turkey as well as Soviet Central Asia the Chinese authorities are believed to be particularly sensitive to disorders in Xinjiang, while surrounding them with a blanket of secrecy.

'illegal religious activities' would doubtless embrace those Islamic marriage and divorce practices which once again have been specifically prohibited.

Developments in Family Law among the Muslims since 1949

Some of the principal developments in the family law of the People's Republic as it affects the Muslim minorities have already been adverted to above. It has been seen that although Article 27 of the Marriage Law of 1950 permitted variations in the national law to be made in respect of national minorities, the legislative powers of Muslim autonomous areas had been used more to strengthen the restrictions on fundamental Islamic marriage rules rather than to accommodate them, at least in relation to polygamy and talaq divorce.[140]

In respect of other rules of Islamic Law the authorities found it prudent in the early 1950s to tread much more carefully. In relation to the customary prohibition on the marriage of Hui women to Hans, for example, the principle of freedom of marriage, though constantly asserted as a fundamental principle of the Marriage Law of 1950, was applied very much along the lines suggested by Wang Huizu some 150 years earlier,[141] namely on the basis of expediency. Where necessary it was to be sacrificed in favour of national unity.

Thus in 1951 the Supreme People's Court instructed the East China Branch Court[142] that although in places where small groups of Hui were living a mixed marriage was possible provided that the head of the Hui woman's family and the Muslim community had no objection, the principle of freedom of marriage for men and women could not be 'mechanically enforced' and must where necessary yield to the principle of racial harmony, at least until such time as the minority peoples had 'attained a higher degree of consciousness'. The courts should thus uphold the objections of Muslims to the marriages of their daughters in such cases.[143]

The fact that objections on the part of the Hui people in East China (an area of the country where fairly small groups of Hui are to be found scattered over several provinces) reached the courts in numbers sufficient to require such a ruling suggests that the customary ban on inter-marriage must have

---

[140]*Supra,* text at n.11.

[141]*Supra,* text at n. 60.

[142]During the initial years of the People's Republic the country was temporarily divided into six large regions, in each of which a branch of the Supreme People's Court functioned.

[143]*Instructive Response of the Supreme People's Court of the Central People's Government Regarding the Problem of Intermarriage of People of Minority Races and People of the Han Race,* 22nd January 1951, in *A Selection of Materials on the Marriage Law of the People's Republic of China,* Vol. 1, Peking, 1982, pp.163-164. Parts of the request for the branch court's opinion stated in the request for this ruling, with which the Supreme Court agreed, are translated in Meijer, *Marriage Law,* p.248. See also the translation in M.H. Van der Valk, 'Documents Concerning Conflicts of Laws in Matters of Marriage in Communist China', *Nederlands Tijdschrift voor Internationaal Recht,* 8, 1961, p. 323.

been a major obstacle to the implementation of the principle of freedom of marriage in areas where much larger Muslim communities predominated. It is thus not surprising to find that in Gansu attempts to assert the principle of free marriage were given even shorter shrift, as illustrated by the following rescript of the Supreme People's Court in 1956:

> To the Superior People's Court of Gansu Province:
> Our court has received the letter from Hu Xiuqin[144] inquiring about 'the problem of intermarriage between Huis and Hans' which was forwarded by the Intermediate People's Court of Yinchuan Prefecture[145] in your province. Our opinion is as follows: in dealing with this question it is necessary to adopt the principle of respecting the habits and customs of the minority nationalities for the benefit of national unity. We hereby return the original letter to you, with the request that you pass it on to the Intermediate People's Court of Yinchuan Prefecture with the reply that they must patiently persuade Hu Xiuqin to think over her own problem on the basis of conforming to the nationalities policy of the Party and State and to the habits and customs of the nationalities of that area.[146]

With the advent of leftist policies in the national minority areas the policy of compromise in this as in other respects was brought to an abrupt halt for some twenty years.[147]

Following the end of the Cultural Revolution a new Marriage Law was enacted in 1980[148] and a Law of Succession in 1985.[149] The Marriage Law of 1980 contains a provision along similar lines to Article 27 of the 1950 law to enable 'adaptations or supplementary provisions' to be made in accordance with 'the specific conditions of the local nationalities in regard to marriage and family' in autonomous areas.[150] Once again, however, notwithstanding a

---

144 It seems clear from the characters Xiuqin ('Elegant Lute') that the writer was a woman.

145 The city of Yinchuan is now the capital of the Ningxia Hui Autonomous Region, which was established by resolution of the National People's Congress on 15th July 1957 (*FGHB*, Vol. 6, 1957, pp. 187-188).

146 *Official letter of Reply of the Supreme People's Court Regarding the Problem of 'Intermarriage Between Huis and Hans'*, 25th August 1956, No. 8436, in *A Selection of Materials on the Marriage Law,* p.65.

147 For the 'disgrace' of mixed marriages in breach of Islamic law in 1958, see Khan, *Islam in China,* p.80; on the change in policy on this point see Meijer, *Marriage Law,* p.250.

148 *Supra,* n. 9.

149 *Law of Succession of the People's Republic of China,* promulgated 10th April 1985, in force 1st October 1985 (*FGHB* [1985], p.1, English text in *Laws,* Vol. 2, p.169).

150 '*Article 36.* The people's congresses of national autonomous areas and their standing committees may formulate certain adaptations or supplementary provisions in keeping with the

climate apparently more favourable to Islamic beliefs at the time when the new law was passed, the supplementary statutes enacted pursuant to this provision by the two autonomous regions with Muslim populations, far from accommodating Islamic law, have sought to suppress it. Before the Marriage Law of 1980 was even in force the Xinjiang legislature passed the *Supplementary Regulations of the Xinjiang Uighur Autonomous Region for the Implementation of the Marriage Law of the People's Republic of China ('the Xinjiang Marriage Regulations')*.[151] Notwithstanding the requirement of equality for all races in Articles 4 and 33 of the Constitution of 1982, the *Xinjiang Marriage Regulations* only apply to members of national minorities in Xinjiang (Article 10).[152]

Some six months later a comparable set of regulations applicable to the Hui and to other minority peoples was introduced in Ningxia.[153]

Under Article 3 of both regulations it is provided that persons related by blood up to the third degree of kinship as prescribed by the Marriage Law of 1980 may not marry.[154]

---

principles of this Law and in the light of the specific conditions of the local nationalities in regard to marriage and family. Provisions formulated by autonomous prefectures and autonomous counties must be submitted to the standing committee of the people's congress of the relevant province or autonomous region for approval. Provisions formulated by autonomous regions must be submitted to the Standing Committee of the National People's Congress as a matter of record.' A similar provision appears in the Law of Succession *(supra,* n. 149), Article 25 of which permits autonomous areas to enact 'adaptive or supplementary provisions' ... 'in accordance with the principles of this Law and the actual practices of the local nationality or nationalities with regard to property inheritance'. No regulations made under this provision have yet come to light.

[151] Adopted by the regional people's congress on 14th December of 1980 to come into force on 1st January 1981 (text in *Zhongguo Falü Nianjian 1987 (Law Yearbook of China 1987)* Peking, 1987, p. 494; translation in *China Law Yearbook 1987,* First English Edition, London, 1989, p. 333). See also Huang Dongyuan, 'The Xinjiang Uighur Autonomous Region Issues Supplementary Regulations for the Enforcement of the Marriage Law', *Guangming Ribao (Guangming Daily),* 19th January 1981. These regulations presumably replace those of 1952, although there is no mention of repeal of the latter.

[152] Article 2 provides, as in the past, for the reduction by 2 years of the higher minimum ages for marriage for both men and women prescribed by the Marriage Law of 1980, so that for Xinjiang minority peoples the ages of marriage are 20 and 18 respectively. It is also provided by Article 9 that planned childbirth is not to be promoted among members of national minorities. This policy was reversed in 1988.

[153] The *Supplementary Regulations of the Ningxia Hui Autonomous Region for the Implementation of the Marriage Law of the People's Republic of China,* adopted by the regional people's congress, 15th June 1981 ('the *Ningxia Marriage Regulations*') (text in *Law Yearbook of China 1987 (supra,* n. 151), p. 495; translation in *China Law Yearbook 1987,* p.334). As in the *Xinjiang Marriage Regulations,* Article 2 provided for the relaxation of the ages of marriage for both sexes, but there was no exemption from the compulsory birth control measures applicable to the Han population.

[154] There was no equivalent provision in the Xinjiang regulations of 1952. In Ningxia the operation of the rule was suspended for 2 years up to 1st January 1983. There is no indication of the status of a marriage celebrated in breach of the national rule between 1st January 1981 (when the Marriage Law of 1980 came into force) and 15th June 1981 (when the *Ningxia Marriage Regulations* came into force).

It does not seem to have been thought necessary in 1980 to repeat the 1952 prohibitions of bigamy and concubinage. On the other hand, although in the *Xinjiang Marriage Regulations* as in the earlier legislation it is provided that people may have a religious ceremony of marriage, it is now laid down that this may not be a substitute for the proper procedure of registration (Articles 6 and 7). Article 4 of the Ningxia legislation is to the same effect. Divorces by talaq are also once again prohibited in Xinjiang (Article 6) but not in Ningxia.

By Article 7 of the *Xinjiang Marriage Regulations* the 'interference of religion in marriage or family [affairs]' is forbidden. At first sight, this may appear to prohibit the parents of Muslim girls from preventing the marriage of their daughters to non-Muslims, but it is doubtful whether the wording of the article is clear enough to have this effect, particularly when contrasted with the wording of Article 4, which provides more specifically that widows are to have 'freedom to re-marry' and that no one else may interfere with this freedom on any pretext.[155]

The first part of Article 6 of the *Ningxia Marriage Regulations* provides:

> *Article 6.* No person shall interfere with a voluntary marriage between a man and a woman one of whom is of the Hui nationality and the other is of a different nationality.

This rule appears to negate the effect of the decision of the Supreme People's Court in the case of Hu Xiuqin,[156] suggesting that a considerable effort must have been made in Ningxia to overcome the old custom.

The second part of Article 6 also deals with a problem on which the Ministry of Justice had previously given a ruling to the People's Court of Qinghai Province, namely the question of the nationality to be given to the children of marriages between Huis and other races:

> The nationality of the children of such a marriage until such time as they become adults shall be determined by their parents but when they are adults shall be determined by the children themselves.[157]

---

155 Judging by the wording of Article 4 of the earlier Xinjiang provisions of 1952, this provision seemed to be aimed at specific customs of the Khalkhas (Kirghiz) and Kazakhs, rather than at any general rule of Islamic law, but there is a similar provision in Article 5 of the *Ningxia Marriage Regulations*.

156 *Supra*, text at n. 146.

157 *Ningxia Marriage Regulations*, Article 6.

In this case, however, the rule laid down by the *Ningxia Marriage Regulations* follows rather than reverses the ruling previously made by the Ministry of Justice.[158]

Although the re-enactment of the local marriage regulations after the entry into force of the Marriage Law of 1980 may suggest that some of the traditional family institutions (based largely on Islamic law) which they seek to prohibit were in fact still very much alive at that date, there is no doubt that the legislation of these two autonomous regions, ostensibly catering for Muslim populations, is designed to restrict the operation of Islamic law.

There are, however, new factors in the latest version of the equation. The apparent willingness even of Party members to be seen as belonging to the Muslim community has already been noted[159] and seems to represent a less overtly hostile attitude to religion on the part of the Communist authorities. While this more friendly attitude may well itself indicate no more than a tactical concession on the part of the Communists designed principally to appeal to the overseas Islamic world in general and its investors in particular, it has unquestionably allowed the material foundations of religious life to be rebuilt.[160] It has also facilitated the development of the study of various aspects of Islam, including Islamic law.

Before the 1980s, even the existence of Islamic law was rarely admitted, let alone discussed;[161] the social practices of Muslims founded on Islamic law were described merely as 'customs' or 'habits', and their religious sanction was ignored. Now, however, Islamic law is regarded as an ordinary part of comparative legal study. Passages from the Qur'an relating to marriage, divorce and the family, for example, are included in one of the principal collections of reference material on family law for law students.[162] Specialized foreign textbooks on the subject have been translated,[163] and in 1984 the first academic symposium ever held in China on Islamic law took place in Urumqi.[164] The symposium included papers on the teaching of Islamic

---

[158]See *Official Letter in Reply of the Ministry of Justice of the People's Republic of China Regarding the Question to Which Nationality the Children of a Man and Woman of Different Nationalities Should Belong, Si-fa-zi* No. 26/829, 15th June 1953, in *A Selection of Materials on the Marriage Law, supra* n. 143, p.250.

[159]*Supra,* n. 136.

[160]In particular the reopening of mosques and the recruitment of clergy. As to the latter, it was said in 1985 that in Ningxia there were 1,500 imams; see Barker,'Where Islam, Marxism meet'.

[161]An exception was the encyclopaedia *Cihai (Sea of Words), supra,* n. 19, in which there is a short article entitled *'Jiaofaxue'* (religious jurisprudence), pp. 138-139.

[162]*Hunyin Lifa Cailiao Xianbian (A Selection of Materials on Matrimonial Legislation),* Peking, 1983, pp. 140, 259.

[163]E.g., Nuo Kuersen (Noel Coulson), *Yisilanjiao Falüshi (A History of Islamic Law),* translated by Wu Yungui, Peking, 1986.

[164]Luo Junqing, 'China's First Symposium on Islamic Law Concludes in Urumqi', *Zhongguo Fazhi Bao (Chinese Legal System News),* 29th August 1984, translated in FBIS-China Report No. CPS-84-085, 11th December 1984, p.35.

law as well as on matters of legal history and substantive law, and it was said at the conclusion that

> all participants agreed that the symposium did much to eliminate old ideas about law and to interpret Islamic law correctly. It also played an important role in legal propaganda and education and in strengthening the solidarity between the various nationalities within China and also between the peoples of China and of various Muslim countries.[165]

The 'correct interpretation' of Islamic law may be an important pointer to the future. On at least one important occasion, it appears, the Chinese government has resorted to Qur'anic interpretation on its own account, calling upon the clergy in Xinjiang not to oppose the imposition of compulsory birth control regulations on Muslim minorities in the region.[166] Although it is unlikely to meet the approval of the guardians of orthodoxy (whether Marxist or Islamic), there is a pragmatic tradition among Chinese Muslims which may find the acceptance of a modern, even Marxist-inspired, interpretation of the law more attractive than confrontation.

[165] *Ibid.* The translation above does not precisely follow that of the FBIS report.
[166] Roche, 'Muslims warned in Xinjiang'. The results of this appeal are not known.

APPENDIX: AREAS IN WHICH NATIONAL AUTONOMY IS ENJOYED BY ISLAMIC MINORITIES

Autonomous Regions (2 out of 5)	**Date of Establishment**
Xinjiang Uighur Autonomous Region	1 Oct. 1955
Ningxia Hui Autonomous Region	25 Oct. 1958
Autonomous Prefectures (5 out of 31)	
Linxia Hui Autonomous Prefecture (Gansu)	19 Nov. 1956
Haixi Mongol-Tibetan-Kazakh Autonomous Prefecture (Qinghai)*	25 Jan. 1954
Kizilsu Kirgiz Autonomous Prefecture (Xinjiang)	14 July 1954
Changi Hui Autonomous Prefecture (Xinjiang)	15 July 1954
Ili Kazakh Autonomous Prefecture (Xinjiang)	27 Nov. 1954
Autonomous Counties (16 out of 80)	
Mengcun Hui Autonomous County (Hebei)	30 Nov. 1955
Dachang Hui Autonomous County (Hebei)	7 Dec. 1955
Dongxiang Autonomous County (Gansu)	25 Sep. 1950
Zhangjiachuan Hui Autonomous County (Gansu)	6 July 1953
Aksay Gazakh Autonomous County (Gansu)	27 Apr. 1954
Jishishan Baoan-Dongxiang-Salar Autonomous County (Gansu)	30 Sep. 1981
Menyuan Hui Autonomous County (Qinghai)	19 Dec. 1953
Hulong Hui Autonomous County (Qinghai)	1 Mar. 1954

Xunhua Salar Autonomous County (Qinghai)	1 Mar. 1954
Yanqi Hui Autonomous County (Xinjiang)	15 Mar. 1954
Mori Kazakh Autonomous County (Xinjiang)	17 July 1954
Taxkorgan Tajik Autonomous County (Xinjiang)	17 Sep. 1954
Barkol Kazakh Autonomous County (Xinjiang)	30 Sep.1954
Weining Yi-Hui-Miao Autonomous County (Guizhou)*	11 Nov. 1954
Weishan Yi-Hui Autonomous County (Yunnan)*	9 Nov. 1956
Xundian Hui-Yi Autonomous County (Yunnan)*	20 Dec. 1979

An * denotes areas shared with non-Muslim predominant nationalities.

INDEX